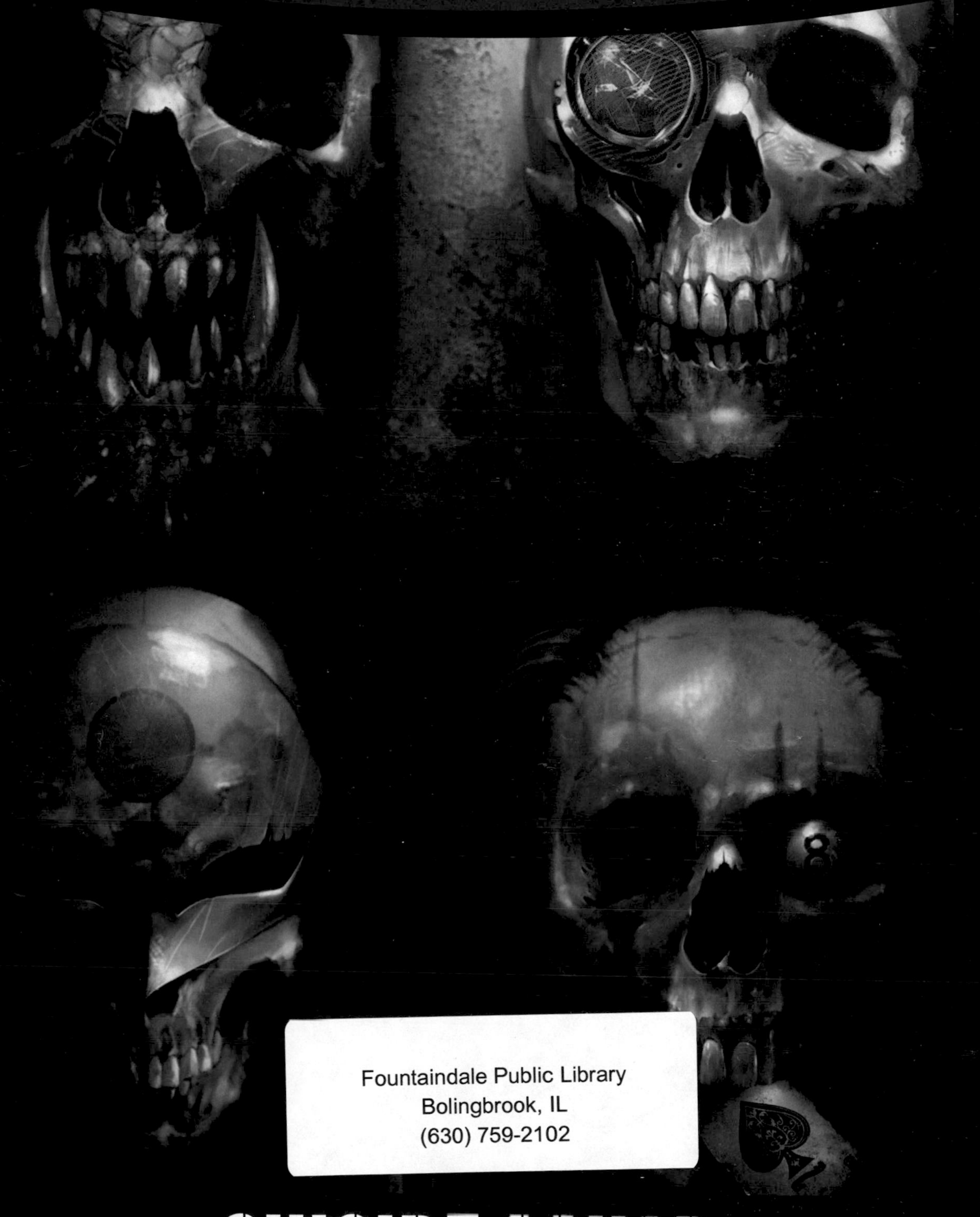

SUICIDE SQUAD

VOL.8 CONSTRICTION

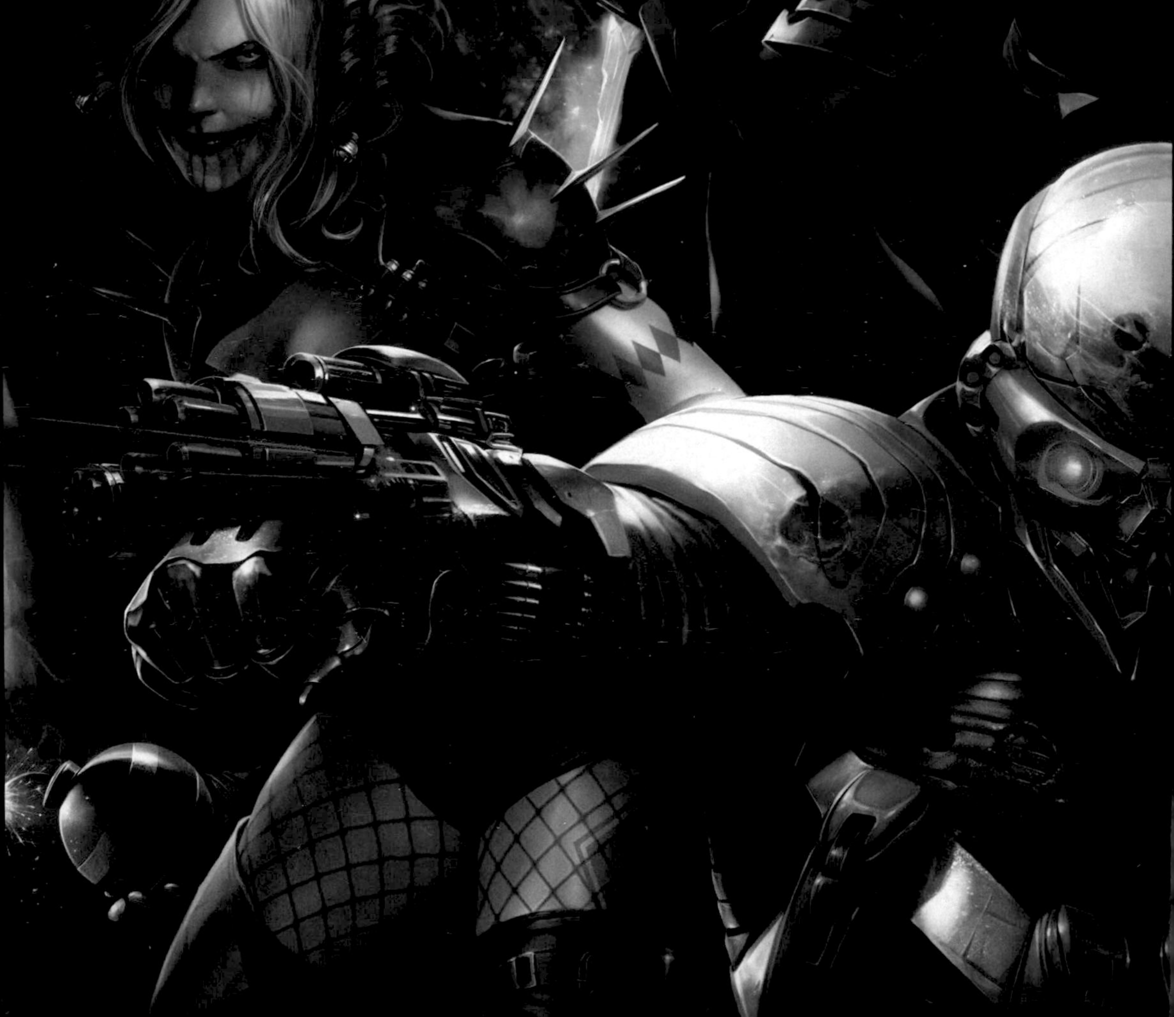

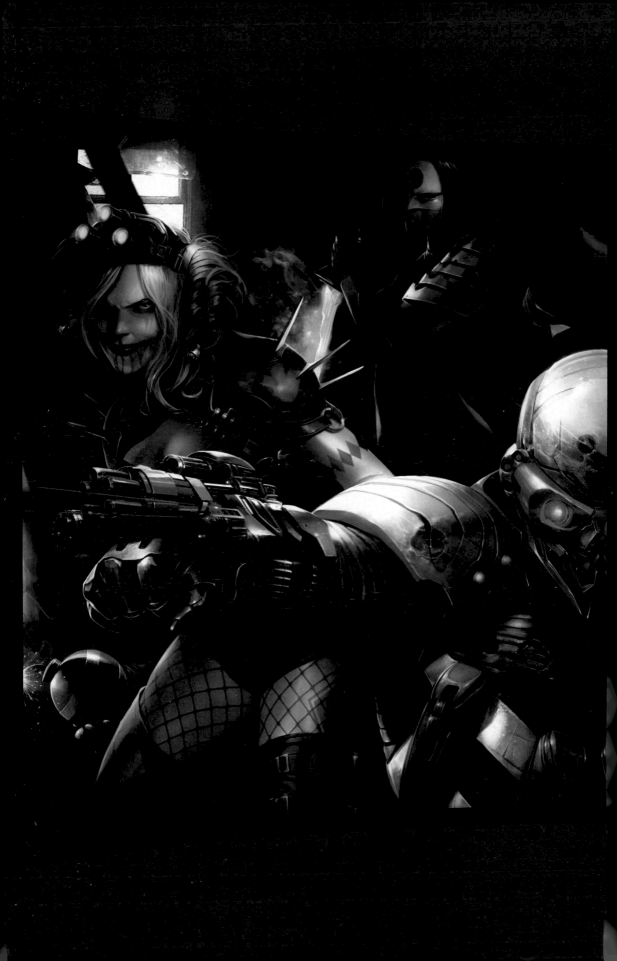

SUICIDE SQUAD
VOL.8 CONSTRICTION

ROB WILLIAMS
CULLEN BUNN
writers

JOE BENNETT * **PHILIPPE BRIONES** * **RONAN CLIQUET** * **WILL CONRAD**
JOSE LUIS * **DIOGENES NEVES** * **EDUARDO PANSICA** * **GERMAN PERALTA**
HUGO PETRUS * **BRENT SCHOONOVER**
VICENTE CIFUENTES * JULIO FERREIRA * MICK GRAY * SCOTT HANNA * JORDI TARRAGONA
artists

GABE ELTAEB * **HI-FI** * **ADRIANO LUCAS** * **JASON WRIGHT**
colorists

PAT BROSSEAU * **DAVE SHARPE**
letterers

JIM LEE, SCOTT WILLIAMS and ALEX SINCLAIR
collection cover artists

MIKE COTTON KATIE KUBERT Editors - Original Series ∗ **ANDREW MARINO ANDREA SHEA** Assistant Editors - Original Series
JEB WOODARD Group Editor - Collected Editions ∗ **ROBIN WILDMAN** Editor - Collected Edition
STEVE COOK Design Director - Books ∗ **ADAM RADO** Publication Production

BOB HARRAS Senior VP - Editor-in-Chief, DC Comics ∗ **PAT McCALLUM** Executive Editor, DC Comics

DAN DiDIO Publisher ∗ **JIM LEE** Publisher & Chief Creative Officer ∗ **BOBBIE CHASE** VP - New Publishing Initiatives & Talent Development
DON FALLETTI VP - Manufacturing Operations & Workflow Management ∗ **LAWRENCE GANEM** VP - Talent Services
ALISON GILL Senior VP - Manufacturing & Operations ∗ **HANK KANALZ** Senior VP - Publishing Strategy & Support Services
DAN MIRON VP - Publishing Operations ∗ **NICK J. NAPOLITANO** VP - Manufacturing Administration & Design
NANCY SPEARS VP - Sales ∗ **MICHELE R. WELLS** VP & Executive Editor, Young Reader

SUICIDE SQUAD VOL. 8: CONSTRICTION

DC Comics, 2900 West Alameda Ave., Burbank, CA 91505
Printed by LSC Communications, Kendallville, IN, USA. 7/12/19. First Printing.
ISBN: 978-1-4012-8887-7

Library of Congress Cataloging-in-Publication Data is available.

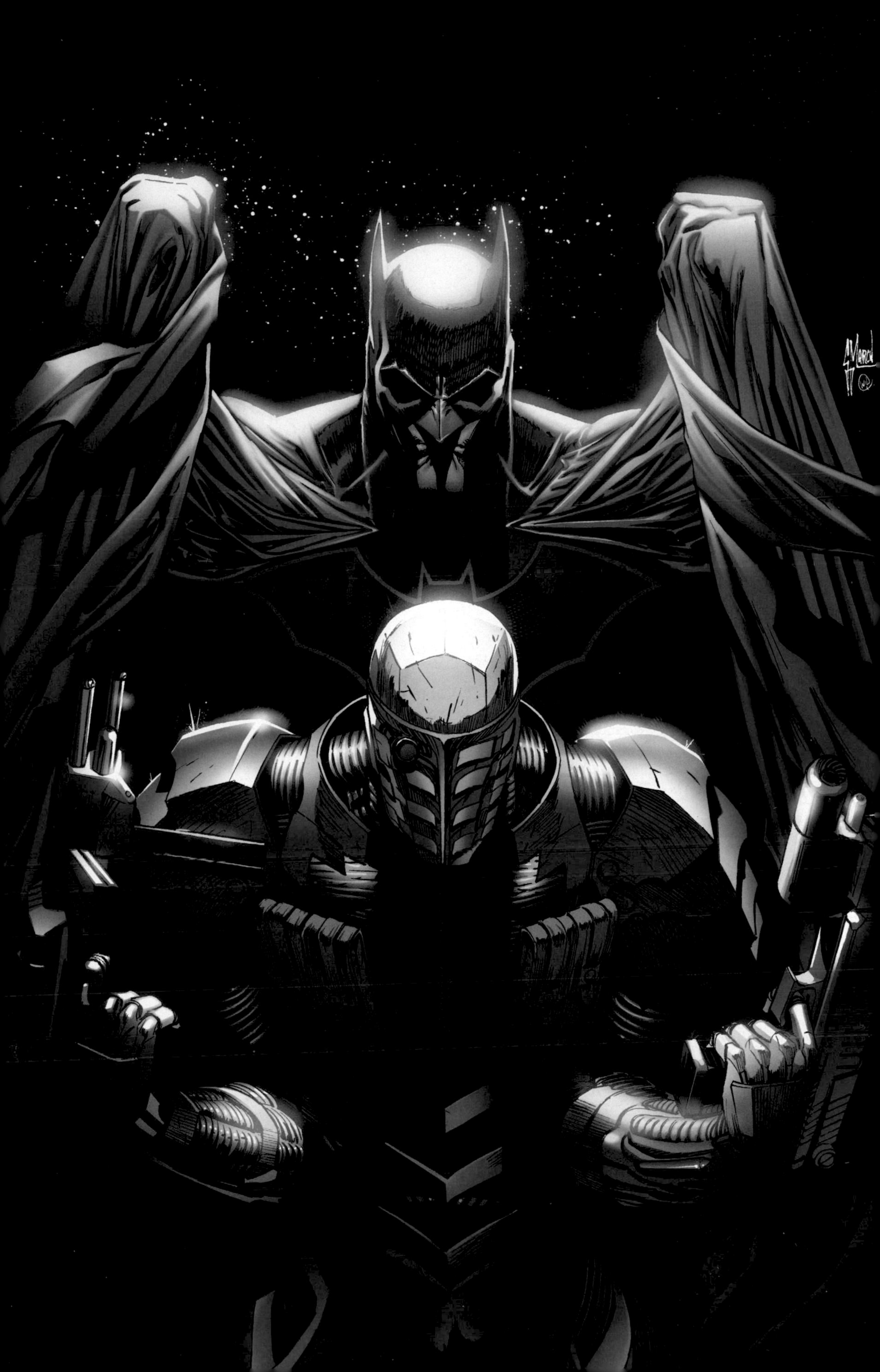

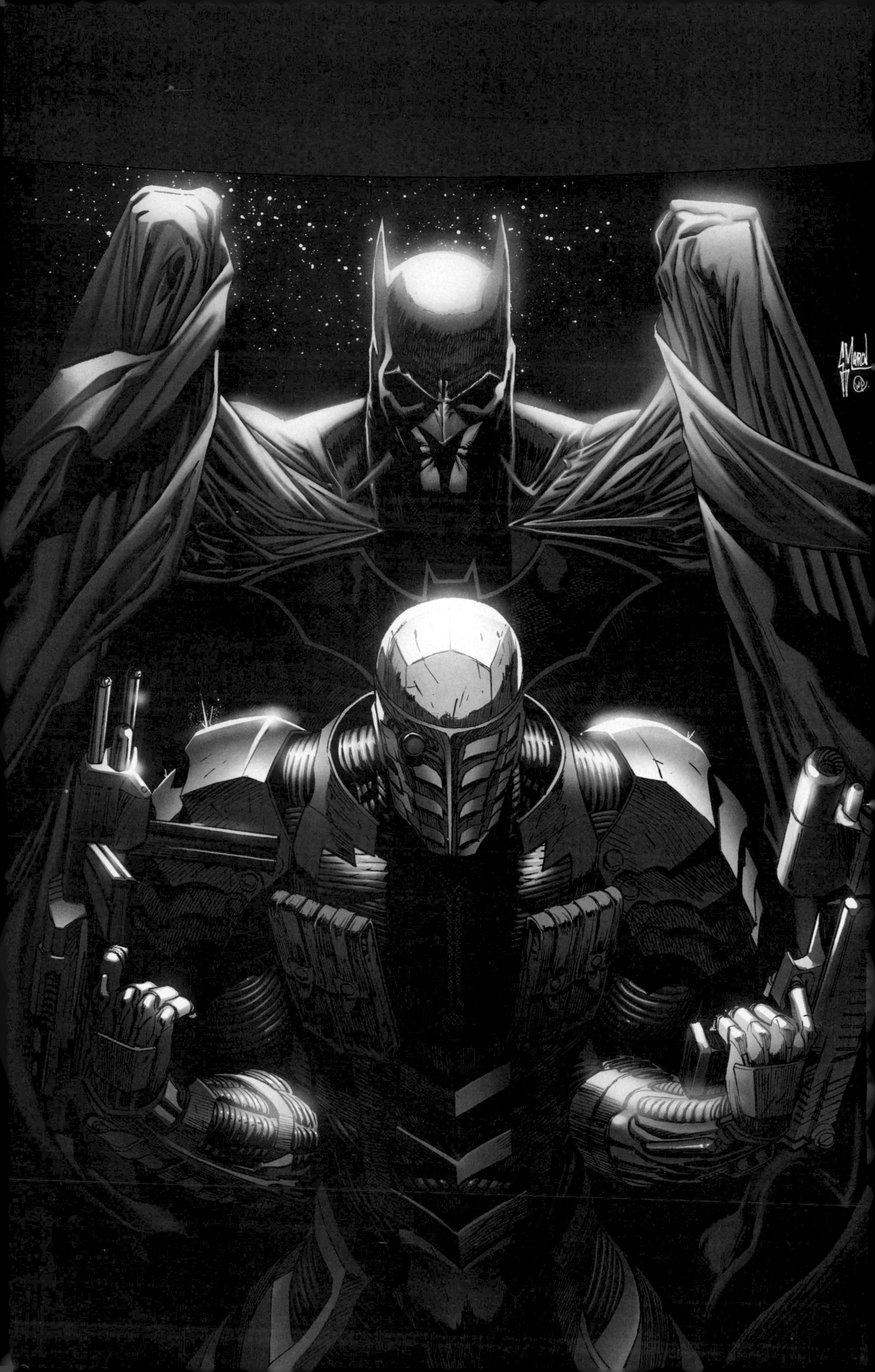

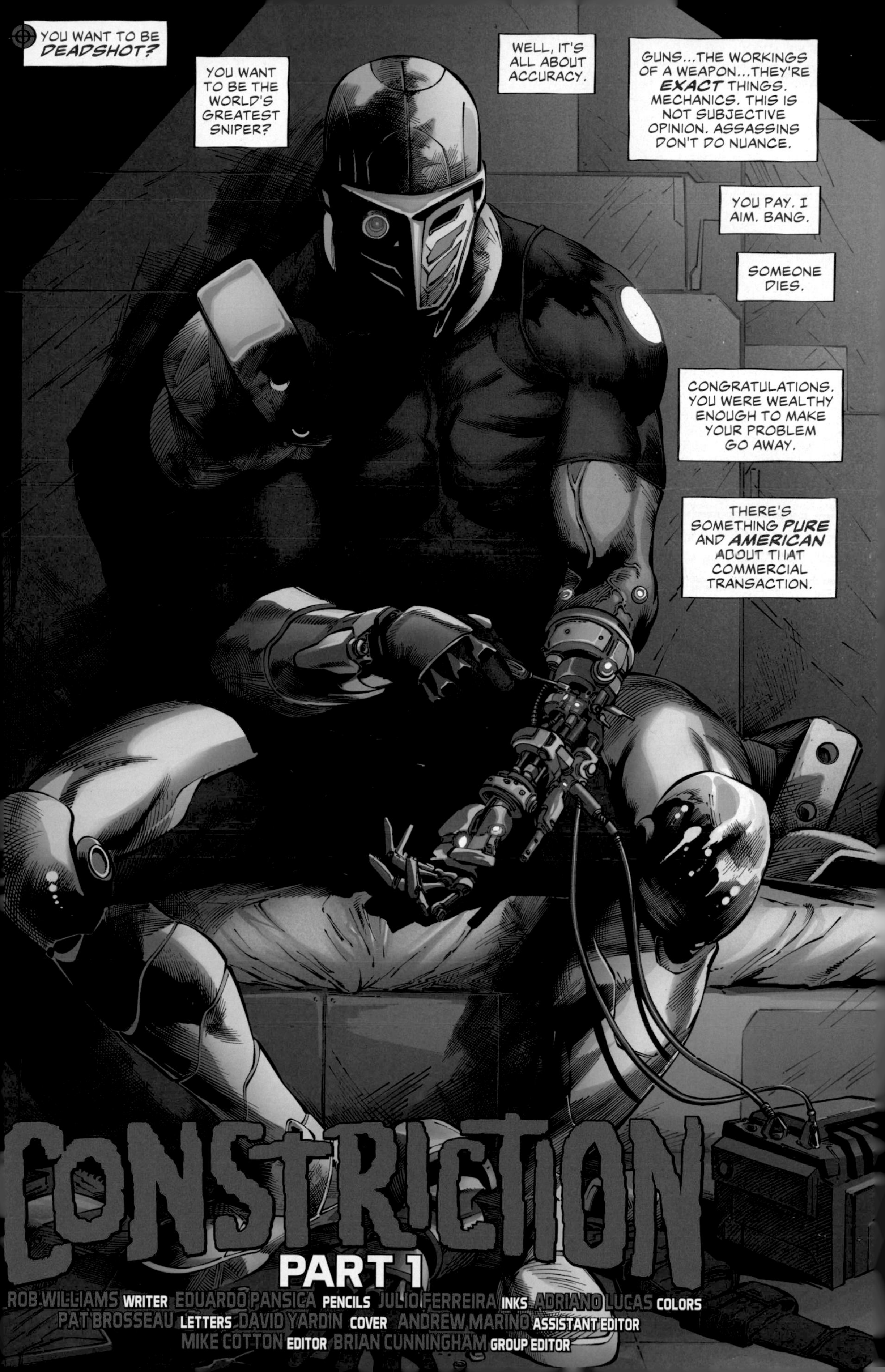
YOU WANT TO BE DEADSHOT?
YOU WANT TO BE THE WORLD'S GREATEST SNIPER?
WELL, IT'S ALL ABOUT ACCURACY.
GUNS...THE WORKINGS OF A WEAPON...THEY'RE EXACT THINGS. MECHANICS. THIS IS NOT SUBJECTIVE OPINION. ASSASSINS DON'T DO NUANCE.
YOU PAY. I AIM. BANG.
SOMEONE DIES.
CONGRATULATIONS. YOU WERE WEALTHY ENOUGH TO MAKE YOUR PROBLEM GO AWAY.
THERE'S SOMETHING PURE AND AMERICAN ABOUT THAT COMMERCIAL TRANSACTION.
CONSTRICTION
PART 1
ROB WILLIAMS WRITER EDUARDO PANSICA PENCILS JULIO FERREIRA INKS ADRIANO LUCAS COLORS
PAT BROSSEAU LETTERS DAVID YARDIN COVER ANDREW MARINO ASSISTANT EDITOR
MIKE COTTON EDITOR BRIAN CUNNINGHAM GROUP EDITOR

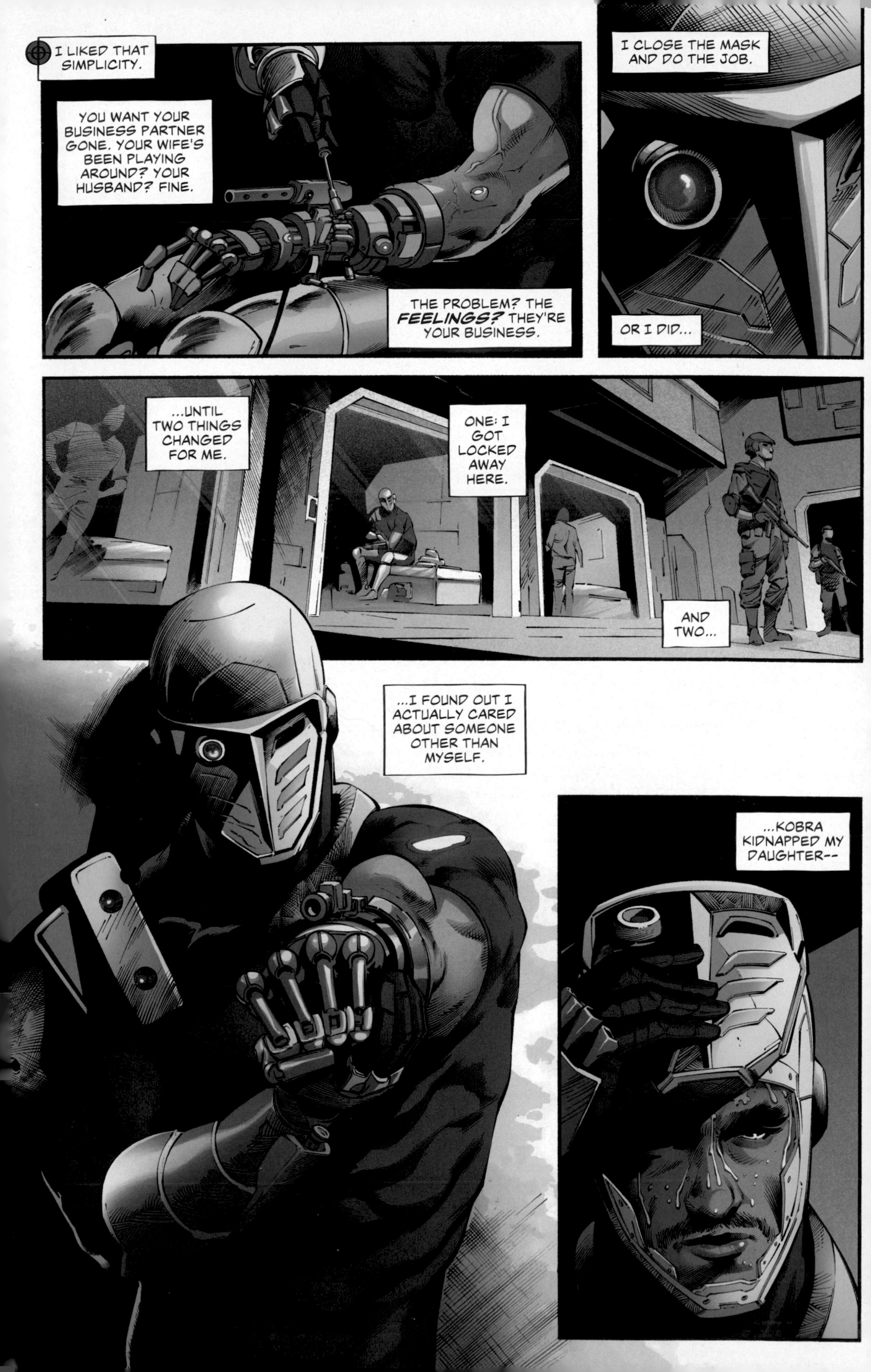
I LIKED THAT SIMPLICITY.
YOU WANT YOUR BUSINESS PARTNER GONE. YOUR WIFE'S BEEN PLAYING AROUND? YOUR HUSBAND? FINE.
THE PROBLEM? THE FEELINGS? THEY'RE YOUR BUSINESS.
I CLOSE THE MASK AND DO THE JOB.
OR I DID...
...UNTIL TWO THINGS CHANGED FOR ME.
ONE: I GOT LOCKED AWAY HERE.
AND TWO...
...I FOUND OUT I ACTUALLY CARED ABOUT SOMEONE OTHER THAN MYSELF.
...KOBRA KIDNAPPED MY DAUGHTER--

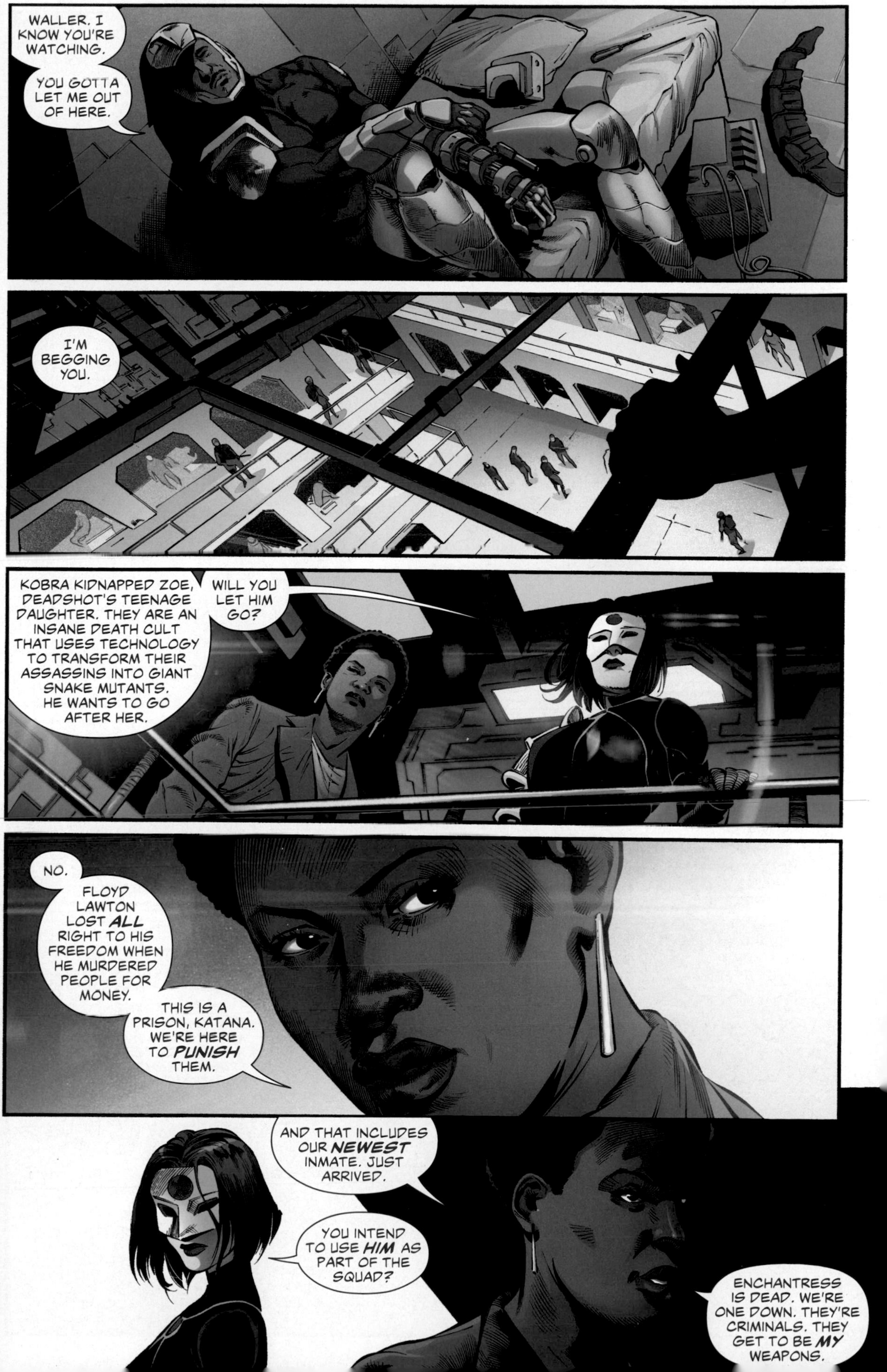
WALLER. I KNOW YOU'RE WATCHING.
YOU GOTTA LET ME OUT OF HERE.
I'M BEGGING YOU.
KOBRA KIDNAPPED ZOE, DEADSHOT'S TEENAGE DAUGHTER. THEY ARE AN INSANE DEATH CULT THAT USES TECHNOLOGY TO TRANSFORM THEIR ASSASSINS INTO GIANT SNAKE MUTANTS. HE WANTS TO GO AFTER HER.
WILL YOU LET HIM GO?
NO.
FLOYD LAWTON LOST ALL RIGHT TO HIS FREEDOM WHEN HE MURDERED PEOPLE FOR MONEY.
THIS IS A PRISON, KATANA. WE'RE HERE TO PUNISH THEM.
AND THAT INCLUDES OUR NEWEST INMATE. JUST ARRIVED.
YOU INTEND TO USE HIM AS PART OF THE SQUAD?
ENCHANTRESS IS DEAD. WE'RE ONE DOWN. THEY'RE CRIMINALS. THEY GET TO BE MY WEAPONS.

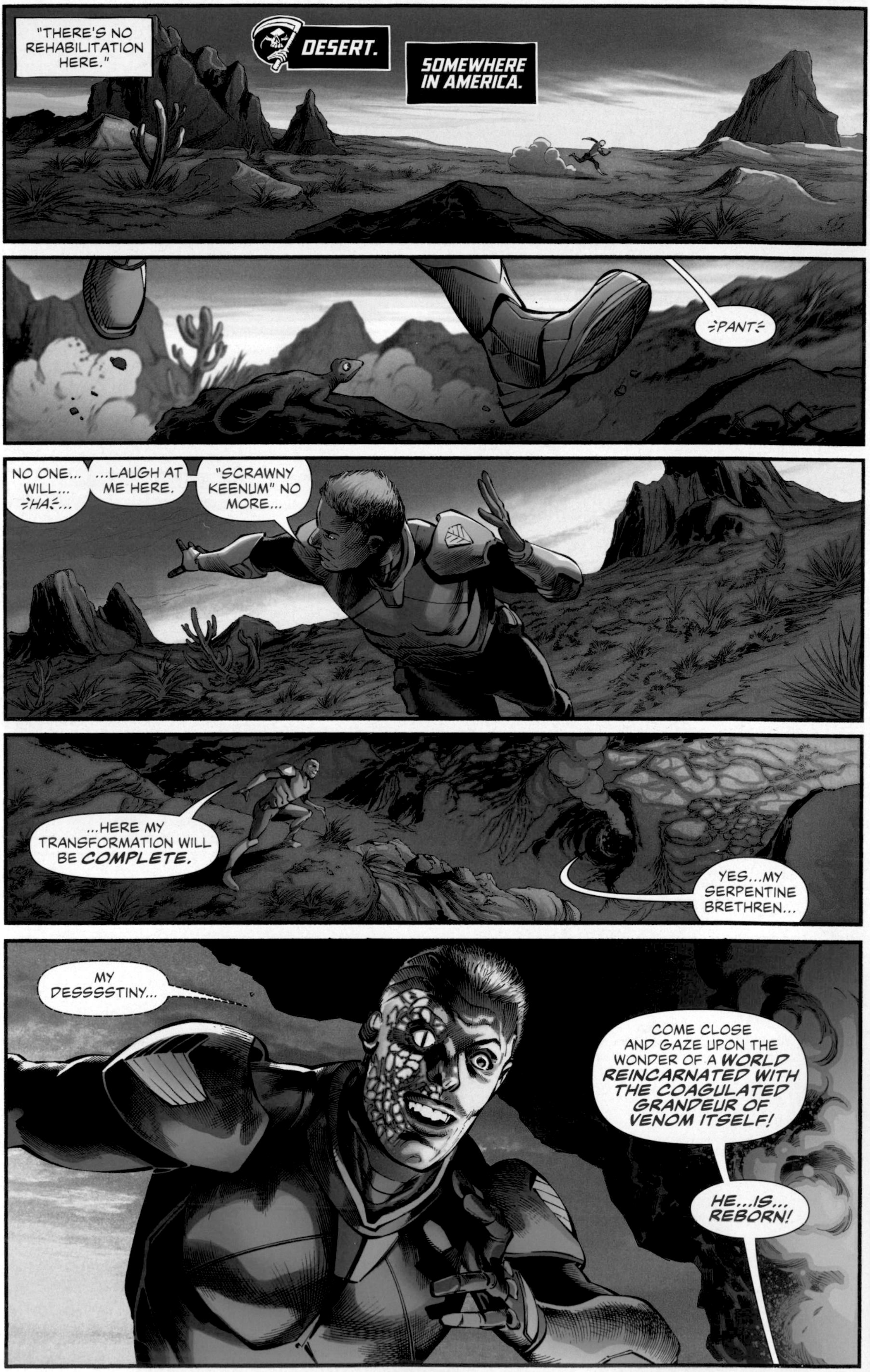
"THERE'S NO REHABILITATION HERE."
DESERT.
SOMEWHERE IN AMERICA.
PANT
NO ONE... WILL... HA...
...LAUGH AT ME HERE.
"SCRAWNY KEENUM" NO MORE...
...HERE MY TRANSFORMATION WILL BE COMPLETE.
YES...MY SERPENTINE BRETHREN...
MY DESSSSTINY...
COME CLOSE AND GAZE UPON THE WONDER OF A WORLD REINCARNATED WITH THE COAGULATED GRANDEUR OF VENOM ITSELF!
HE...IS... REBORN!

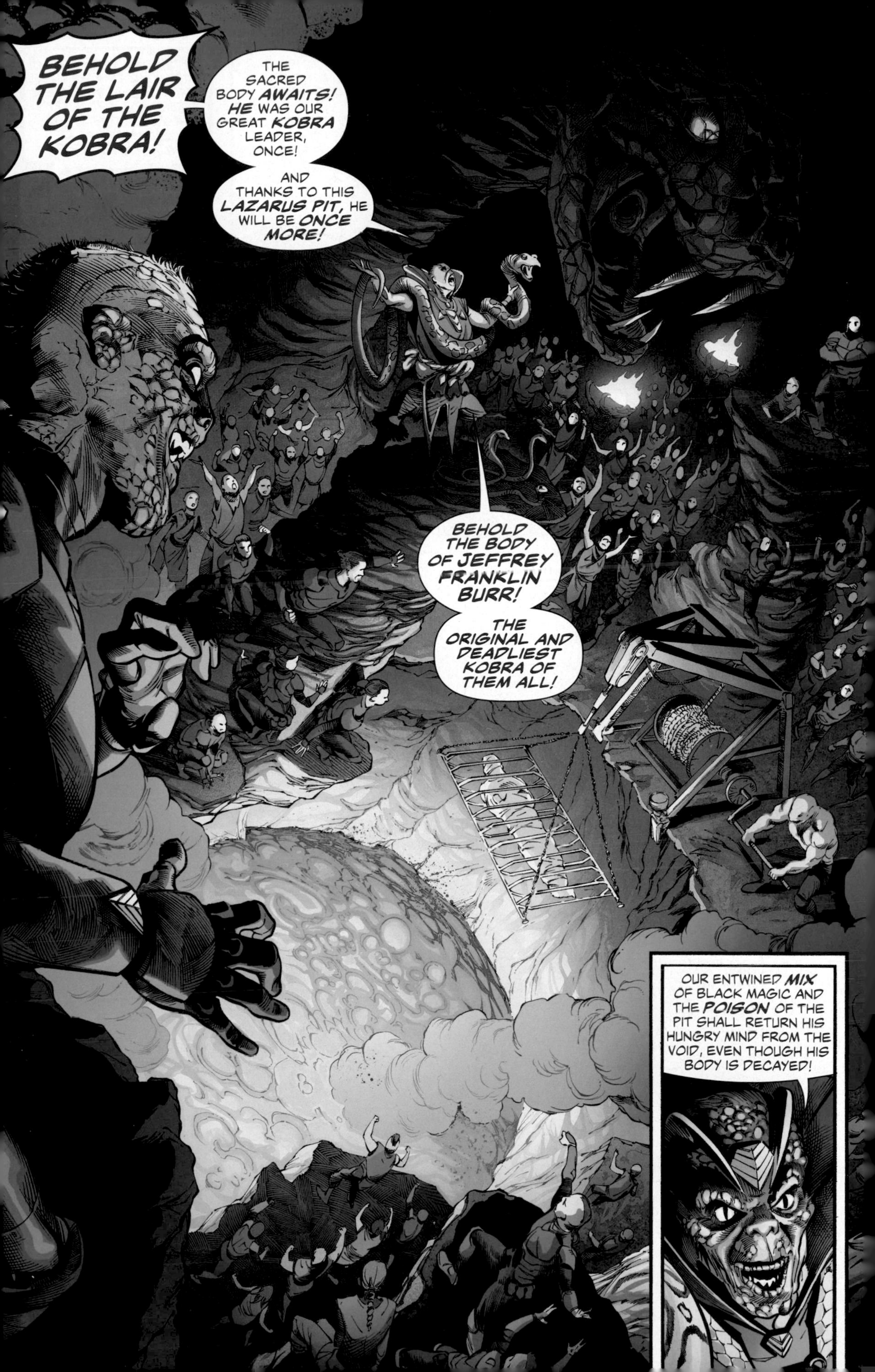
BEHOLD THE LAIR OF THE KOBRA!
THE SACRED BODY AWAITS! HE WAS OUR GREAT KOBRA LEADER, ONCE!
AND THANKS TO THIS LAZARUS PIT, HE WILL BE ONCE MORE!
BEHOLD THE BODY OF JEFFREY FRANKLIN BURR!
THE ORIGINAL AND DEADLIEST KOBRA OF THEM ALL!
OUR ENTWINED MIX OF BLACK MAGIC AND THE POISON OF THE PIT SHALL RETURN HIS HUNGRY MIND FROM THE VOID, EVEN THOUGH HIS BODY IS DECAYED!

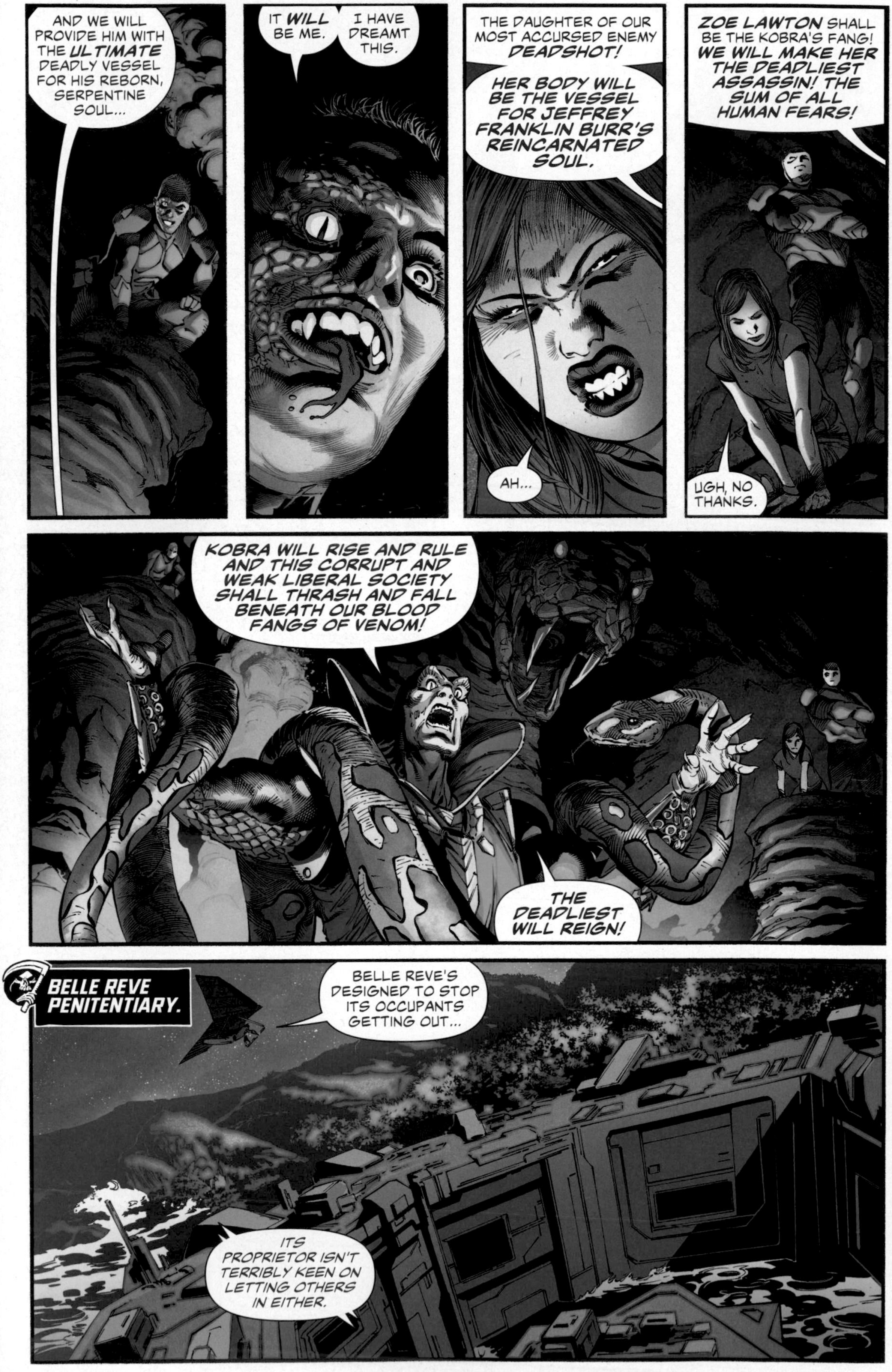
AND WE WILL PROVIDE HIM WITH THE ULTIMATE DEADLY VESSEL FOR HIS REBORN, SERPENTINE SOUL...
IT WILL BE ME.
I HAVE DREAMT THIS.
THE DAUGHTER OF OUR MOST ACCURSED ENEMY DEADSHOT!
HER BODY WILL BE THE VESSEL FOR JEFFREY FRANKLIN BURR'S REINCARNATED SOUL.
AH...
ZOE LAWTON SHALL BE THE KOBRA'S FANG! WE WILL MAKE HER THE DEADLIEST ASSASSIN! THE SUM OF ALL HUMAN FEARS!
UGH, NO THANKS.
KOBRA WILL RISE AND RULE AND THIS CORRUPT AND WEAK LIBERAL SOCIETY SHALL THRASH AND FALL BENEATH OUR BLOOD FANGS OF VENOM!
THE DEADLIEST WILL REIGN!
BELLE REVE PENITENTIARY.
BELLE REVE'S DESIGNED TO STOP ITS OCCUPANTS GETTING OUT...
ITS PROPRIETOR ISN'T TERRIBLY KEEN ON LETTING OTHERS IN EITHER.

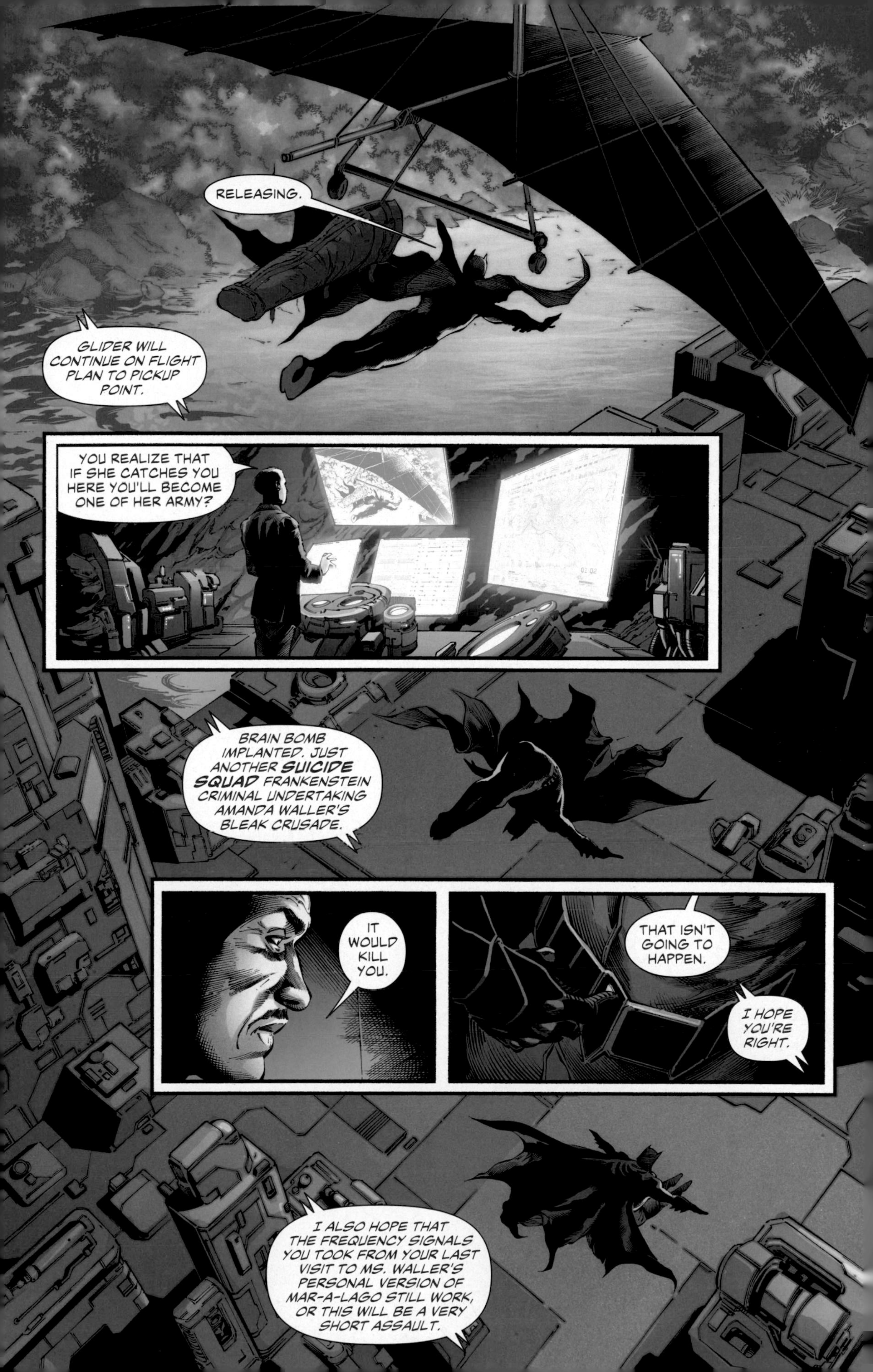
RELEASING.
GLIDER WILL CONTINUE ON FLIGHT PLAN TO PICKUP POINT.
YOU REALIZE THAT IF SHE CATCHES YOU HERE YOU'LL BECOME ONE OF HER ARMY?
BRAIN BOMB IMPLANTED. JUST ANOTHER SUICIDE SQUAD FRANKENSTEIN CRIMINAL UNDERTAKING AMANDA WALLER'S BLEAK CRUSADE.
IT WOULD KILL YOU.
THAT ISN'T GOING TO HAPPEN.
I HOPE YOU'RE RIGHT.
I ALSO HOPE THAT THE FREQUENCY SIGNALS YOU TOOK FROM YOUR LAST VISIT TO MS. WALLER'S PERSONAL VERSION OF MAR-A-LAGO STILL WORK, OR THIS WILL BE A VERY SHORT ASSAULT.

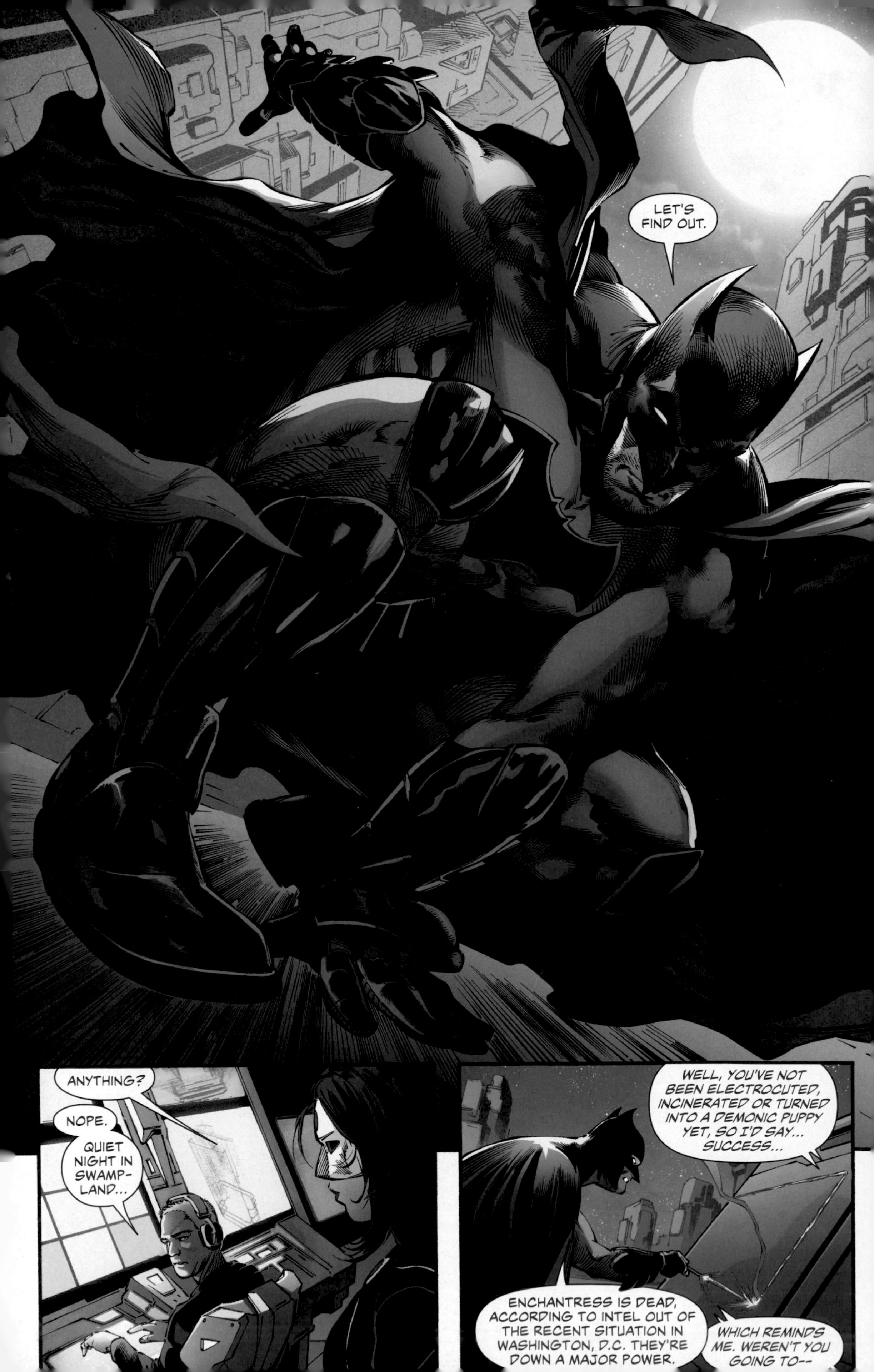
LET'S FIND OUT.
ANYTHING?
NOPE.
QUIET NIGHT IN SWAMP-LAND...
WELL, YOU'VE NOT BEEN ELECTROCUTED, INCINERATED OR TURNED INTO A DEMONIC PUPPY YET, SO I'D SAY... SUCCESS...
ENCHANTRESS IS DEAD, ACCORDING TO INTEL OUT OF THE RECENT SITUATION IN WASHINGTON, D.C. THEY'RE DOWN A MAJOR POWER.
WHICH REMINDS ME. WEREN'T YOU GOING TO--

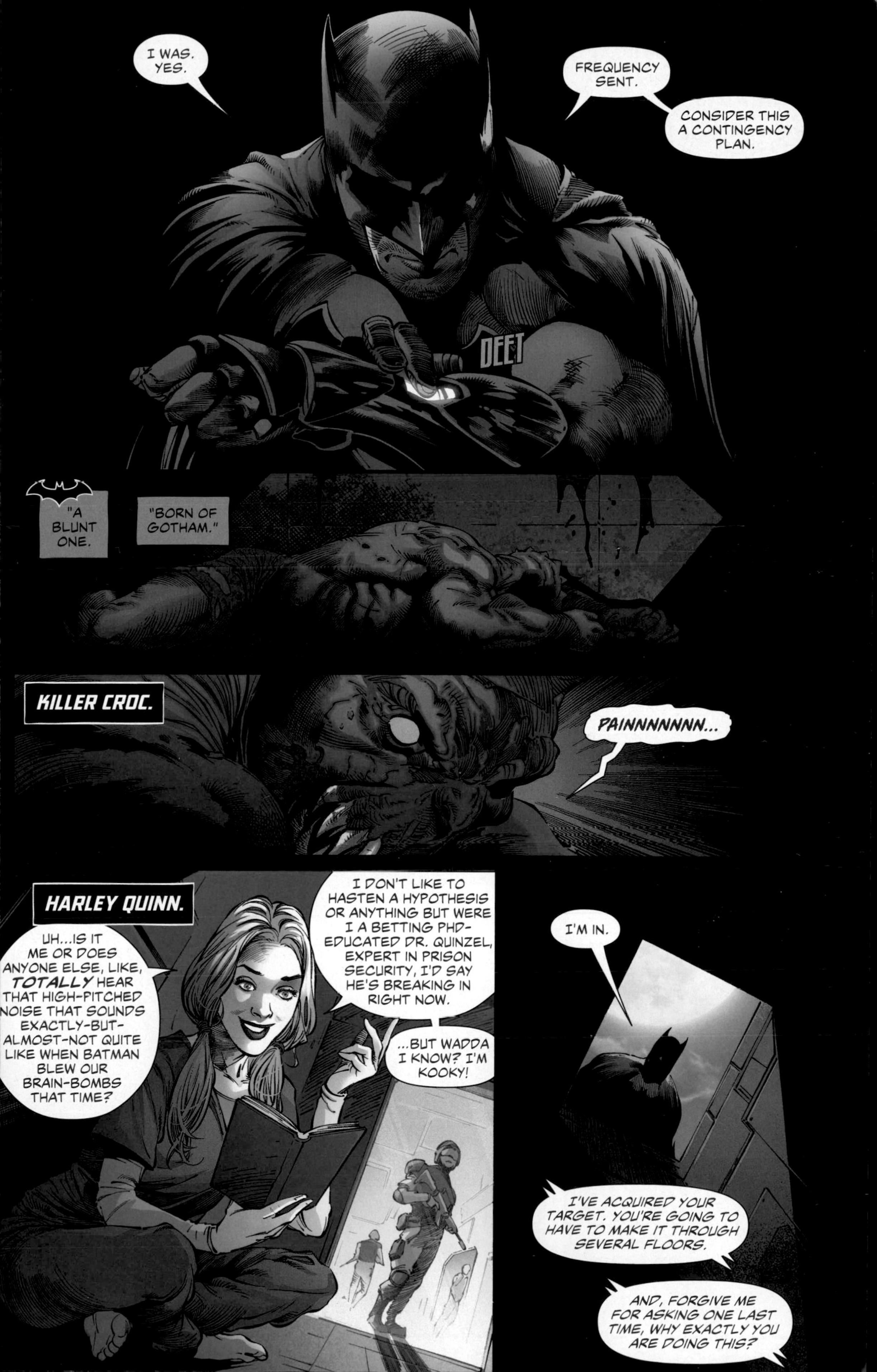

I WAS. YES.
FREQUENCY SENT.
CONSIDER THIS A CONTINGENCY PLAN.
DEET
"A BLUNT ONE.
"BORN OF GOTHAM."
KILLER CROC.
PAINNNNNNN...
HARLEY QUINN.
UH...IS IT ME OR DOES ANYONE ELSE, LIKE, TOTALLY HEAR THAT HIGH-PITCHED NOISE THAT SOUNDS EXACTLY-BUT-ALMOST-NOT QUITE LIKE WHEN BATMAN BLEW OUR BRAIN-BOMBS THAT TIME?
I DON'T LIKE TO HASTEN A HYPOTHESIS OR ANYTHING BUT WERE I A BETTING PHD-EDUCATED DR. QUINZEL, EXPERT IN PRISON SECURITY, I'D SAY HE'S BREAKING IN RIGHT NOW.
...BUT WADDA I KNOW? I'M KOOKY!
I'M IN.
I'VE ACQUIRED YOUR TARGET. YOU'RE GOING TO HAVE TO MAKE IT THROUGH SEVERAL FLOORS.
AND, FORGIVE ME FOR ASKING ONE LAST TIME, WHY EXACTLY YOU ARE DOING THIS?

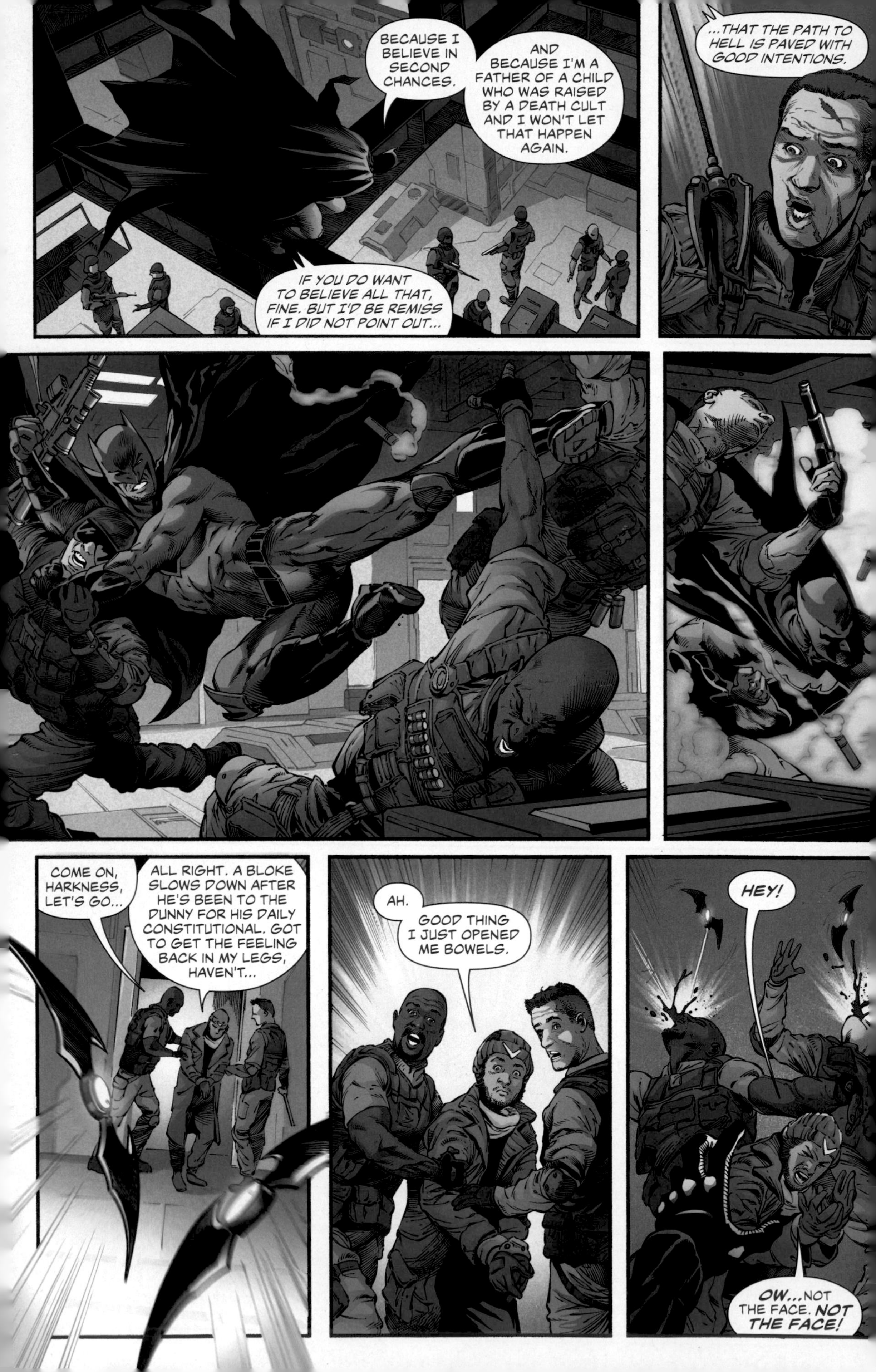
BECAUSE I BELIEVE IN SECOND CHANCES.
AND BECAUSE I'M A FATHER OF A CHILD WHO WAS RAISED BY A DEATH CULT AND I WON'T LET THAT HAPPEN AGAIN.
IF YOU DO WANT TO BELIEVE ALL THAT, FINE. BUT I'D BE REMISS IF I DID NOT POINT OUT...
...THAT THE PATH TO HELL IS PAVED WITH GOOD INTENTIONS.
COME ON, HARKNESS, LET'S GO...
ALL RIGHT. A BLOKE SLOWS DOWN AFTER HE'S BEEN TO THE DUNNY FOR HIS DAILY CONSTITUTIONAL. GOT TO GET THE FEELING BACK IN MY LEGS, HAVEN'T...
AH.
GOOD THING I JUST OPENED ME BOWELS.
HEY!
OW... NOT THE FACE. NOT THE FACE!

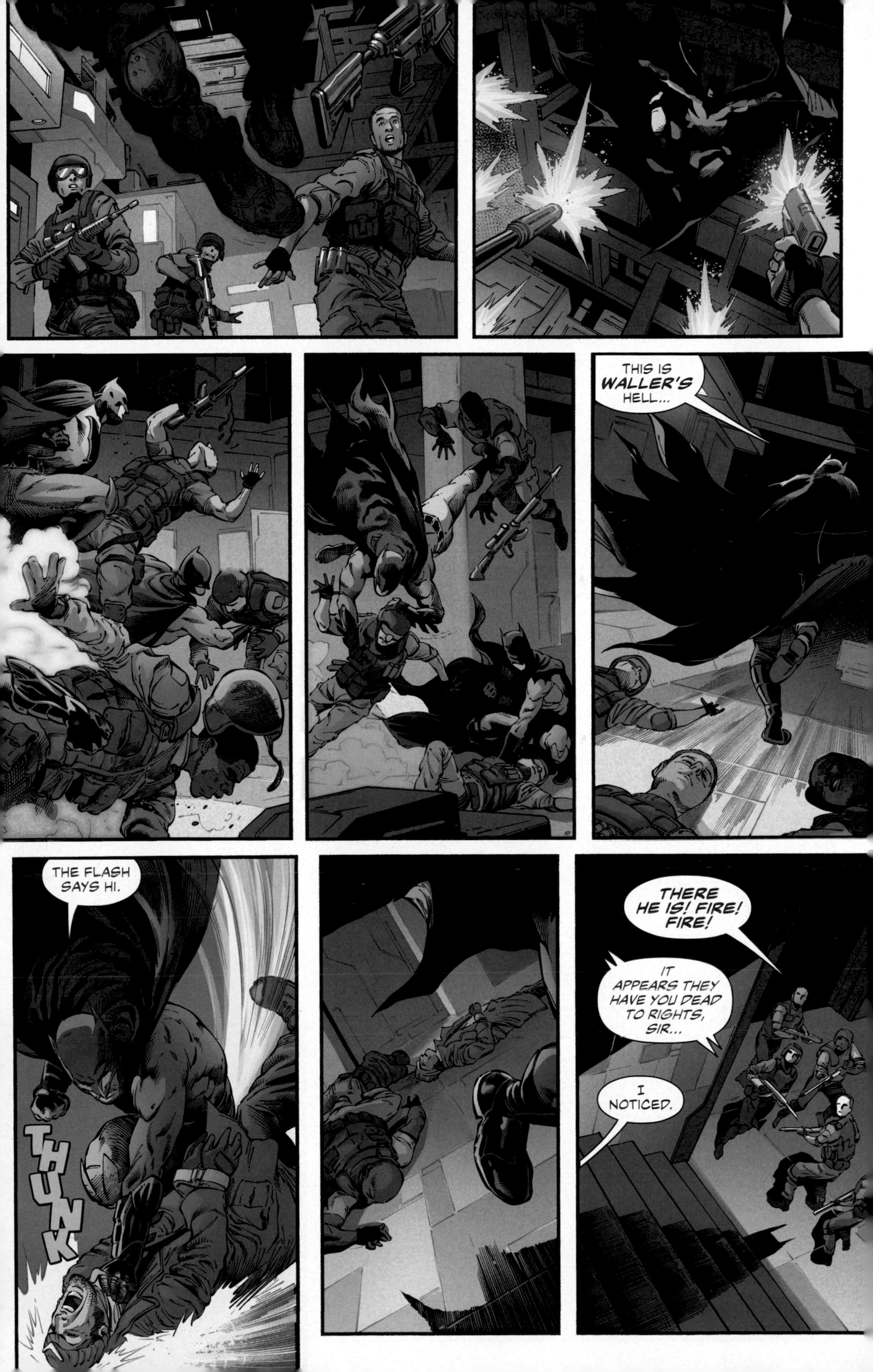

THIS IS WALLER'S HELL...
THE FLASH SAYS HI.
THUNK
THERE HE IS! FIRE! FIRE!
IT APPEARS THEY HAVE YOU DEAD TO RIGHTS, SIR...
I NOTICED.

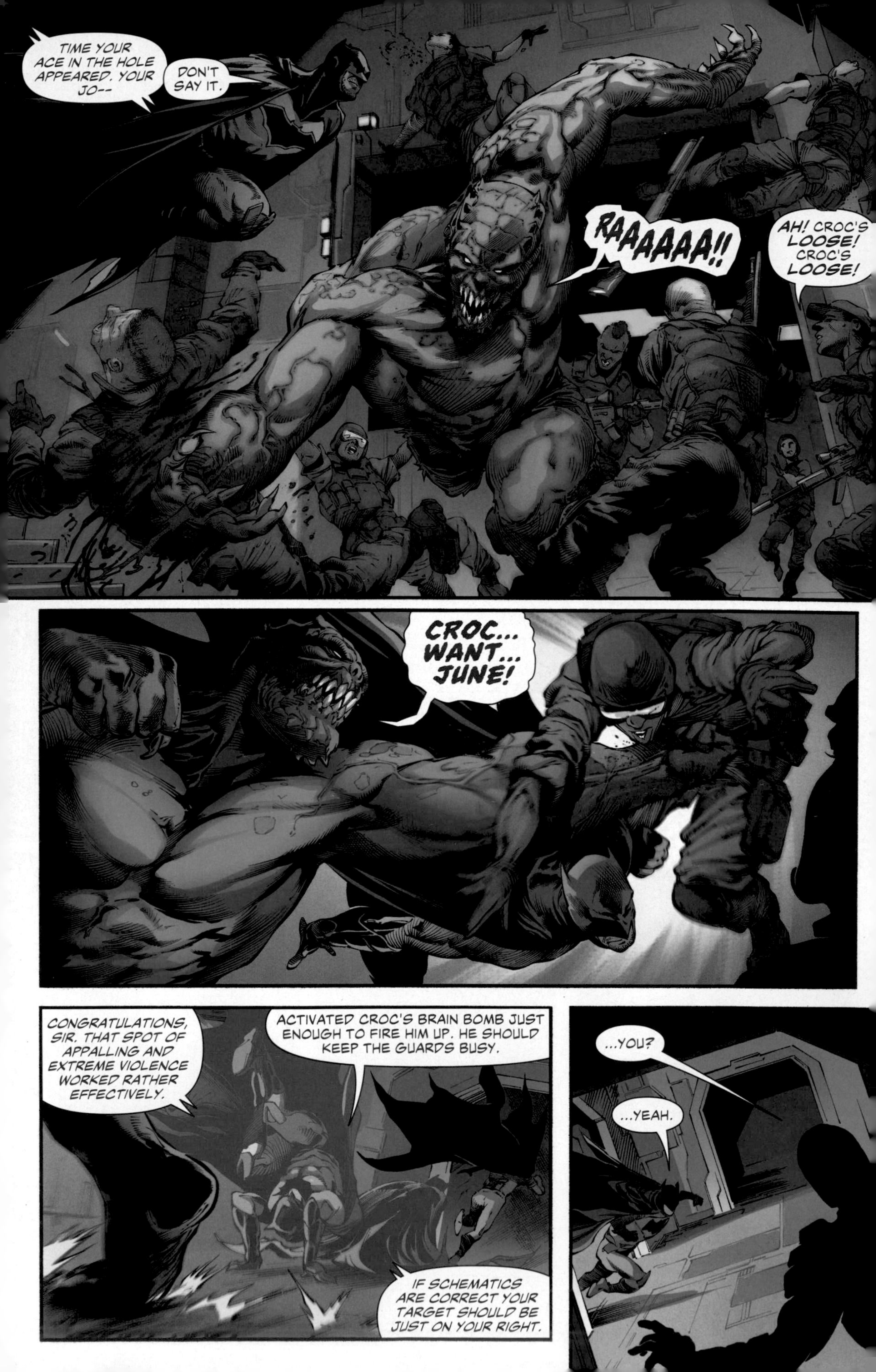
TIME YOUR ACE IN THE HOLE APPEARED. YOUR JO--
DON'T SAY IT.
RAAAAAA!!
AH! CROC'S LOOSE! CROC'S LOOSE!
CROC... WANT... JUNE!
CONGRATULATIONS, SIR. THAT SPOT OF APPALLING AND EXTREME VIOLENCE WORKED RATHER EFFECTIVELY.
ACTIVATED CROC'S BRAIN BOMB JUST ENOUGH TO FIRE HIM UP. HE SHOULD KEEP THE GUARDS BUSY.
IF SCHEMATICS ARE CORRECT YOUR TARGET SHOULD BE JUST ON YOUR RIGHT.
...YOU?
...YEAH.

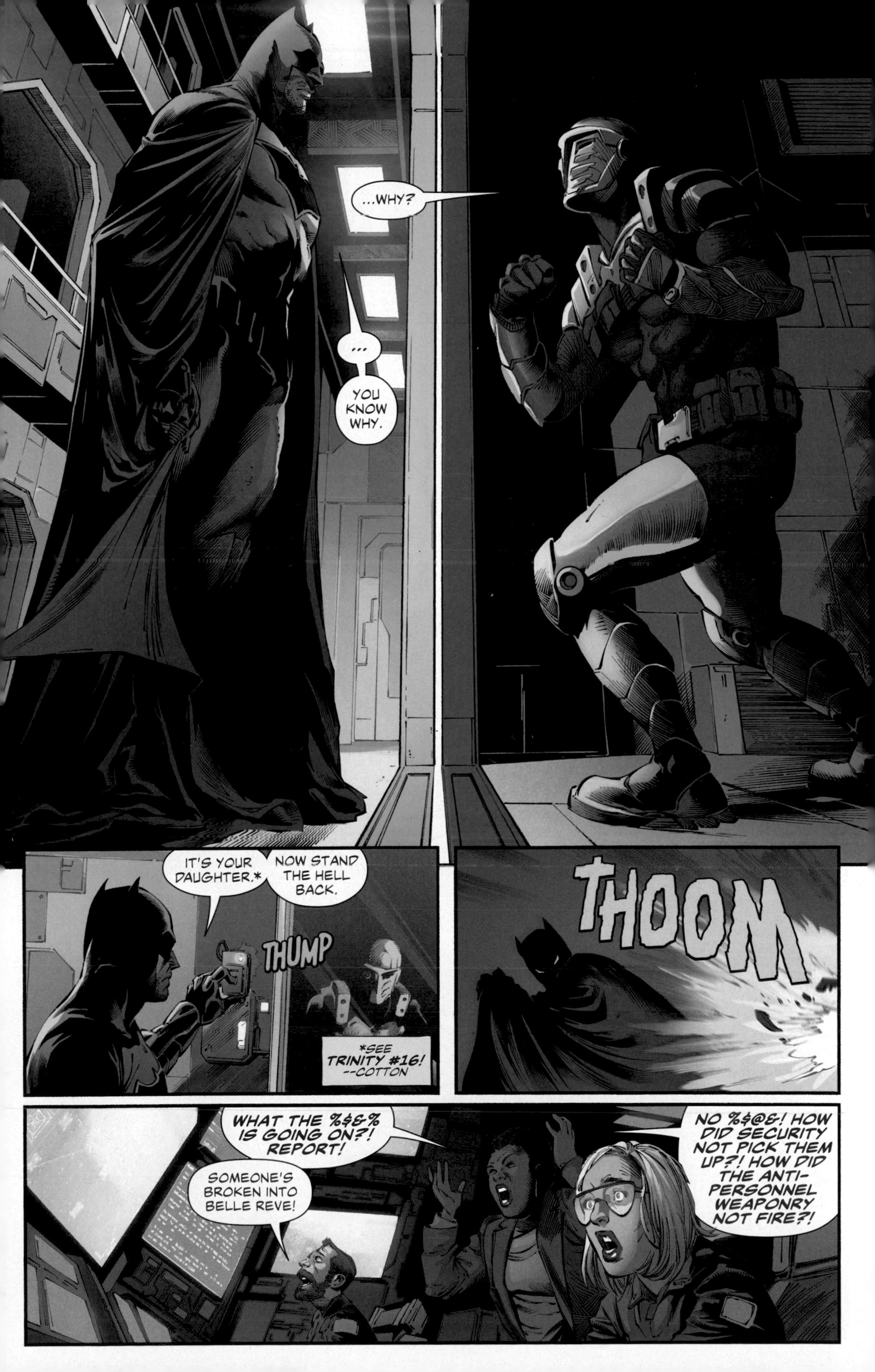

...WHY?
...
YOU KNOW WHY.
IT'S YOUR DAUGHTER.*
NOW STAND THE HELL BACK.
THUMP
*SEE TRINITY #16! --COTTON
THOOM
WHAT THE %$&% IS GOING ON?! REPORT!
SOMEONE'S BROKEN INTO BELLE REVE!
NO %$@&! HOW DID SECURITY NOT PICK THEM UP?! HOW DID THE ANTI-PERSONNEL WEAPONRY NOT FIRE?!

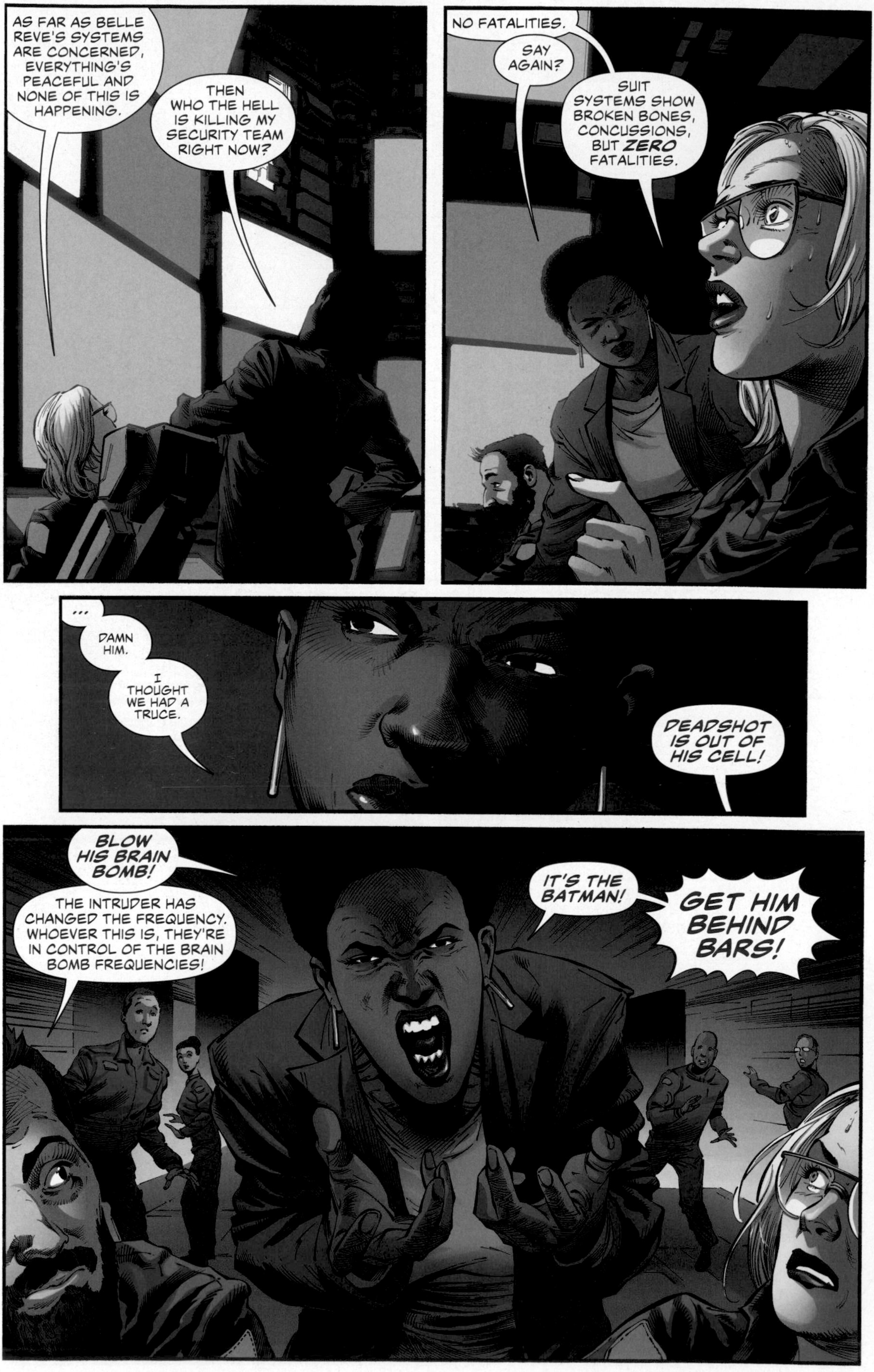
AS FAR AS BELLE REVE'S SYSTEMS ARE CONCERNED, EVERYTHING'S PEACEFUL AND NONE OF THIS IS HAPPENING.
THEN WHO THE HELL IS KILLING MY SECURITY TEAM RIGHT NOW?
NO FATALITIES.
SAY AGAIN?
SUIT SYSTEMS SHOW BROKEN BONES, CONCUSSIONS, BUT ZERO FATALITIES.
...
DAMN HIM.
I THOUGHT WE HAD A TRUCE.
DEADSHOT IS OUT OF HIS CELL!
BLOW HIS BRAIN BOMB!
THE INTRUDER HAS CHANGED THE FREQUENCY. WHOEVER THIS IS, THEY'RE IN CONTROL OF THE BRAIN BOMB FREQUENCIES!
IT'S THE BATMAN!
GET HIM BEHIND BARS!

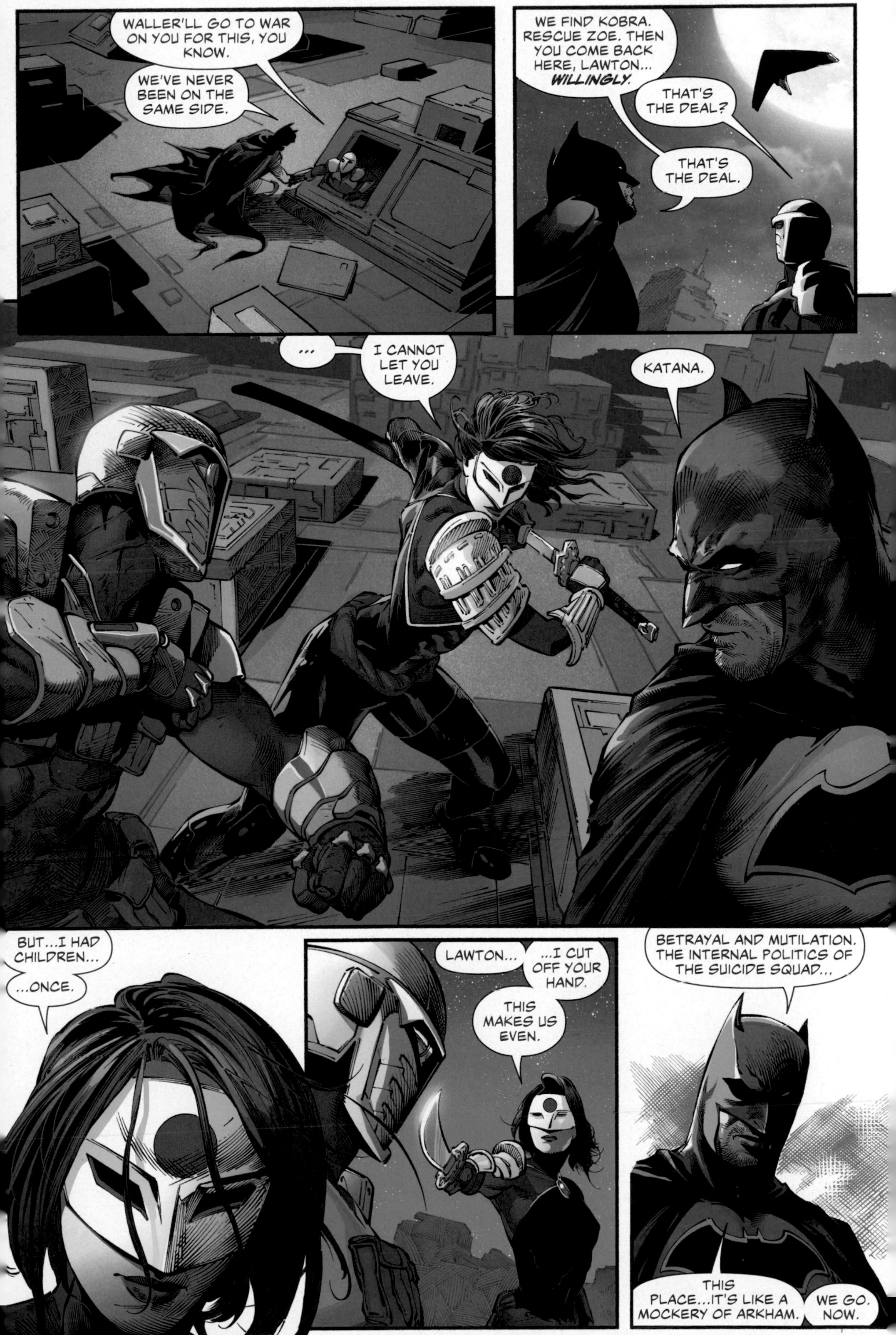
WALLER'LL GO TO WAR ON YOU FOR THIS, YOU KNOW.
WE'VE NEVER BEEN ON THE SAME SIDE.
WE FIND KOBRA. RESCUE ZOE. THEN YOU COME BACK HERE, LAWTON... WILLINGLY.
THAT'S THE DEAL?
THAT'S THE DEAL.
...
I CANNOT LET YOU LEAVE.
KATANA.
BUT...I HAD CHILDREN...
...ONCE.
LAWTON...
...I CUT OFF YOUR HAND.
THIS MAKES US EVEN.
BETRAYAL AND MUTILATION. THE INTERNAL POLITICS OF THE SUICIDE SQUAD...
THIS PLACE...IT'S LIKE A MOCKERY OF ARKHAM.
WE GO. NOW.

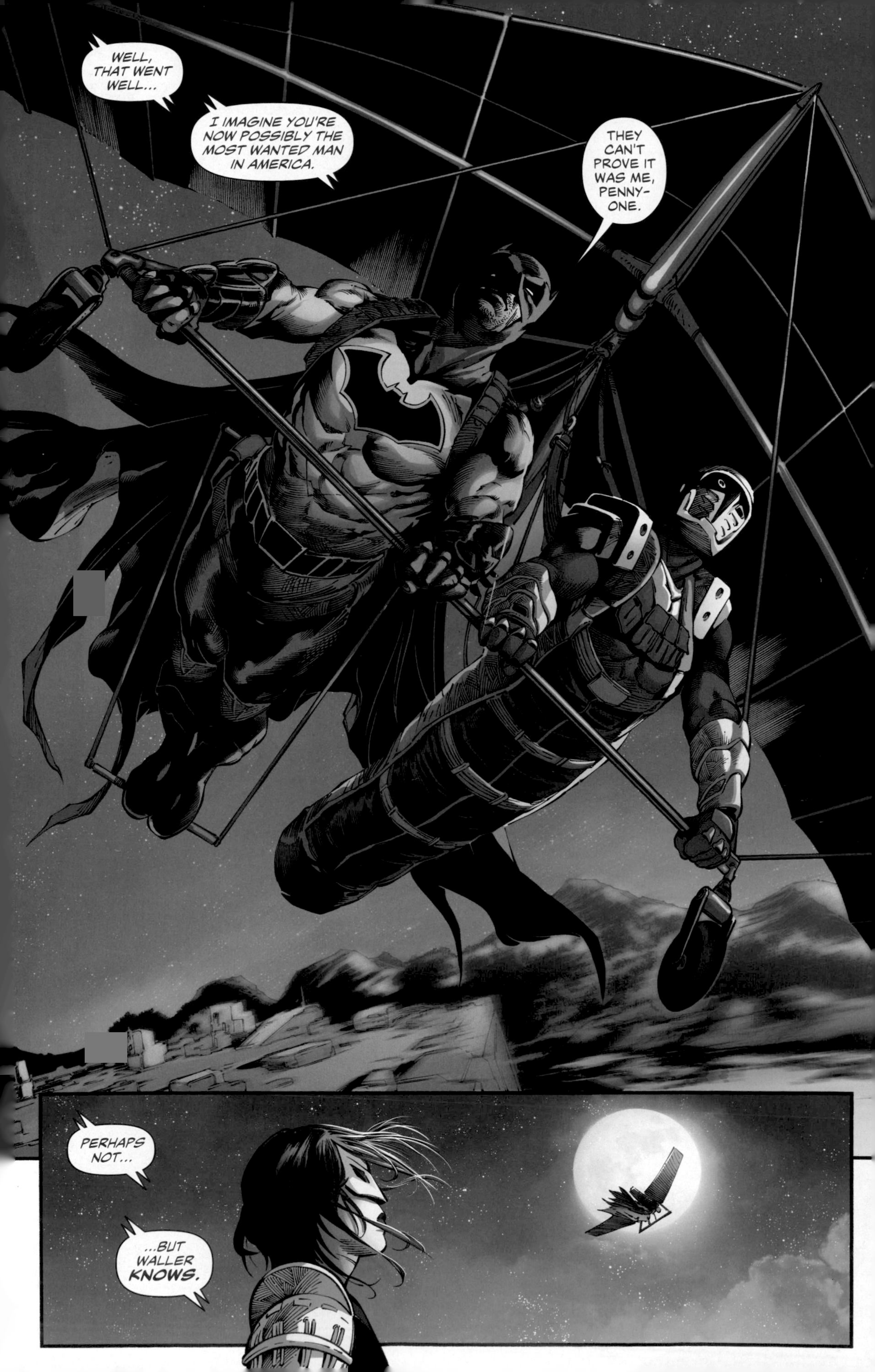
WELL, THAT WENT WELL...
I IMAGINE YOU'RE NOW POSSIBLY THE MOST WANTED MAN IN AMERICA.
THEY CAN'T PROVE IT WAS ME, PENNY-ONE.
PERHAPS NOT...
...BUT WALLER KNOWS.

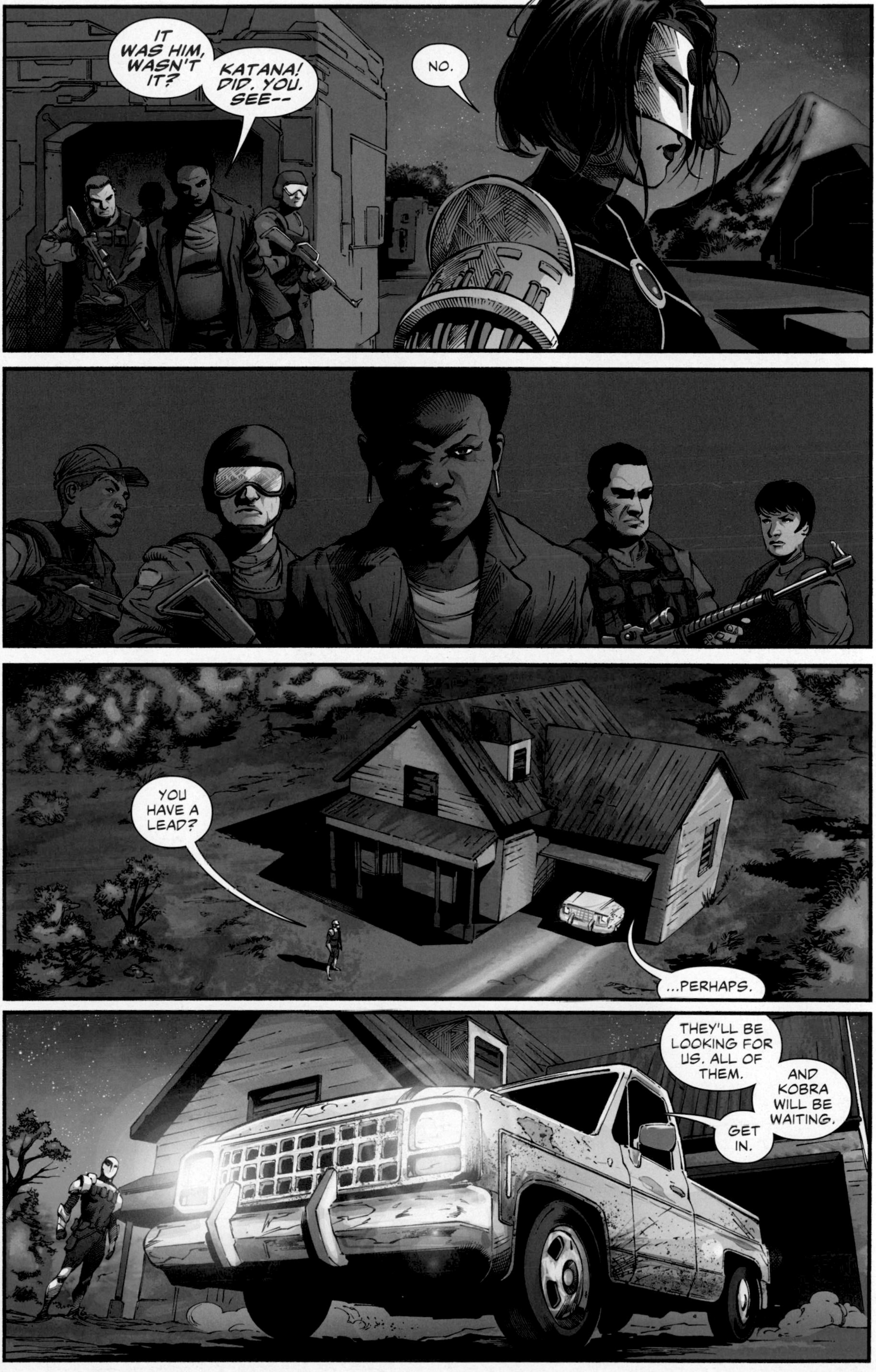
IT WAS HIM, WASN'T IT?
KATANA! DID. YOU. SEE--
NO.
YOU HAVE A LEAD?
...PERHAPS.
THEY'LL BE LOOKING FOR US. ALL OF THEM.
AND KOBRA WILL BE WAITING.
GET IN.

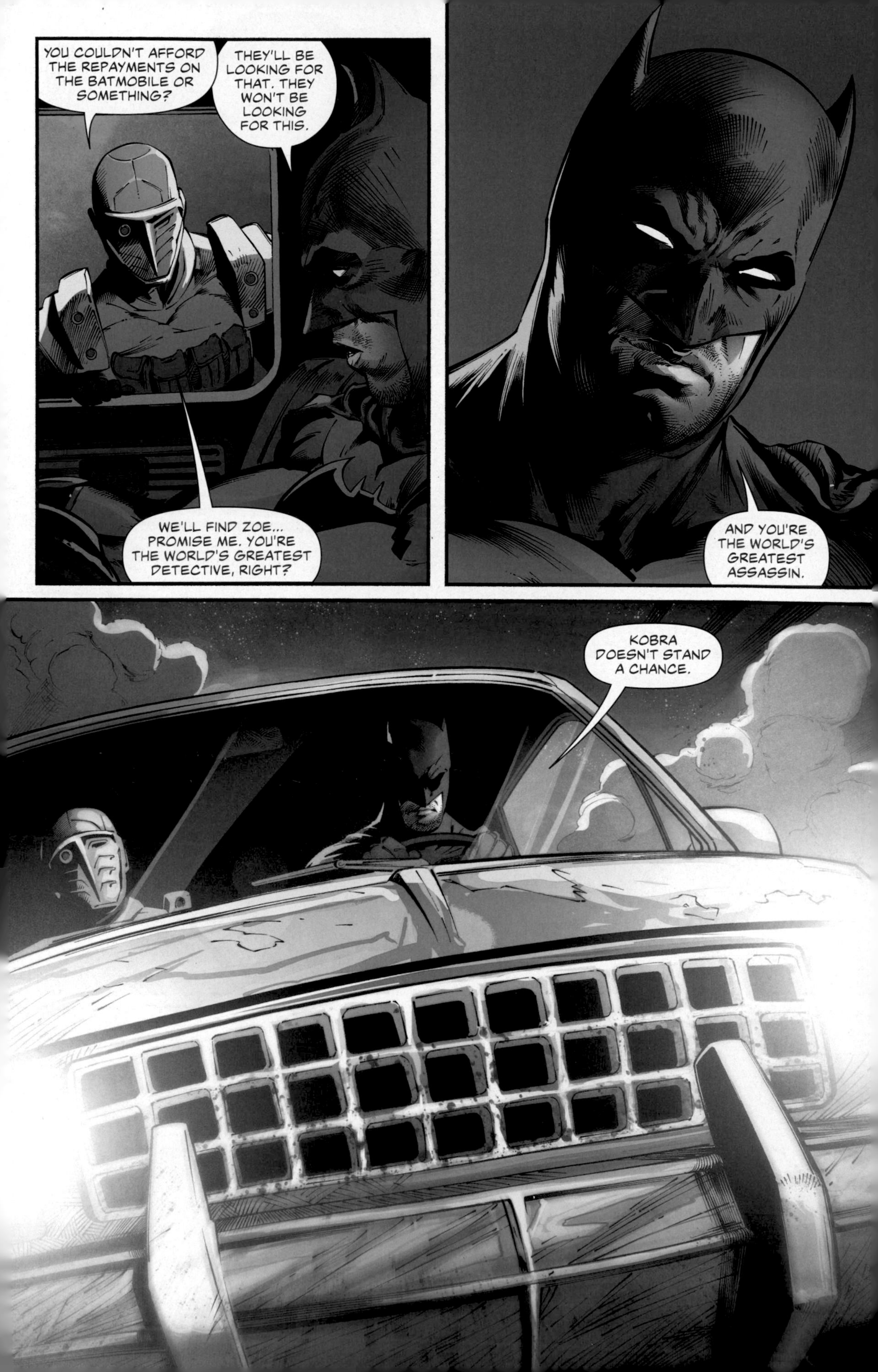
YOU COULDN'T AFFORD THE REPAYMENTS ON THE BATMOBILE OR SOMETHING?
THEY'LL BE LOOKING FOR THAT. THEY WON'T BE LOOKING FOR THIS.
WE'LL FIND ZOE... PROMISE ME. YOU'RE THE WORLD'S GREATEST DETECTIVE, RIGHT?
AND YOU'RE THE WORLD'S GREATEST ASSASSIN.
KOBRA DOESN'T STAND A CHANCE.

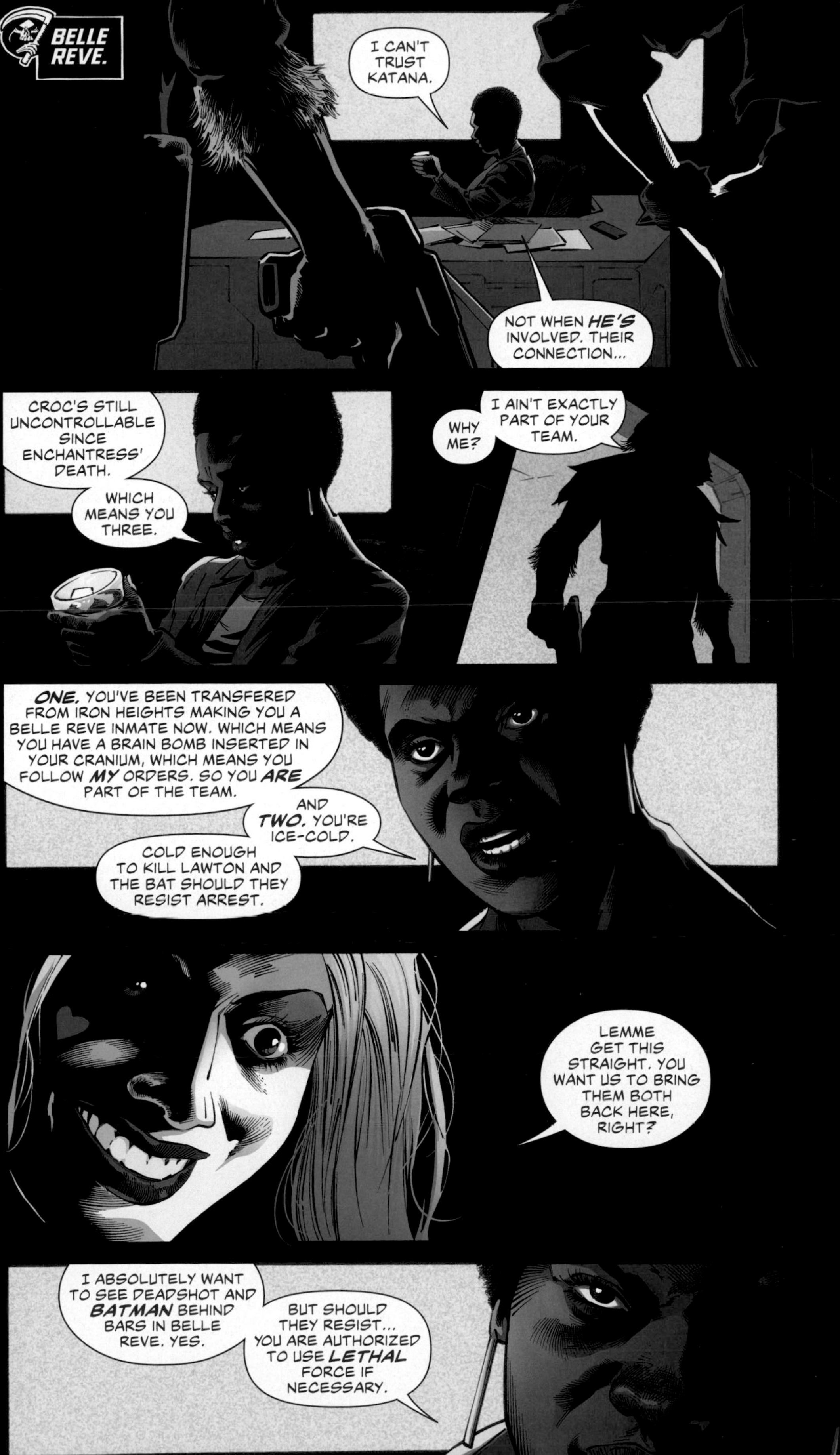
BELLE REVE.
I CAN'T TRUST KATANA.
NOT WHEN HE'S INVOLVED. THEIR CONNECTION...
CROC'S STILL UNCONTROLLABLE SINCE ENCHANTRESS' DEATH.
WHICH MEANS YOU THREE.
WHY ME?
I AIN'T EXACTLY PART OF YOUR TEAM.
ONE. YOU'VE BEEN TRANSFERED FROM IRON HEIGHTS MAKING YOU A BELLE REVE INMATE NOW. WHICH MEANS YOU HAVE A BRAIN BOMB INSERTED IN YOUR CRANIUM, WHICH MEANS YOU FOLLOW MY ORDERS. SO YOU ARE PART OF THE TEAM.
AND TWO. YOU'RE ICE-COLD.
COLD ENOUGH TO KILL LAWTON AND THE BAT SHOULD THEY RESIST ARREST.
LEMME GET THIS STRAIGHT. YOU WANT US TO BRING THEM BOTH BACK HERE, RIGHT?
I ABSOLUTELY WANT TO SEE DEADSHOT AND BATMAN BEHIND BARS IN BELLE REVE. YES.
BUT SHOULD THEY RESIST... YOU ARE AUTHORIZED TO USE LETHAL FORCE IF NECESSARY.

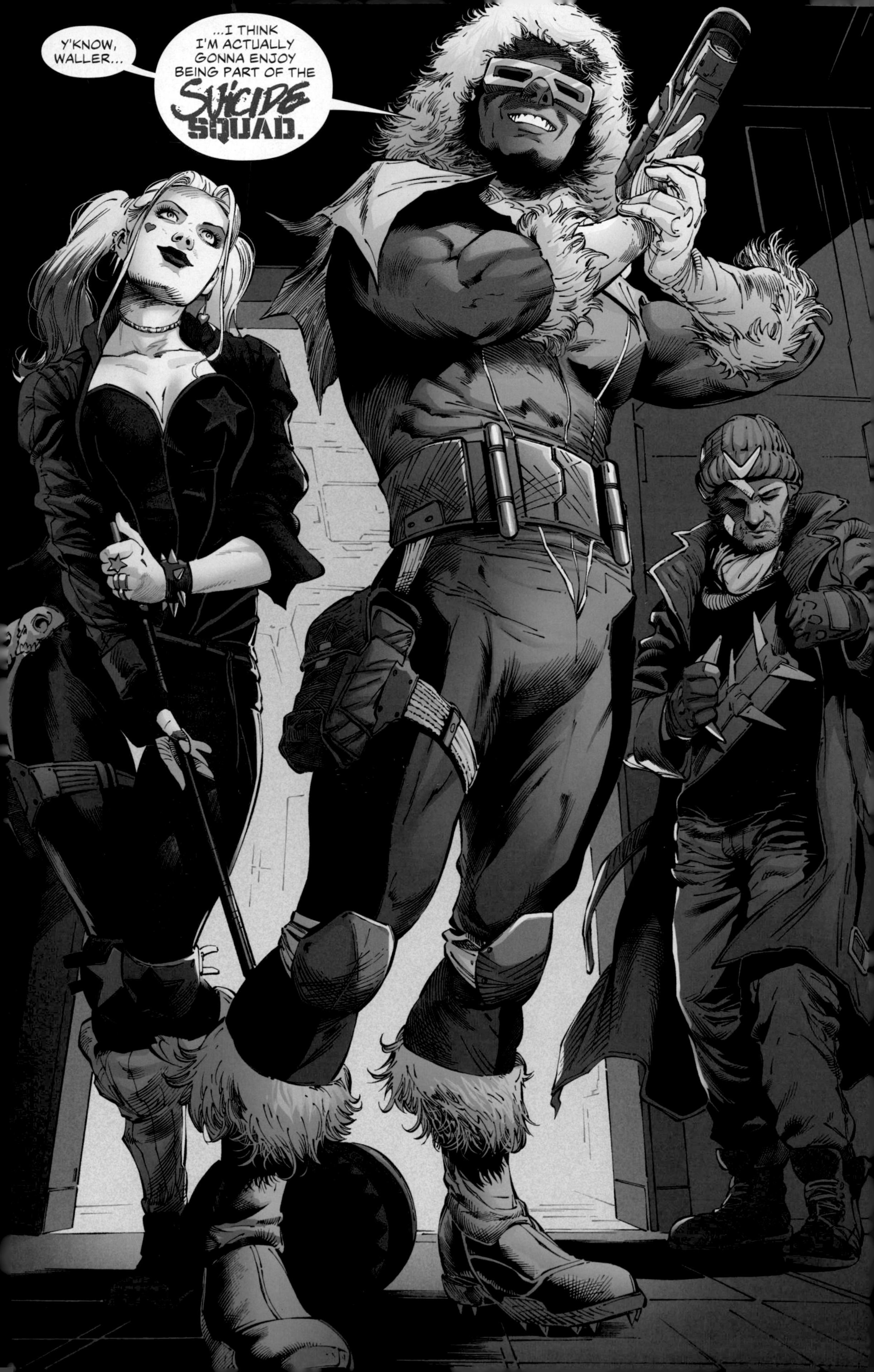
Y'KNOW, WALLER...
...I THINK I'M ACTUALLY GONNA ENJOY BEING PART OF THE
SUICIDE SQUAD.

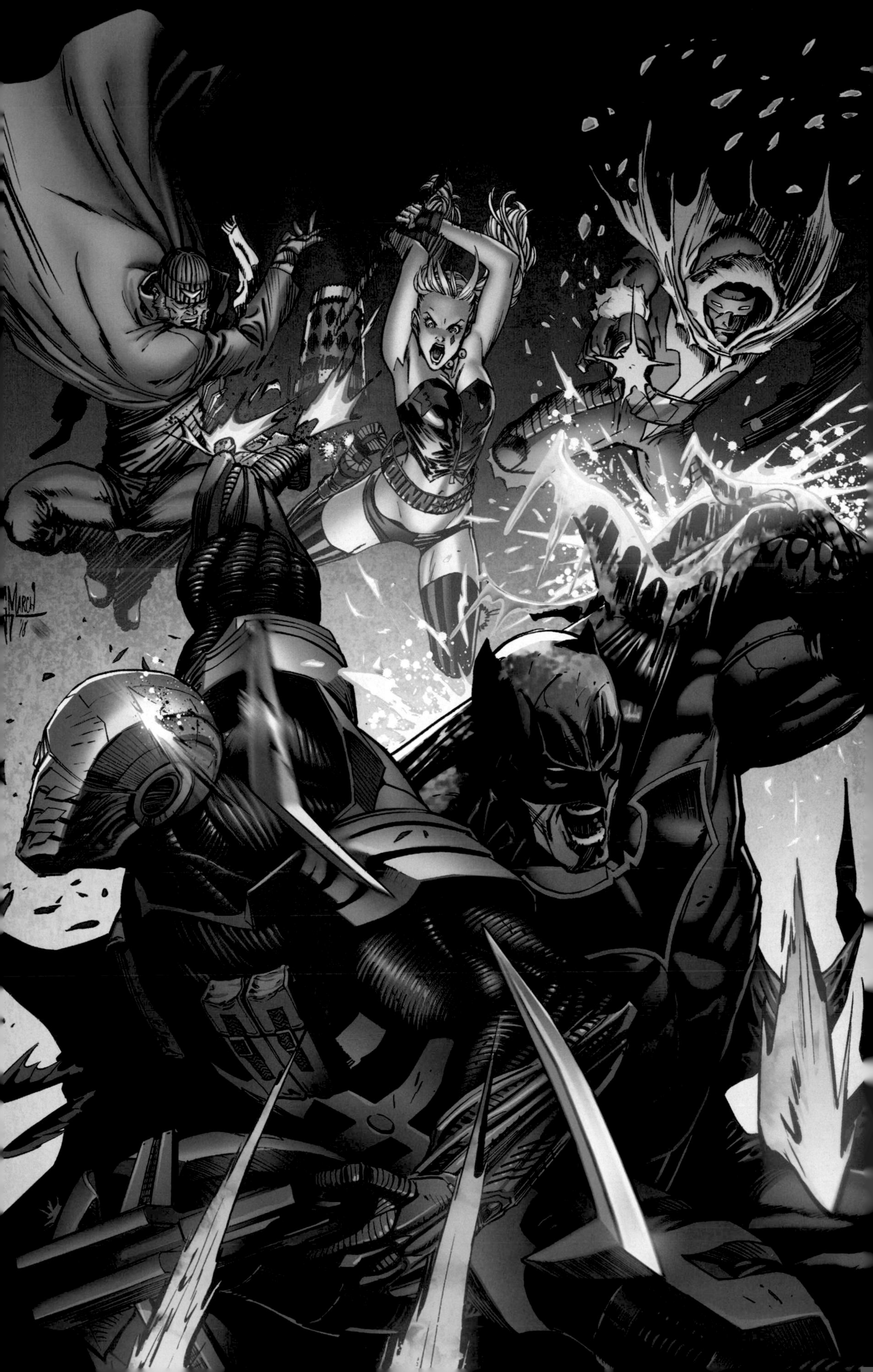

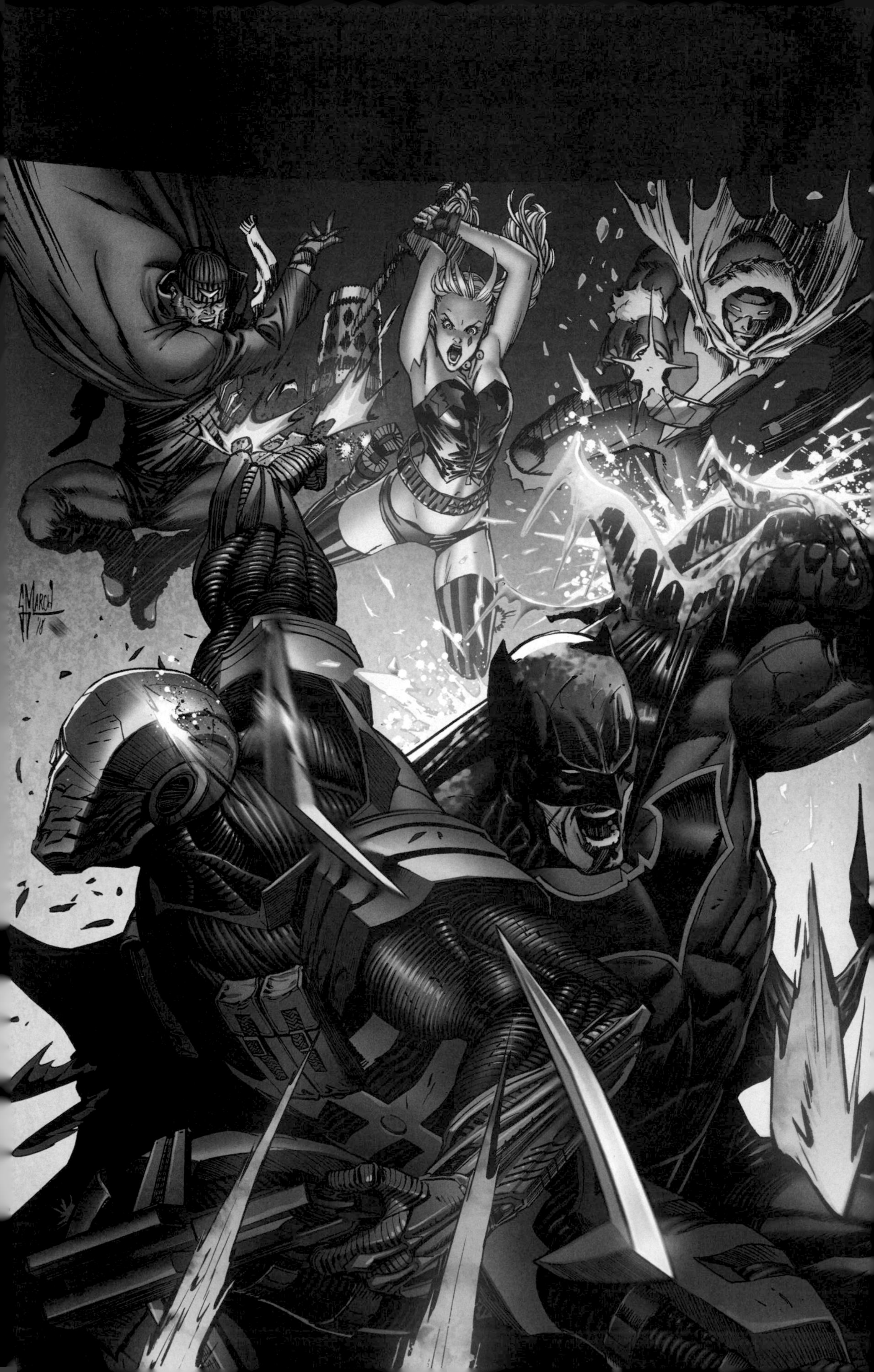

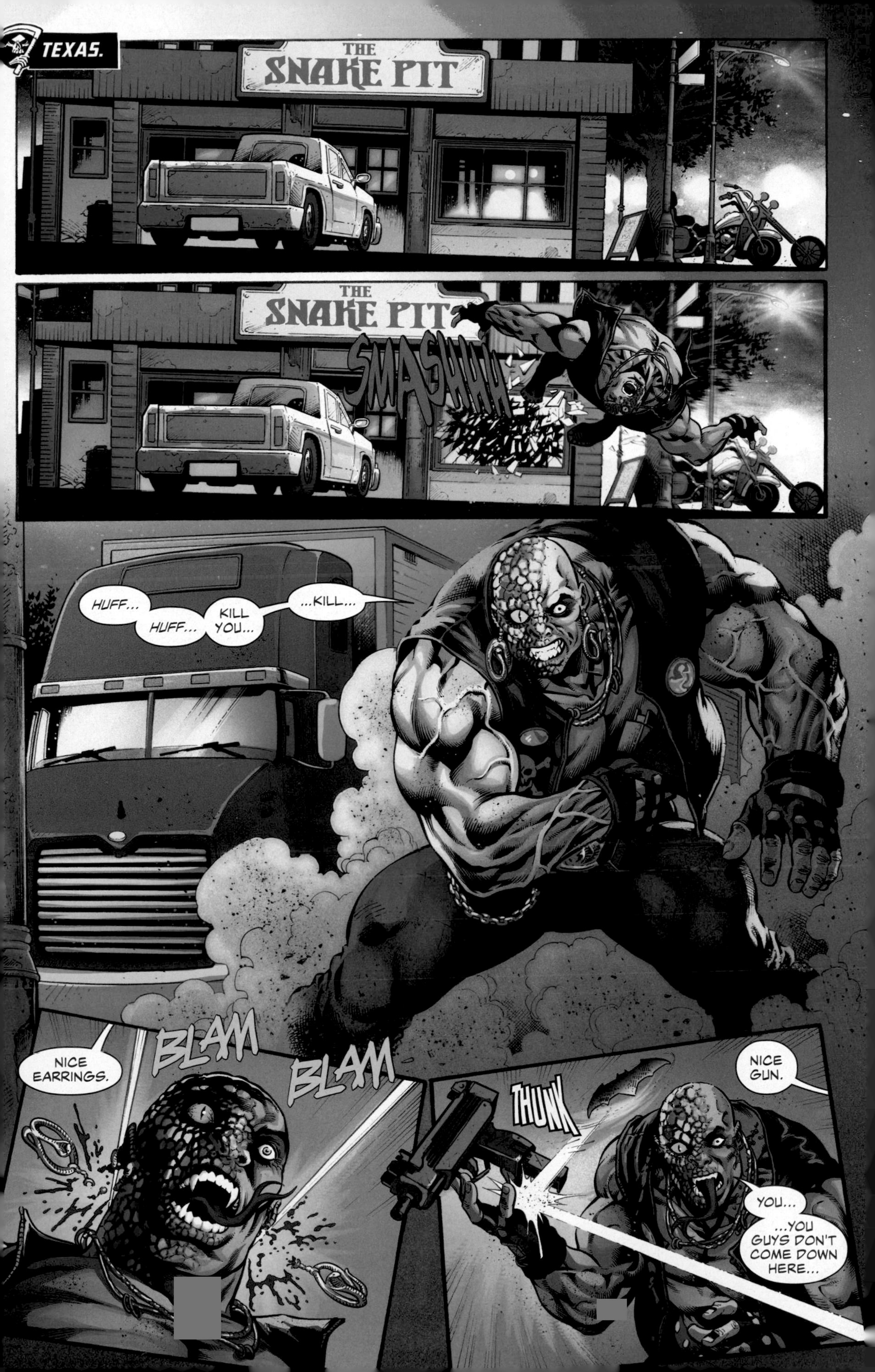
TEXAS.
THE SNAKE PIT
THE SNAKE PIT
SMASHHH
HUFF...
HUFF...
KILL YOU...
...KILL...
NICE EARRINGS.
BLAM
BLAM
THUNK
NICE GUN.
YOU...
...YOU GUYS DON'T COME DOWN HERE...

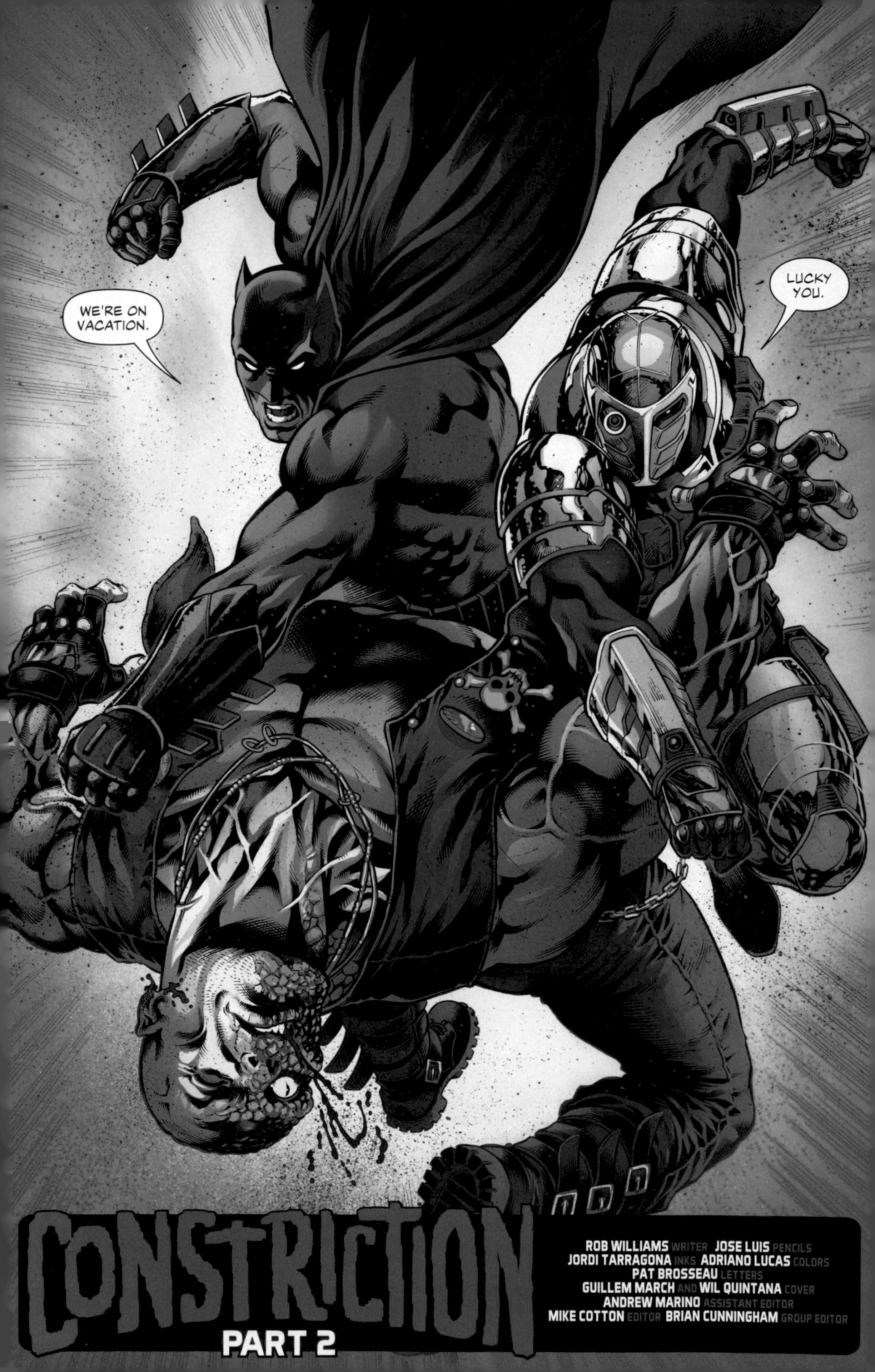
WE'RE ON VACATION.
LUCKY YOU.
CONSTRICTION
PART 2
ROB WILLIAMS WRITER JOSE LUIS PENCILS
JORDI TARRAGONA INKS ADRIANO LUCAS COLORS
PAT BROSSEAU LETTERS
GUILLEM MARCH AND WIL QUINTANA COVER
ANDREW MARINO ASSISTANT EDITOR
MIKE COTTON EDITOR BRIAN CUNNINGHAM GROUP EDITOR

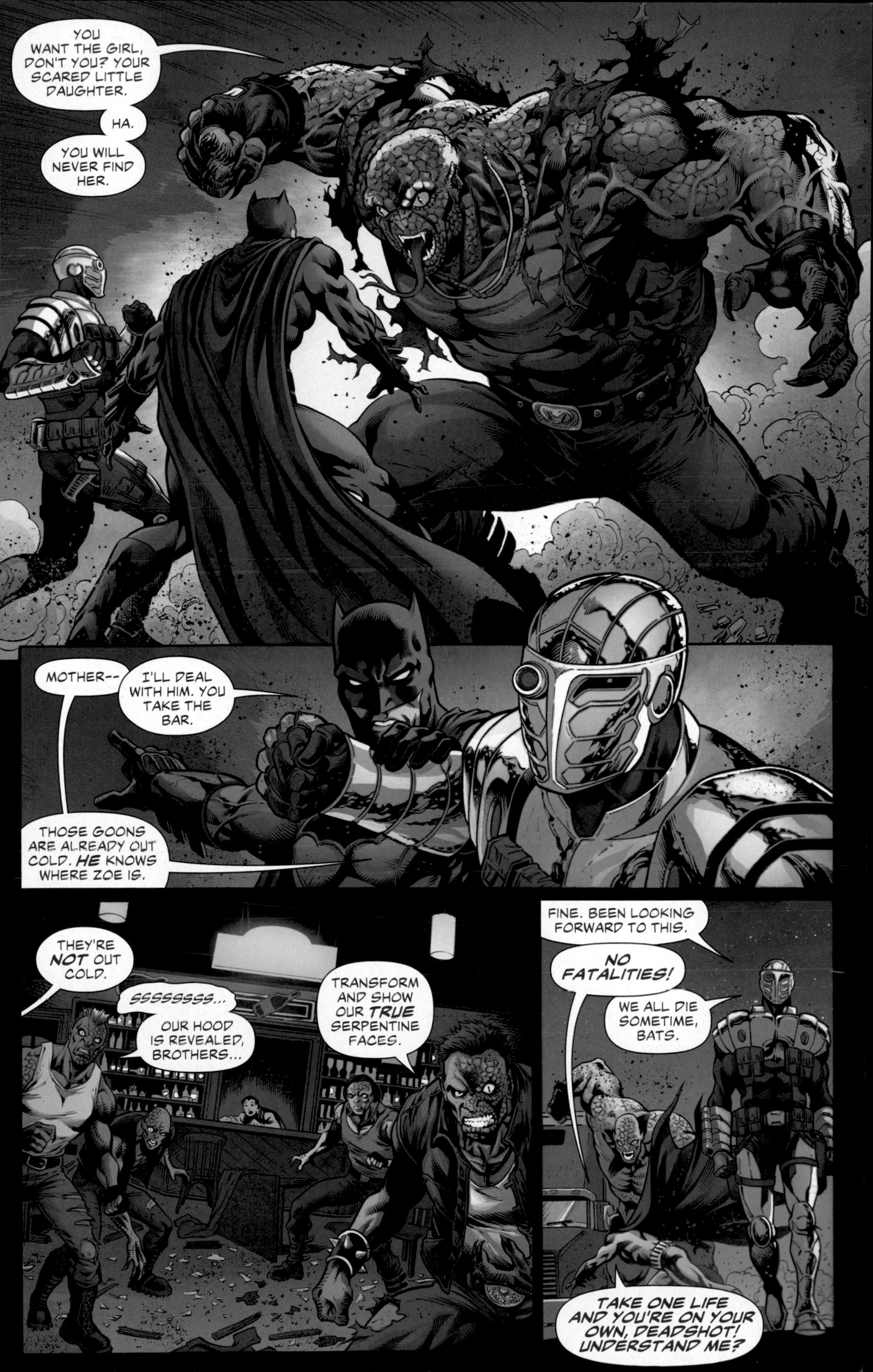
YOU WANT THE GIRL, DON'T YOU? YOUR SCARED LITTLE DAUGHTER.
HA.
YOU WILL NEVER FIND HER.
MOTHER--
I'LL DEAL WITH HIM. YOU TAKE THE BAR.
THOSE GOONS ARE ALREADY OUT COLD. **HE** KNOWS WHERE ZOE IS.
THEY'RE **NOT** OUT COLD.
SSSSSSSS...
OUR HOOD IS REVEALED, BROTHERS...
TRANSFORM AND SHOW OUR **TRUE** SERPENTINE FACES.
FINE. BEEN LOOKING FORWARD TO THIS.
NO FATALITIES!
WE ALL DIE SOMETIME, BATS.
TAKE ONE LIFE AND YOU'RE ON YOUR OWN, DEADSHOT! UNDERSTAND ME?

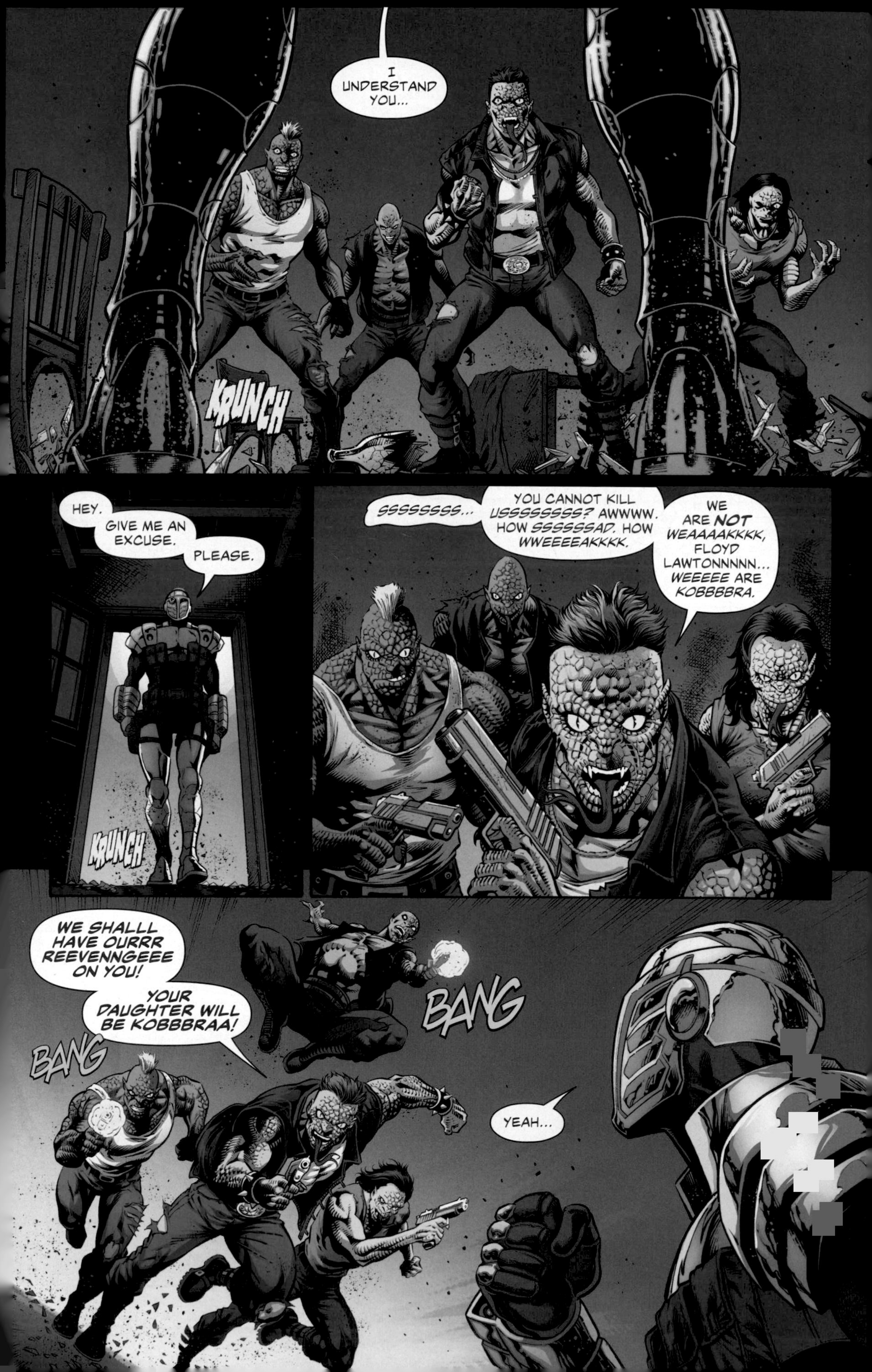
I UNDERSTAND YOU...
KRUNCH
HEY.
GIVE ME AN EXCUSE.
PLEASE.
KRUNCH
SSSSSSSS...
YOU CANNOT KILL USSSSSSSS? AWWWW. HOW SSSSSSAD. HOW WWEEEEAKKKK.
WE ARE NOT WEAAAAKKKK, FLOYD LAWTONNNNN... WEEEEE ARE KOBBBBRA.
WE SHALLL HAVE OURRR REEVENNGEEE ON YOU!
YOUR DAUGHTER WILL BE KOBBBRAA!
BANG
BANG
YEAH...

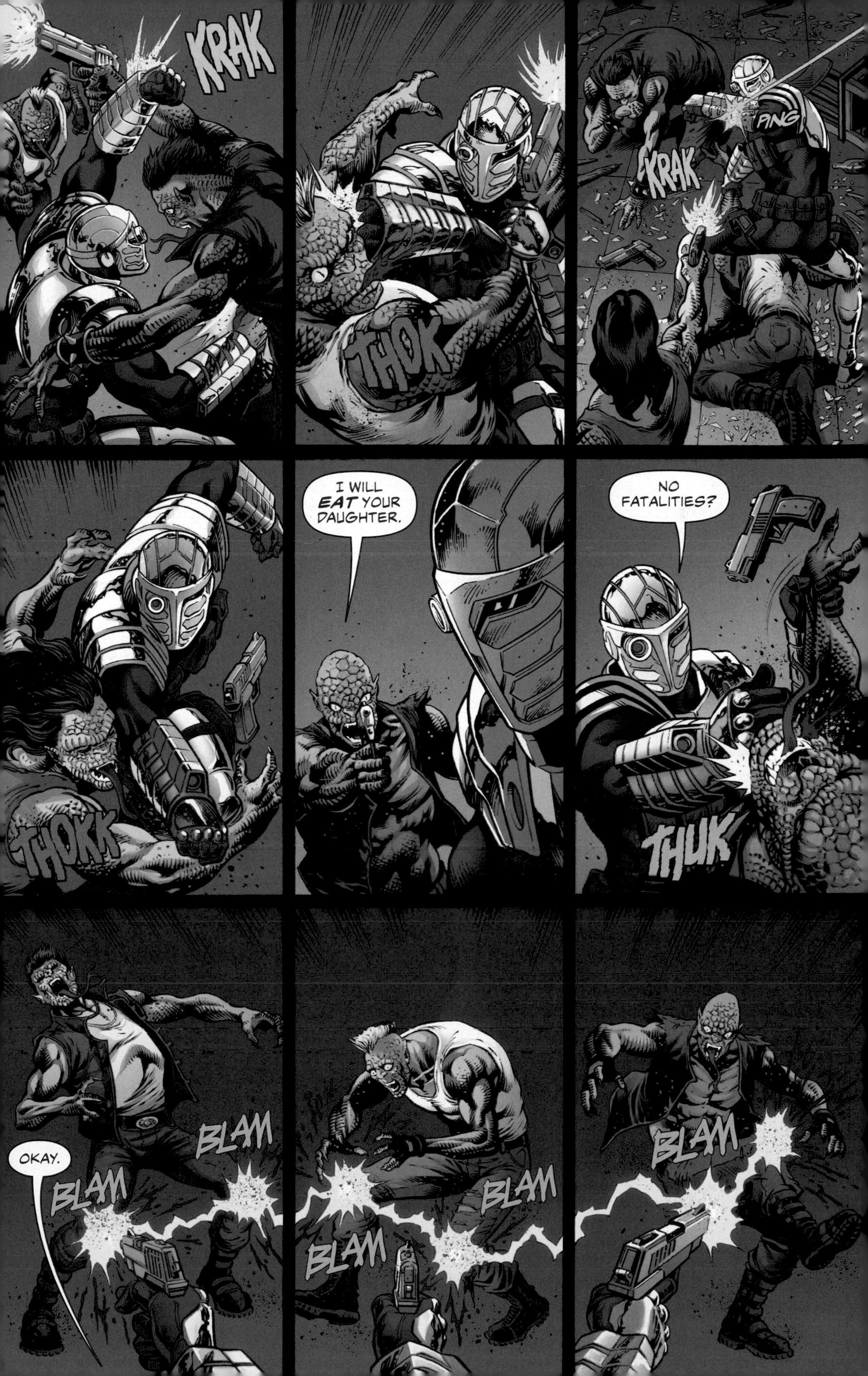
KRAK
THOK
KRAK
PING
THOKK
I WILL EAT YOUR DAUGHTER.
NO FATALITIES?
THUK
OKAY.
BLAM
BLAM
BLAM
BLAM
BLAM

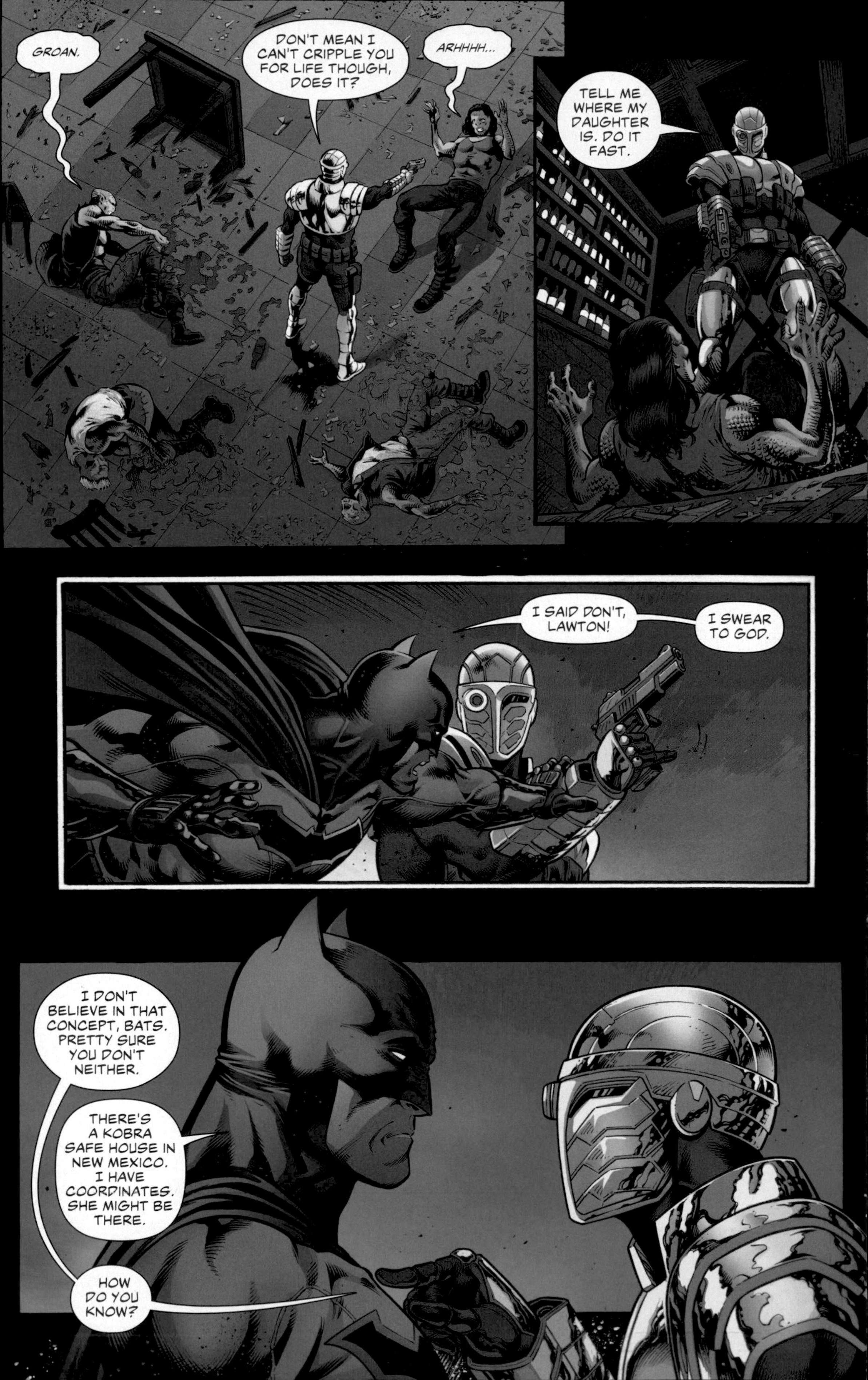
GROAN.
DON'T MEAN I CAN'T CRIPPLE YOU FOR LIFE THOUGH, DOES IT?
ARHHHH...
TELL ME WHERE MY DAUGHTER IS. DO IT FAST.
I SAID DON'T, LAWTON!
I SWEAR TO GOD.
I DON'T BELIEVE IN THAT CONCEPT, BATS. PRETTY SURE YOU DON'T NEITHER.
THERE'S A KOBRA SAFE HOUSE IN NEW MEXICO. I HAVE COORDINATES. SHE MIGHT BE THERE.
HOW DO YOU KNOW?

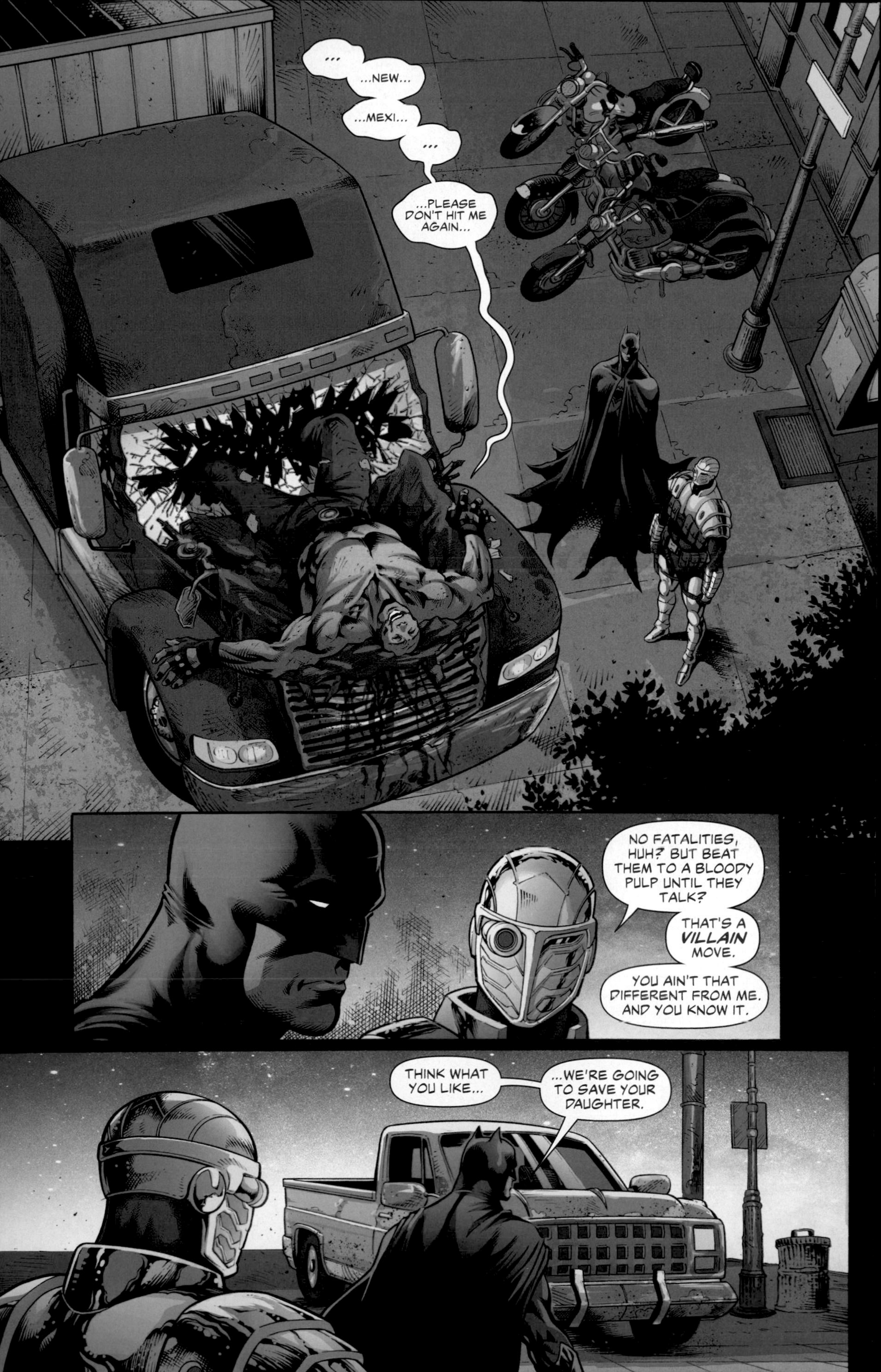
...
...NEW...
...MEXI...
...
...PLEASE DON'T HIT ME AGAIN...
NO FATALITIES, HUH? BUT BEAT THEM TO A BLOODY PULP UNTIL THEY TALK?
THAT'S A VILLAIN MOVE.
YOU AIN'T THAT DIFFERENT FROM ME. AND YOU KNOW IT.
THINK WHAT YOU LIKE...
...WE'RE GOING TO SAVE YOUR DAUGHTER.

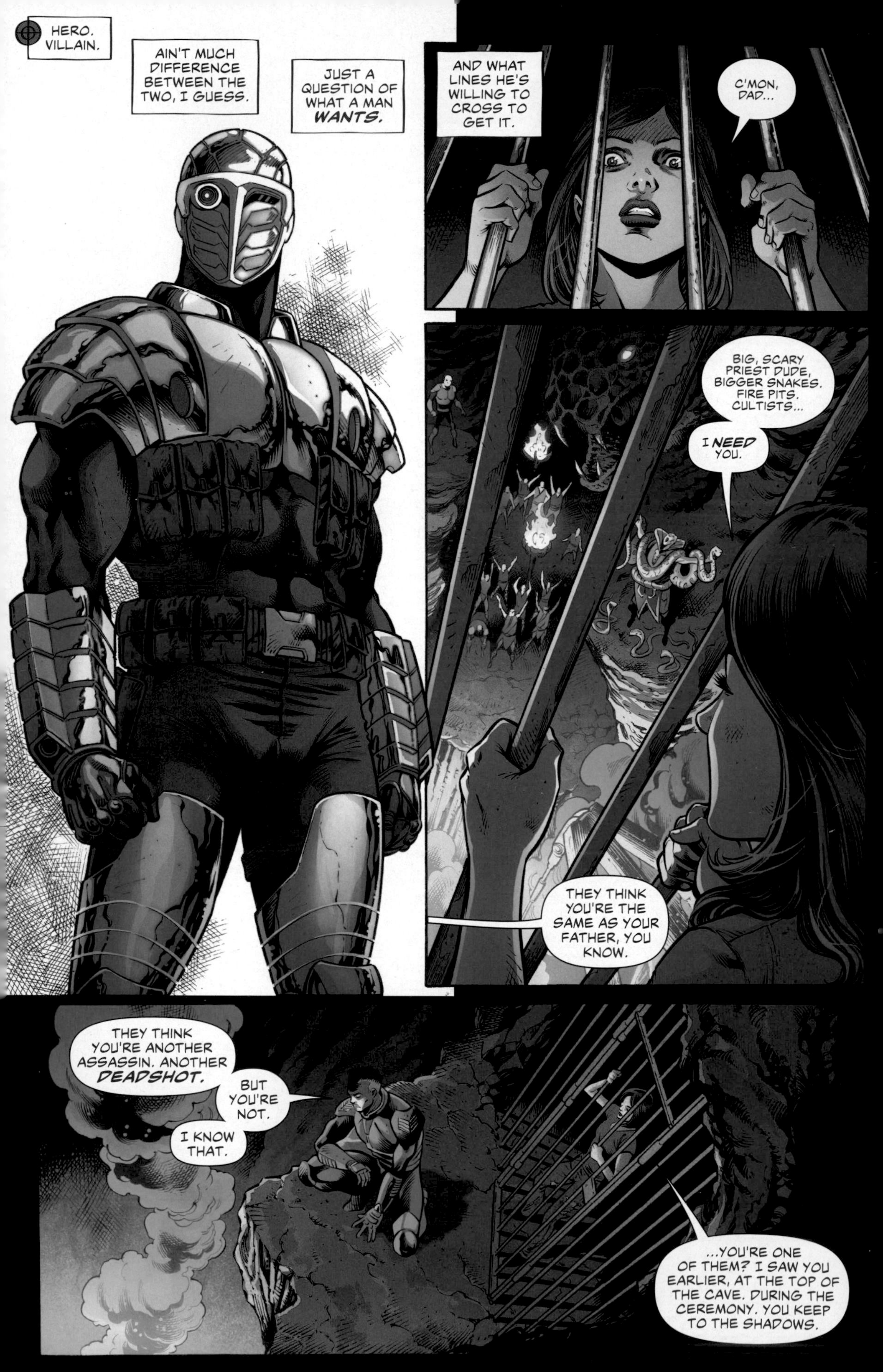
HERO. VILLAIN.
AIN'T MUCH DIFFERENCE BETWEEN THE TWO, I GUESS.
JUST A QUESTION OF WHAT A MAN WANTS.
AND WHAT LINES HE'S WILLING TO CROSS TO GET IT.
C'MON, DAD...
BIG, SCARY PRIEST DUDE, BIGGER SNAKES. FIRE PITS. CULTISTS...
I NEED YOU.
THEY THINK YOU'RE THE SAME AS YOUR FATHER, YOU KNOW.
THEY THINK YOU'RE ANOTHER ASSASSIN. ANOTHER DEADSHOT.
BUT YOU'RE NOT.
I KNOW THAT.
...YOU'RE ONE OF THEM? I SAW YOU EARLIER, AT THE TOP OF THE CAVE. DURING THE CEREMONY. YOU KEEP TO THE SHADOWS.

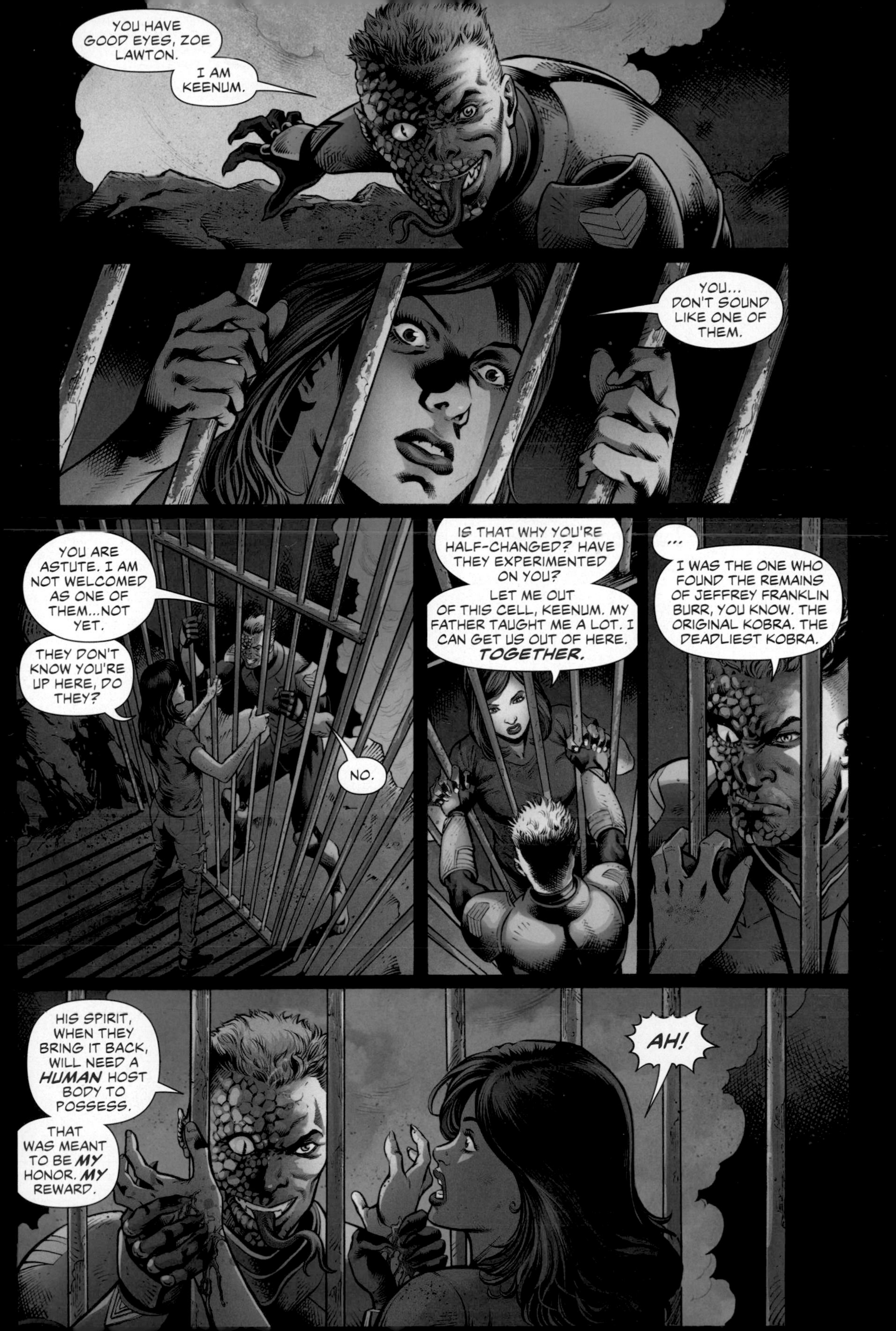
YOU HAVE GOOD EYES, ZOE LAWTON.
I AM KEENUM.
YOU... DON'T SOUND LIKE ONE OF THEM.
YOU ARE ASTUTE. I AM NOT WELCOMED AS ONE OF THEM...NOT YET.
THEY DON'T KNOW YOU'RE UP HERE, DO THEY?
NO.
IS THAT WHY YOU'RE HALF-CHANGED? HAVE THEY EXPERIMENTED ON YOU?
LET ME OUT OF THIS CELL, KEENUM. MY FATHER TAUGHT ME A LOT. I CAN GET US OUT OF HERE. TOGETHER.
...
I WAS THE ONE WHO FOUND THE REMAINS OF JEFFREY FRANKLIN BURR, YOU KNOW. THE ORIGINAL KOBRA. THE DEADLIEST KOBRA.
HIS SPIRIT, WHEN THEY BRING IT BACK, WILL NEED A HUMAN HOST BODY TO POSSESS.
THAT WAS MEANT TO BE MY HONOR. MY REWARD.
AH!

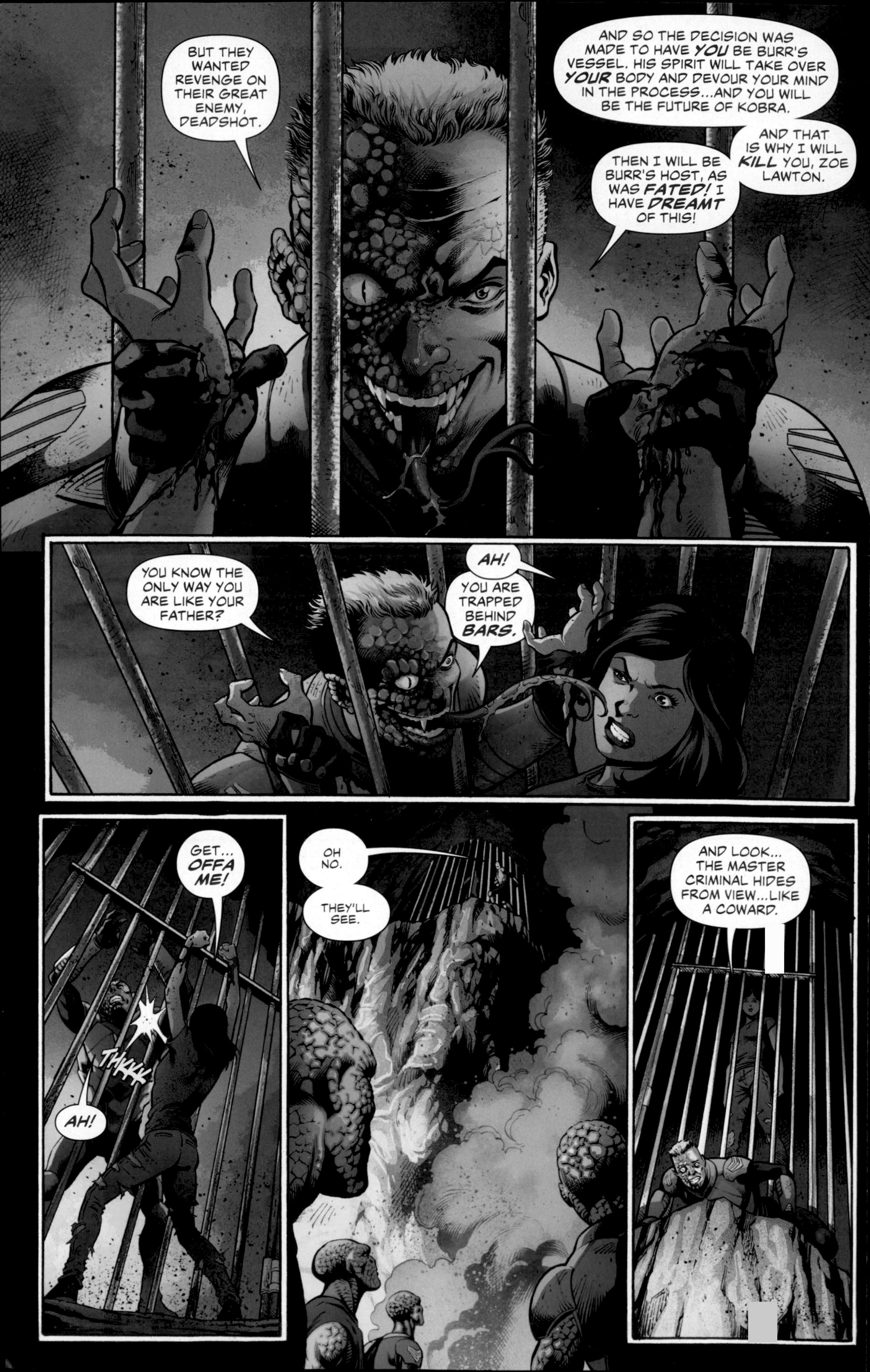
BUT THEY WANTED REVENGE ON THEIR GREAT ENEMY, DEADSHOT.
AND SO THE DECISION WAS MADE TO HAVE *YOU* BE BURR'S VESSEL. HIS SPIRIT WILL TAKE OVER *YOUR* BODY AND DEVOUR YOUR MIND IN THE PROCESS...AND YOU WILL BE THE FUTURE OF KOBRA.
THEN I WILL BE BURR'S HOST, AS WAS *FATED!* I HAVE *DREAMT* OF THIS!
AND THAT IS WHY I WILL *KILL* YOU, ZOE LAWTON.
YOU KNOW THE ONLY WAY YOU ARE LIKE YOUR FATHER?
AH!
YOU ARE TRAPPED BEHIND *BARS.*
GET... *OFFA ME!*
THKKK
AH!
OH NO.
THEY'LL SEE.
AND LOOK... THE MASTER CRIMINAL HIDES FROM VIEW...LIKE A COWARD.

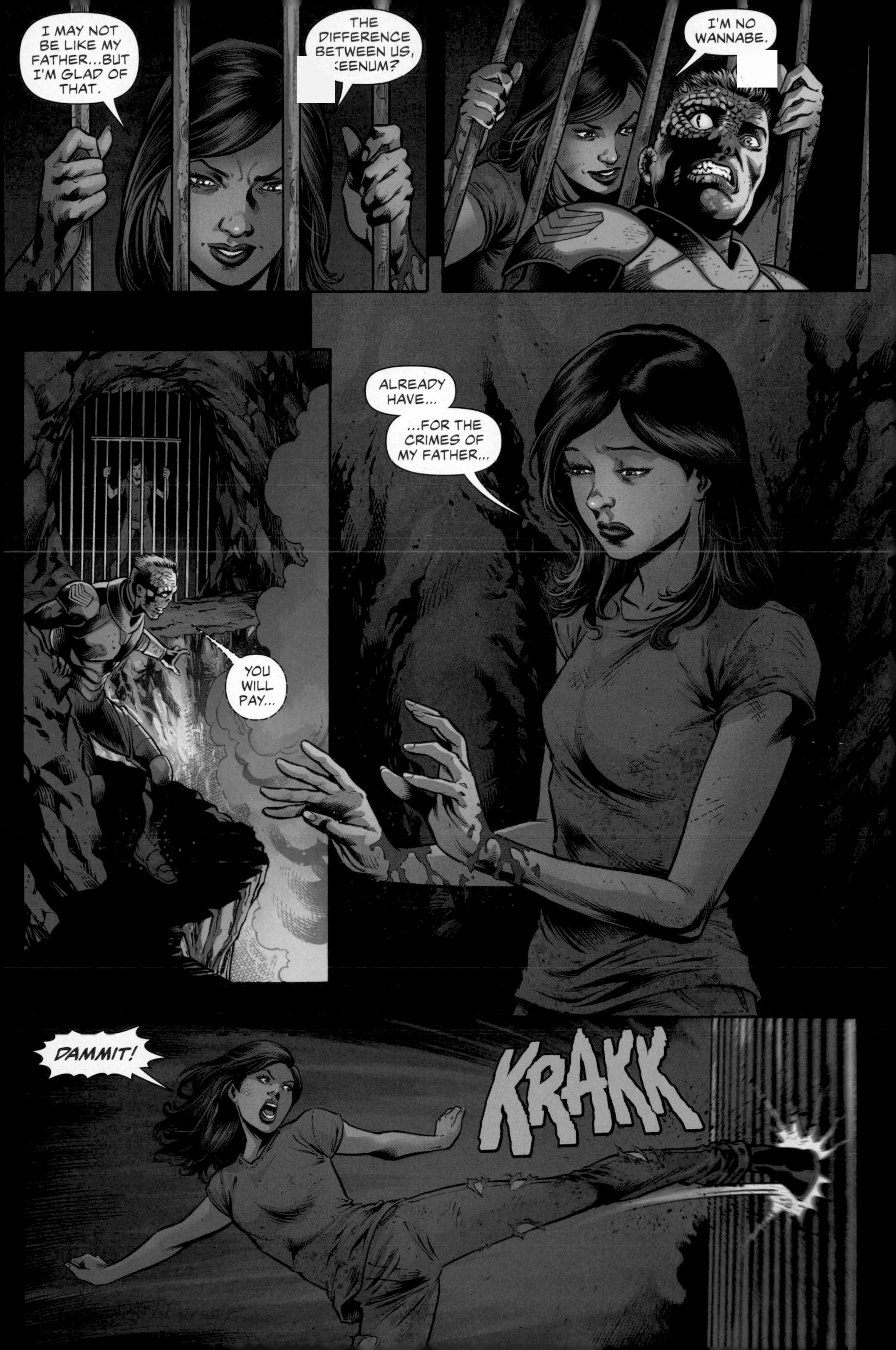
I MAY NOT BE LIKE MY FATHER...BUT I'M GLAD OF THAT.
THE DIFFERENCE BETWEEN US, EENUM?
I'M NO WANNABE.
ALREADY HAVE...
...FOR THE CRIMES OF MY FATHER...
YOU WILL PAY...
DAMMIT!
KRAKK

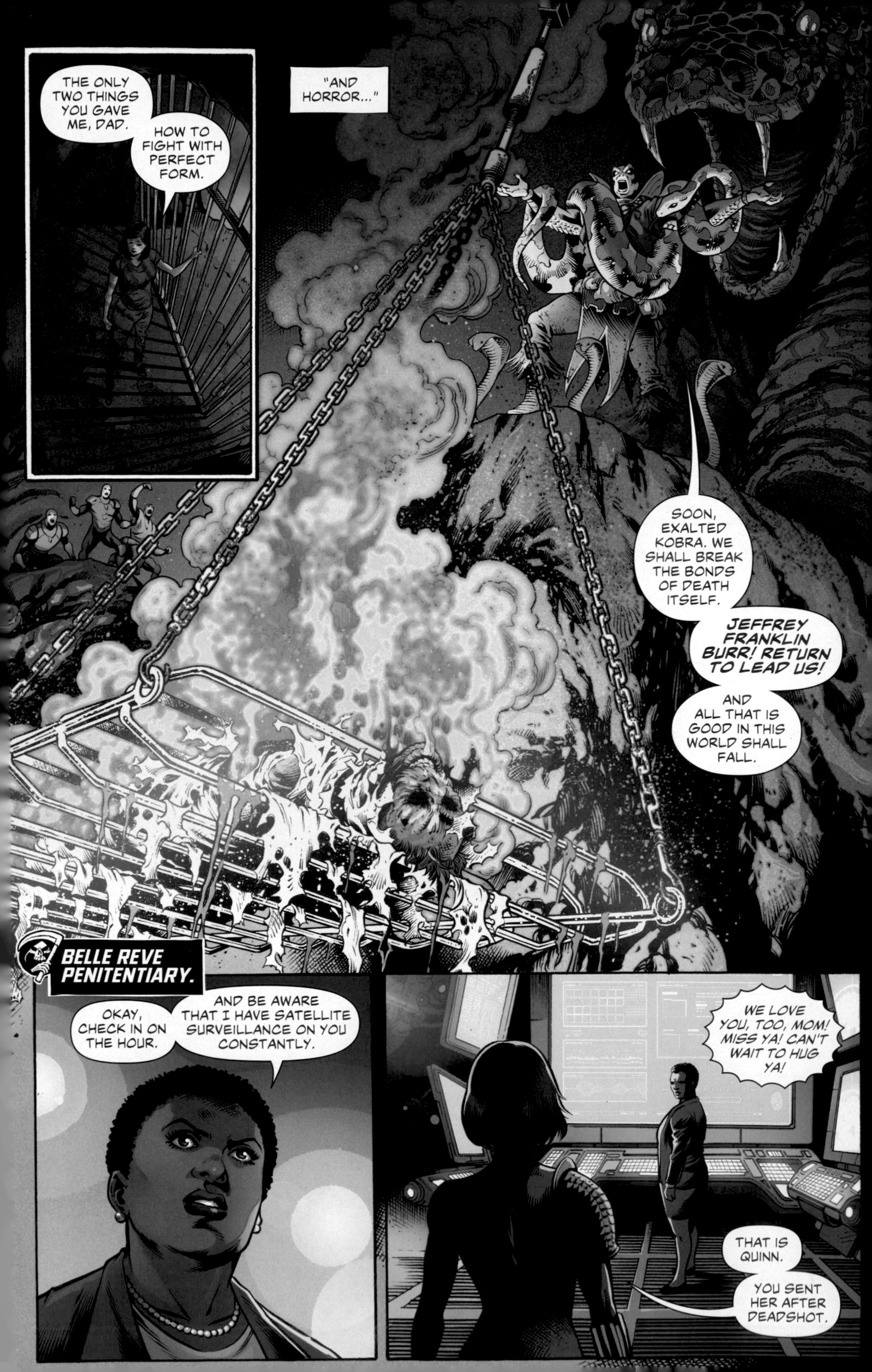
THE ONLY TWO THINGS YOU GAVE ME, DAD.
HOW TO FIGHT WITH PERFECT FORM.
"AND HORROR..."
SOON, EXALTED KOBRA. WE SHALL BREAK THE BONDS OF DEATH ITSELF.
JEFFREY FRANKLIN BURR! RETURN TO LEAD US!
AND ALL THAT IS GOOD IN THIS WORLD SHALL FALL.
BELLE REVE PENITENTIARY.
OKAY, CHECK IN ON THE HOUR.
AND BE AWARE THAT I HAVE SATELLITE SURVEILLANCE ON YOU CONSTANTLY.
WE LOVE YOU, TOO, MOM! MISS YA! CAN'T WAIT TO HUG YA!
THAT IS QUINN.
YOU SENT HER AFTER DEADSHOT.

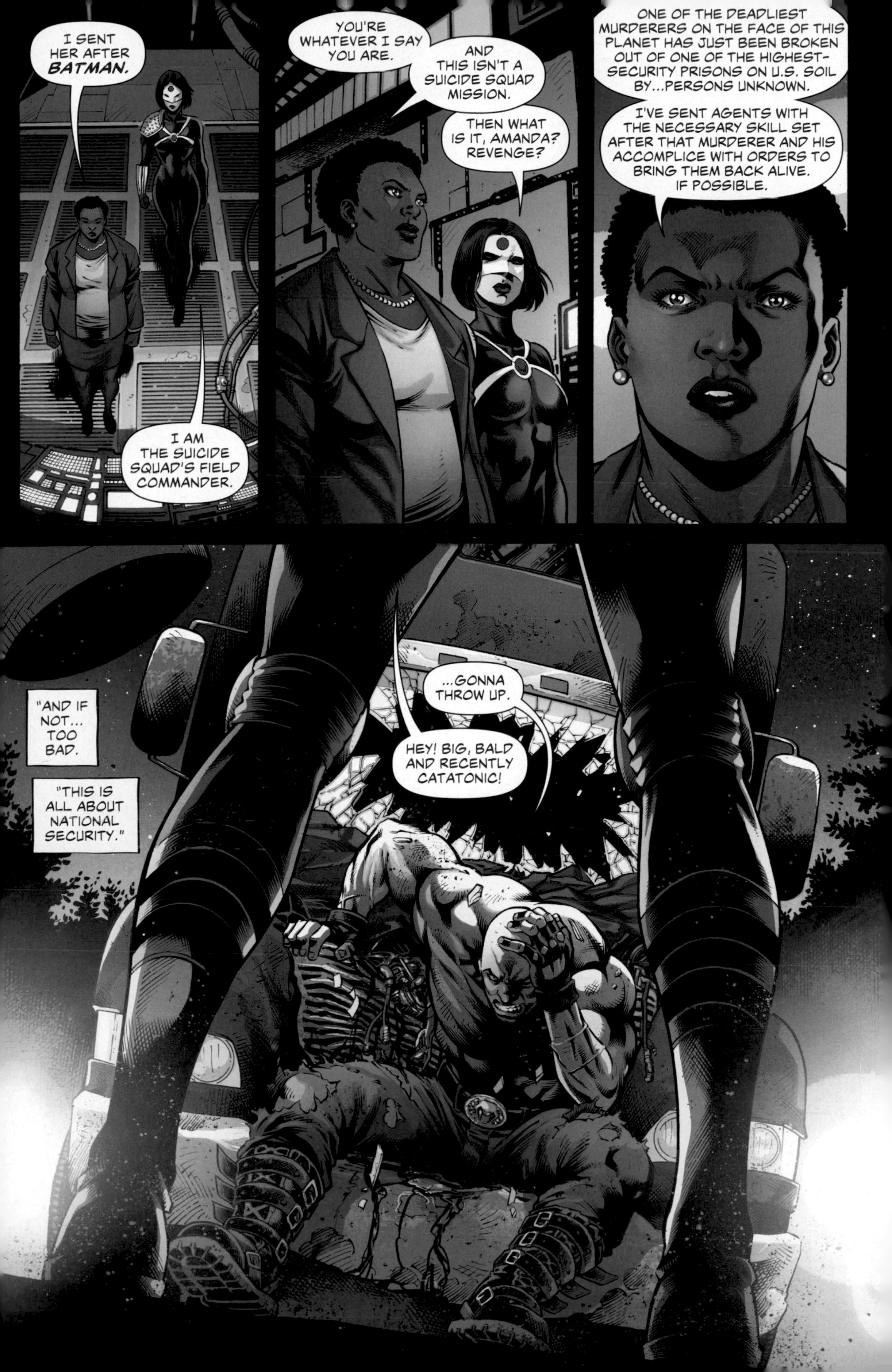
I SENT HER AFTER **BATMAN.**
I AM THE SUICIDE SQUAD'S FIELD COMMANDER.
YOU'RE WHATEVER I SAY YOU ARE.
AND THIS ISN'T A SUICIDE SQUAD MISSION.
THEN WHAT IS IT, AMANDA? REVENGE?
ONE OF THE DEADLIEST MURDERERS ON THE FACE OF THIS PLANET HAS JUST BEEN BROKEN OUT OF ONE OF THE HIGHEST-SECURITY PRISONS ON U.S. SOIL BY...PERSONS UNKNOWN.
I'VE SENT AGENTS WITH THE NECESSARY SKILL SET AFTER THAT MURDERER AND HIS ACCOMPLICE WITH ORDERS TO BRING THEM BACK ALIVE. IF POSSIBLE.
"AND IF NOT... TOO BAD.
"THIS IS ALL ABOUT NATIONAL SECURITY."
...GONNA THROW UP.
HEY! BIG, BALD AND RECENTLY CATATONIC!

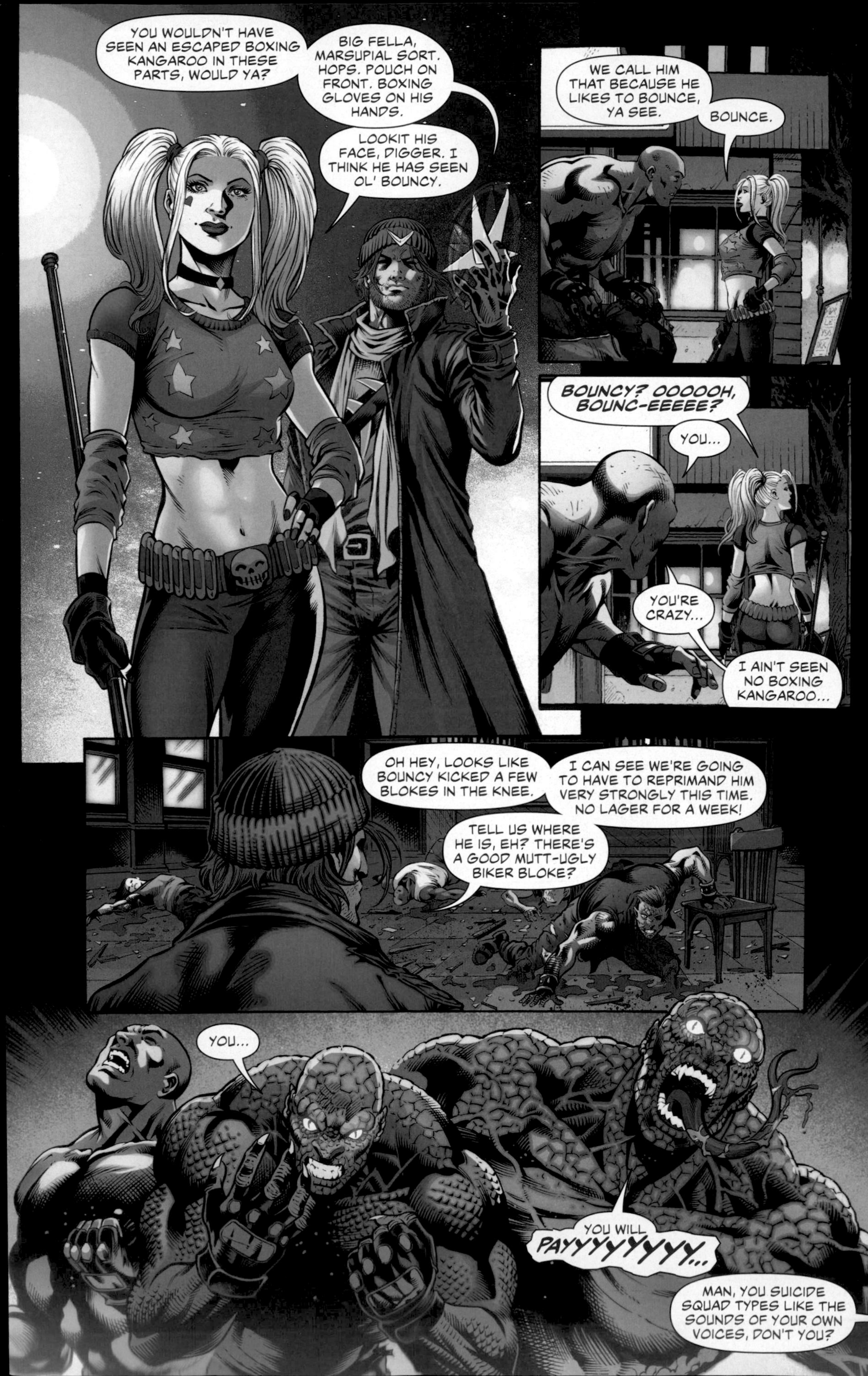
YOU WOULDN'T HAVE SEEN AN ESCAPED BOXING KANGAROO IN THESE PARTS, WOULD YA?
BIG FELLA, MARSUPIAL SORT. HOPS. POUCH ON FRONT. BOXING GLOVES ON HIS HANDS.
LOOKIT HIS FACE, DIGGER. I THINK HE HAS SEEN OL' BOUNCY.
WE CALL HIM THAT BECAUSE HE LIKES TO BOUNCE, YA SEE.
BOUNCE.
BOUNCY? OOOOOH, BOUNC-EEEEE?
YOU...
YOU'RE CRAZY...
I AIN'T SEEN NO BOXING KANGAROO...
OH HEY, LOOKS LIKE BOUNCY KICKED A FEW BLOKES IN THE KNEE.
I CAN SEE WE'RE GOING TO HAVE TO REPRIMAND HIM VERY STRONGLY THIS TIME. NO LAGER FOR A WEEK!
TELL US WHERE HE IS, EH? THERE'S A GOOD MUTT-UGLY BIKER BLOKE?
YOU...
YOU WILL PAYYYYYYY...
MAN, YOU SUICIDE SQUAD TYPES LIKE THE SOUNDS OF YOUR OWN VOICES, DON'T YOU?

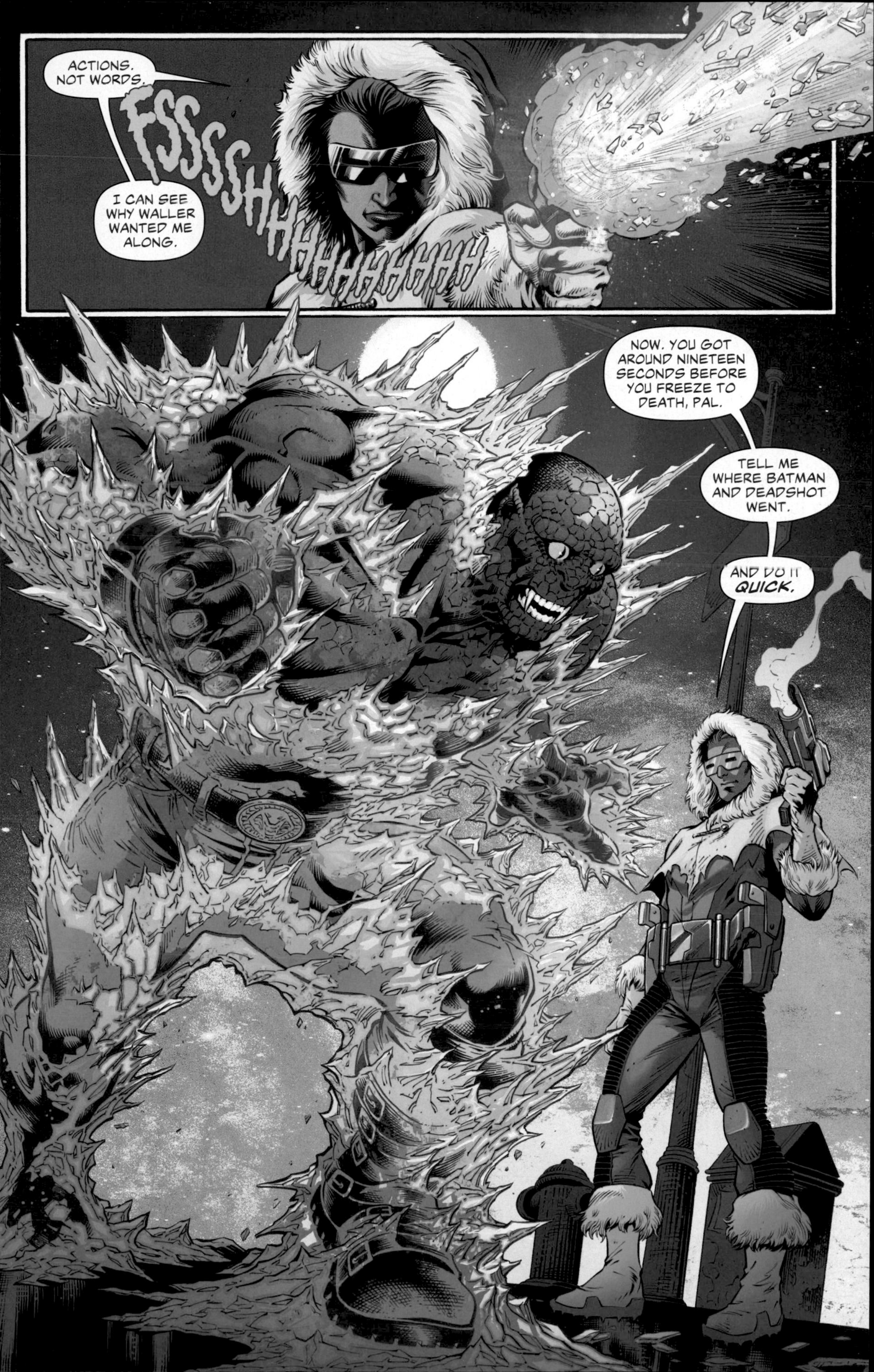
ACTIONS. NOT WORDS.
FSSSSHHHHHHHHHHHH
I CAN SEE WHY WALLER WANTED ME ALONG.
NOW. YOU GOT AROUND NINETEEN SECONDS BEFORE YOU FREEZE TO DEATH, PAL.
TELL ME WHERE BATMAN AND DEADSHOT WENT.
AND DO IT *QUICK.*

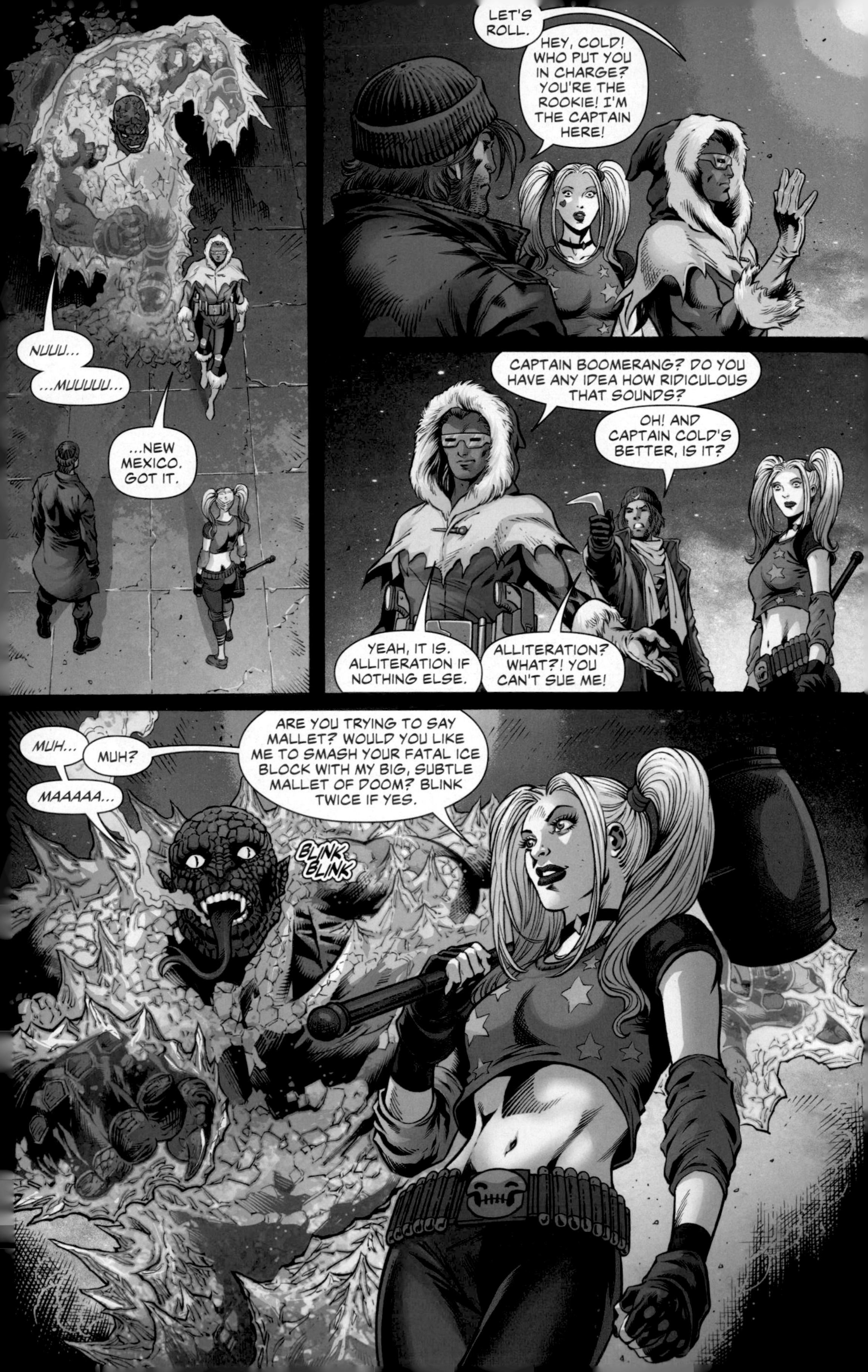
NUUU...
...MUUUUU...
...NEW MEXICO. GOT IT.
LET'S ROLL.
HEY, COLD! WHO PUT YOU IN CHARGE? YOU'RE THE ROOKIE! I'M THE CAPTAIN HERE!
CAPTAIN BOOMERANG? DO YOU HAVE ANY IDEA HOW RIDICULOUS THAT SOUNDS?
OH! AND CAPTAIN COLD'S BETTER, IS IT?
YEAH, IT IS. ALLITERATION IF NOTHING ELSE.
ALLITERATION? WHAT?! YOU CAN'T SUE ME!
MUH...
MUH?
MAAAAA...
ARE YOU TRYING TO SAY MALLET? WOULD YOU LIKE ME TO SMASH YOUR FATAL ICE BLOCK WITH MY BIG, SUBTLE MALLET OF DOOM? BLINK TWICE IF YES.
BLINK BLINK

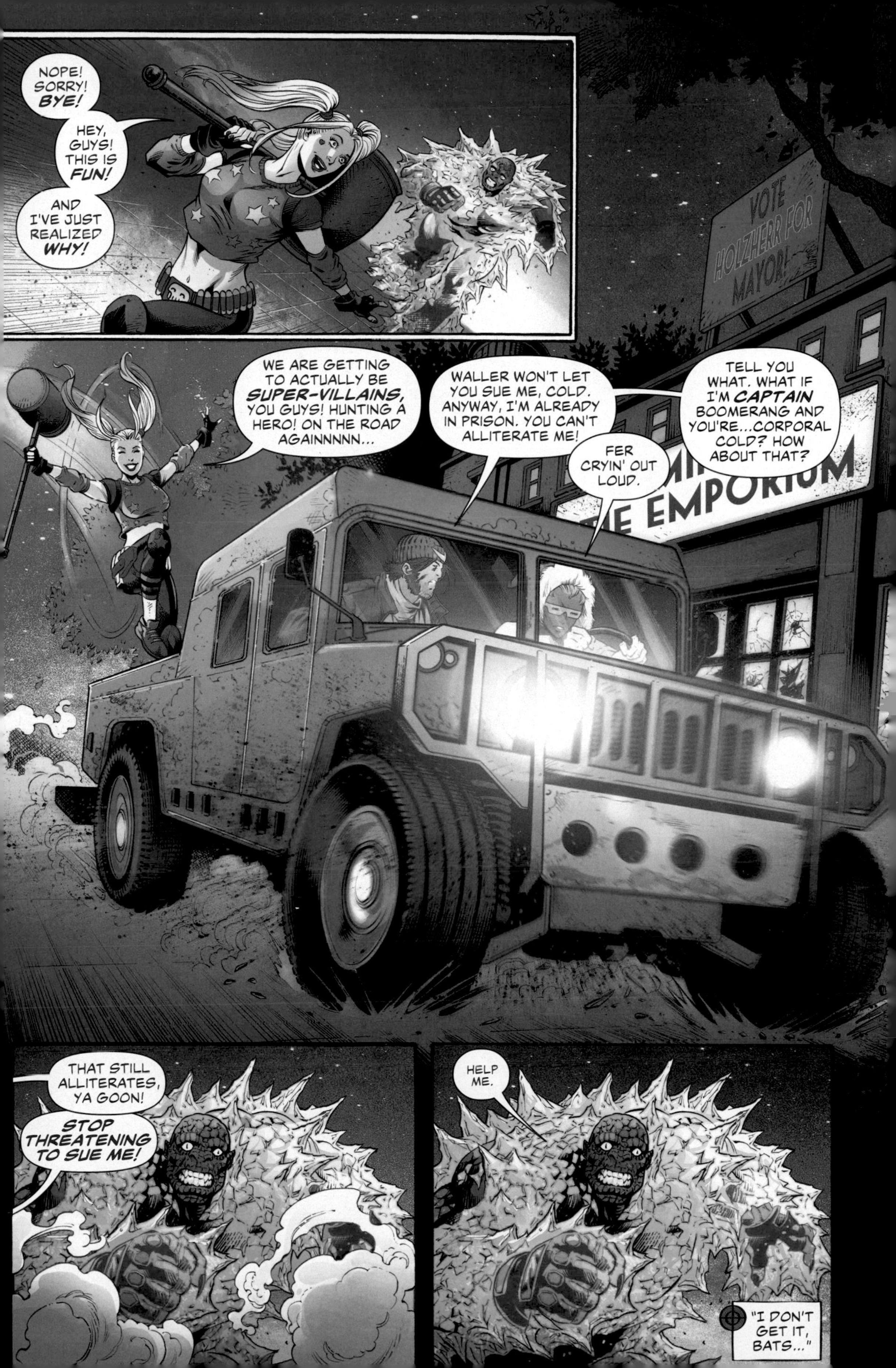
NOPE! SORRY! BYE!
HEY, GUYS! THIS IS FUN!
AND I'VE JUST REALIZED WHY!
VOTE HOLZHERR FOR MAYOR!
WE ARE GETTING TO ACTUALLY BE SUPER-VILLAINS, YOU GUYS! HUNTING A HERO! ON THE ROAD AGAINNNNN...
WALLER WON'T LET YOU SUE ME, COLD. ANYWAY, I'M ALREADY IN PRISON. YOU CAN'T ALLITERATE ME!
TELL YOU WHAT. WHAT IF I'M CAPTAIN BOOMERANG AND YOU'RE...CORPORAL COLD? HOW ABOUT THAT?
FER CRYIN' OUT LOUD.
EMPORIUM
THAT STILL ALLITERATES, YA GOON!
STOP THREATENING TO SUE ME!
HELP ME.
"I DON'T GET IT, BATS..."

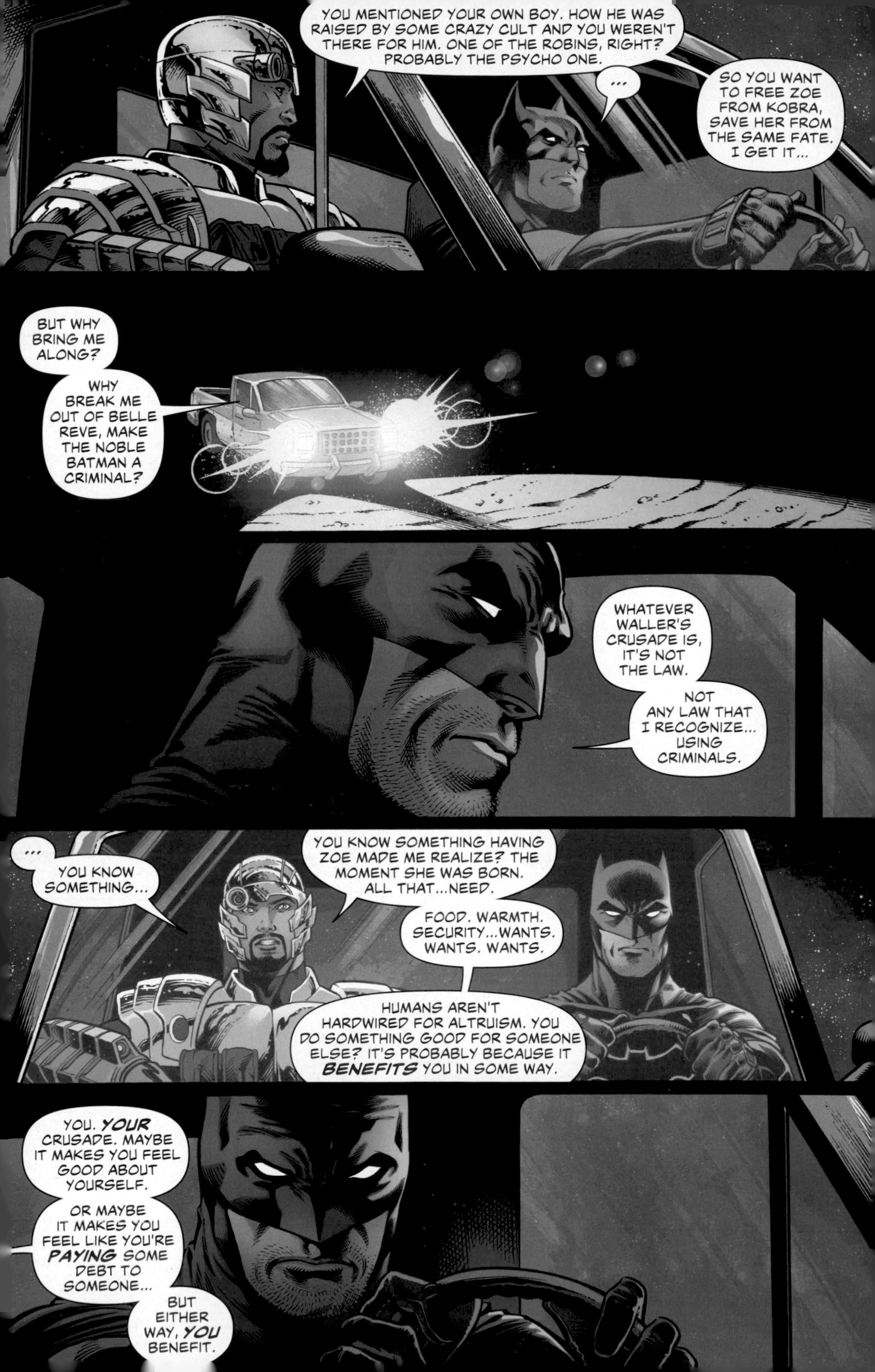
YOU MENTIONED YOUR OWN BOY. HOW HE WAS RAISED BY SOME CRAZY CULT AND YOU WEREN'T THERE FOR HIM. ONE OF THE ROBINS, RIGHT? PROBABLY THE PSYCHO ONE.
...
SO YOU WANT TO FREE ZOE FROM KOBRA, SAVE HER FROM THE SAME FATE. I GET IT...
BUT WHY BRING ME ALONG?
WHY BREAK ME OUT OF BELLE REVE, MAKE THE NOBLE BATMAN A CRIMINAL?
WHATEVER WALLER'S CRUSADE IS, IT'S NOT THE LAW.
NOT ANY LAW THAT I RECOGNIZE... USING CRIMINALS.
...
YOU KNOW SOMETHING...
YOU KNOW SOMETHING HAVING ZOE MADE ME REALIZE? THE MOMENT SHE WAS BORN. ALL THAT...NEED.
FOOD. WARMTH. SECURITY...WANTS. WANTS. WANTS.
HUMANS AREN'T HARDWIRED FOR ALTRUISM. YOU DO SOMETHING GOOD FOR SOMEONE ELSE? IT'S PROBABLY BECAUSE IT BENEFITS YOU IN SOME WAY.
YOU. YOUR CRUSADE. MAYBE IT MAKES YOU FEEL GOOD ABOUT YOURSELF.
OR MAYBE IT MAKES YOU FEEL LIKE YOU'RE PAYING SOME DEBT TO SOMEONE...
BUT EITHER WAY, YOU BENEFIT.

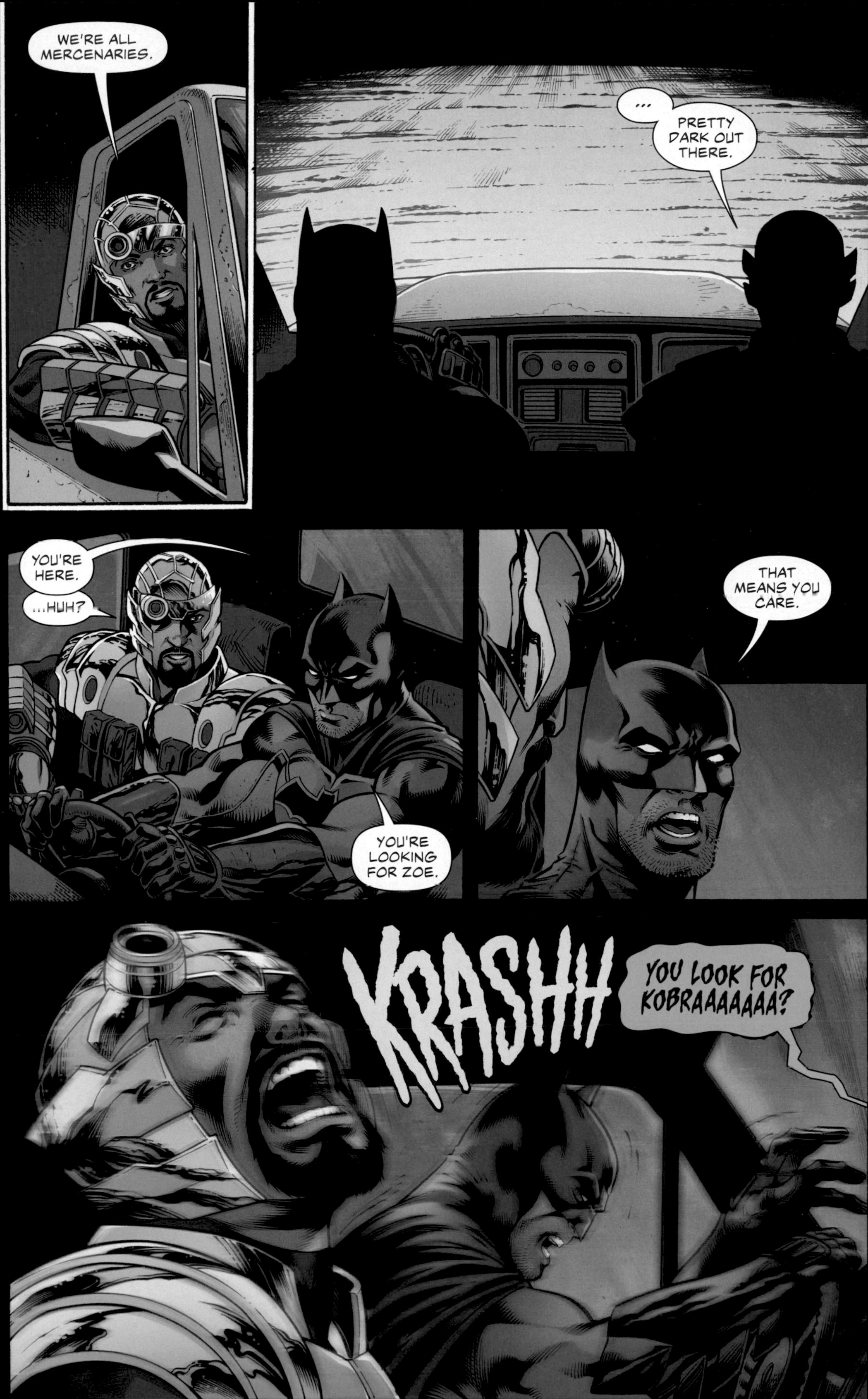
WE'RE ALL MERCENARIES.
...
PRETTY DARK OUT THERE.
YOU'RE HERE.
...HUH?
YOU'RE LOOKING FOR ZOE.
THAT MEANS YOU CARE.
KRASHH
YOU LOOK FOR KOBRAAAAAAA?

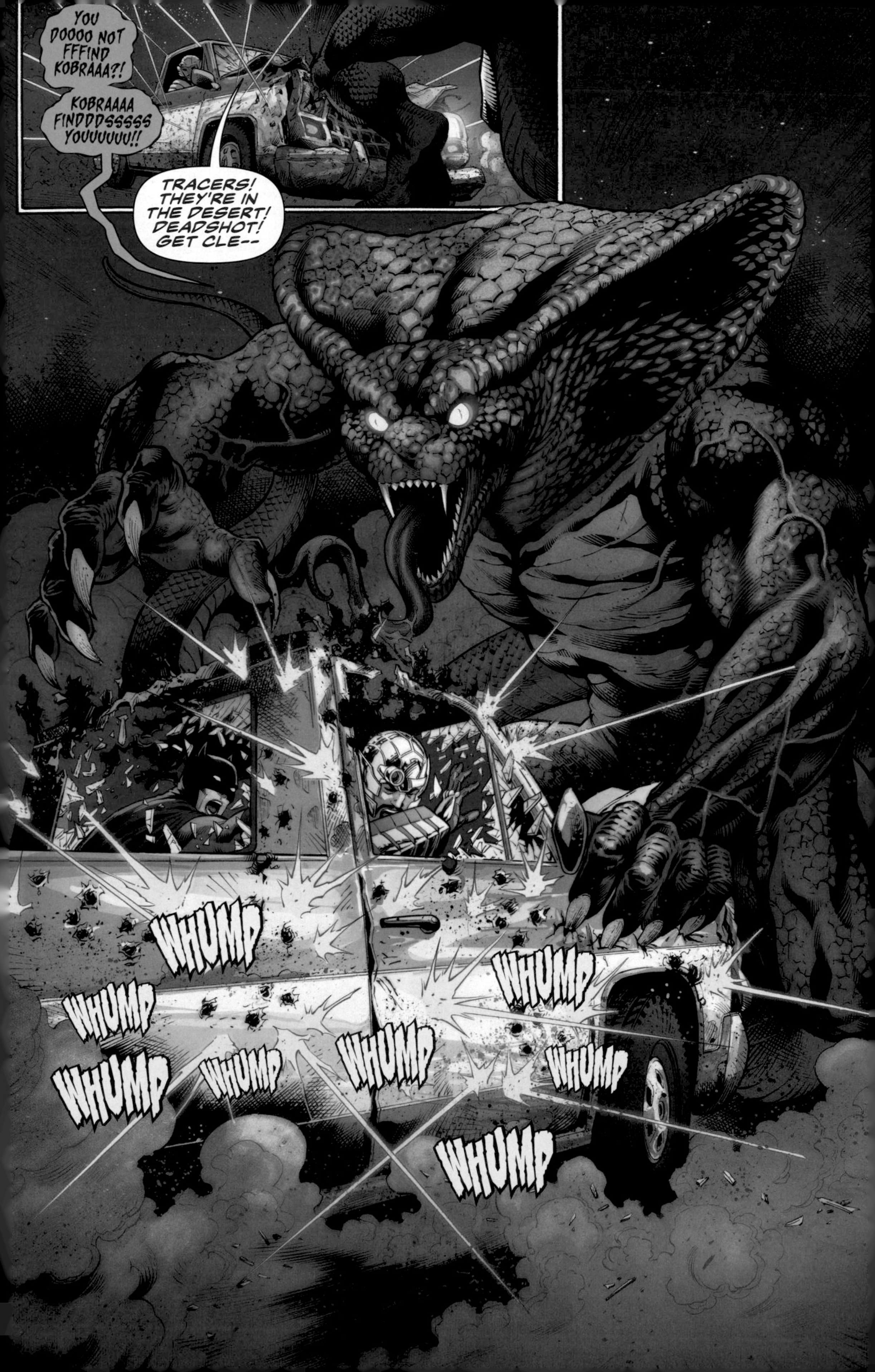

YOU DOOOO NOT FFFIND KOBRAAA?!
KOBRAAAA FINDDDSSSSS YOUUUUUU!!
TRACERS! THEY'RE IN THE DESERT! DEADSHOT! GET CLE--
WHUMP
WHUMP
WHUMP
WHUMP
WHUMP
WHUMP
WHUMP
WHUMP

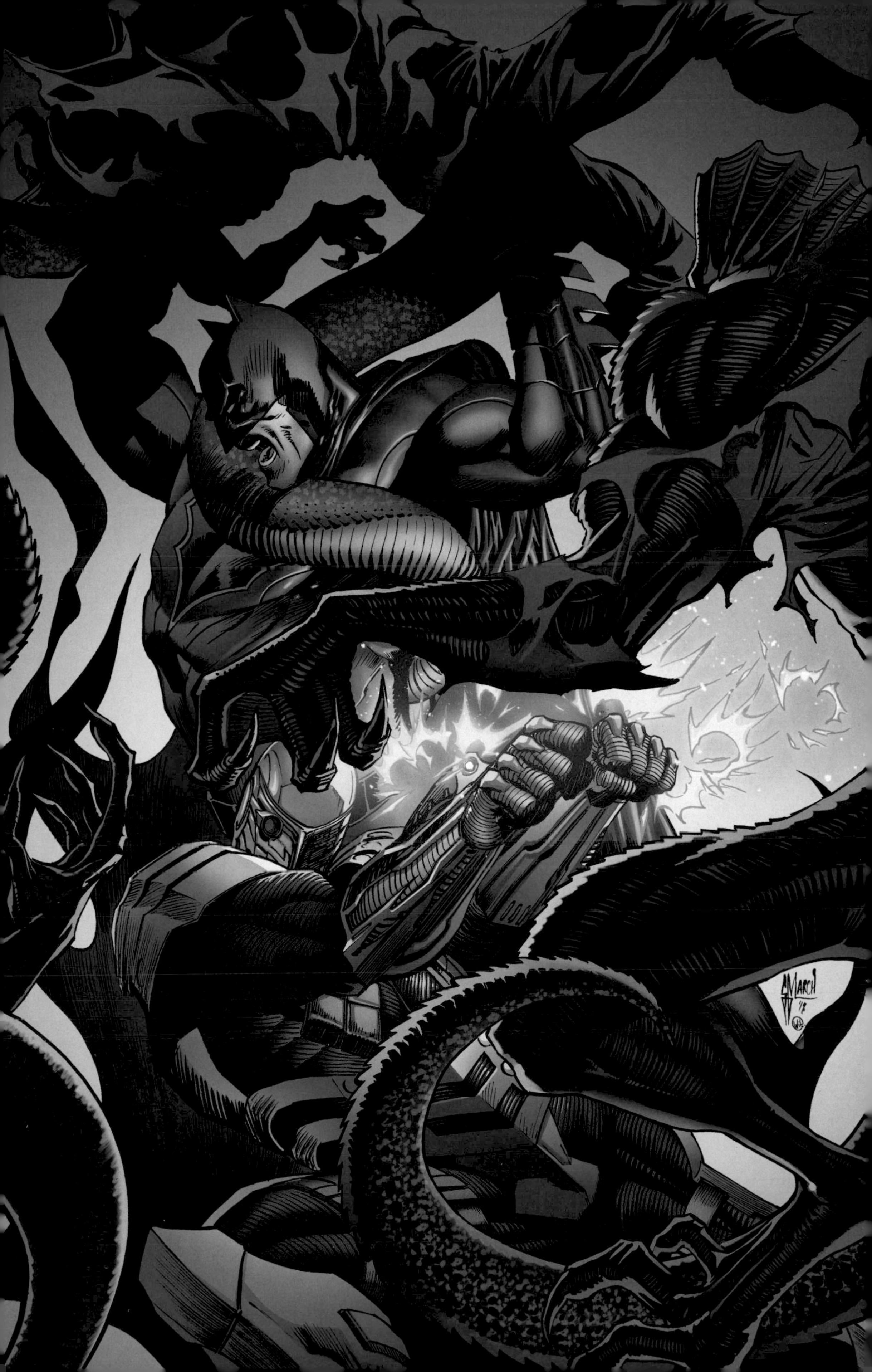

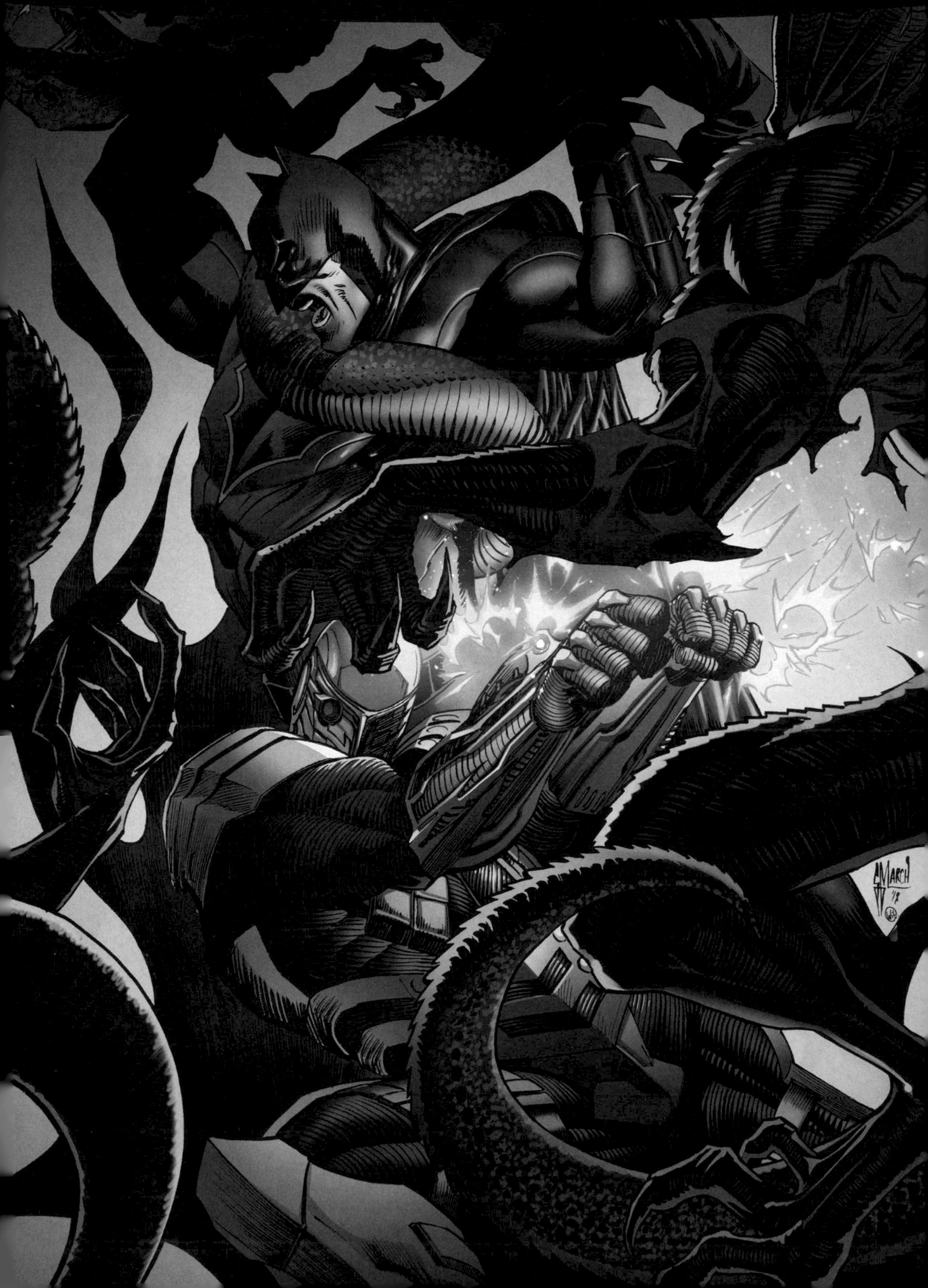

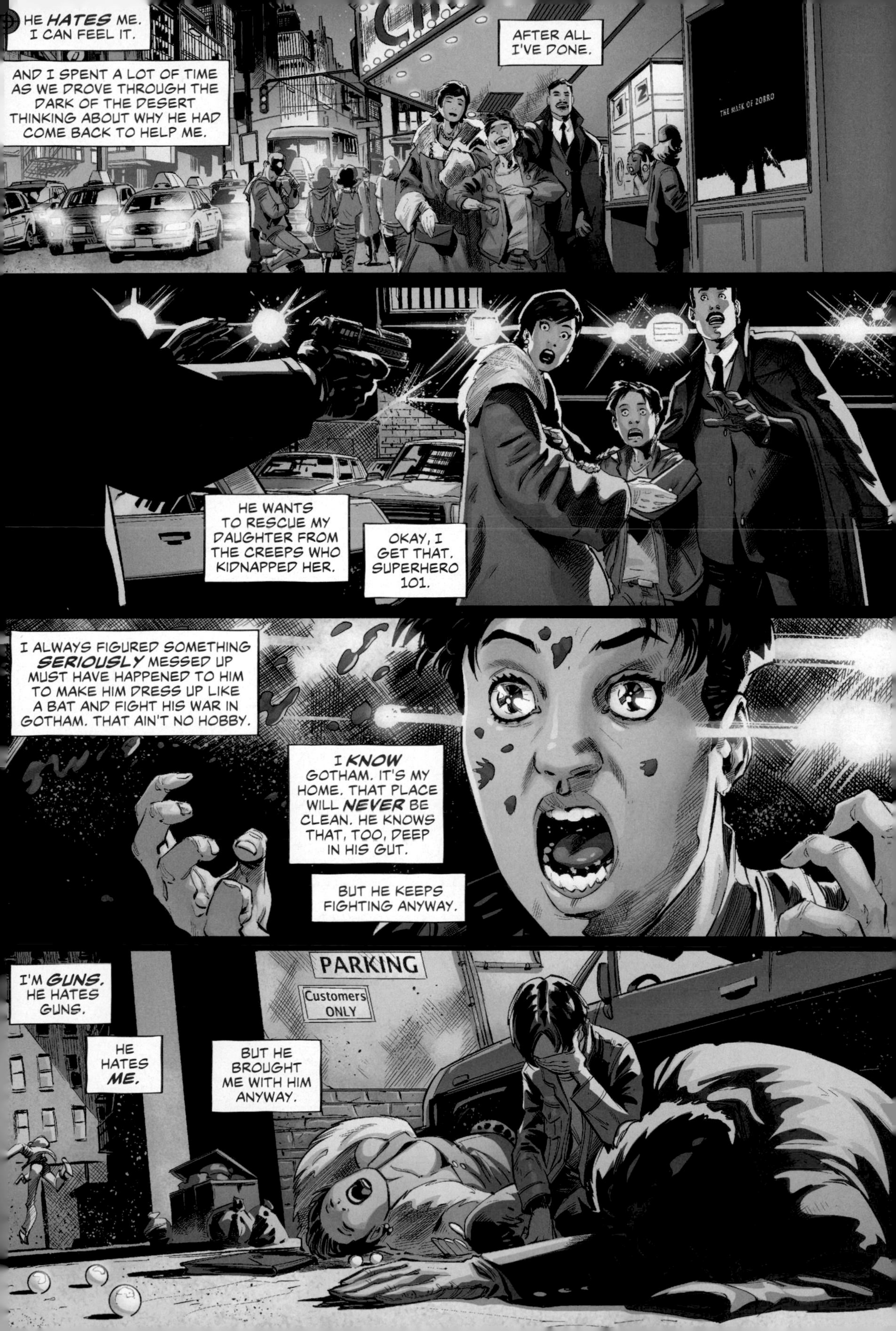
HE HATES ME. I CAN FEEL IT.
AFTER ALL I'VE DONE.
AND I SPENT A LOT OF TIME AS WE DROVE THROUGH THE DARK OF THE DESERT THINKING ABOUT WHY HE HAD COME BACK TO HELP ME.
THE MASK OF ZORRO
HE WANTS TO RESCUE MY DAUGHTER FROM THE CREEPS WHO KIDNAPPED HER.
OKAY, I GET THAT. SUPERHERO 101.
I ALWAYS FIGURED SOMETHING SERIOUSLY MESSED UP MUST HAVE HAPPENED TO HIM TO MAKE HIM DRESS UP LIKE A BAT AND FIGHT HIS WAR IN GOTHAM. THAT AIN'T NO HOBBY.
I KNOW GOTHAM. IT'S MY HOME. THAT PLACE WILL NEVER BE CLEAN. HE KNOWS THAT, TOO, DEEP IN HIS GUT.
BUT HE KEEPS FIGHTING ANYWAY.
PARKING
Customers ONLY
I'M GUNS. HE HATES GUNS.
HE HATES ME.
BUT HE BROUGHT ME WITH HIM ANYWAY.

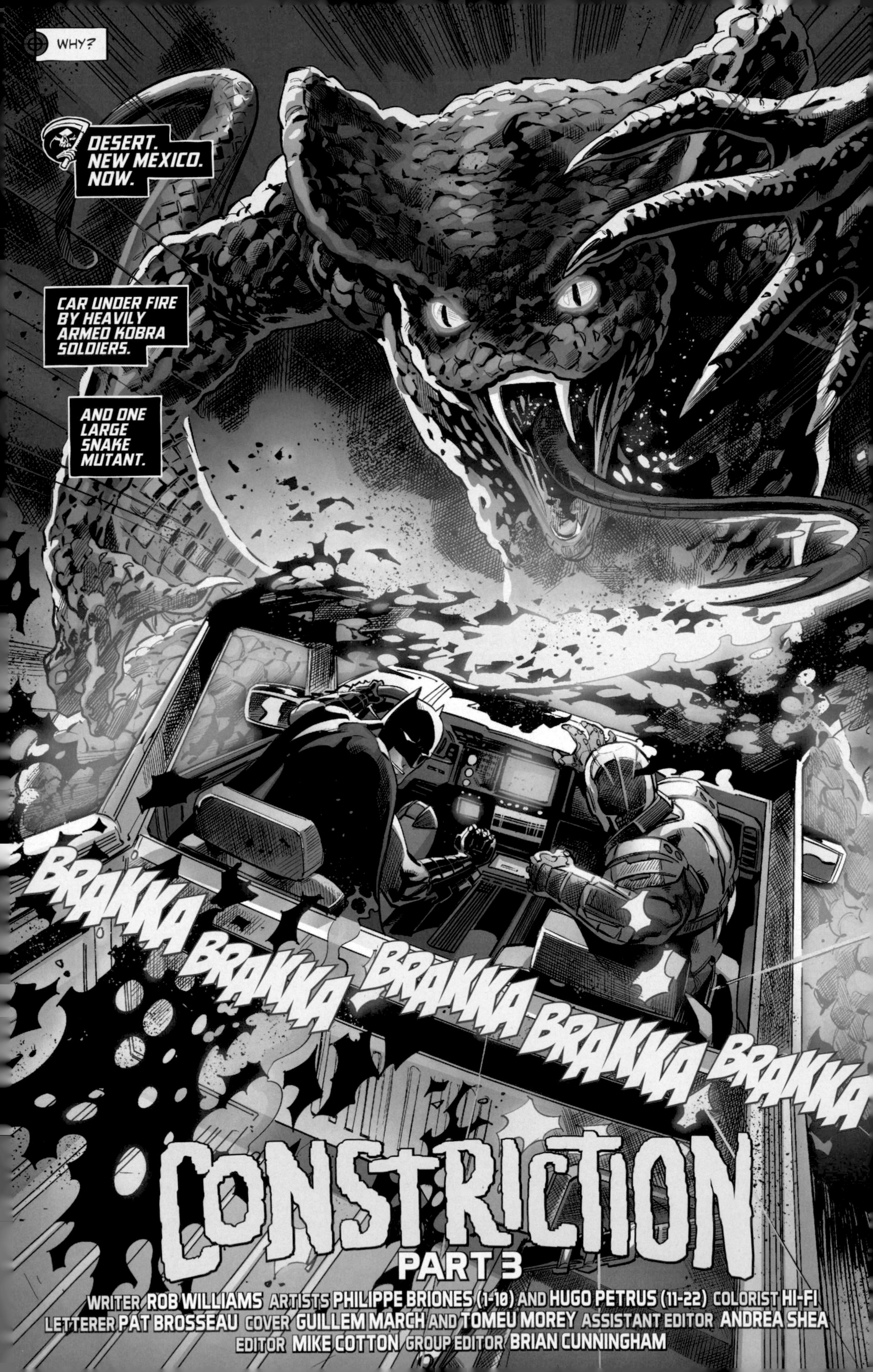
WHY?
DESERT. NEW MEXICO. NOW.
CAR UNDER FIRE BY HEAVILY ARMED KOBRA SOLDIERS.
AND ONE LARGE SNAKE MUTANT.
BRAKKA BRAKKA BRAKKA BRAKKA BRAKKA BRAKKA
CONSTRICTION
PART 3
WRITER ROB WILLIAMS ARTISTS PHILIPPE BRIONES (1-10) AND HUGO PETRUS (11-22) COLORIST HI-FI
LETTERER PAT BROSSEAU COVER GUILLEM MARCH AND TOMEU MOREY ASSISTANT EDITOR ANDREA SHEA
EDITOR MIKE COTTON GROUP EDITOR BRIAN CUNNINGHAM

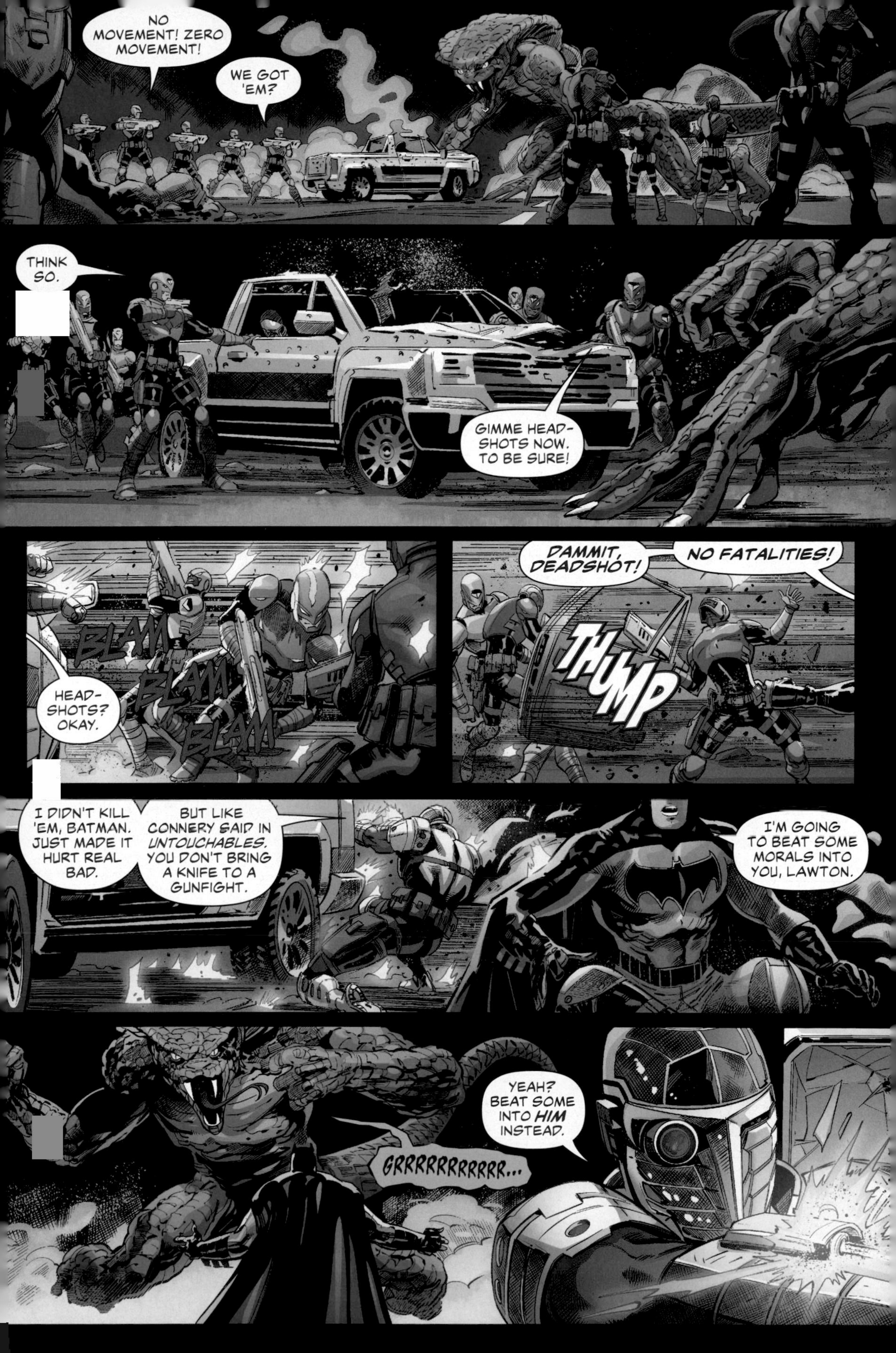
NO MOVEMENT! ZERO MOVEMENT!
WE GOT 'EM?
THINK SO.
GIMME HEAD-SHOTS NOW. TO BE SURE!
BLAM
BLAM
BLAM
HEAD-SHOTS? OKAY.
DAMMIT, DEADSHOT!
NO FATALITIES!
THUMP
I DIDN'T KILL 'EM, BATMAN. JUST MADE IT HURT REAL BAD.
BUT LIKE CONNERY SAID IN *UNTOUCHABLES.* YOU DON'T BRING A KNIFE TO A GUNFIGHT.
I'M GOING TO BEAT SOME MORALS INTO YOU, LAWTON.
YEAH? BEAT SOME INTO *HIM* INSTEAD.
GRRRRRRRRRRR...

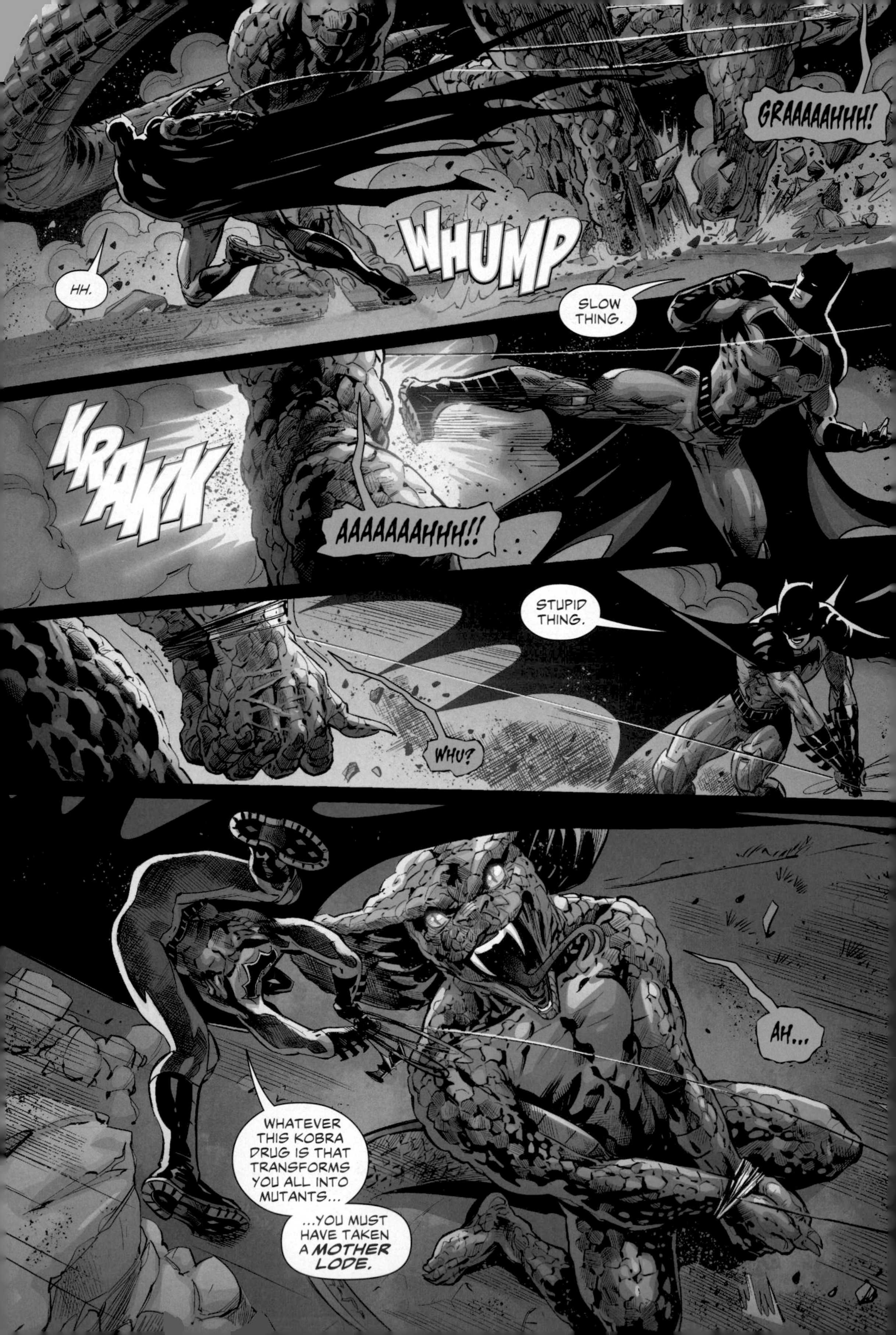
GRAAAAAHHH!
HH.
WHUMP
SLOW THING.
KRAKK
AAAAAAAHHH!!
STUPID THING.
WHU?
AH...
WHATEVER THIS KOBRA DRUG IS THAT TRANSFORMS YOU ALL INTO MUTANTS...
...YOU MUST HAVE TAKEN A MOTHER LODE.

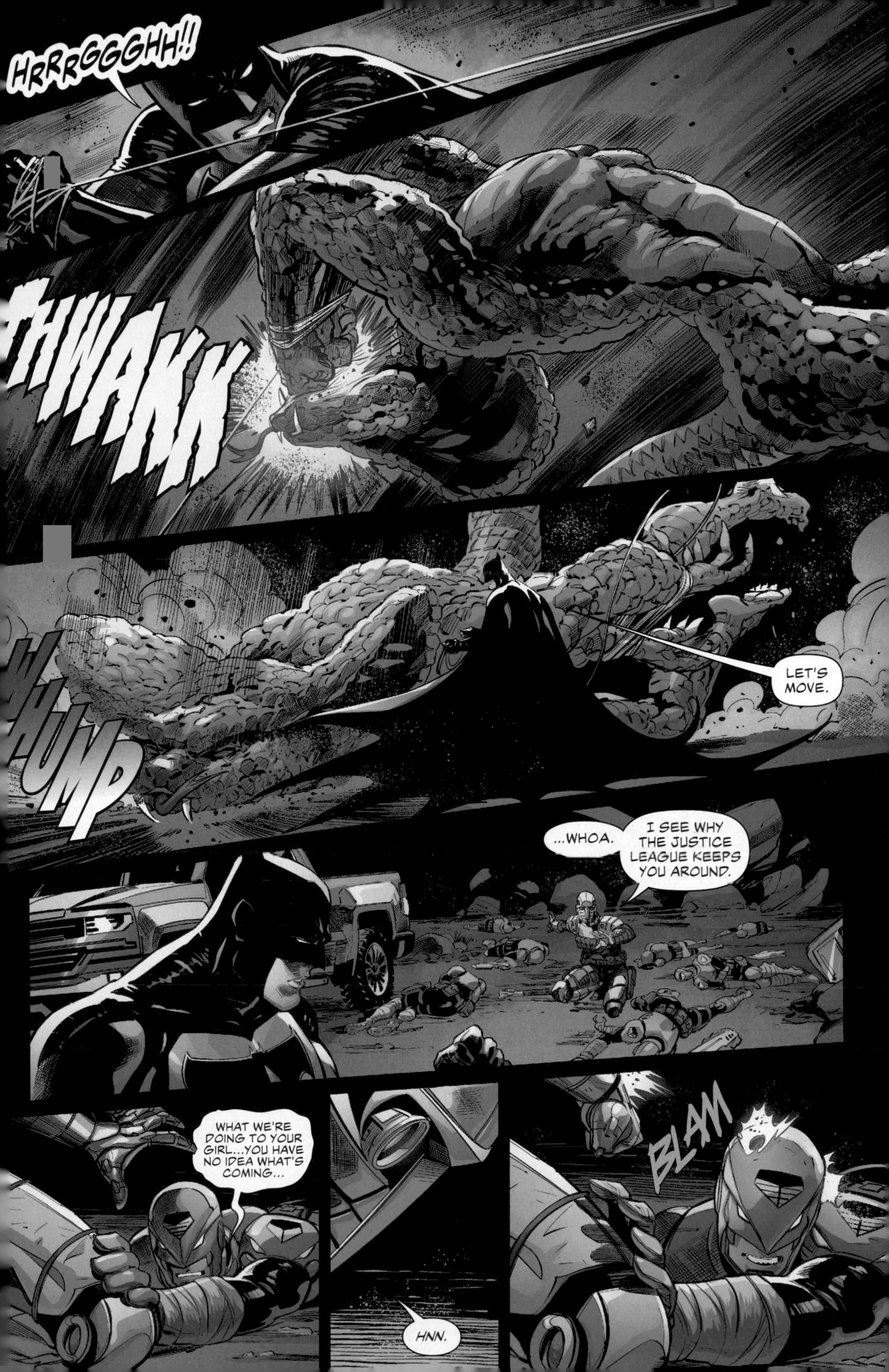
HRRRGGGHH!!
THWAKK
WHUMP
LET'S MOVE.
...WHOA.
I SEE WHY THE JUSTICE LEAGUE KEEPS YOU AROUND.
WHAT WE'RE DOING TO YOUR GIRL...YOU HAVE NO IDEA WHAT'S COMING...
HNN.
BLAM

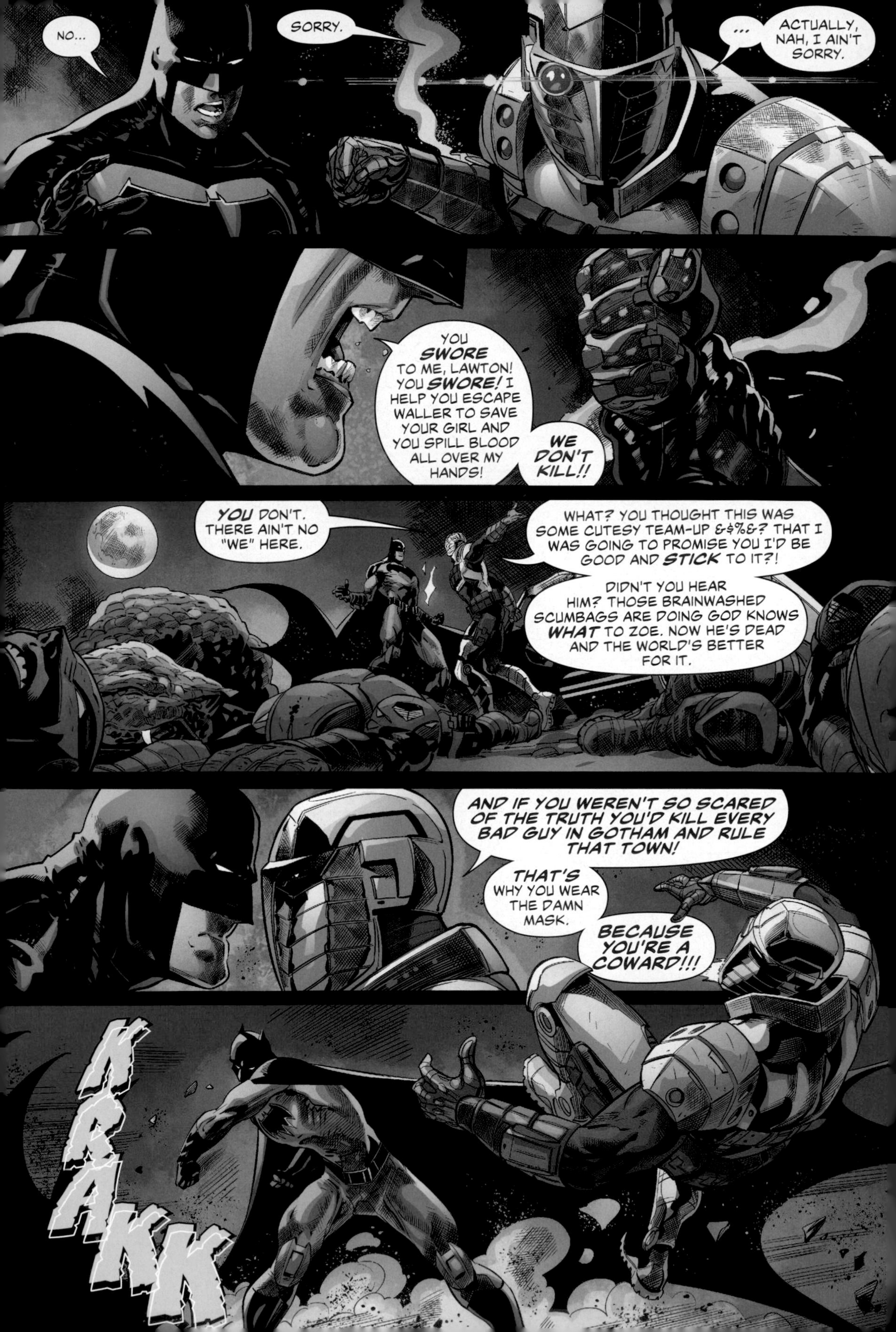
NO...
SORRY.
...
ACTUALLY, NAH, I AIN'T SORRY.
YOU SWORE TO ME, LAWTON! YOU SWORE! I HELP YOU ESCAPE WALLER TO SAVE YOUR GIRL AND YOU SPILL BLOOD ALL OVER MY HANDS!
WE DON'T KILL!!
YOU DON'T. THERE AIN'T NO "WE" HERE.
WHAT? YOU THOUGHT THIS WAS SOME CUTESY TEAM-UP &$%&? THAT I WAS GOING TO PROMISE YOU I'D BE GOOD AND STICK TO IT?!
DIDN'T YOU HEAR HIM? THOSE BRAINWASHED SCUMBAGS ARE DOING GOD KNOWS WHAT TO ZOE. NOW HE'S DEAD AND THE WORLD'S BETTER FOR IT.
AND IF YOU WEREN'T SO SCARED OF THE TRUTH YOU'D KILL EVERY BAD GUY IN GOTHAM AND RULE THAT TOWN!
THAT'S WHY YOU WEAR THE DAMN MASK.
BECAUSE YOU'RE A COWARD!!!
KRAKK

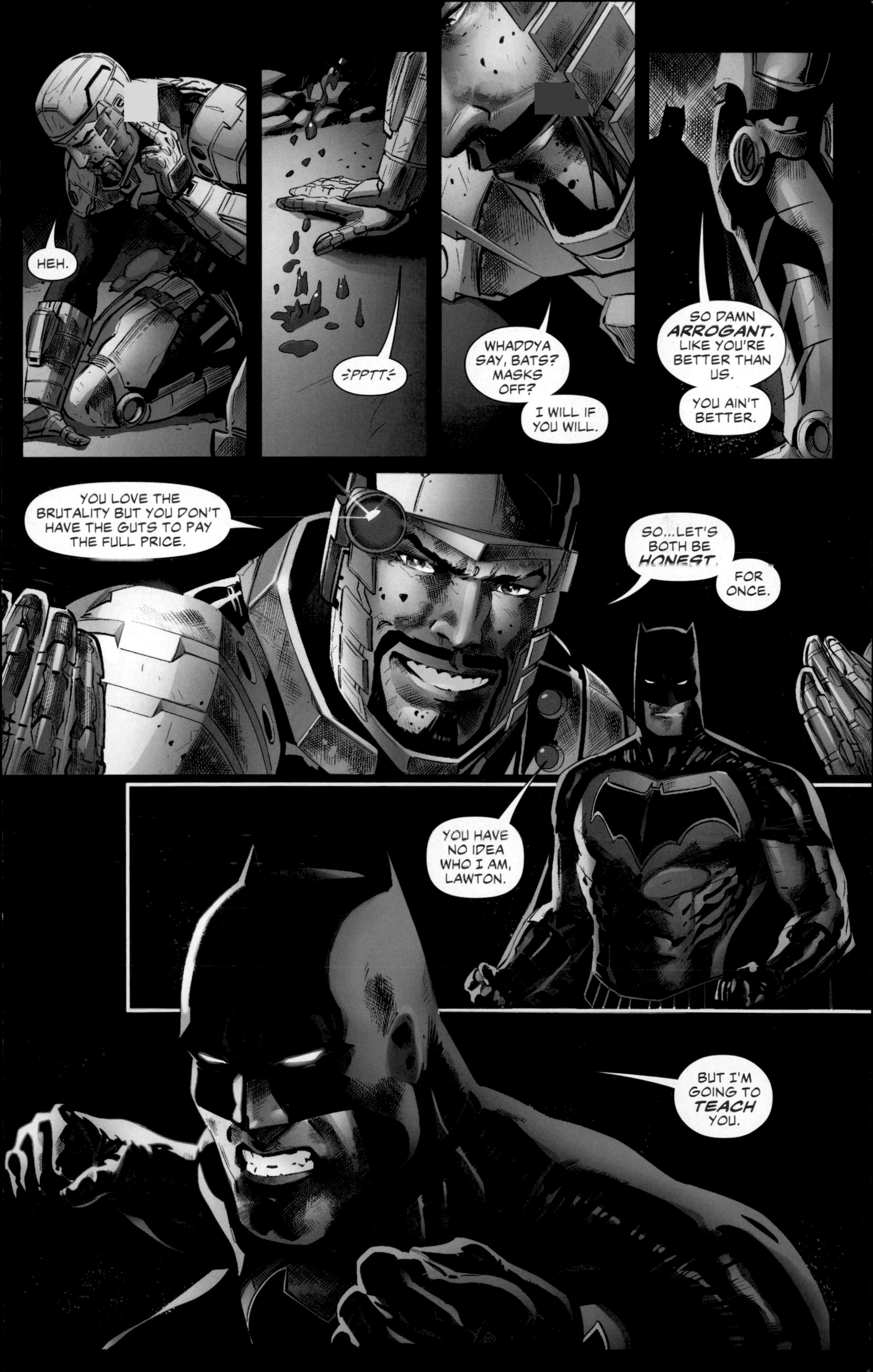
HEH.
PPTT
WHADDYA SAY, BATS? MASKS OFF?
I WILL IF YOU WILL.
SO DAMN *ARROGANT.* LIKE YOU'RE BETTER THAN US.
YOU AIN'T BETTER.
YOU LOVE THE BRUTALITY BUT YOU DON'T HAVE THE GUTS TO PAY THE FULL PRICE.
SO...LET'S BOTH BE *HONEST*.
FOR ONCE.
YOU HAVE NO IDEA WHO I AM, LAWTON.
BUT I'M GOING TO *TEACH* YOU.

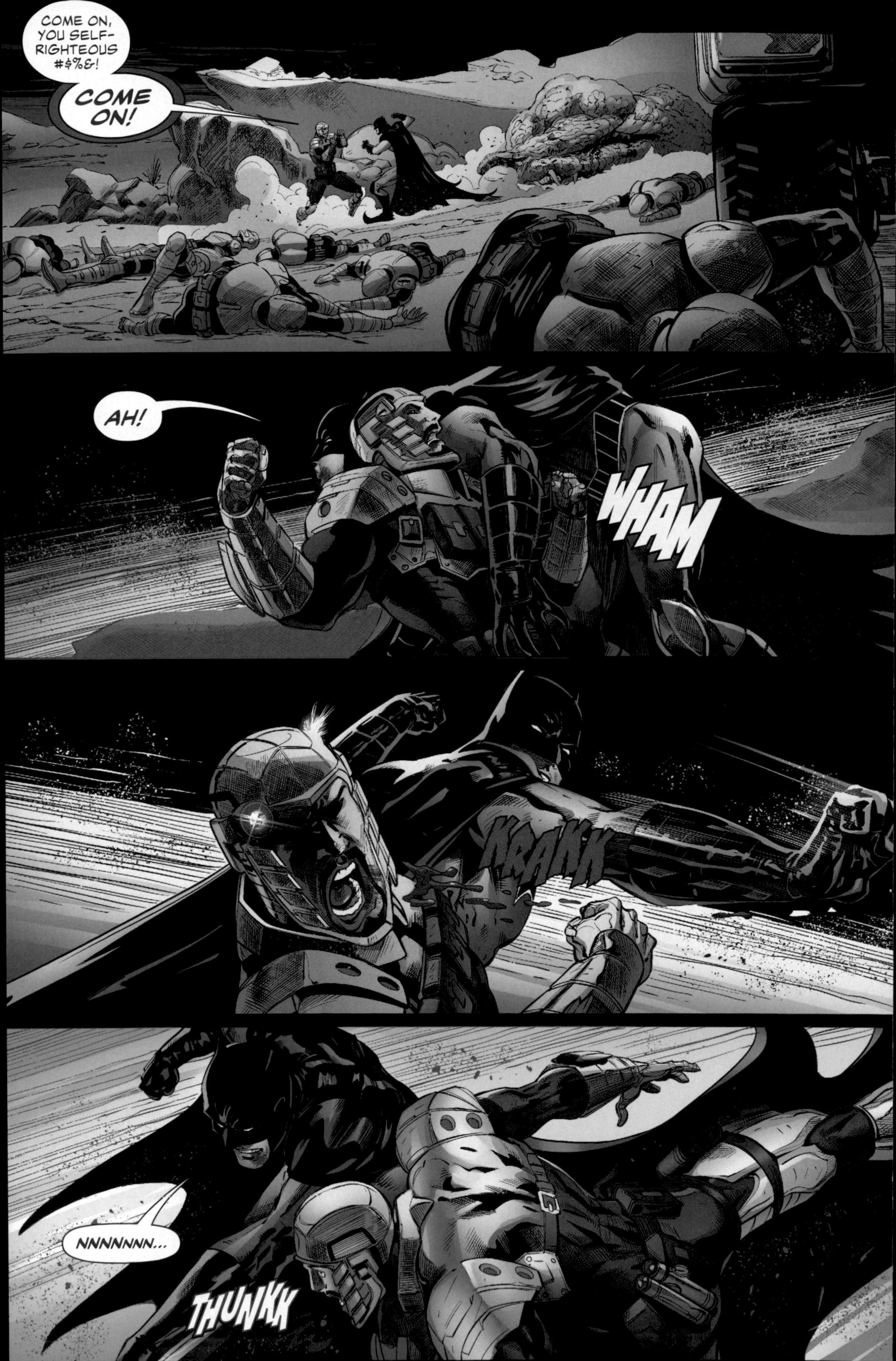
COME ON, YOU SELF-RIGHTEOUS #$%&!
COME ON!
AH!
WHAM
KRAKK
NNNNNNN...
THUNKK

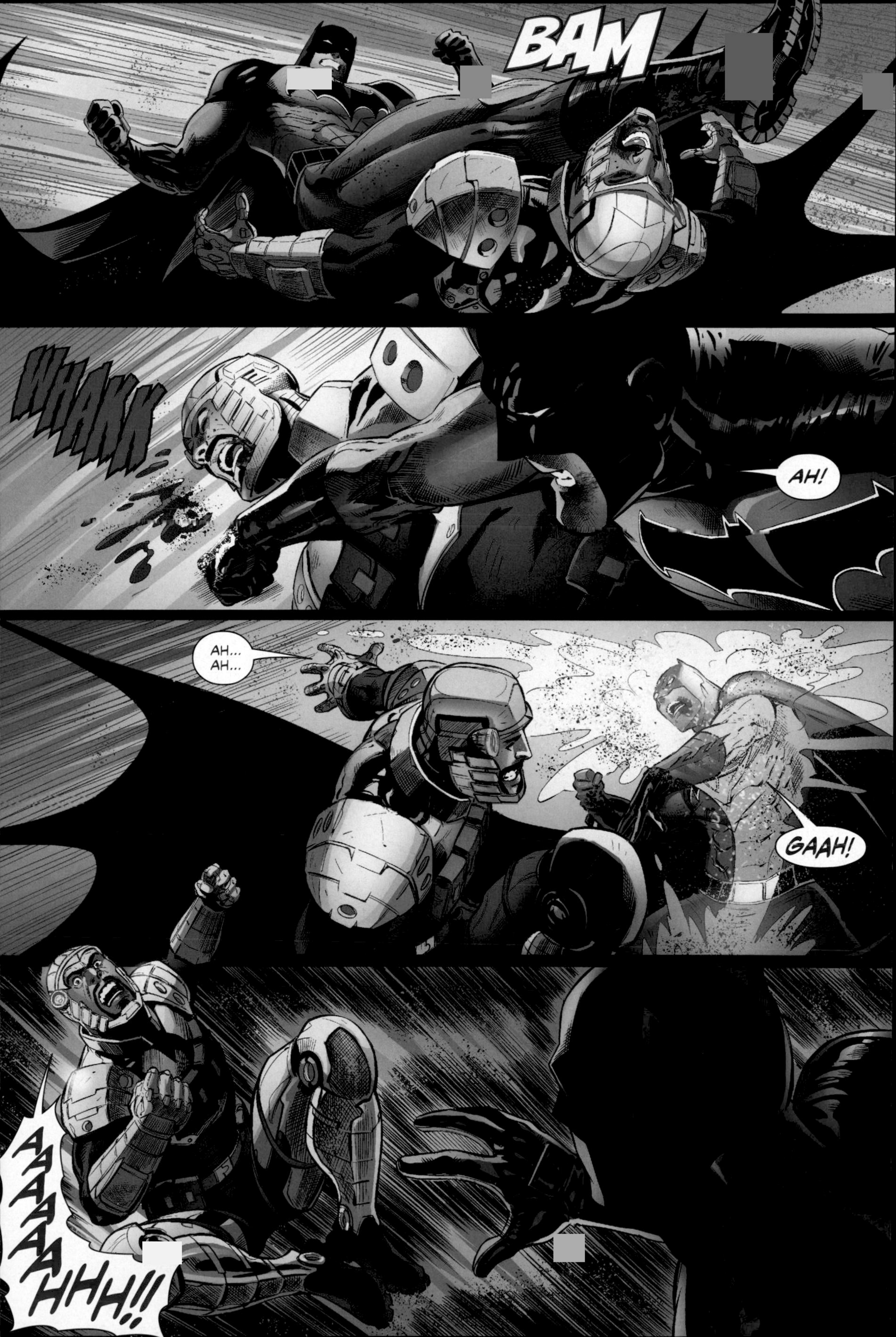
BAM
WHAKK
AH!
AH... AH...
GAAH!
AAAAAAHHH!!

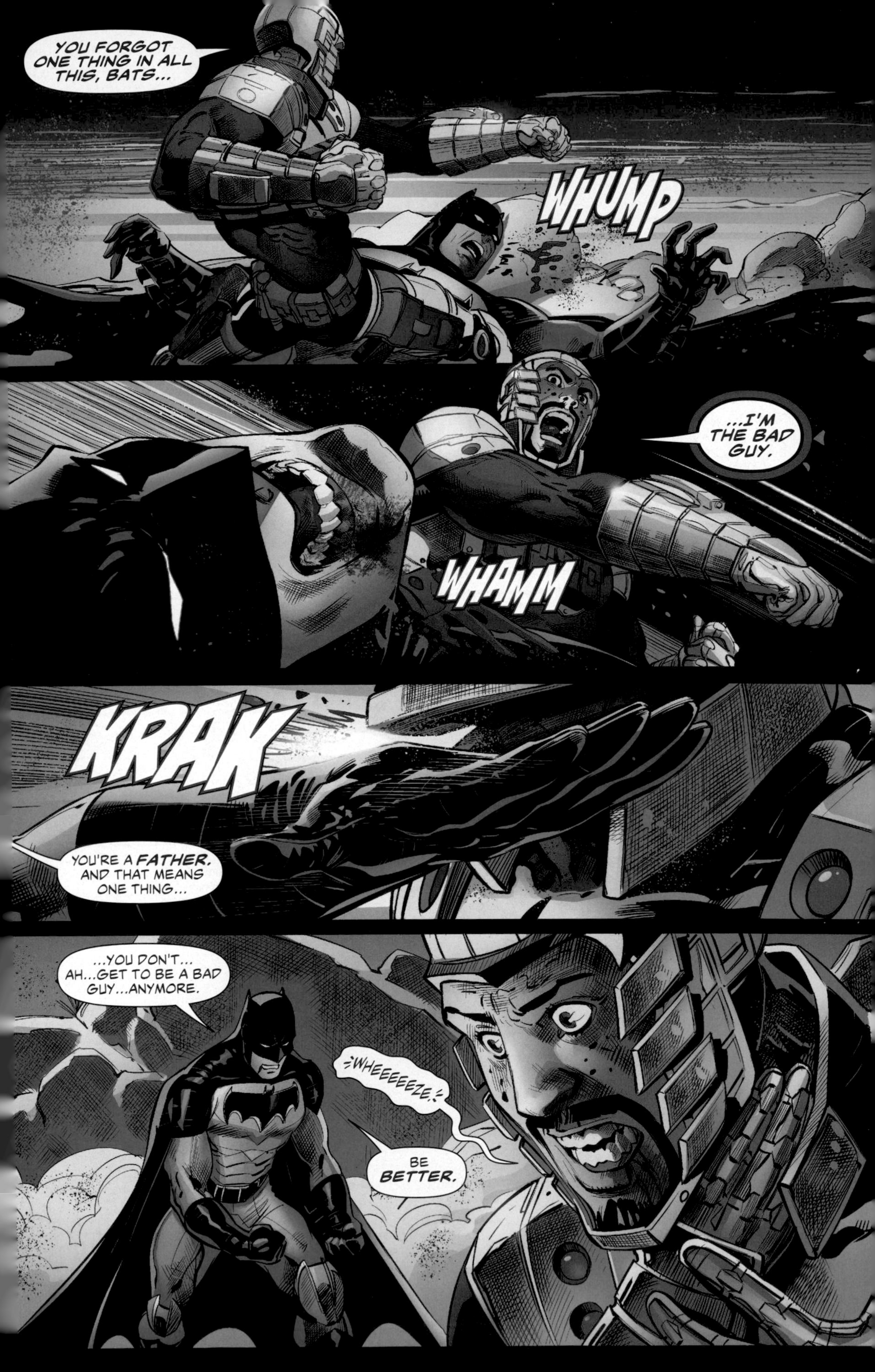

YOU FORGOT ONE THING IN ALL THIS, BATS...
WHUMP
...I'M THE BAD GUY.
WHAMM
KRAK
YOU'RE A FATHER. AND THAT MEANS ONE THING...
...YOU DON'T... AH...GET TO BE A BAD GUY...ANYMORE.
WHEEEEEZE
BE BETTER.

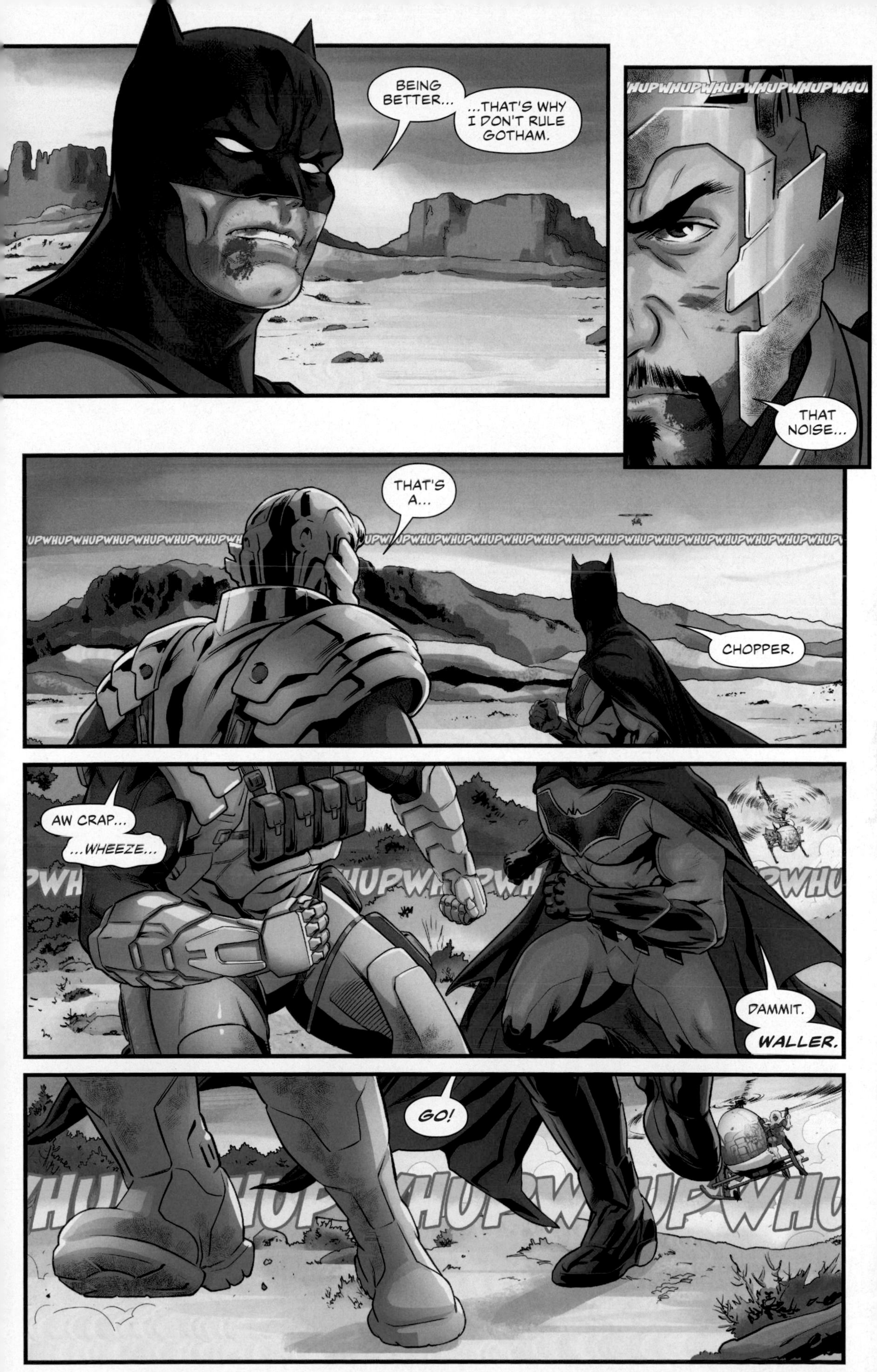
WHUPWHUPWHUPWHUPWHU
BEING BETTER...
...THAT'S WHY I DON'T RULE GOTHAM.
THAT NOISE...
THAT'S A...
WHUPWHUPWHUPWHUPWHUPWHUPWHUPWHUPWHUPWHUPWHUPWHUPWHUPWHUPWH
CHOPPER.
AW CRAP...
...WHEEZE...
DAMMIT.
WALLER.
GO!

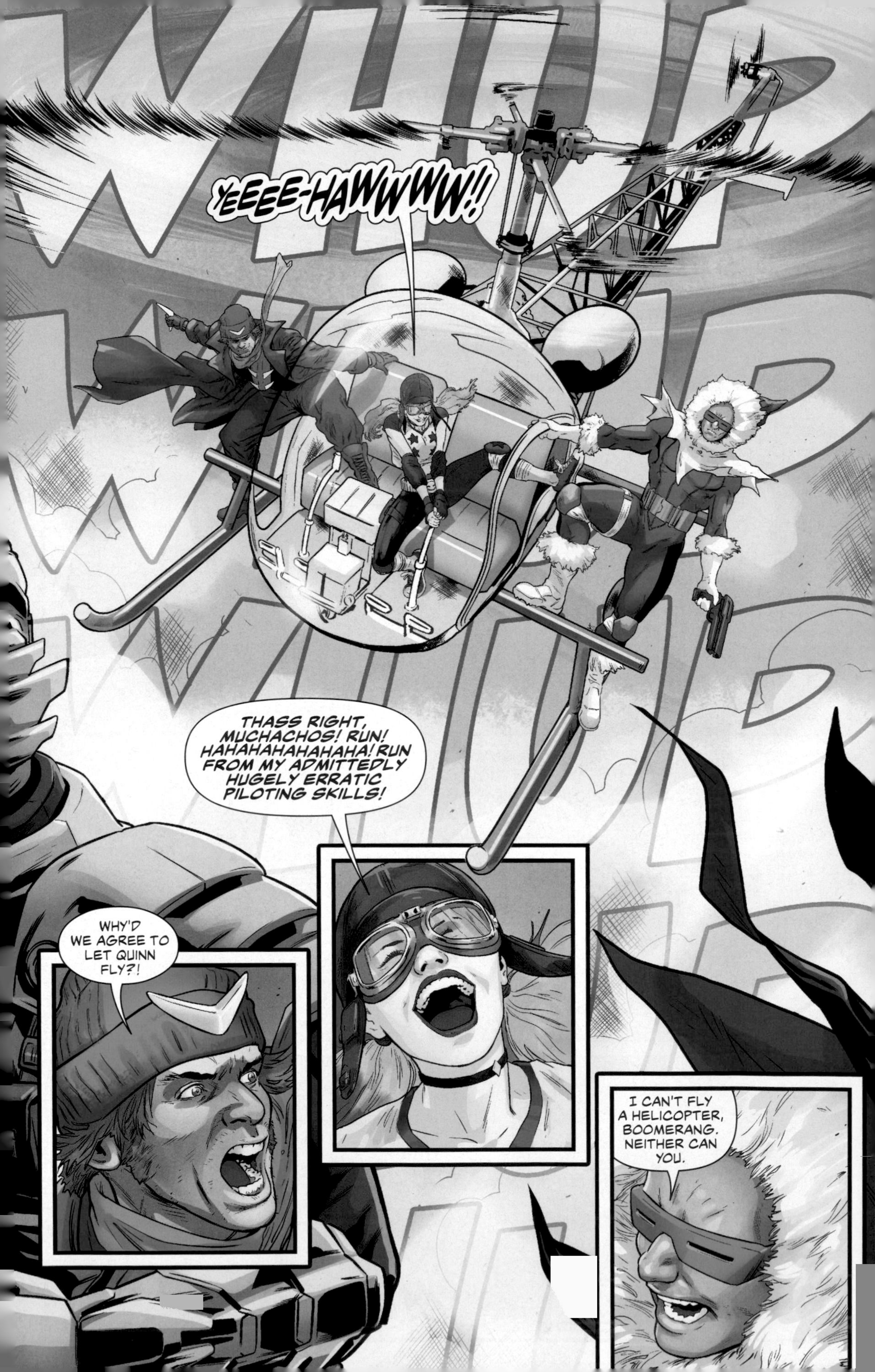
YEEEE-HAWWWW!!
THASS RIGHT, MUCHACHOS! RUN! HAHAHAHAHAHAHA! RUN FROM MY ADMITTEDLY HUGELY ERRATIC PILOTING SKILLS!
WHY'D WE AGREE TO LET QUINN FLY?!
I CAN'T FLY A HELICOPTER, BOOMERANG. NEITHER CAN YOU.

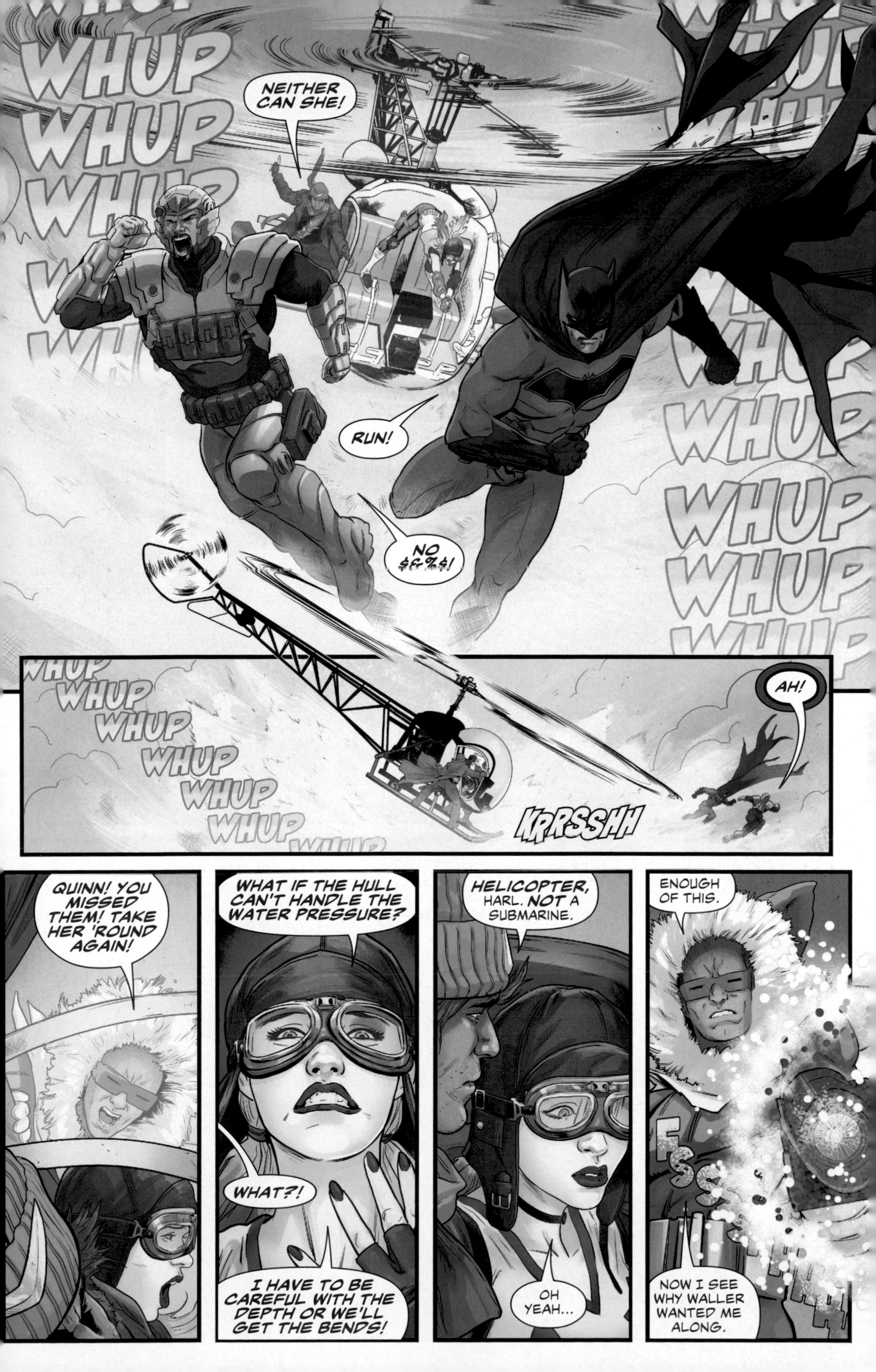
WHUP
WHUP
WHUP
NEITHER CAN SHE!
RUN!
NO $&%$!
WHUP
WHUP
WHUP
WHUP
WHUP
WHUP
WHUP
WHUP
AH!
KRRSSHH
QUINN! YOU MISSED THEM! TAKE HER 'ROUND AGAIN!
WHAT IF THE HULL CAN'T HANDLE THE WATER PRESSURE?
WHAT?!
I HAVE TO BE CAREFUL WITH THE DEPTH OR WE'LL GET THE BENDS!
HELICOPTER, HARL. NOT A SUBMARINE.
OH YEAH...
ENOUGH OF THIS.
NOW I SEE WHY WALLER WANTED ME ALONG.

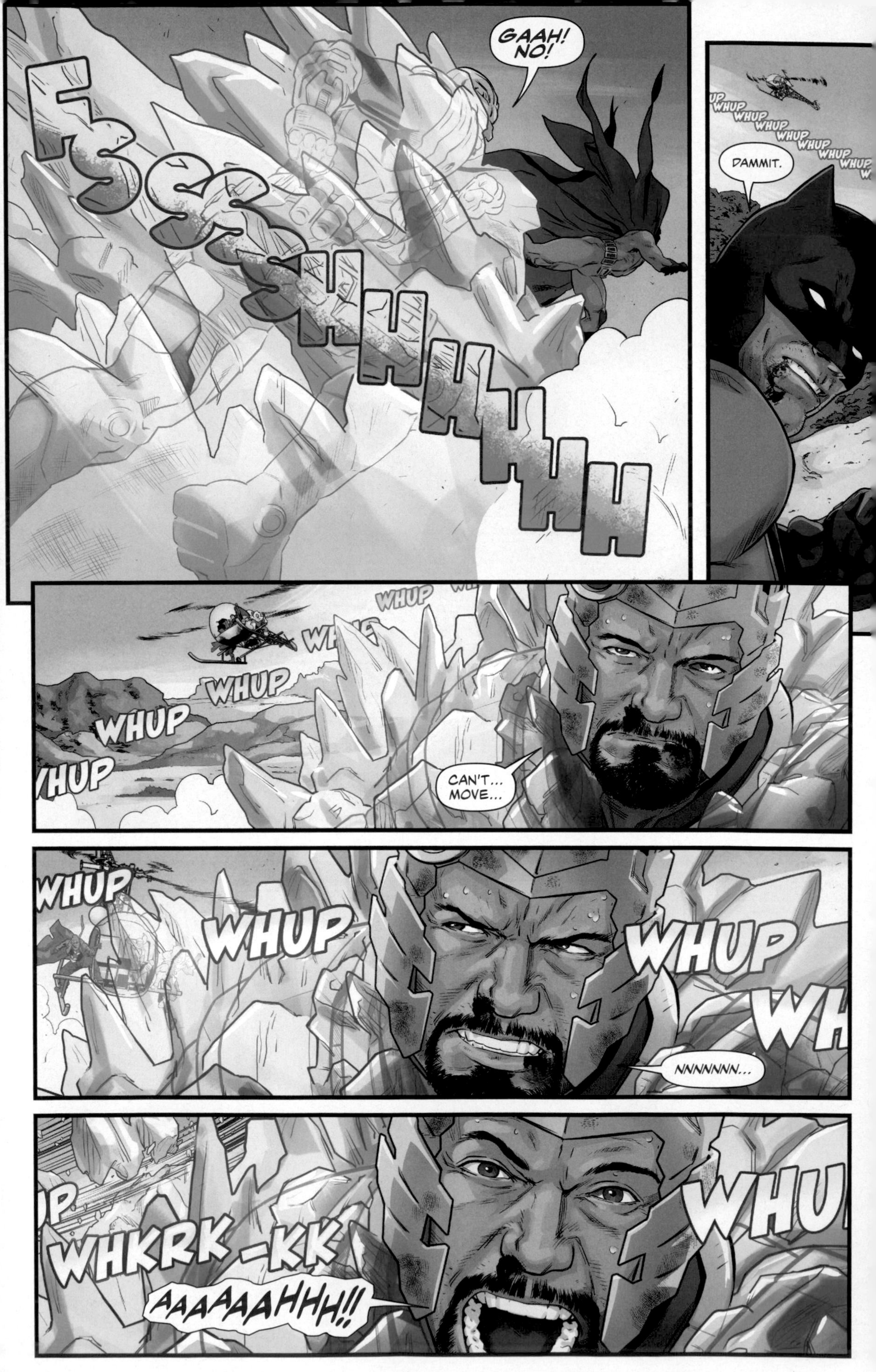
GAAH! NO!
FSSSSHHHHHHH
WHUP WHUP WHUP WHUP WHUP WHUP WHUP
DAMMIT.
WHUP
WHUP
WHUP
WHUP
CAN'T... MOVE...
WHUP
WHUP
WHUP
NNNNNNN...
WHKRK-KK
AAAAAAHHH!!

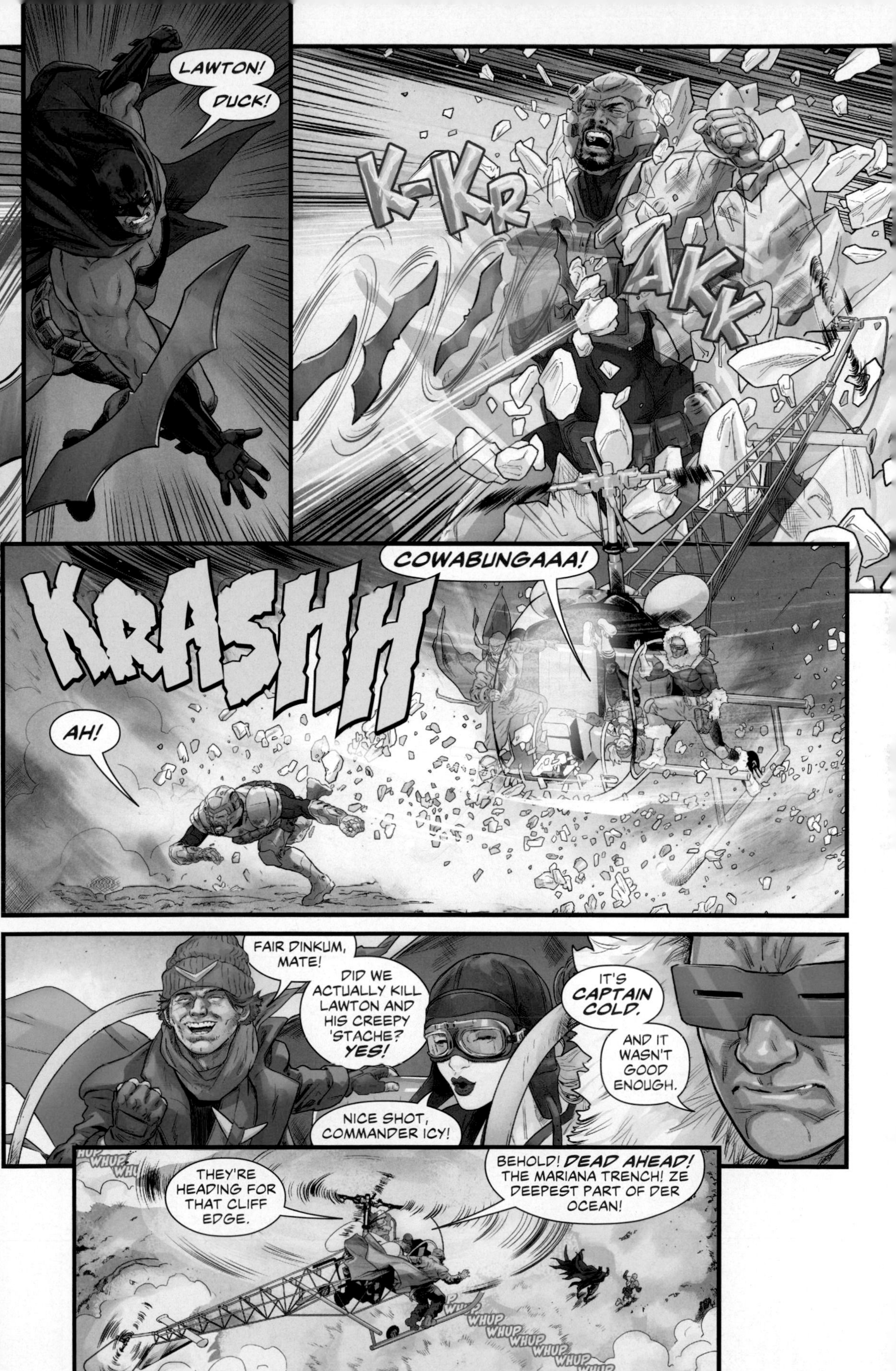
LAWTON!
DUCK!
K-KR
AKK
KRASHH
COWABUNGAAA!
AH!
FAIR DINKUM, MATE!
DID WE ACTUALLY KILL LAWTON AND HIS CREEPY 'STACHE? YES!
NICE SHOT, COMMANDER ICY!
IT'S CAPTAIN COLD.
AND IT WASN'T GOOD ENOUGH.
THEY'RE HEADING FOR THAT CLIFF EDGE.
BEHOLD! DEAD AHEAD! THE MARIANA TRENCH! ZE DEEPEST PART OF DER OCEAN!
WHUP WHUP
WHUP WHUP WHUP WHUP WHUP WHUP WHUP

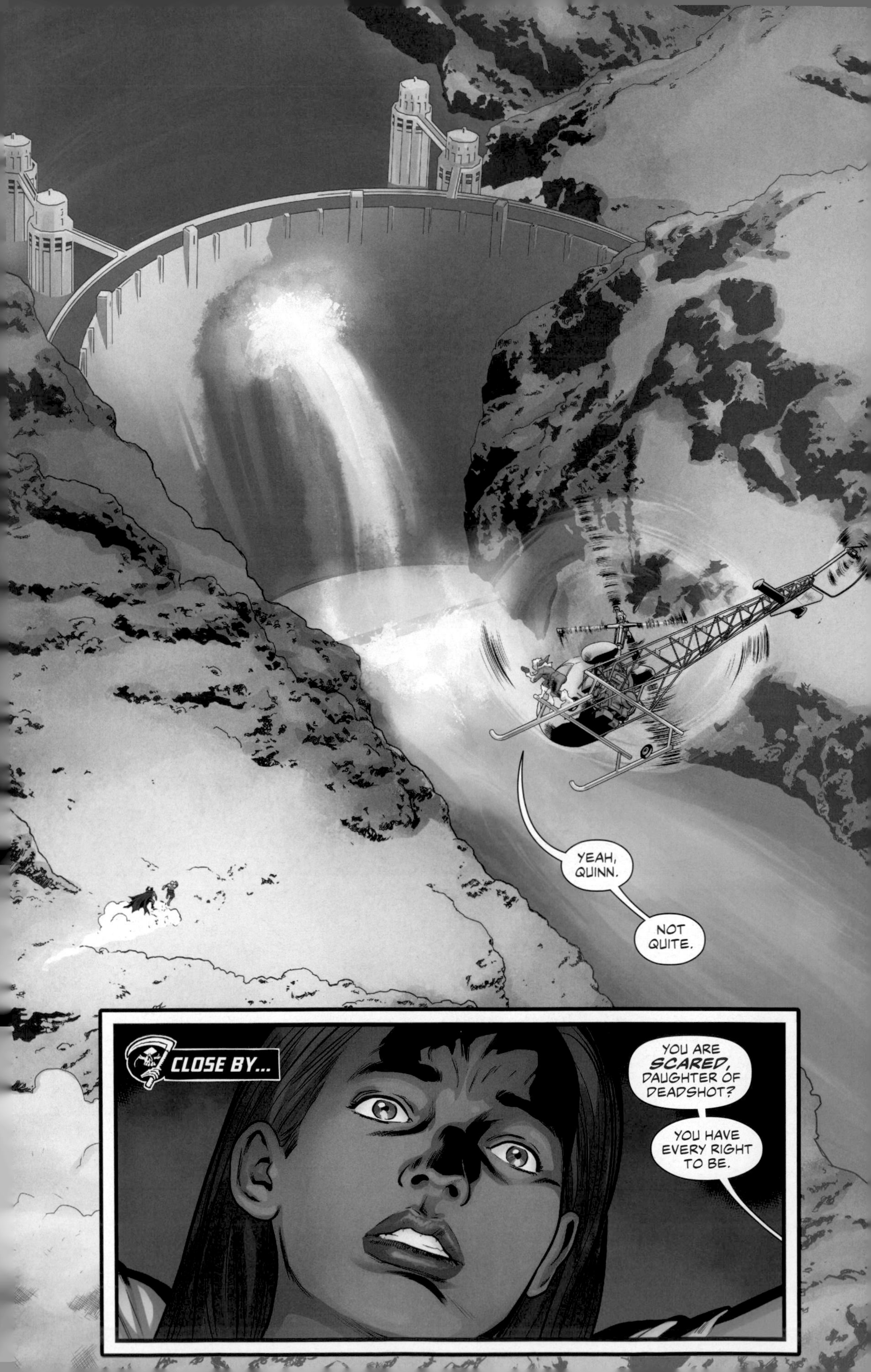
YEAH, QUINN.
NOT QUITE.
CLOSE BY...
YOU ARE SCARED, DAUGHTER OF DEADSHOT?
YOU HAVE EVERY RIGHT TO BE.

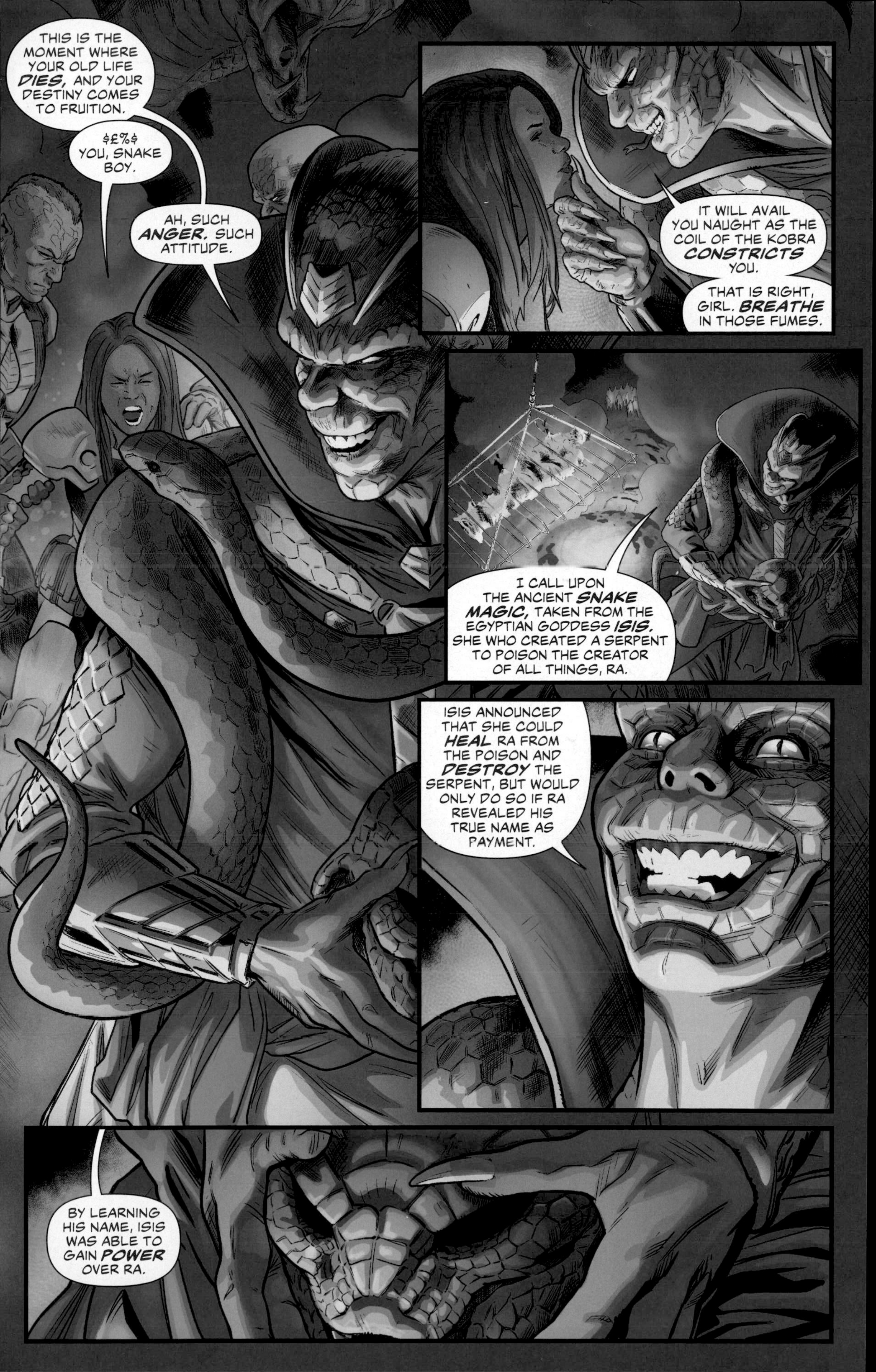
THIS IS THE MOMENT WHERE YOUR OLD LIFE DIES, AND YOUR DESTINY COMES TO FRUITION.
$£%$ YOU, SNAKE BOY.
AH, SUCH ANGER. SUCH ATTITUDE.
IT WILL AVAIL YOU NAUGHT AS THE COIL OF THE KOBRA CONSTRICTS YOU.
THAT IS RIGHT, GIRL. BREATHE IN THOSE FUMES.
I CALL UPON THE ANCIENT SNAKE MAGIC, TAKEN FROM THE EGYPTIAN GODDESS ISIS. SHE WHO CREATED A SERPENT TO POISON THE CREATOR OF ALL THINGS, RA.
ISIS ANNOUNCED THAT SHE COULD HEAL RA FROM THE POISON AND DESTROY THE SERPENT, BUT WOULD ONLY DO SO IF RA REVEALED HIS TRUE NAME AS PAYMENT.
BY LEARNING HIS NAME, ISIS WAS ABLE TO GAIN POWER OVER RA.

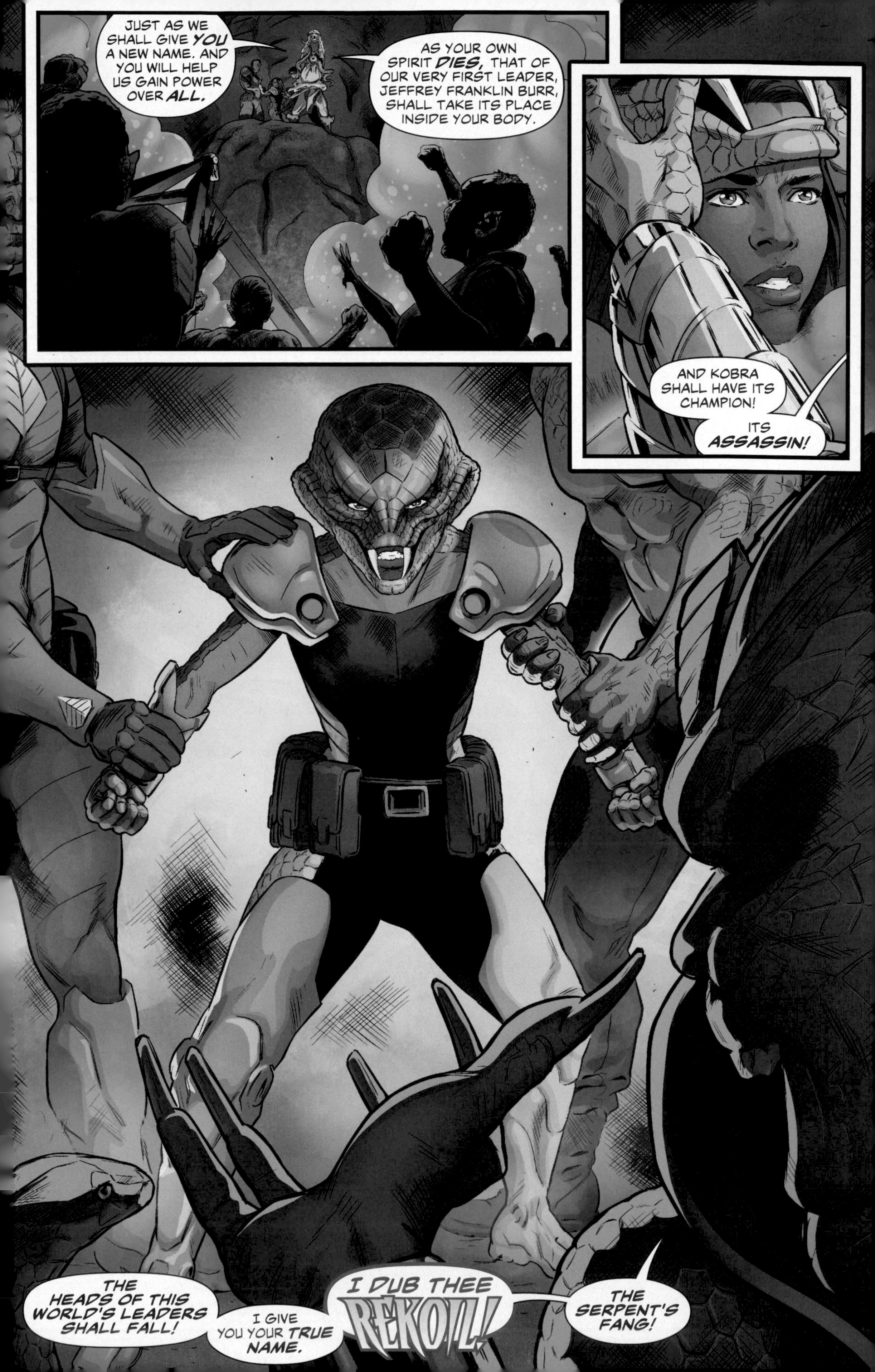
JUST AS WE SHALL GIVE YOU A NEW NAME. AND YOU WILL HELP US GAIN POWER OVER ALL.
AS YOUR OWN SPIRIT DIES, THAT OF OUR VERY FIRST LEADER, JEFFREY FRANKLIN BURR, SHALL TAKE ITS PLACE INSIDE YOUR BODY.
AND KOBRA SHALL HAVE ITS CHAMPION!
ITS ASSASSIN!
THE HEADS OF THIS WORLD'S LEADERS SHALL FALL!
I GIVE YOU YOUR TRUE NAME.
I DUB THEE REKOIL!
THE SERPENT'S FANG!

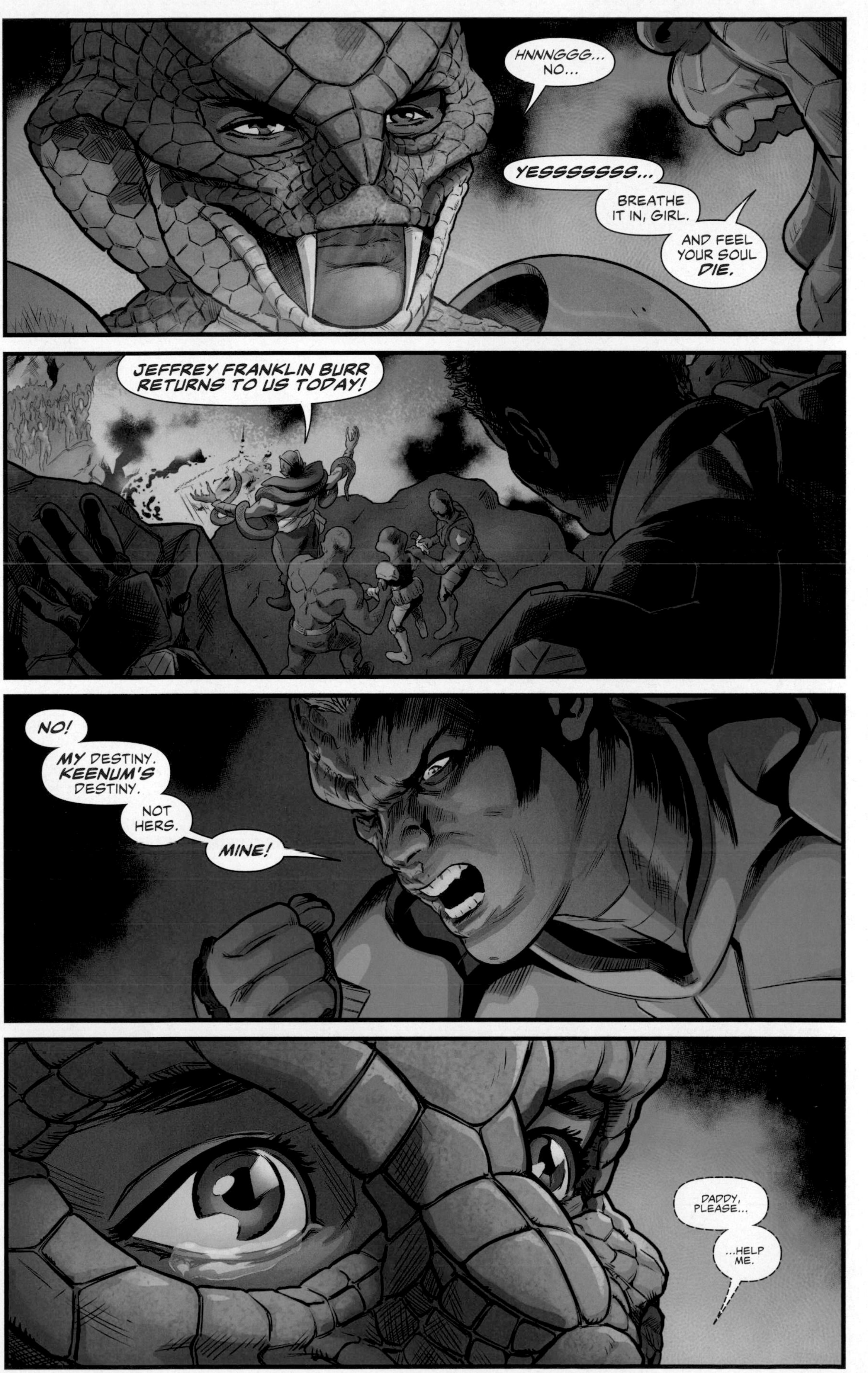
HNNNGGG... NO...
YESSSSSSS...
BREATHE IT IN, GIRL.
AND FEEL YOUR SOUL DIE.
JEFFREY FRANKLIN BURR RETURNS TO US TODAY!
NO!
MY DESTINY. KEENUM'S DESTINY.
NOT HERS.
MINE!
DADDY, PLEASE...
...HELP ME.

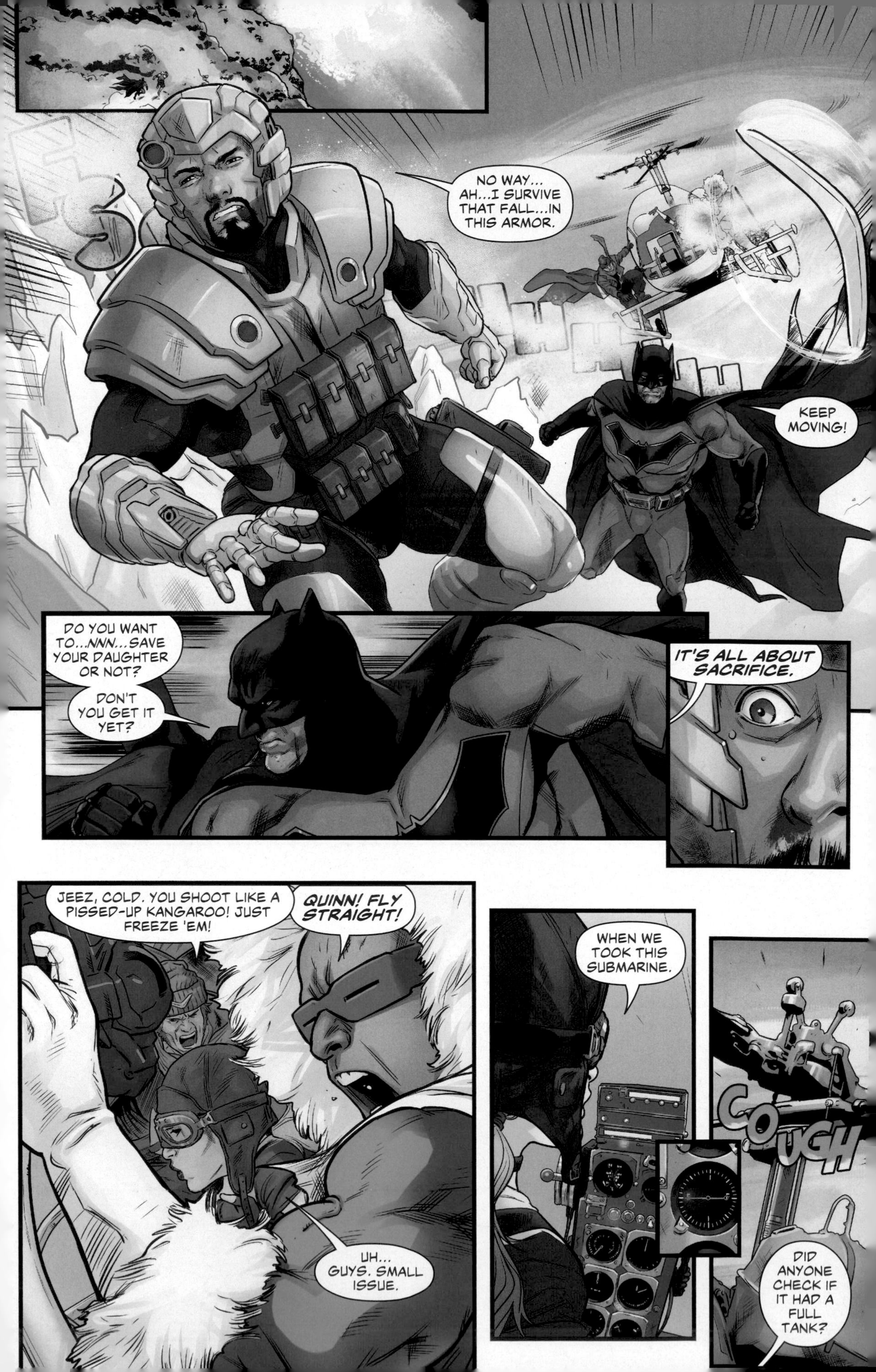
NO WAY... AH...I SURVIVE THAT FALL...IN THIS ARMOR.
KEEP MOVING!
DO YOU WANT TO...NNN...SAVE YOUR DAUGHTER OR NOT?
DON'T YOU GET IT YET?
IT'S ALL ABOUT SACRIFICE.
JEEZ, COLD. YOU SHOOT LIKE A PISSED-UP KANGAROO! JUST FREEZE 'EM!
QUINN! FLY STRAIGHT!
UH... GUYS. SMALL ISSUE.
WHEN WE TOOK THIS SUBMARINE.
COUGH
DID ANYONE CHECK IF IT HAD A FULL TANK?

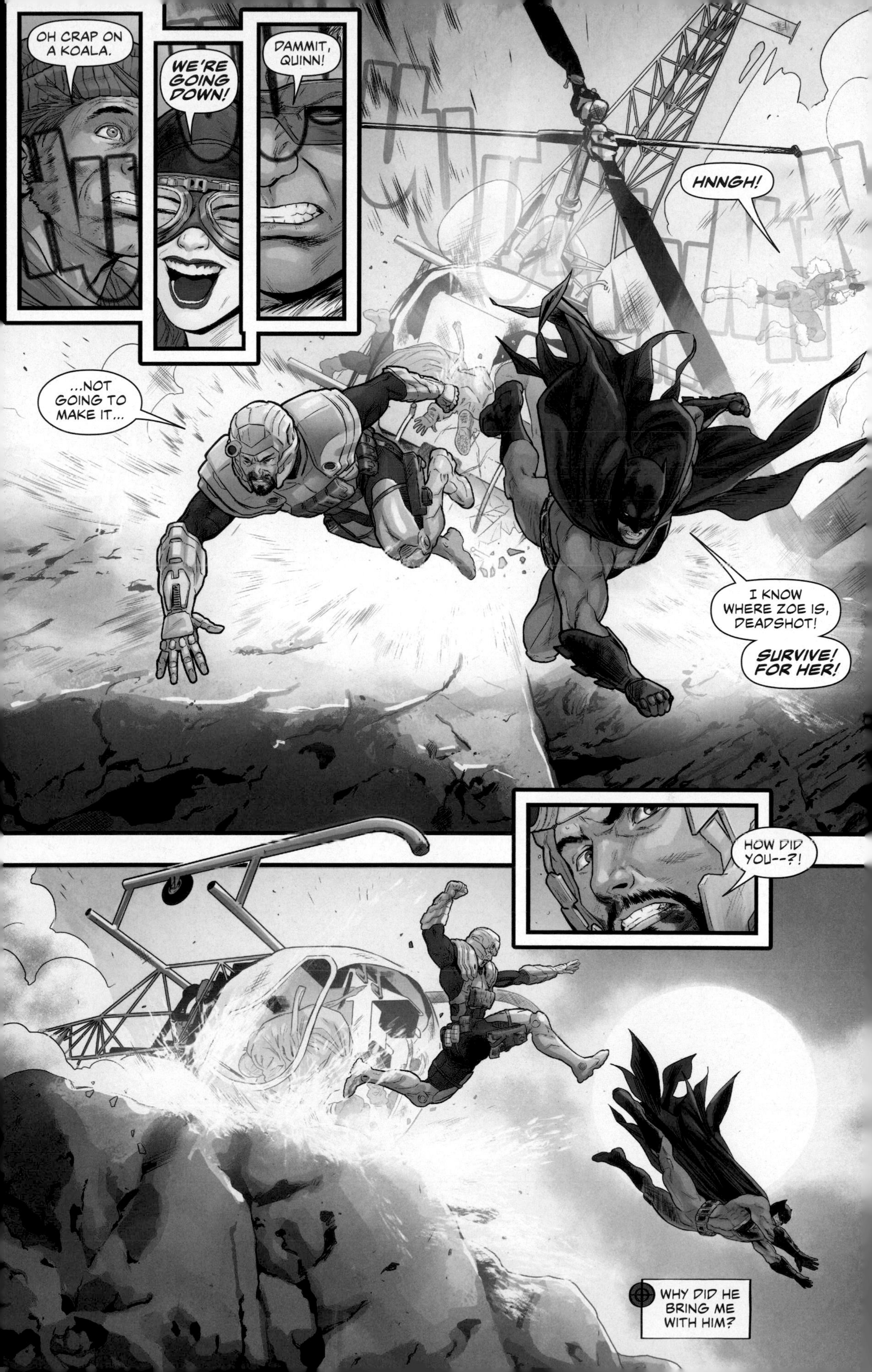
OH CRAP ON A KOALA.
WE'RE GOING DOWN!
DAMMIT, QUINN!
HNNGH!
...NOT GOING TO MAKE IT...
I KNOW WHERE ZOE IS, DEADSHOT!
SURVIVE! FOR HER!
HOW DID YOU--?!
WHY DID HE BRING ME WITH HIM?

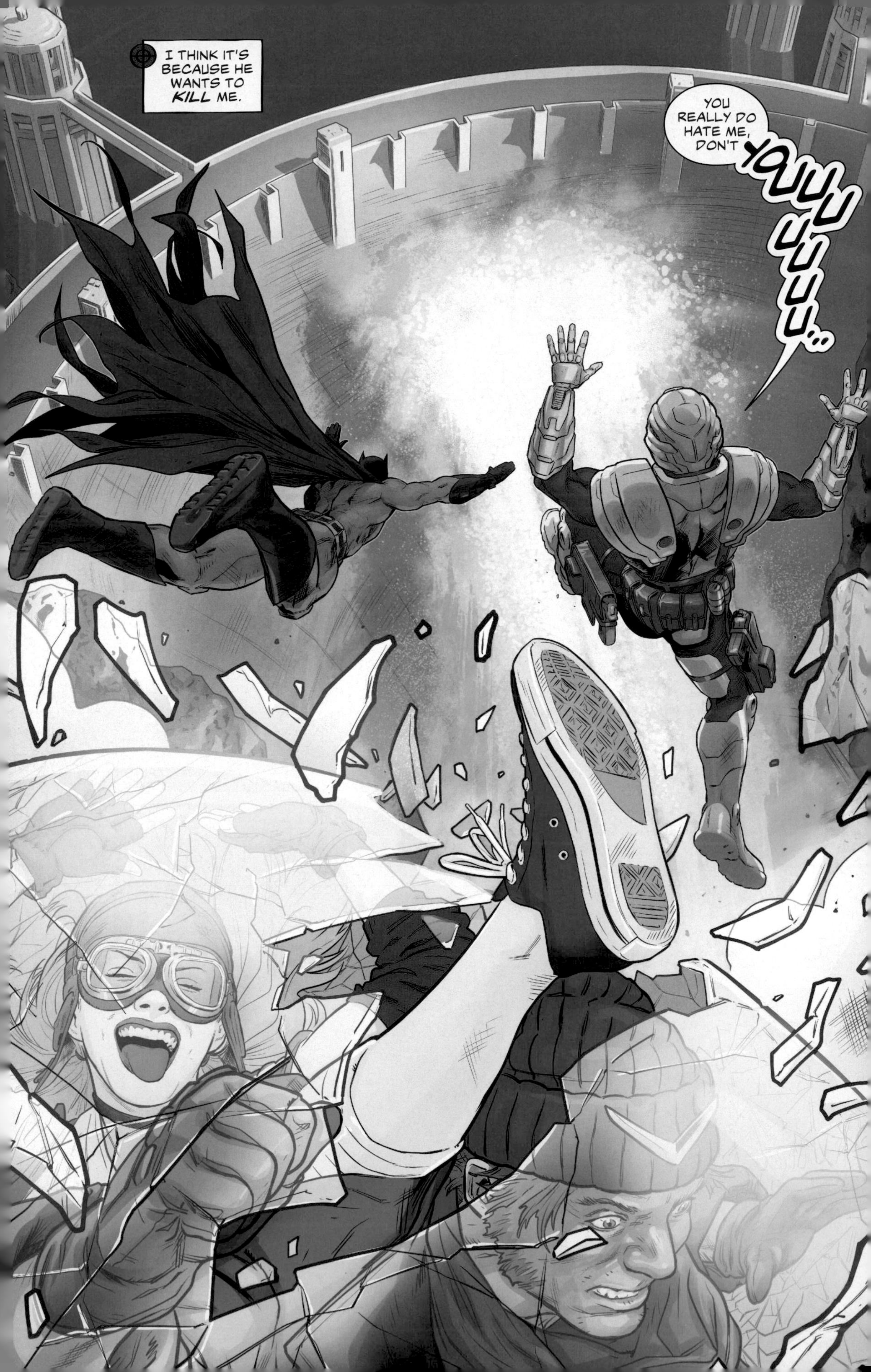
I THINK IT'S BECAUSE HE WANTS TO *KILL* ME.
YOU REALLY DO HATE ME, DON'T YOUUUUUUU...

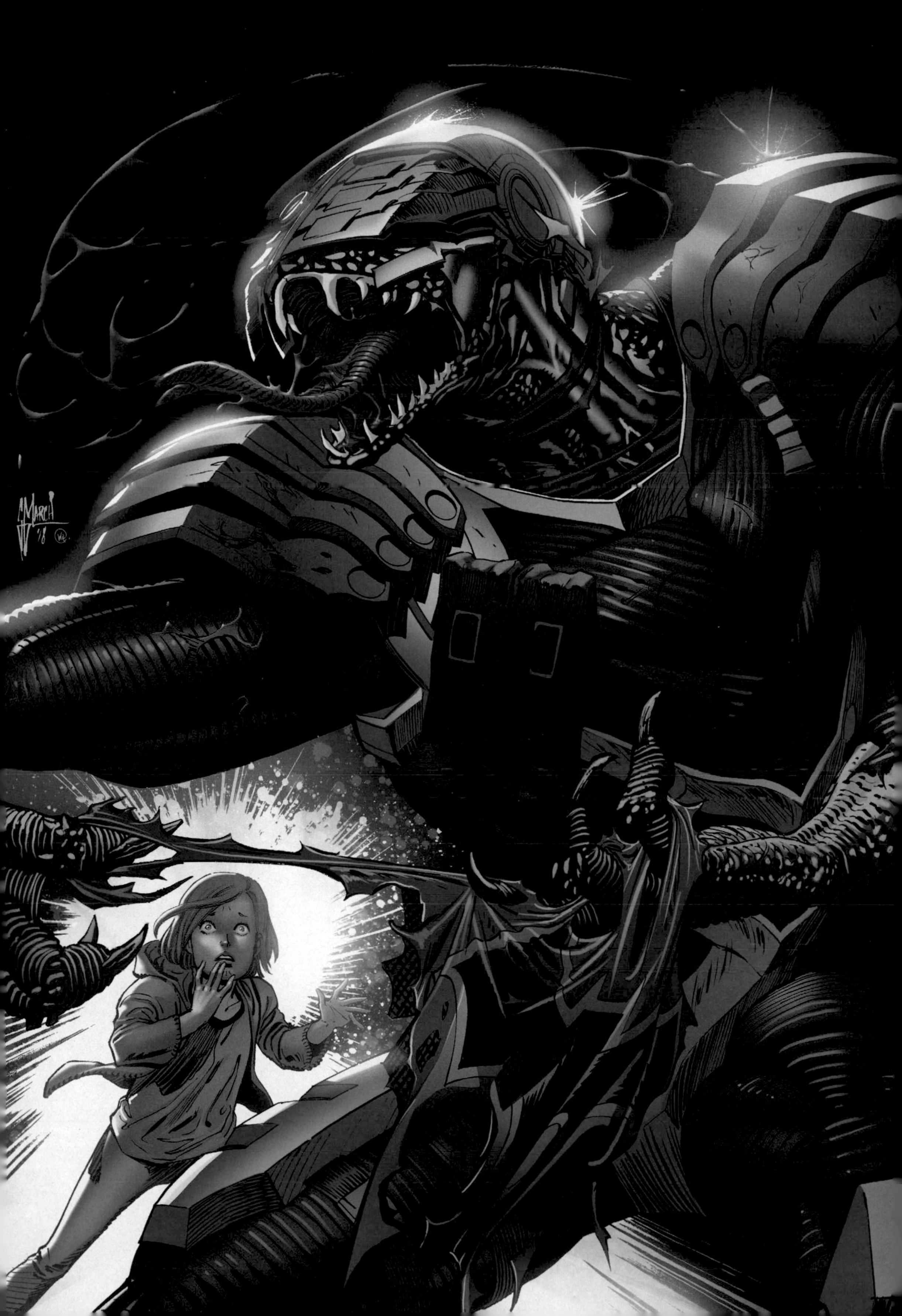

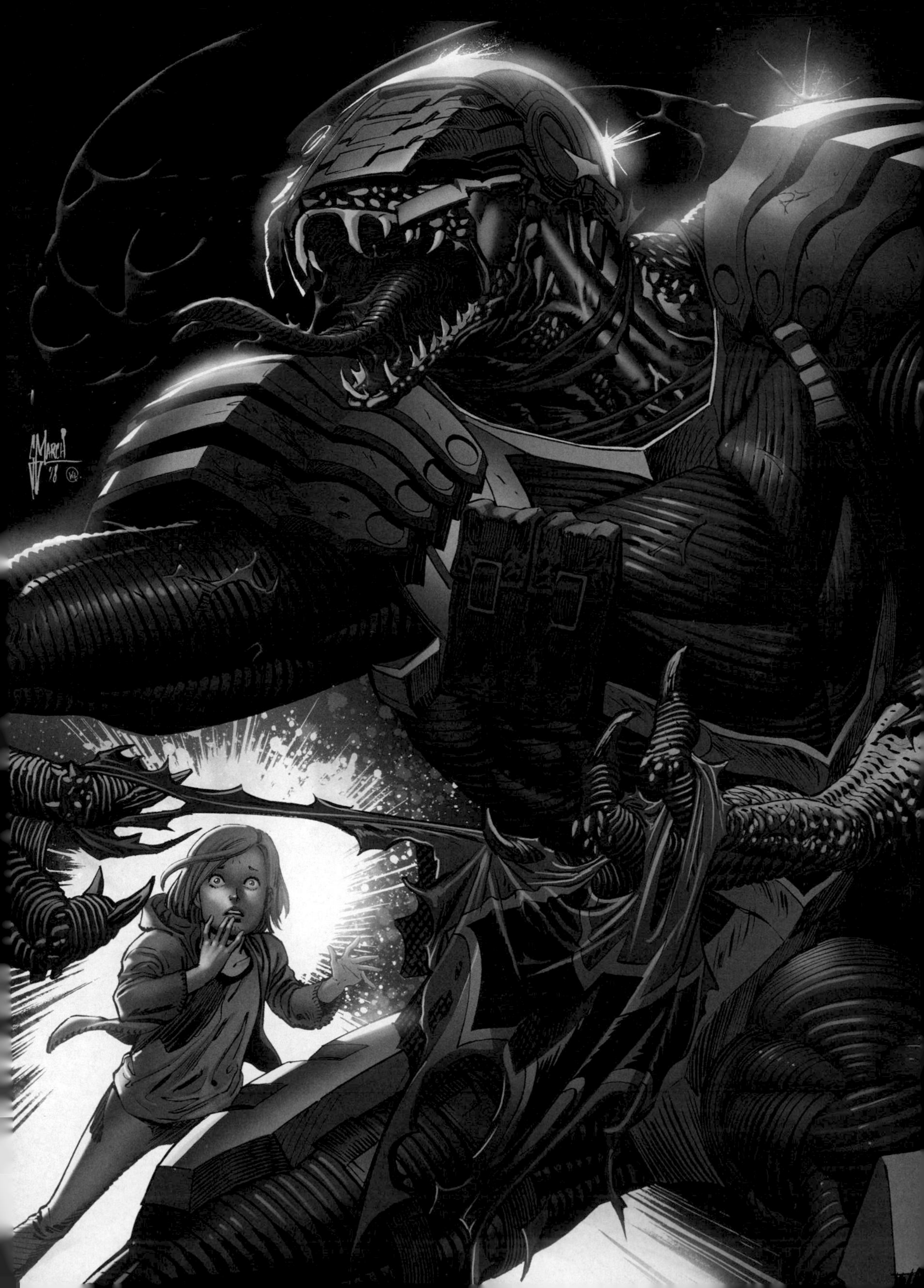

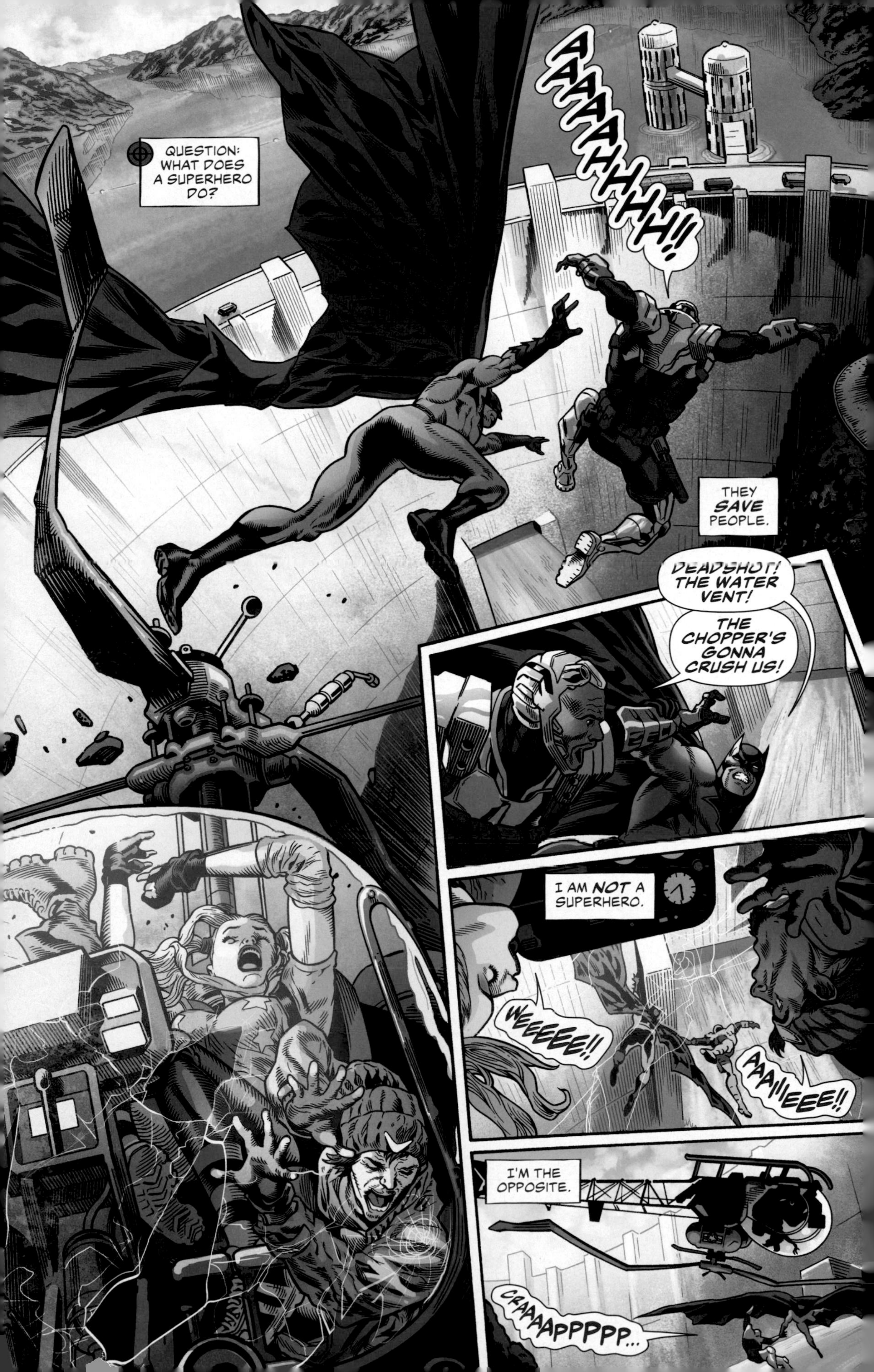
QUESTION: WHAT DOES A SUPERHERO DO?
AAAAAHHHH!!
THEY SAVE PEOPLE.
DEADSHOT! THE WATER VENT!
THE CHOPPER'S GONNA CRUSH US!
I AM NOT A SUPERHERO.
WEEEEE!!
AAAIIIEEE!!
I'M THE OPPOSITE.
CRAAAAPPPPP...

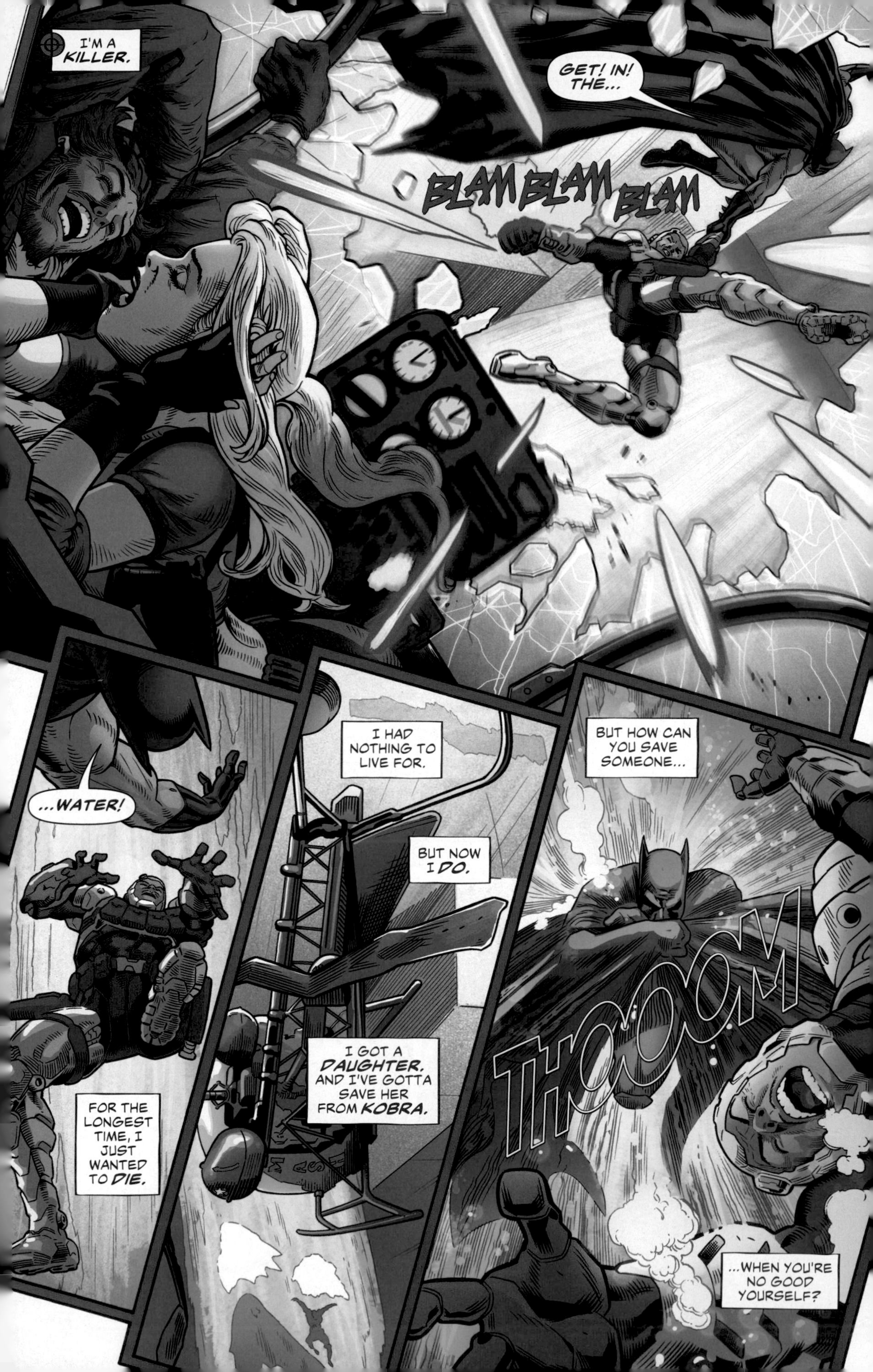
I'M A KILLER.
GET! IN! THE...
BLAM BLAM BLAM
...WATER!
FOR THE LONGEST TIME, I JUST WANTED TO DIE.
I HAD NOTHING TO LIVE FOR.
BUT NOW I DO.
I GOT A DAUGHTER. AND I'VE GOTTA SAVE HER FROM KOBRA.
BUT HOW CAN YOU SAVE SOMEONE...
THOOOM
...WHEN YOU'RE NO GOOD YOURSELF?

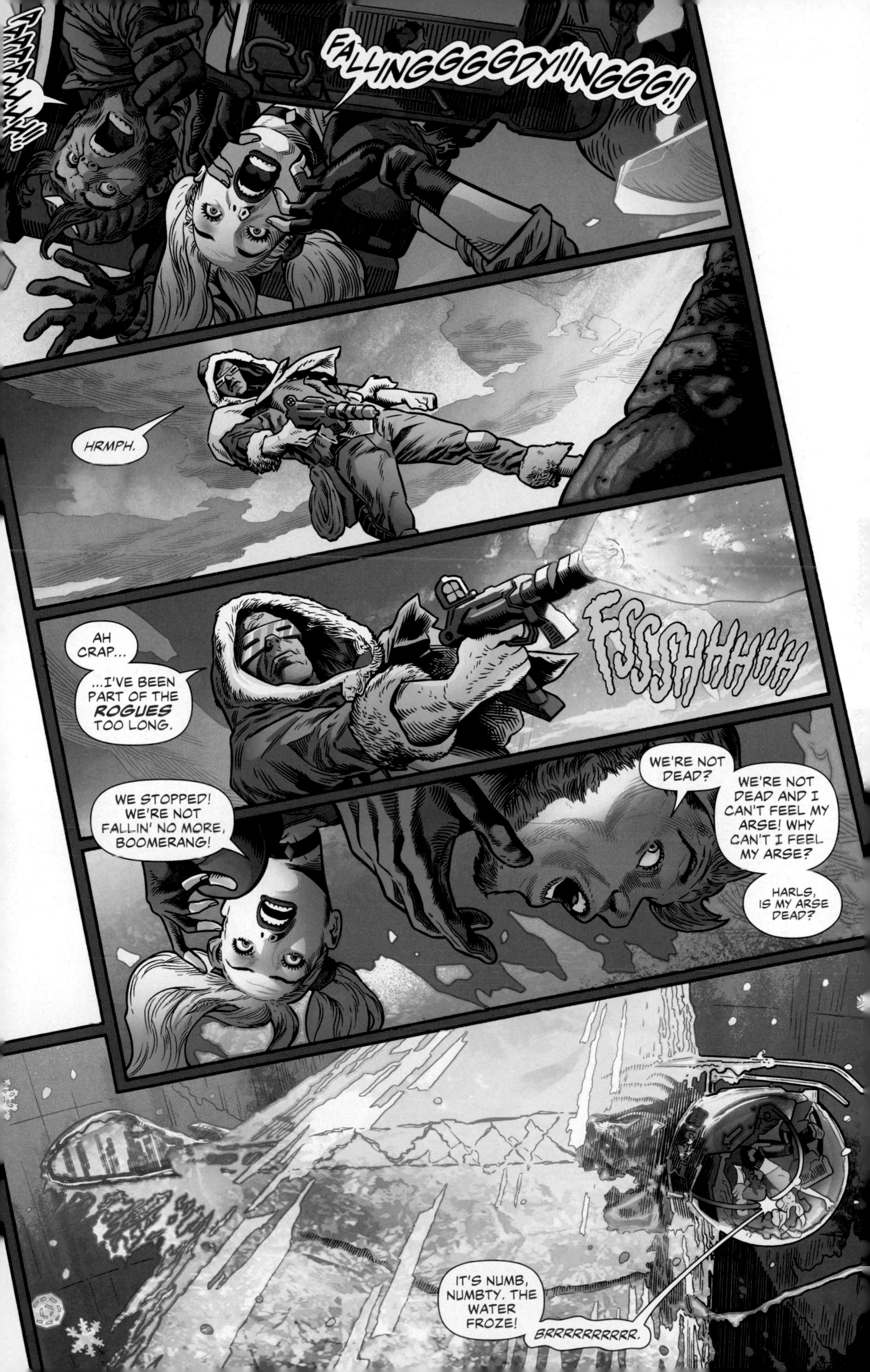
AAAAAAAAAAHHH!!
FALLINGGGGGDYIIINGGGG!!
HRMPH.
AH CRAP...
...I'VE BEEN PART OF THE ROGUES TOO LONG.
FSSSHHHHH
WE STOPPED! WE'RE NOT FALLIN' NO MORE, BOOMERANG!
WE'RE NOT DEAD?
WE'RE NOT DEAD AND I CAN'T FEEL MY ARSE! WHY CAN'T I FEEL MY ARSE?
HARLS, IS MY ARSE DEAD?
IT'S NUMB, NUMBTY. THE WATER FROZE!
BRRRRRRRRRR.

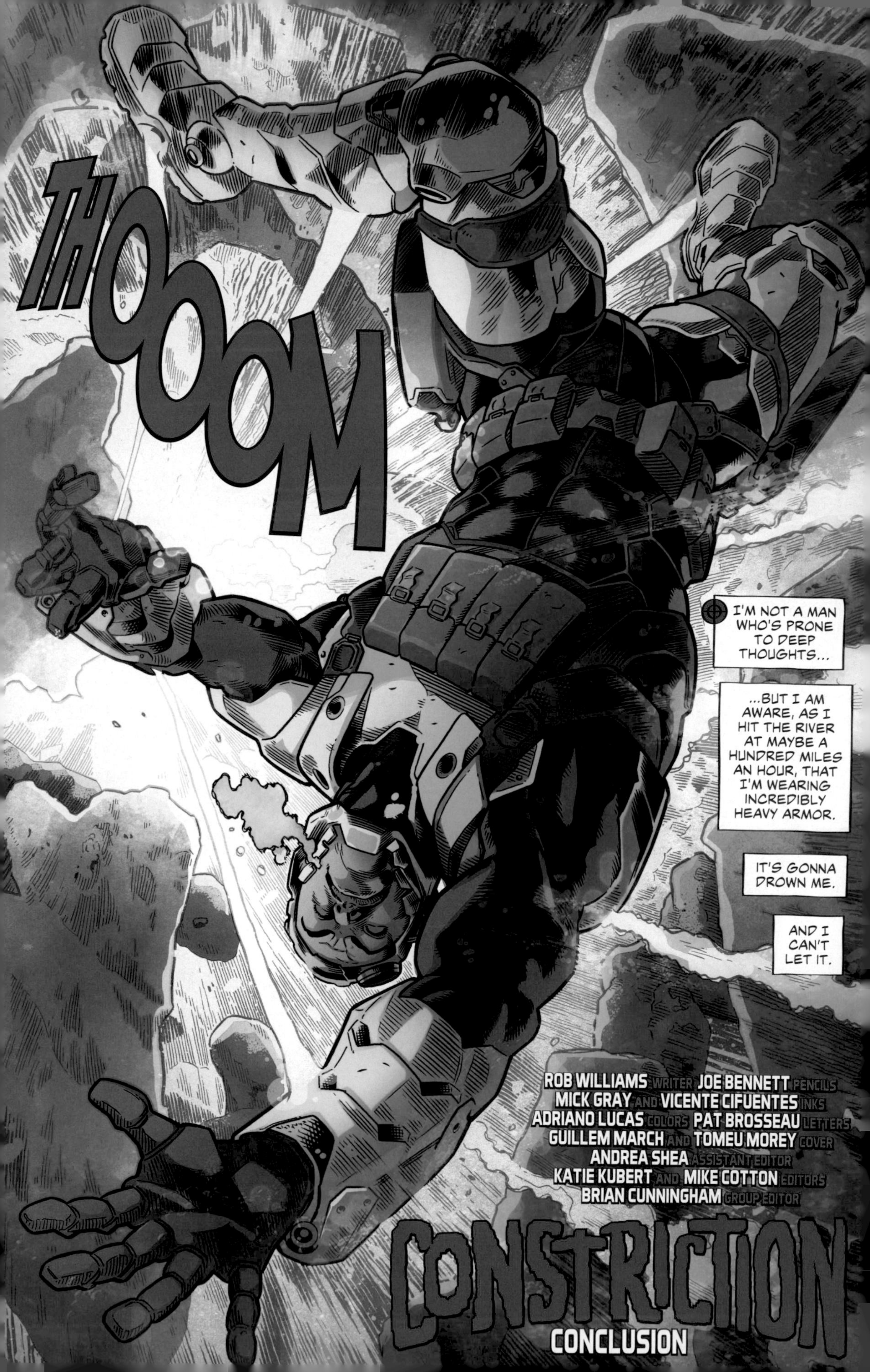
THOOOOM
I'M NOT A MAN WHO'S PRONE TO DEEP THOUGHTS...
...BUT I AM AWARE, AS I HIT THE RIVER AT MAYBE A HUNDRED MILES AN HOUR, THAT I'M WEARING INCREDIBLY HEAVY ARMOR.
IT'S GONNA DROWN ME.
AND I CAN'T LET IT.
ROB WILLIAMS WRITER JOE BENNETT PENCILS
MICK GRAY AND VICENTE CIFUENTES INKS
ADRIANO LUCAS COLORS PAT BROSSEAU LETTERS
GUILLEM MARCH AND TOMEU MOREY COVER
ANDREA SHEA ASSISTANT EDITOR
KATIE KUBERT AND MIKE COTTON EDITORS
BRIAN CUNNINGHAM GROUP EDITOR
CONSTRICTION
CONCLUSION

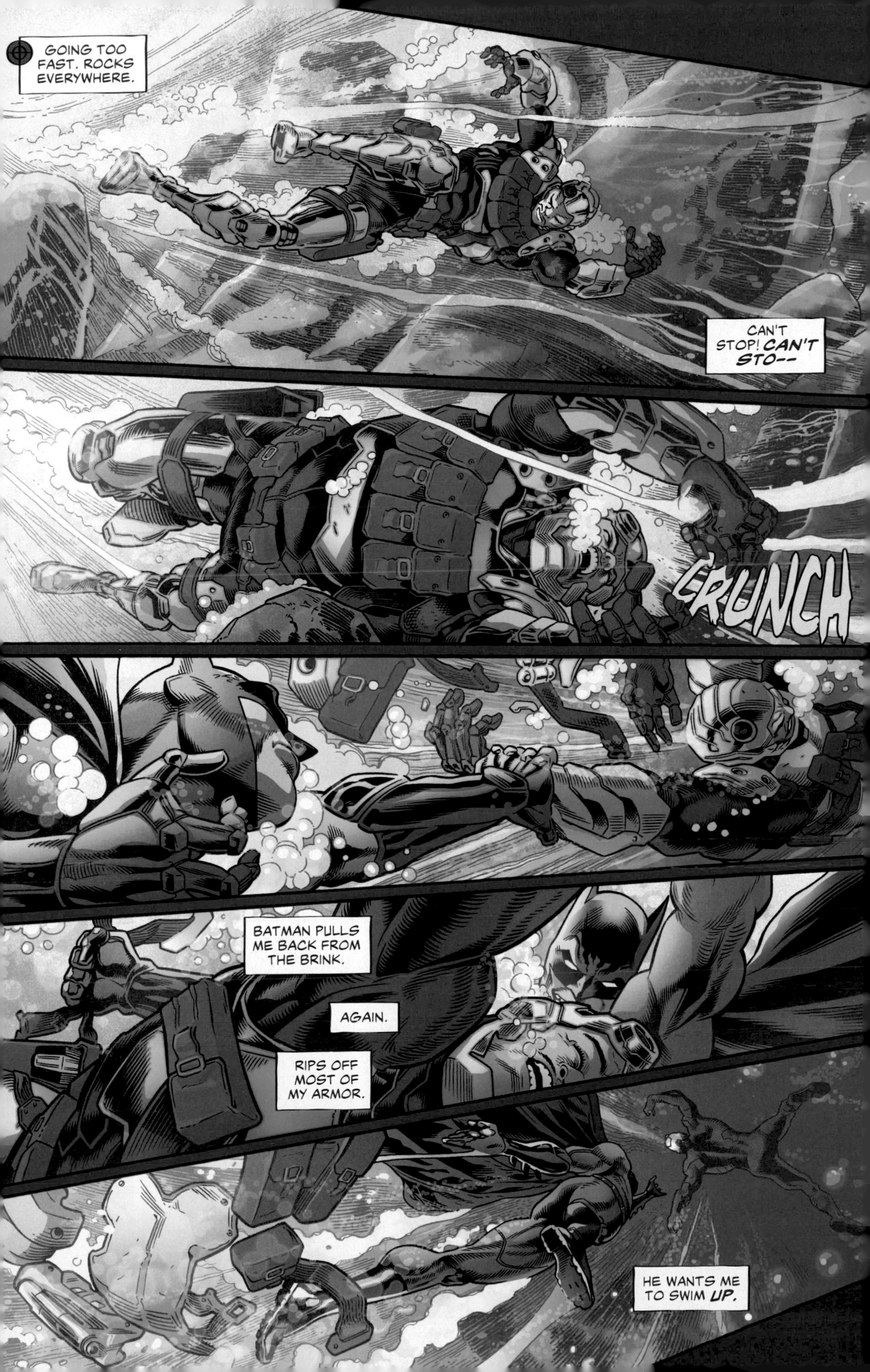
GOING TOO FAST. ROCKS EVERYWHERE.
CAN'T STOP! CAN'T STO--
CRUNCH
BATMAN PULLS ME BACK FROM THE BRINK.
AGAIN.
RIPS OFF MOST OF MY ARMOR.
HE WANTS ME TO SWIM UP.

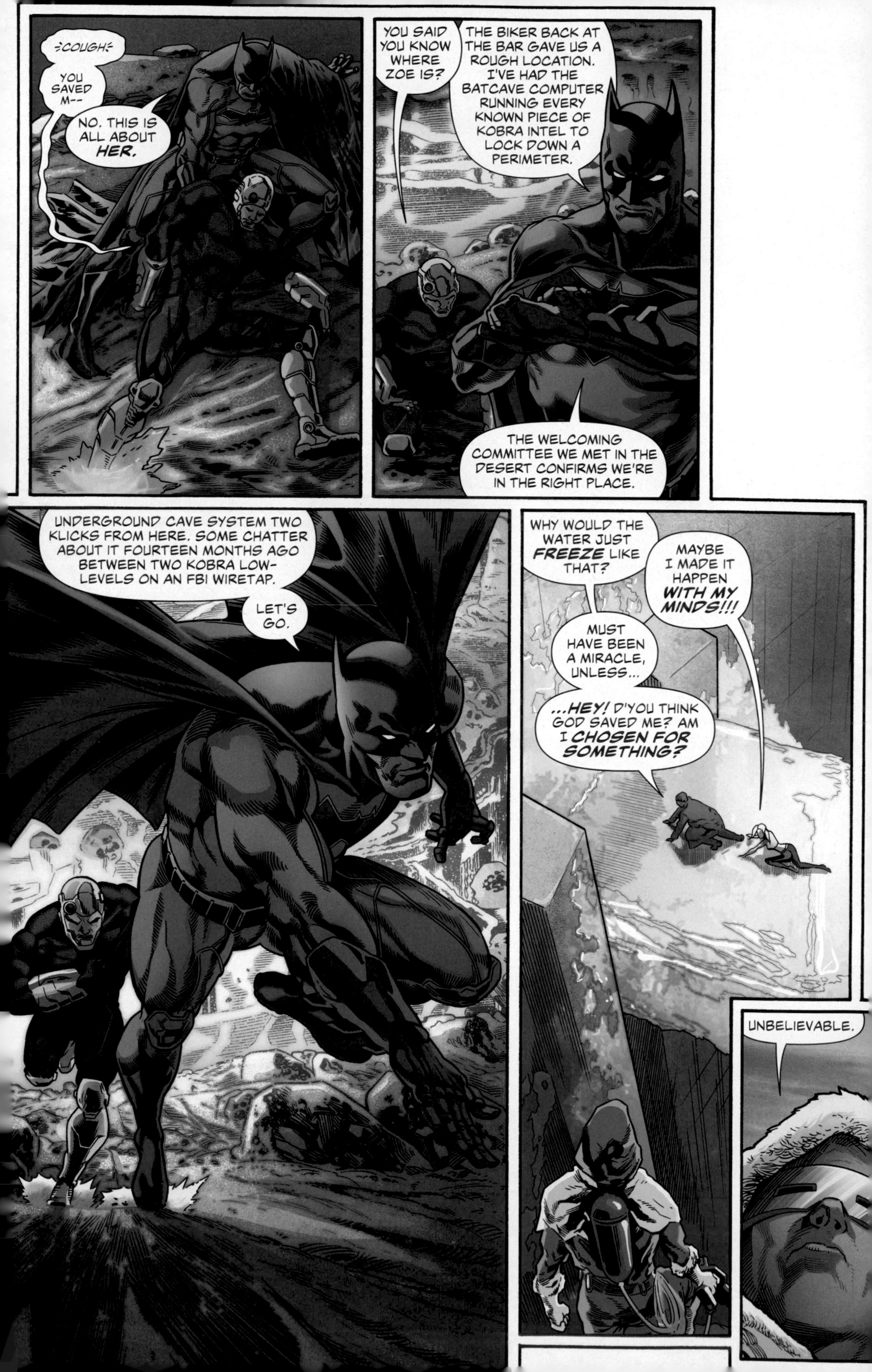

COUGH
YOU SAVED M--
NO. THIS IS ALL ABOUT HER.
YOU SAID YOU KNOW WHERE ZOE IS?
THE BIKER BACK AT THE BAR GAVE US A ROUGH LOCATION. I'VE HAD THE BATCAVE COMPUTER RUNNING EVERY KNOWN PIECE OF KOBRA INTEL TO LOCK DOWN A PERIMETER.
THE WELCOMING COMMITTEE WE MET IN THE DESERT CONFIRMS WE'RE IN THE RIGHT PLACE.
UNDERGROUND CAVE SYSTEM TWO KLICKS FROM HERE. SOME CHATTER ABOUT IT FOURTEEN MONTHS AGO BETWEEN TWO KOBRA LOW-LEVELS ON AN FBI WIRETAP.
LET'S GO.
WHY WOULD THE WATER JUST FREEZE LIKE THAT?
MAYBE I MADE IT HAPPEN WITH MY MINDS!!!
MUST HAVE BEEN A MIRACLE, UNLESS...
...HEY! D'YOU THINK GOD SAVED ME? AM I CHOSEN FOR SOMETHING?
UNBELIEVABLE.

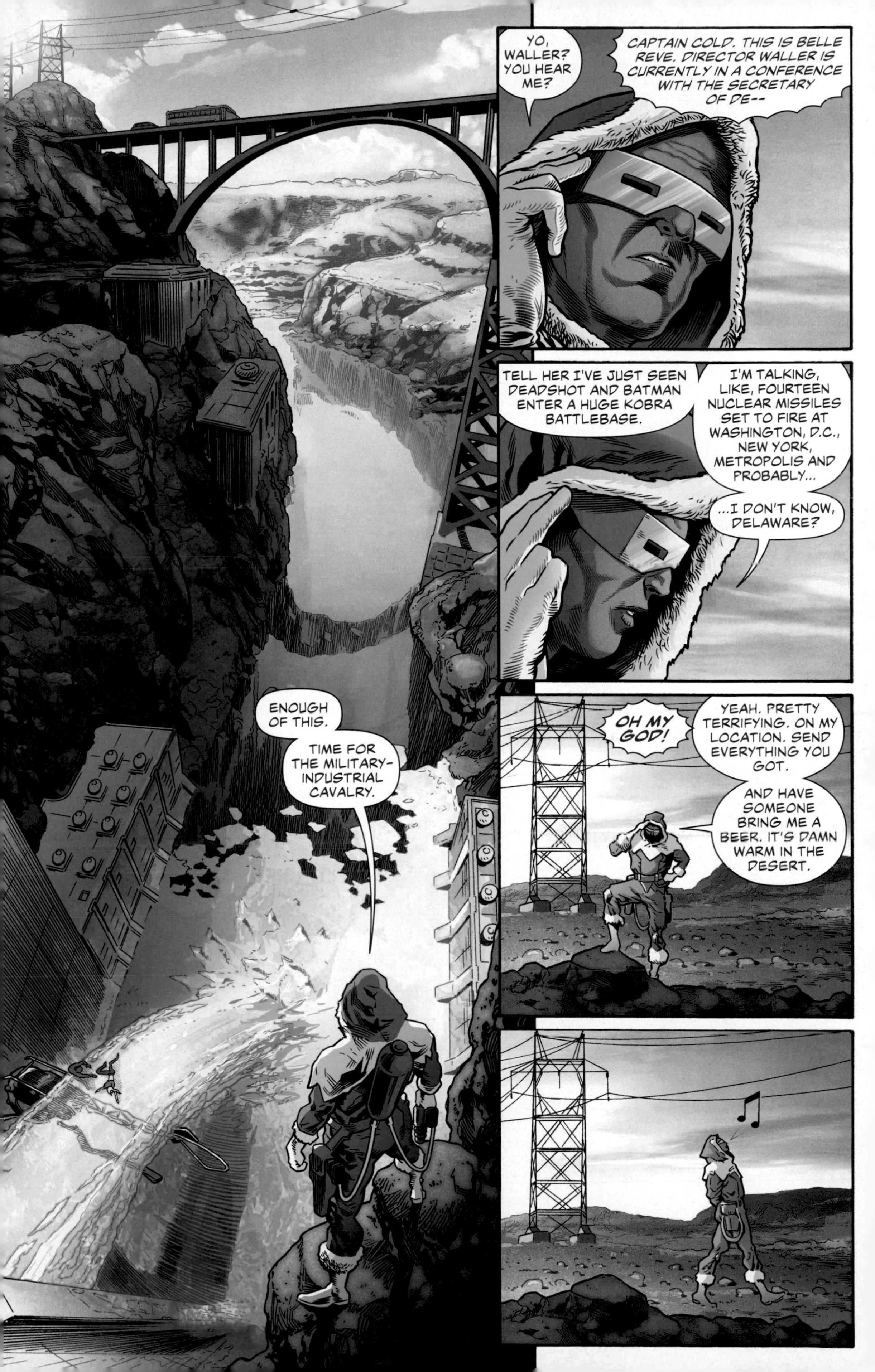
YO, WALLER? YOU HEAR ME?
CAPTAIN COLD. THIS IS BELLE REVE. DIRECTOR WALLER IS CURRENTLY IN A CONFERENCE WITH THE SECRETARY OF DE--
TELL HER I'VE JUST SEEN DEADSHOT AND BATMAN ENTER A HUGE KOBRA BATTLEBASE.
I'M TALKING, LIKE, FOURTEEN NUCLEAR MISSILES SET TO FIRE AT WASHINGTON, D.C., NEW YORK, METROPOLIS AND PROBABLY...
...I DON'T KNOW, DELAWARE?
OH MY GOD!
YEAH. PRETTY TERRIFYING. ON MY LOCATION. SEND EVERYTHING YOU GOT.
AND HAVE SOMEONE BRING ME A BEER. IT'S DAMN WARM IN THE DESERT.
ENOUGH OF THIS.
TIME FOR THE MILITARY-INDUSTRIAL CAVALRY.

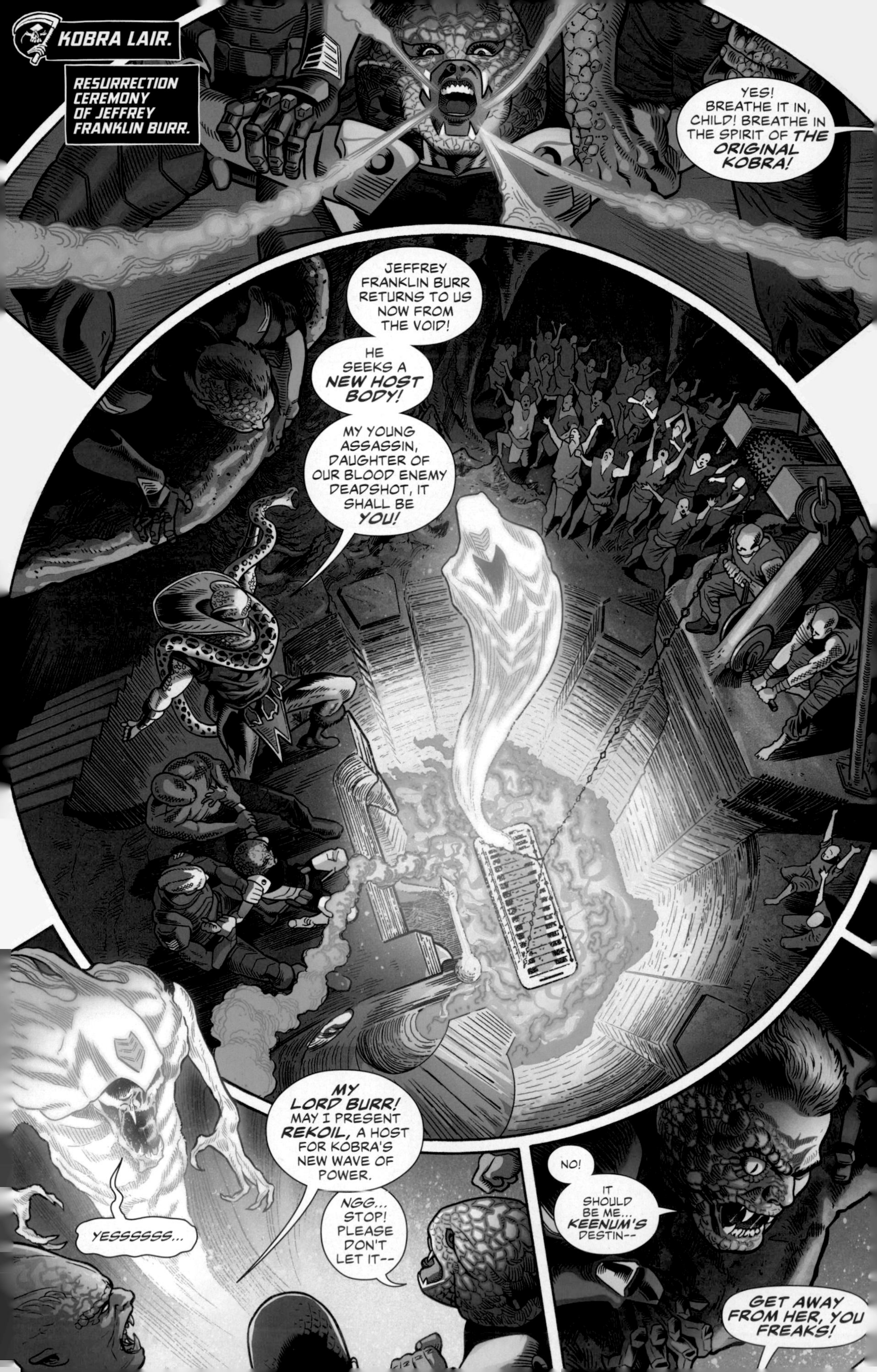
KOBRA LAIR.
RESURRECTION CEREMONY OF JEFFREY FRANKLIN BURR.
YES! BREATHE IT IN, CHILD! BREATHE IN THE SPIRIT OF THE ORIGINAL KOBRA!
JEFFREY FRANKLIN BURR RETURNS TO US NOW FROM THE VOID!
HE SEEKS A NEW HOST BODY!
MY YOUNG ASSASSIN, DAUGHTER OF OUR BLOOD ENEMY DEADSHOT, IT SHALL BE YOU!
MY LORD BURR! MAY I PRESENT REKOIL, A HOST FOR KOBRA'S NEW WAVE OF POWER.
YESSSSSS...
NGG... STOP! PLEASE DON'T LET IT--
NO!
IT SHOULD BE ME... KEENUM'S DESTIN--
GET AWAY FROM HER, YOU FREAKS!

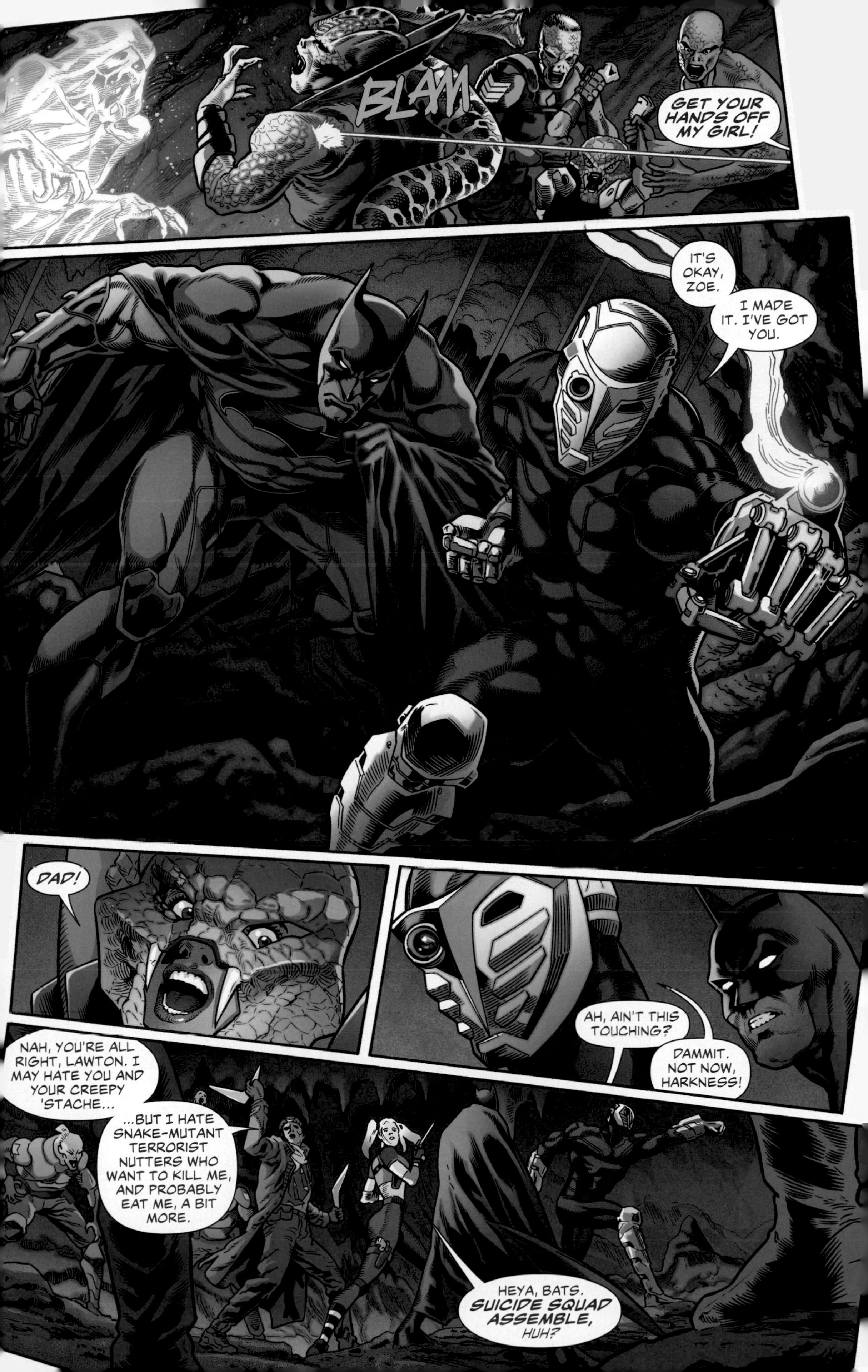
BLAM
GET YOUR HANDS OFF MY GIRL!
IT'S OKAY, ZOE.
I MADE IT. I'VE GOT YOU.
DAD!
AH, AIN'T THIS TOUCHING?
DAMMIT. NOT NOW, HARKNESS!
NAH, YOU'RE ALL RIGHT, LAWTON. I MAY HATE YOU AND YOUR CREEPY 'STACHE...
...BUT I HATE SNAKE-MUTANT TERRORIST NUTTERS WHO WANT TO KILL ME, AND PROBABLY EAT ME, A BIT MORE.
HEYA, BATS. SUICIDE SQUAD ASSEMBLE, HUH?

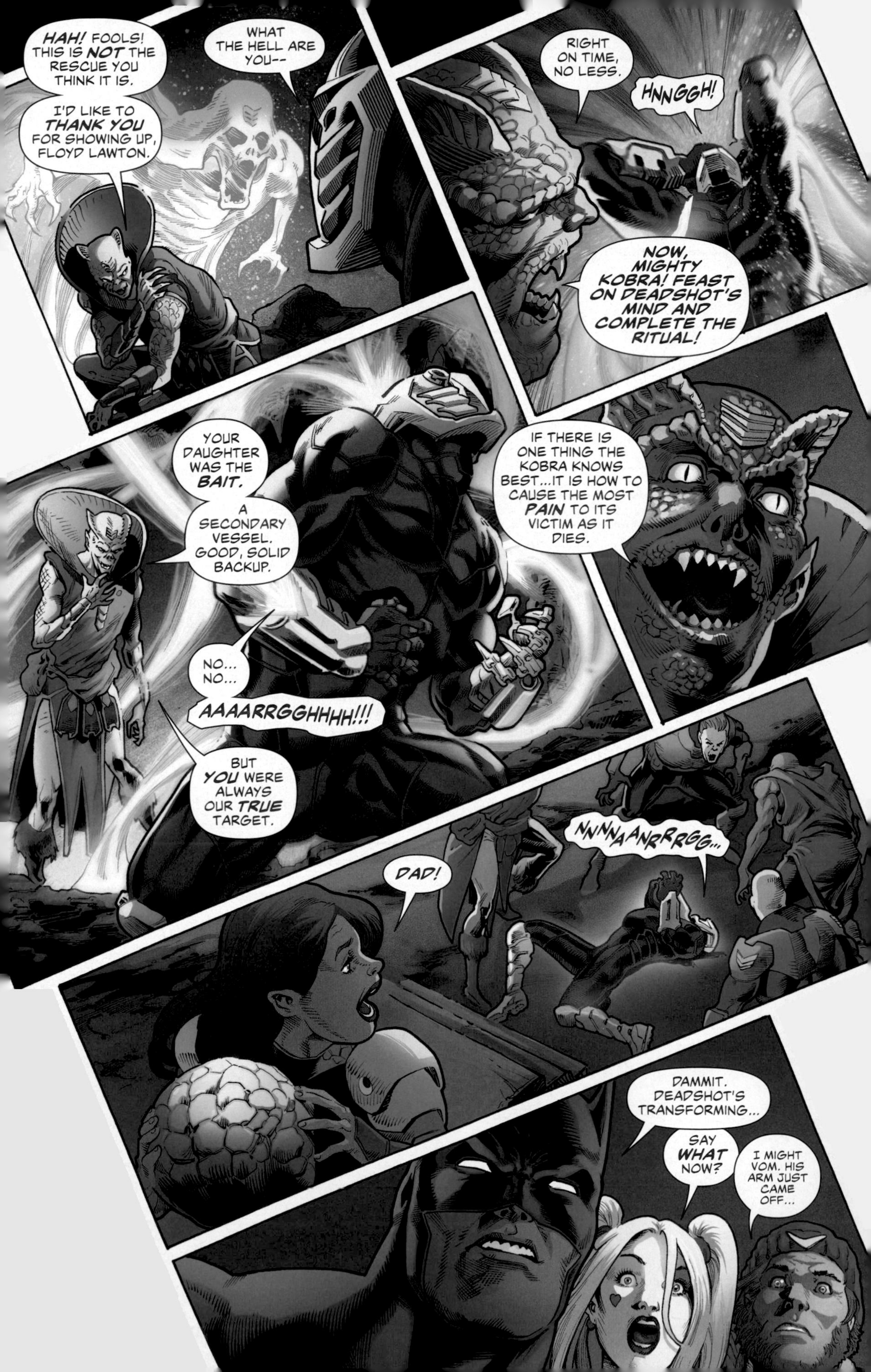
HAH! FOOLS! THIS IS NOT THE RESCUE YOU THINK IT IS.
I'D LIKE TO THANK YOU FOR SHOWING UP, FLOYD LAWTON.
WHAT THE HELL ARE YOU--
RIGHT ON TIME, NO LESS.
HNNGGH!
NOW, MIGHTY KOBRA! FEAST ON DEADSHOT'S MIND AND COMPLETE THE RITUAL!
YOUR DAUGHTER WAS THE BAIT.
A SECONDARY VESSEL. GOOD, SOLID BACKUP.
NO... NO...
AAAARRGGHHHH!!!
BUT YOU WERE ALWAYS OUR TRUE TARGET.
IF THERE IS ONE THING THE KOBRA KNOWS BEST...IT IS HOW TO CAUSE THE MOST PAIN TO ITS VICTIM AS IT DIES.
NNNNAANRRRGG...
DAD!
DAMMIT. DEADSHOT'S TRANSFORMING...
SAY WHAT NOW?
I MIGHT VOM. HIS ARM JUST CAME OFF...

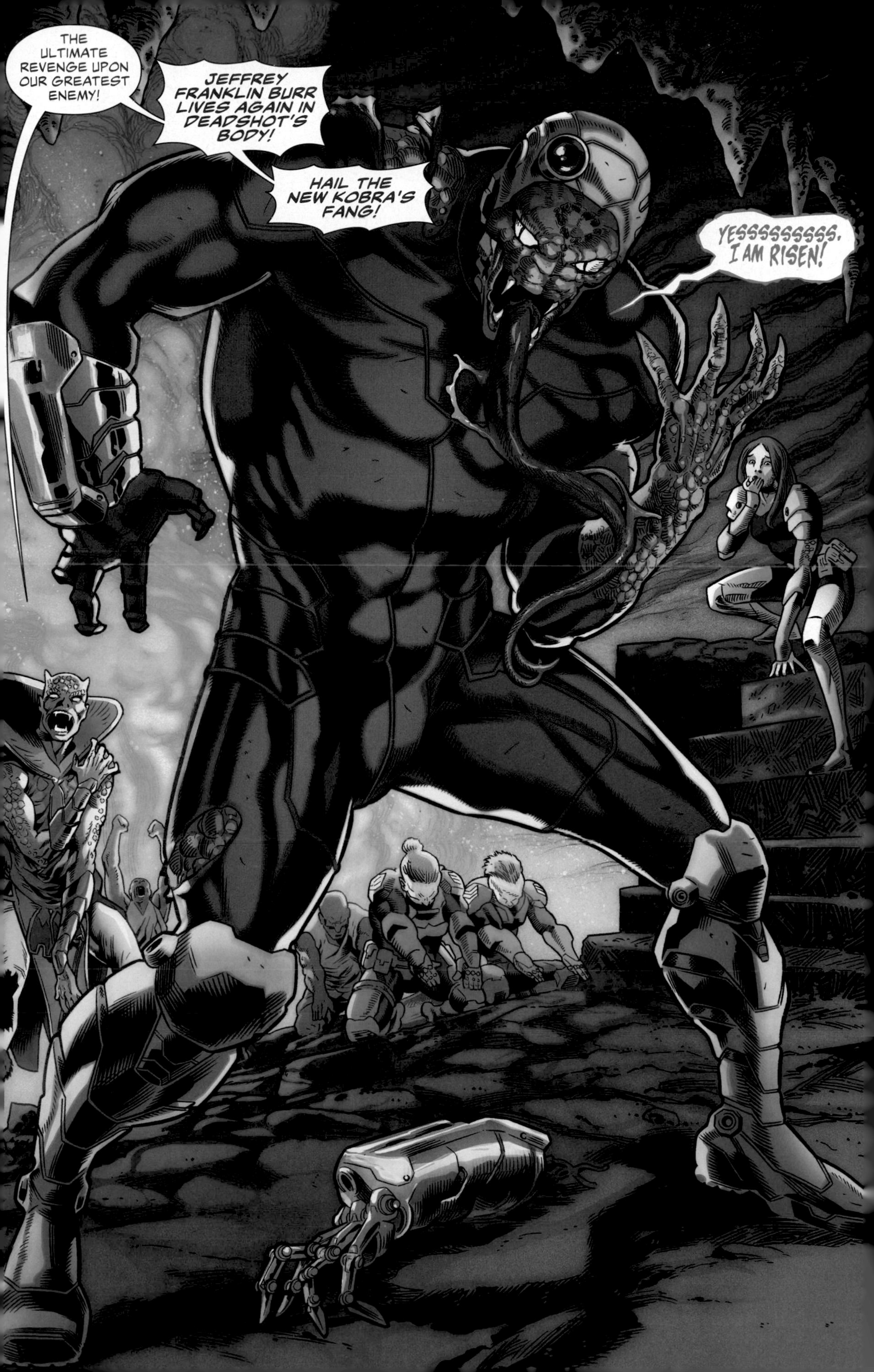
THE ULTIMATE REVENGE UPON OUR GREATEST ENEMY!
JEFFREY FRANKLIN BURR LIVES AGAIN IN DEADSHOT'S BODY!
HAIL THE NEW KOBRA'S FANG!
YESSSSSSSSS. I AM RISEN!

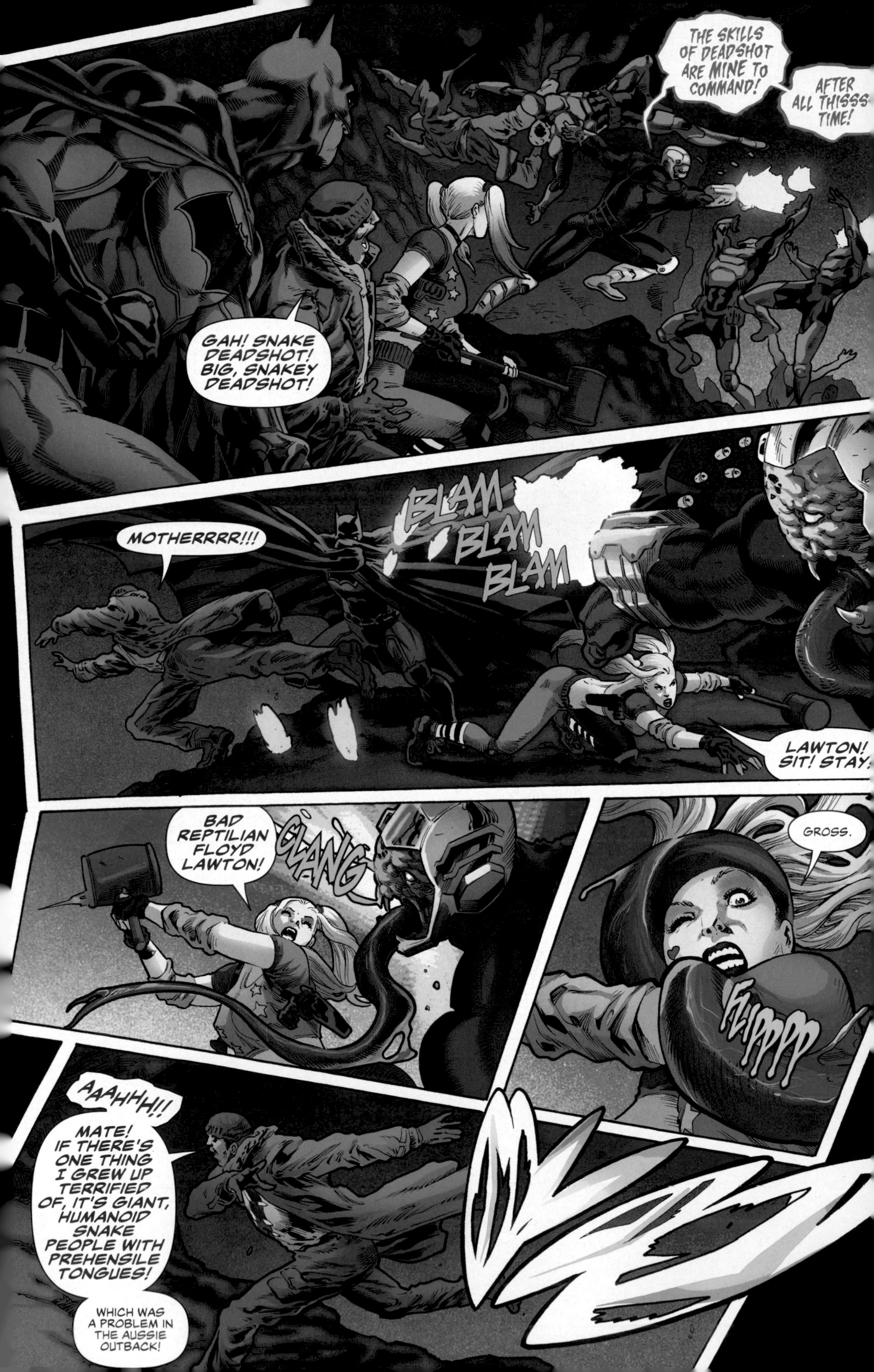
THE SKILLS OF DEADSHOT ARE MINE TO COMMAND!
AFTER ALL THISSS TIME!
GAH! SNAKE DEADSHOT! BIG, SNAKEY DEADSHOT!
BLAM BLAM BLAM
MOTHERRRR!!!
LAWTON! SIT! STAY!
BAD REPTILIAN FLOYD LAWTON!
CLANG
GROSS.
FLLLPPPP
AAAHHH!!
MATE! IF THERE'S ONE THING I GREW UP TERRIFIED OF, IT'S GIANT, HUMANOID SNAKE PEOPLE WITH PREHENSILE TONGUES!
WHICH WAS A PROBLEM IN THE AUSSIE OUTBACK!

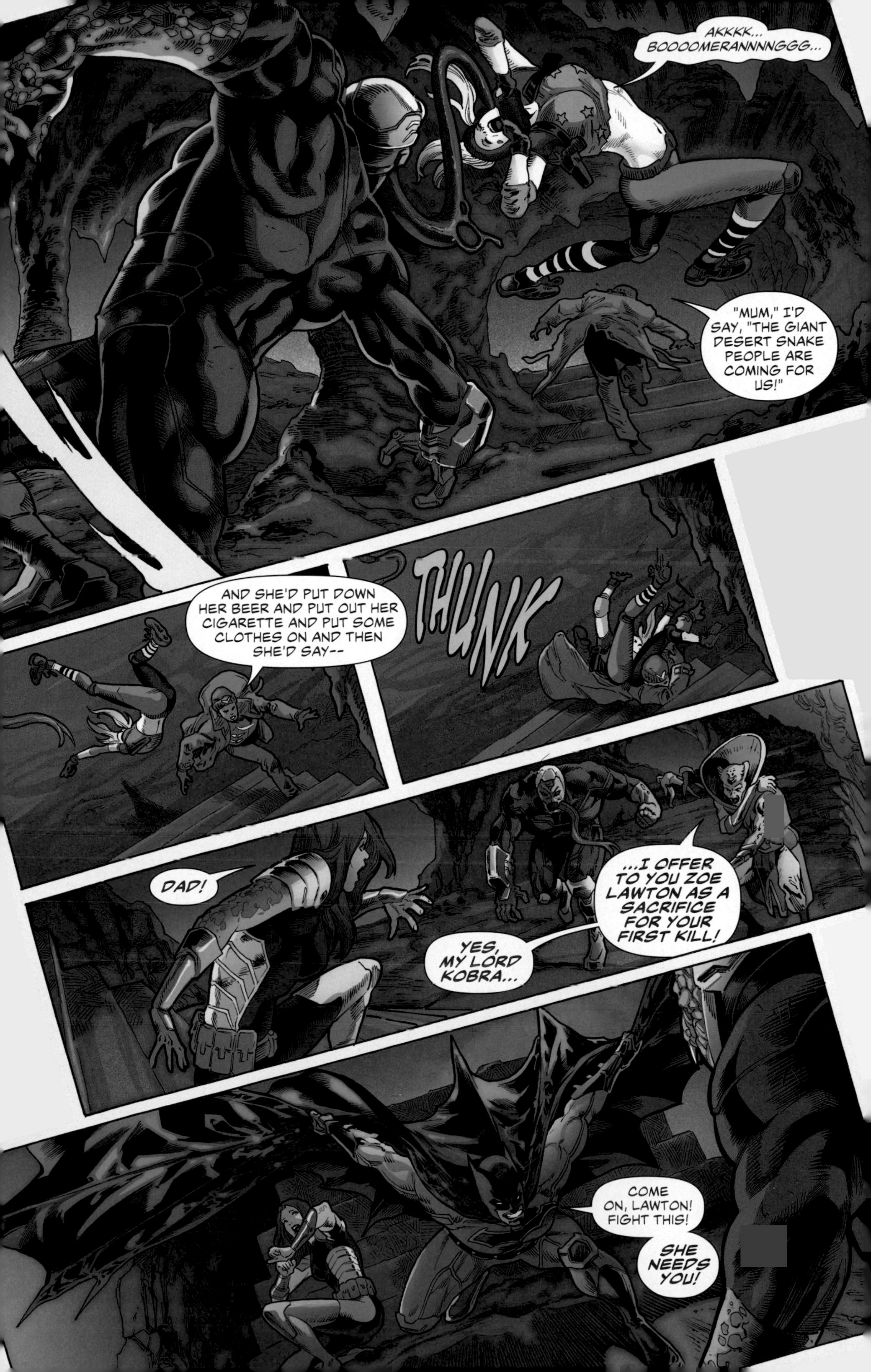
AKKKK... BOOOOMERANNNNGGG...
"MUM," I'D SAY, "THE GIANT DESERT SNAKE PEOPLE ARE COMING FOR US!"
AND SHE'D PUT DOWN HER BEER AND PUT OUT HER CIGARETTE AND PUT SOME CLOTHES ON AND THEN SHE'D SAY--
THUNK
DAD!
...I OFFER TO YOU ZOE LAWTON AS A SACRIFICE FOR YOUR FIRST KILL!
YES, MY LORD KOBRA...
COME ON, LAWTON! FIGHT THIS!
SHE NEEDS YOU!

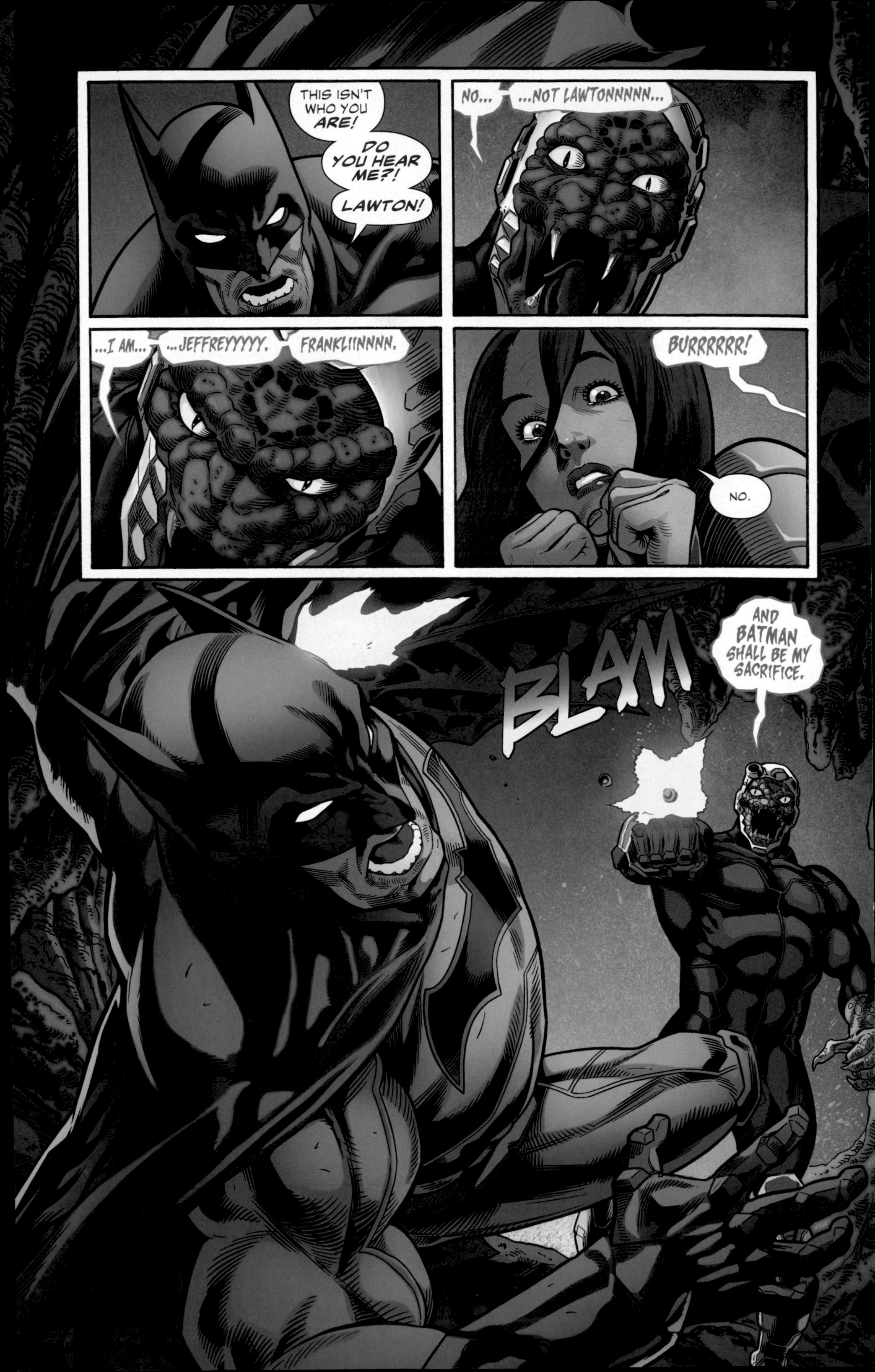
THIS ISN'T WHO YOU ARE!
DO YOU HEAR ME?!
LAWTON!
NO...
...NOT LAWTONNNNN...
...I AM...
...JEFFREYYYYY.
FRANKLIINNNN.
BURRRRRR!
NO.
BLAM
AND BATMAN SHALL BE MY SACRIFICE.

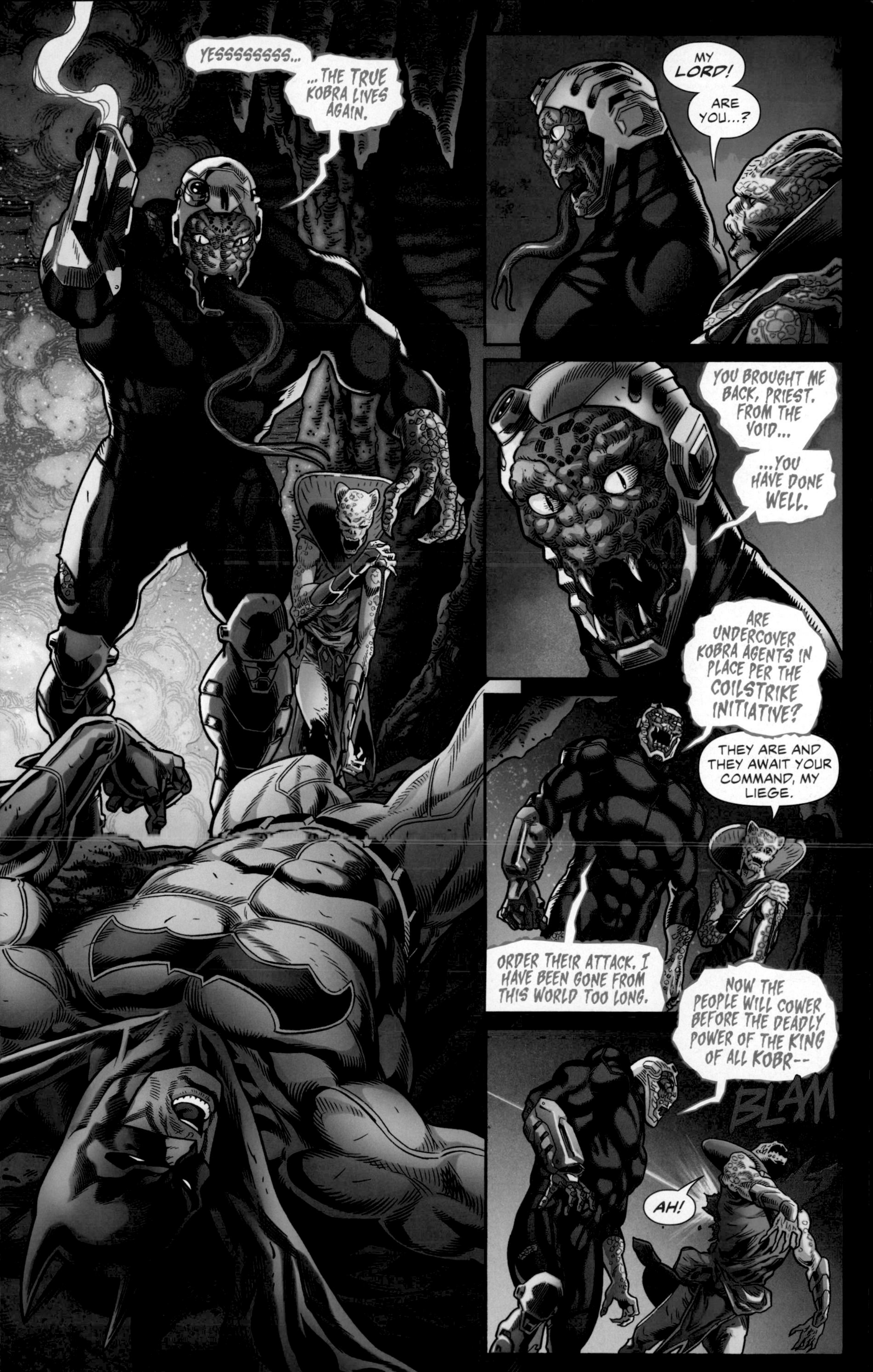
YESSSSSSSS...
...THE TRUE KOBRA LIVES AGAIN.
MY LORD!
ARE YOU...?
YOU BROUGHT ME BACK, PRIEST. FROM THE VOID...
...YOU HAVE DONE WELL.
ARE UNDERCOVER KOBRA AGENTS IN PLACE PER THE COILSTRIKE INITIATIVE?
THEY ARE AND THEY AWAIT YOUR COMMAND, MY LIEGE.
ORDER THEIR ATTACK. I HAVE BEEN GONE FROM THIS WORLD TOO LONG.
NOW THE PEOPLE WILL COWER BEFORE THE DEADLY POWER OF THE KING OF ALL KOBR--
BLAM
AH!

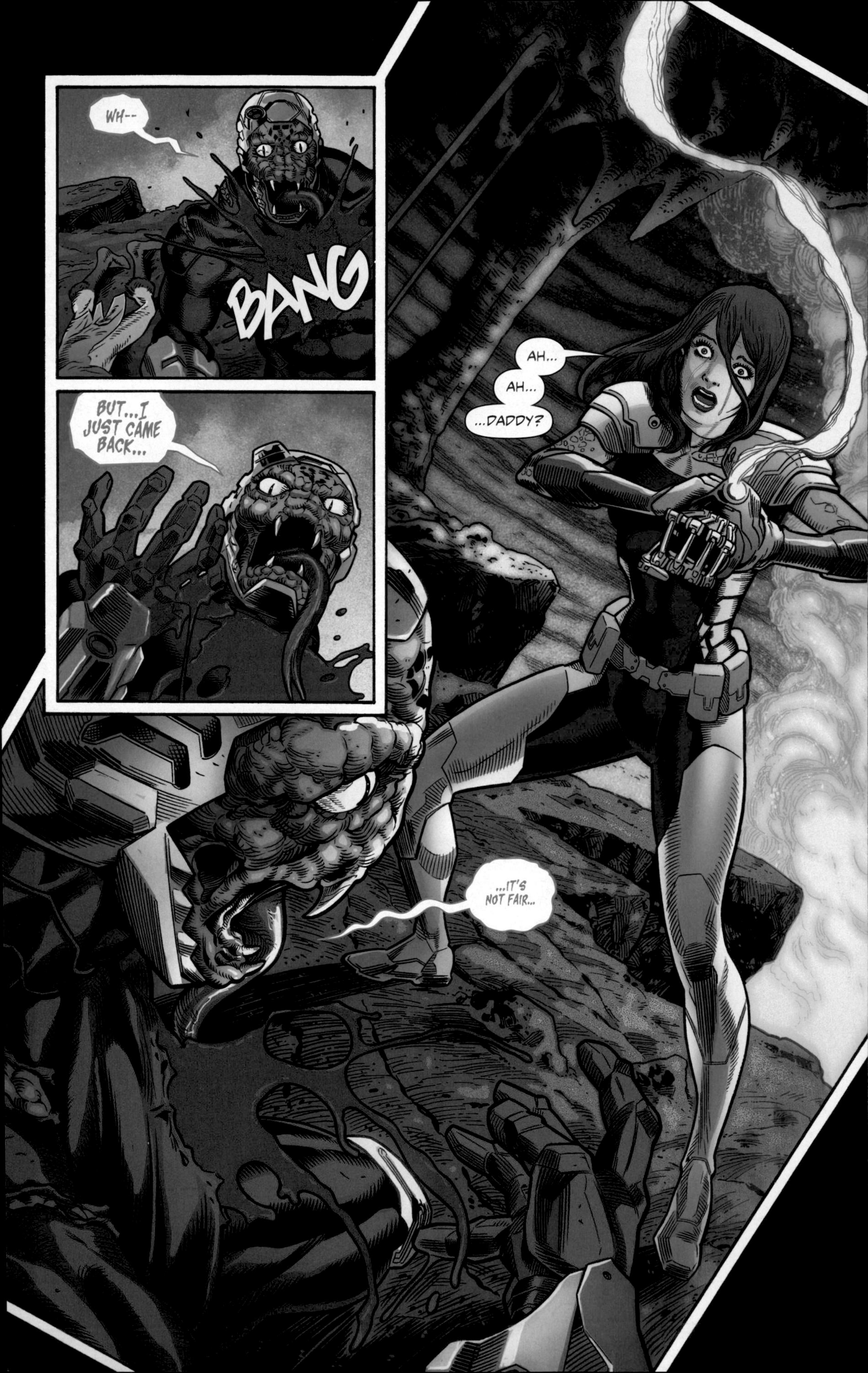
WH--
BANG
BUT...I JUST CAME BACK...
AH...
AH...
...DADDY?
...IT'S NOT FAIR...

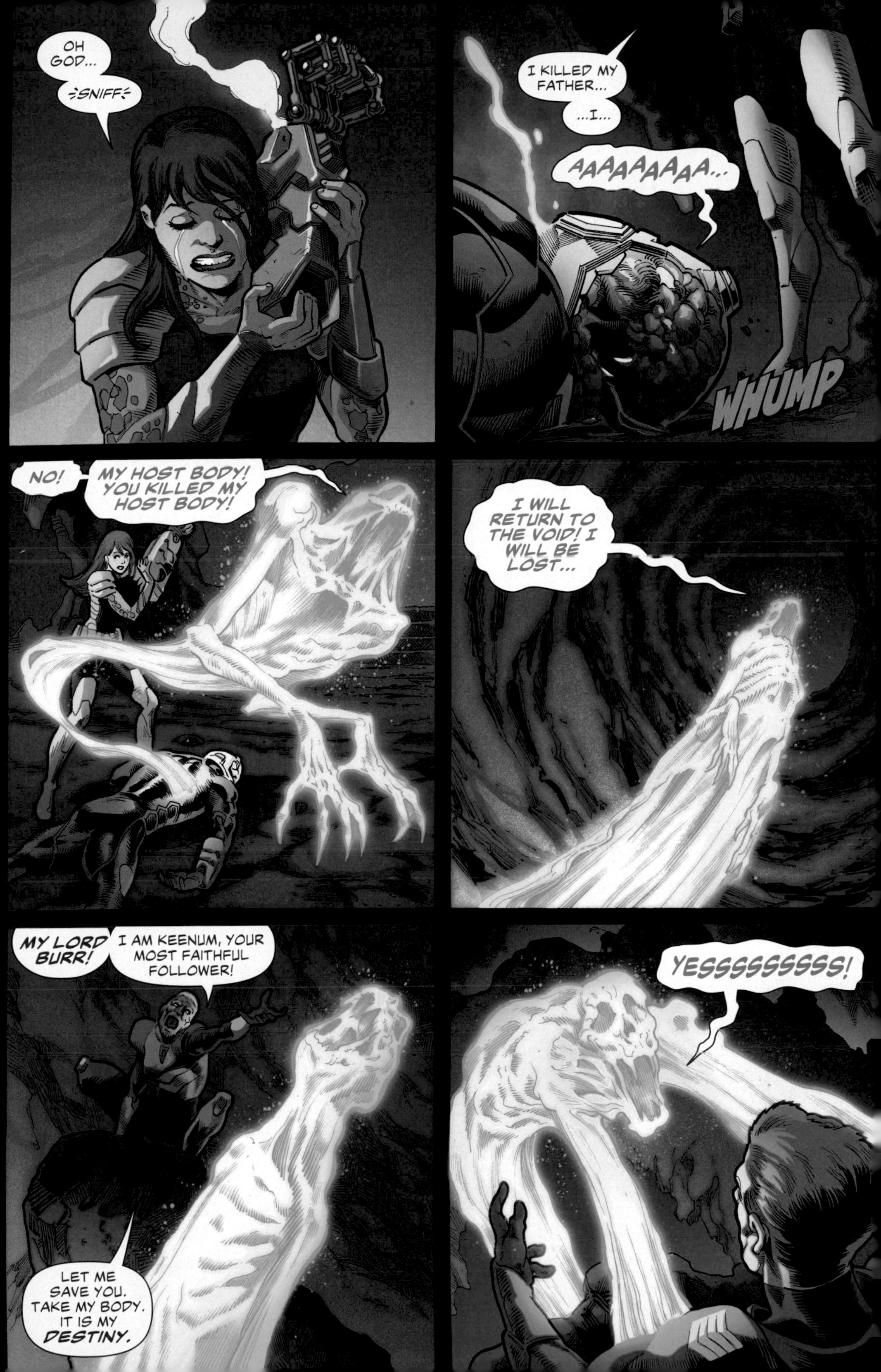
OH GOD...
SNIFF
I KILLED MY FATHER...
...I...
AAAAAAAAA...
WHUMP
NO!
MY HOST BODY! YOU KILLED MY HOST BODY!
I WILL RETURN TO THE VOID! I WILL BE LOST...
MY LORD BURR!
I AM KEENUM, YOUR MOST FAITHFUL FOLLOWER!
LET ME SAVE YOU. TAKE MY BODY. IT IS MY DESTINY.
YESSSSSSSSS!

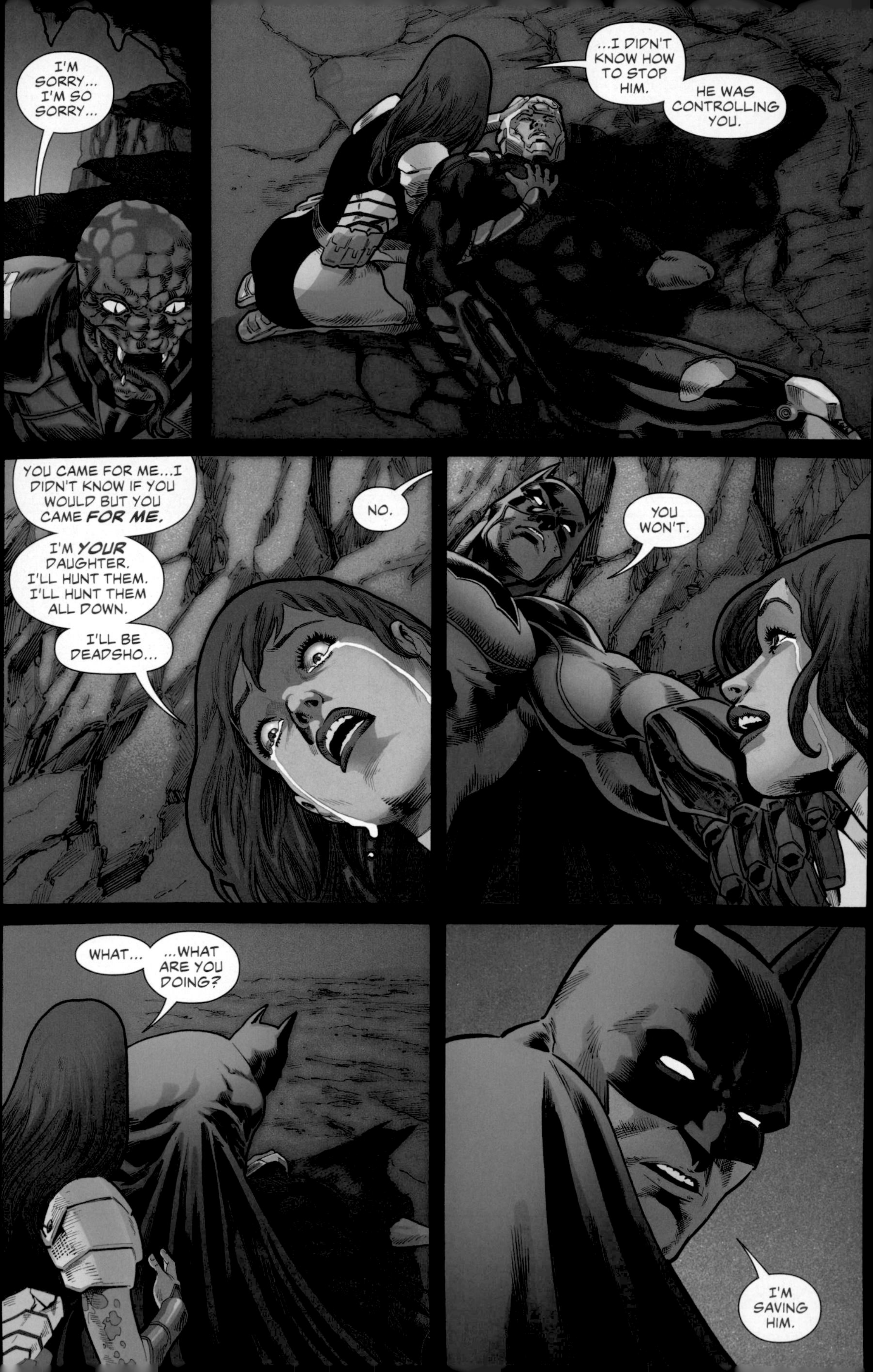
I'M SORRY... I'M SO SORRY...
...I DIDN'T KNOW HOW TO STOP HIM.
HE WAS CONTROLLING YOU.
YOU CAME FOR ME...I DIDN'T KNOW IF YOU WOULD BUT YOU CAME FOR ME.
I'M YOUR DAUGHTER. I'LL HUNT THEM. I'LL HUNT THEM ALL DOWN.
I'LL BE DEADSHO...
NO.
YOU WON'T.
WHAT...
...WHAT ARE YOU DOING?
I'M SAVING HIM.

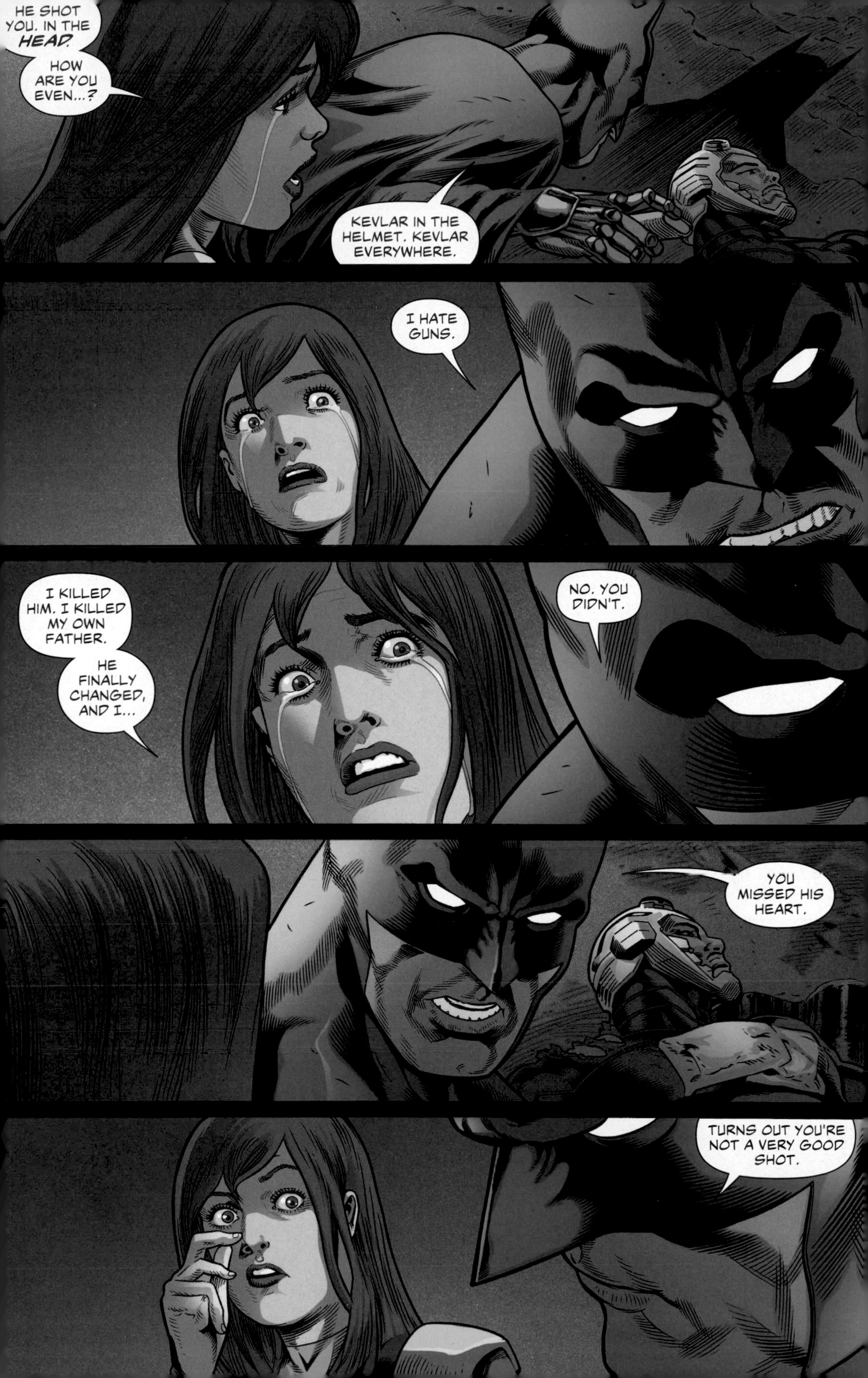
HE SHOT YOU. IN THE HEAD.
HOW ARE YOU EVEN...?
KEVLAR IN THE HELMET. KEVLAR EVERYWHERE.
I HATE GUNS.
I KILLED HIM. I KILLED MY OWN FATHER.
HE FINALLY CHANGED, AND I...
NO. YOU DIDN'T.
YOU MISSED HIS HEART.
TURNS OUT YOU'RE NOT A VERY GOOD SHOT.

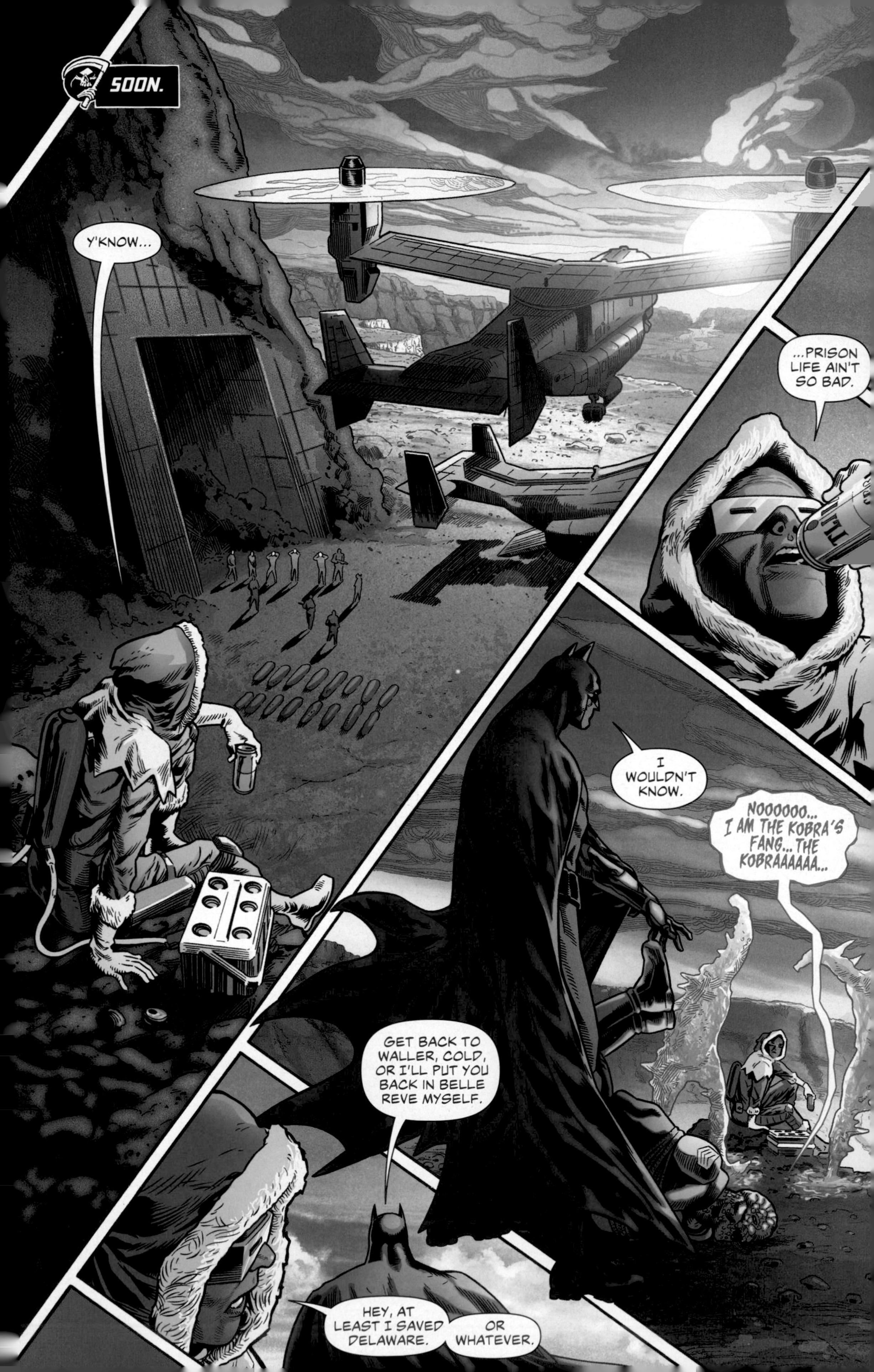
SOON.
Y'KNOW...
...PRISON LIFE AIN'T SO BAD.
I WOULDN'T KNOW.
NOOOOOO... I AM THE KOBRA'S FANG...THE KOBRAAAAAA...
GET BACK TO WALLER, COLD, OR I'LL PUT YOU BACK IN BELLE REVE MYSELF.
HEY, AT LEAST I SAVED DELAWARE.
OR WHATEVER.

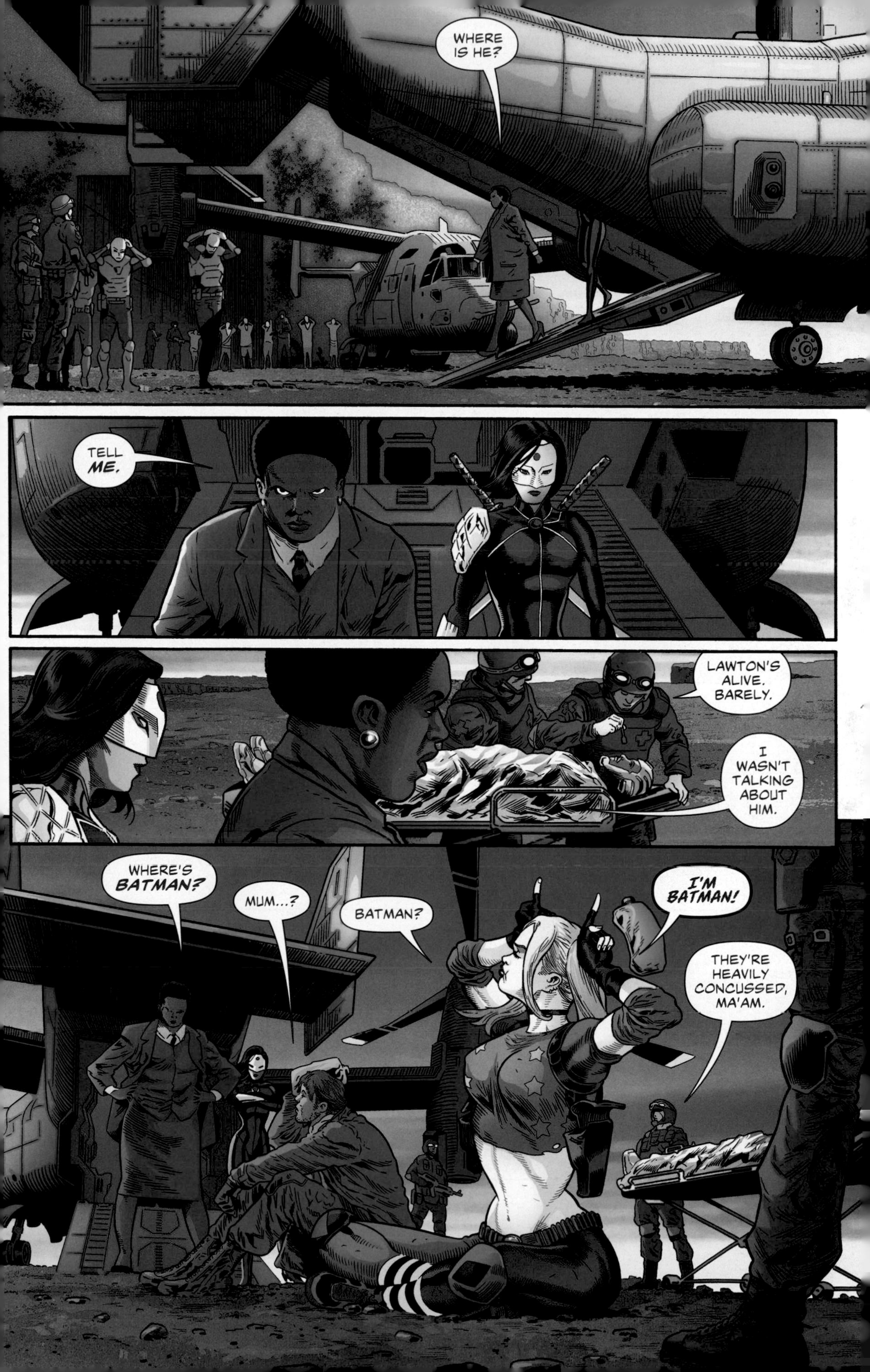
WHERE IS HE?
TELL ME.
LAWTON'S ALIVE. BARELY.
I WASN'T TALKING ABOUT HIM.
WHERE'S BATMAN?
MUM...?
BATMAN?
I'M BATMAN!
THEY'RE HEAVILY CONCUSSED, MA'AM.

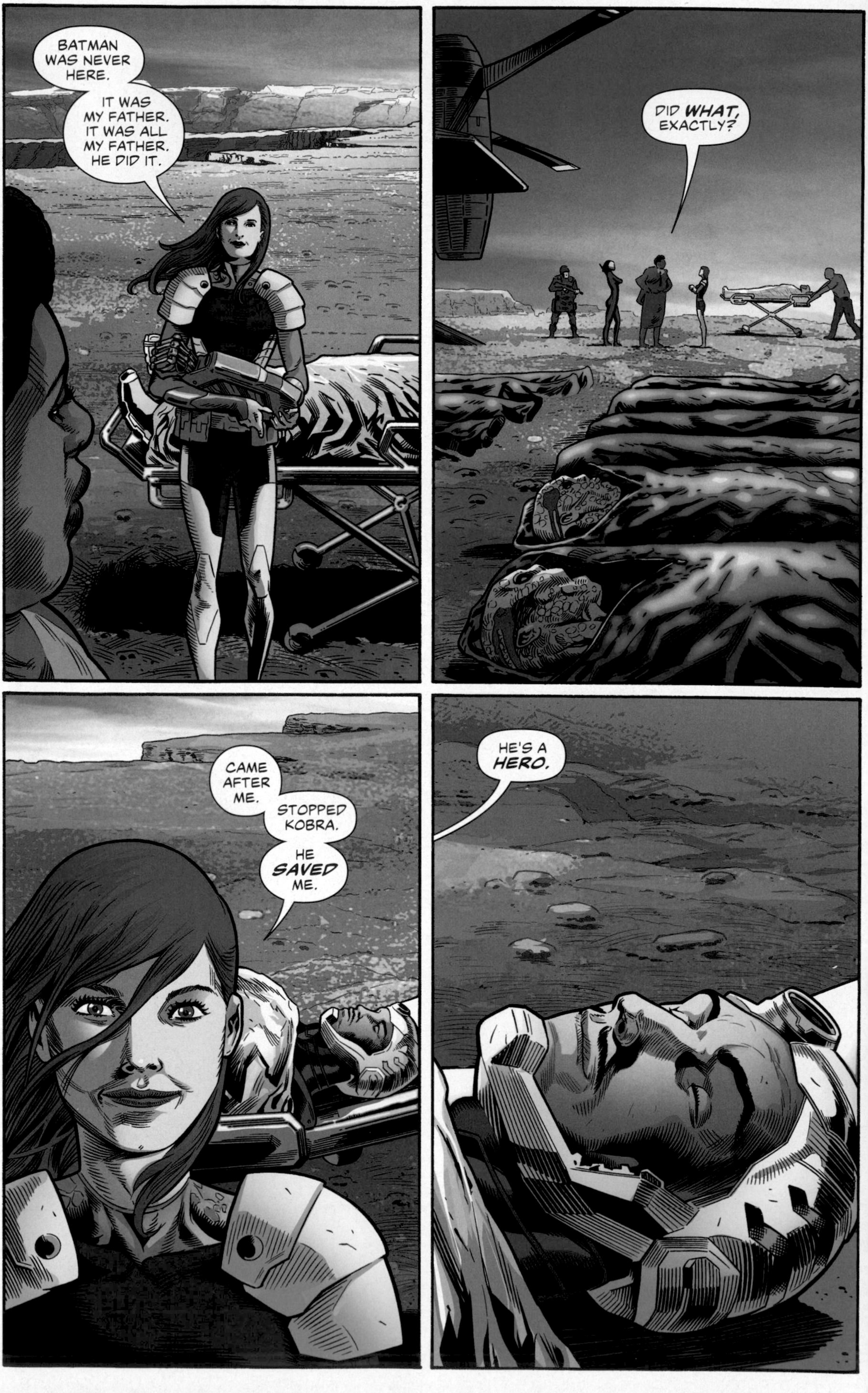
BATMAN WAS NEVER HERE.
IT WAS MY FATHER. IT WAS ALL MY FATHER. HE DID IT.
DID WHAT, EXACTLY?
CAME AFTER ME.
STOPPED KOBRA.
HE SAVED ME.
HE'S A HERO.

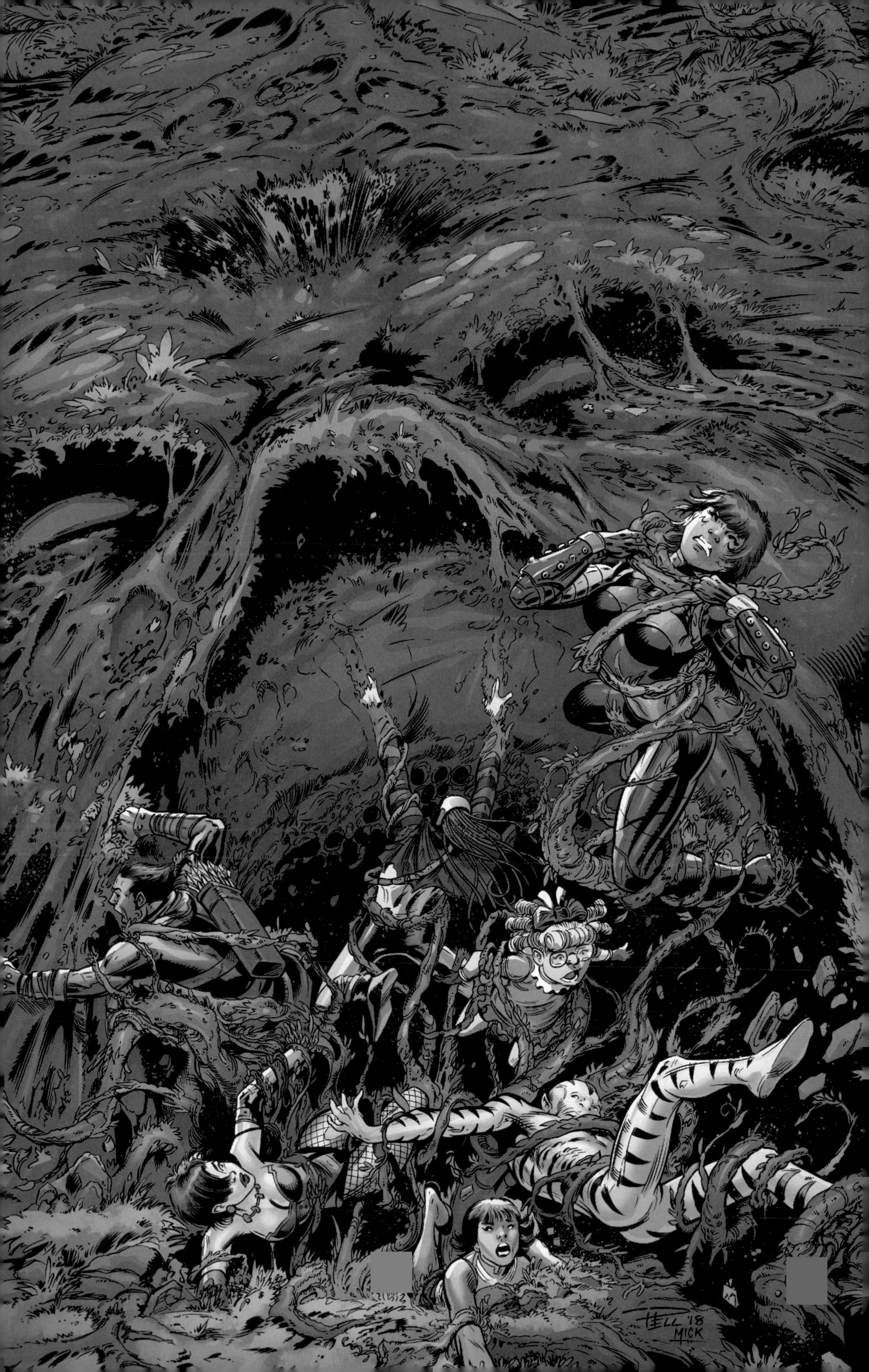

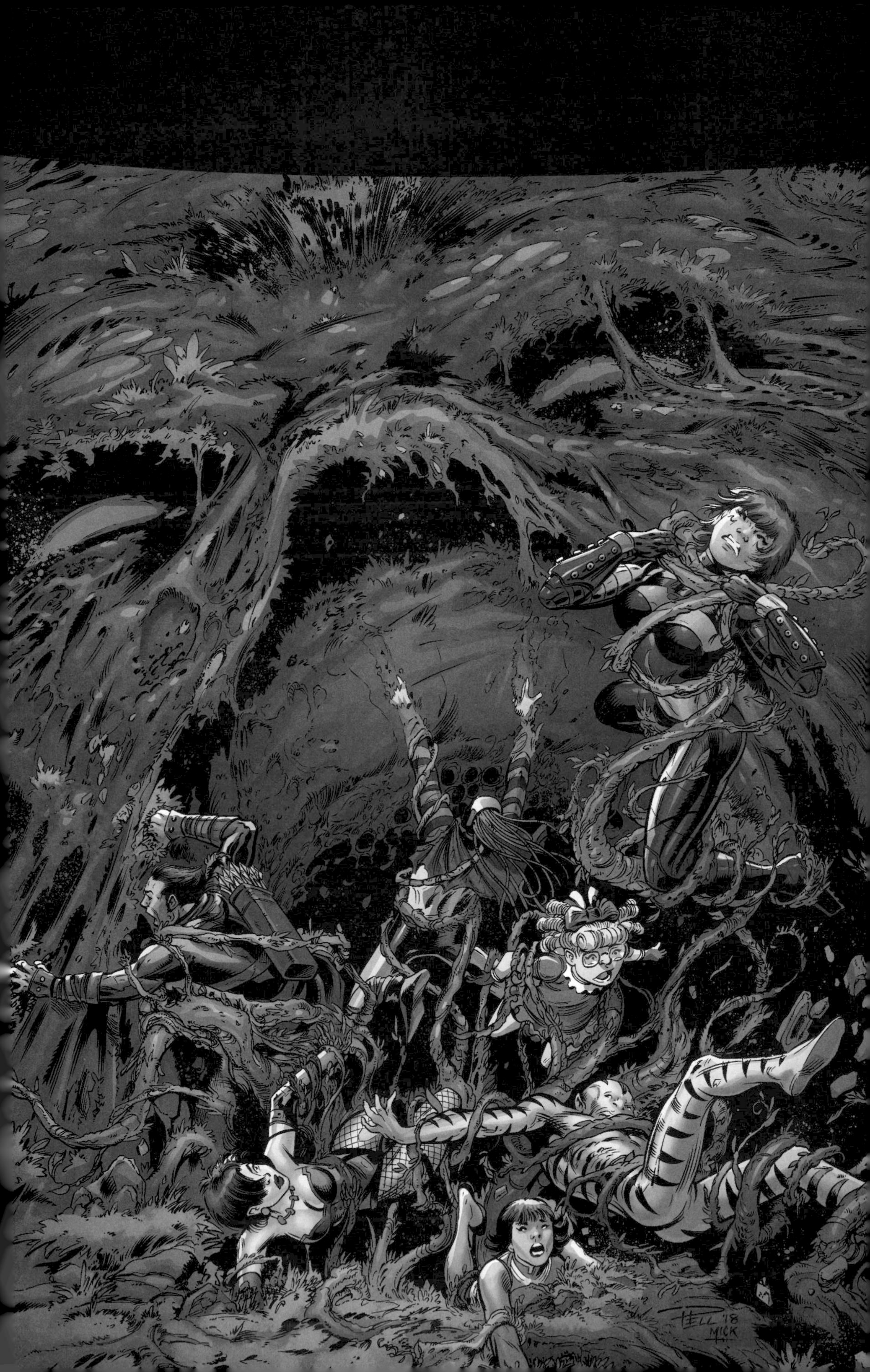
'18
MICK

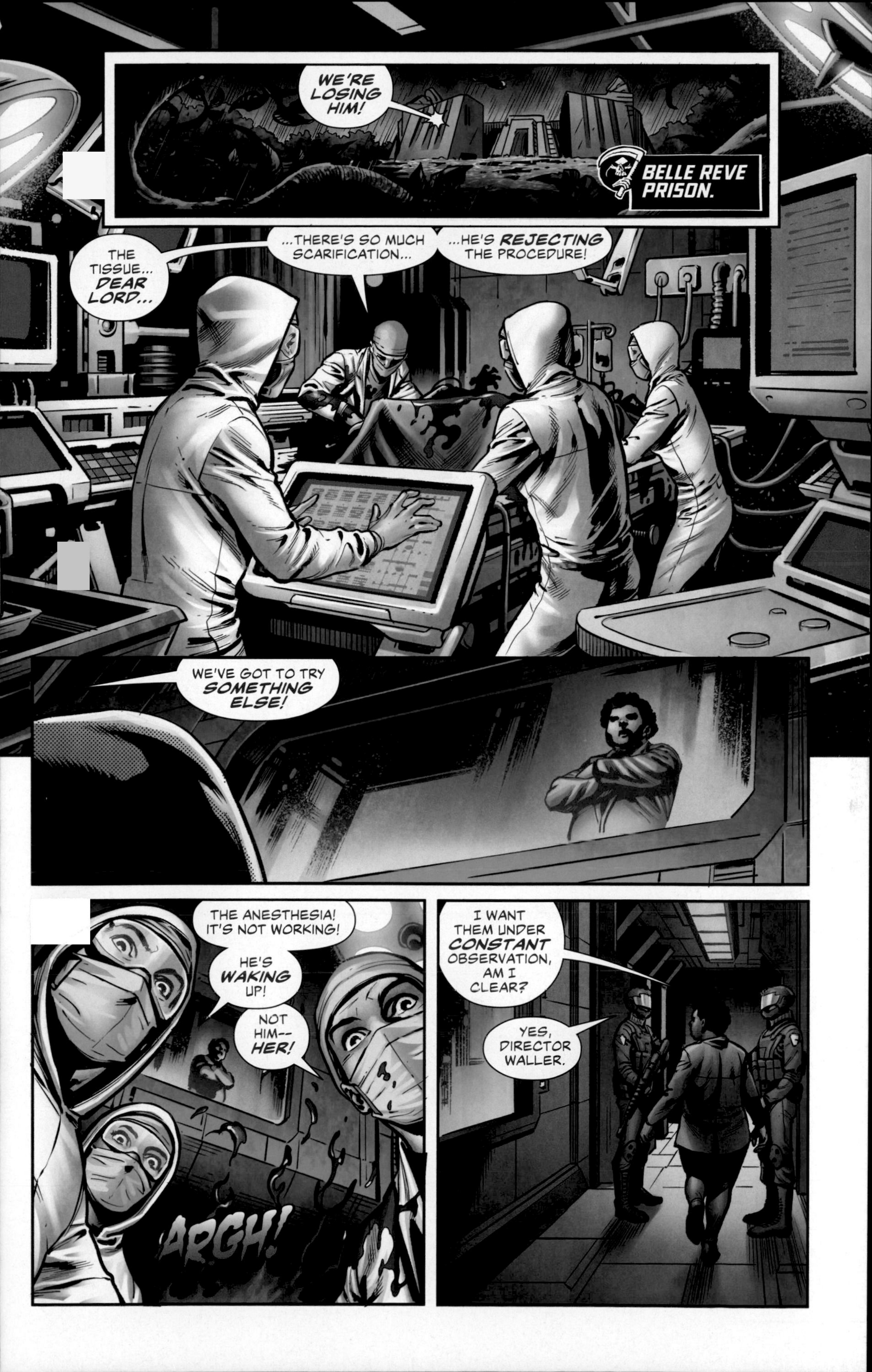
WE'RE LOSING HIM!
BELLE REVE PRISON.
THE TISSUE... DEAR LORD...
...THERE'S SO MUCH SCARIFICATION...
...HE'S REJECTING THE PROCEDURE!
WE'VE GOT TO TRY SOMETHING ELSE!
THE ANESTHESIA! IT'S NOT WORKING!
HE'S WAKING UP!
NOT HIM-- HER!
ARGH!
I WANT THEM UNDER CONSTANT OBSERVATION, AM I CLEAR?
YES, DIRECTOR WALLER.

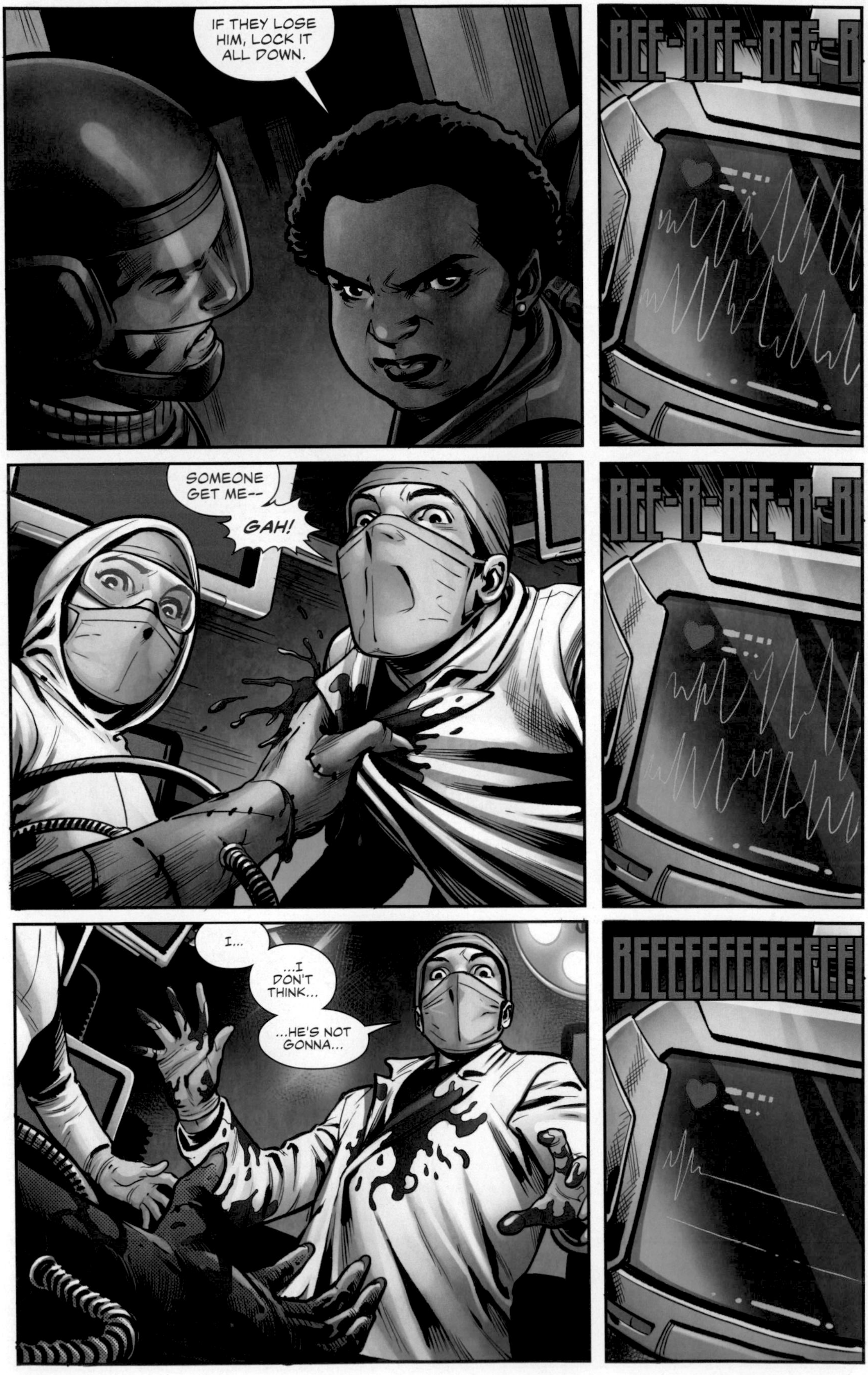
IF THEY LOSE HIM, LOCK IT ALL DOWN.
BEE-BEE-BEE-B
SOMEONE GET ME--
GAH!
BEE-B-BEE-B-B
I...
...I DON'T THINK...
...HE'S NOT GONNA...
BEEEEEEEEEEEE

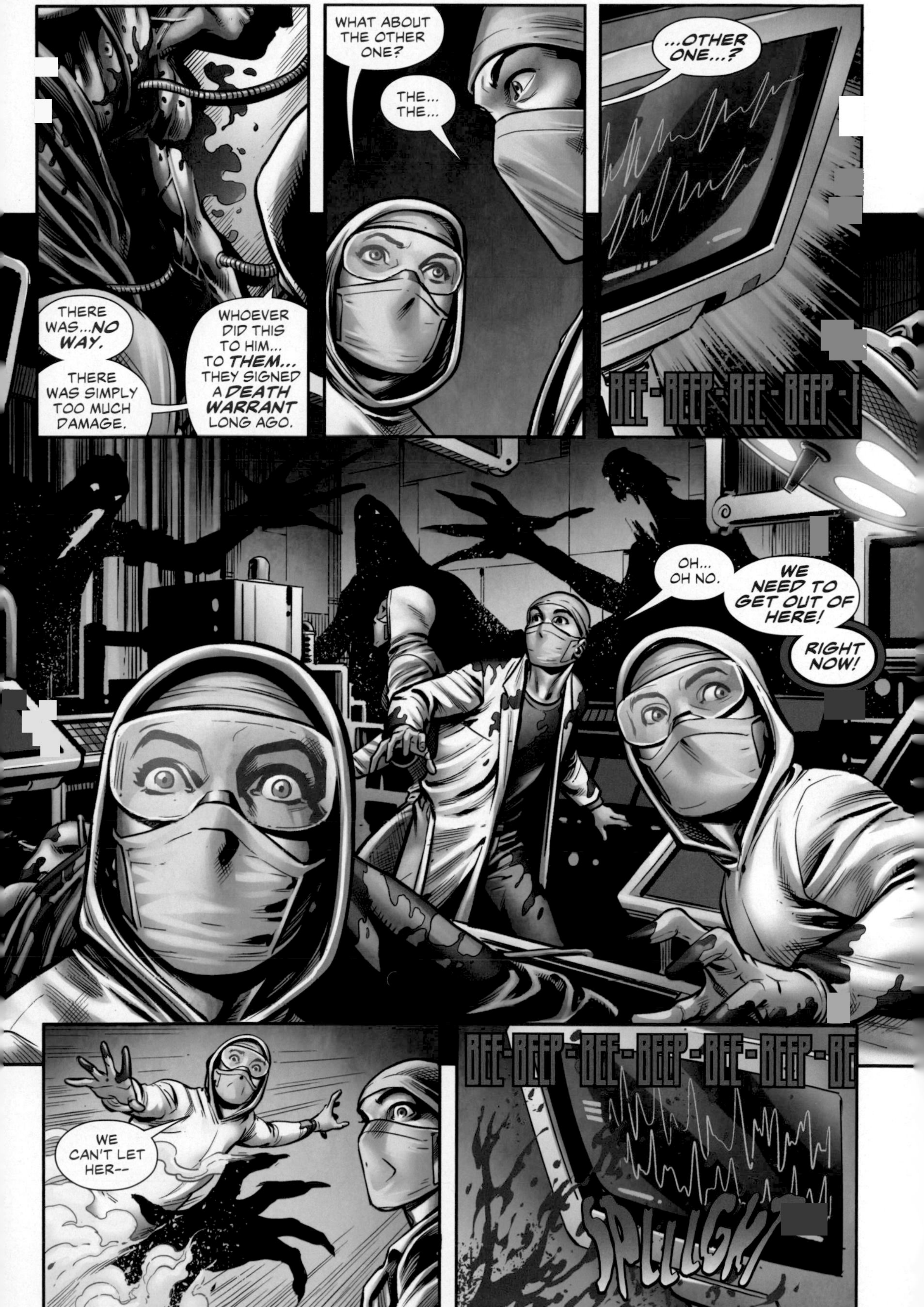

THERE WAS...NO WAY.
THERE WAS SIMPLY TOO MUCH DAMAGE.
WHOEVER DID THIS TO HIM... TO THEM... THEY SIGNED A DEATH WARRANT LONG AGO.
WHAT ABOUT THE OTHER ONE?
THE... THE...
...OTHER ONE...?
BEE-BEEP-BEE-BEEP-
OH... OH NO.
WE NEED TO GET OUT OF HERE!
RIGHT NOW!
WE CAN'T LET HER--
BEE-BEEP-BEE-BEEP-BEE-BEEP-BE
SPLLLGH!

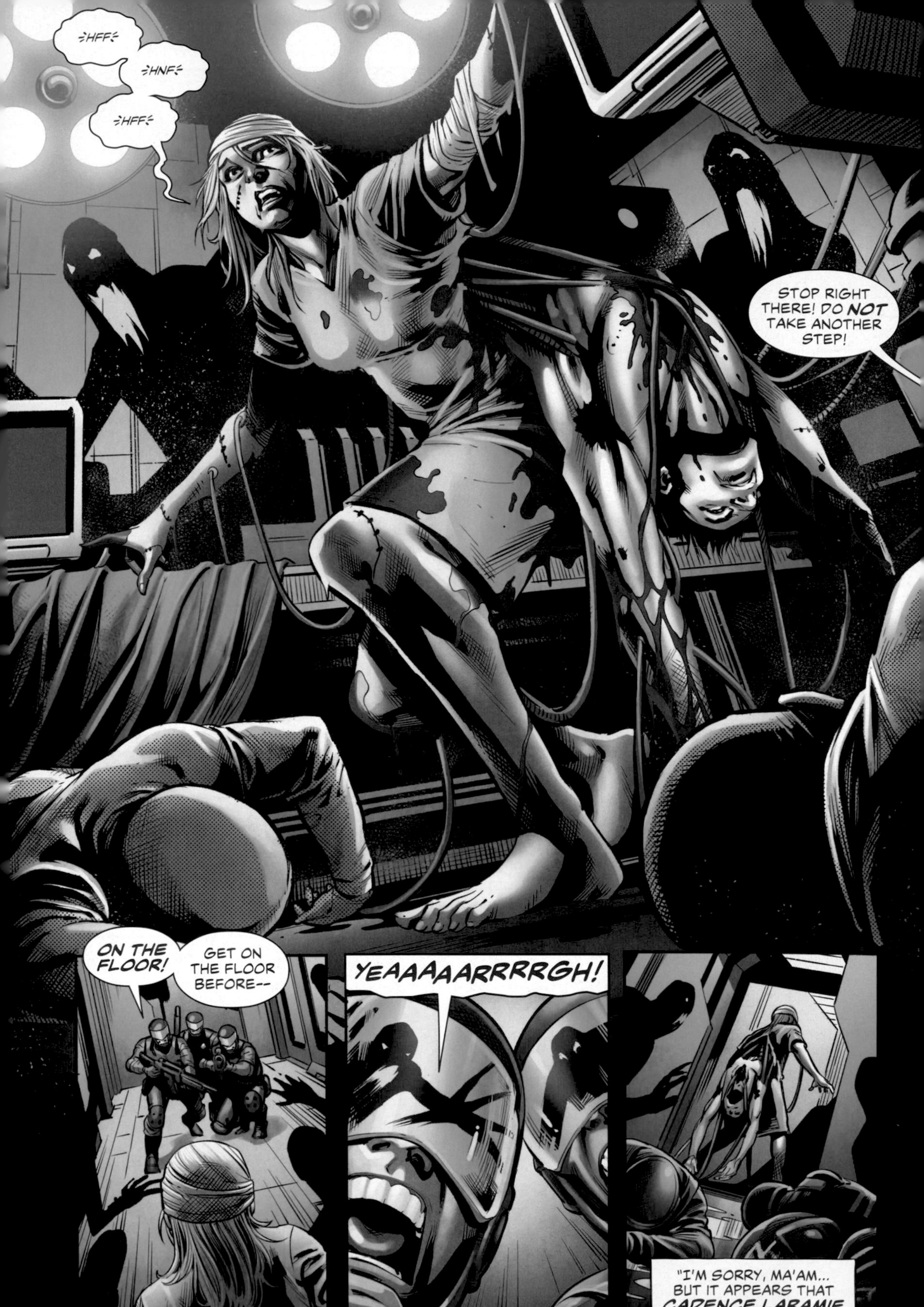

HFF
HNF
HFF
STOP RIGHT THERE! DO NOT TAKE ANOTHER STEP!
ON THE FLOOR!
GET ON THE FLOOR BEFORE--
YEAAAAARRRRGH!
"I'M SORRY, MA'AM... BUT IT APPEARS THAT CADENCE LARAMIE HAS ESCAPED."

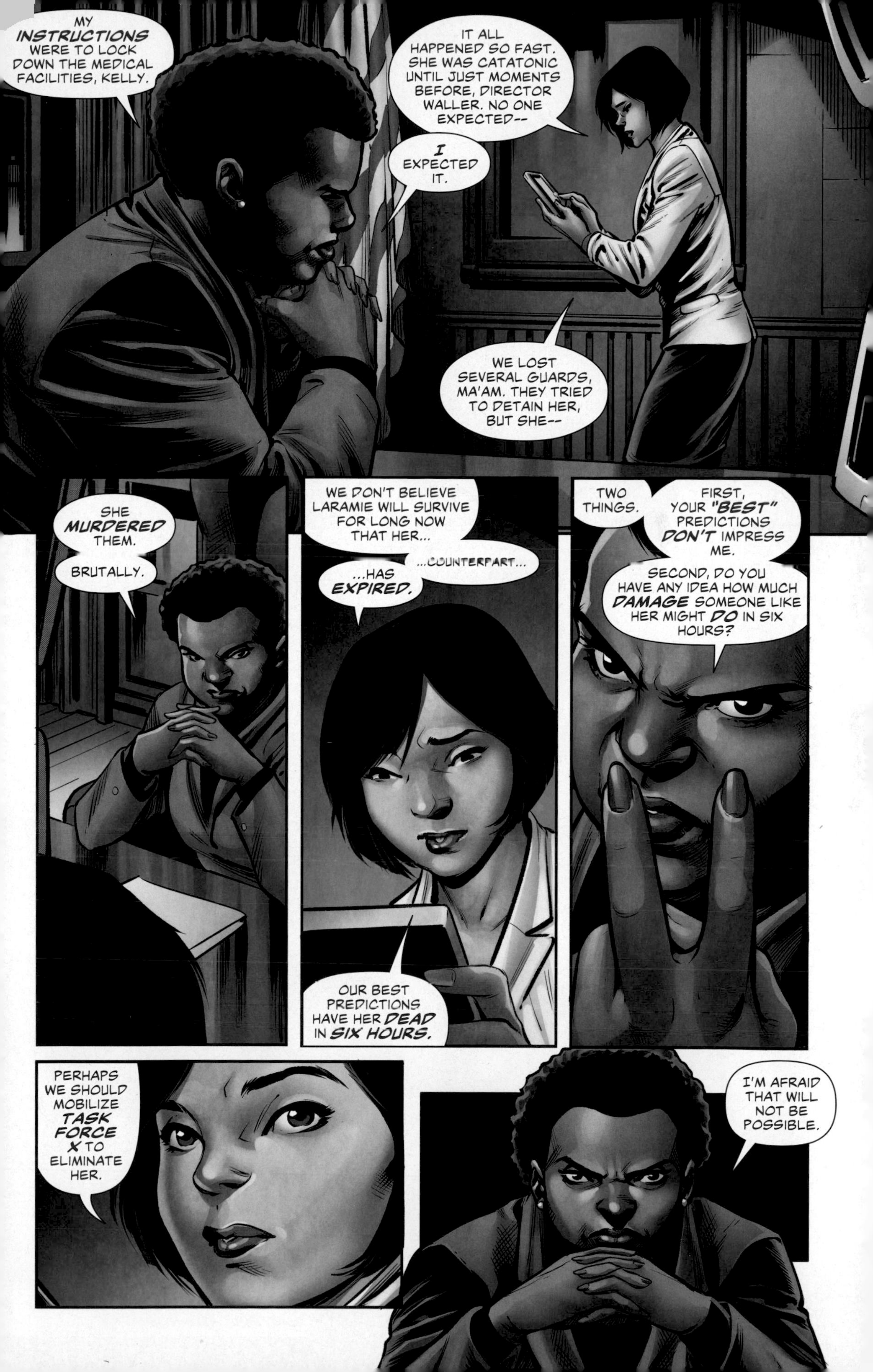

MY INSTRUCTIONS WERE TO LOCK DOWN THE MEDICAL FACILITIES, KELLY.
IT ALL HAPPENED SO FAST. SHE WAS CATATONIC UNTIL JUST MOMENTS BEFORE, DIRECTOR WALLER. NO ONE EXPECTED--
I EXPECTED IT.
WE LOST SEVERAL GUARDS, MA'AM. THEY TRIED TO DETAIN HER, BUT SHE--
SHE MURDERED THEM.
BRUTALLY.
WE DON'T BELIEVE LARAMIE WILL SURVIVE FOR LONG NOW THAT HER...
...COUNTERPART...
...HAS EXPIRED.
OUR BEST PREDICTIONS HAVE HER DEAD IN SIX HOURS.
TWO THINGS.
FIRST, YOUR "BEST" PREDICTIONS DON'T IMPRESS ME.
SECOND, DO YOU HAVE ANY IDEA HOW MUCH DAMAGE SOMEONE LIKE HER MIGHT DO IN SIX HOURS?
PERHAPS WE SHOULD MOBILIZE TASK FORCE X TO ELIMINATE HER.
I'M AFRAID THAT WILL NOT BE POSSIBLE.

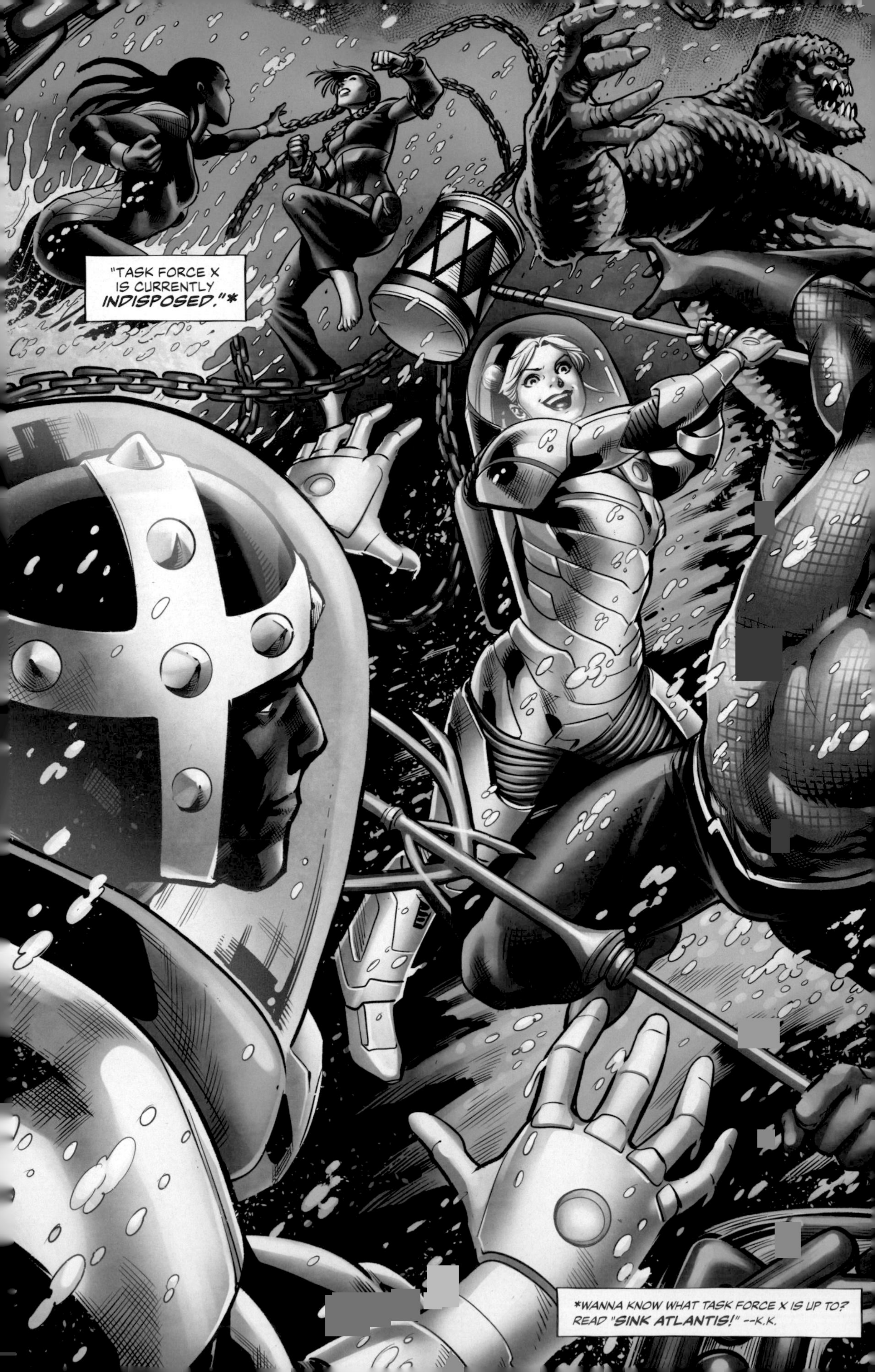
"TASK FORCE X IS CURRENTLY INDISPOSED."*
*WANNA KNOW WHAT TASK FORCE X IS UP TO? READ "SINK ATLANTIS!" --K.K.

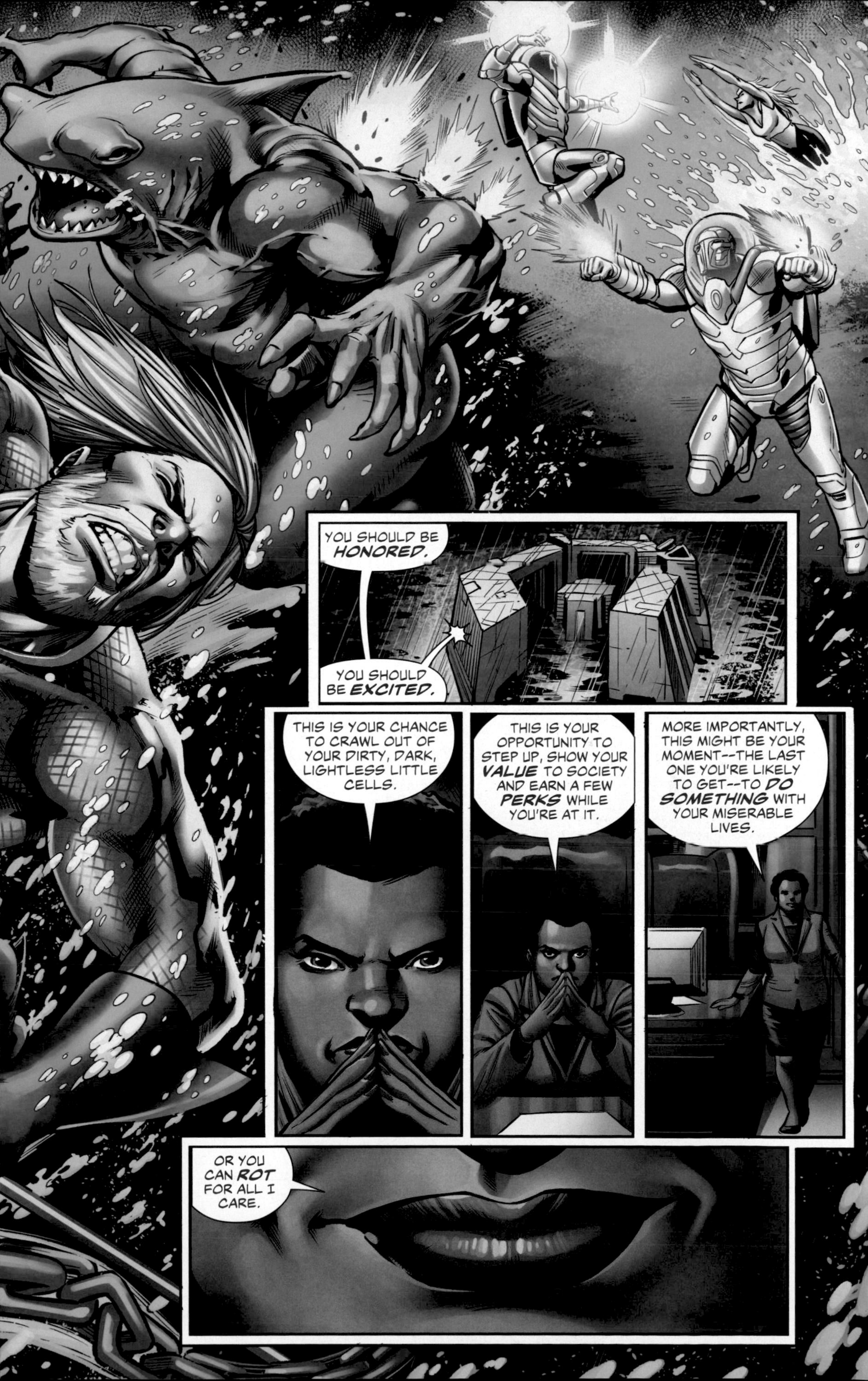
YOU SHOULD BE HONORED.
YOU SHOULD BE EXCITED.
THIS IS YOUR CHANCE TO CRAWL OUT OF YOUR DIRTY, DARK, LIGHTLESS LITTLE CELLS.
THIS IS YOUR OPPORTUNITY TO STEP UP, SHOW YOUR VALUE TO SOCIETY AND EARN A FEW PERKS WHILE YOU'RE AT IT.
MORE IMPORTANTLY, THIS MIGHT BE YOUR MOMENT--THE LAST ONE YOU'RE LIKELY TO GET--TO DO SOMETHING WITH YOUR MISERABLE LIVES.
OR YOU CAN ROT FOR ALL I CARE.

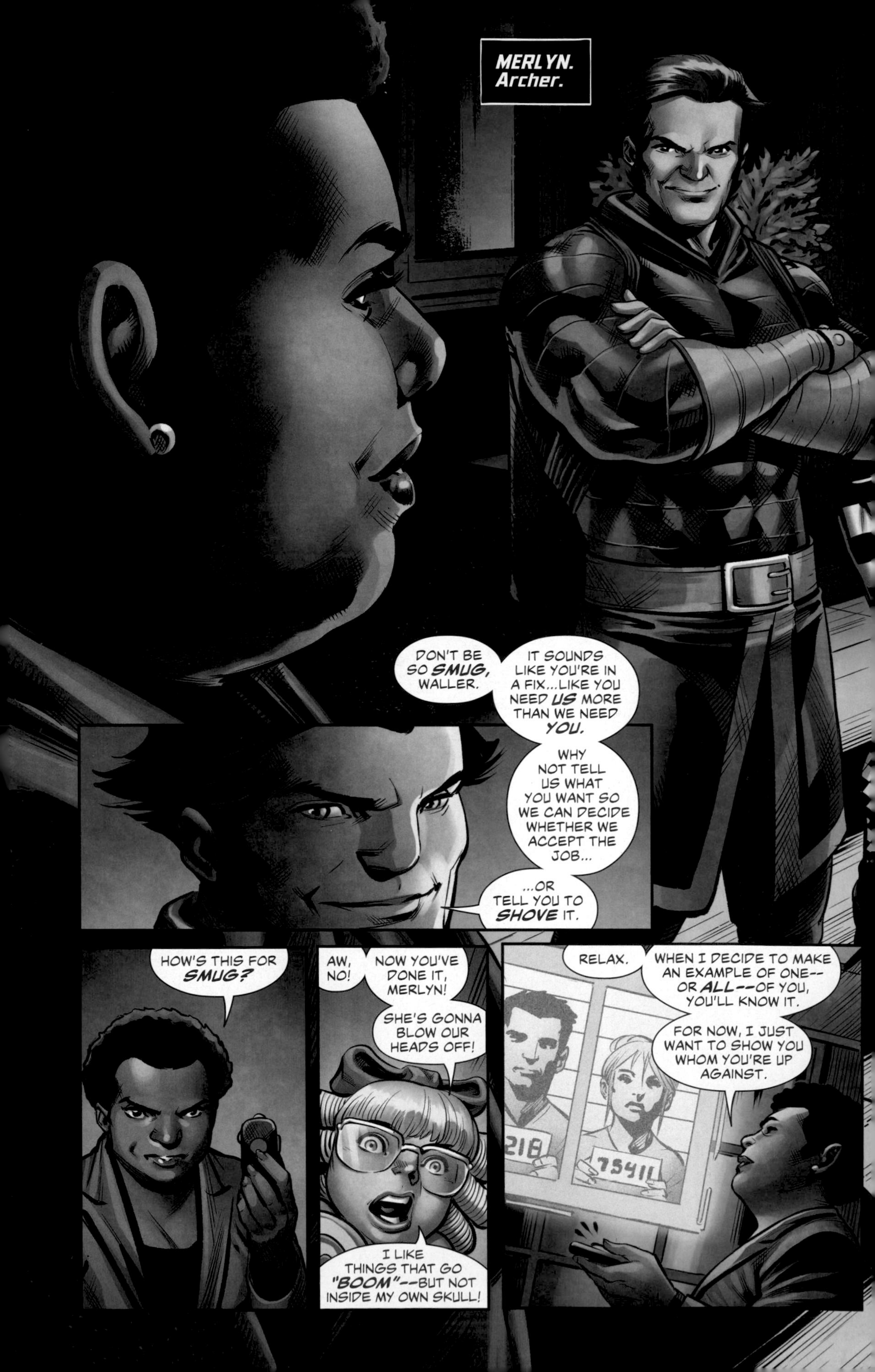
MERLYN. Archer.
DON'T BE SO SMUG, WALLER.
IT SOUNDS LIKE YOU'RE IN A FIX...LIKE YOU NEED US MORE THAN WE NEED YOU.
WHY NOT TELL US WHAT YOU WANT SO WE CAN DECIDE WHETHER WE ACCEPT THE JOB...
...OR TELL YOU TO SHOVE IT.
HOW'S THIS FOR SMUG?
AW, NO!
NOW YOU'VE DONE IT, MERLYN!
SHE'S GONNA BLOW OUR HEADS OFF!
I LIKE THINGS THAT GO "BOOM"--BUT NOT INSIDE MY OWN SKULL!
RELAX.
WHEN I DECIDE TO MAKE AN EXAMPLE OF ONE--OR ALL--OF YOU, YOU'LL KNOW IT.
FOR NOW, I JUST WANT TO SHOW YOU WHOM YOU'RE UP AGAINST.
218
75411

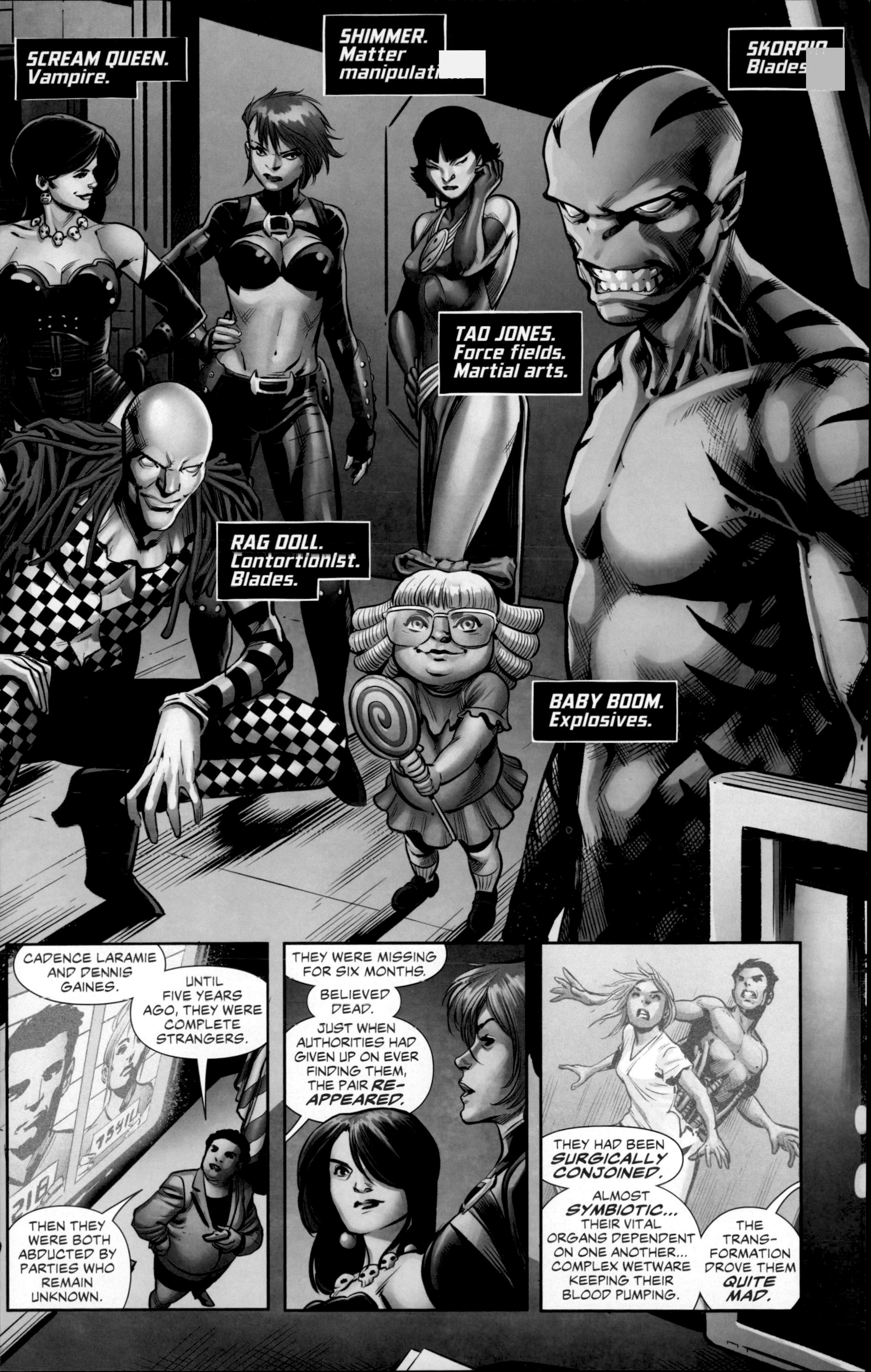
SCREAM QUEEN. Vampire.
SHIMMER. Matter manipulati
SKORPIO Blades
TAO JONES. Force fields. Martial arts.
RAG DOLL. Contortionist. Blades.
BABY BOOM. Explosives.
CADENCE LARAMIE AND DENNIS GAINES.
UNTIL FIVE YEARS AGO, THEY WERE COMPLETE STRANGERS.
THEN THEY WERE BOTH ABDUCTED BY PARTIES WHO REMAIN UNKNOWN.
THEY WERE MISSING FOR SIX MONTHS.
BELIEVED DEAD.
JUST WHEN AUTHORITIES HAD GIVEN UP ON EVER FINDING THEM, THE PAIR RE-APPEARED.
THEY HAD BEEN SURGICALLY CONJOINED.
ALMOST SYMBIOTIC... THEIR VITAL ORGANS DEPENDENT ON ONE ANOTHER... COMPLEX WETWARE KEEPING THEIR BLOOD PUMPING.
THE TRANS-FORMATION DROVE THEM QUITE MAD.

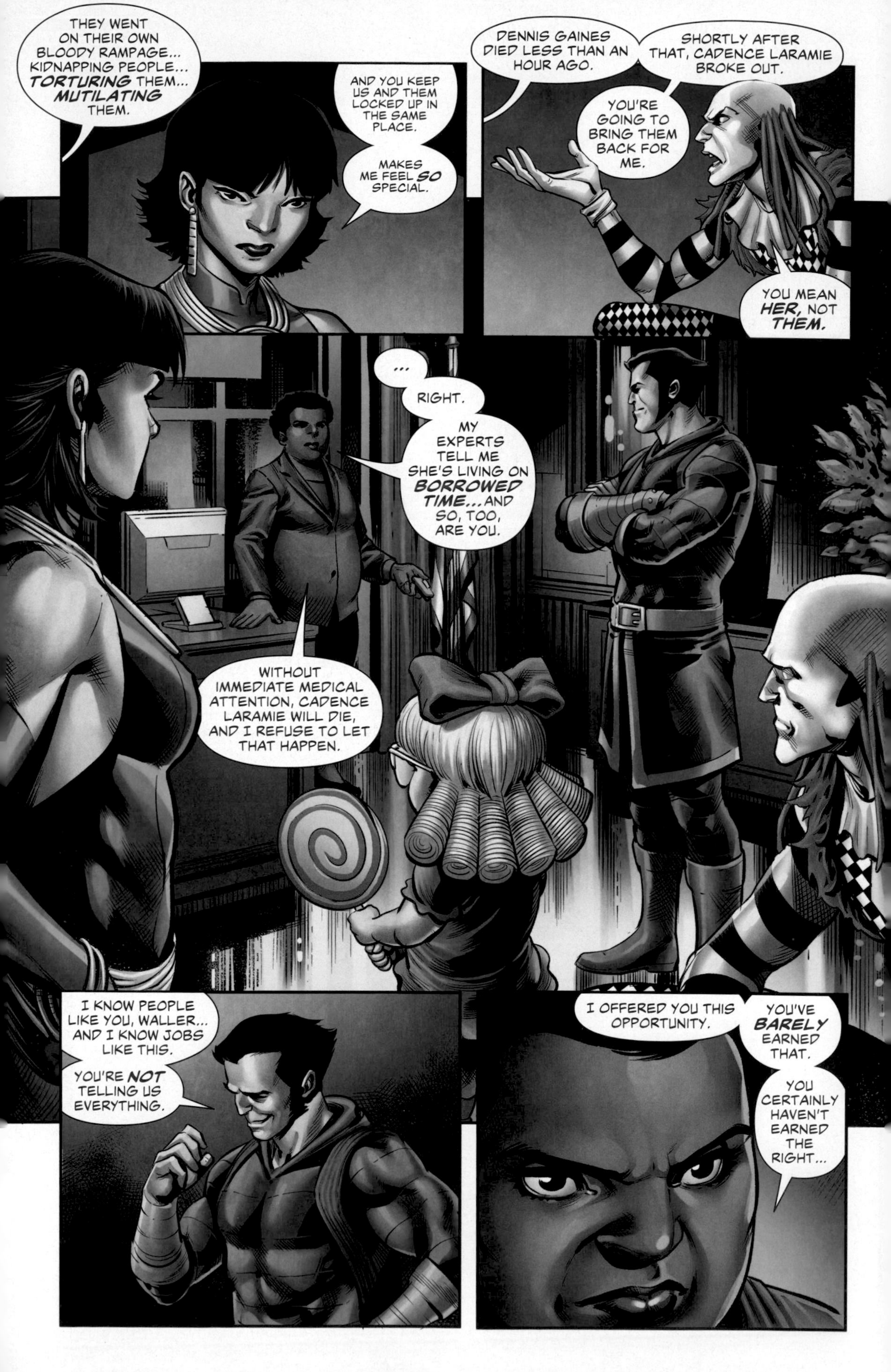
THEY WENT ON THEIR OWN BLOODY RAMPAGE... KIDNAPPING PEOPLE... TORTURING THEM... MUTILATING THEM.
AND YOU KEEP US AND THEM LOCKED UP IN THE SAME PLACE.
MAKES ME FEEL SO SPECIAL.
DENNIS GAINES DIED LESS THAN AN HOUR AGO.
SHORTLY AFTER THAT, CADENCE LARAMIE BROKE OUT.
YOU'RE GOING TO BRING THEM BACK FOR ME.
YOU MEAN HER, NOT THEM.
...
RIGHT.
MY EXPERTS TELL ME SHE'S LIVING ON BORROWED TIME... AND SO, TOO, ARE YOU.
WITHOUT IMMEDIATE MEDICAL ATTENTION, CADENCE LARAMIE WILL DIE, AND I REFUSE TO LET THAT HAPPEN.
I KNOW PEOPLE LIKE YOU, WALLER... AND I KNOW JOBS LIKE THIS.
YOU'RE NOT TELLING US EVERYTHING.
I OFFERED YOU THIS OPPORTUNITY.
YOU'VE BARELY EARNED THAT.
YOU CERTAINLY HAVEN'T EARNED THE RIGHT...

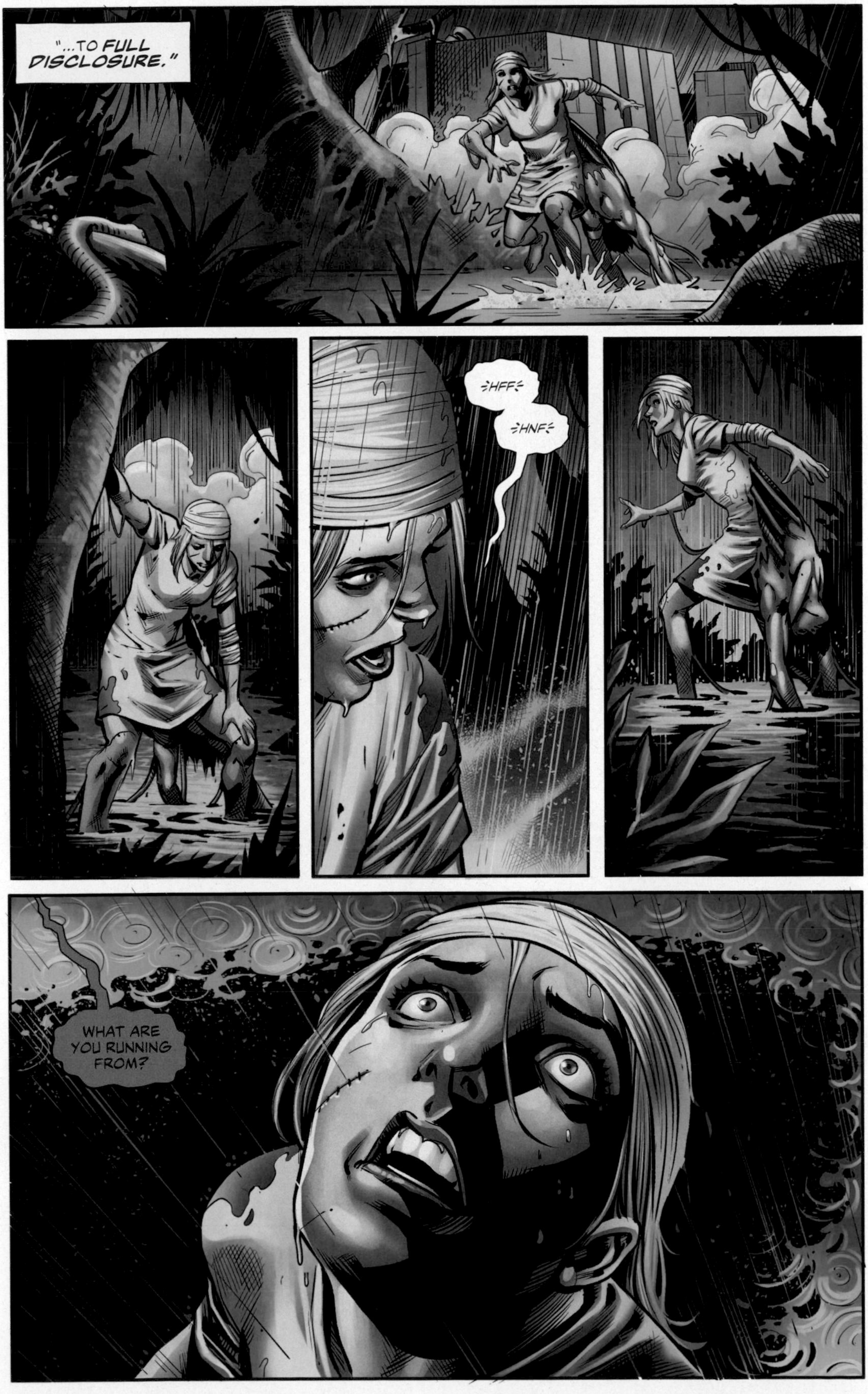
"...TO FULL DISCLOSURE."
HFF
HNF
WHAT ARE YOU RUNNING FROM?

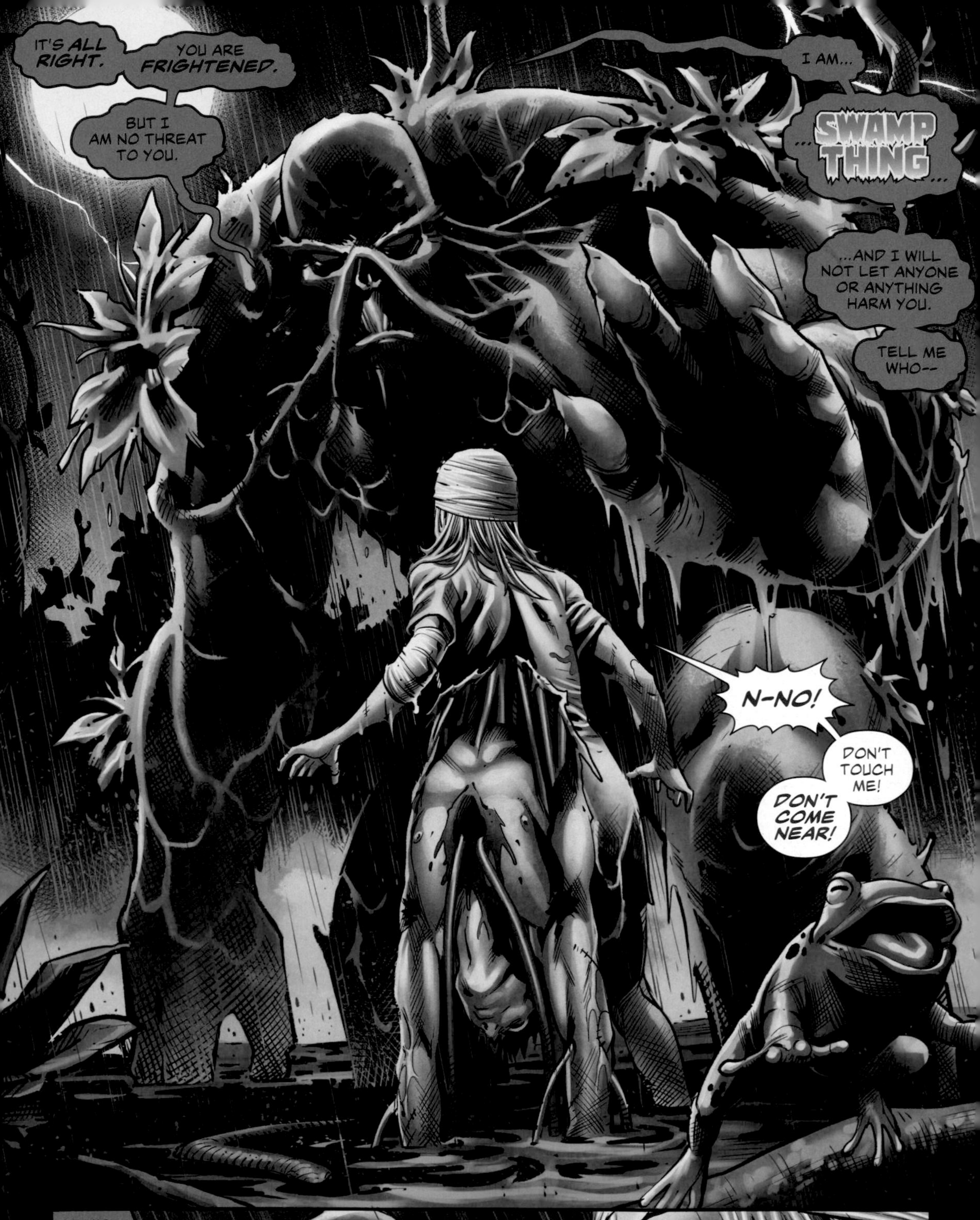
IT'S ALL RIGHT.
YOU ARE FRIGHTENED.
BUT I AM NO THREAT TO YOU.
I AM...
...SWAMP THING...
...AND I WILL NOT LET ANYONE OR ANYTHING HARM YOU.
TELL ME WHO--
N-NO!
DON'T TOUCH ME!
DON'T COME NEAR!

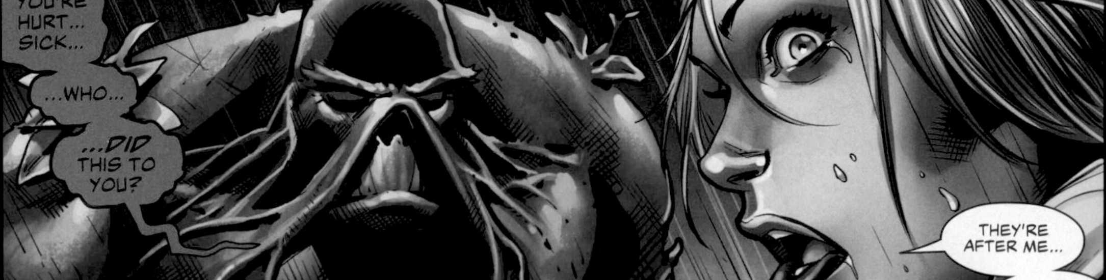
YOU'RE HURT... SICK...
...WHO...
...DID THIS TO YOU?
THEY'RE AFTER ME...
...I KNOW IT...

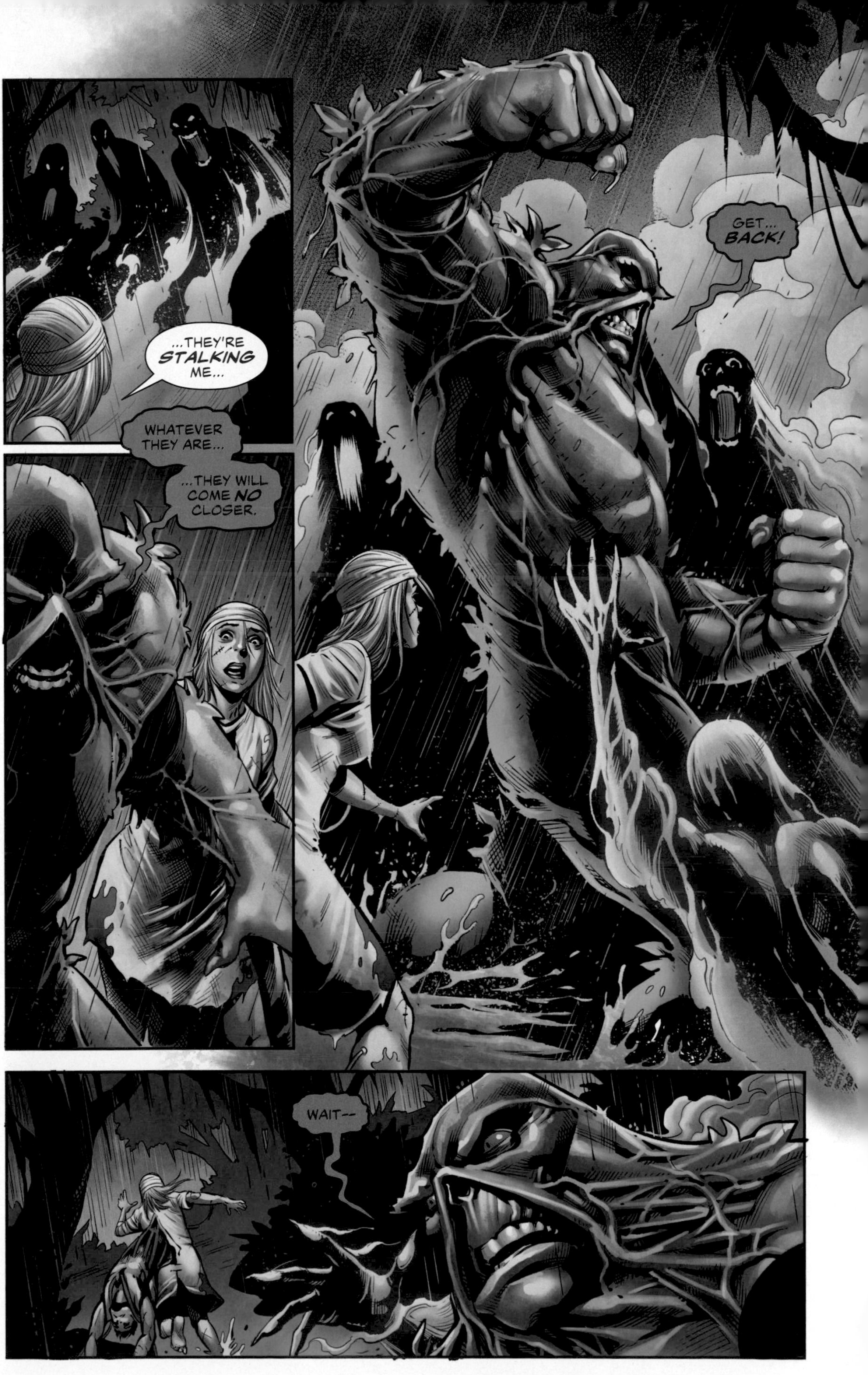
...THEY'RE STALKING ME...
WHATEVER THEY ARE...
...THEY WILL COME NO CLOSER.
GET... BACK!
WAIT--

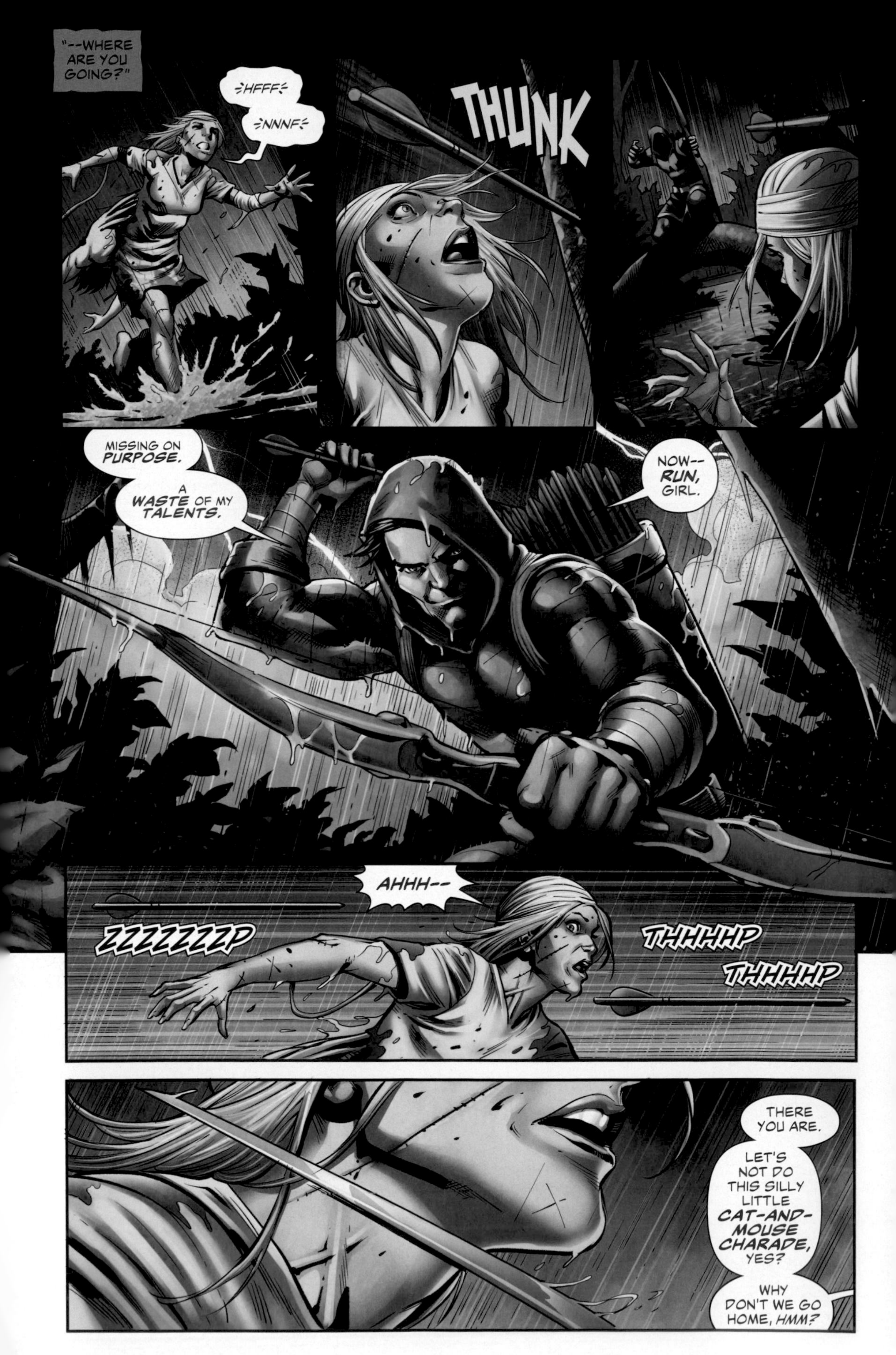
"--WHERE ARE YOU GOING?"
HFFF
NNNF
THUNK
MISSING ON PURPOSE.
A WASTE OF MY TALENTS.
NOW-- RUN, GIRL.
AHHH--
ZZZZZZZP
THHHHP
THHHHP
THERE YOU ARE.
LET'S NOT DO THIS SILLY LITTLE CAT-AND-MOUSE CHARADE, YES?
WHY DON'T WE GO HOME, HMM?

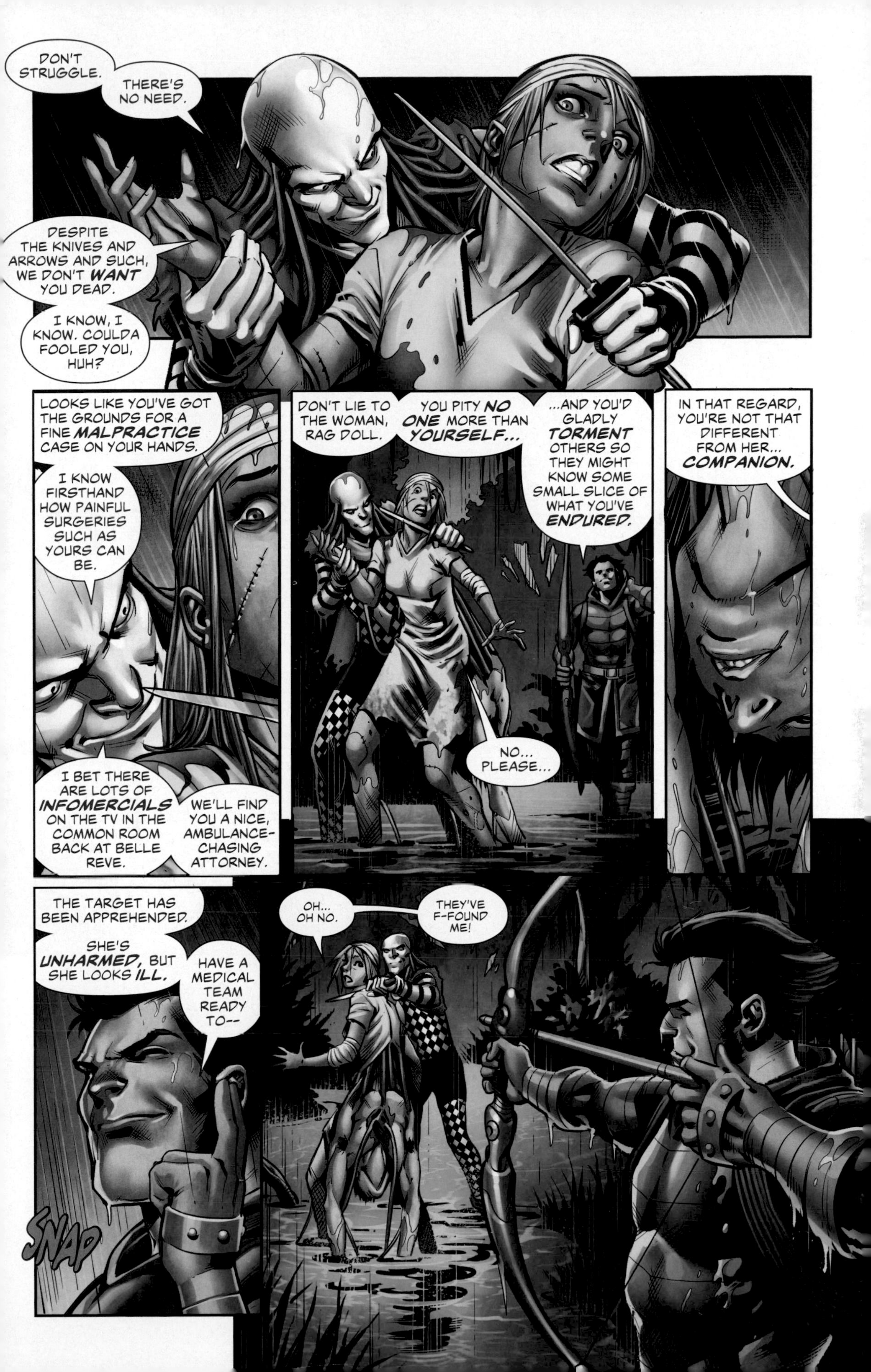
DON'T STRUGGLE.
THERE'S NO NEED.
DESPITE THE KNIVES AND ARROWS AND SUCH, WE DON'T WANT YOU DEAD.
I KNOW, I KNOW. COULDA FOOLED YOU, HUH?
LOOKS LIKE YOU'VE GOT THE GROUNDS FOR A FINE MALPRACTICE CASE ON YOUR HANDS.
I KNOW FIRSTHAND HOW PAINFUL SURGERIES SUCH AS YOURS CAN BE.
I BET THERE ARE LOTS OF INFOMERCIALS ON THE TV IN THE COMMON ROOM BACK AT BELLE REVE.
WE'LL FIND YOU A NICE, AMBULANCE-CHASING ATTORNEY.
DON'T LIE TO THE WOMAN, RAG DOLL.
YOU PITY NO ONE MORE THAN YOURSELF...
...AND YOU'D GLADLY TORMENT OTHERS SO THEY MIGHT KNOW SOME SMALL SLICE OF WHAT YOU'VE ENDURED.
NO... PLEASE...
IN THAT REGARD, YOU'RE NOT THAT DIFFERENT FROM HER... COMPANION.
THE TARGET HAS BEEN APPREHENDED.
SHE'S UNHARMED, BUT SHE LOOKS ILL.
HAVE A MEDICAL TEAM READY TO--
SNAP
OH... OH NO.
THEY'VE F-FOUND ME!

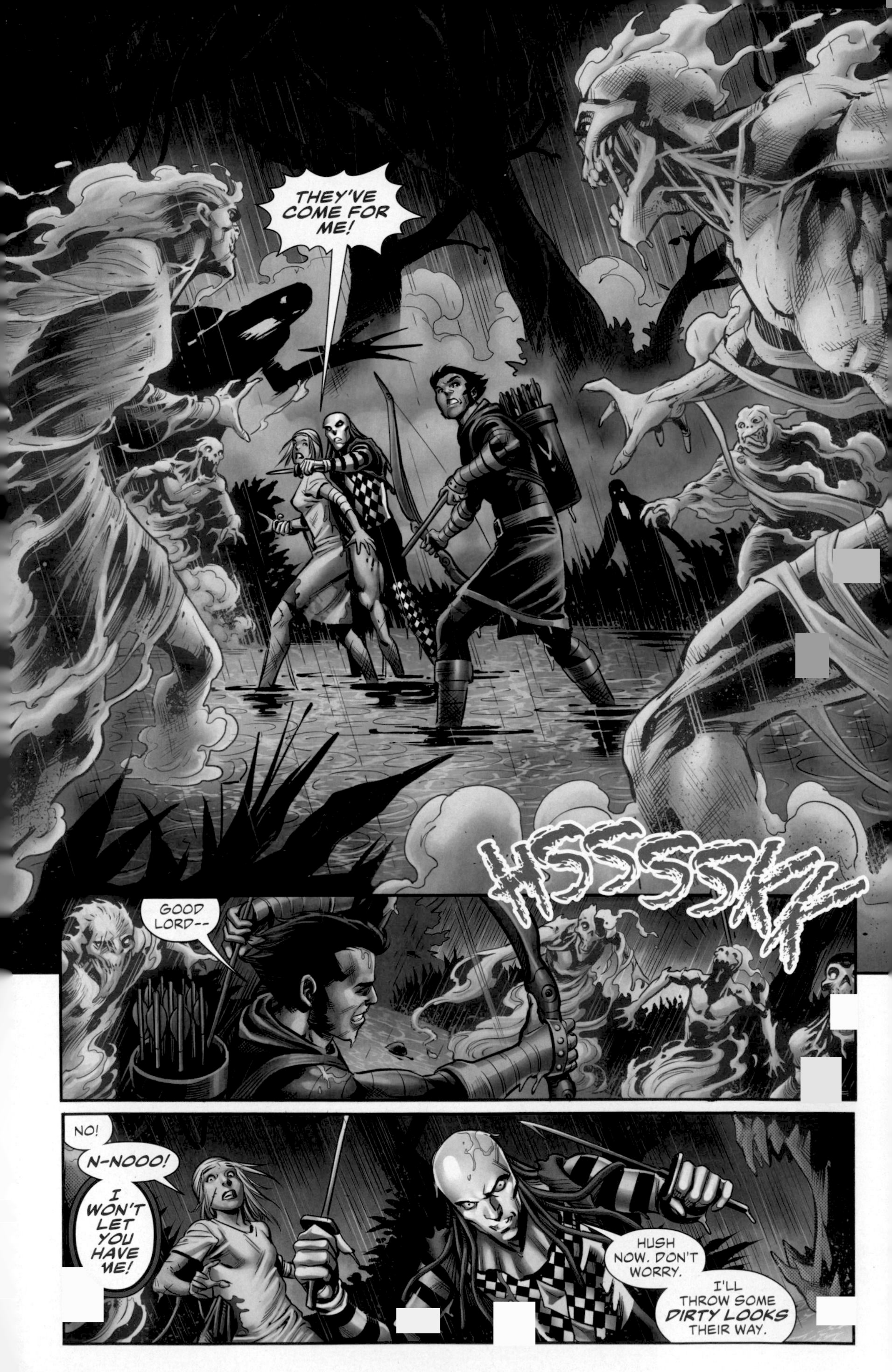
THEY'VE COME FOR ME!
HSSSSKZ
GOOD LORD--
NO!
N-NOOO!
I WON'T LET YOU HAVE ME!
HUSH NOW. DON'T WORRY.
I'LL THROW SOME DIRTY LOOKS THEIR WAY.

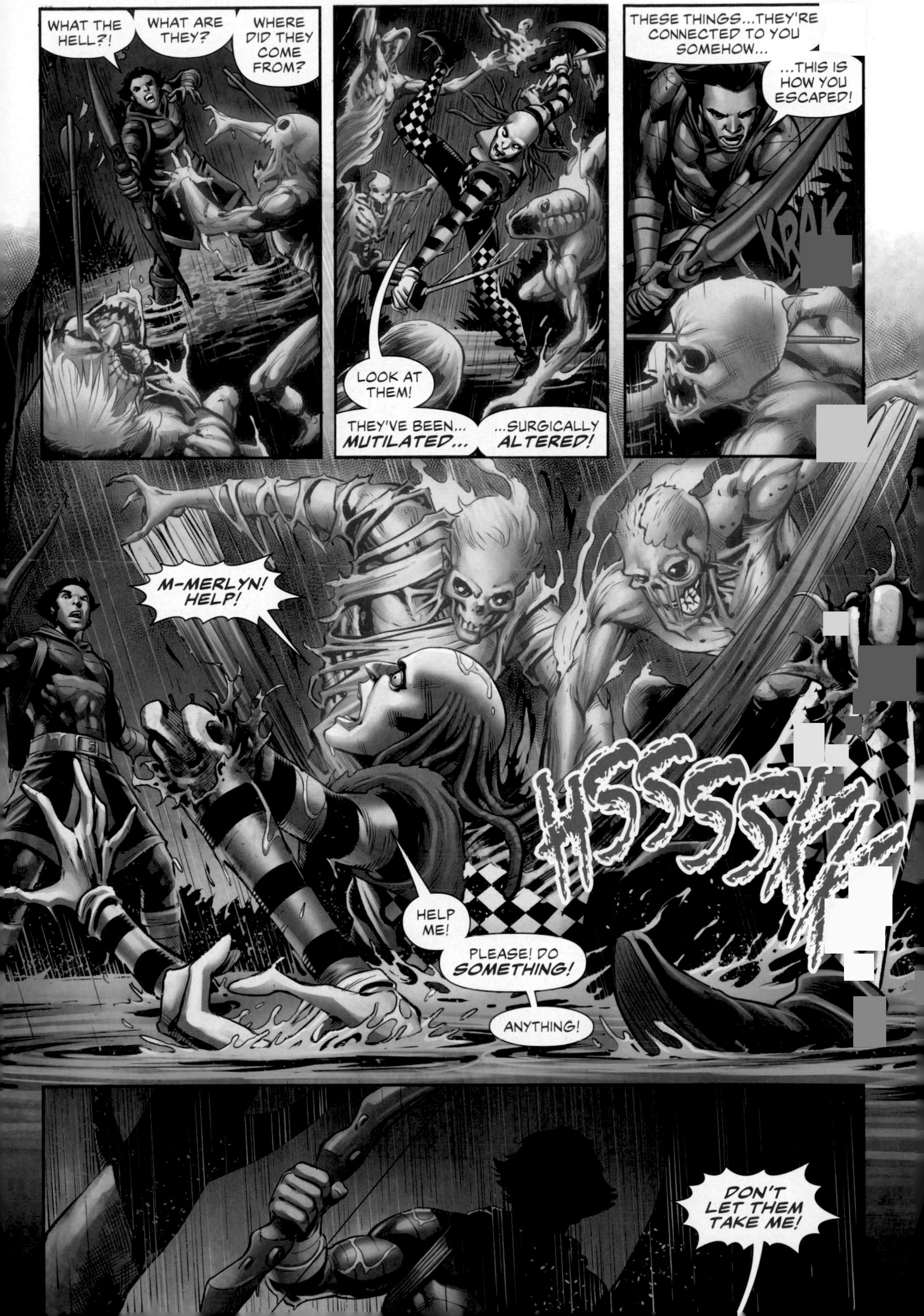
WHAT THE HELL?!
WHAT ARE THEY?
WHERE DID THEY COME FROM?
LOOK AT THEM!
THEY'VE BEEN... MUTILATED...
...SURGICALLY ALTERED!
THESE THINGS...THEY'RE CONNECTED TO YOU SOMEHOW...
...THIS IS HOW YOU ESCAPED!
KRAK
M-MERLYN! HELP!
HELP ME!
PLEASE! DO SOMETHING!
ANYTHING!
DON'T LET THEM TAKE ME!

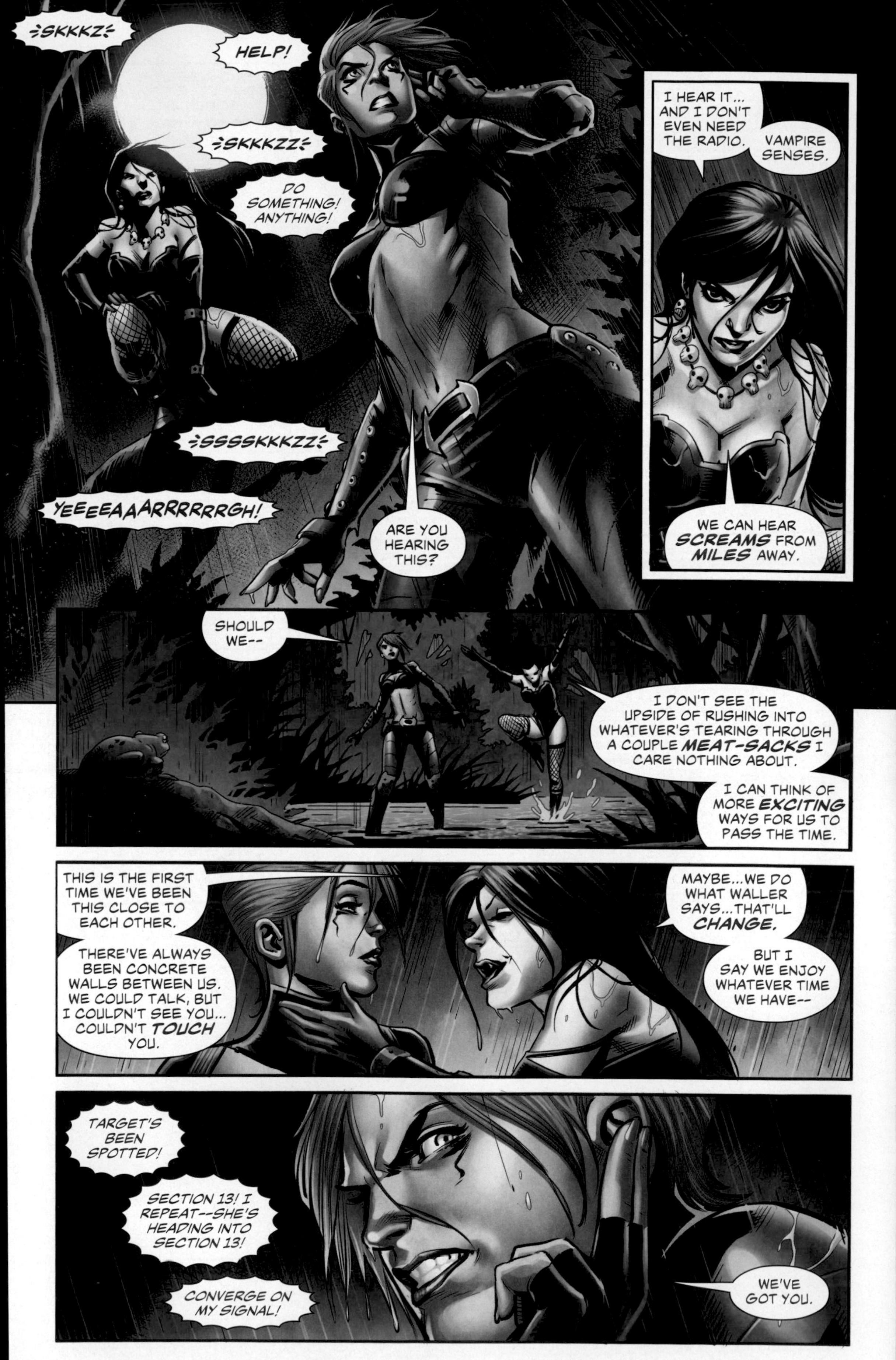
SKKKZ
HELP!
SKKKZZ
DO SOMETHING! ANYTHING!
SSSSKKKZZ
YEEEEAAARRRRRRGH!
ARE YOU HEARING THIS?
I HEAR IT... AND I DON'T EVEN NEED THE RADIO.
VAMPIRE SENSES.
WE CAN HEAR SCREAMS FROM MILES AWAY.
SHOULD WE--
I DON'T SEE THE UPSIDE OF RUSHING INTO WHATEVER'S TEARING THROUGH A COUPLE MEAT-SACKS I CARE NOTHING ABOUT.
I CAN THINK OF MORE EXCITING WAYS FOR US TO PASS THE TIME.
THIS IS THE FIRST TIME WE'VE BEEN THIS CLOSE TO EACH OTHER.
THERE'VE ALWAYS BEEN CONCRETE WALLS BETWEEN US. WE COULD TALK, BUT I COULDN'T SEE YOU... COULDN'T TOUCH YOU.
MAYBE...WE DO WHAT WALLER SAYS...THAT'LL CHANGE.
BUT I SAY WE ENJOY WHATEVER TIME WE HAVE--
TARGET'S BEEN SPOTTED!
SECTION 13! I REPEAT--SHE'S HEADING INTO SECTION 13!
CONVERGE ON MY SIGNAL!
WE'VE GOT YOU.

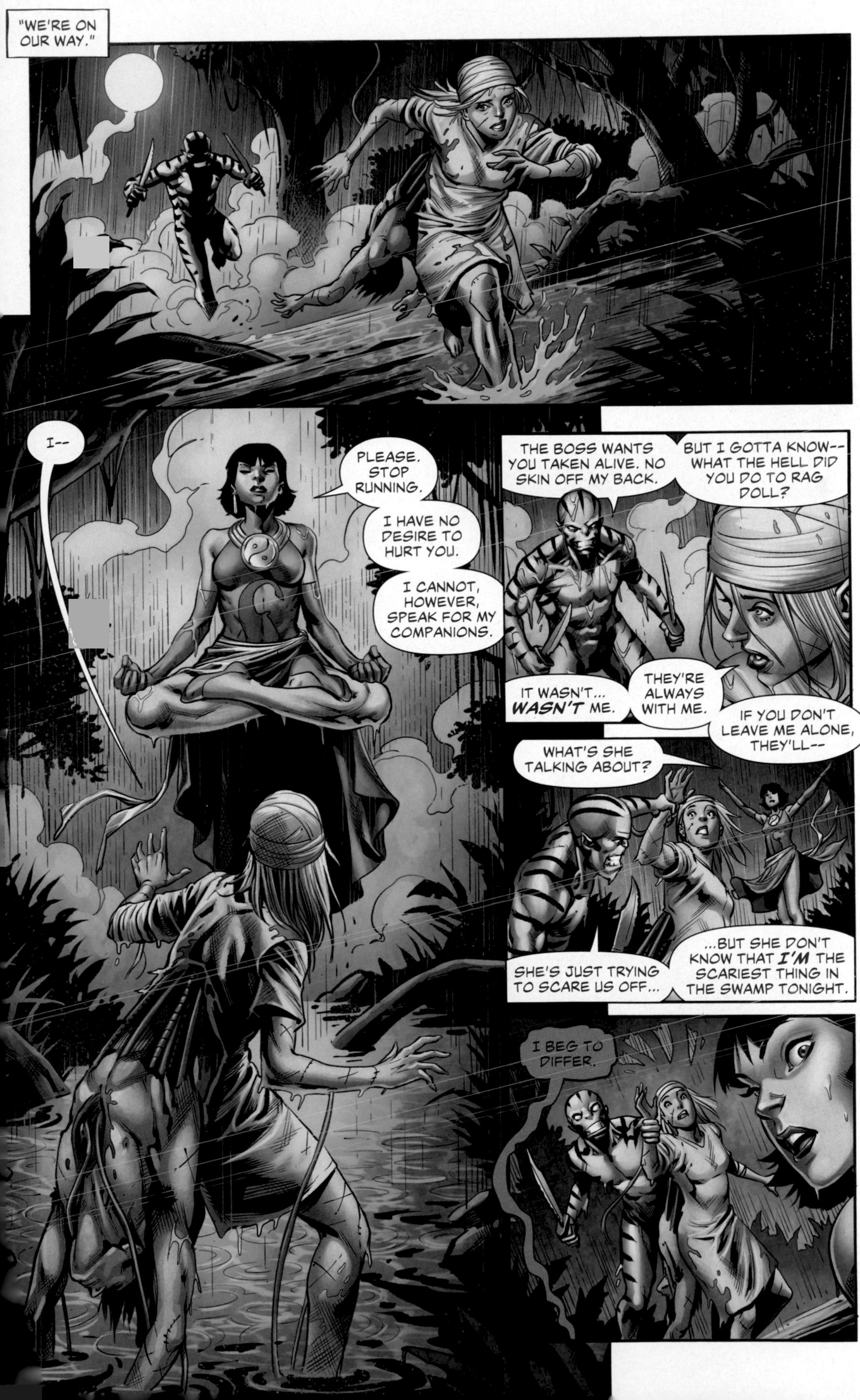
"WE'RE ON OUR WAY."
I--
PLEASE. STOP RUNNING.
I HAVE NO DESIRE TO HURT YOU.
I CANNOT, HOWEVER, SPEAK FOR MY COMPANIONS.
THE BOSS WANTS YOU TAKEN ALIVE. NO SKIN OFF MY BACK.
BUT I GOTTA KNOW-- WHAT THE HELL DID YOU DO TO RAG DOLL?
IT WASN'T... WASN'T ME.
THEY'RE ALWAYS WITH ME.
IF YOU DON'T LEAVE ME ALONE, THEY'LL--
WHAT'S SHE TALKING ABOUT?
SHE'S JUST TRYING TO SCARE US OFF...
...BUT SHE DON'T KNOW THAT I'M THE SCARIEST THING IN THE SWAMP TONIGHT.
I BEG TO DIFFER.

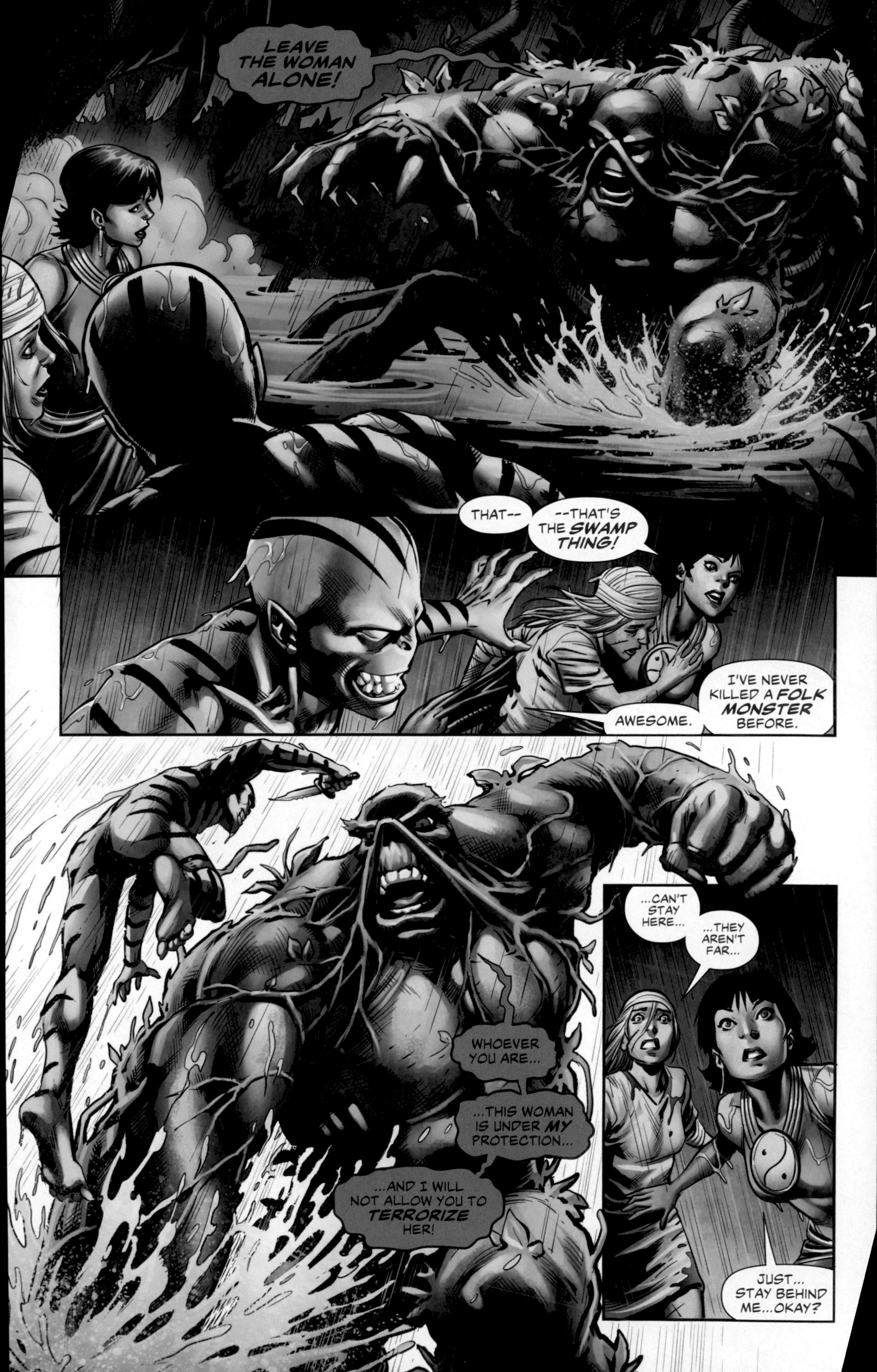
LEAVE THE WOMAN ALONE!
THAT--
--THAT'S THE SWAMP THING!
AWESOME.
I'VE NEVER KILLED A FOLK MONSTER BEFORE.
WHOEVER YOU ARE...
...THIS WOMAN IS UNDER MY PROTECTION...
...AND I WILL NOT ALLOW YOU TO TERRORIZE HER!
...CAN'T STAY HERE...
...THEY AREN'T FAR...
JUST... STAY BEHIND ME...OKAY?

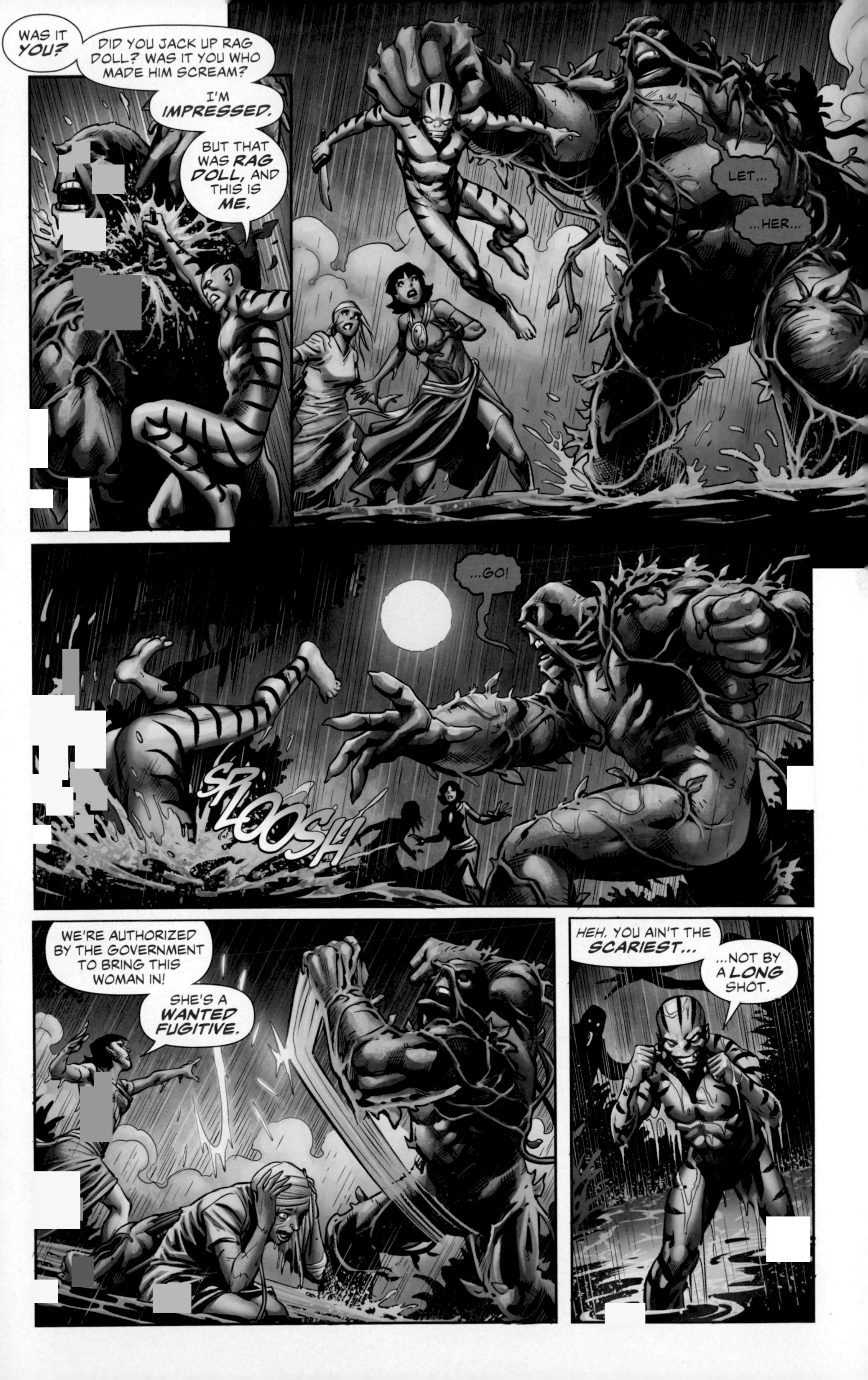
WAS IT YOU?
DID YOU JACK UP RAG DOLL? WAS IT YOU WHO MADE HIM SCREAM?
I'M IMPRESSED.
BUT THAT WAS RAG DOLL, AND THIS IS ME.
LET...
...HER...
...GO!
SPLOOSH
WE'RE AUTHORIZED BY THE GOVERNMENT TO BRING THIS WOMAN IN!
SHE'S A WANTED FUGITIVE.
HEH. YOU AIN'T THE SCARIEST...
...NOT BY A LONG SHOT.

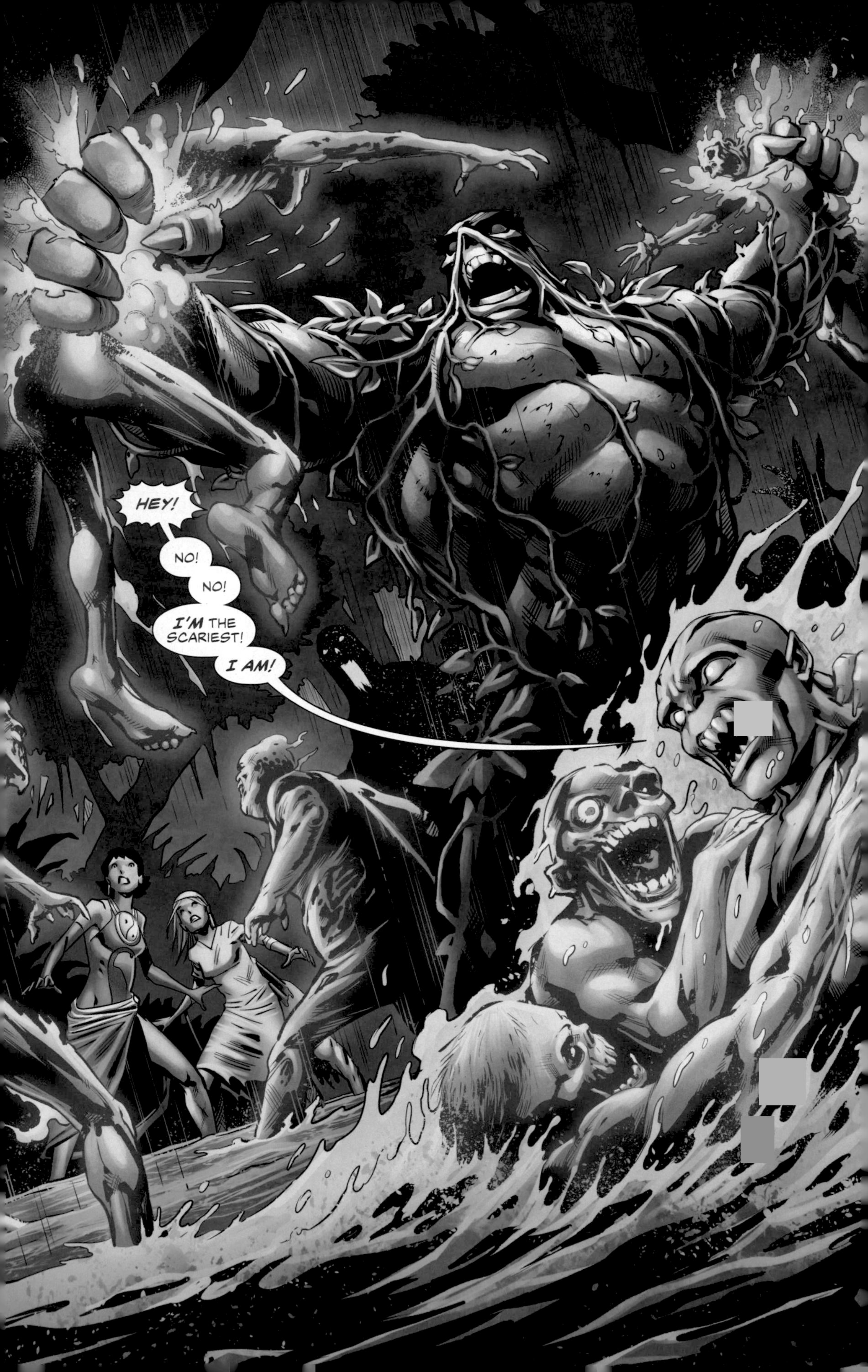
HEY!
NO!
NO!
I'M THE SCARIEST!
I AM!

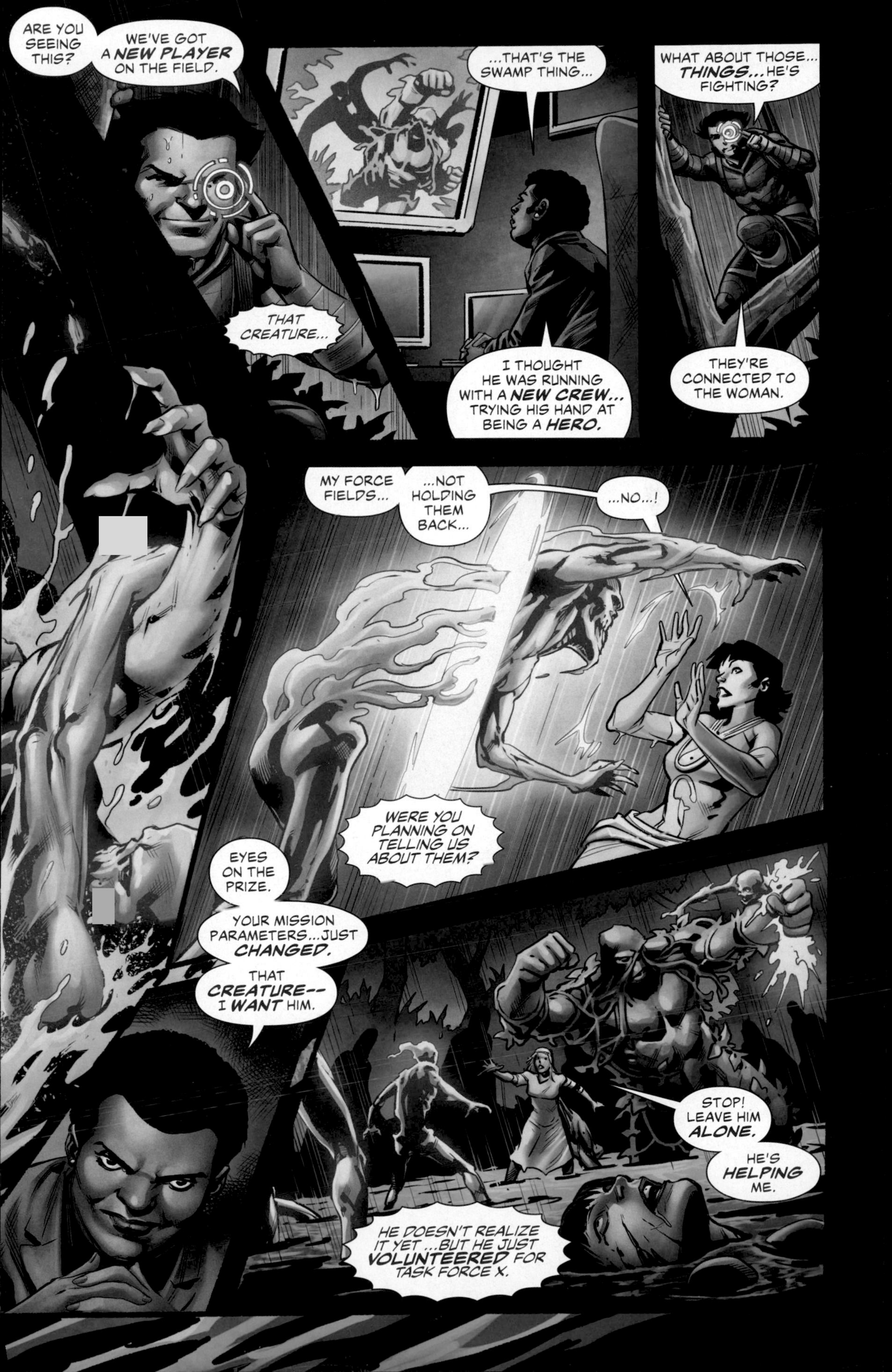

ARE YOU SEEING THIS?
WE'VE GOT A NEW PLAYER ON THE FIELD.
THAT CREATURE...
...THAT'S THE SWAMP THING...
I THOUGHT HE WAS RUNNING WITH A NEW CREW... TRYING HIS HAND AT BEING A HERO.
WHAT ABOUT THOSE... THINGS... HE'S FIGHTING?
THEY'RE CONNECTED TO THE WOMAN.
MY FORCE FIELDS...
...NOT HOLDING THEM BACK...
...NO...!
WERE YOU PLANNING ON TELLING US ABOUT THEM?
EYES ON THE PRIZE.
YOUR MISSION PARAMETERS...JUST CHANGED.
THAT CREATURE-- I WANT HIM.
STOP! LEAVE HIM ALONE.
HE'S HELPING ME.
HE DOESN'T REALIZE IT YET ...BUT HE JUST VOLUNTEERED FOR TASK FORCE X.

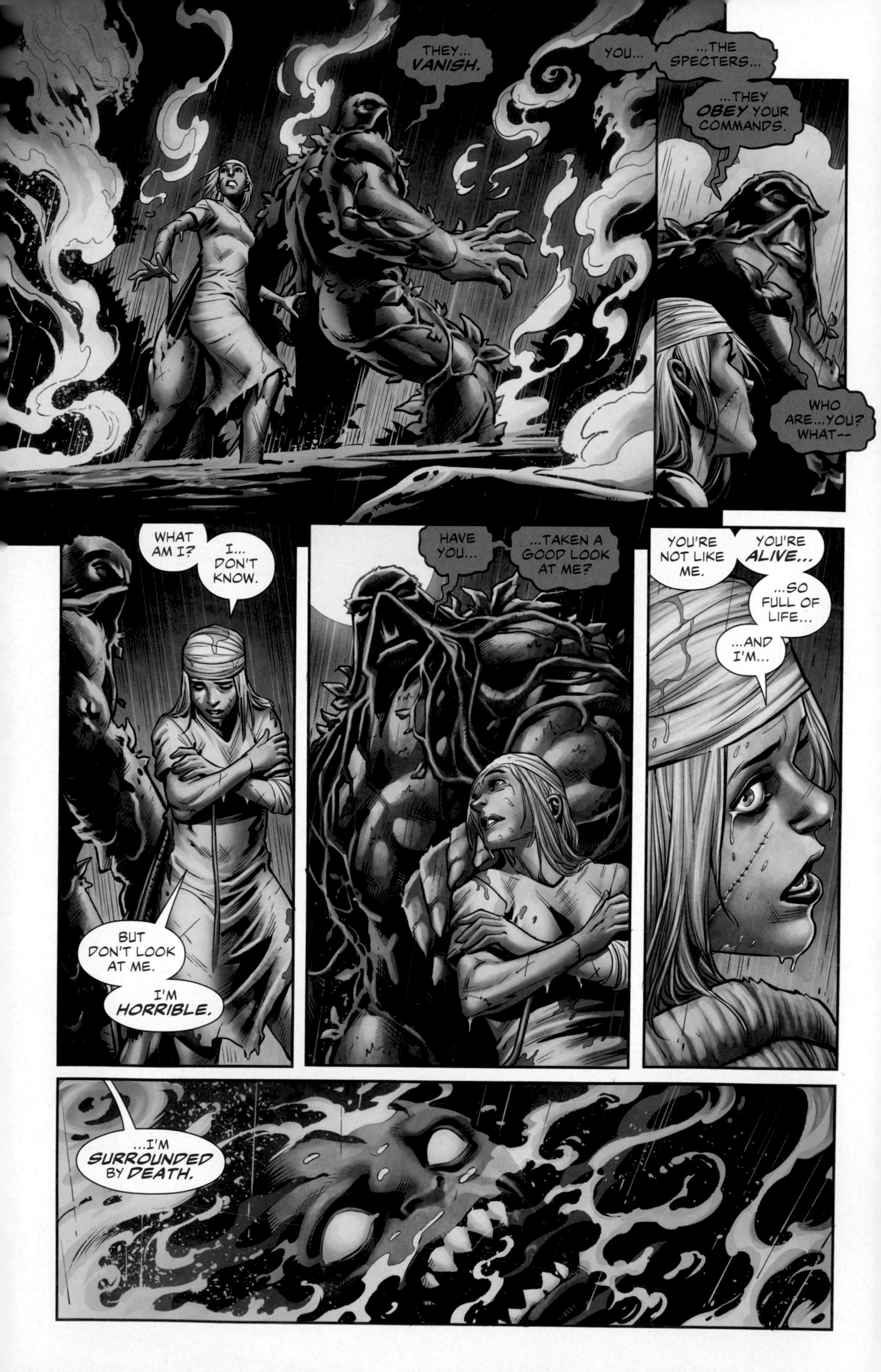
THEY... VANISH.
YOU...
...THE SPECTERS...
...THEY OBEY YOUR COMMANDS.
WHO ARE...YOU? WHAT--
WHAT AM I?
I... DON'T KNOW.
BUT DON'T LOOK AT ME.
I'M HORRIBLE.
HAVE YOU...
...TAKEN A GOOD LOOK AT ME?
YOU'RE NOT LIKE ME.
YOU'RE ALIVE...
...SO FULL OF LIFE...
...AND I'M...
...I'M SURROUNDED BY DEATH.

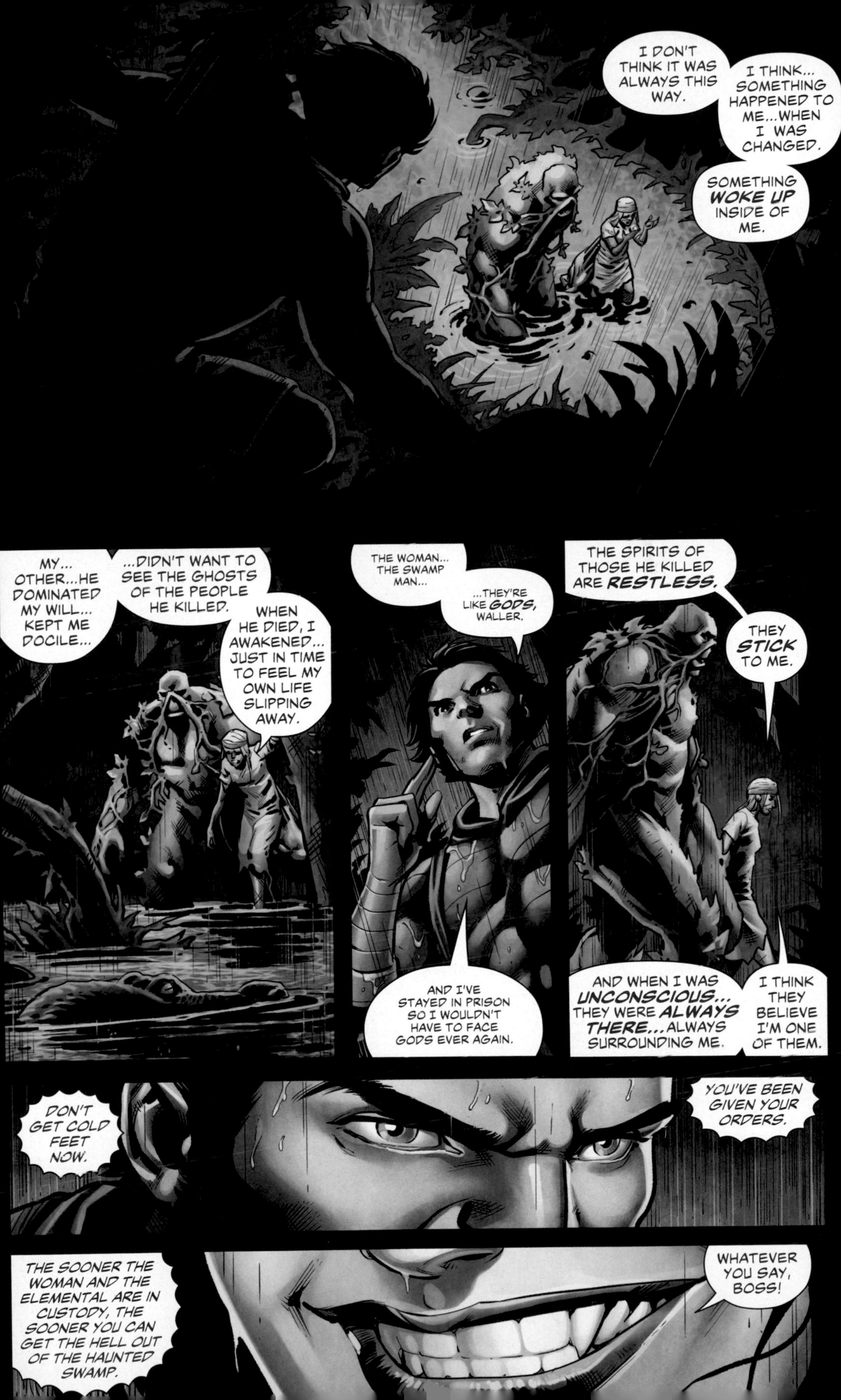
I DON'T THINK IT WAS ALWAYS THIS WAY.
I THINK... SOMETHING HAPPENED TO ME...WHEN I WAS CHANGED.
SOMETHING WOKE UP INSIDE OF ME.
MY... OTHER...HE DOMINATED MY WILL... KEPT ME DOCILE...
...DIDN'T WANT TO SEE THE GHOSTS OF THE PEOPLE HE KILLED.
WHEN HE DIED, I AWAKENED... JUST IN TIME TO FEEL MY OWN LIFE SLIPPING AWAY.
THE WOMAN... THE SWAMP MAN...
...THEY'RE LIKE GODS, WALLER.
AND I'VE STAYED IN PRISON SO I WOULDN'T HAVE TO FACE GODS EVER AGAIN.
THE SPIRITS OF THOSE HE KILLED ARE RESTLESS.
THEY STICK TO ME.
AND WHEN I WAS UNCONSCIOUS... THEY WERE ALWAYS THERE... ALWAYS SURROUNDING ME.
I THINK THEY BELIEVE I'M ONE OF THEM.
DON'T GET COLD FEET NOW.
YOU'VE BEEN GIVEN YOUR ORDERS.
THE SOONER THE WOMAN AND THE ELEMENTAL ARE IN CUSTODY, THE SOONER YOU CAN GET THE HELL OUT OF THE HAUNTED SWAMP.
WHATEVER YOU SAY, BOSS!

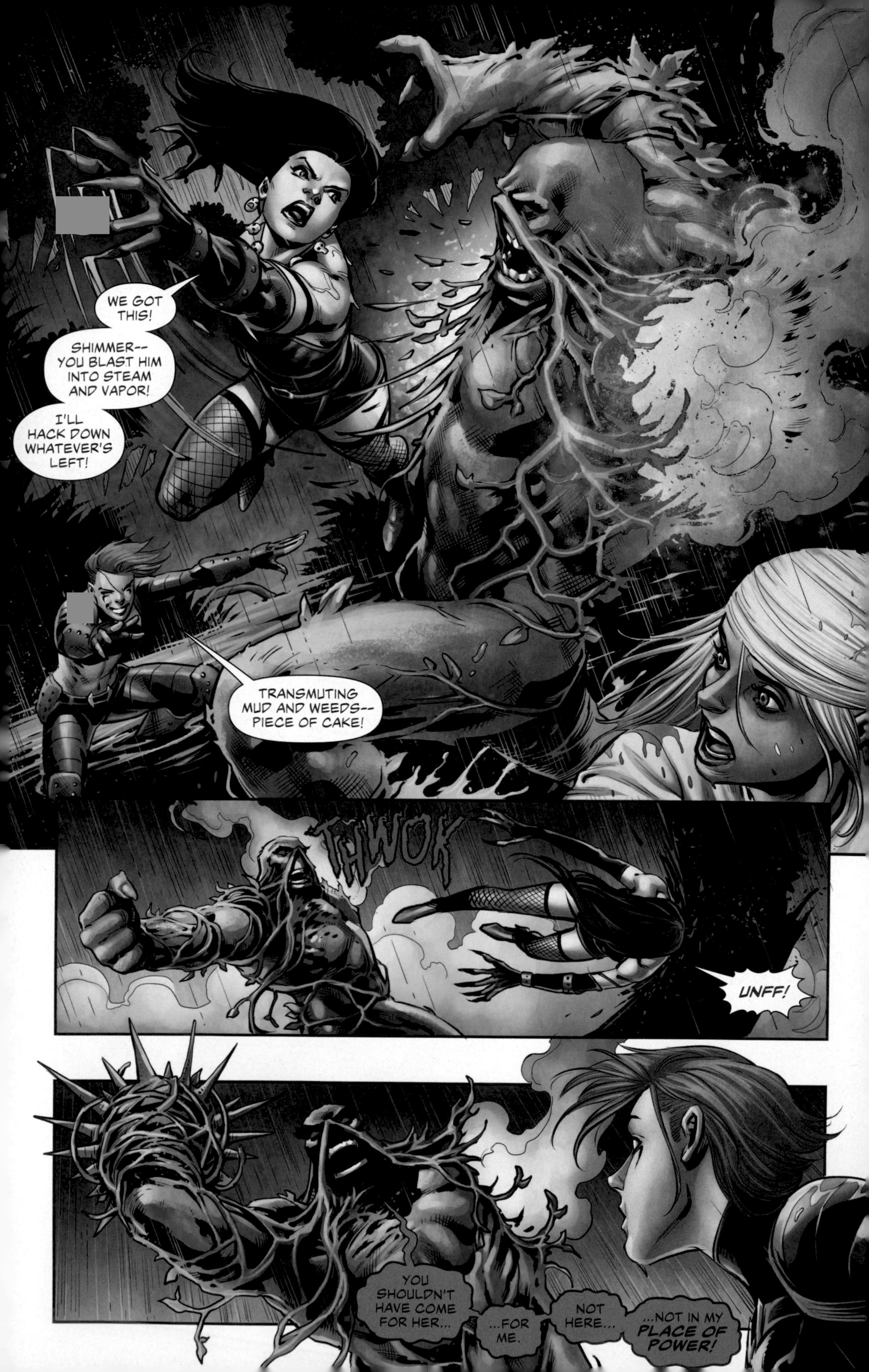
WE GOT THIS!
SHIMMER-- YOU BLAST HIM INTO STEAM AND VAPOR!
I'LL HACK DOWN WHATEVER'S LEFT!
TRANSMUTING MUD AND WEEDS-- PIECE OF CAKE!
THWOK
UNFF!
YOU SHOULDN'T HAVE COME FOR HER...
...FOR ME.
NOT HERE...
...NOT IN MY PLACE OF POWER!

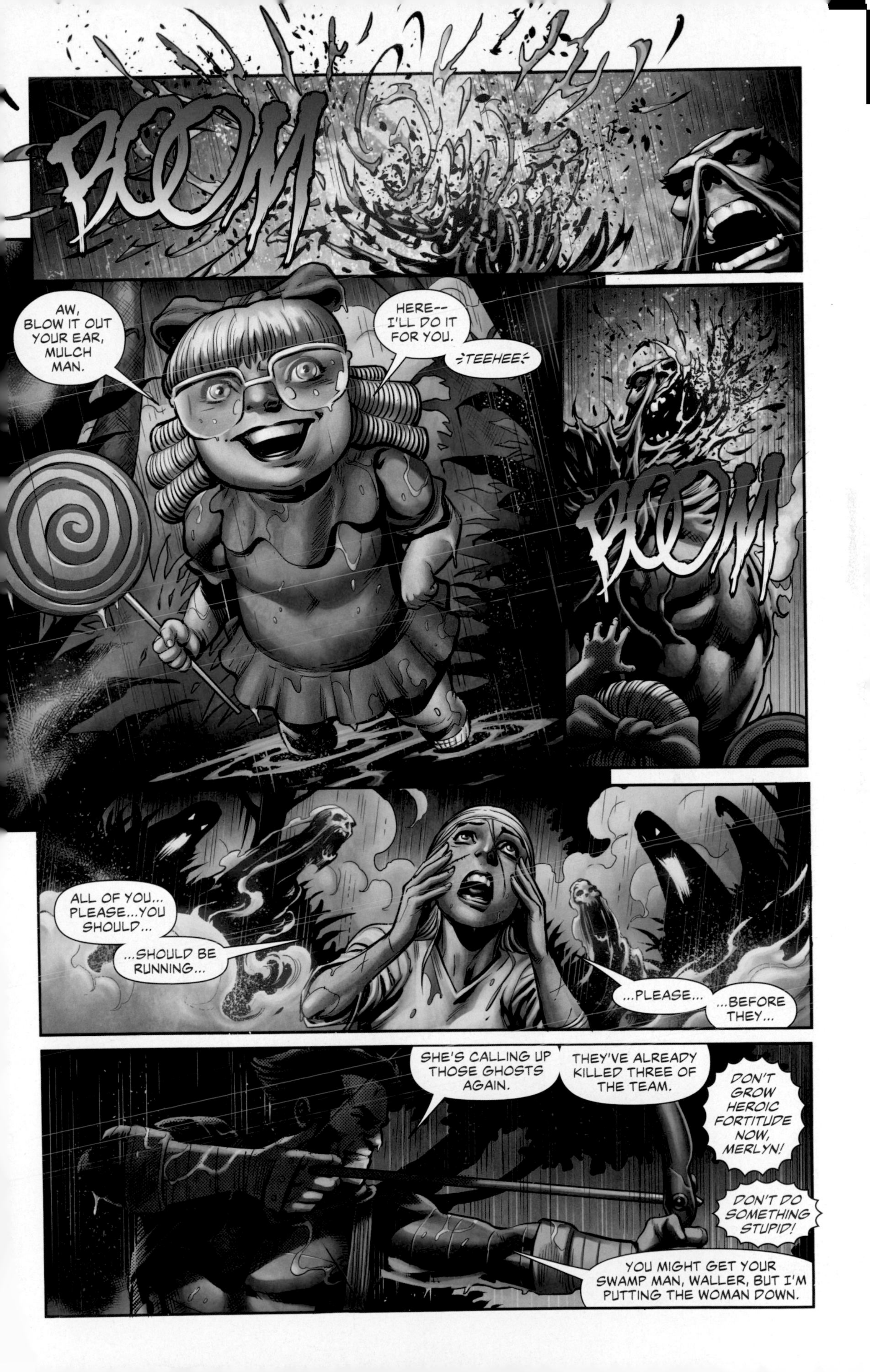
BOOM
AW, BLOW IT OUT YOUR EAR, MULCH MAN.
HERE-- I'LL DO IT FOR YOU.
TEEHEE
BOOM
ALL OF YOU... PLEASE...YOU SHOULD...
...SHOULD BE RUNNING...
...PLEASE...
...BEFORE THEY...
SHE'S CALLING UP THOSE GHOSTS AGAIN.
THEY'VE ALREADY KILLED THREE OF THE TEAM.
DON'T GROW HEROIC FORTITUDE NOW, MERLYN!
DON'T DO SOMETHING STUPID!
YOU MIGHT GET YOUR SWAMP MAN, WALLER, BUT I'M PUTTING THE WOMAN DOWN.

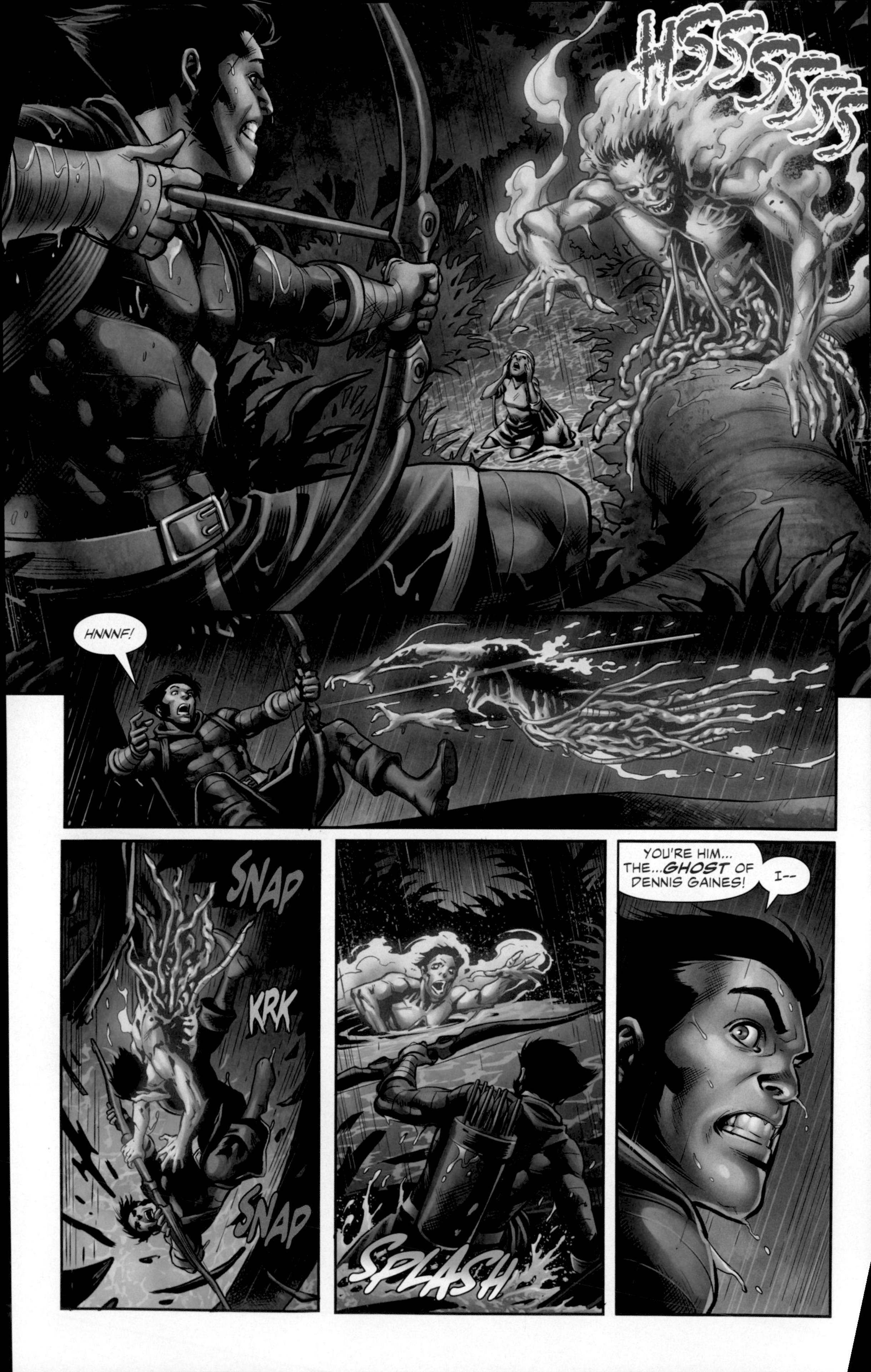
HSSSSSS
HNNNF!
SNAP
KRK
SNAP
SPLASH
YOU'RE HIM... THE...GHOST OF DENNIS GAINES!
I--

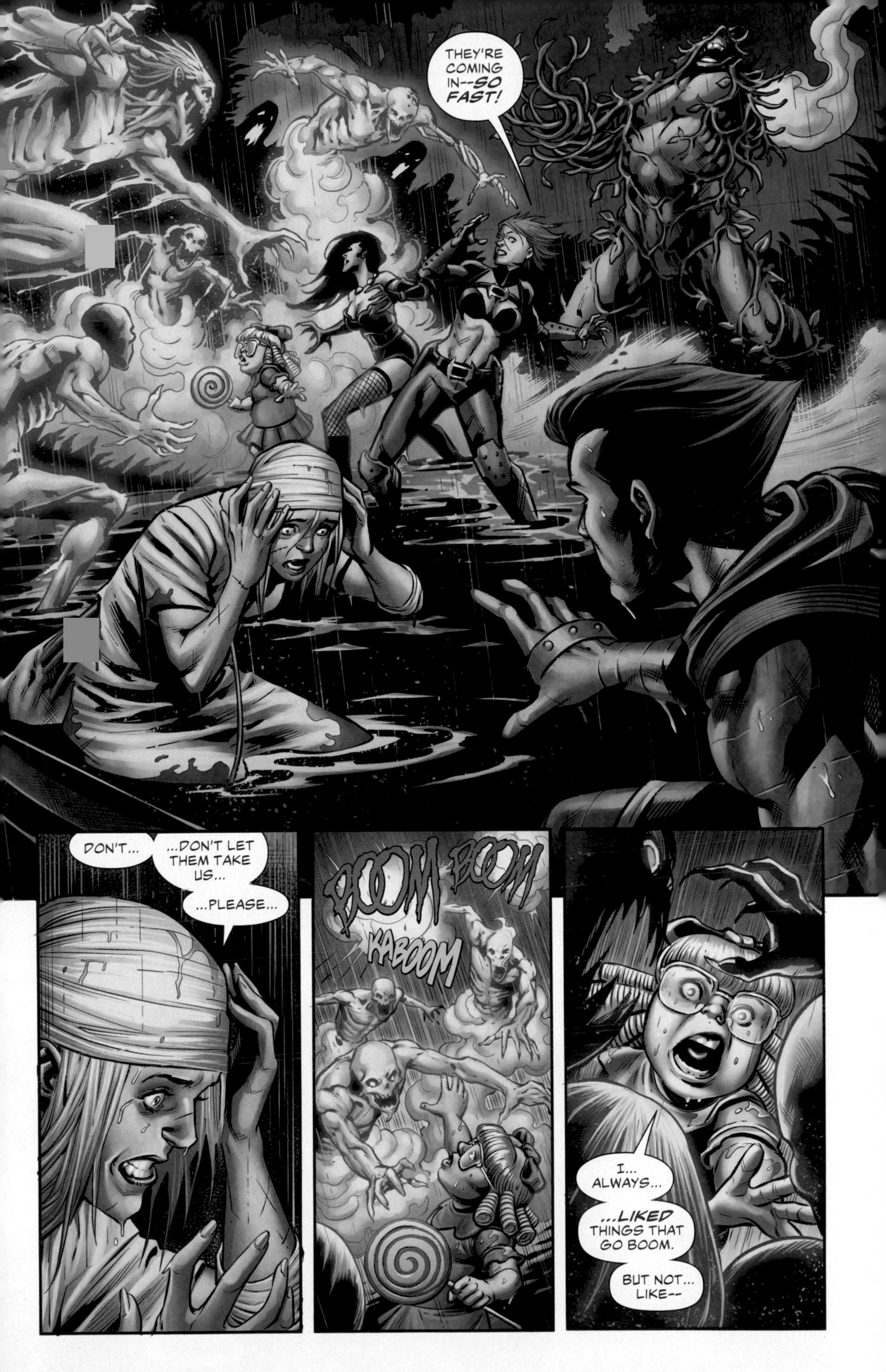
THEY'RE COMING IN--SO FAST!
DON'T...
...DON'T LET THEM TAKE US...
...PLEASE...
BOOM BOOM
KABOOM
I... ALWAYS...
...LIKED THINGS THAT GO BOOM.
BUT NOT... LIKE--

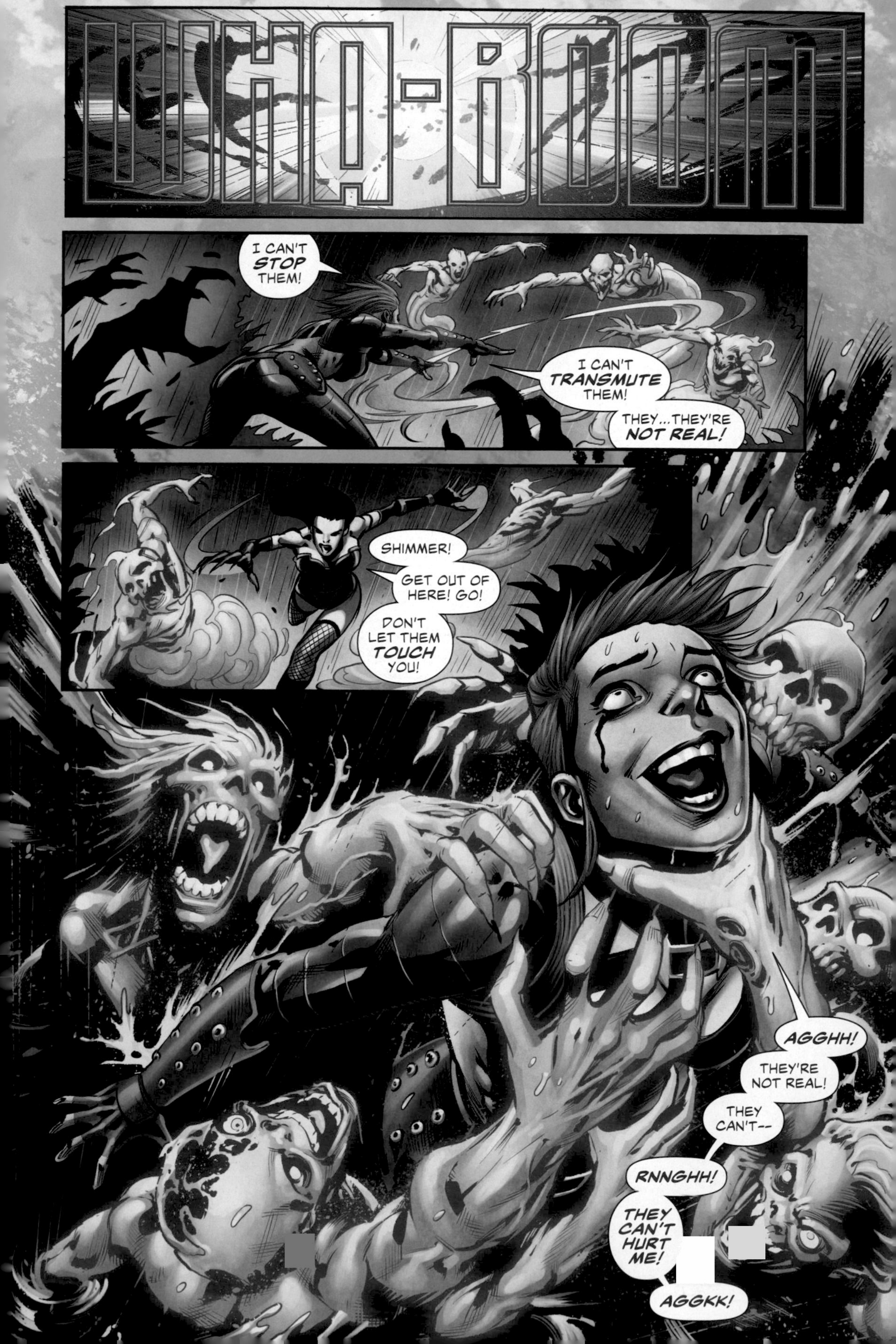
WHA-BOOM
I CAN'T STOP THEM!
I CAN'T TRANSMUTE THEM!
THEY...THEY'RE NOT REAL!
SHIMMER!
GET OUT OF HERE! GO!
DON'T LET THEM TOUCH YOU!
AGGHH!
THEY'RE NOT REAL!
THEY CAN'T--
RNNGHH!
THEY CAN'T HURT ME!
AGGKK!

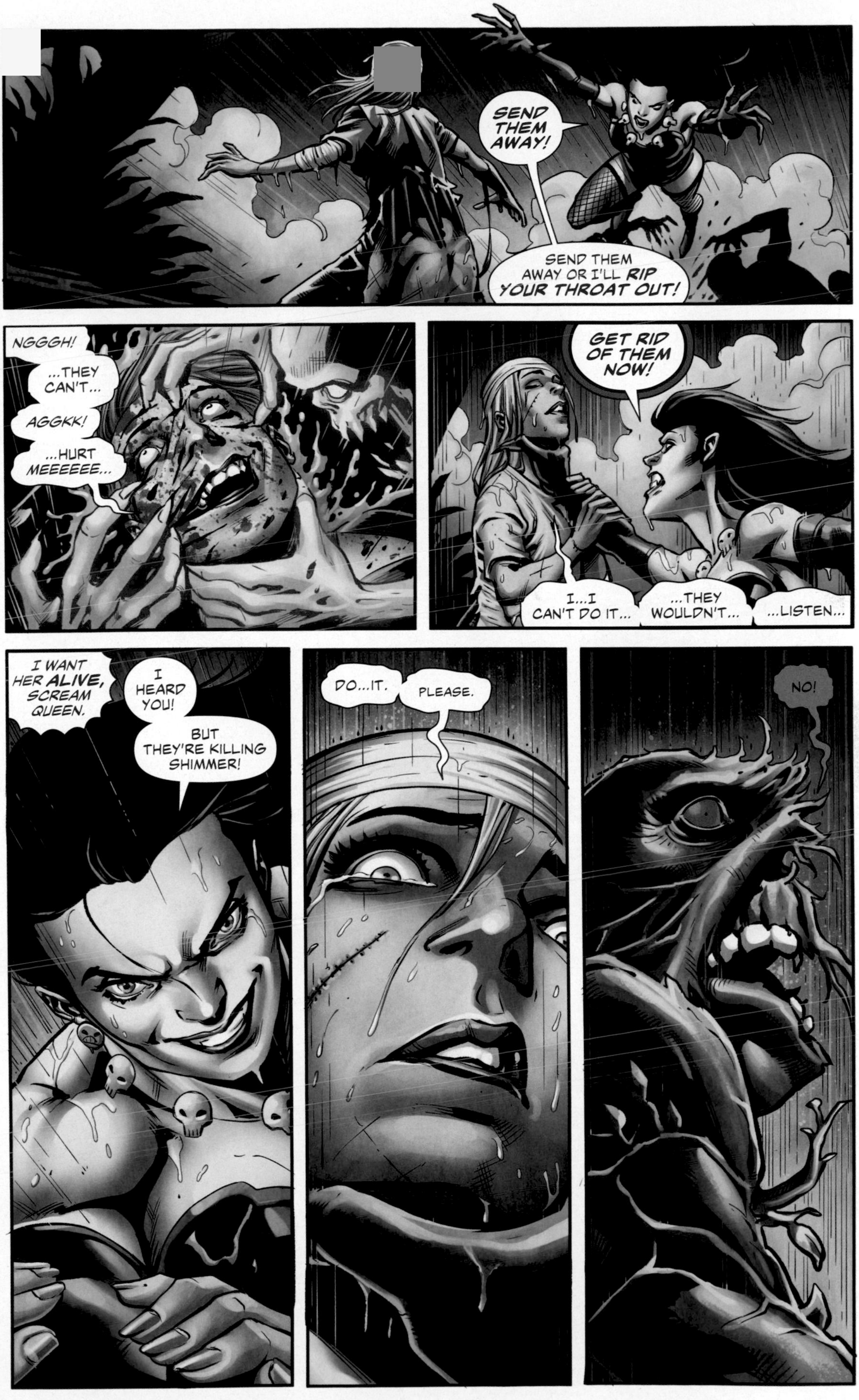
SEND THEM AWAY!
SEND THEM AWAY OR I'LL RIP YOUR THROAT OUT!
NGGGH!
...THEY CAN'T...
AGGKK!
...HURT MEEEEEE...
GET RID OF THEM NOW!
I...I CAN'T DO IT...
...THEY WOULDN'T...
...LISTEN...
I WANT HER ALIVE, SCREAM QUEEN.
I HEARD YOU!
BUT THEY'RE KILLING SHIMMER!
DO...IT.
PLEASE.
NO!

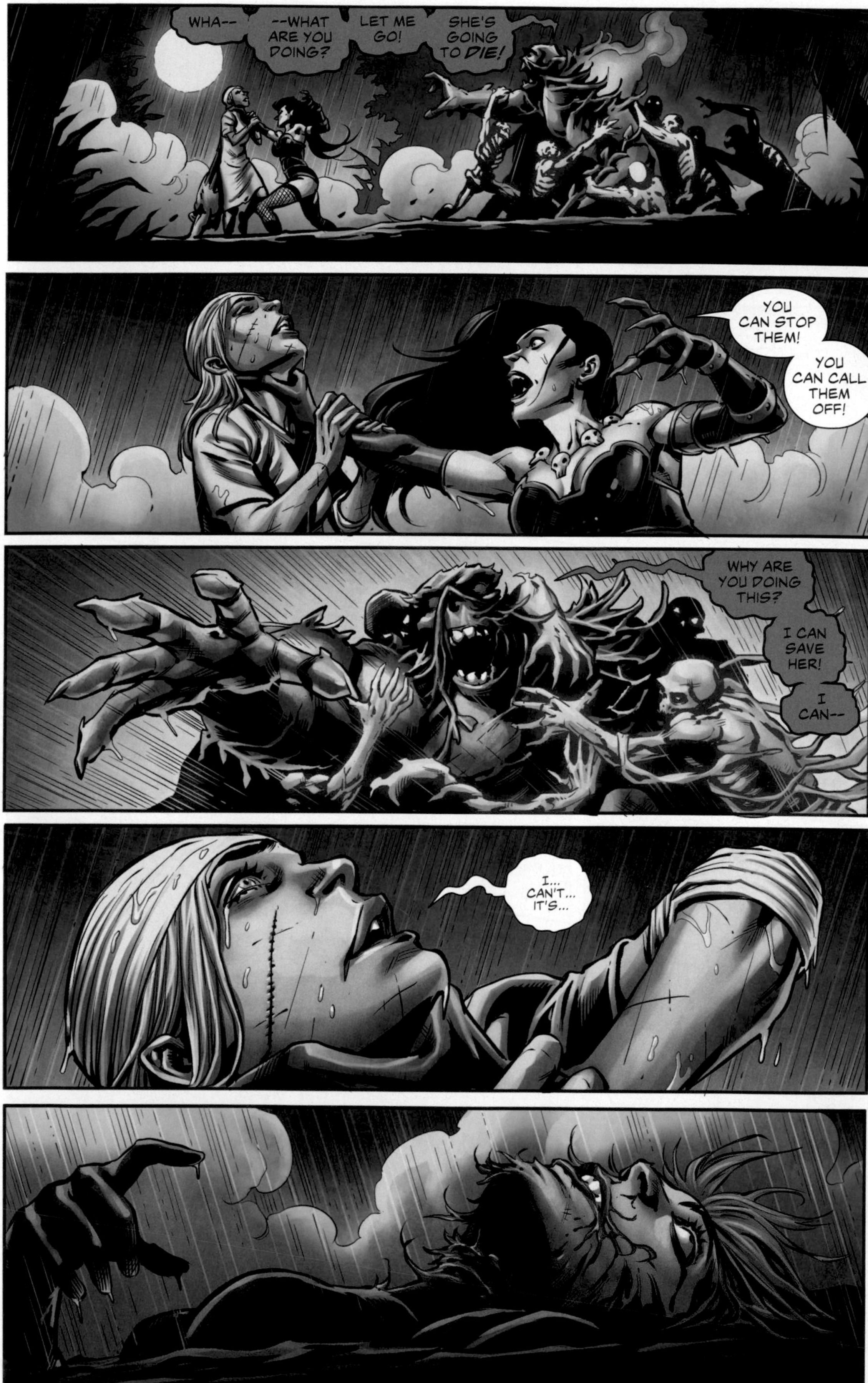
WHA--
--WHAT ARE YOU DOING?
LET ME GO!
SHE'S GOING TO DIE!
YOU CAN STOP THEM!
YOU CAN CALL THEM OFF!
WHY ARE YOU DOING THIS?
I CAN SAVE HER!
I CAN--
I... CAN'T... IT'S...

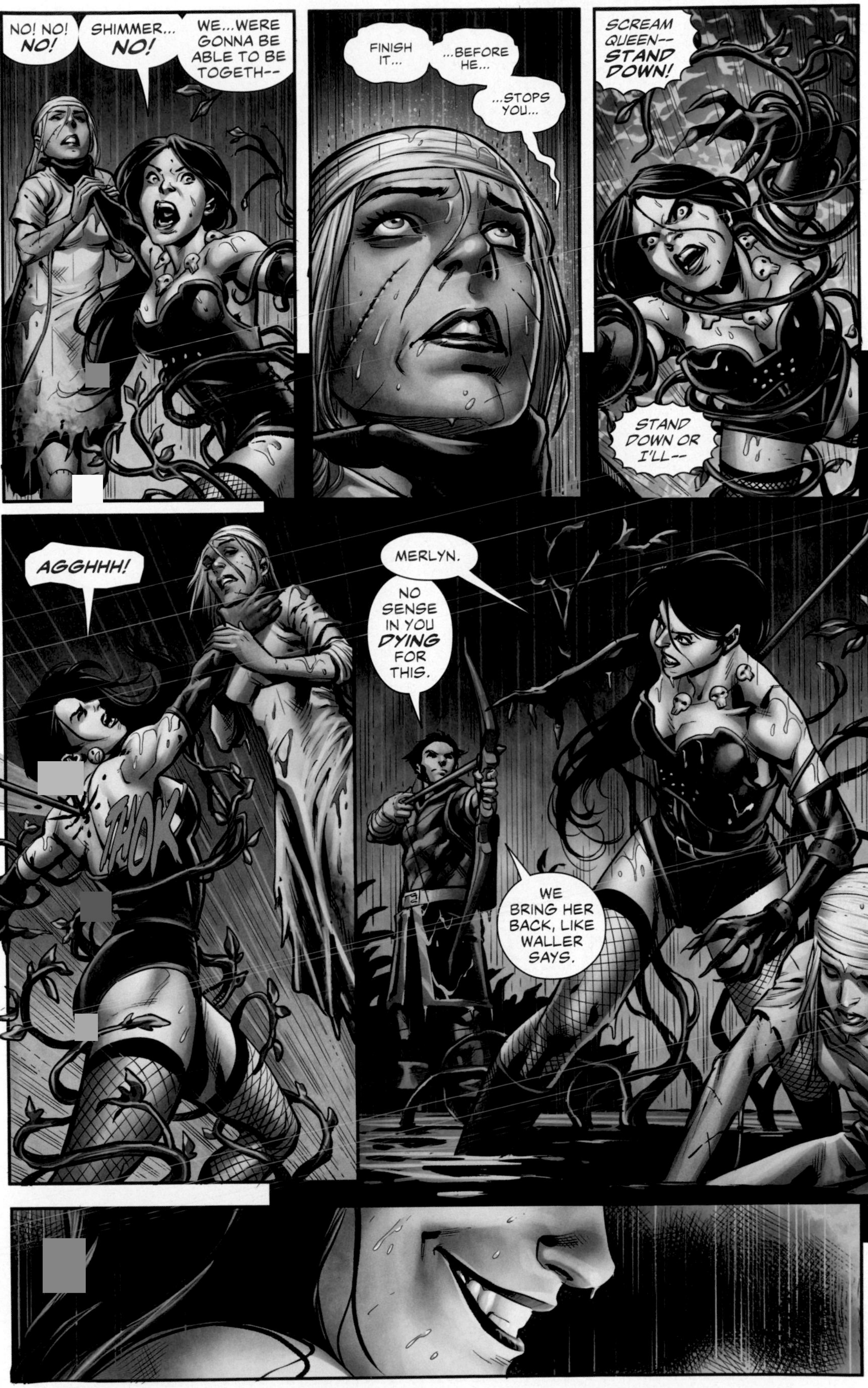
NO! NO! NO!
SHIMMER... NO!
WE...WERE GONNA BE ABLE TO BE TOGETH--
FINISH IT...
...BEFORE HE...
...STOPS YOU...
SCREAM QUEEN-- STAND DOWN!
STAND DOWN OR I'LL--
AGGHHH!
THOK
MERLYN.
NO SENSE IN YOU DYING FOR THIS.
WE BRING HER BACK, LIKE WALLER SAYS.

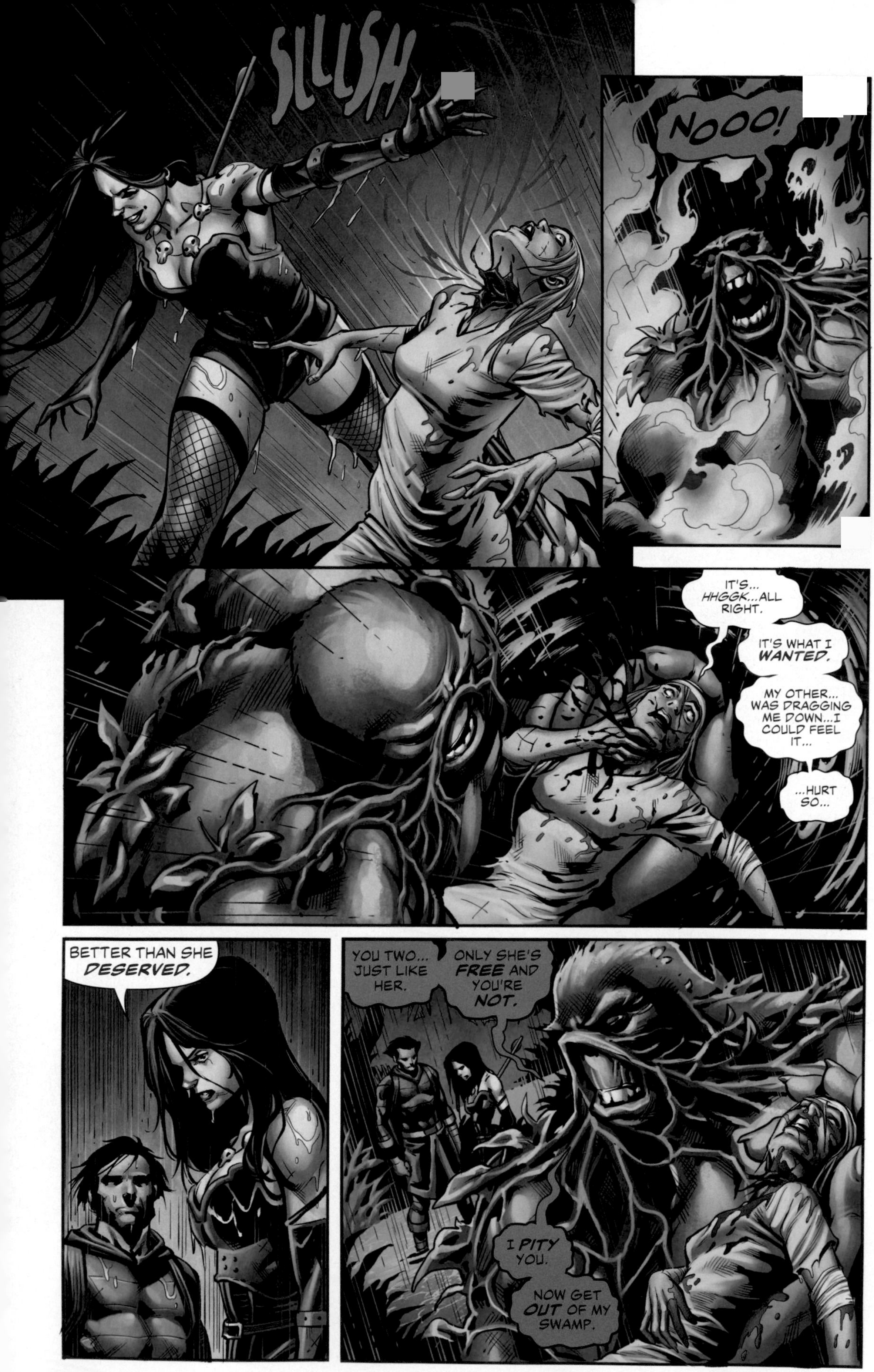
SLLLSH
NOOO!
IT'S... HHGGK...ALL RIGHT.
IT'S WHAT I WANTED.
MY OTHER... WAS DRAGGING ME DOWN...I COULD FEEL IT...
...HURT SO...
BETTER THAN SHE DESERVED.
YOU TWO... JUST LIKE HER.
ONLY SHE'S FREE AND YOU'RE NOT.
I PITY YOU.
NOW GET OUT OF MY SWAMP.

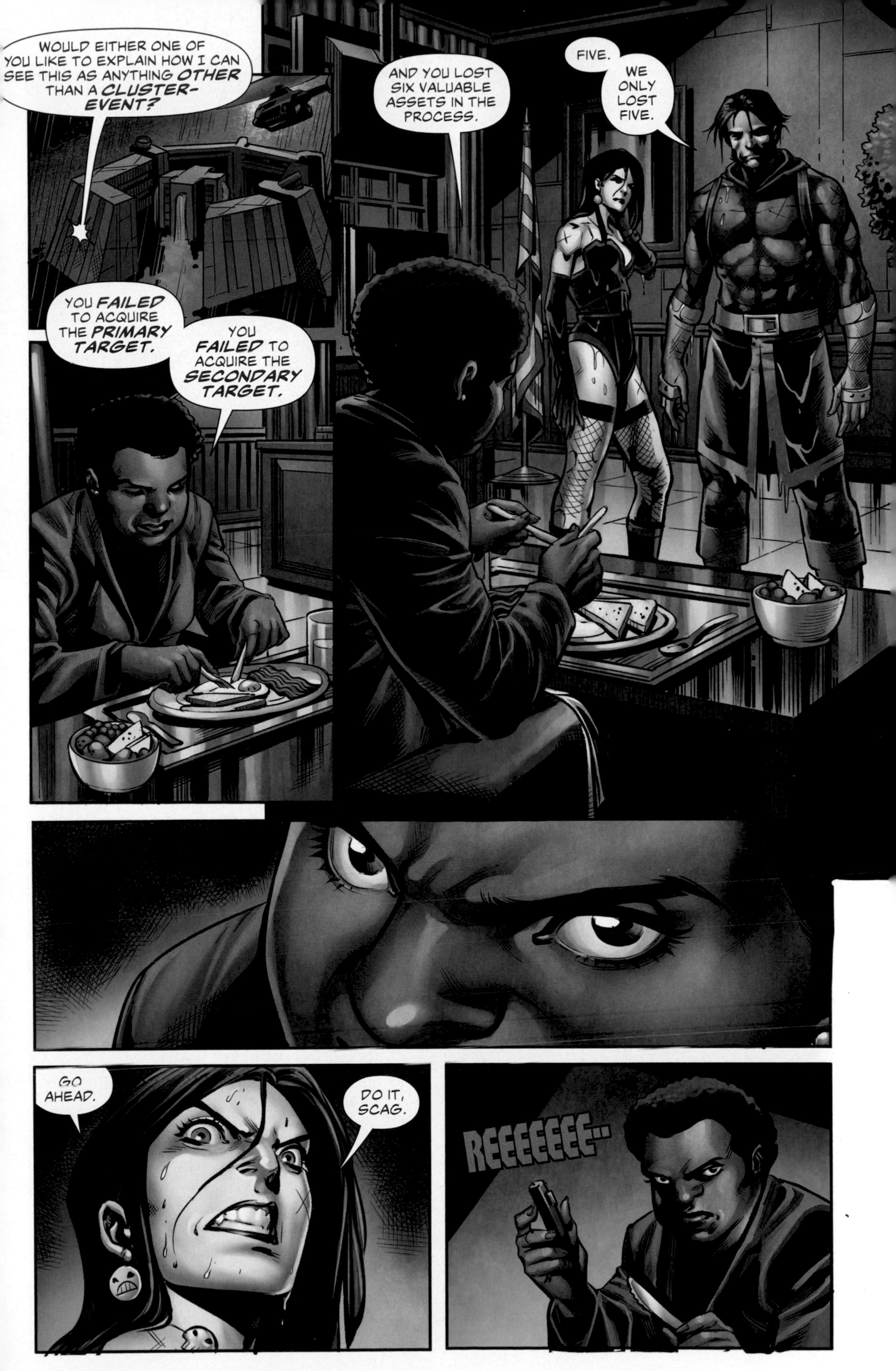
WOULD EITHER ONE OF YOU LIKE TO EXPLAIN HOW I CAN SEE THIS AS ANYTHING OTHER THAN A CLUSTER-EVENT?
AND YOU LOST SIX VALUABLE ASSETS IN THE PROCESS.
FIVE.
WE ONLY LOST FIVE.
YOU FAILED TO ACQUIRE THE PRIMARY TARGET.
YOU FAILED TO ACQUIRE THE SECONDARY TARGET.
GO AHEAD.
DO IT, SCAG.
REEEEEEE--

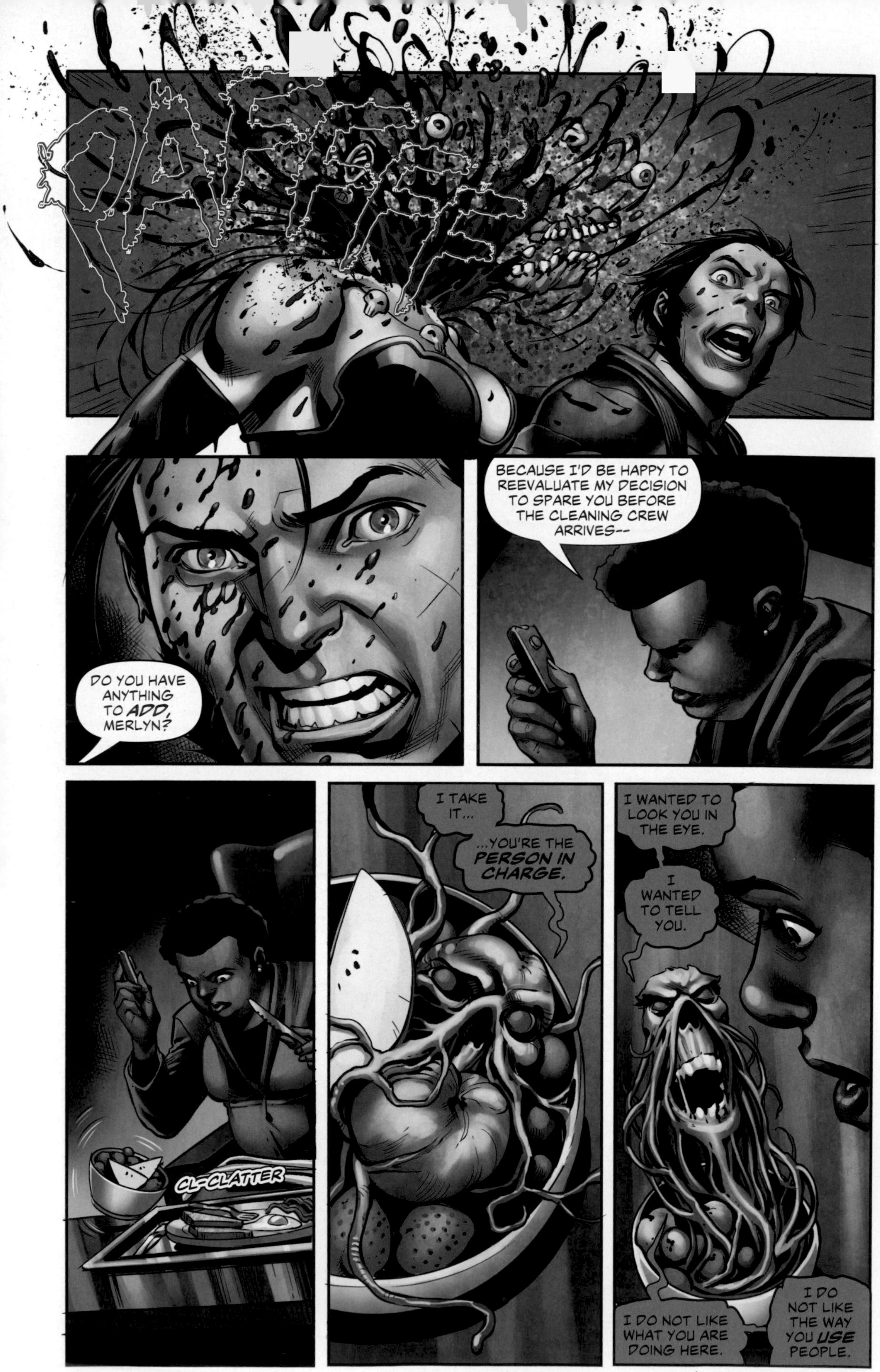
DO YOU HAVE ANYTHING TO ADD, MERLYN?
BECAUSE I'D BE HAPPY TO REEVALUATE MY DECISION TO SPARE YOU BEFORE THE CLEANING CREW ARRIVES--
CL-CLATTER
I TAKE IT...
...YOU'RE THE PERSON IN CHARGE.
I WANTED TO LOOK YOU IN THE EYE.
I WANTED TO TELL YOU.
I DO NOT LIKE WHAT YOU ARE DOING HERE.
I DO NOT LIKE THE WAY YOU USE PEOPLE.

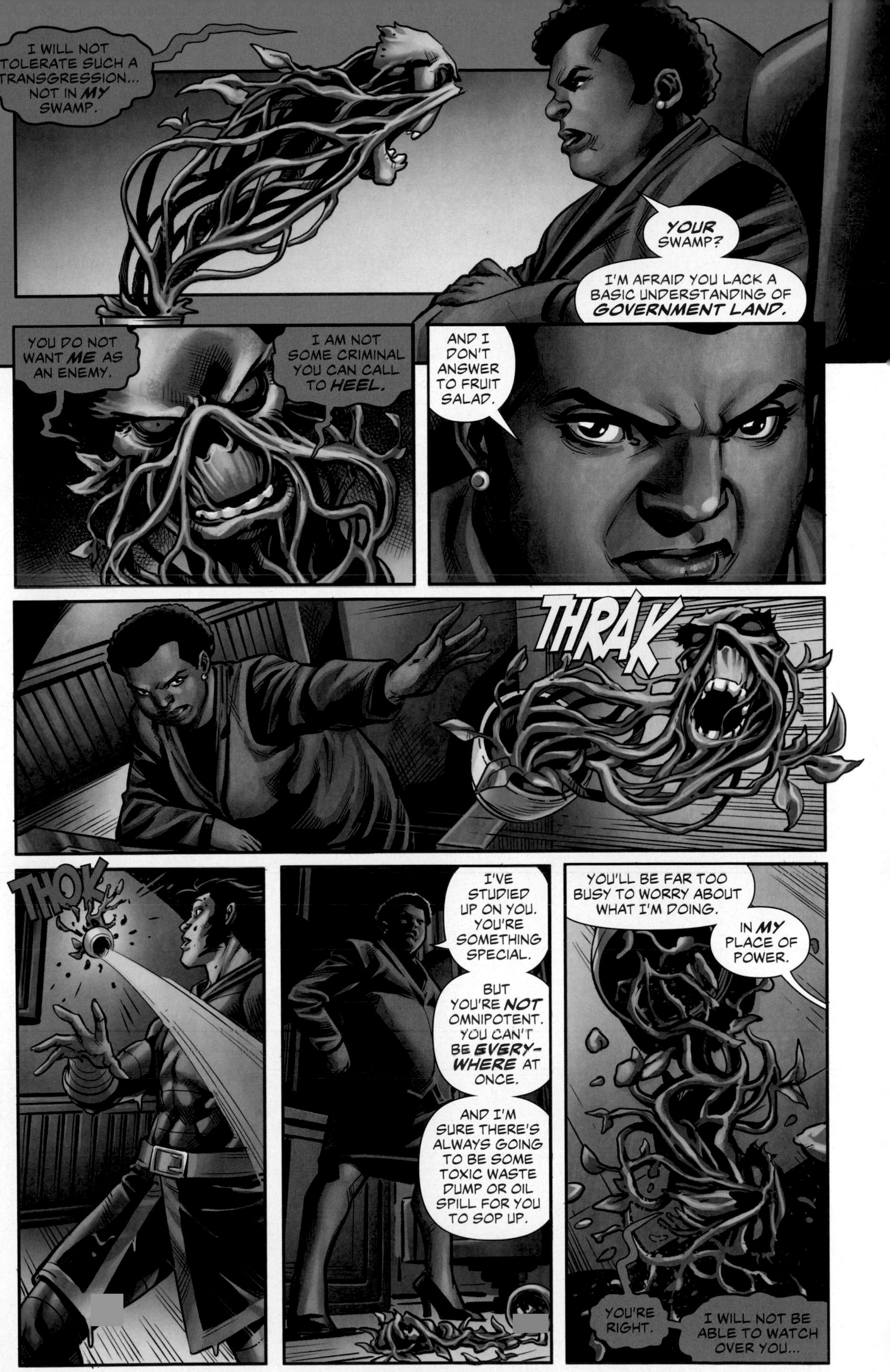
I WILL NOT TOLERATE SUCH A TRANSGRESSION... NOT IN MY SWAMP.
YOUR SWAMP?
I'M AFRAID YOU LACK A BASIC UNDERSTANDING OF GOVERNMENT LAND.
YOU DO NOT WANT ME AS AN ENEMY.
I AM NOT SOME CRIMINAL YOU CAN CALL TO HEEL.
AND I DON'T ANSWER TO FRUIT SALAD.
THRAK
THOK
I'VE STUDIED UP ON YOU. YOU'RE SOMETHING SPECIAL.
BUT YOU'RE NOT OMNIPOTENT. YOU CAN'T BE EVERY-WHERE AT ONCE.
AND I'M SURE THERE'S ALWAYS GOING TO BE SOME TOXIC WASTE DUMP OR OIL SPILL FOR YOU TO SOP UP.
YOU'LL BE FAR TOO BUSY TO WORRY ABOUT WHAT I'M DOING.
IN MY PLACE OF POWER.
YOU'RE RIGHT.
I WILL NOT BE ABLE TO WATCH OVER YOU...

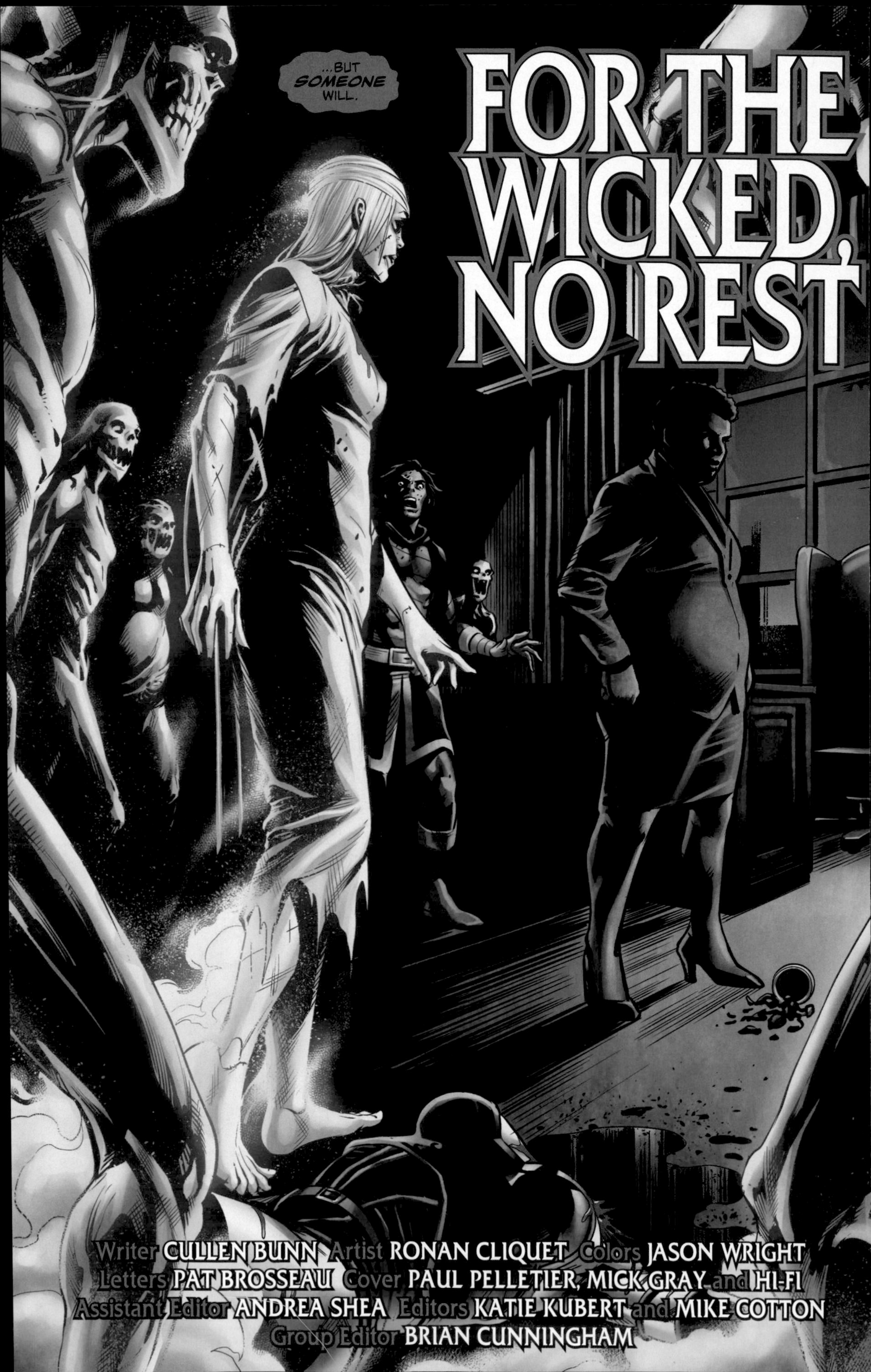
...BUT SOMEONE WILL.
FOR THE WICKED, NO REST
Writer CULLEN BUNN Artist RONAN CLIQUET Colors JASON WRIGHT
Letters PAT BROSSEAU Cover PAUL PELLETIER, MICK GRAY and HI-FI
Assistant Editor ANDREA SHEA Editors KATIE KUBERT and MIKE COTTON
Group Editor BRIAN CUNNINGHAM

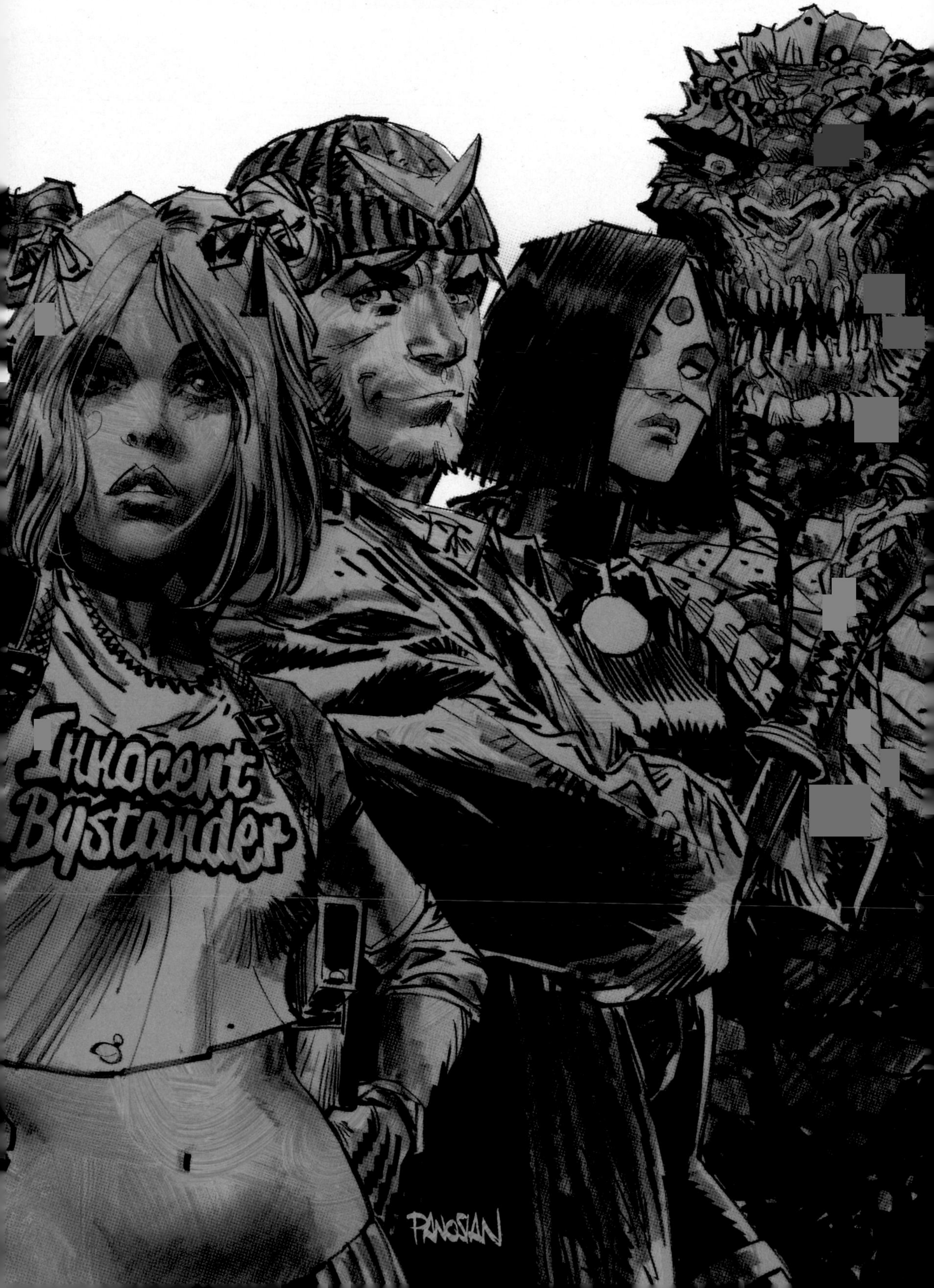
Innocent Bystander
PANOSIAN

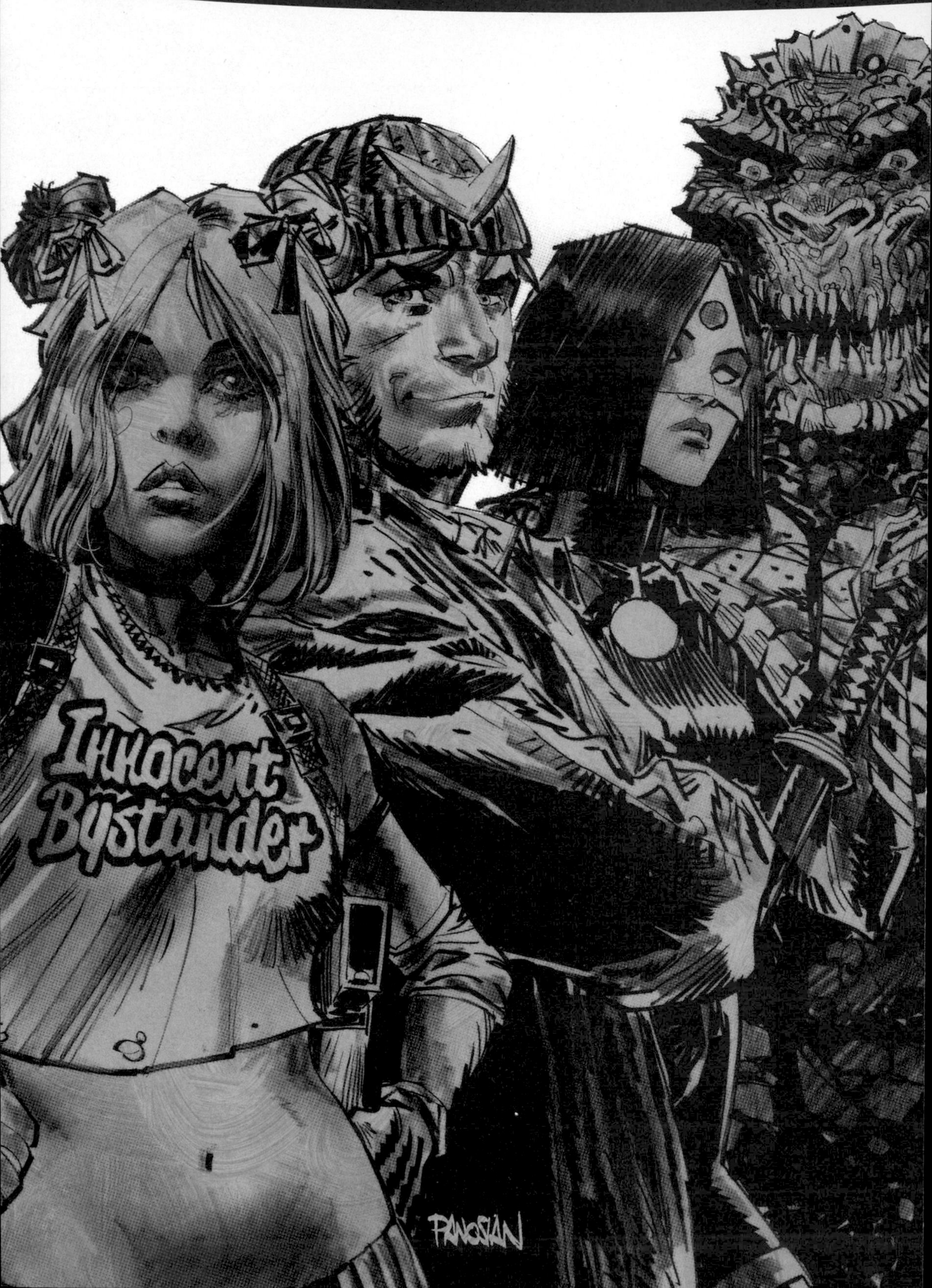
Innocent Bystander
PANOSIAN

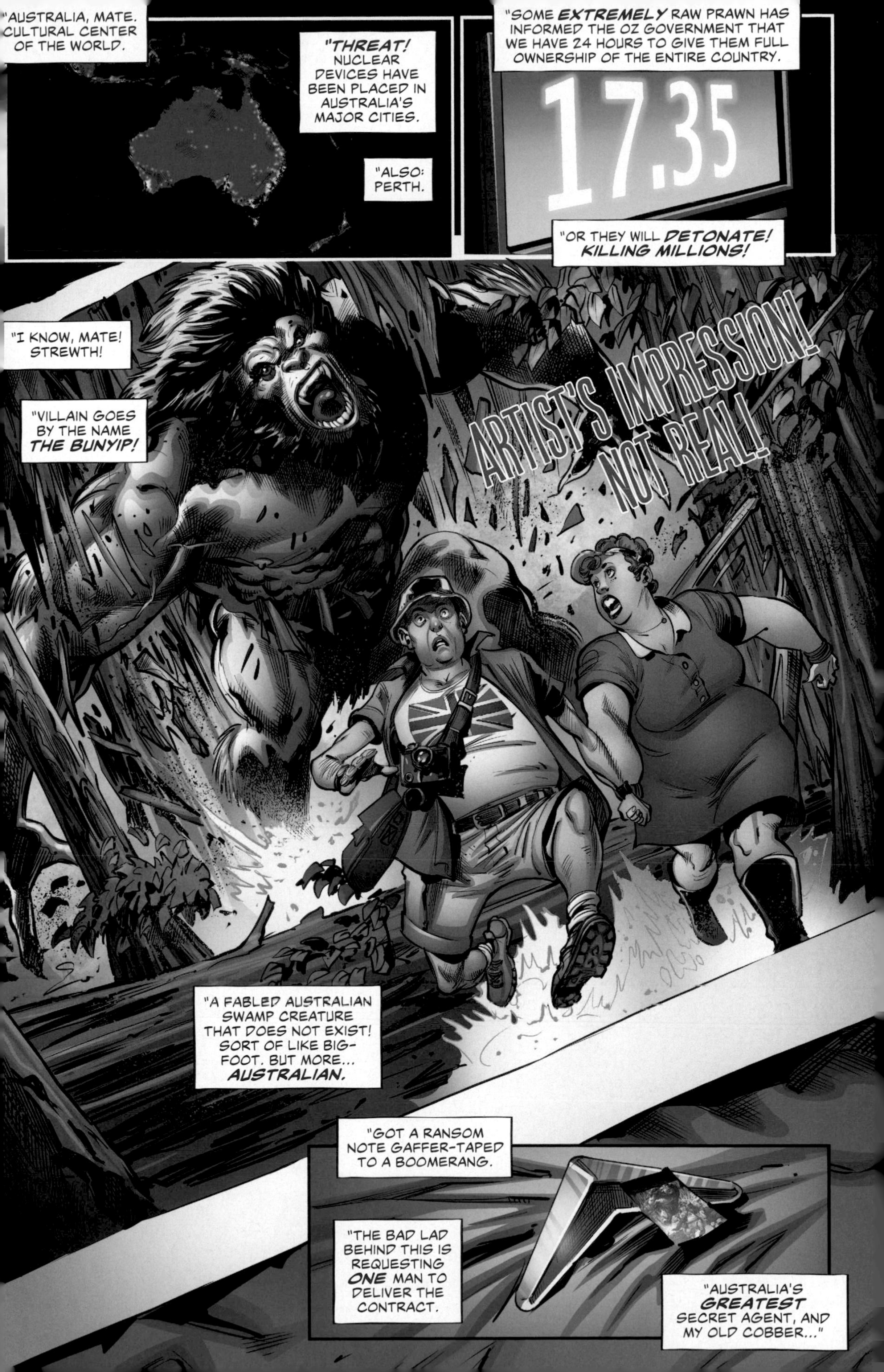
"AUSTRALIA, MATE. CULTURAL CENTER OF THE WORLD.
"THREAT! NUCLEAR DEVICES HAVE BEEN PLACED IN AUSTRALIA'S MAJOR CITIES.
"ALSO: PERTH.
"SOME EXTREMELY RAW PRAWN HAS INFORMED THE OZ GOVERNMENT THAT WE HAVE 24 HOURS TO GIVE THEM FULL OWNERSHIP OF THE ENTIRE COUNTRY.
17.35
"OR THEY WILL DETONATE! KILLING MILLIONS!
"I KNOW, MATE! STREWTH!
"VILLAIN GOES BY THE NAME THE BUNYIP!
ARTIST'S IMPRESSION! NOT REAL!
"A FABLED AUSTRALIAN SWAMP CREATURE THAT DOES NOT EXIST! SORT OF LIKE BIG-FOOT. BUT MORE... AUSTRALIAN.
"GOT A RANSOM NOTE GAFFER-TAPED TO A BOOMERANG.
"THE BAD LAD BEHIND THIS IS REQUESTING ONE MAN TO DELIVER THE CONTRACT.
"AUSTRALIA'S GREATEST SECRET AGENT, AND MY OLD COBBER..."

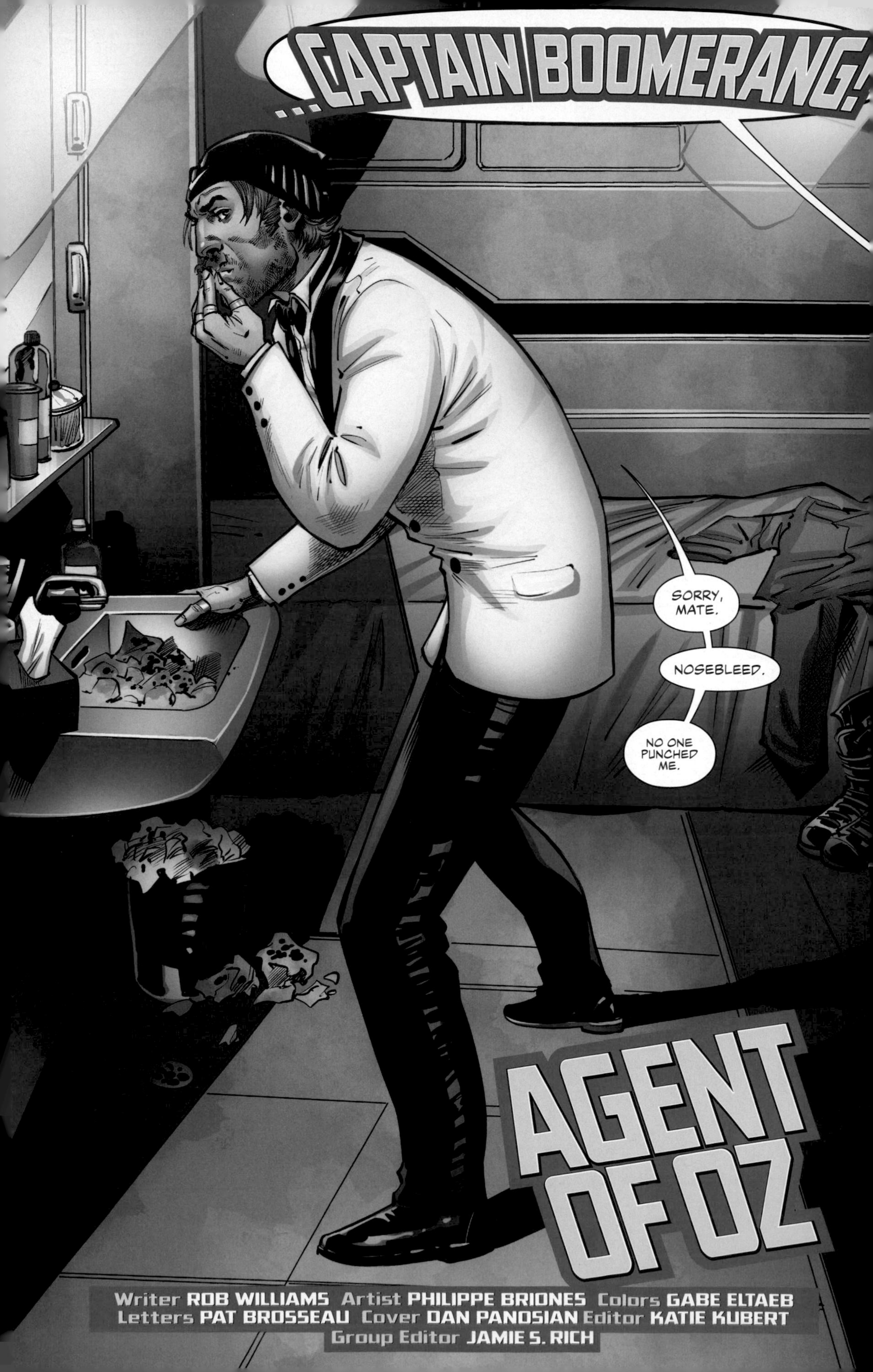
...CAPTAIN BOOMERANG!
SORRY, MATE.
NOSEBLEED.
NO ONE PUNCHED ME.
AGENT OF OZ
Writer ROB WILLIAMS Artist PHILIPPE BRIONES Colors GABE ELTAEB
Letters PAT BROSSEAU Cover DAN PANOSIAN Editor KATIE KUBERT
Group Editor JAMIE S. RICH

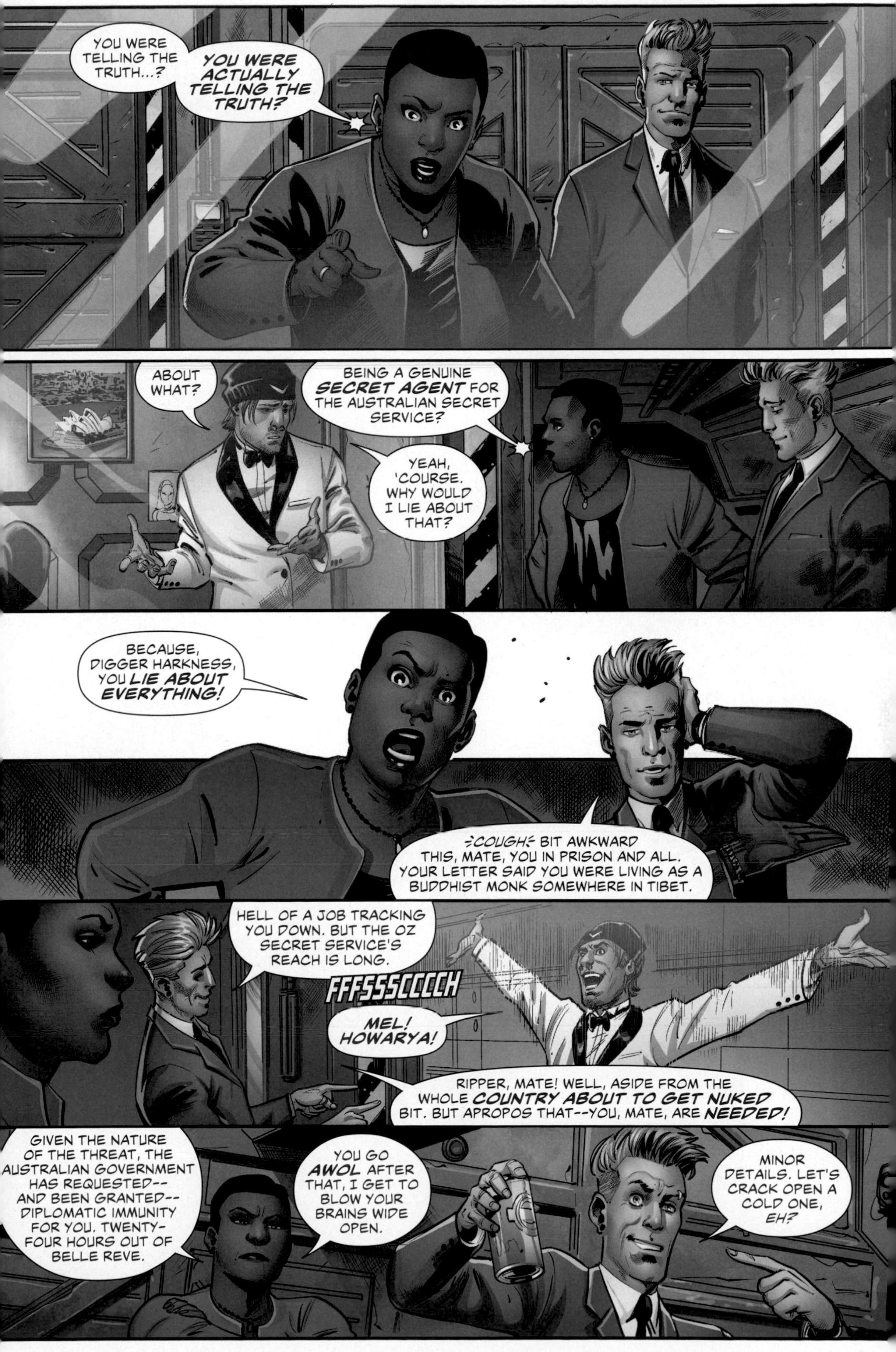
YOU WERE TELLING THE TRUTH...?
YOU WERE ACTUALLY TELLING THE TRUTH?
ABOUT WHAT?
BEING A GENUINE SECRET AGENT FOR THE AUSTRALIAN SECRET SERVICE?
YEAH, 'COURSE. WHY WOULD I LIE ABOUT THAT?
BECAUSE, DIGGER HARKNESS, YOU LIE ABOUT EVERYTHING!
COUGH BIT AWKWARD THIS, MATE, YOU IN PRISON AND ALL. YOUR LETTER SAID YOU WERE LIVING AS A BUDDHIST MONK SOMEWHERE IN TIBET.
HELL OF A JOB TRACKING YOU DOWN. BUT THE OZ SECRET SERVICE'S REACH IS LONG.
FFFSSSCCCCH
MEL! HOWARYA!
RIPPER, MATE! WELL, ASIDE FROM THE WHOLE COUNTRY ABOUT TO GET NUKED BIT. BUT APROPOS THAT--YOU, MATE, ARE NEEDED!
GIVEN THE NATURE OF THE THREAT, THE AUSTRALIAN GOVERNMENT HAS REQUESTED--AND BEEN GRANTED--DIPLOMATIC IMMUNITY FOR YOU. TWENTY-FOUR HOURS OUT OF BELLE REVE.
YOU GO AWOL AFTER THAT, I GET TO BLOW YOUR BRAINS WIDE OPEN.
MINOR DETAILS. LET'S CRACK OPEN A COLD ONE, EH?

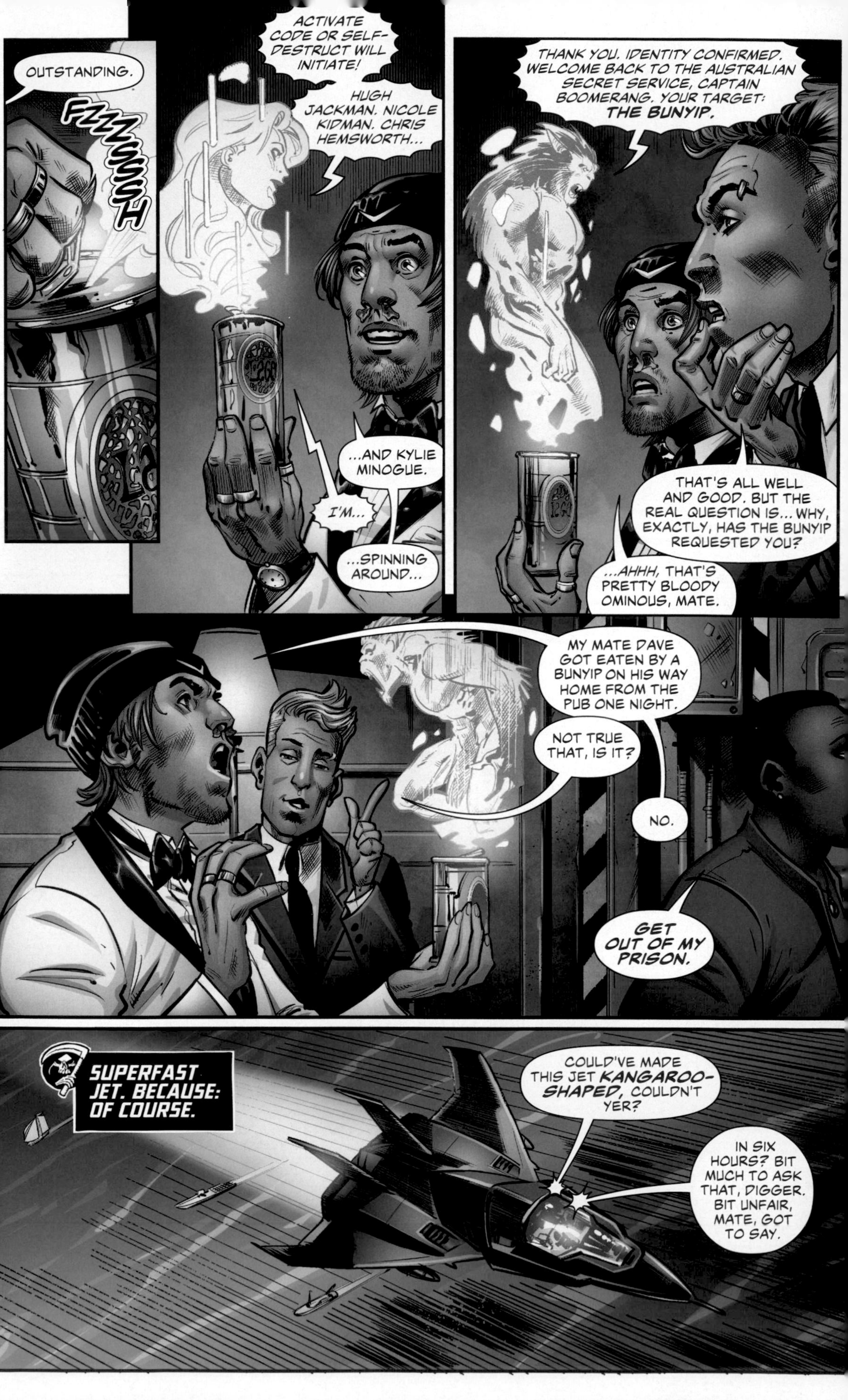
OUTSTANDING.
FZZZSSSH
ACTIVATE CODE OR SELF-DESTRUCT WILL INITIATE!
HUGH JACKMAN. NICOLE KIDMAN. CHRIS HEMSWORTH...
...AND KYLIE MINOGUE.
I'M...
...SPINNING AROUND...
THANK YOU. IDENTITY CONFIRMED. WELCOME BACK TO THE AUSTRALIAN SECRET SERVICE, CAPTAIN BOOMERANG. YOUR TARGET: THE BUNYIP.
THAT'S ALL WELL AND GOOD. BUT THE REAL QUESTION IS... WHY, EXACTLY, HAS THE BUNYIP REQUESTED YOU?
...AHHH, THAT'S PRETTY BLOODY OMINOUS, MATE.
MY MATE DAVE GOT EATEN BY A BUNYIP ON HIS WAY HOME FROM THE PUB ONE NIGHT.
NOT TRUE THAT, IS IT?
NO.
GET OUT OF MY PRISON.
SUPERFAST JET. BECAUSE: OF COURSE.
COULD'VE MADE THIS JET KANGAROO-SHAPED, COULDN'T YER?
IN SIX HOURS? BIT MUCH TO ASK THAT, DIGGER. BIT UNFAIR, MATE, GOT TO SAY.

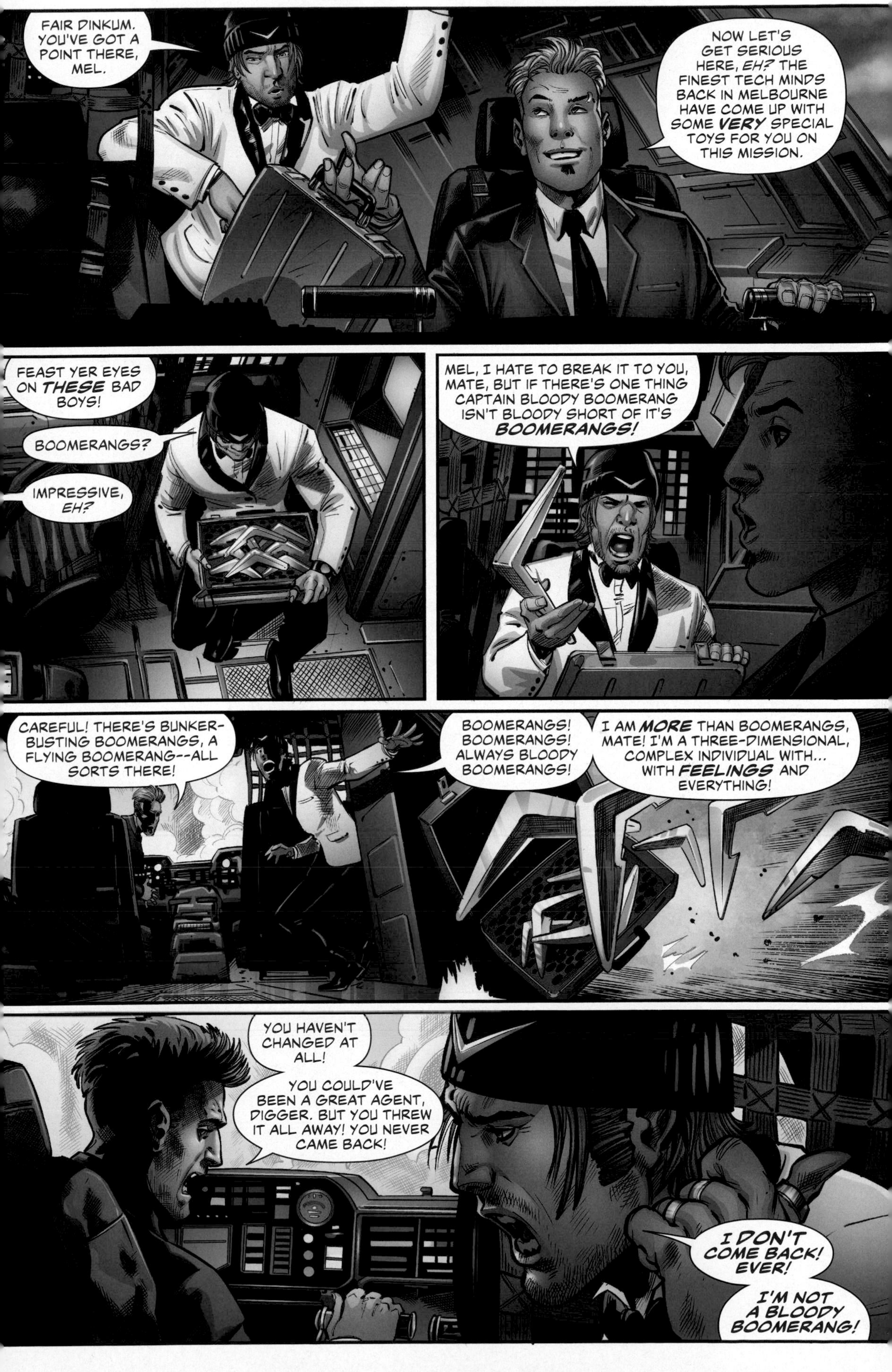
FAIR DINKUM. YOU'VE GOT A POINT THERE, MEL.
NOW LET'S GET SERIOUS HERE, *EH?* THE FINEST TECH MINDS BACK IN MELBOURNE HAVE COME UP WITH SOME **VERY** SPECIAL TOYS FOR YOU ON THIS MISSION.
FEAST YER EYES ON ***THESE*** BAD BOYS!
BOOMERANGS?
IMPRESSIVE, *EH?*
MEL, I HATE TO BREAK IT TO YOU, MATE, BUT IF THERE'S ONE THING CAPTAIN BLOODY BOOMERANG ISN'T BLOODY SHORT OF IT'S ***BOOMERANGS!***
CAREFUL! THERE'S BUNKER-BUSTING BOOMERANGS, A FLYING BOOMERANG--ALL SORTS THERE!
BOOMERANGS! BOOMERANGS! ALWAYS BLOODY BOOMERANGS!
I AM ***MORE*** THAN BOOMERANGS, MATE! I'M A THREE-DIMENSIONAL, COMPLEX INDIVIDUAL WITH... WITH ***FEELINGS*** AND EVERYTHING!
YOU HAVEN'T CHANGED AT ALL!
YOU COULD'VE BEEN A GREAT AGENT, DIGGER. BUT YOU THREW IT ALL AWAY! YOU NEVER CAME BACK!
I DON'T COME BACK! EVER!
I'M NOT A BLOODY BOOMERANG!

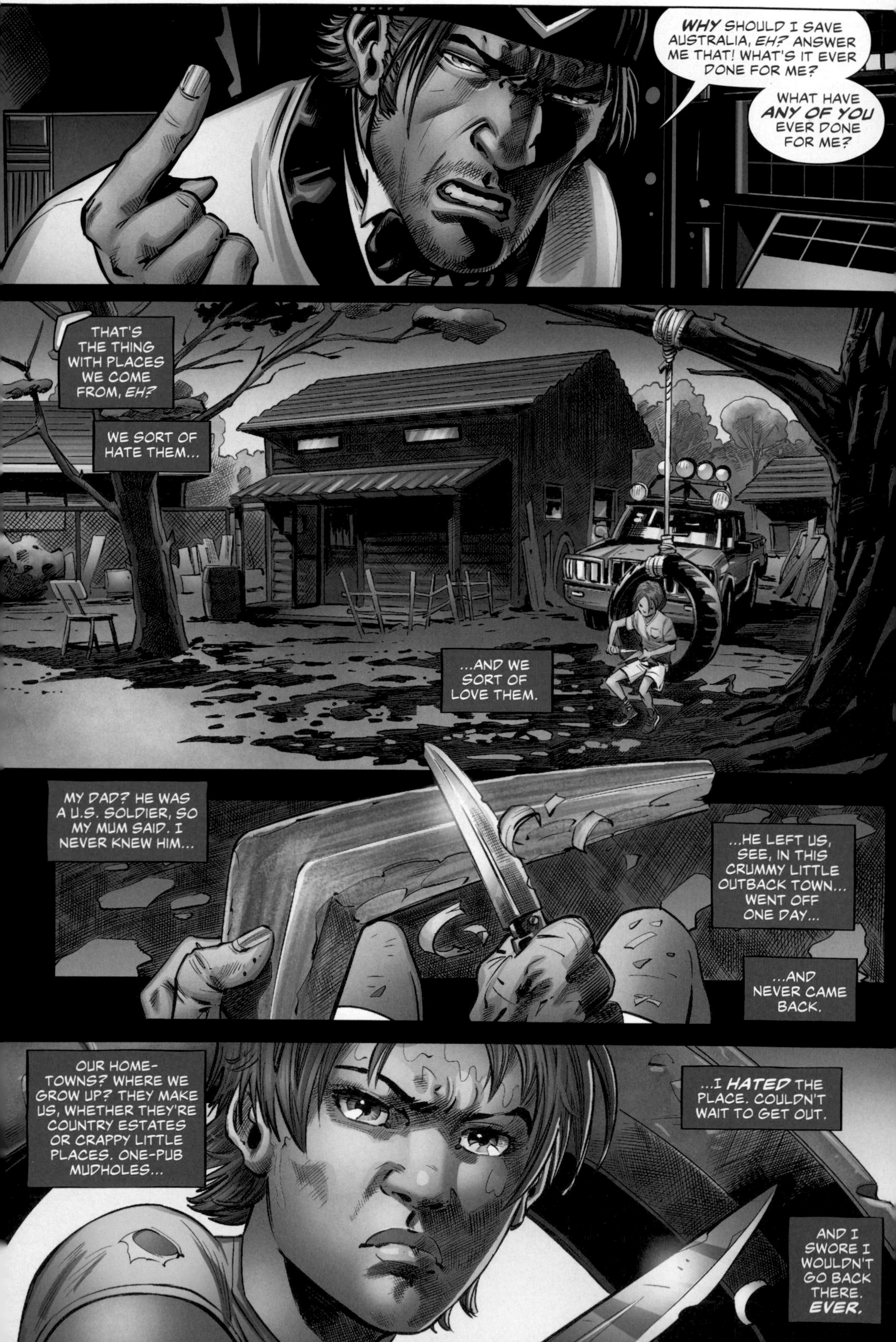
WHY SHOULD I SAVE AUSTRALIA, EH? ANSWER ME THAT! WHAT'S IT EVER DONE FOR ME?
WHAT HAVE ANY OF YOU EVER DONE FOR ME?
THAT'S THE THING WITH PLACES WE COME FROM, EH?
WE SORT OF HATE THEM...
...AND WE SORT OF LOVE THEM.
MY DAD? HE WAS A U.S. SOLDIER, SO MY MUM SAID. I NEVER KNEW HIM...
...HE LEFT US, SEE, IN THIS CRUMMY LITTLE OUTBACK TOWN... WENT OFF ONE DAY...
...AND NEVER CAME BACK.
OUR HOME-TOWNS? WHERE WE GROW UP? THEY MAKE US, WHETHER THEY'RE COUNTRY ESTATES OR CRAPPY LITTLE PLACES. ONE-PUB MUDHOLES...
...I HATED THE PLACE. COULDN'T WAIT TO GET OUT.
AND I SWORE I WOULDN'T GO BACK THERE. EVER.

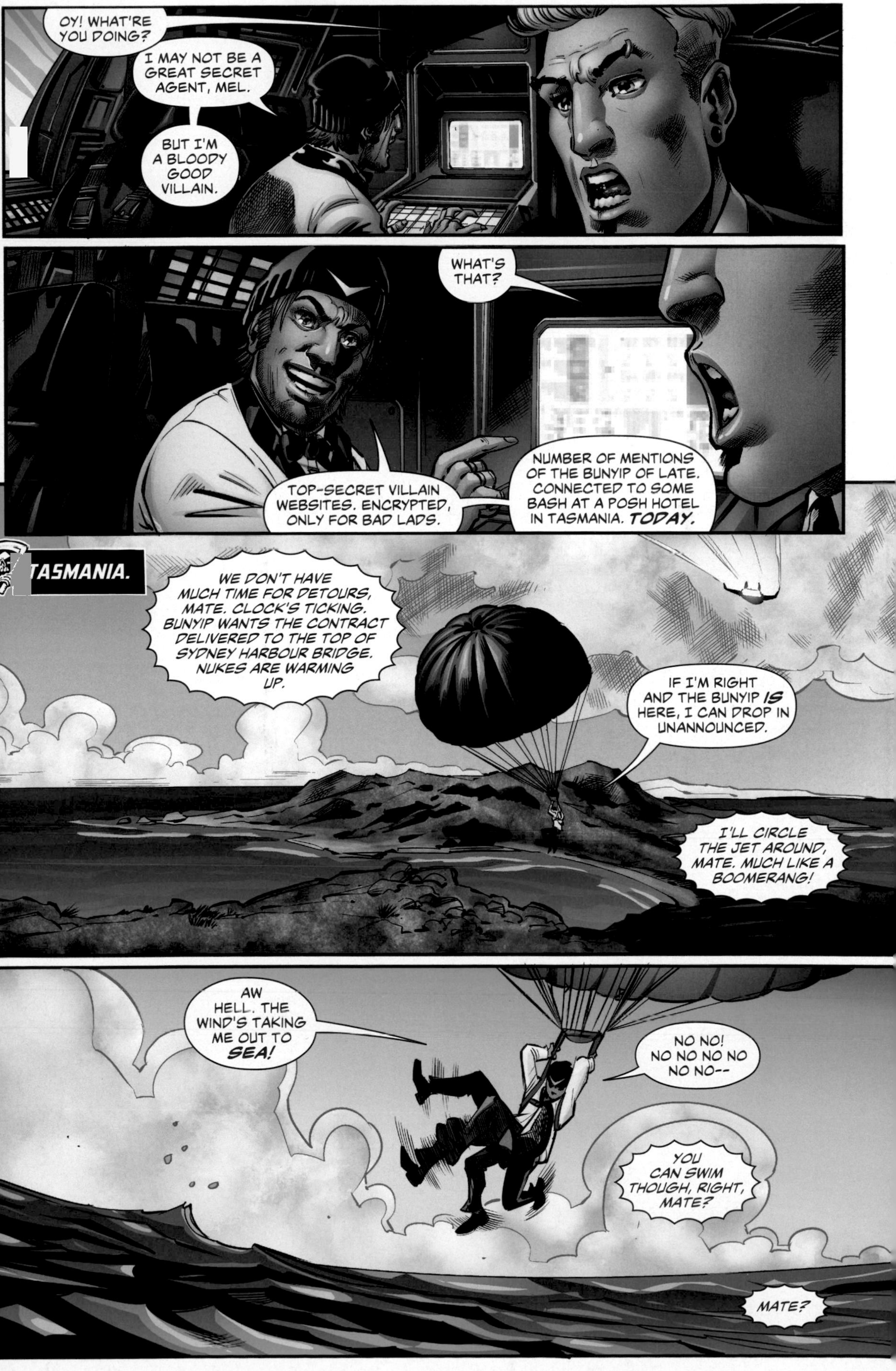
OY! WHAT'RE YOU DOING?
I MAY NOT BE A GREAT SECRET AGENT, MEL.
BUT I'M A BLOODY GOOD VILLAIN.
WHAT'S THAT?
TOP-SECRET VILLAIN WEBSITES. ENCRYPTED, ONLY FOR BAD LADS.
NUMBER OF MENTIONS OF THE BUNYIP OF LATE. CONNECTED TO SOME BASH AT A POSH HOTEL IN TASMANIA. TODAY.
TASMANIA.
WE DON'T HAVE MUCH TIME FOR DETOURS, MATE. CLOCK'S TICKING. BUNYIP WANTS THE CONTRACT DELIVERED TO THE TOP OF SYDNEY HARBOUR BRIDGE. NUKES ARE WARMING UP.
IF I'M RIGHT AND THE BUNYIP IS HERE, I CAN DROP IN UNANNOUNCED.
I'LL CIRCLE THE JET AROUND, MATE. MUCH LIKE A BOOMERANG!
AW HELL. THE WIND'S TAKING ME OUT TO SEA!
NO NO! NO NO NO NO NO NO--
YOU CAN SWIM THOUGH, RIGHT, MATE?
MATE?

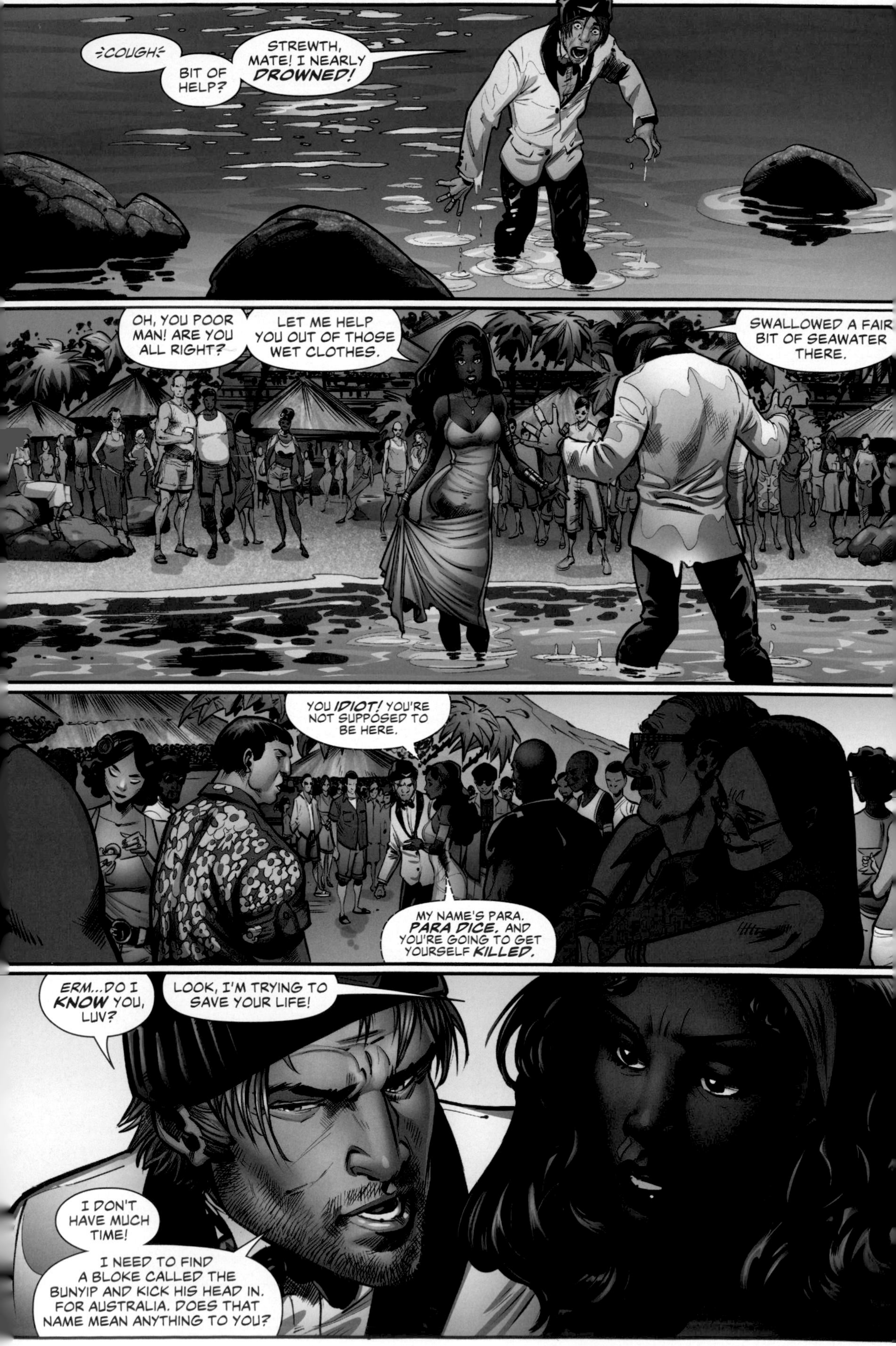

COUGH
BIT OF HELP?
STREWTH, MATE! I NEARLY DROWNED!
OH, YOU POOR MAN! ARE YOU ALL RIGHT?
LET ME HELP YOU OUT OF THOSE WET CLOTHES.
SWALLOWED A FAIR BIT OF SEAWATER THERE.
YOU IDIOT! YOU'RE NOT SUPPOSED TO BE HERE.
MY NAME'S PARA. PARA DICE. AND YOU'RE GOING TO GET YOURSELF KILLED.
ERM...DO I KNOW YOU, LUV?
LOOK, I'M TRYING TO SAVE YOUR LIFE!
I DON'T HAVE MUCH TIME!
I NEED TO FIND A BLOKE CALLED THE BUNYIP AND KICK HIS HEAD IN. FOR AUSTRALIA. DOES THAT NAME MEAN ANYTHING TO YOU?

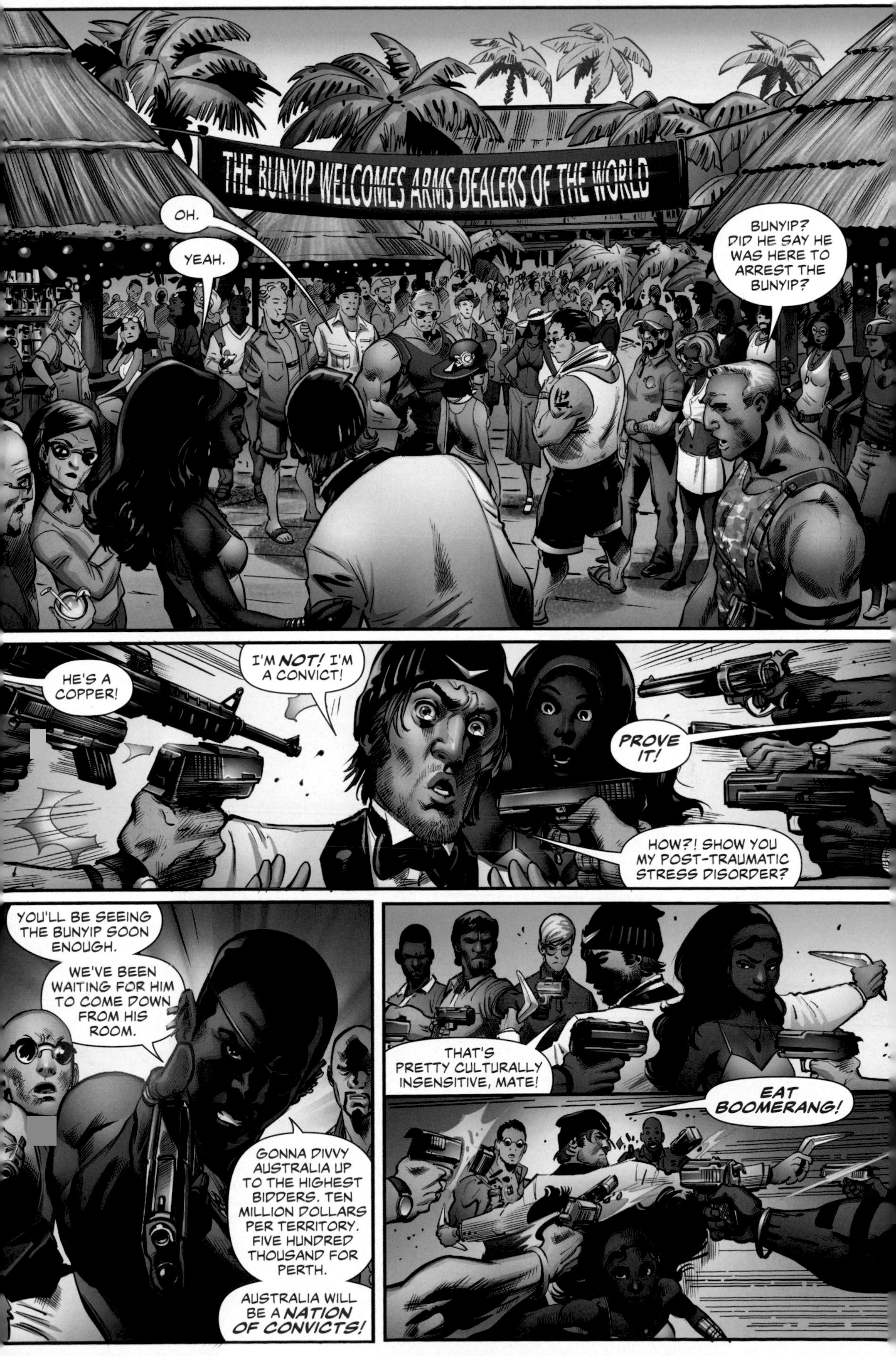
THE BUNYIP WELCOMES ARMS DEALERS OF THE WORLD
OH.
YEAH.
BUNYIP? DID HE SAY HE WAS HERE TO ARREST THE BUNYIP?
HE'S A COPPER!
I'M NOT! I'M A CONVICT!
PROVE IT!
HOW?! SHOW YOU MY POST-TRAUMATIC STRESS DISORDER?
YOU'LL BE SEEING THE BUNYIP SOON ENOUGH.
WE'VE BEEN WAITING FOR HIM TO COME DOWN FROM HIS ROOM.
GONNA DIVVY AUSTRALIA UP TO THE HIGHEST BIDDERS. TEN MILLION DOLLARS PER TERRITORY. FIVE HUNDRED THOUSAND FOR PERTH.
AUSTRALIA WILL BE A NATION OF CONVICTS!
THAT'S PRETTY CULTURALLY INSENSITIVE, MATE!
EAT BOOMERANG!

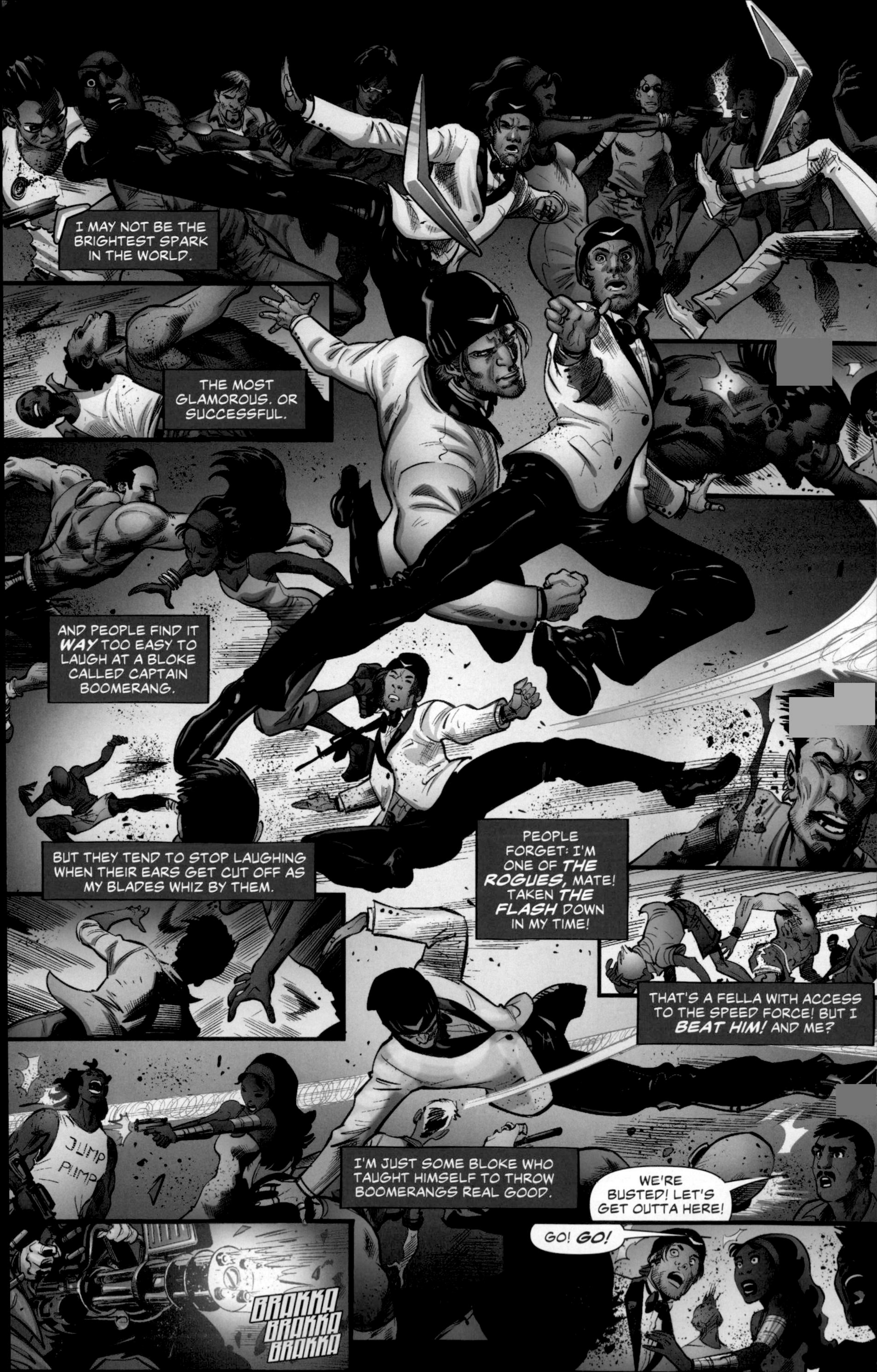
I MAY NOT BE THE BRIGHTEST SPARK IN THE WORLD.
THE MOST GLAMOROUS. OR SUCCESSFUL.
AND PEOPLE FIND IT WAY TOO EASY TO LAUGH AT A BLOKE CALLED CAPTAIN BOOMERANG.
BUT THEY TEND TO STOP LAUGHING WHEN THEIR EARS GET CUT OFF AS MY BLADES WHIZ BY THEM.
PEOPLE FORGET: I'M ONE OF THE ROGUES, MATE! TAKEN THE FLASH DOWN IN MY TIME!
THAT'S A FELLA WITH ACCESS TO THE SPEED FORCE! BUT I BEAT HIM! AND ME?
JUMP PUMP
I'M JUST SOME BLOKE WHO TAUGHT HIMSELF TO THROW BOOMERANGS REAL GOOD.
WE'RE BUSTED! LET'S GET OUTTA HERE!
GO! GO!
BRAKKA BRAKKA BRAKKA

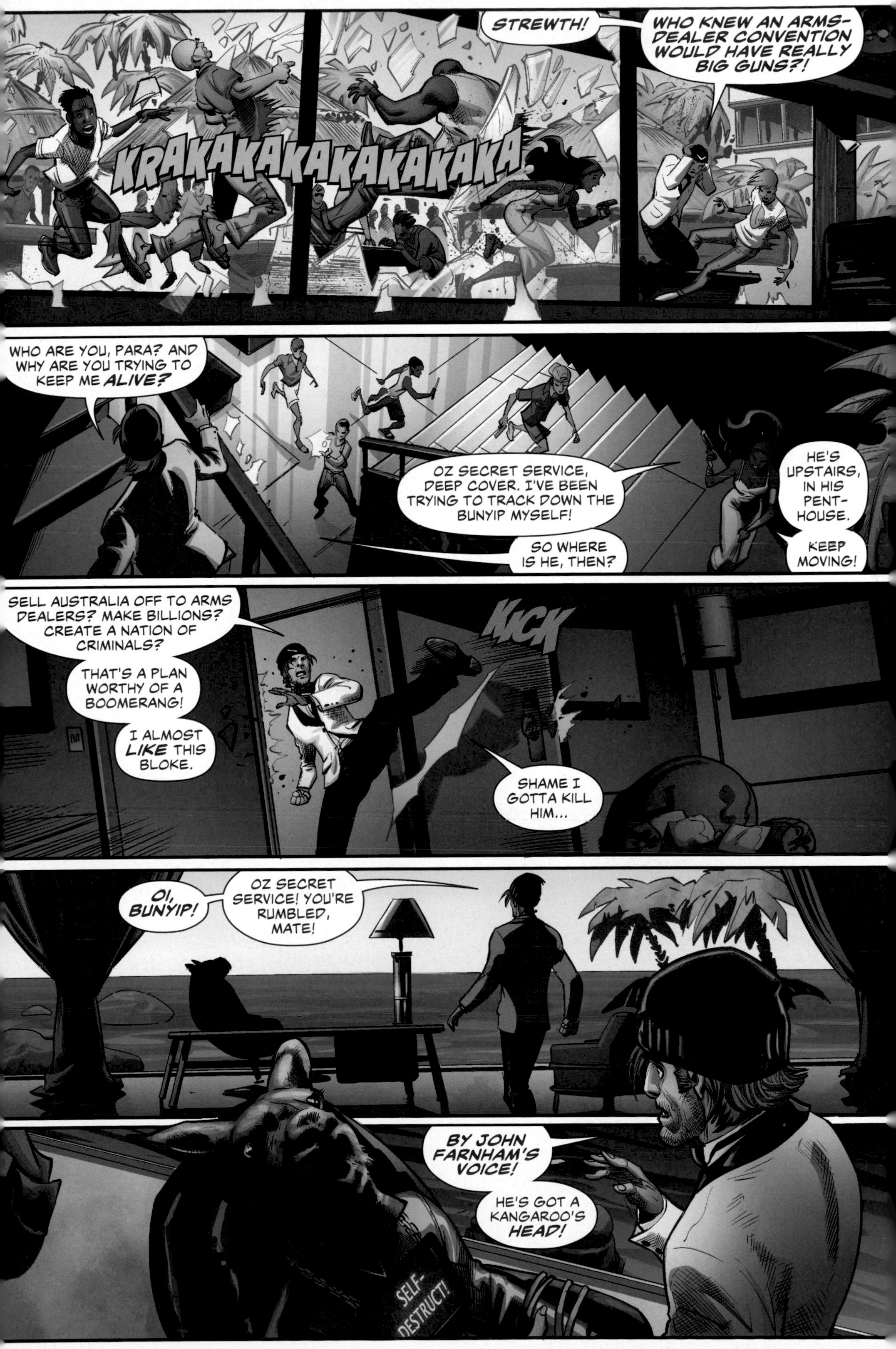
KRAKAKAKAKAKAKAKAKA
STREWTH!
WHO KNEW AN ARMS-DEALER CONVENTION WOULD HAVE REALLY BIG GUNS?!
WHO ARE YOU, PARA? AND WHY ARE YOU TRYING TO KEEP ME ALIVE?
OZ SECRET SERVICE, DEEP COVER. I'VE BEEN TRYING TO TRACK DOWN THE BUNYIP MYSELF!
SO WHERE IS HE, THEN?
HE'S UPSTAIRS, IN HIS PENT-HOUSE.
KEEP MOVING!
SELL AUSTRALIA OFF TO ARMS DEALERS? MAKE BILLIONS? CREATE A NATION OF CRIMINALS?
THAT'S A PLAN WORTHY OF A BOOMERANG!
I ALMOST LIKE THIS BLOKE.
KICK
SHAME I GOTTA KILL HIM...
OI, BUNYIP!
OZ SECRET SERVICE! YOU'RE RUMBLED, MATE!
BY JOHN FARNHAM'S VOICE!
HE'S GOT A KANGAROO'S HEAD!
SELF-DESTRUCT!

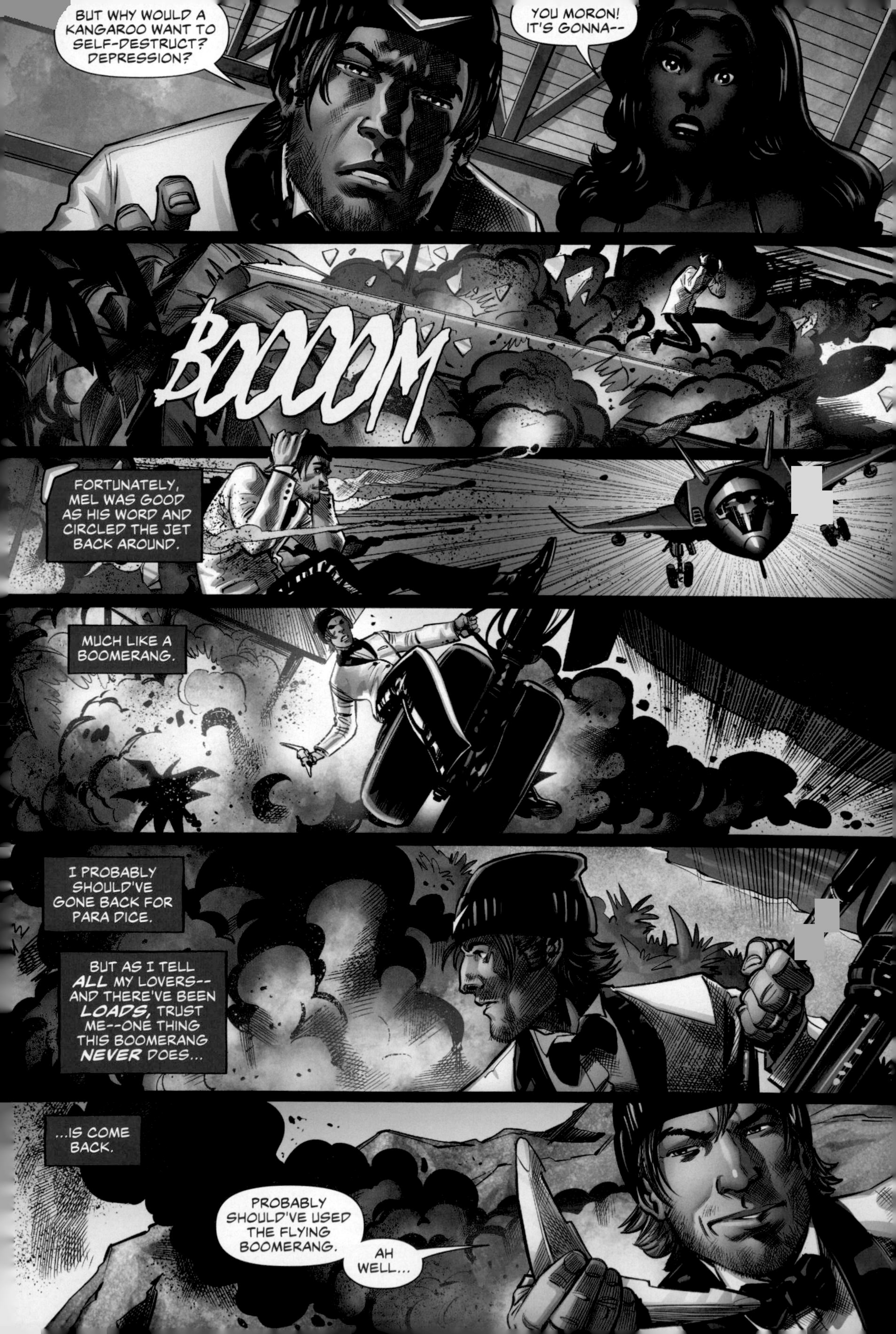
BUT WHY WOULD A KANGAROO WANT TO SELF-DESTRUCT? DEPRESSION?
YOU MORON! IT'S GONNA--
BOOOOM
FORTUNATELY, MEL WAS GOOD AS HIS WORD AND CIRCLED THE JET BACK AROUND.
MUCH LIKE A BOOMERANG.
I PROBABLY SHOULD'VE GONE BACK FOR PARA DICE.
BUT AS I TELL ALL MY LOVERS--AND THERE'VE BEEN LOADS, TRUST ME--ONE THING THIS BOOMERANG NEVER DOES...
...IS COME BACK.
PROBABLY SHOULD'VE USED THE FLYING BOOMERANG.
AH WELL...

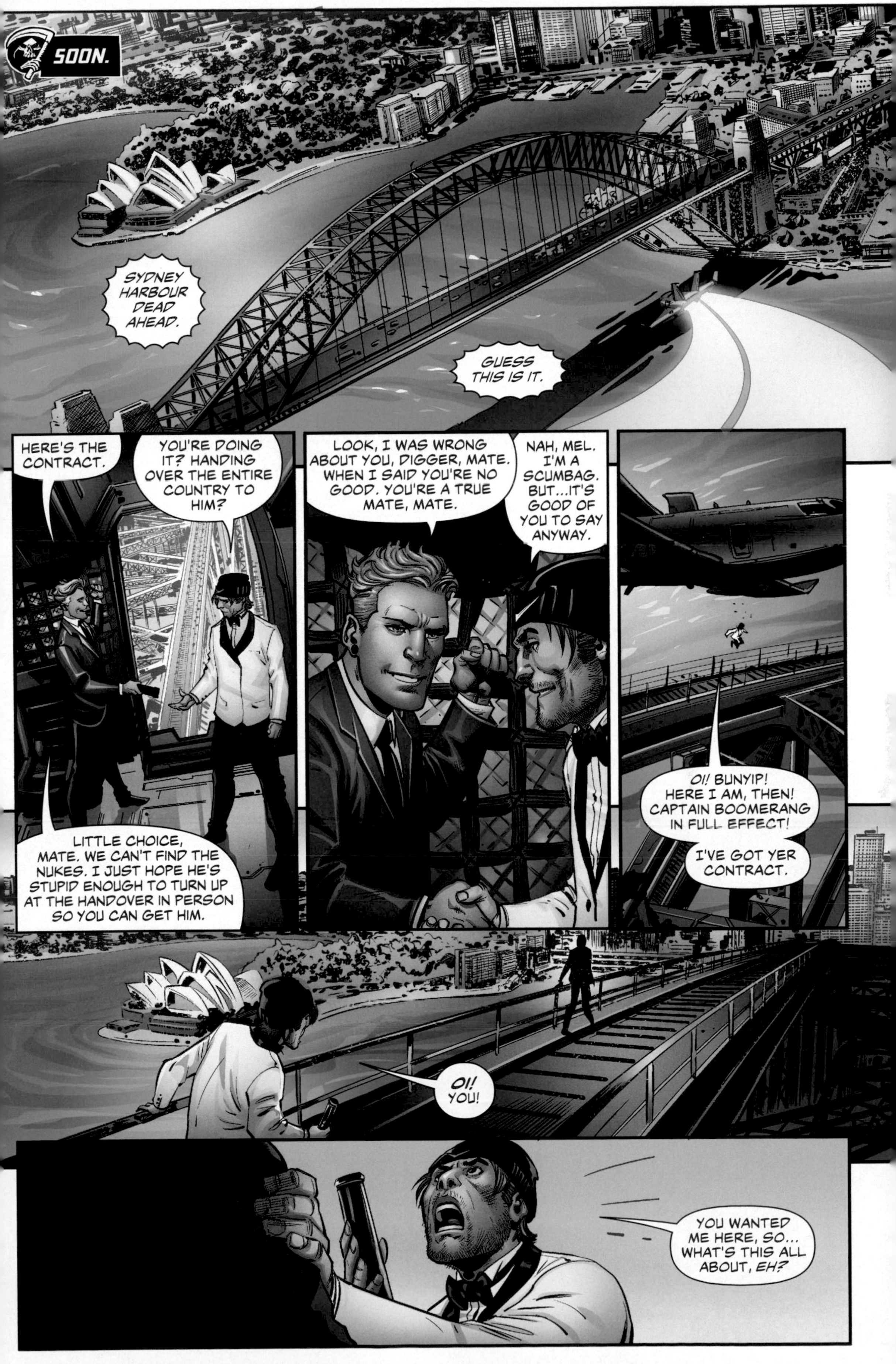
SOON.
SYDNEY HARBOUR DEAD AHEAD.
GUESS THIS IS IT.
HERE'S THE CONTRACT.
YOU'RE DOING IT? HANDING OVER THE ENTIRE COUNTRY TO HIM?
LITTLE CHOICE, MATE. WE CAN'T FIND THE NUKES. I JUST HOPE HE'S STUPID ENOUGH TO TURN UP AT THE HANDOVER IN PERSON SO YOU CAN GET HIM.
LOOK, I WAS WRONG ABOUT YOU, DIGGER, MATE. WHEN I SAID YOU'RE NO GOOD. YOU'RE A TRUE MATE, MATE.
NAH, MEL. I'M A SCUMBAG. BUT...IT'S GOOD OF YOU TO SAY ANYWAY.
OI! BUNYIP! HERE I AM, THEN! CAPTAIN BOOMERANG IN FULL EFFECT!
I'VE GOT YER CONTRACT.
OI! YOU!
YOU WANTED ME HERE, SO... WHAT'S THIS ALL ABOUT, EH?

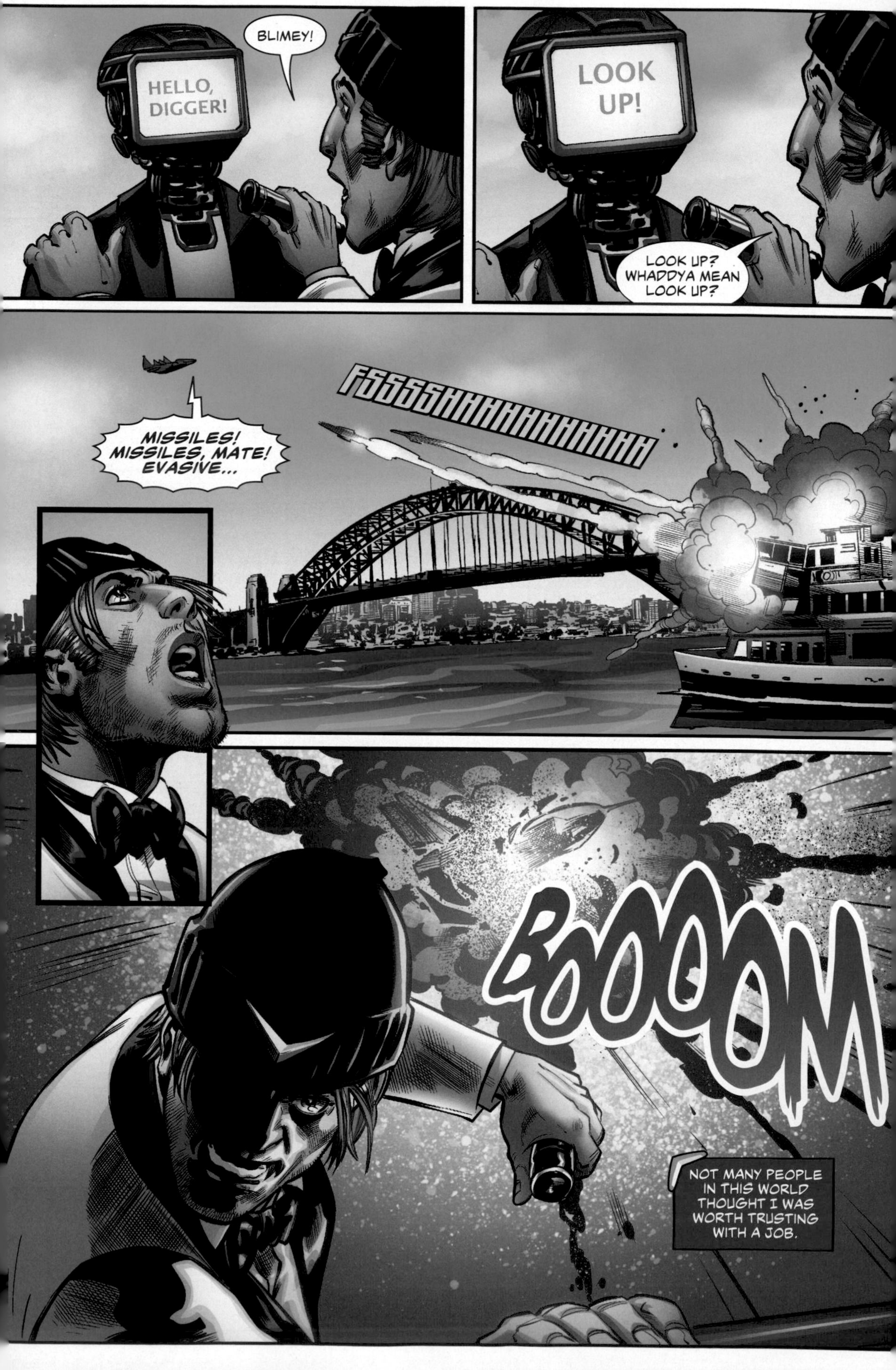
HELLO, DIGGER!
BLIMEY!
LOOK UP!
LOOK UP? WHADDYA MEAN LOOK UP?
FSSSSHHHHHHHHHHHH
MISSILES! MISSILES, MATE! EVASIVE...
BOOOOM
NOT MANY PEOPLE IN THIS WORLD THOUGHT I WAS WORTH TRUSTING WITH A JOB.

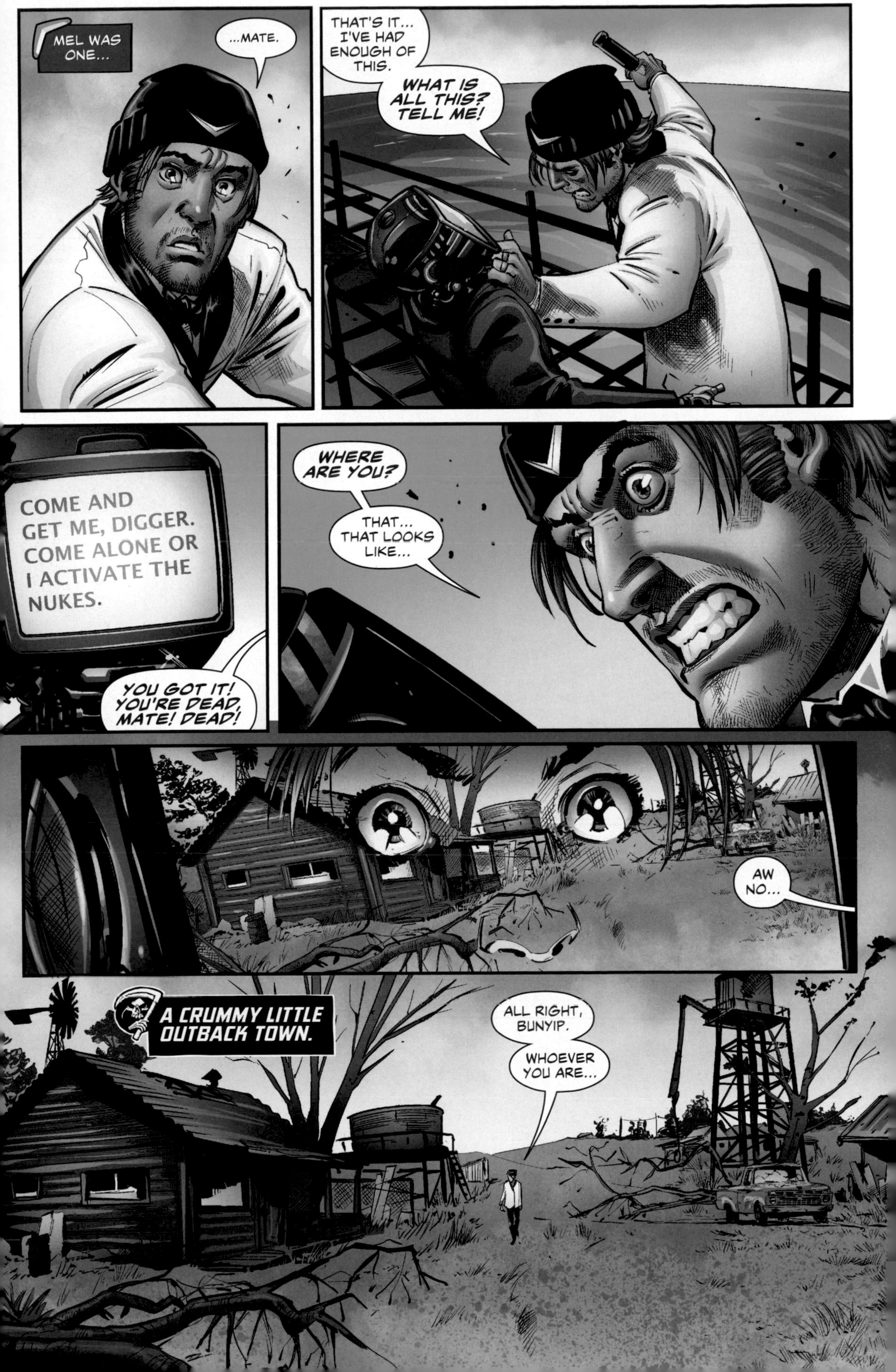
MEL WAS ONE...
...MATE.
THAT'S IT... I'VE HAD ENOUGH OF THIS.
WHAT IS ALL THIS? TELL ME!
COME AND GET ME, DIGGER. COME ALONE OR I ACTIVATE THE NUKES.
WHERE ARE YOU?
THAT... THAT LOOKS LIKE...
YOU GOT IT! YOU'RE DEAD, MATE! DEAD!
AW NO...
A CRUMMY LITTLE OUTBACK TOWN.
ALL RIGHT, BUNYIP.
WHOEVER YOU ARE...

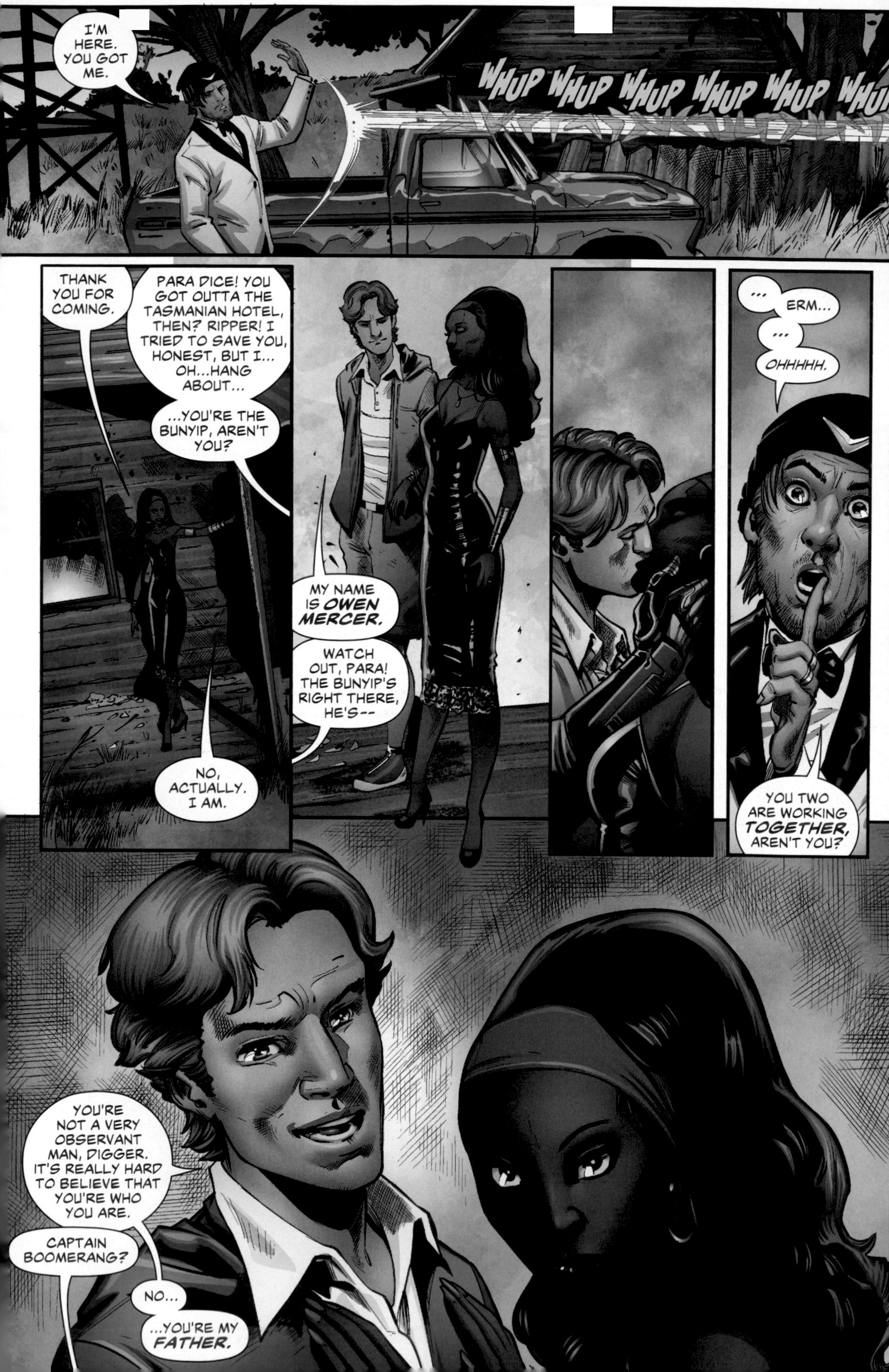
I'M HERE. YOU GOT ME.
WHUP WHUP WHUP WHUP WHUP WHU
THANK YOU FOR COMING.
PARA DICE! YOU GOT OUTTA THE TASMANIAN HOTEL, THEN? RIPPER! I TRIED TO SAVE YOU, HONEST, BUT I... OH...HANG ABOUT...
...YOU'RE THE BUNYIP, AREN'T YOU?
MY NAME IS OWEN MERCER.
WATCH OUT, PARA! THE BUNYIP'S RIGHT THERE, HE'S--
NO, ACTUALLY. I AM.
... ERM...
...
OHHHHH.
YOU TWO ARE WORKING TOGETHER, AREN'T YOU?
YOU'RE NOT A VERY OBSERVANT MAN, DIGGER. IT'S REALLY HARD TO BELIEVE THAT YOU'RE WHO YOU ARE.
CAPTAIN BOOMERANG?
NO...
...YOU'RE MY FATHER.

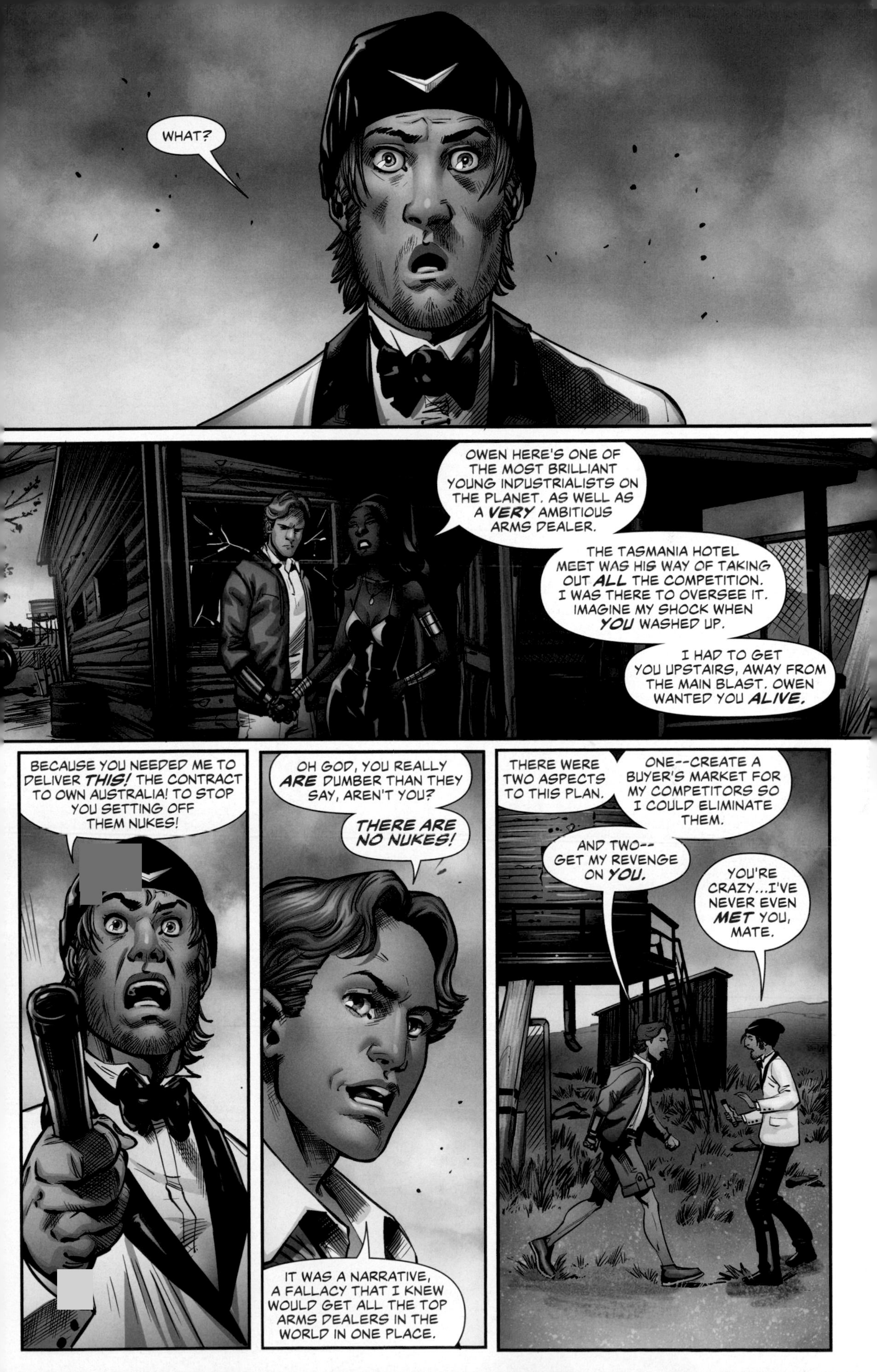
WHAT?
OWEN HERE'S ONE OF THE MOST BRILLIANT YOUNG INDUSTRIALISTS ON THE PLANET. AS WELL AS A *VERY* AMBITIOUS ARMS DEALER.
THE TASMANIA HOTEL MEET WAS HIS WAY OF TAKING OUT *ALL* THE COMPETITION. I WAS THERE TO OVERSEE IT. IMAGINE MY SHOCK WHEN *YOU* WASHED UP.
I HAD TO GET YOU UPSTAIRS, AWAY FROM THE MAIN BLAST. OWEN WANTED YOU *ALIVE.*
BECAUSE YOU NEEDED ME TO DELIVER *THIS!* THE CONTRACT TO OWN AUSTRALIA! TO STOP YOU SETTING OFF THEM NUKES!
OH GOD, YOU REALLY *ARE* DUMBER THAN THEY SAY, AREN'T YOU?
THERE ARE NO NUKES!
IT WAS A NARRATIVE, A FALLACY THAT I KNEW WOULD GET ALL THE TOP ARMS DEALERS IN THE WORLD IN ONE PLACE.
THERE WERE TWO ASPECTS TO THIS PLAN.
ONE--CREATE A BUYER'S MARKET FOR MY COMPETITORS SO I COULD ELIMINATE THEM.
AND TWO-- GET MY REVENGE ON *YOU.*
YOU'RE CRAZY...I'VE NEVER EVEN *MET* YOU, MATE.

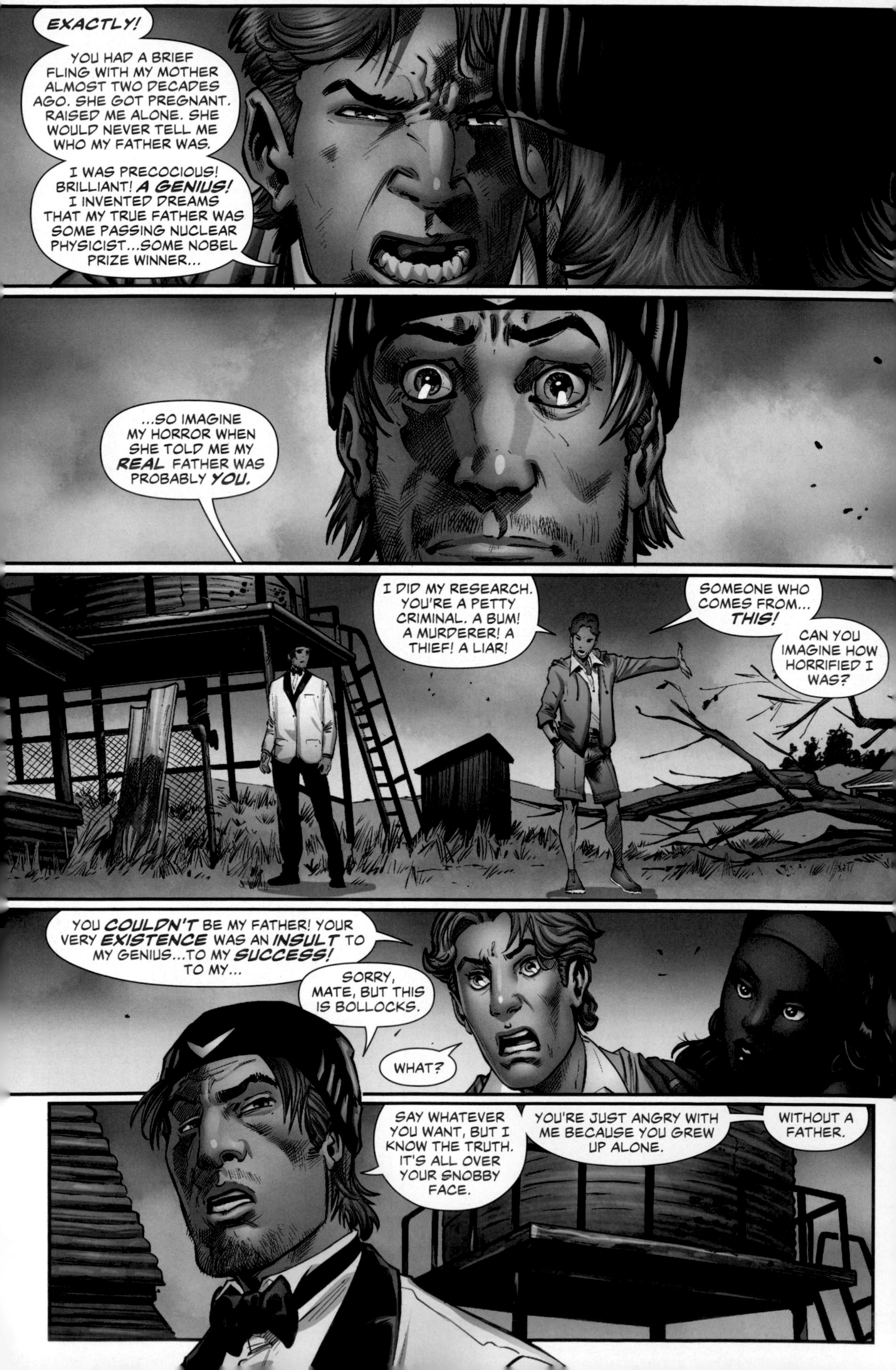
EXACTLY!
YOU HAD A BRIEF FLING WITH MY MOTHER ALMOST TWO DECADES AGO. SHE GOT PREGNANT. RAISED ME ALONE. SHE WOULD NEVER TELL ME WHO MY FATHER WAS.
I WAS PRECOCIOUS! BRILLIANT! A GENIUS! I INVENTED DREAMS THAT MY TRUE FATHER WAS SOME PASSING NUCLEAR PHYSICIST...SOME NOBEL PRIZE WINNER...
...SO IMAGINE MY HORROR WHEN SHE TOLD ME MY REAL FATHER WAS PROBABLY YOU.
I DID MY RESEARCH. YOU'RE A PETTY CRIMINAL. A BUM! A MURDERER! A THIEF! A LIAR!
SOMEONE WHO COMES FROM... THIS!
CAN YOU IMAGINE HOW HORRIFIED I WAS?
YOU COULDN'T BE MY FATHER! YOUR VERY EXISTENCE WAS AN INSULT TO MY GENIUS...TO MY SUCCESS! TO MY...
SORRY, MATE, BUT THIS IS BOLLOCKS.
WHAT?
SAY WHATEVER YOU WANT, BUT I KNOW THE TRUTH. IT'S ALL OVER YOUR SNOBBY FACE.
YOU'RE JUST ANGRY WITH ME BECAUSE YOU GREW UP ALONE.
WITHOUT A FATHER.

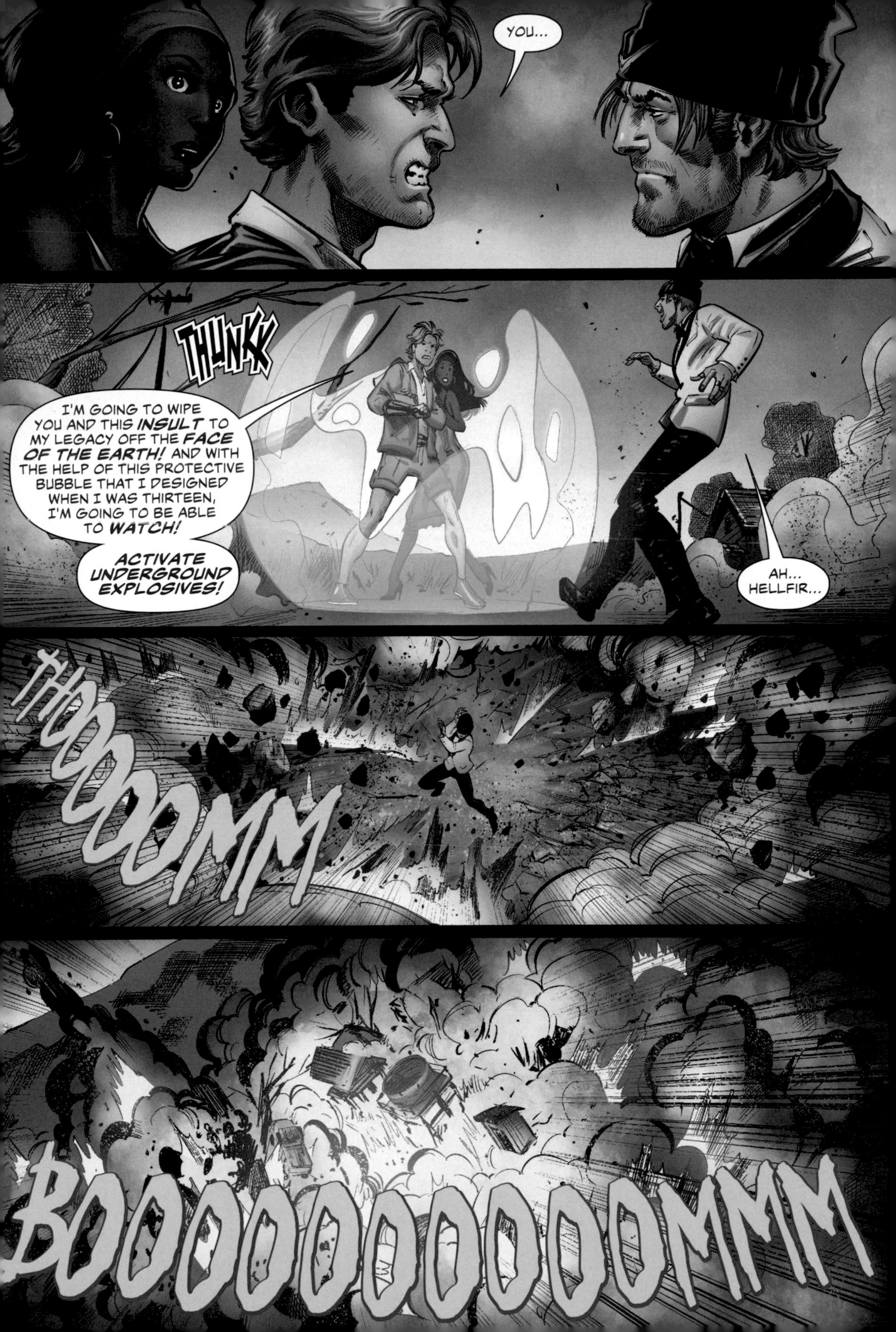
YOU...
THUNK
I'M GOING TO WIPE YOU AND THIS INSULT TO MY LEGACY OFF THE FACE OF THE EARTH! AND WITH THE HELP OF THIS PROTECTIVE BUBBLE THAT I DESIGNED WHEN I WAS THIRTEEN, I'M GOING TO BE ABLE TO WATCH!
ACTIVATE UNDERGROUND EXPLOSIVES!
AH... HELLFIR...
THOOOOMM
BOOOOOOOOOMMM

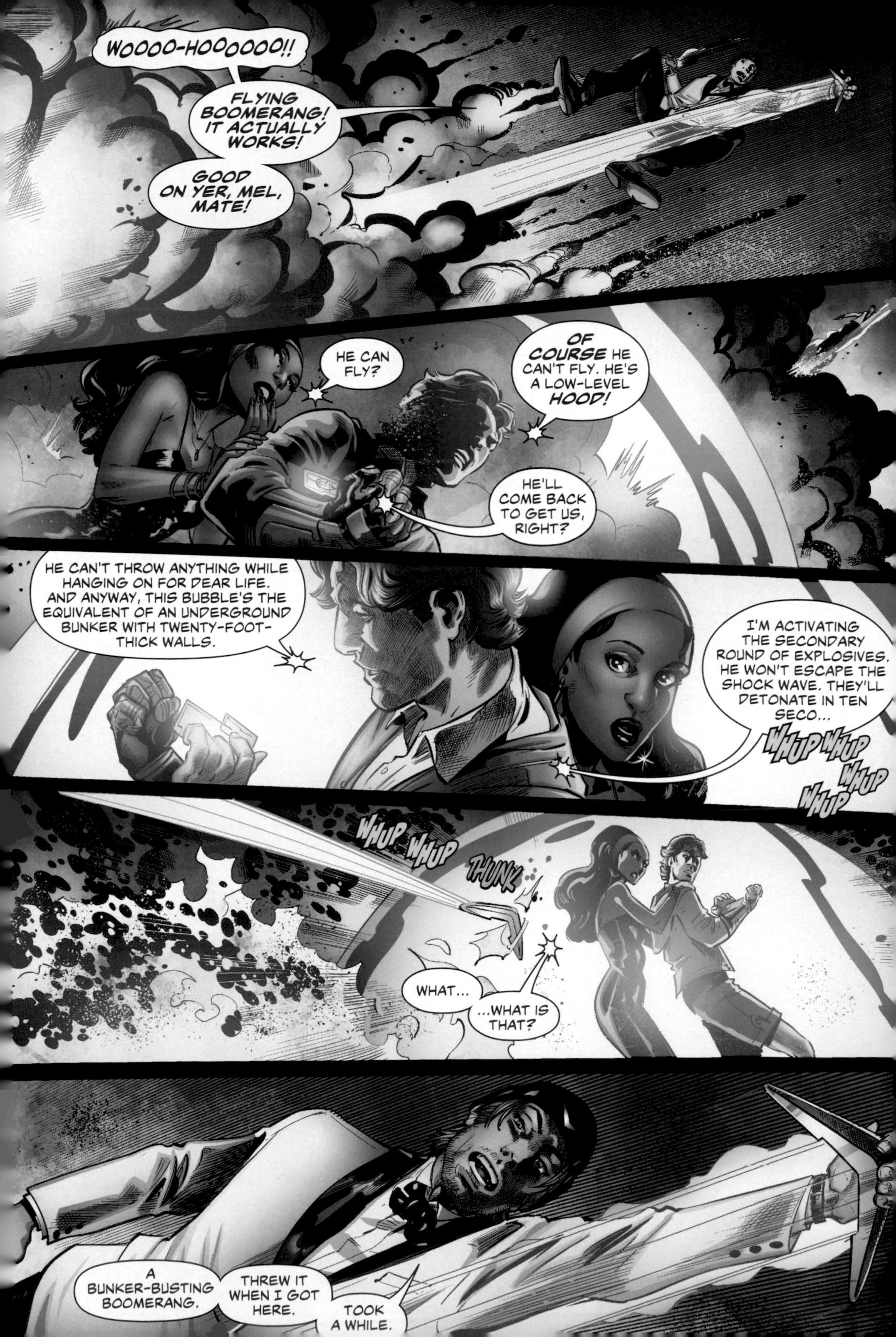
WOOOO-HOOOOOO!!
FLYING BOOMERANG! IT ACTUALLY WORKS!
GOOD ON YER, MEL, MATE!
HE CAN FLY?
OF COURSE HE CAN'T FLY. HE'S A LOW-LEVEL HOOD!
HE'LL COME BACK TO GET US, RIGHT?
HE CAN'T THROW ANYTHING WHILE HANGING ON FOR DEAR LIFE. AND ANYWAY, THIS BUBBLE'S THE EQUIVALENT OF AN UNDERGROUND BUNKER WITH TWENTY-FOOT-THICK WALLS.
I'M ACTIVATING THE SECONDARY ROUND OF EXPLOSIVES. HE WON'T ESCAPE THE SHOCK WAVE. THEY'LL DETONATE IN TEN SECO...
WHUP WHUP WHUP WHUP
WHUP WHUP
THUNK
WHAT...
...WHAT IS THAT?
A BUNKER-BUSTING BOOMERANG.
THREW IT WHEN I GOT HERE.
TOOK A WHILE.

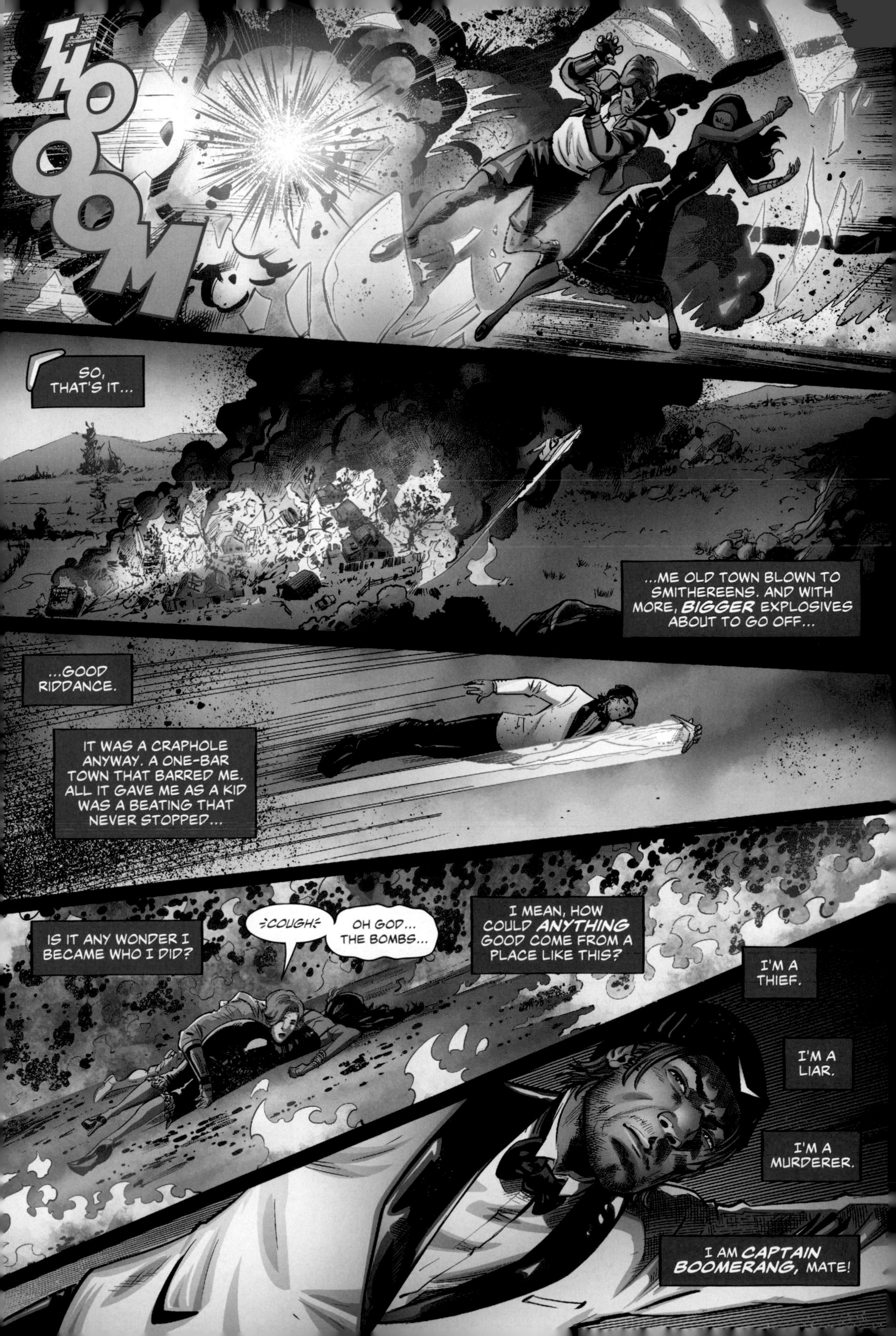
THOOOM
SO, THAT'S IT...
...ME OLD TOWN BLOWN TO SMITHEREENS. AND WITH MORE, BIGGER EXPLOSIVES ABOUT TO GO OFF...
...GOOD RIDDANCE.
IT WAS A CRAPHOLE ANYWAY. A ONE-BAR TOWN THAT BARRED ME. ALL IT GAVE ME AS A KID WAS A BEATING THAT NEVER STOPPED...
IS IT ANY WONDER I BECAME WHO I DID?
COUGH
OH GOD... THE BOMBS...
I MEAN, HOW COULD ANYTHING GOOD COME FROM A PLACE LIKE THIS?
I'M A THIEF.
I'M A LIAR.
I'M A MURDERER.
I AM CAPTAIN BOOMERANG, MATE!

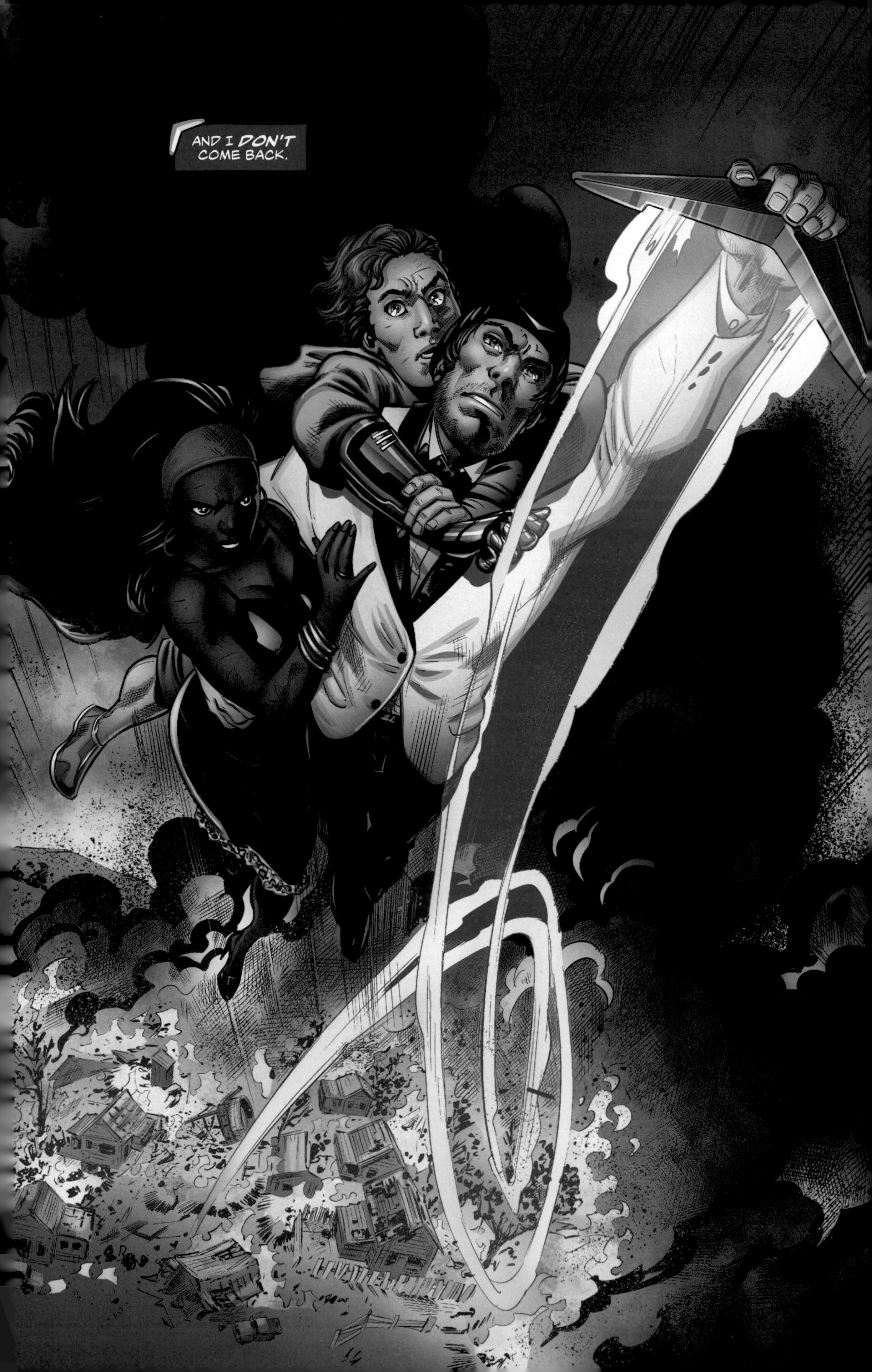
AND I DON'T COME BACK.

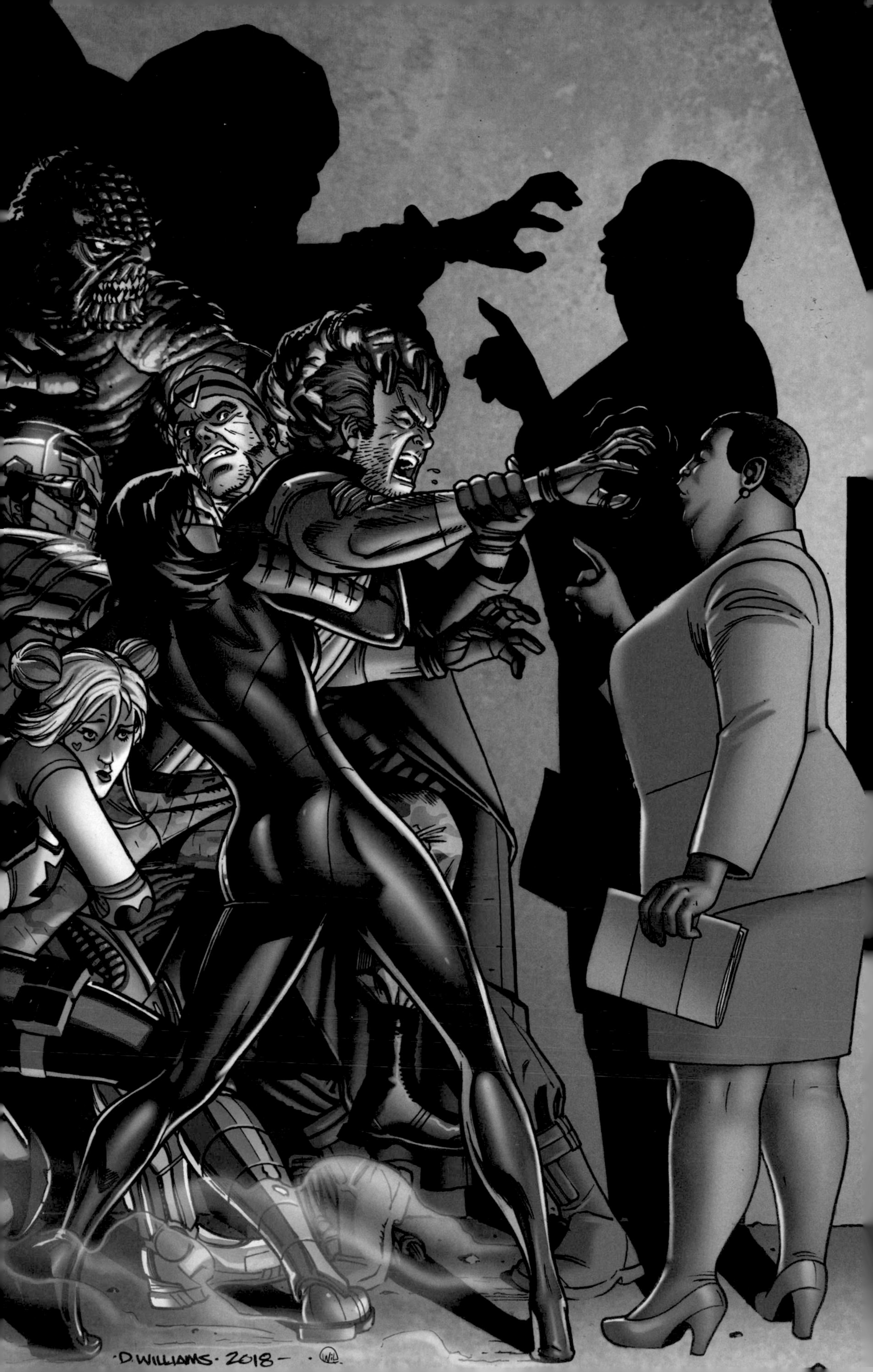
·D.WILLIAMS·2018–

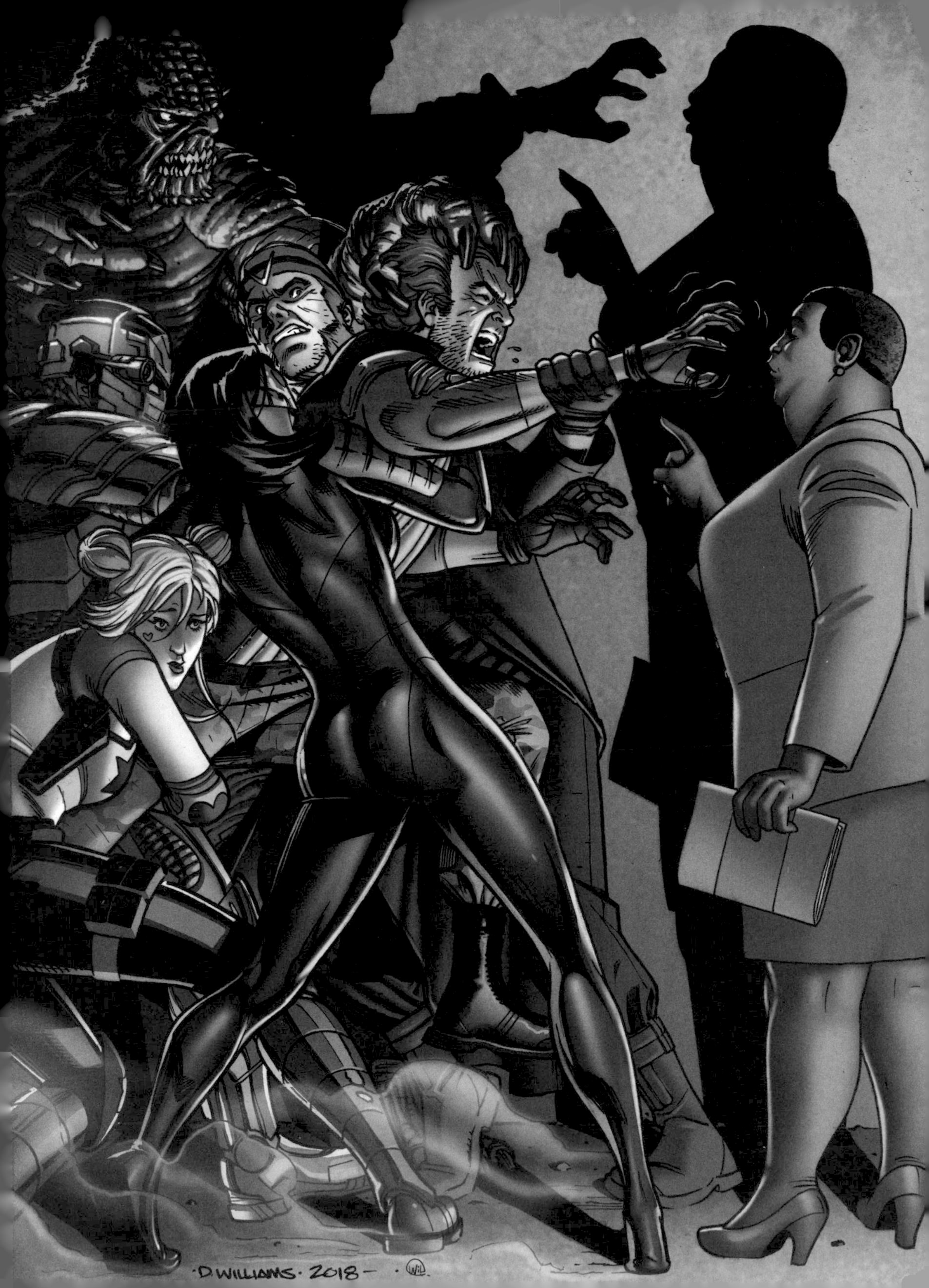
D. WILLIAMS · 2018 ·

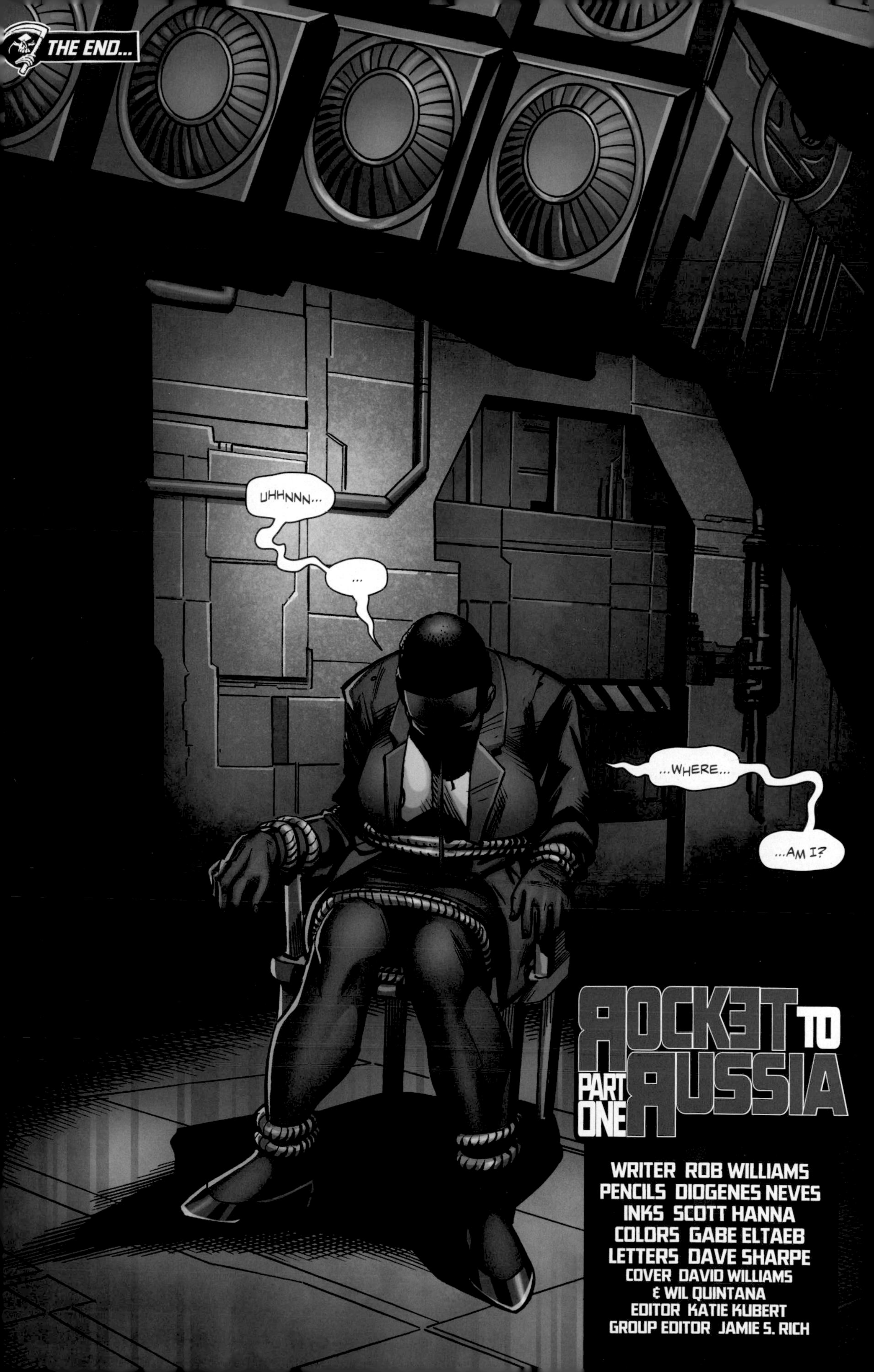
THE END...
UHHNNN...
...
...WHERE...
...AM I?
ROCKET TO RUSSIA
PART ONE
WRITER ROB WILLIAMS
PENCILS DIOGENES NEVES
INKS SCOTT HANNA
COLORS GABE ELTAEB
LETTERS DAVE SHARPE
COVER DAVID WILLIAMS
& WIL QUINTANA
EDITOR KATIE KUBERT
GROUP EDITOR JAMIE S. RICH

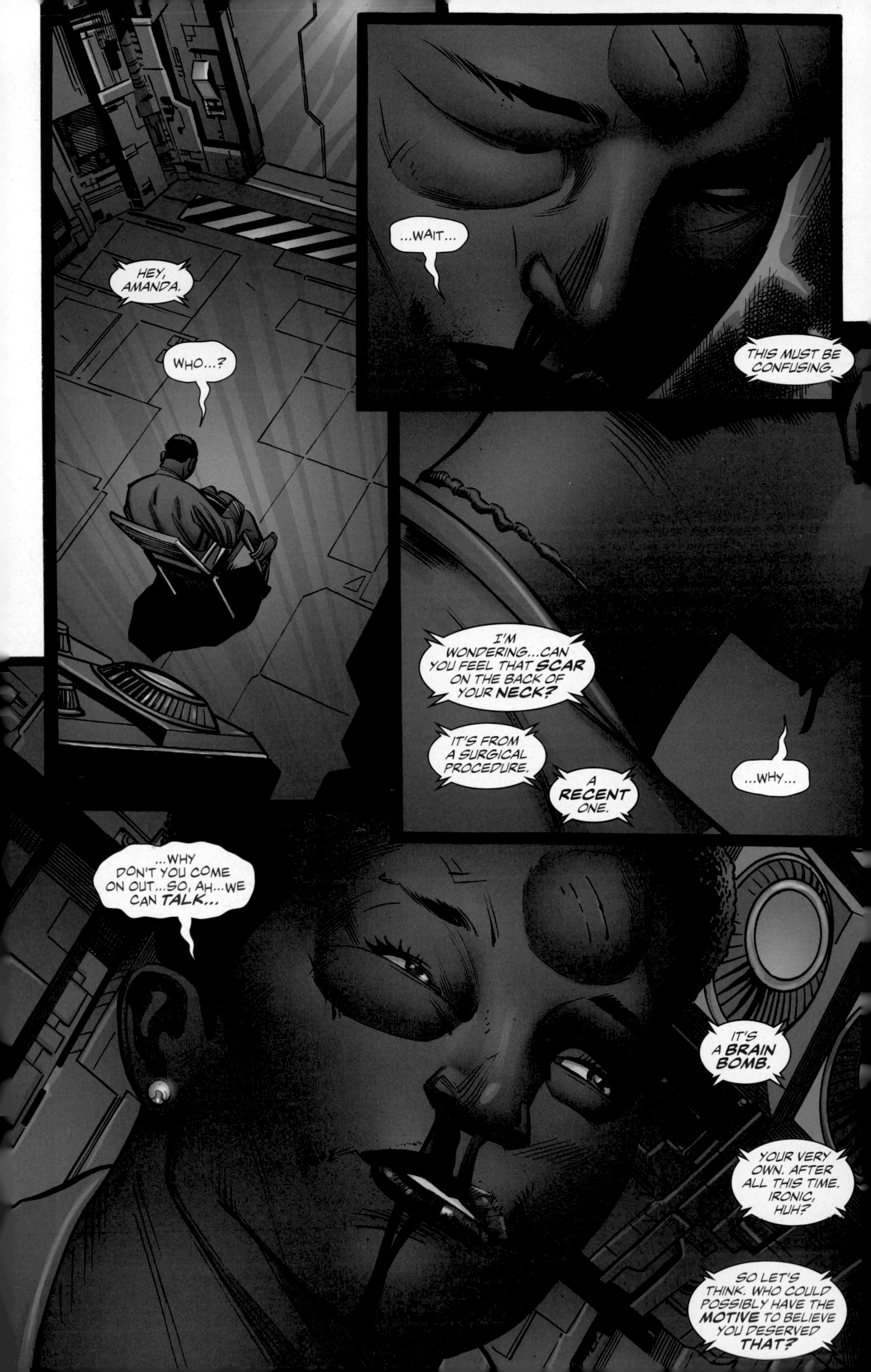
HEY, AMANDA.
WHO...?
...WAIT...
THIS MUST BE CONFUSING.
I'M WONDERING...CAN YOU FEEL THAT SCAR ON THE BACK OF YOUR NECK?
IT'S FROM A SURGICAL PROCEDURE.
A RECENT ONE.
...WHY...
...WHY DON'T YOU COME ON OUT...SO, AH...WE CAN TALK...
IT'S A BRAIN BOMB.
YOUR VERY OWN. AFTER ALL THIS TIME. IRONIC, HUH?
SO LET'S THINK. WHO COULD POSSIBLY HAVE THE MOTIVE TO BELIEVE YOU DESERVED THAT?

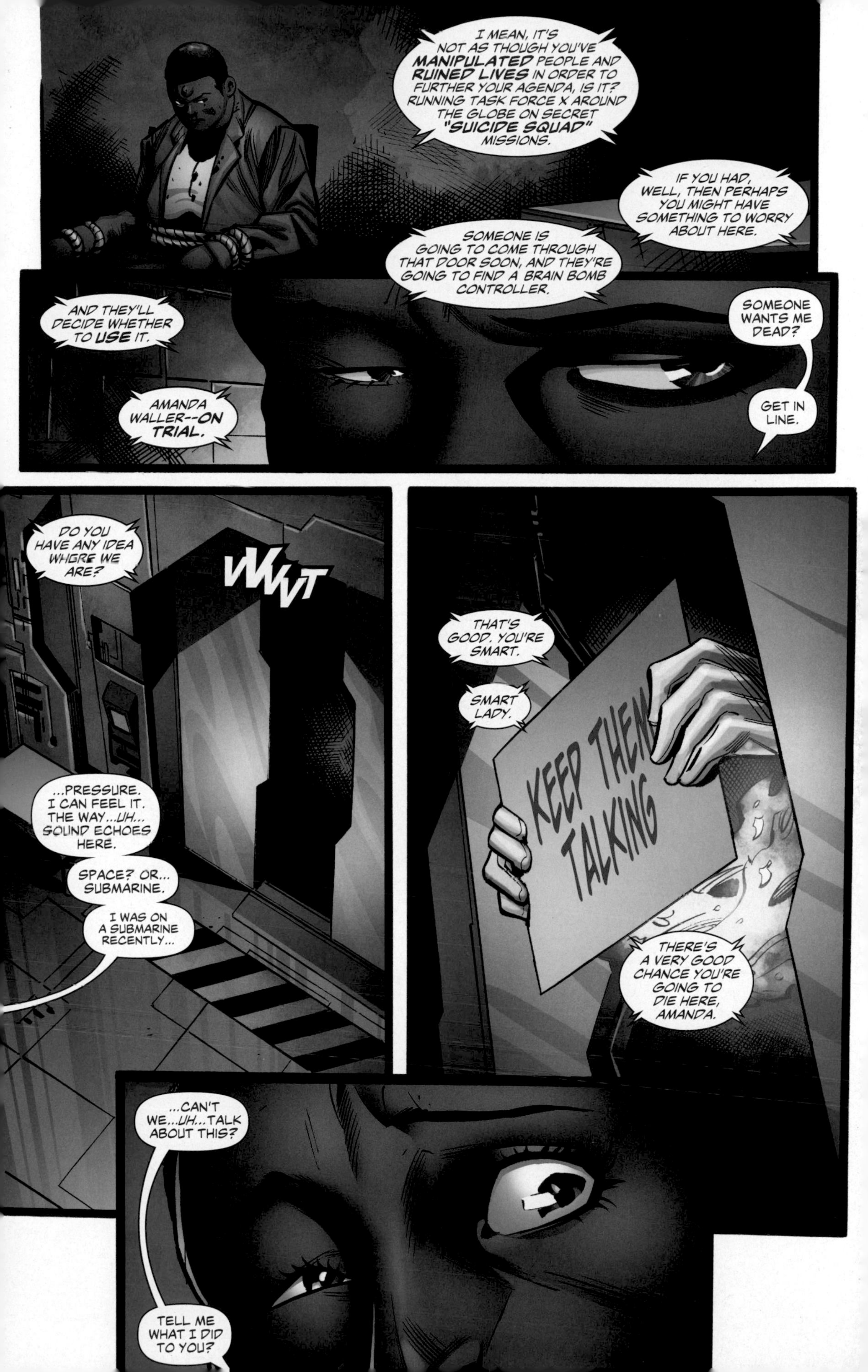
I MEAN, IT'S NOT AS THOUGH YOU'VE MANIPULATED PEOPLE AND RUINED LIVES IN ORDER TO FURTHER YOUR AGENDA, IS IT? RUNNING TASK FORCE X AROUND THE GLOBE ON SECRET "SUICIDE SQUAD" MISSIONS.
IF YOU HAD, WELL, THEN PERHAPS YOU MIGHT HAVE SOMETHING TO WORRY ABOUT HERE.
SOMEONE IS GOING TO COME THROUGH THAT DOOR SOON, AND THEY'RE GOING TO FIND A BRAIN BOMB CONTROLLER.
AND THEY'LL DECIDE WHETHER TO USE IT.
AMANDA WALLER--ON TRIAL.
SOMEONE WANTS ME DEAD?
GET IN LINE.
DO YOU HAVE ANY IDEA WHERE WE ARE?
VWVT
...PRESSURE. I CAN FEEL IT. THE WAY...UH... SOUND ECHOES HERE.
SPACE? OR... SUBMARINE.
I WAS ON A SUBMARINE RECENTLY...
THAT'S GOOD. YOU'RE SMART.
SMART LADY.
KEEP THEM TALKING
THERE'S A VERY GOOD CHANCE YOU'RE GOING TO DIE HERE, AMANDA.
...CAN'T WE...UH...TALK ABOUT THIS?
TELL ME WHAT I DID TO YOU?

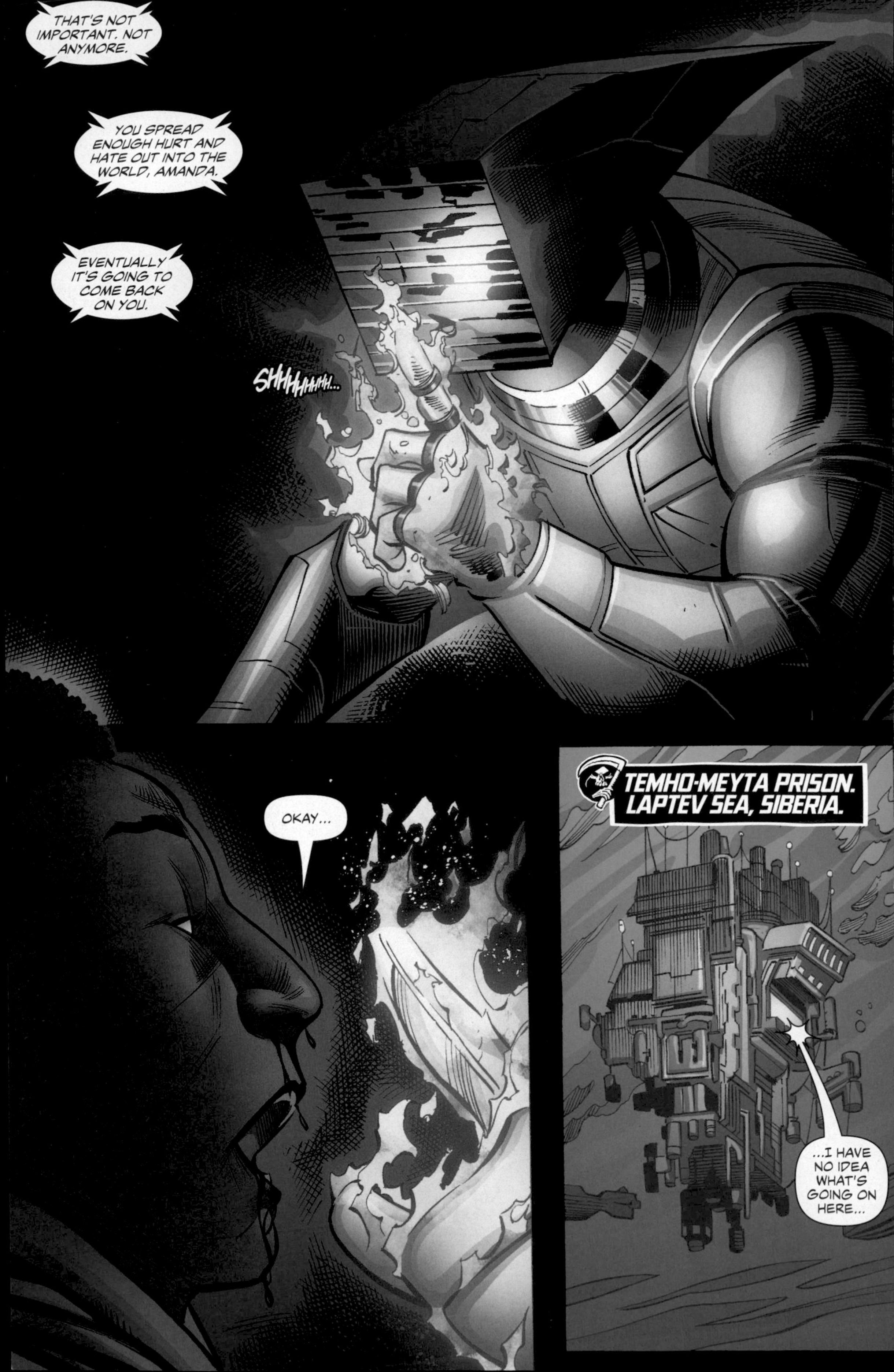
THAT'S NOT IMPORTANT. NOT ANYMORE.
YOU SPREAD ENOUGH HURT AND HATE OUT INTO THE WORLD, AMANDA.
EVENTUALLY IT'S GOING TO COME BACK ON YOU.
SHHHHHHH...
OKAY...
TEMHO-MEYTA PRISON. LAPTEV SEA, SIBERIA.
...I HAVE NO IDEA WHAT'S GOING ON HERE...

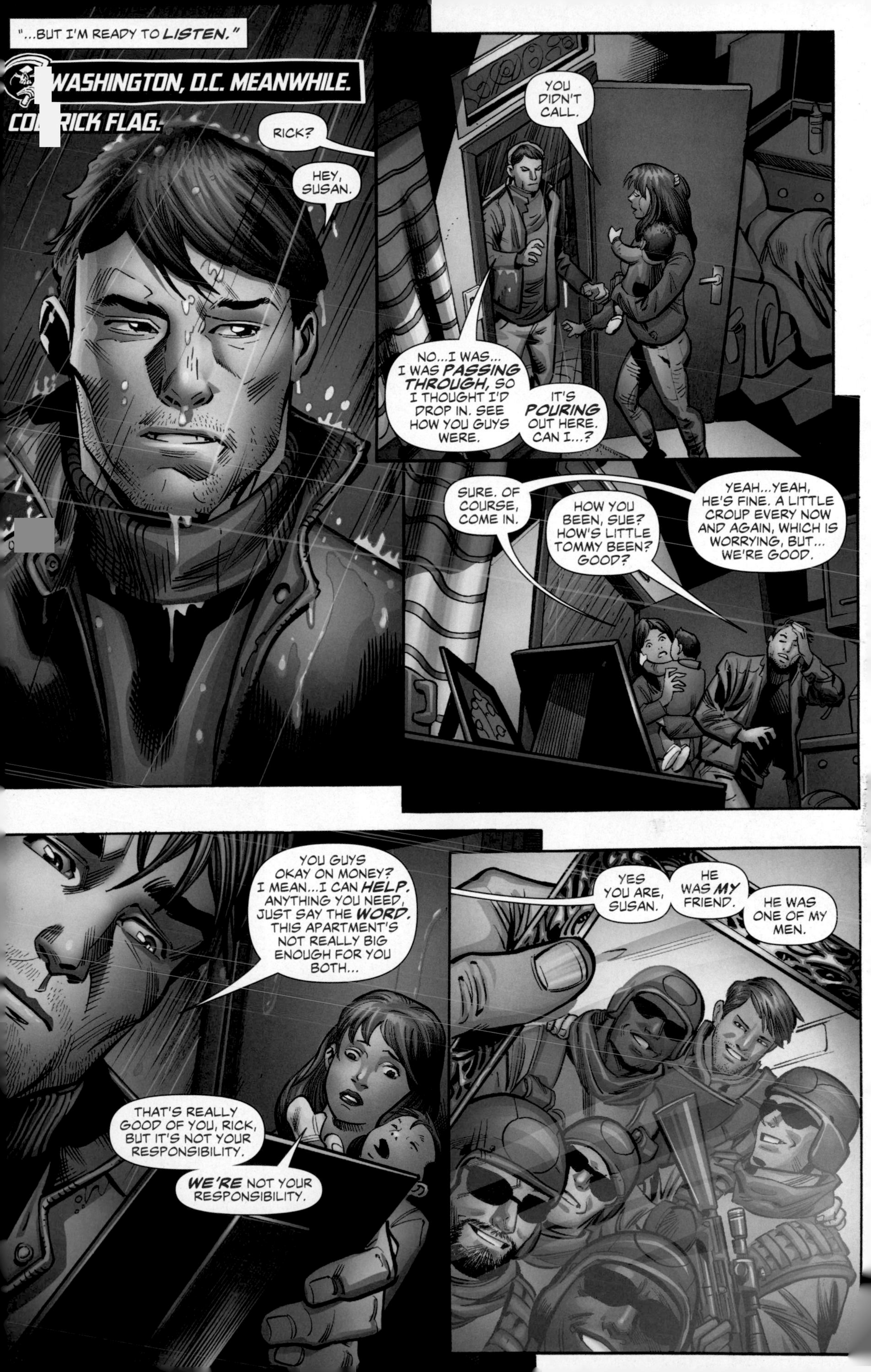
"...BUT I'M READY TO LISTEN."
WASHINGTON, D.C. MEANWHILE.
CO RICK FLAG.
RICK?
HEY, SUSAN.
YOU DIDN'T CALL.
NO...I WAS... I WAS PASSING THROUGH, SO I THOUGHT I'D DROP IN. SEE HOW YOU GUYS WERE.
IT'S POURING OUT HERE. CAN I...?
SURE. OF COURSE, COME IN.
HOW YOU BEEN, SUE? HOW'S LITTLE TOMMY BEEN? GOOD?
YEAH...YEAH, HE'S FINE. A LITTLE CROUP EVERY NOW AND AGAIN, WHICH IS WORRYING, BUT... WE'RE GOOD.
YOU GUYS OKAY ON MONEY? I MEAN...I CAN HELP. ANYTHING YOU NEED, JUST SAY THE WORD. THIS APARTMENT'S NOT REALLY BIG ENOUGH FOR YOU BOTH...
THAT'S REALLY GOOD OF YOU, RICK, BUT IT'S NOT YOUR RESPONSIBILITY.
WE'RE NOT YOUR RESPONSIBILITY.
YES YOU ARE, SUSAN.
HE WAS MY FRIEND.
HE WAS ONE OF MY MEN.

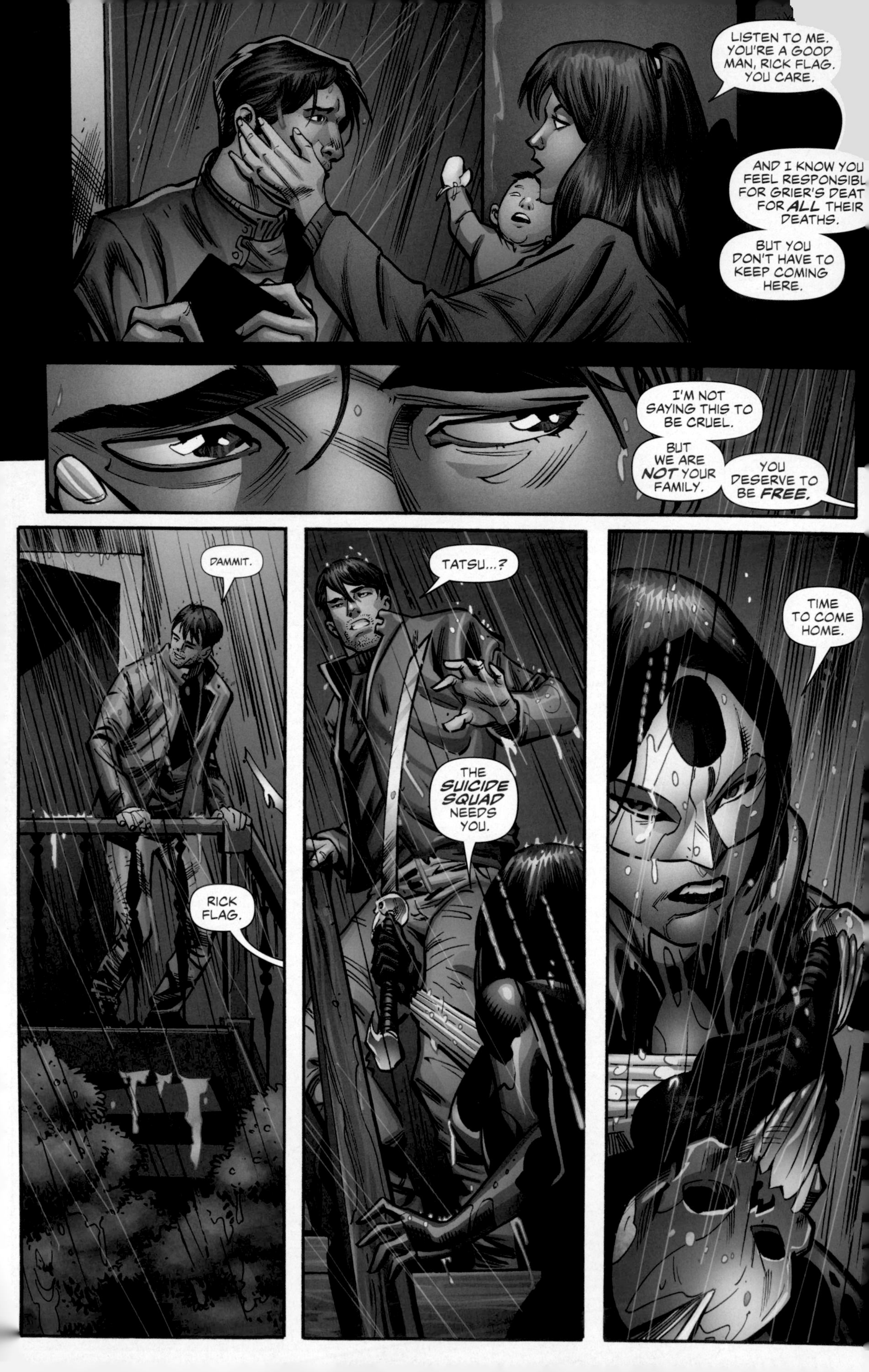
LISTEN TO ME. YOU'RE A GOOD MAN, RICK FLAG. YOU CARE.
AND I KNOW YOU FEEL RESPONSIBL FOR GRIER'S DEAT FOR ALL THEIR DEATHS.
BUT YOU DON'T HAVE TO KEEP COMING HERE.
I'M NOT SAYING THIS TO BE CRUEL.
BUT WE ARE NOT YOUR FAMILY.
YOU DESERVE TO BE FREE.
DAMMIT.
RICK FLAG.
TATSU...?
THE SUICIDE SQUAD NEEDS YOU.
TIME TO COME HOME.

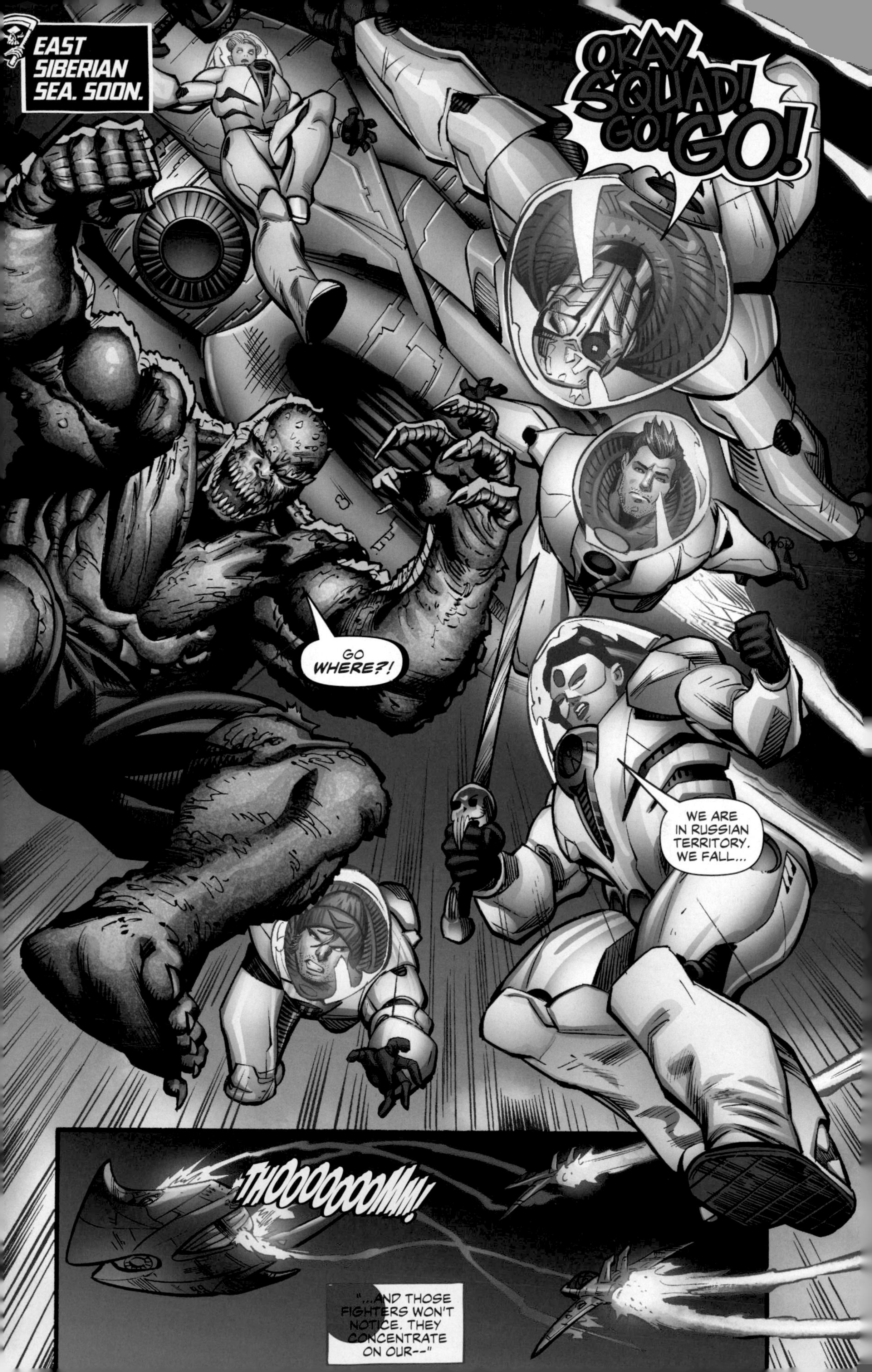
EAST SIBERIAN SEA. SOON.
OKAY, SQUAD! GO! GO!
GO WHERE?!
WE ARE IN RUSSIAN TERRITORY. WE FALL...
THOOOOOOOMM!
"...AND THOSE FIGHTERS WON'T NOTICE. THEY CONCENTRATE ON OUR--"

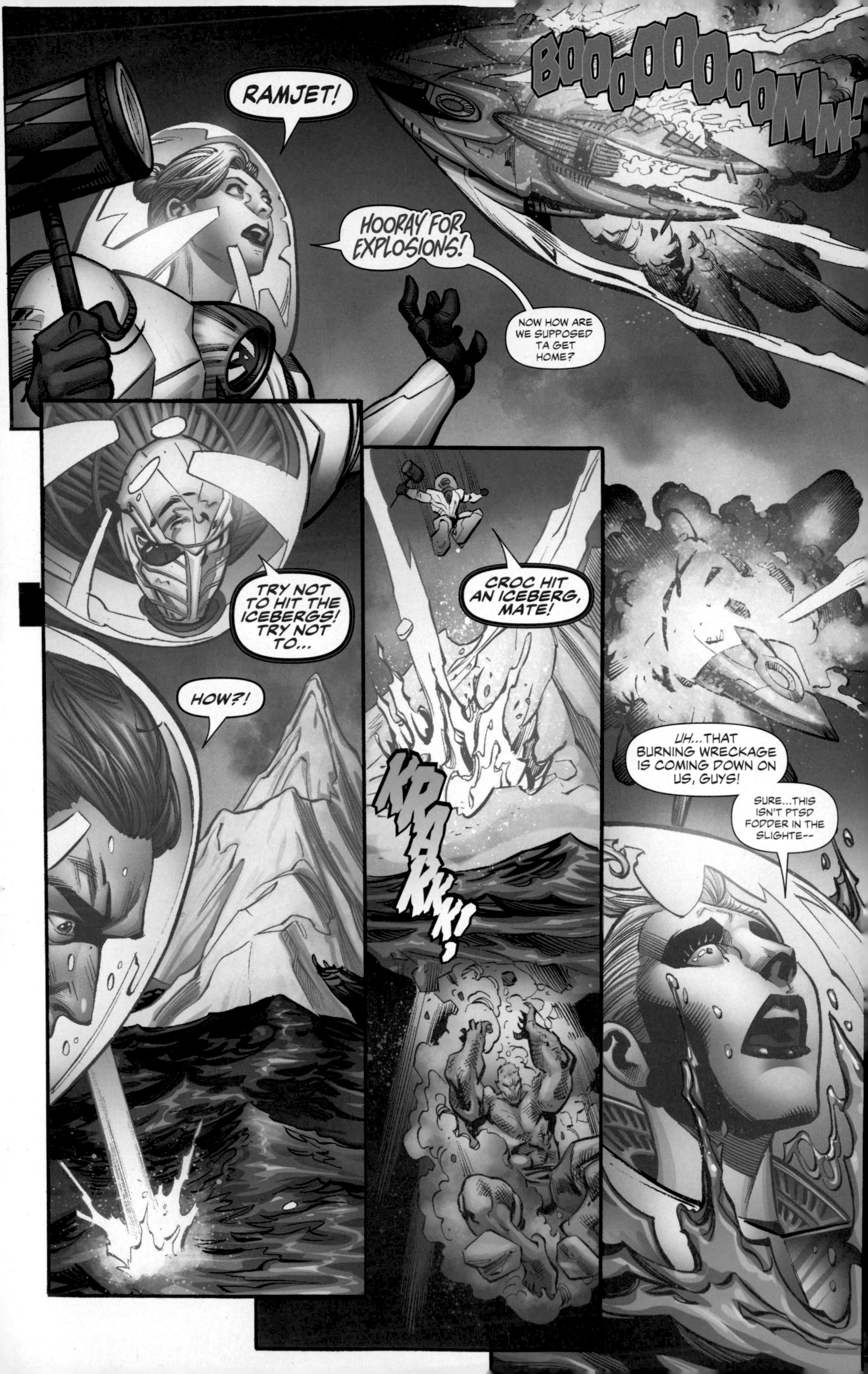
RAMJET!
BOOOOOOOOOMM!
HOORAY FOR EXPLOSIONS!
NOW HOW ARE WE SUPPOSED TA GET HOME?
TRY NOT TO HIT THE ICEBERGS! TRY NOT TO...
HOW?!
CROC HIT AN ICEBERG, MATE!
KRAKKKK!
UH...THAT BURNING WRECKAGE IS COMING DOWN ON US, GUYS!
SURE...THIS ISN'T PTSD FODDER IN THE SLIGHTE--

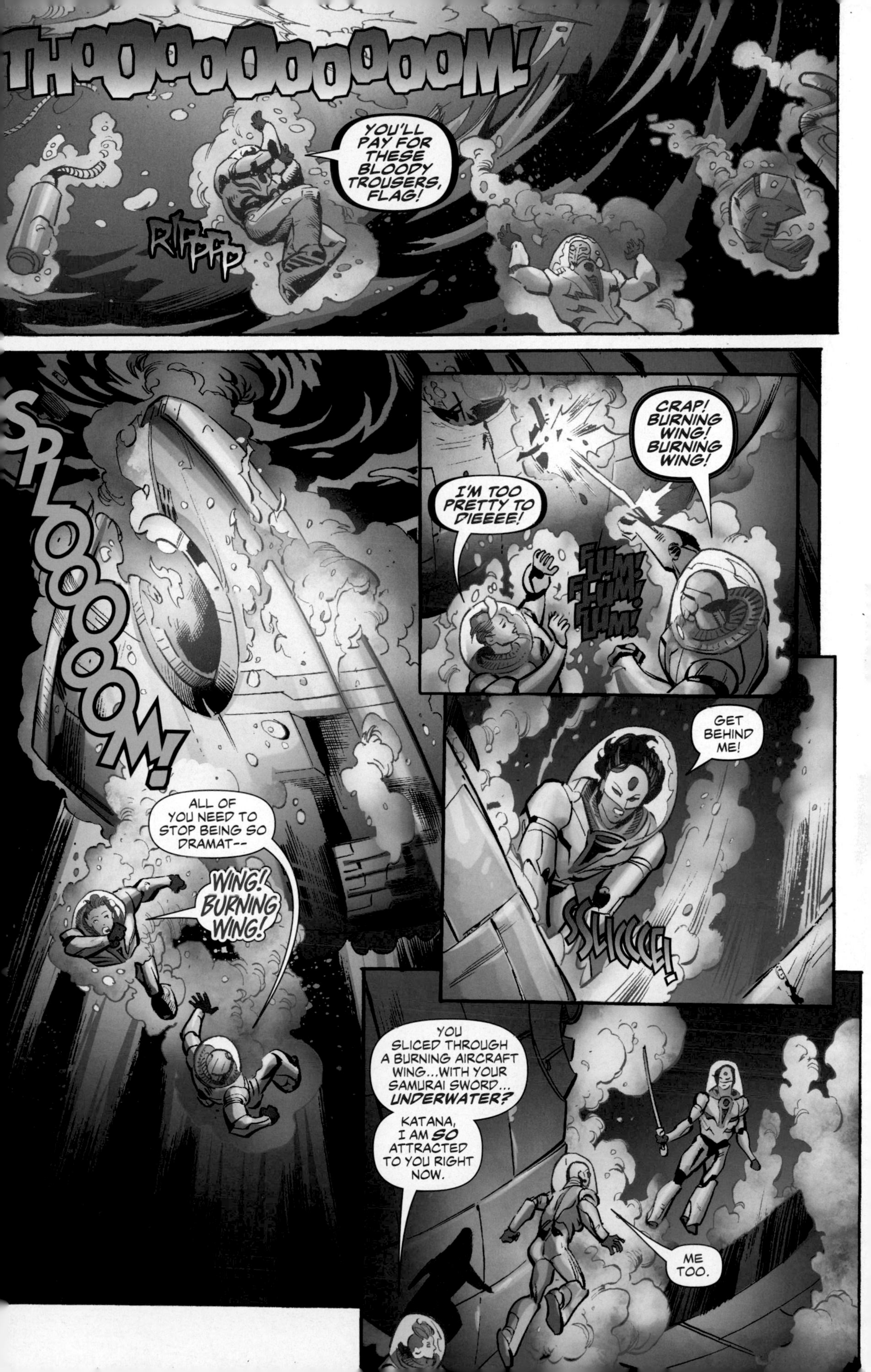
THOOOOOOOOOOM!
YOU'LL PAY FOR THESE BLOODY TROUSERS, FLAG!
RIPPP
SPLOOOOOOOM!
CRAP! BURNING WING! BURNING WING!
I'M TOO PRETTY TO DIEEEE!
FLUM! FLUM! FLUM!
ALL OF YOU NEED TO STOP BEING SO DRAMAT--
WING! BURNING WING!
GET BEHIND ME!
SSLICCCE!
YOU SLICED THROUGH A BURNING AIRCRAFT WING...WITH YOUR SAMURAI SWORD... UNDERWATER?
KATANA, I AM SO ATTRACTED TO YOU RIGHT NOW.
ME TOO.

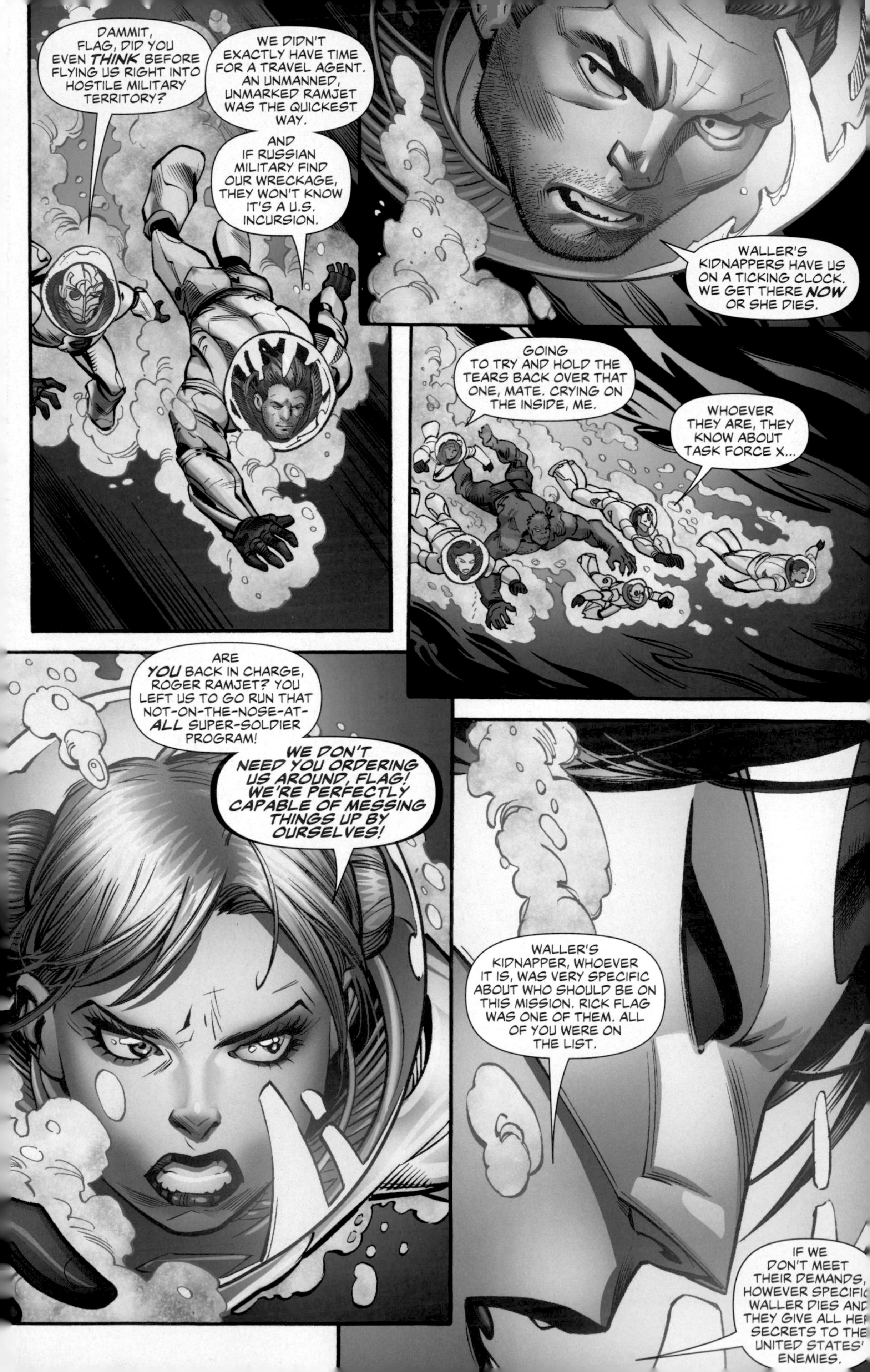
DAMMIT, FLAG, DID YOU EVEN THINK BEFORE FLYING US RIGHT INTO HOSTILE MILITARY TERRITORY?
WE DIDN'T EXACTLY HAVE TIME FOR A TRAVEL AGENT. AN UNMANNED, UNMARKED RAMJET WAS THE QUICKEST WAY.
AND IF RUSSIAN MILITARY FIND OUR WRECKAGE, THEY WON'T KNOW IT'S A U.S. INCURSION.
WALLER'S KIDNAPPERS HAVE US ON A TICKING CLOCK. WE GET THERE NOW OR SHE DIES.
GOING TO TRY AND HOLD THE TEARS BACK OVER THAT ONE, MATE. CRYING ON THE INSIDE, ME.
WHOEVER THEY ARE, THEY KNOW ABOUT TASK FORCE X...
ARE YOU BACK IN CHARGE, ROGER RAMJET? YOU LEFT US TO GO RUN THAT NOT-ON-THE-NOSE-AT-ALL SUPER-SOLDIER PROGRAM!
WE DON'T NEED YOU ORDERING US AROUND, FLAG! WE'RE PERFECTLY CAPABLE OF MESSING THINGS UP BY OURSELVES!
WALLER'S KIDNAPPER, WHOEVER IT IS, WAS VERY SPECIFIC ABOUT WHO SHOULD BE ON THIS MISSION. RICK FLAG WAS ONE OF THEM. ALL OF YOU WERE ON THE LIST.
IF WE DON'T MEET THEIR DEMANDS, HOWEVER SPECIFIC, WALLER DIES AND THEY GIVE ALL HER SECRETS TO THE UNITED STATES' ENEMIES.

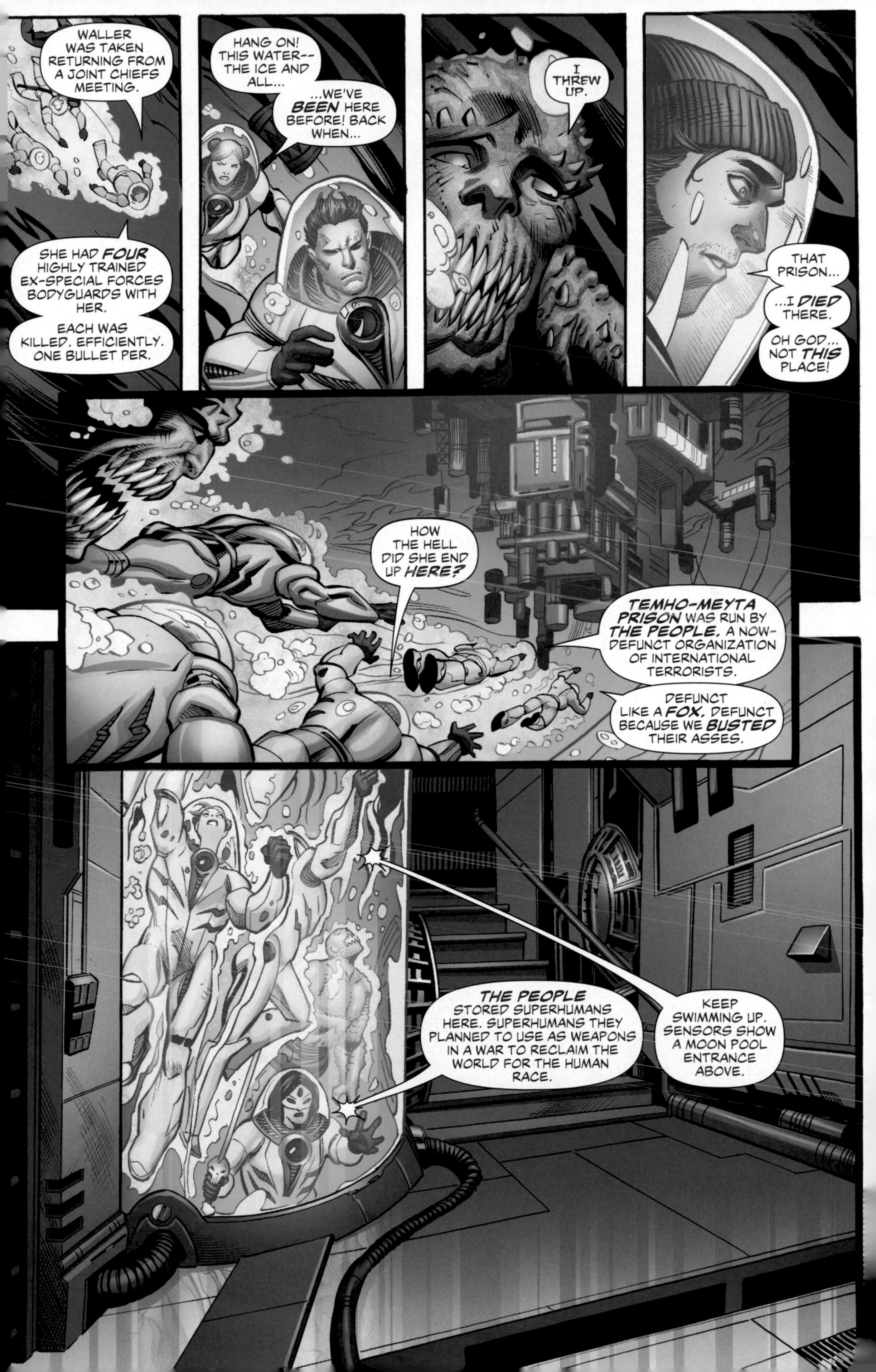

WALLER WAS TAKEN RETURNING FROM A JOINT CHIEFS MEETING.
SHE HAD FOUR HIGHLY TRAINED EX-SPECIAL FORCES BODYGUARDS WITH HER.
EACH WAS KILLED. EFFICIENTLY. ONE BULLET PER.
HANG ON! THIS WATER-- THE ICE AND ALL...
...WE'VE BEEN HERE BEFORE! BACK WHEN...
I THREW UP.
THAT PRISON...
...I DIED THERE.
OH GOD... NOT THIS PLACE!
HOW THE HELL DID SHE END UP HERE?
TEMHO-MEYTA PRISON WAS RUN BY THE PEOPLE. A NOW-DEFUNCT ORGANIZATION OF INTERNATIONAL TERRORISTS.
DEFUNCT LIKE A FOX. DEFUNCT BECAUSE WE BUSTED THEIR ASSES.
THE PEOPLE STORED SUPERHUMANS HERE. SUPERHUMANS THEY PLANNED TO USE AS WEAPONS IN A WAR TO RECLAIM THE WORLD FOR THE HUMAN RACE.
KEEP SWIMMING UP. SENSORS SHOW A MOON POOL ENTRANCE ABOVE.

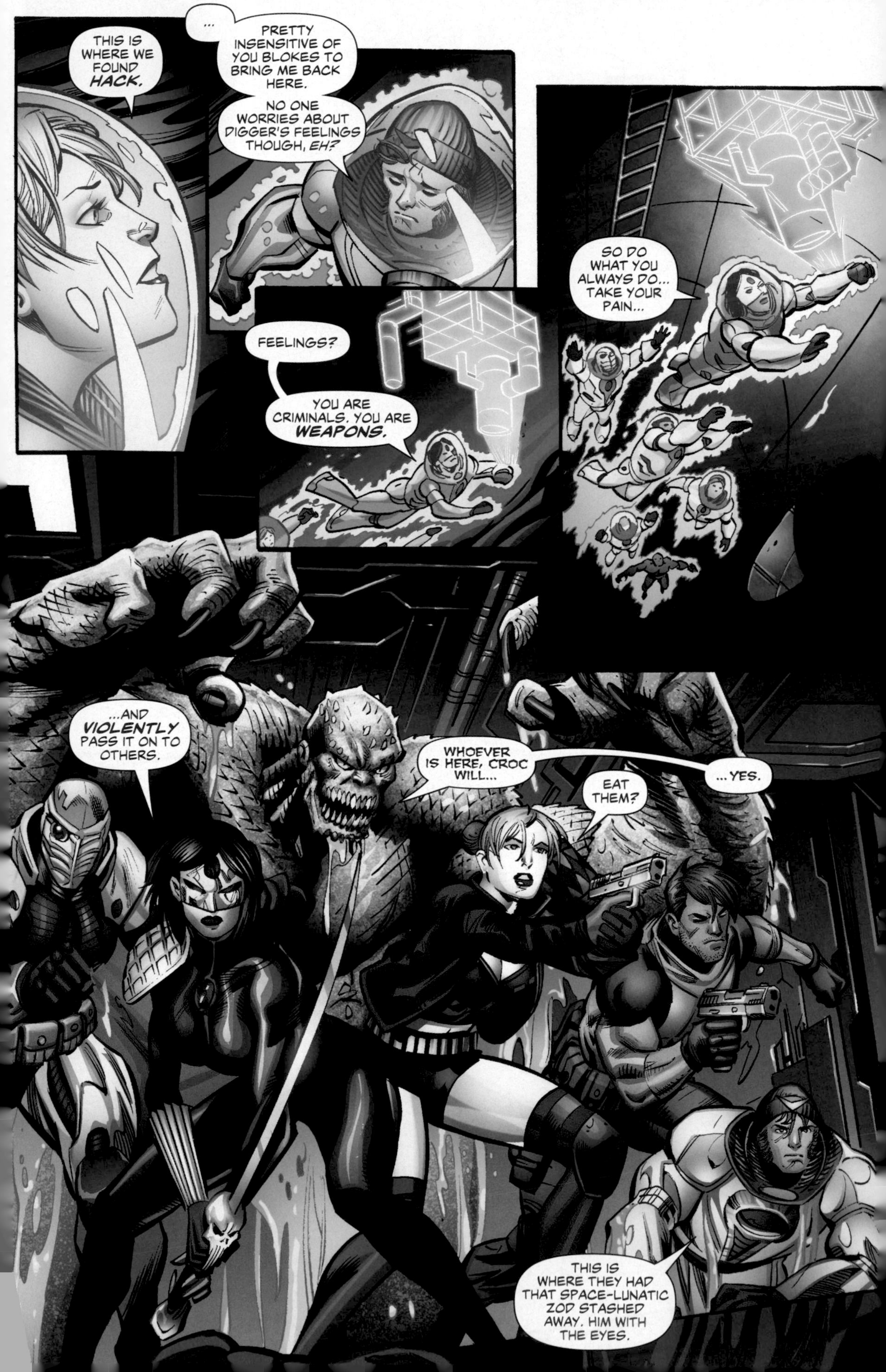
THIS IS WHERE WE FOUND HACK.
...
PRETTY INSENSITIVE OF YOU BLOKES TO BRING ME BACK HERE.
NO ONE WORRIES ABOUT DIGGER'S FEELINGS THOUGH, EH?
FEELINGS?
YOU ARE CRIMINALS. YOU ARE WEAPONS.
SO DO WHAT YOU ALWAYS DO... TAKE YOUR PAIN...
...AND VIOLENTLY PASS IT ON TO OTHERS.
WHOEVER IS HERE, CROC WILL...
EAT THEM?
...YES.
THIS IS WHERE THEY HAD THAT SPACE-LUNATIC ZOD STASHED AWAY. HIM WITH THE EYES.

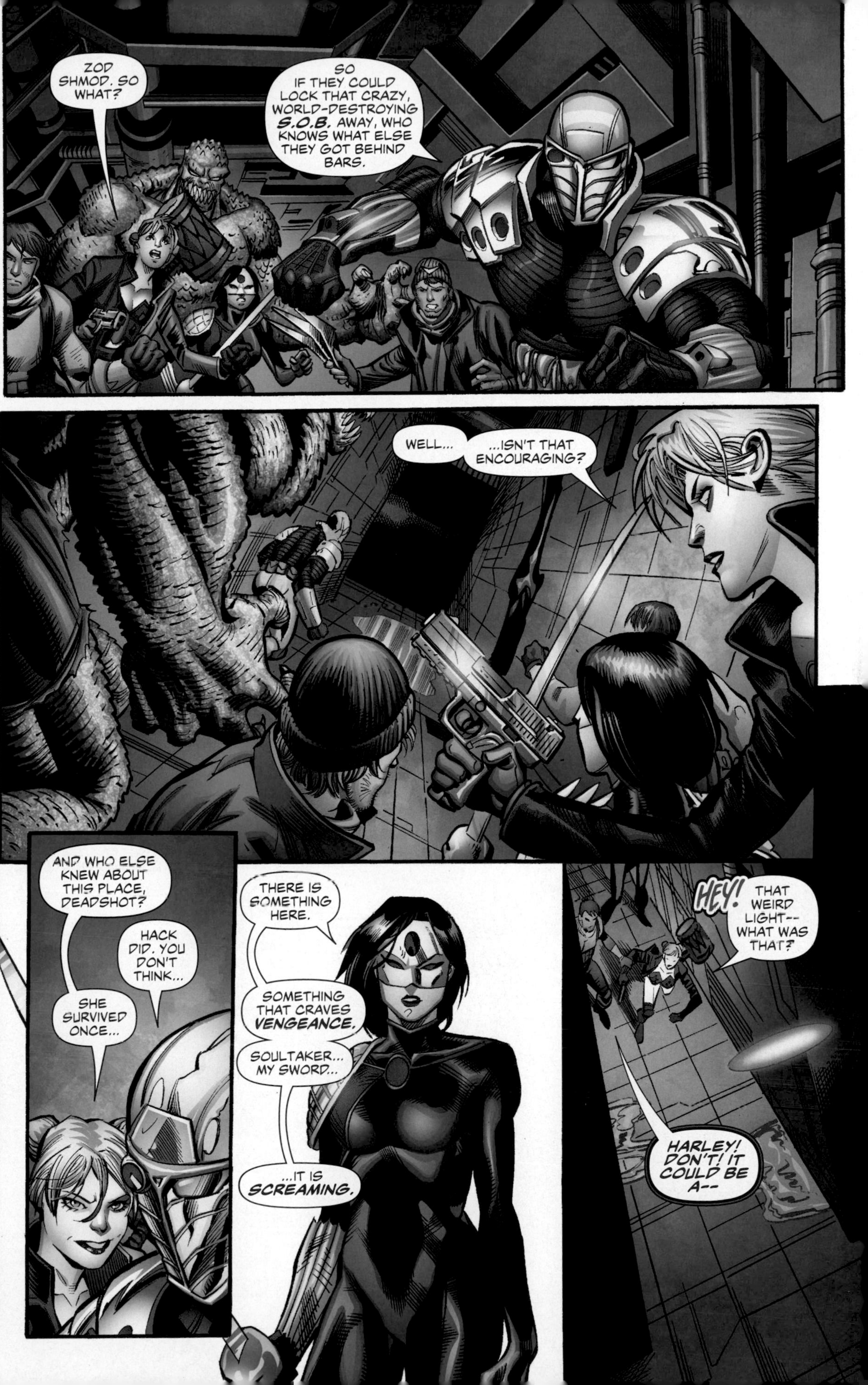
ZOD SHMOD. SO WHAT?
SO IF THEY COULD LOCK THAT CRAZY, WORLD-DESTROYING S.O.B. AWAY, WHO KNOWS WHAT ELSE THEY GOT BEHIND BARS.
WELL...
...ISN'T THAT ENCOURAGING?
AND WHO ELSE KNEW ABOUT THIS PLACE, DEADSHOT?
HACK DID. YOU DON'T THINK...
SHE SURVIVED ONCE...
THERE IS SOMETHING HERE.
SOMETHING THAT CRAVES VENGEANCE.
SOULTAKER... MY SWORD...
...IT IS SCREAMING.
HEY!
THAT WEIRD LIGHT-- WHAT WAS THAT?
HARLEY! DON'T! IT COULD BE A--

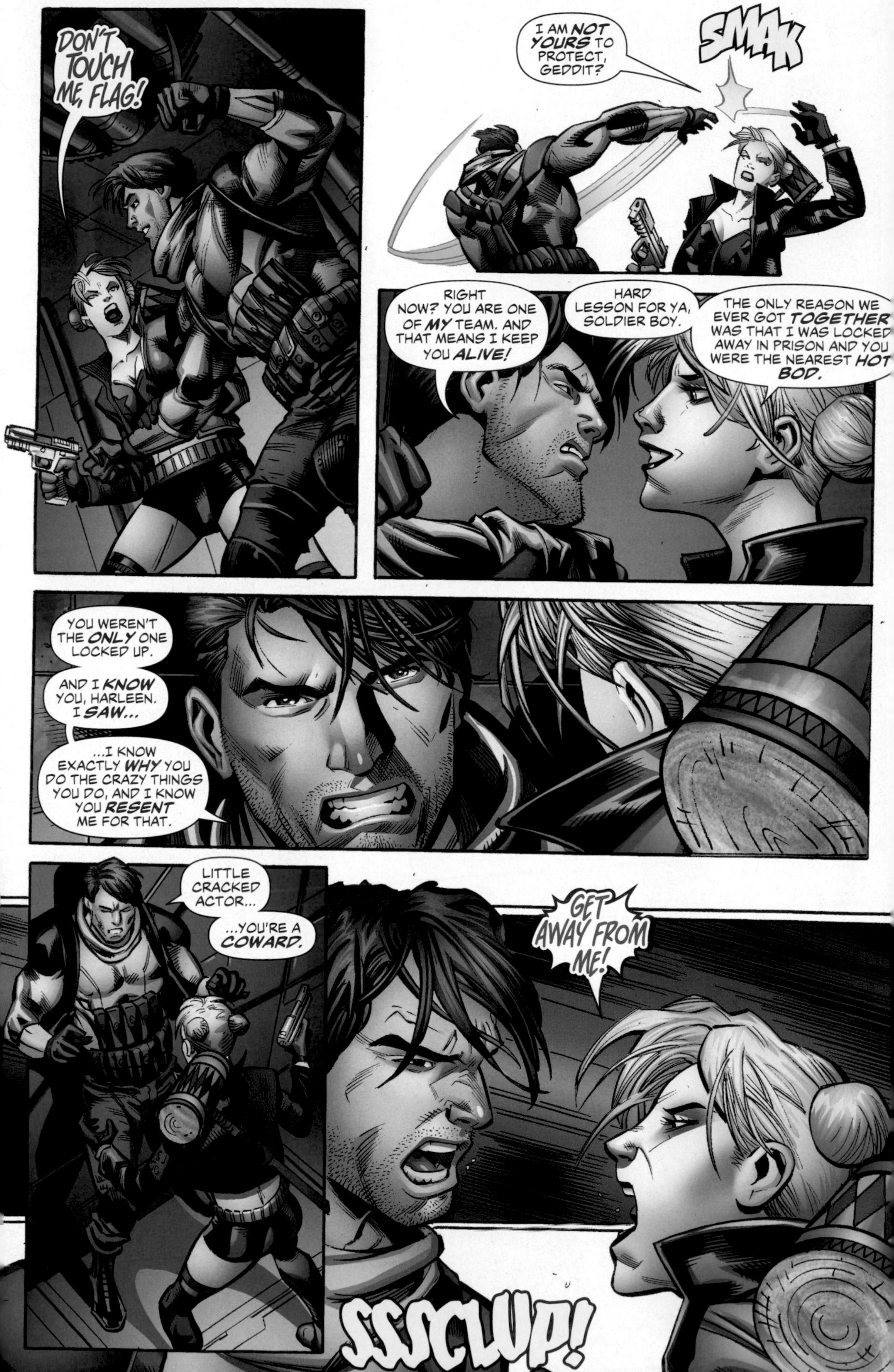
DON'T TOUCH ME, FLAG!
I AM NOT YOURS TO PROTECT, GEDDIT?
SMAK
RIGHT NOW? YOU ARE ONE OF MY TEAM. AND THAT MEANS I KEEP YOU ALIVE!
HARD LESSON FOR YA, SOLDIER BOY.
THE ONLY REASON WE EVER GOT TOGETHER WAS THAT I WAS LOCKED AWAY IN PRISON AND YOU WERE THE NEAREST HOT BOD.
YOU WEREN'T THE ONLY ONE LOCKED UP.
AND I KNOW YOU, HARLEEN. I SAW...
...I KNOW EXACTLY WHY YOU DO THE CRAZY THINGS YOU DO, AND I KNOW YOU RESENT ME FOR THAT.
LITTLE CRACKED ACTOR...
...YOU'RE A COWARD.
GET AWAY FROM ME!
SSSCLUP!

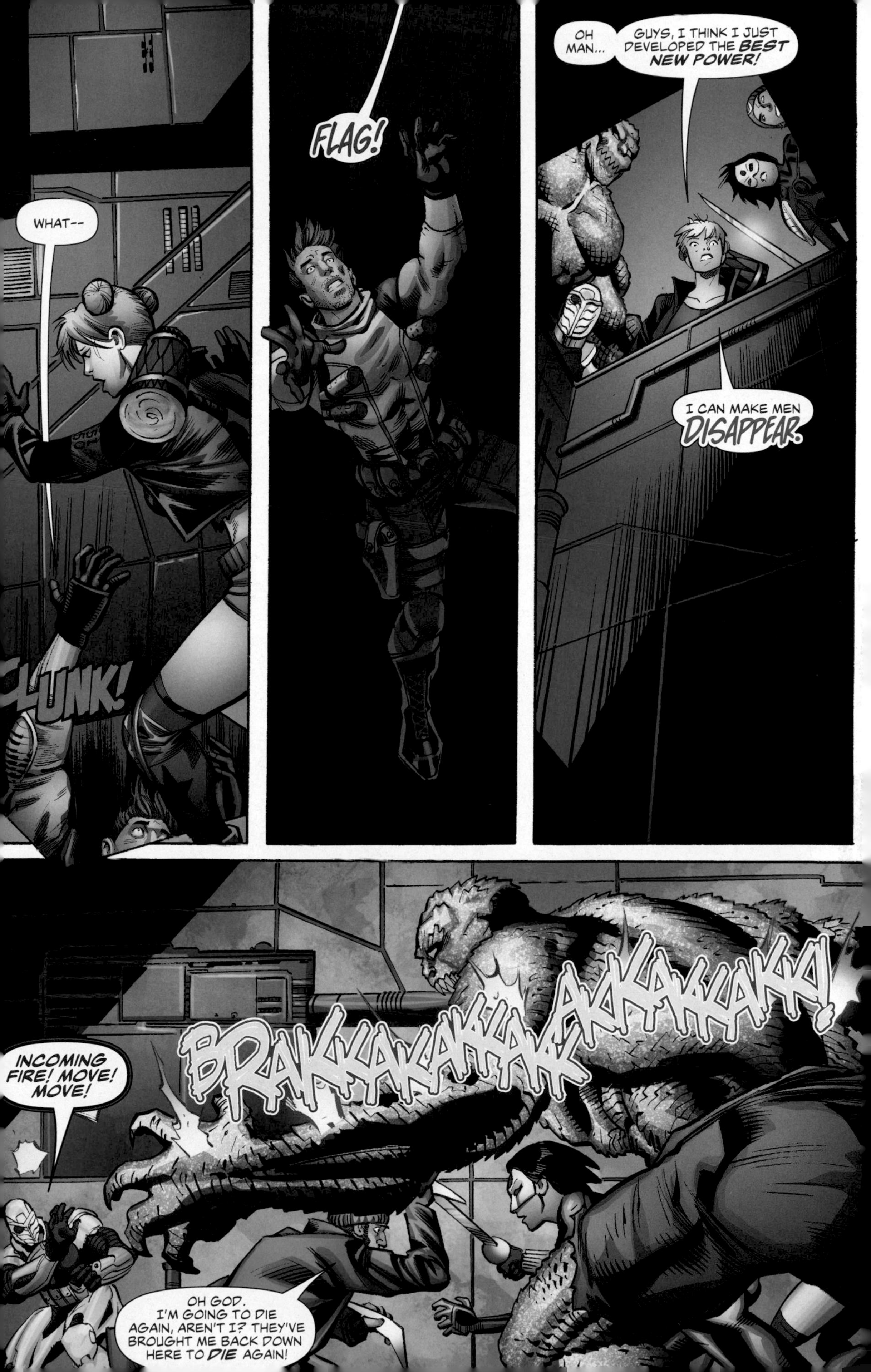
WHAT--
CLUNK!
FLAG!
OH MAN...
GUYS, I THINK I JUST DEVELOPED THE BEST NEW POWER!
I CAN MAKE MEN DISAPPEAR.
BRAKKAKAKAKAKAKAKAKAKAKAKA!
INCOMING FIRE! MOVE! MOVE!
OH GOD. I'M GOING TO DIE AGAIN, AREN'T I? THEY'VE BROUGHT ME BACK DOWN HERE TO DIE AGAIN!

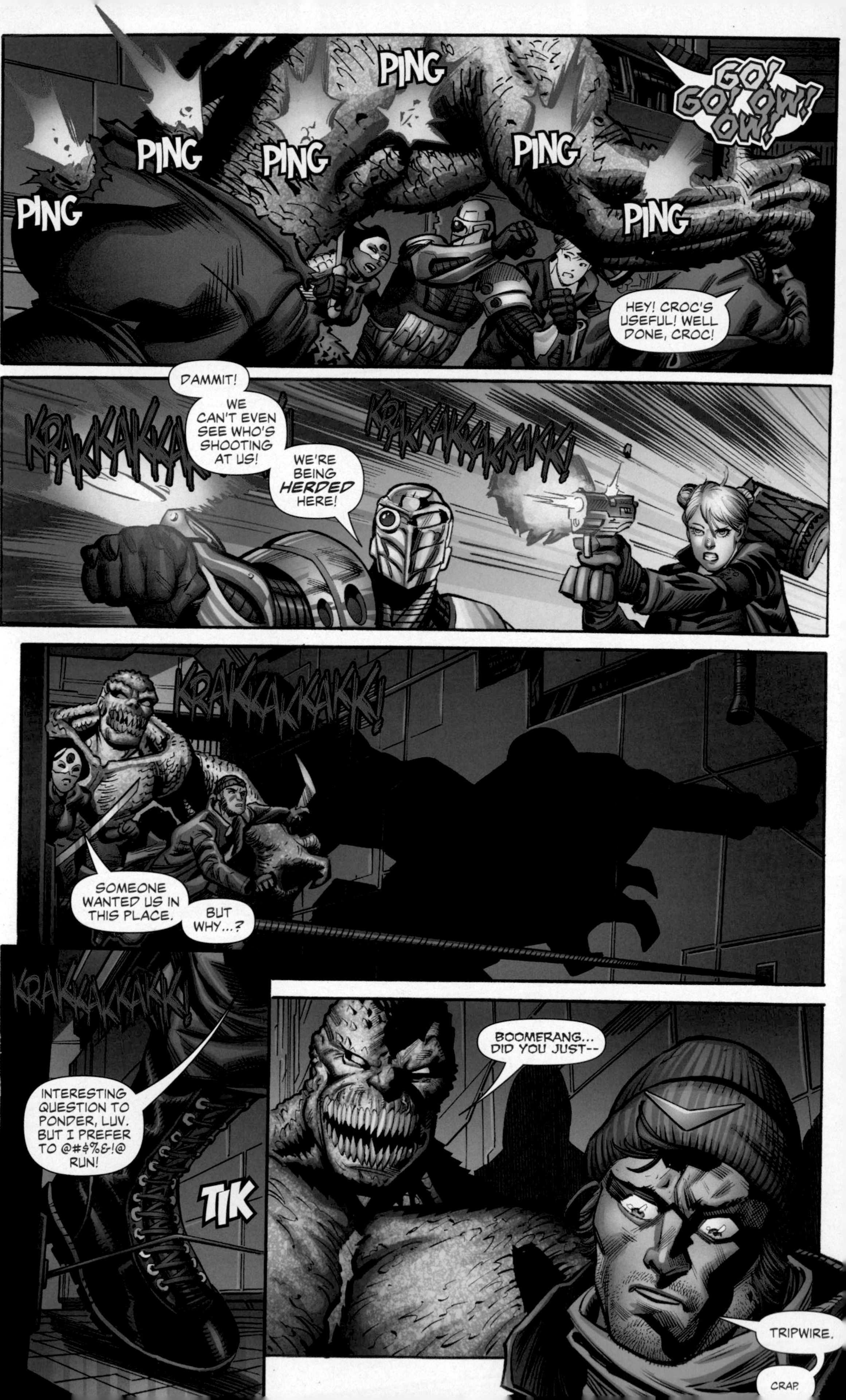
PING
PING
PING
PING
PING
PING
GO! GO! OW! OW!
HEY! CROC'S USEFUL! WELL DONE, CROC!
KRAKKAKKAK
DAMMIT!
WE CAN'T EVEN SEE WHO'S SHOOTING AT US!
WE'RE BEING HERDED HERE!
KRAKKAKKAKKAKK!
KRAKKAKKAKK!
SOMEONE WANTED US IN THIS PLACE.
BUT WHY...?
KRAKKAKKAKK!
INTERESTING QUESTION TO PONDER, LUV. BUT I PREFER TO @#$%&!@ RUN!
TIK
BOOMERANG... DID YOU JUST--
TRIPWIRE.
CRAP.

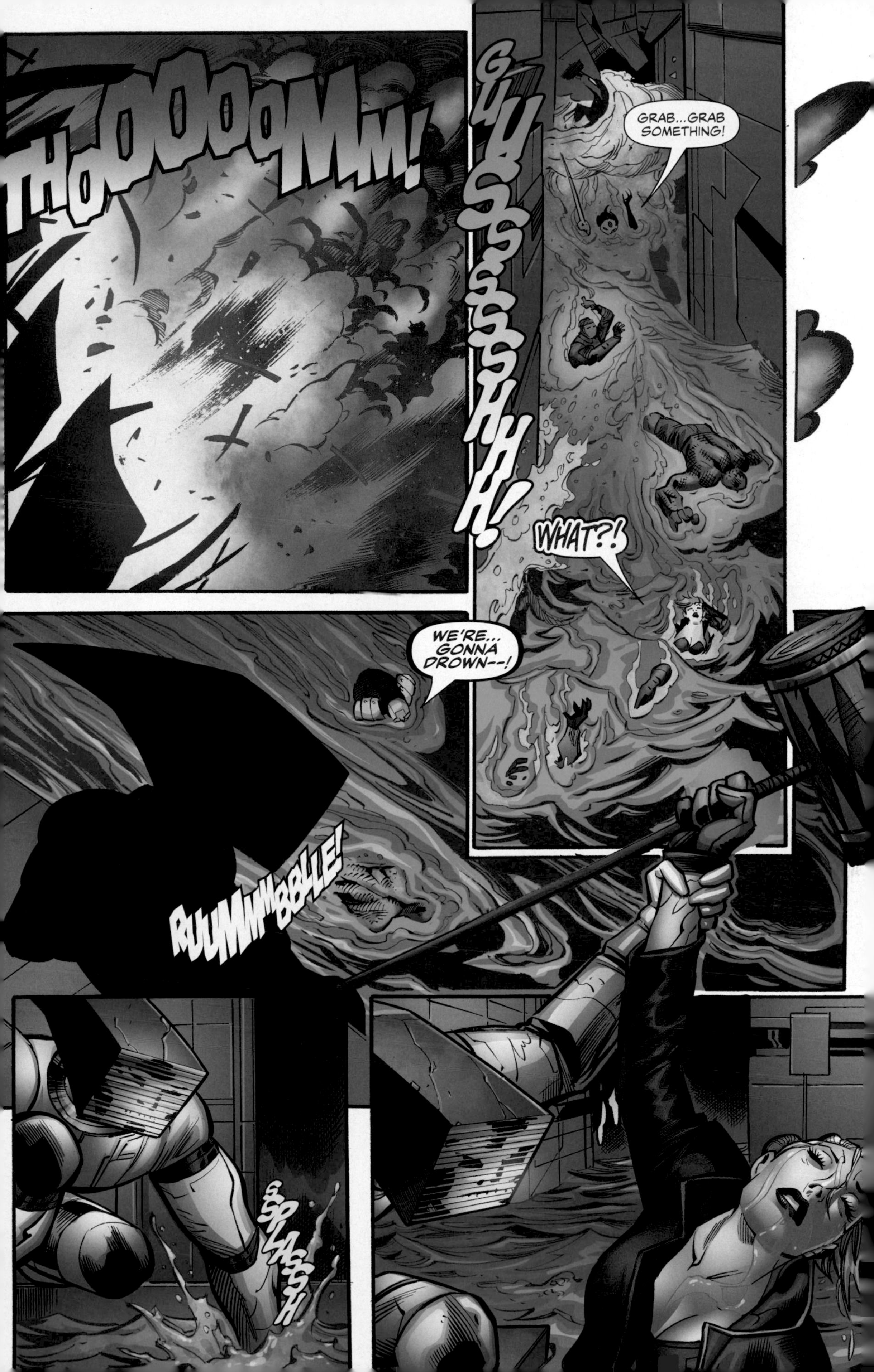
THOOOOOOMMM!
GUUSSSSSHHHH!
GRAB...GRAB SOMETHING!
WHAT?!
WE'RE... GONNA DROWN--!
RUUMMMBBLLE!
SSPLASSH

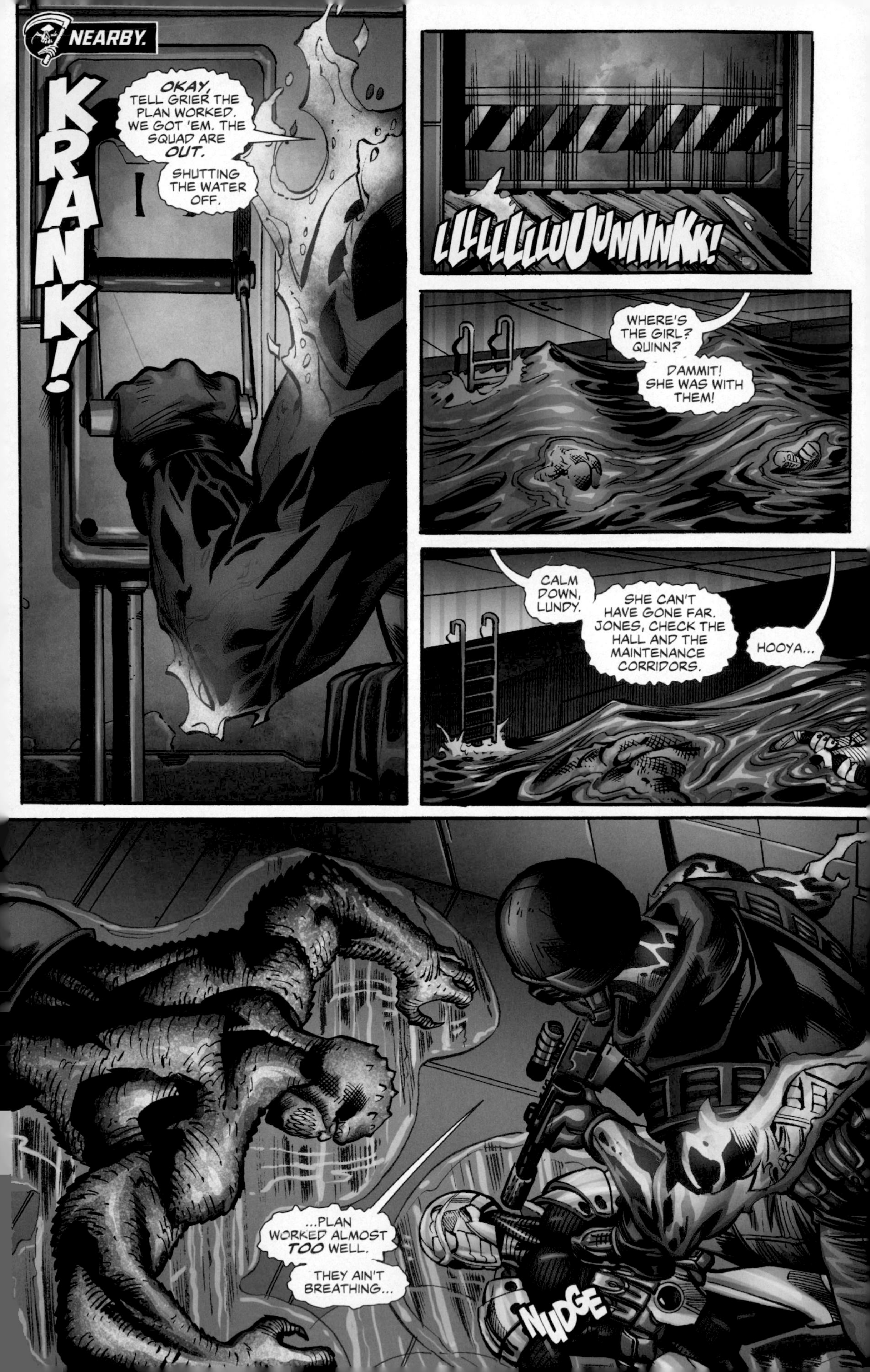
NEARBY.
KRANK!
OKAY, TELL GRIER THE PLAN WORKED. WE GOT 'EM. THE SQUAD ARE OUT.
SHUTTING THE WATER OFF.
LLLLLLLLUUUNNNKK!
WHERE'S THE GIRL? QUINN?
DAMMIT! SHE WAS WITH THEM!
CALM DOWN, LUNDY.
SHE CAN'T HAVE GONE FAR. JONES, CHECK THE HALL AND THE MAINTENANCE CORRIDORS.
HOOYA...
...PLAN WORKED ALMOST TOO WELL.
THEY AIN'T BREATHING...
NUDGE

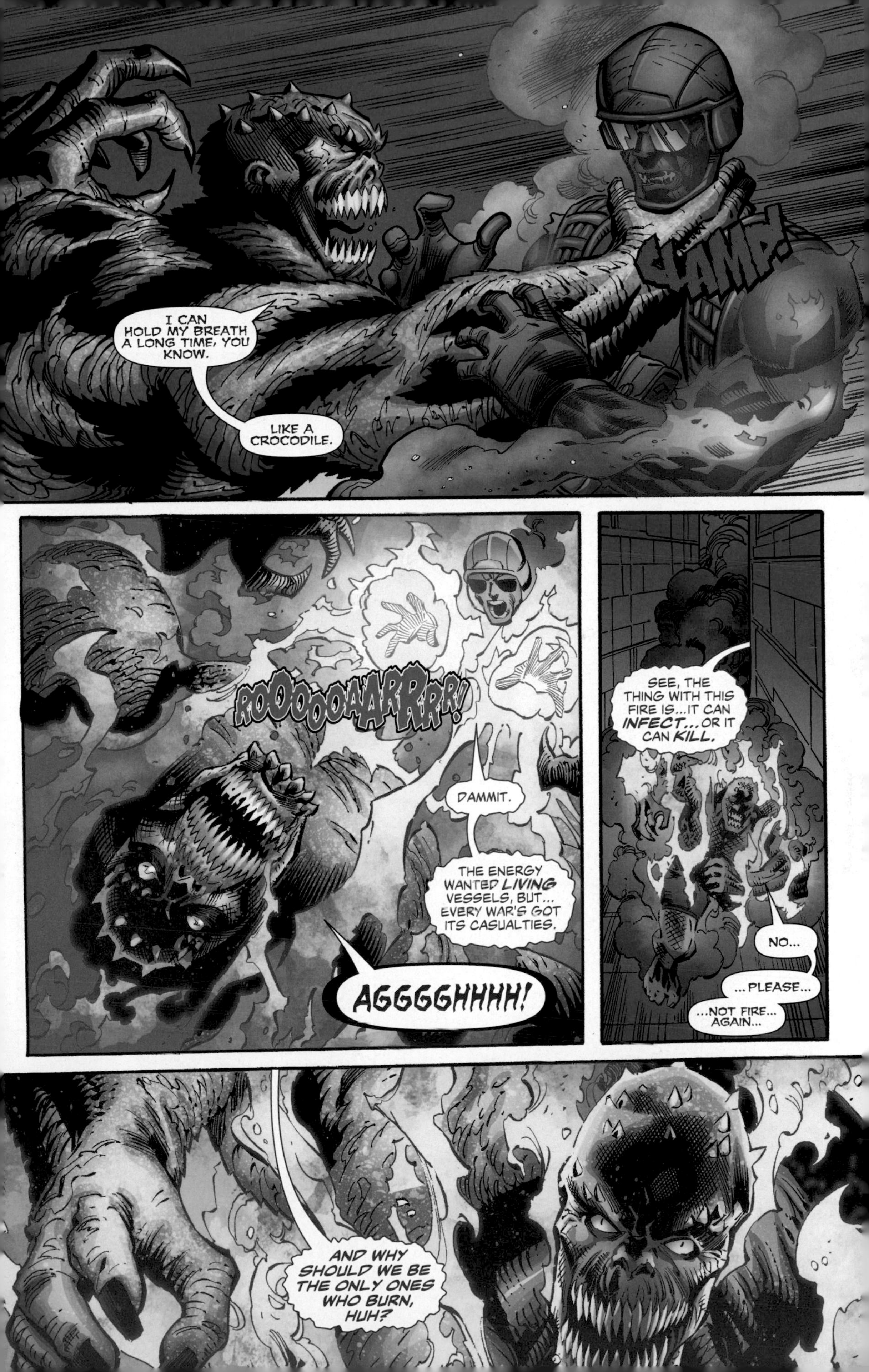

I CAN HOLD MY BREATH A LONG TIME, YOU KNOW.
LIKE A CROCODILE.
CLAMP!
ROOOOOOAARRRR!
DAMMIT.
THE ENERGY WANTED *LIVING* VESSELS, BUT... EVERY WAR'S GOT ITS CASUALTIES.
AGGGGHHHH!
SEE, THE THING WITH THIS FIRE IS...IT CAN *INFECT...* OR IT CAN *KILL.*
NO...
...PLEASE...
...NOT FIRE... AGAIN...
AND WHY SHOULD WE BE THE ONLY ONES WHO BURN, HUH?

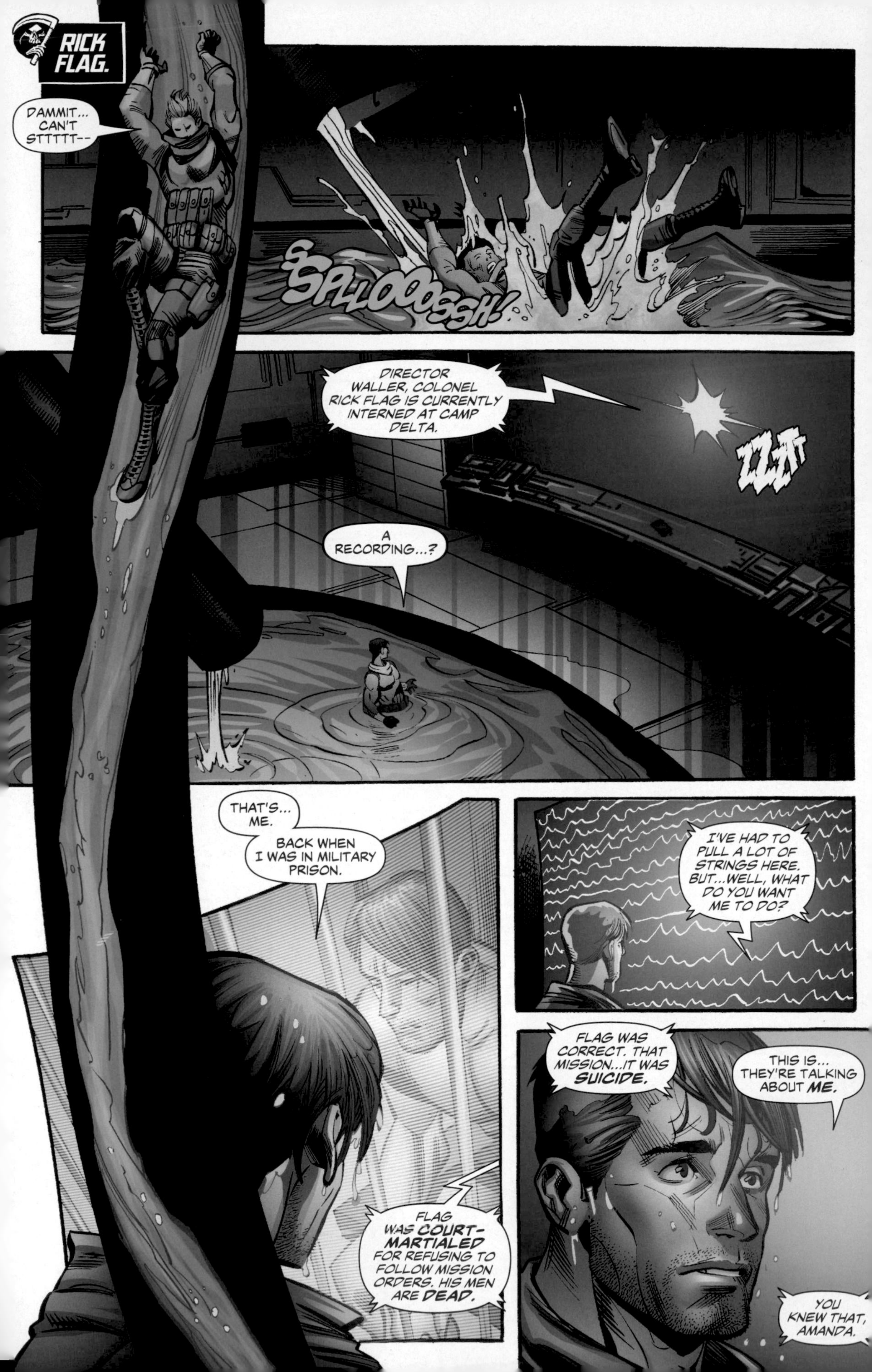
RICK FLAG.
DAMMIT... CAN'T STTTTT--
S-SPLLOOOOSSH!
DIRECTOR WALLER, COLONEL RICK FLAG IS CURRENTLY INTERNED AT CAMP DELTA.
ZZZT
A RECORDING...?
THAT'S... ME.
BACK WHEN I WAS IN MILITARY PRISON.
I'VE HAD TO PULL A LOT OF STRINGS HERE. BUT...WELL, WHAT DO YOU WANT ME TO DO?
FLAG WAS CORRECT. THAT MISSION...IT WAS SUICIDE.
THIS IS... THEY'RE TALKING ABOUT ME.
FLAG WAS COURT-MARTIALED FOR REFUSING TO FOLLOW MISSION ORDERS. HIS MEN ARE DEAD.
YOU KNEW THAT, AMANDA.

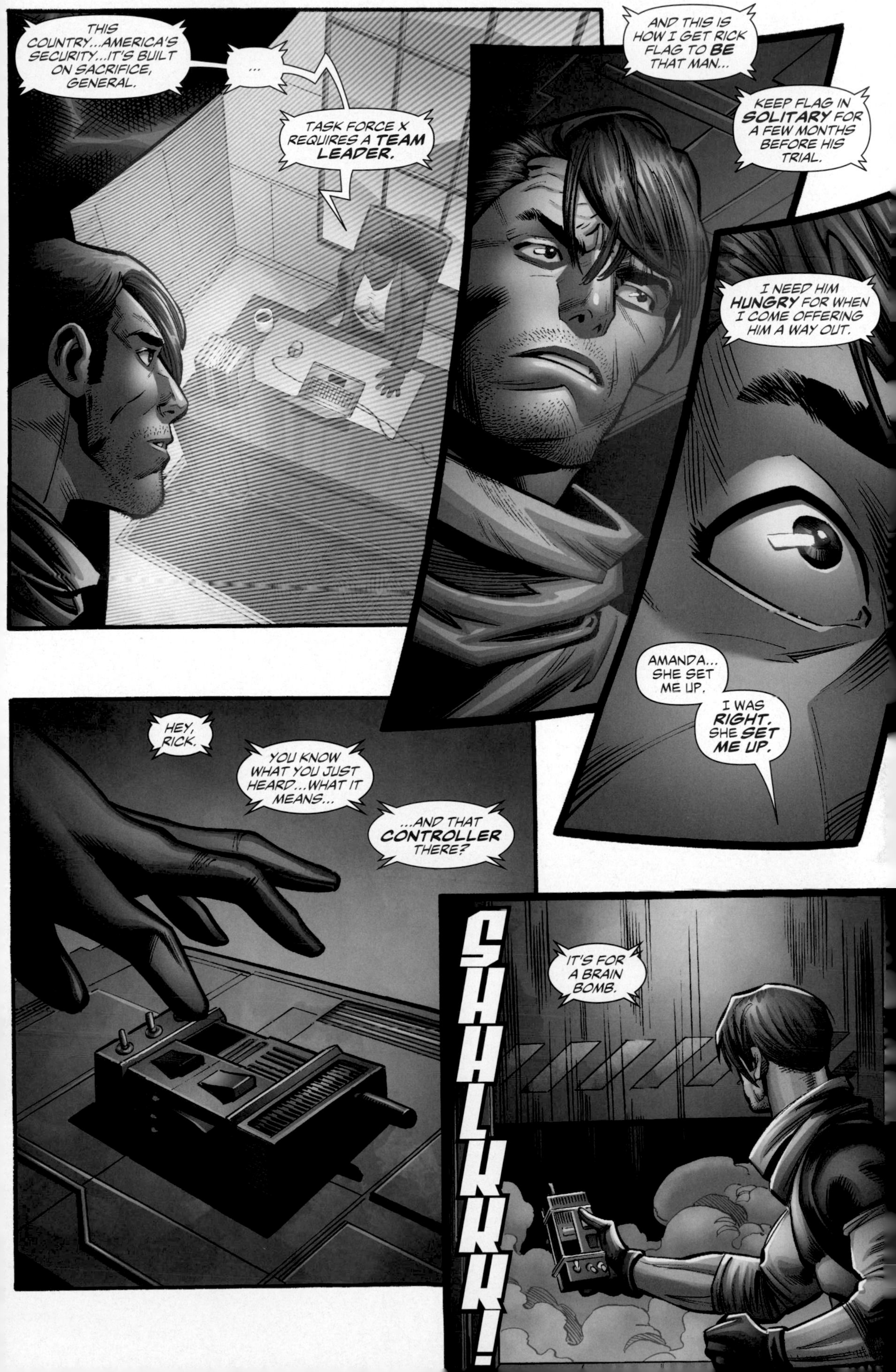
THIS COUNTRY...AMERICA'S SECURITY...IT'S BUILT ON SACRIFICE, GENERAL.
...
TASK FORCE X REQUIRES A TEAM LEADER.
AND THIS IS HOW I GET RICK FLAG TO BE THAT MAN...
KEEP FLAG IN SOLITARY FOR A FEW MONTHS BEFORE HIS TRIAL.
I NEED HIM HUNGRY FOR WHEN I COME OFFERING HIM A WAY OUT.
AMANDA... SHE SET ME UP.
I WAS RIGHT. SHE SET ME UP.
HEY, RICK.
YOU KNOW WHAT YOU JUST HEARD...WHAT IT MEANS...
...AND THAT CONTROLLER THERE?
SHHLKKK!
IT'S FOR A BRAIN BOMB.

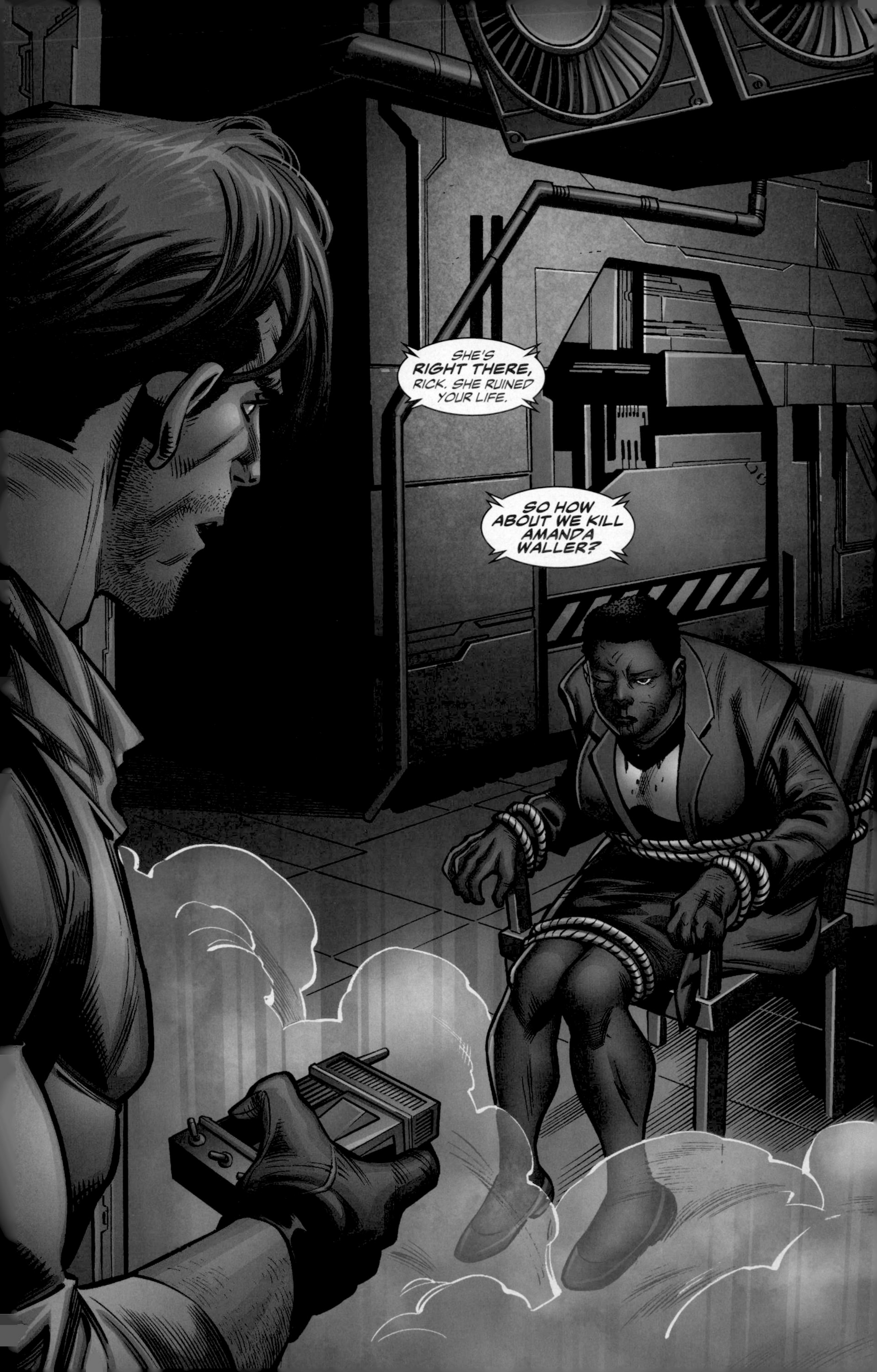
SHE'S RIGHT THERE, RICK. SHE RUINED YOUR LIFE.
SO HOW ABOUT WE KILL AMANDA WALLER?

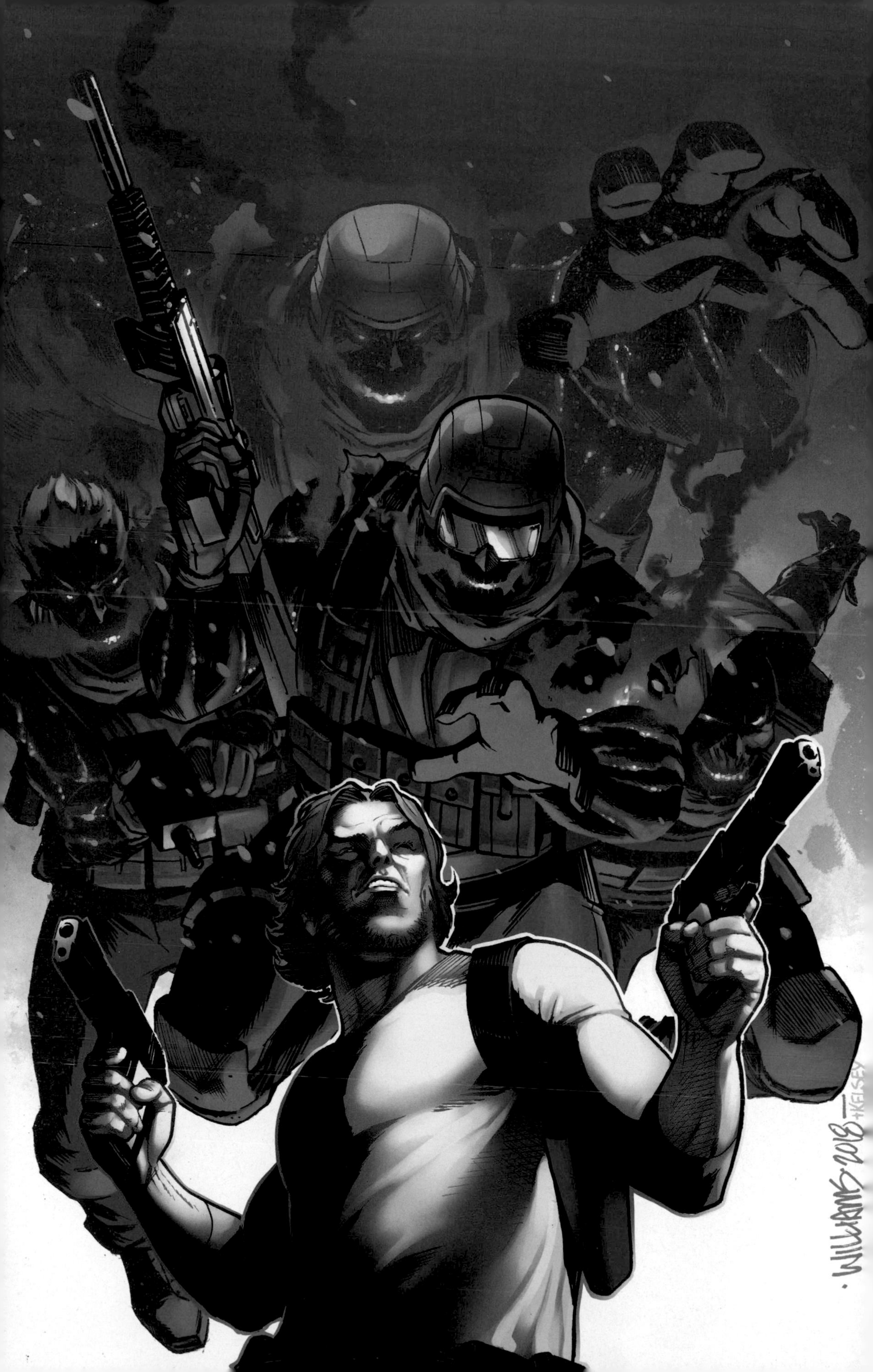
WILLIAMS 2018
+KELSEY

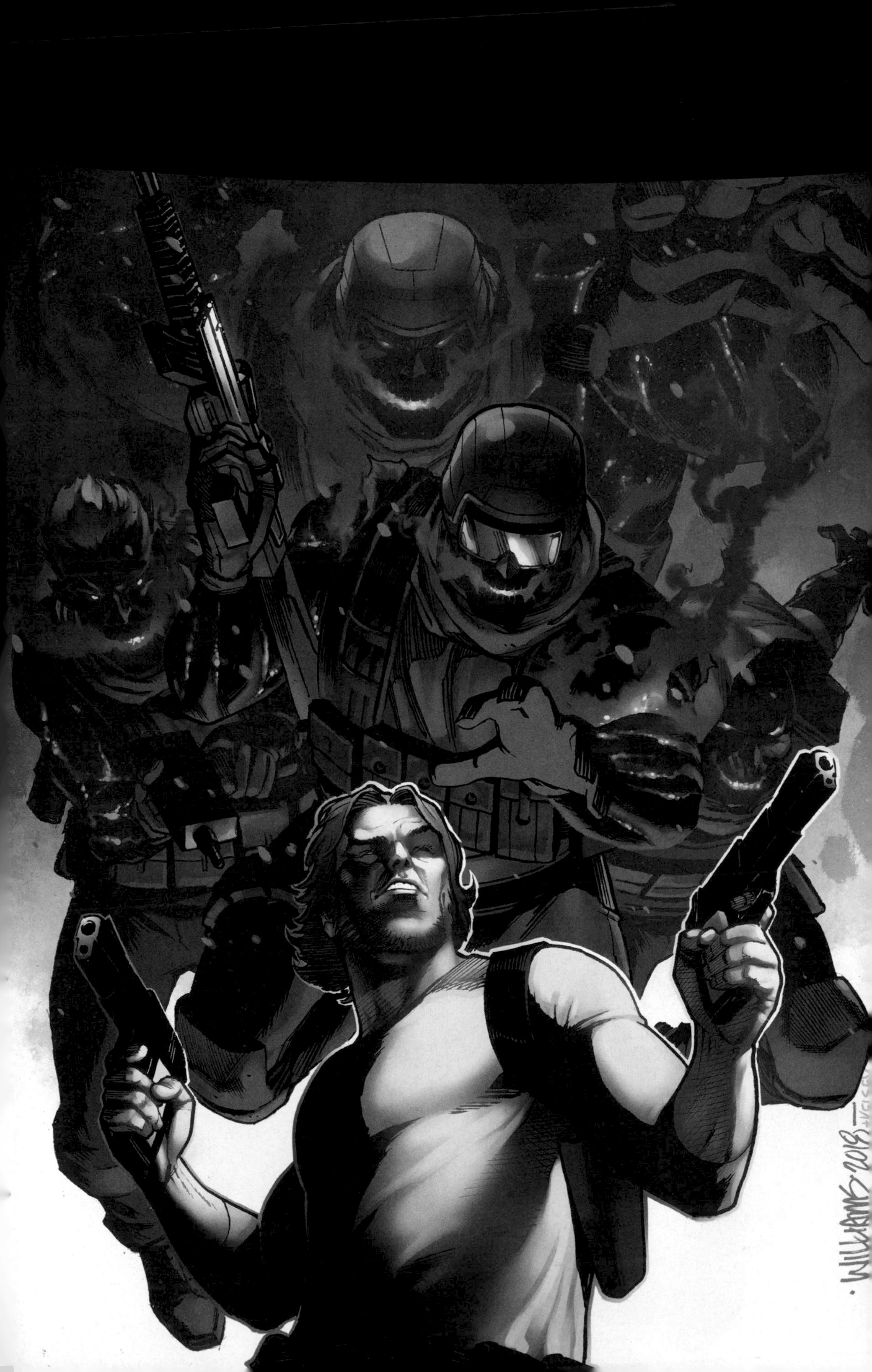
WILLIAMS 2018

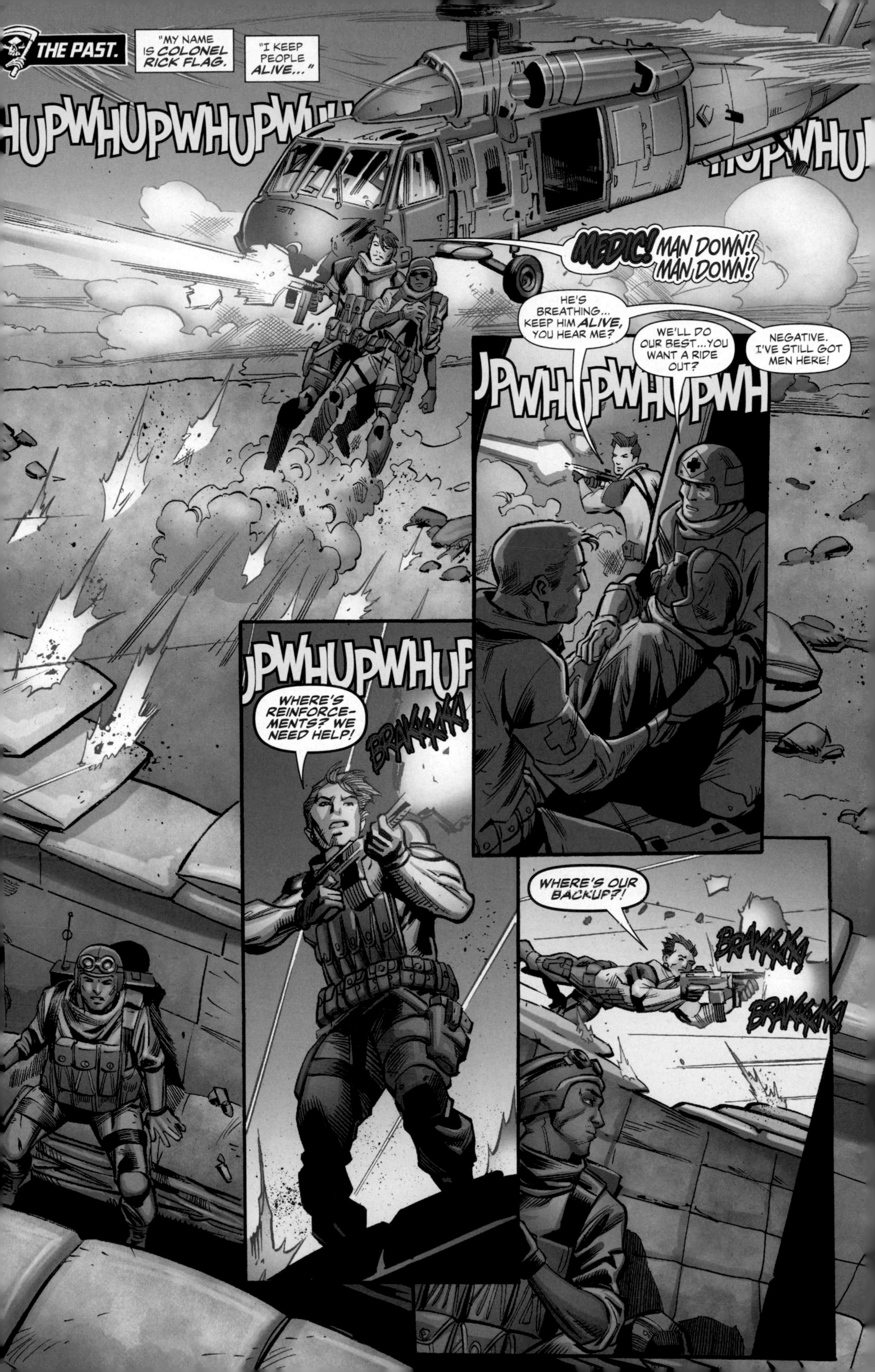
THE PAST.
"MY NAME IS COLONEL RICK FLAG.
"I KEEP PEOPLE ALIVE..."
WHUPWHUPWHUPWHU
WHUPWHU
MEDIC! MAN DOWN! MAN DOWN!
UPWHUPWHUPWH
HE'S BREATHING... KEEP HIM ALIVE, YOU HEAR ME?
WE'LL DO OUR BEST...YOU WANT A RIDE OUT?
NEGATIVE. I'VE STILL GOT MEN HERE!
UPWHUPWHUP
WHERE'S REINFORCE-MENTS? WE NEED HELP!
BRAKKAKKA!
WHERE'S OUR BACKUP?!
BRAKKAKKA
BRAKKAKKA!

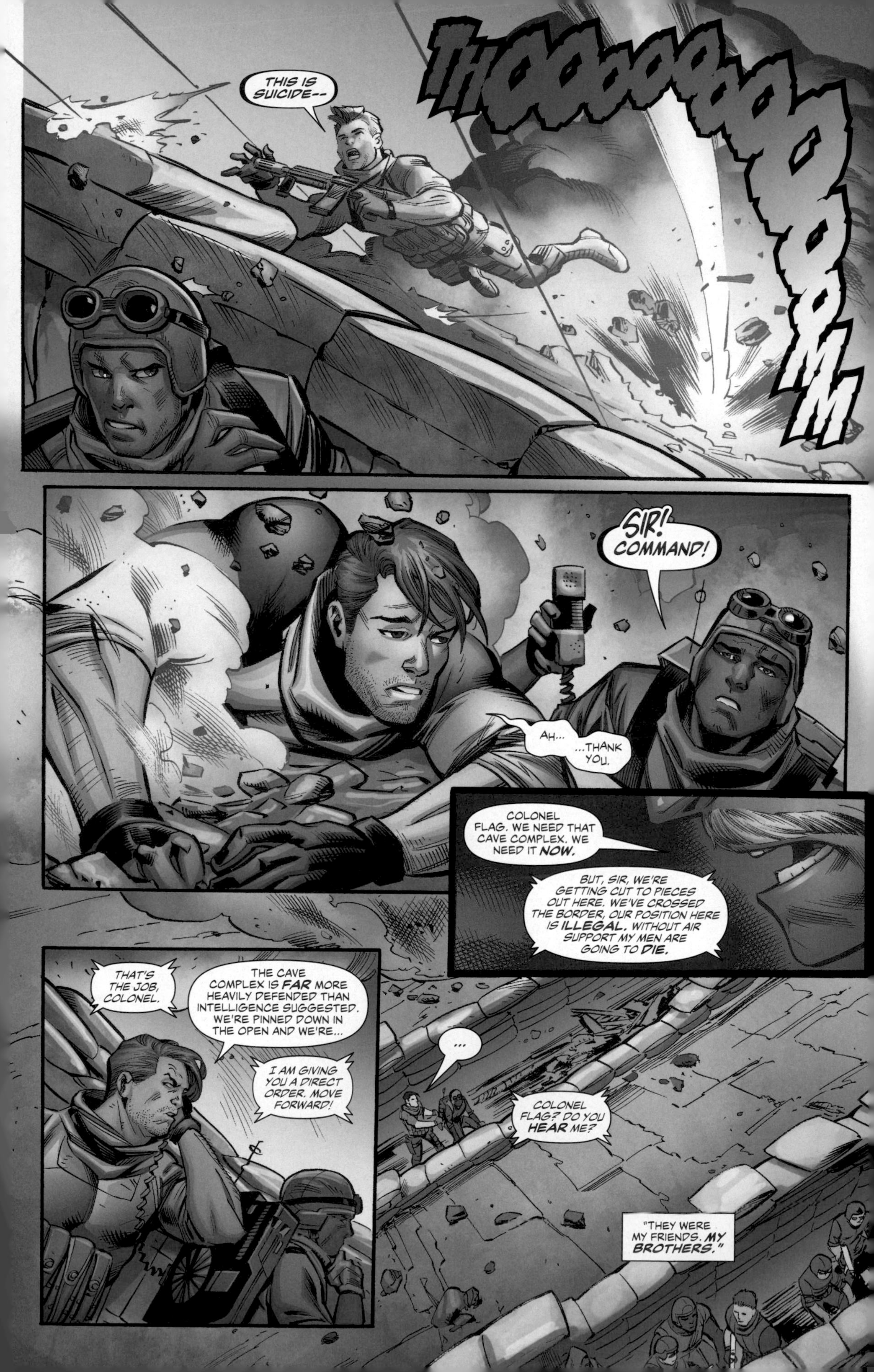
THIS IS SUICIDE--
THOOOOOOOOOOM
SIR! COMMAND!
AH...
...THANK YOU.
COLONEL FLAG. WE NEED THAT CAVE COMPLEX. WE NEED IT NOW.
BUT, SIR, WE'RE GETTING CUT TO PIECES OUT HERE. WE'VE CROSSED THE BORDER, OUR POSITION HERE IS ILLEGAL. WITHOUT AIR SUPPORT MY MEN ARE GOING TO DIE.
THAT'S THE JOB, COLONEL.
THE CAVE COMPLEX IS FAR MORE HEAVILY DEFENDED THAN INTELLIGENCE SUGGESTED. WE'RE PINNED DOWN IN THE OPEN AND WE'RE...
I AM GIVING YOU A DIRECT ORDER. MOVE FORWARD!
...
COLONEL FLAG? DO YOU HEAR ME?
"THEY WERE MY FRIENDS. MY BROTHERS."

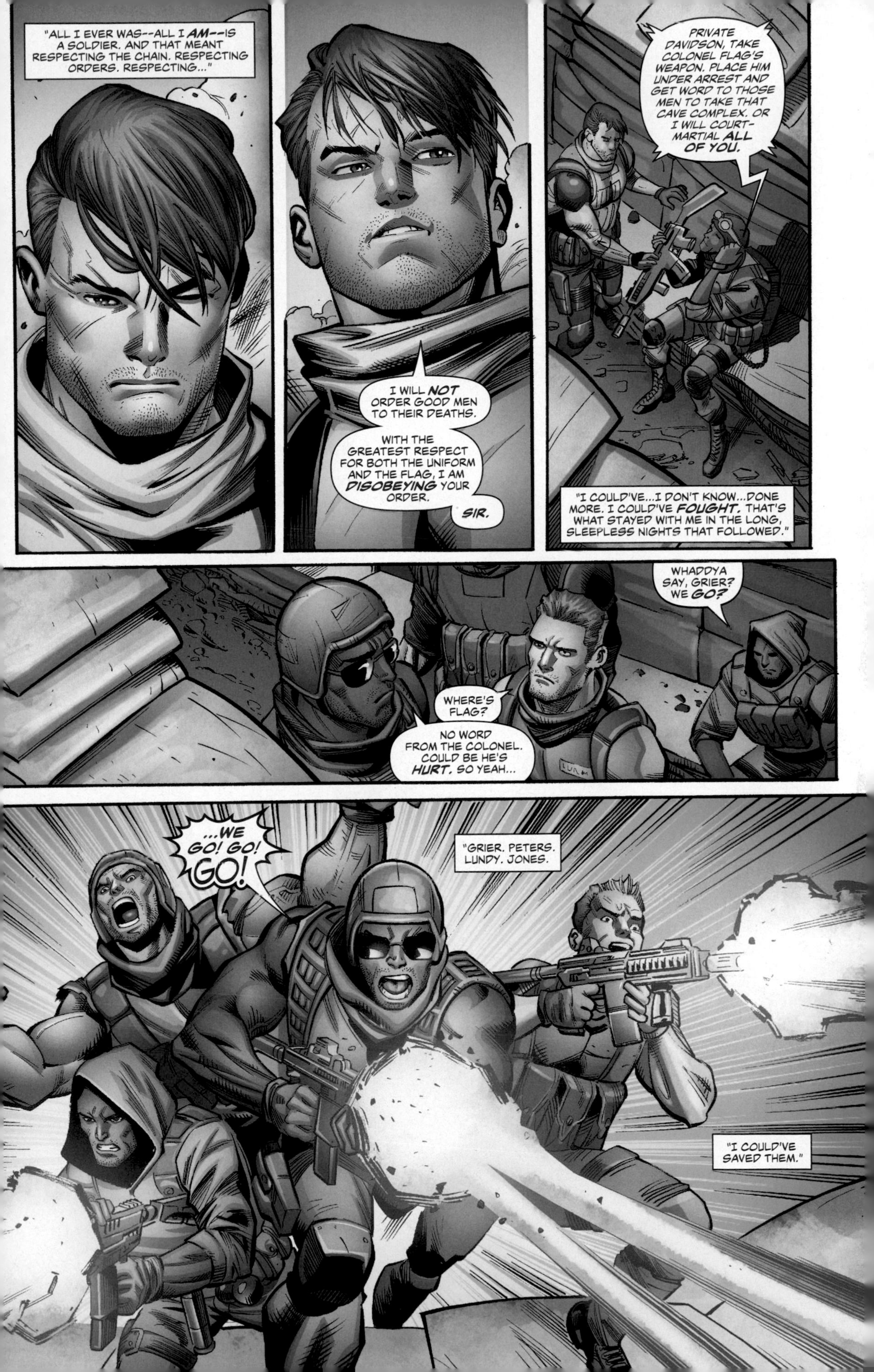
"ALL I EVER WAS--ALL I AM--IS A SOLDIER. AND THAT MEANT RESPECTING THE CHAIN. RESPECTING ORDERS. RESPECTING..."
I WILL NOT ORDER GOOD MEN TO THEIR DEATHS.
WITH THE GREATEST RESPECT FOR BOTH THE UNIFORM AND THE FLAG, I AM DISOBEYING YOUR ORDER.
SIR.
PRIVATE DAVIDSON, TAKE COLONEL FLAG'S WEAPON. PLACE HIM UNDER ARREST AND GET WORD TO THOSE MEN TO TAKE THAT CAVE COMPLEX. OR I WILL COURT-MARTIAL ALL OF YOU.
"I COULD'VE...I DON'T KNOW...DONE MORE. I COULD'VE FOUGHT. THAT'S WHAT STAYED WITH ME IN THE LONG, SLEEPLESS NIGHTS THAT FOLLOWED."
WHADDYA SAY, GRIER? WE GO?
WHERE'S FLAG?
NO WORD FROM THE COLONEL. COULD BE HE'S HURT. SO YEAH...
...WE GO! GO! GO!
"GRIER. PETERS. LUNDY. JONES.
"I COULD'VE SAVED THEM."

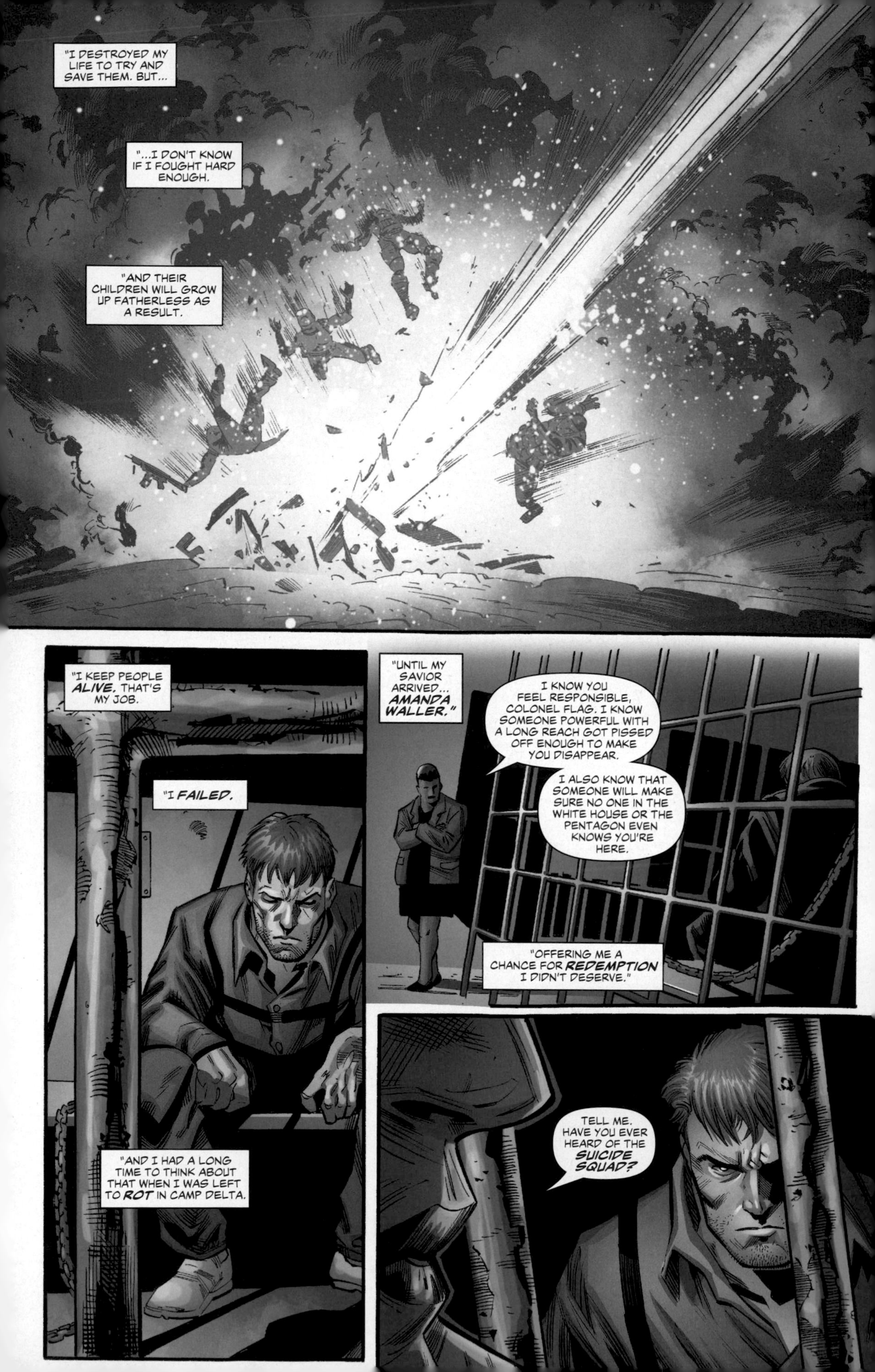
"I DESTROYED MY LIFE TO TRY AND SAVE THEM. BUT...
"...I DON'T KNOW IF I FOUGHT HARD ENOUGH.
"AND THEIR CHILDREN WILL GROW UP FATHERLESS AS A RESULT.
"I KEEP PEOPLE ALIVE. THAT'S MY JOB.
"I FAILED.
"AND I HAD A LONG TIME TO THINK ABOUT THAT WHEN I WAS LEFT TO ROT IN CAMP DELTA.
"UNTIL MY SAVIOR ARRIVED... AMANDA WALLER."
I KNOW YOU FEEL RESPONSIBLE, COLONEL FLAG. I KNOW SOMEONE POWERFUL WITH A LONG REACH GOT PISSED OFF ENOUGH TO MAKE YOU DISAPPEAR.
I ALSO KNOW THAT SOMEONE WILL MAKE SURE NO ONE IN THE WHITE HOUSE OR THE PENTAGON EVEN KNOWS YOU'RE HERE.
"OFFERING ME A CHANCE FOR REDEMPTION I DIDN'T DESERVE."
TELL ME. HAVE YOU EVER HEARD OF THE SUICIDE SQUAD?

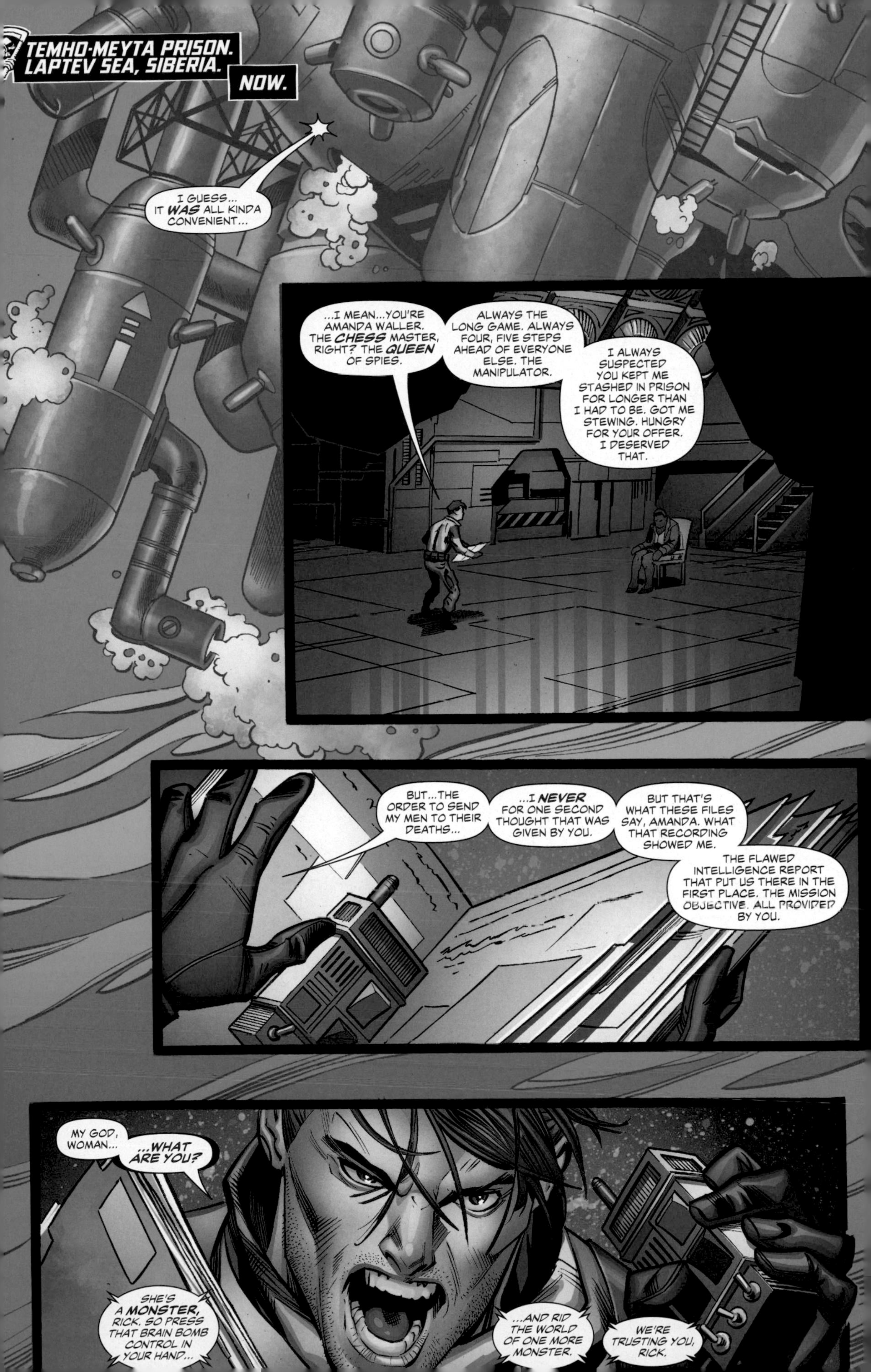
TEMHO-MEYTA PRISON. LAPTEV SEA, SIBERIA.
NOW.
I GUESS... IT WAS ALL KINDA CONVENIENT...
...I MEAN...YOU'RE AMANDA WALLER. THE CHESS MASTER, RIGHT? THE QUEEN OF SPIES.
ALWAYS THE LONG GAME. ALWAYS FOUR, FIVE STEPS AHEAD OF EVERYONE ELSE. THE MANIPULATOR.
I ALWAYS SUSPECTED YOU KEPT ME STASHED IN PRISON FOR LONGER THAN I HAD TO BE. GOT ME STEWING. HUNGRY FOR YOUR OFFER. I DESERVED THAT.
BUT...THE ORDER TO SEND MY MEN TO THEIR DEATHS...
...I NEVER FOR ONE SECOND THOUGHT THAT WAS GIVEN BY YOU.
BUT THAT'S WHAT THESE FILES SAY, AMANDA. WHAT THAT RECORDING SHOWED ME.
THE FLAWED INTELLIGENCE REPORT THAT PUT US THERE IN THE FIRST PLACE. THE MISSION OBJECTIVE. ALL PROVIDED BY YOU.
MY GOD, WOMAN...
...WHAT ARE YOU?
SHE'S A MONSTER, RICK, SO PRESS THAT BRAIN BOMB CONTROL IN YOUR HAND...
...AND RID THE WORLD OF ONE MORE MONSTER.
WE'RE TRUSTING YOU, RICK.

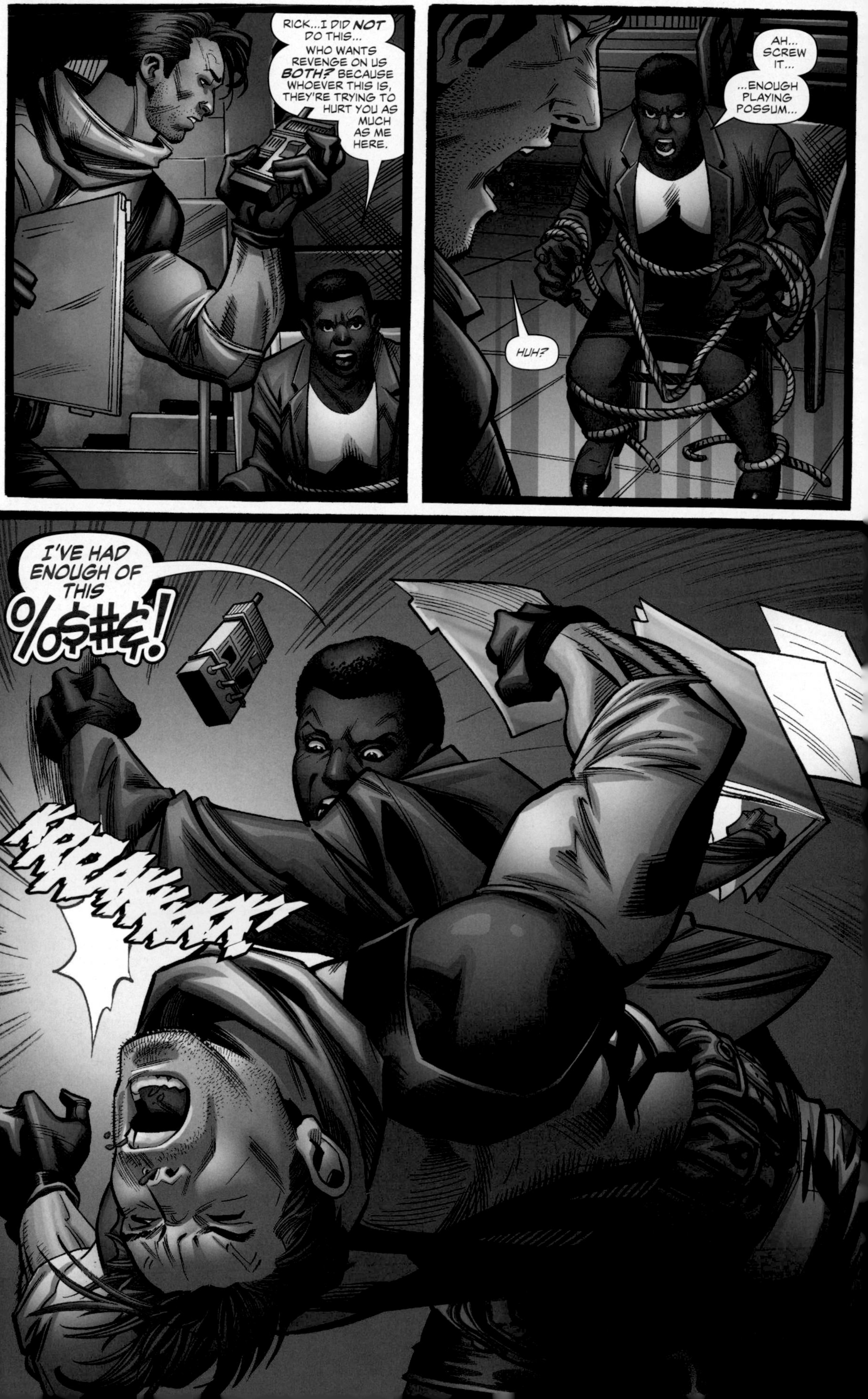
RICK...I DID NOT DO THIS... WHO WANTS REVENGE ON US BOTH? BECAUSE WHOEVER THIS IS, THEY'RE TRYING TO HURT YOU AS MUCH AS ME HERE.
AH... SCREW IT...
...ENOUGH PLAYING POSSUM...
HUH?
I'VE HAD ENOUGH OF THIS %$#&!
KRRAKKKK!

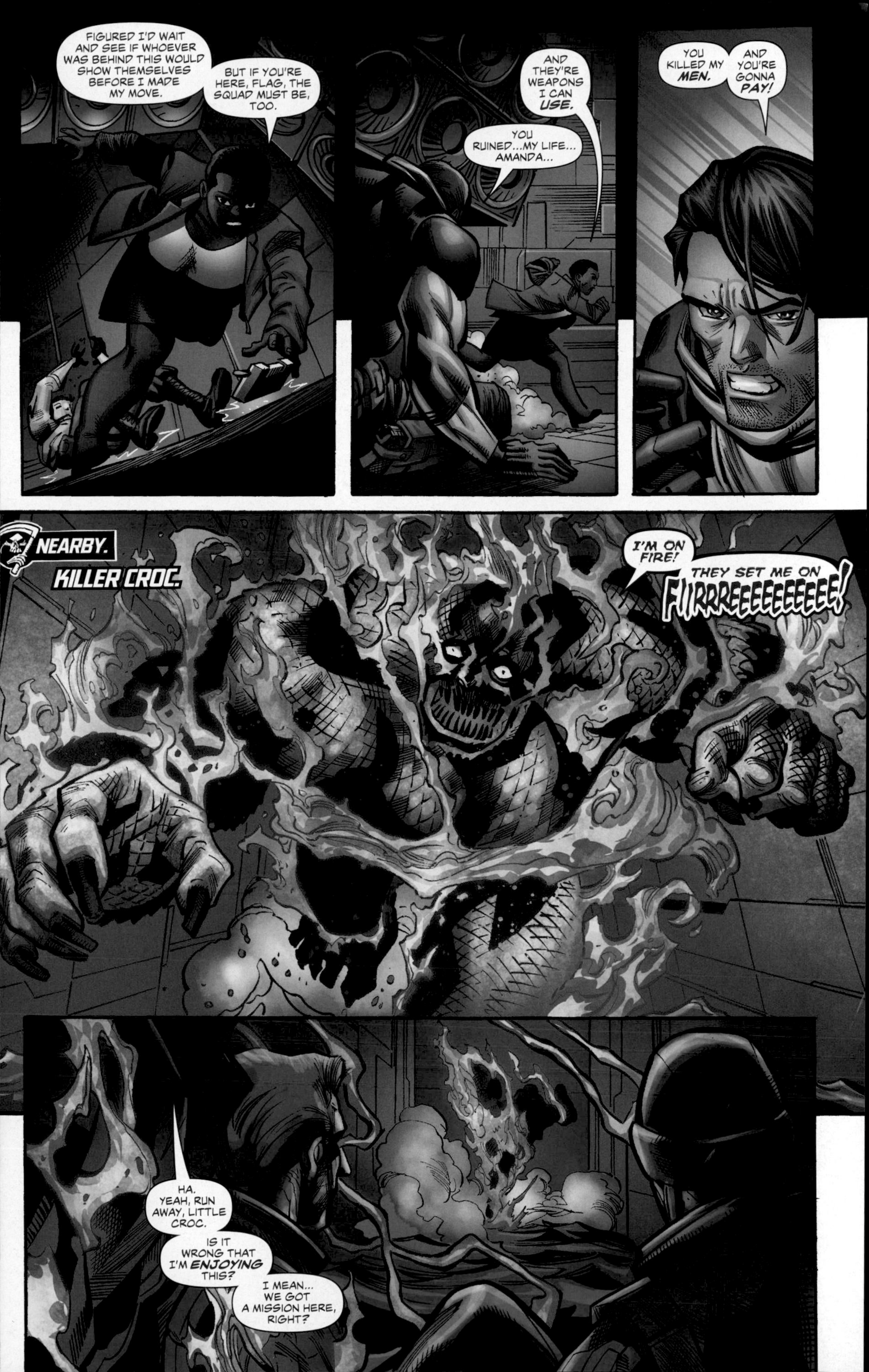
FIGURED I'D WAIT AND SEE IF WHOEVER WAS BEHIND THIS WOULD SHOW THEMSELVES BEFORE I MADE MY MOVE.
BUT IF YOU'RE HERE, FLAG, THE SQUAD MUST BE, TOO.
AND THEY'RE WEAPONS I CAN USE.
YOU RUINED...MY LIFE... AMANDA...
YOU KILLED MY MEN.
AND YOU'RE GONNA PAY!
NEARBY.
KILLER CROC.
I'M ON FIRE!
THEY SET ME ON FIIRRREEEEEEEEEE!
HA. YEAH, RUN AWAY, LITTLE CROC.
IS IT WRONG THAT I'M ENJOYING THIS?
I MEAN... WE GOT A MISSION HERE, RIGHT?

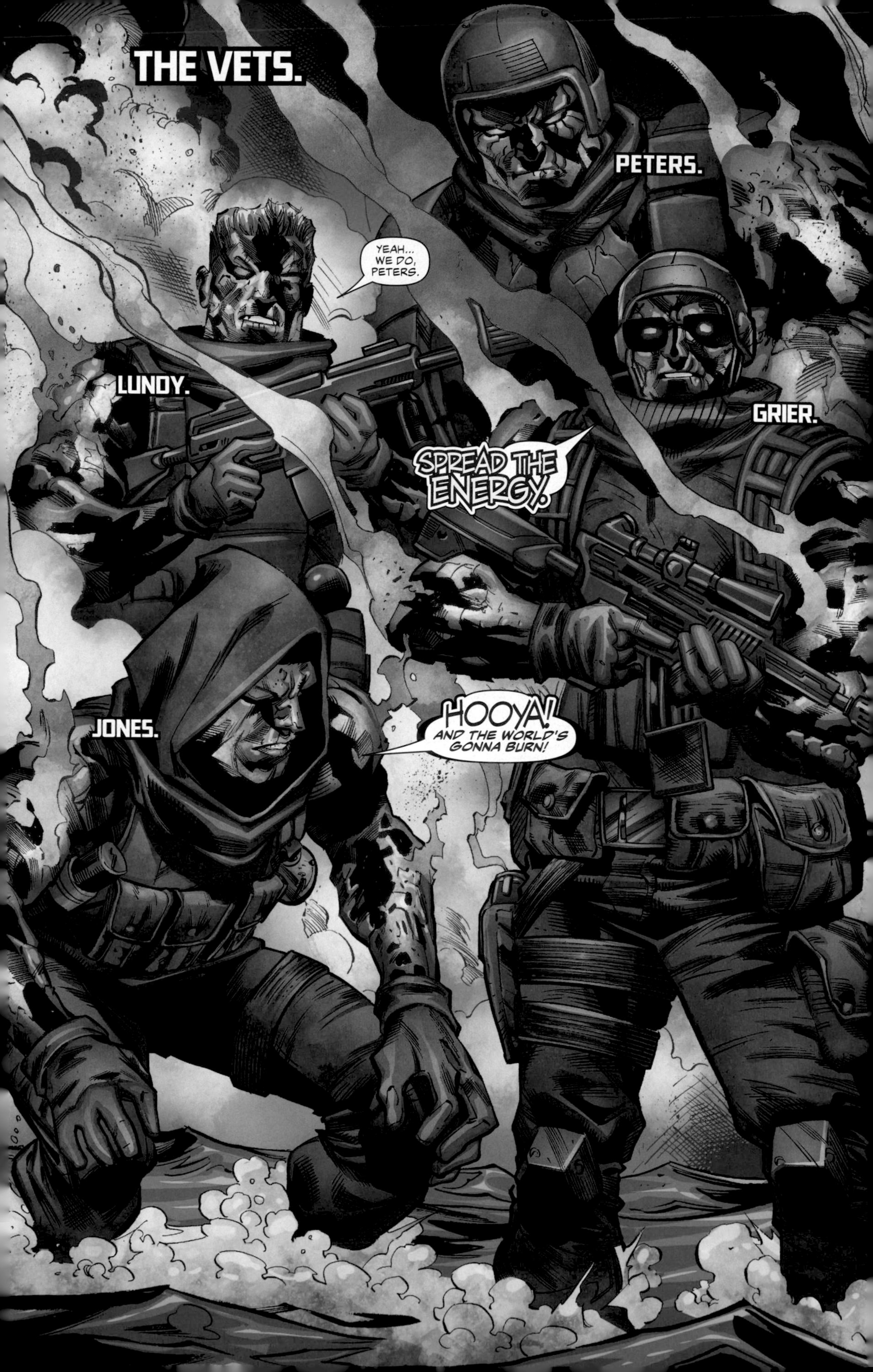
THE VETS.
PETERS.
YEAH... WE DO, PETERS.
LUNDY.
GRIER.
SPREAD THE ENERGY.
JONES.
HOOYA! AND THE WORLD'S GONNA BURN!

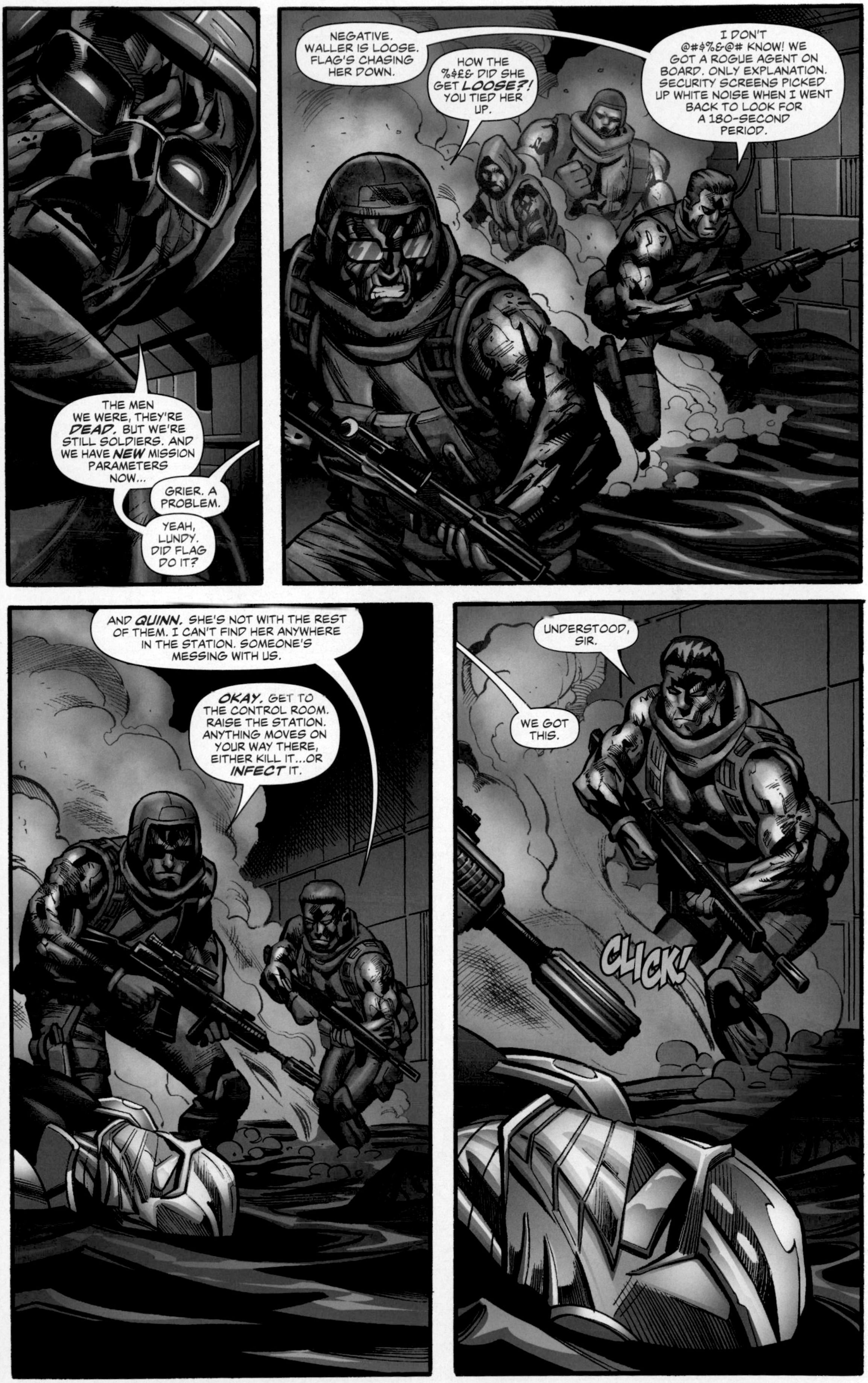

THE MEN WE WERE, THEY'RE DEAD. BUT WE'RE STILL SOLDIERS. AND WE HAVE NEW MISSION PARAMETERS NOW...
GRIER. A PROBLEM.
YEAH, LUNDY. DID FLAG DO IT?
NEGATIVE. WALLER IS LOOSE. FLAG'S CHASING HER DOWN.
HOW THE %$££ DID SHE GET LOOSE?! YOU TIED HER UP.
I DON'T @#$%&@# KNOW! WE GOT A ROGUE AGENT ON BOARD. ONLY EXPLANATION. SECURITY SCREENS PICKED UP WHITE NOISE WHEN I WENT BACK TO LOOK FOR A 180-SECOND PERIOD.
AND QUINN. SHE'S NOT WITH THE REST OF THEM. I CAN'T FIND HER ANYWHERE IN THE STATION. SOMEONE'S MESSING WITH US.
OKAY. GET TO THE CONTROL ROOM. RAISE THE STATION. ANYTHING MOVES ON YOUR WAY THERE, EITHER KILL IT...OR INFECT IT.
UNDERSTOOD, SIR.
WE GOT THIS.
CLICK!

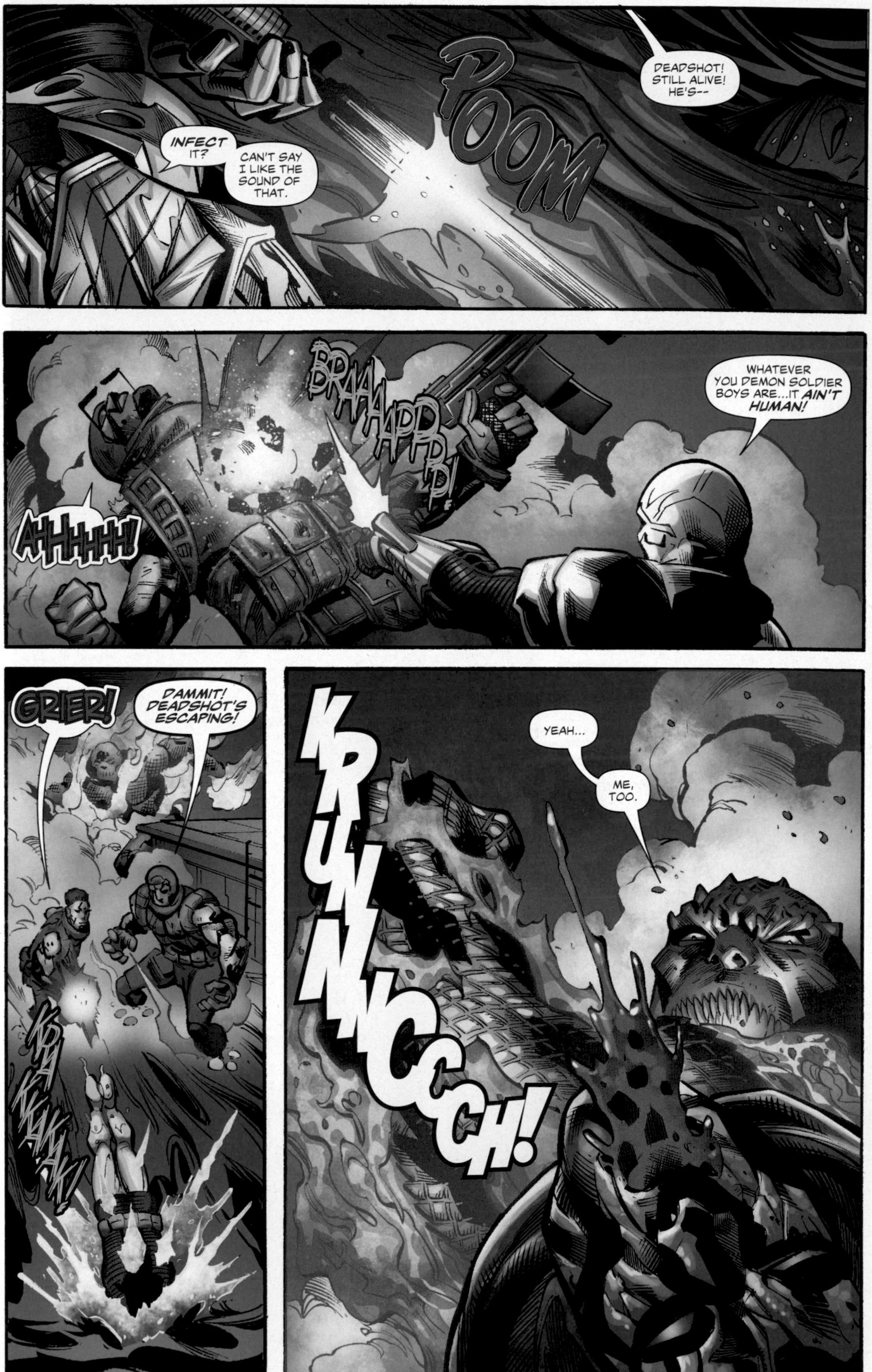
INFECT IT?
CAN'T SAY I LIKE THE SOUND OF THAT.
POOM
DEADSHOT! STILL ALIVE! HE'S--
BRAAAAPPPPP!
WHATEVER YOU DEMON SOLDIER BOYS ARE...IT AIN'T HUMAN!
AHHHHHH!
GRIER!
DAMMIT! DEADSHOT'S ESCAPING!
KRAKAKAKAK!
KRUNNCCCH!
YEAH...
ME, TOO.

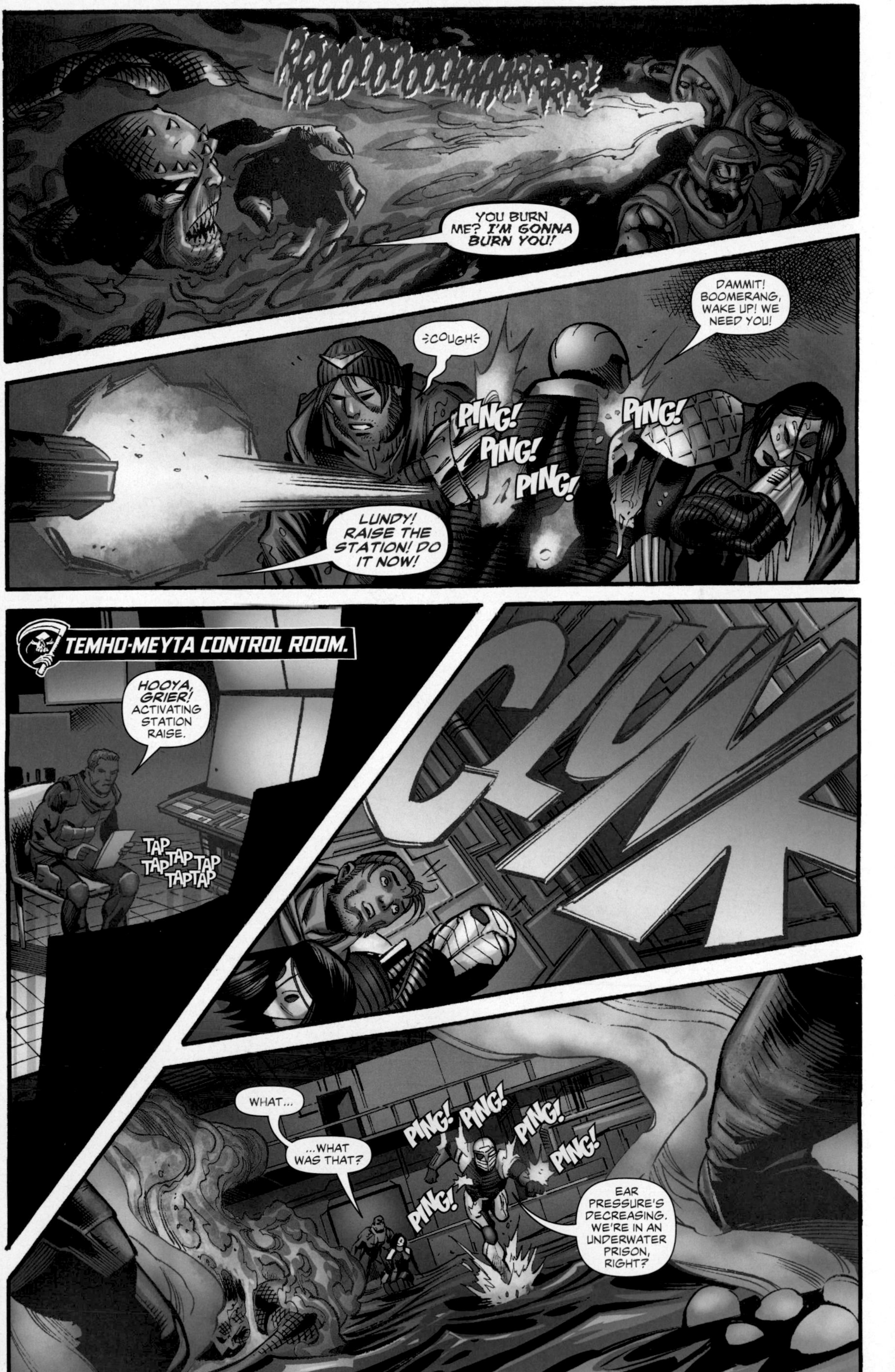
RROOOOOOOAARRRR!
YOU BURN ME? I'M GONNA BURN YOU!
DAMMIT! BOOMERANG, WAKE UP! WE NEED YOU!
COUGH
PING! PING! PING! PING!
LUNDY! RAISE THE STATION! DO IT NOW!
TEMHO-MEYTA CONTROL ROOM.
HOOYA, GRIER! ACTIVATING STATION RAISE.
TAP TAP TAP TAP TAPTAP
CLUNK
WHAT...
...WHAT WAS THAT?
PING! PING! PING! PING! PING!
EAR PRESSURE'S DECREASING. WE'RE IN AN UNDERWATER PRISON, RIGHT?

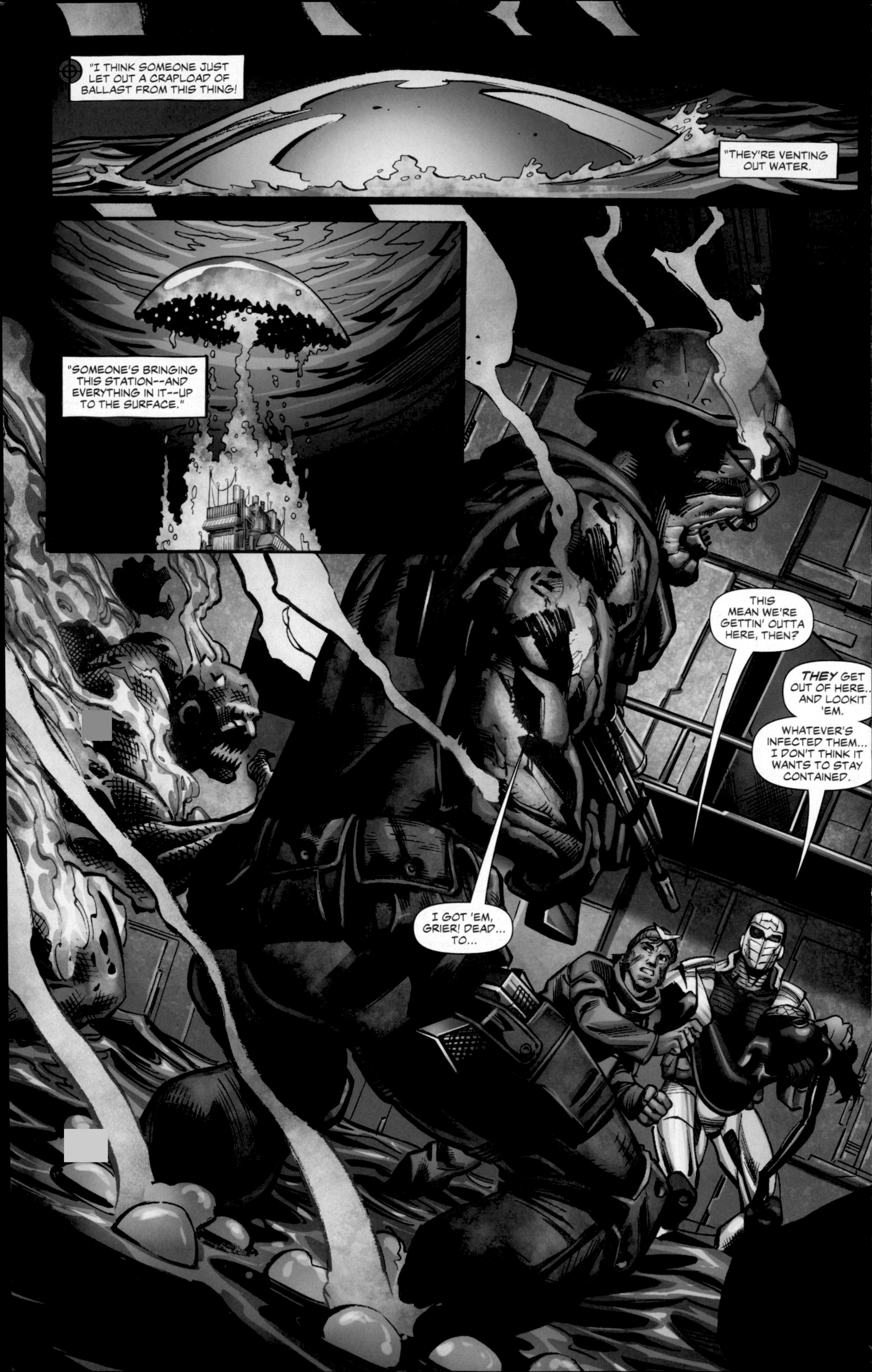
"I THINK SOMEONE JUST LET OUT A CRAPLOAD OF BALLAST FROM THIS THING!
"THEY'RE VENTING OUT WATER.
"SOMEONE'S BRINGING THIS STATION--AND EVERYTHING IN IT--UP TO THE SURFACE."
THIS MEAN WE'RE GETTIN' OUTTA HERE, THEN?
THEY GET OUT OF HERE... AND LOOKIT 'EM.
WHATEVER'S INFECTED THEM... I DON'T THINK IT WANTS TO STAY CONTAINED.
I GOT 'EM, GRIER! DEAD... TO...

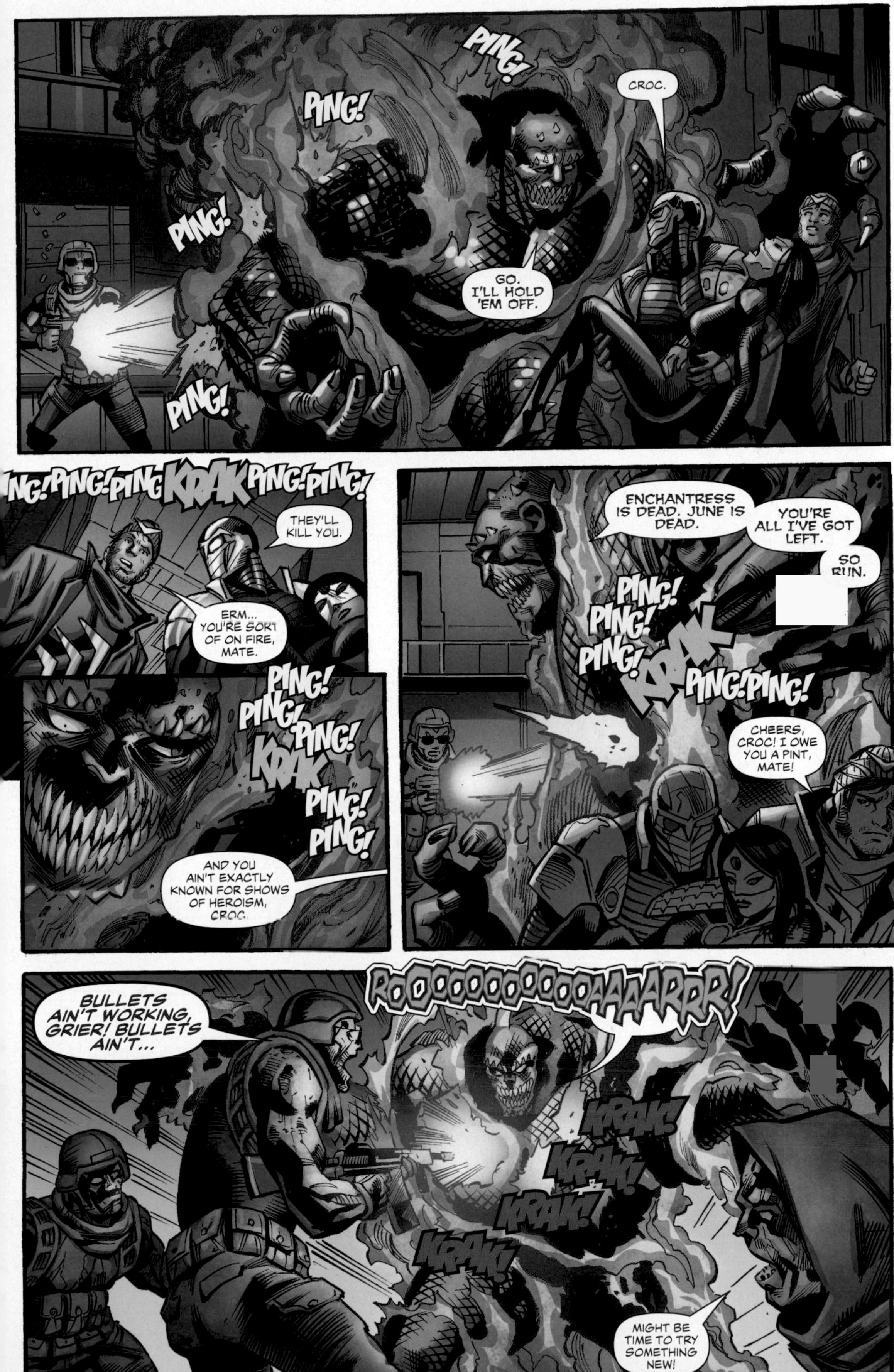
PING!
PING!
CROC.
PING!
GO. I'LL HOLD 'EM OFF.
PING!
NG!PING!PING KRAK PING!PING!
THEY'LL KILL YOU.
ERM... YOU'RE SORT OF ON FIRE, MATE.
PING!
PING!
PING!
KRAK
PING!
PING!
AND YOU AIN'T EXACTLY KNOWN FOR SHOWS OF HEROISM, CROC.
ENCHANTRESS IS DEAD. JUNE IS DEAD.
YOU'RE ALL I'VE GOT LEFT.
SO RUN.
PING!
PING!
PING!
KRAK
PING!PING!
CHEERS, CROC! I OWE YOU A PINT, MATE!
BULLETS AIN'T WORKING, GRIER! BULLETS AIN'T...
ROOOOOOOOOOOOAAAARRR!
KRAK!
KRAK!
KRAK!
KRAK!
MIGHT BE TIME TO TRY SOMETHING NEW!

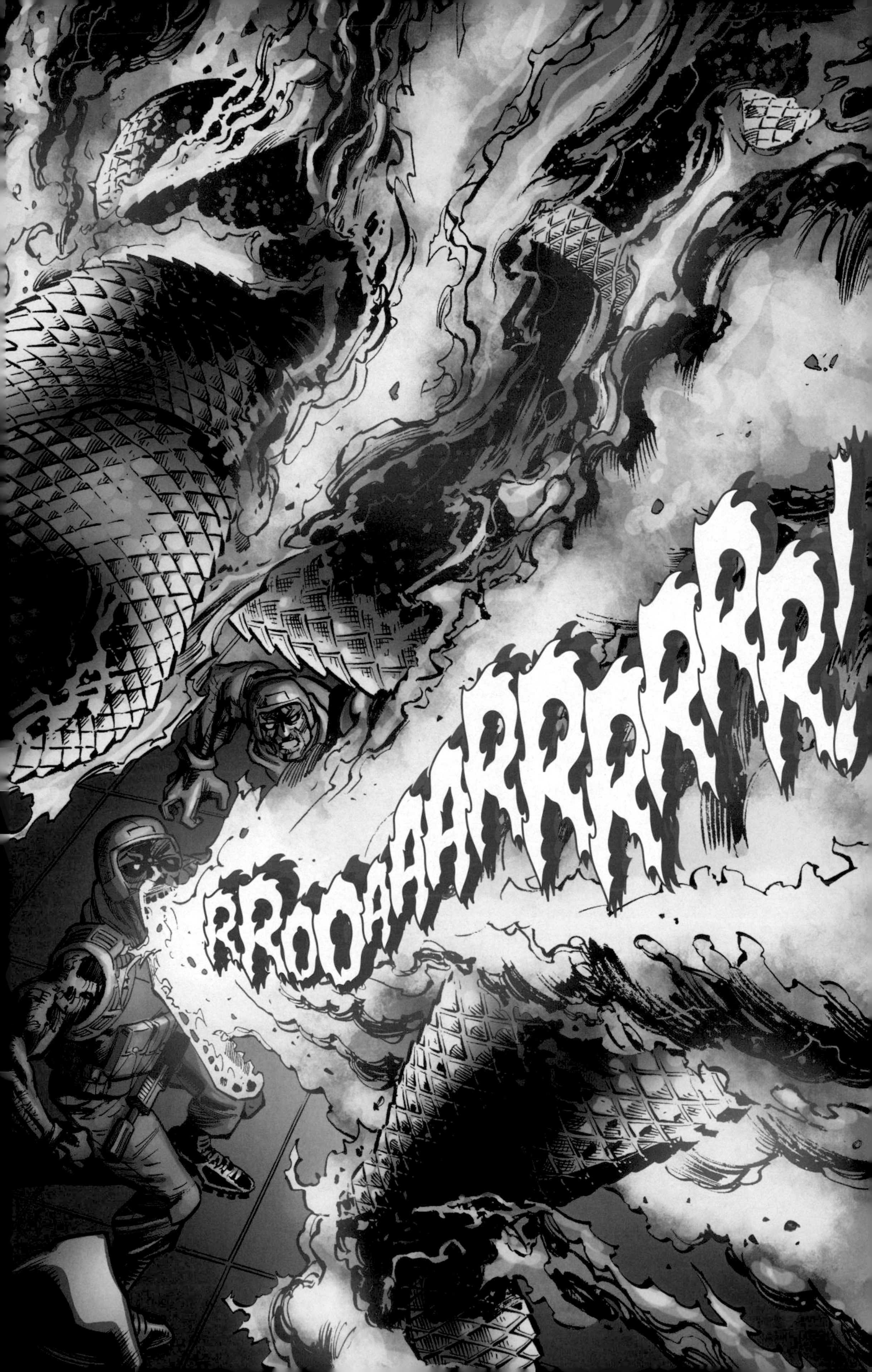
RROOAHRRRRRR!

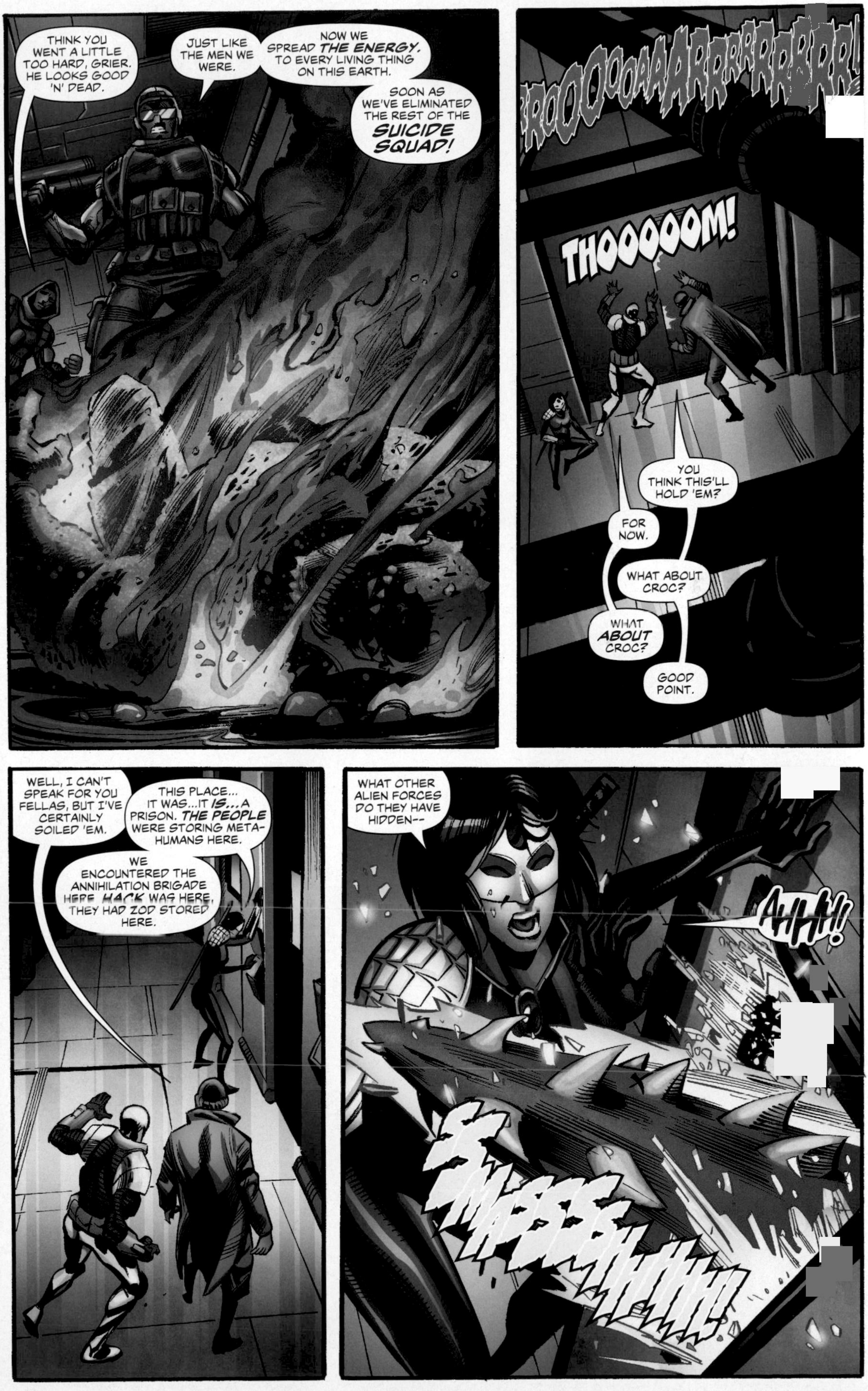
THINK YOU WENT A LITTLE TOO HARD, GRIER. HE LOOKS GOOD 'N' DEAD.
JUST LIKE THE MEN WE WERE.
NOW WE SPREAD THE ENERGY. TO EVERY LIVING THING ON THIS EARTH.
SOON AS WE'VE ELIMINATED THE REST OF THE SUICIDE SQUAD!
RROOOOOAAARRRRRRRRR!
THOOOOOM!
YOU THINK THIS'LL HOLD 'EM?
FOR NOW.
WHAT ABOUT CROC?
WHAT ABOUT CROC?
GOOD POINT.
WELL, I CAN'T SPEAK FOR YOU FELLAS, BUT I'VE CERTAINLY SOILED 'EM.
THIS PLACE... IT WAS...IT IS... A PRISON. THE PEOPLE WERE STORING META-HUMANS HERE.
WE ENCOUNTERED THE ANNIHILATION BRIGADE HERE. HACK WAS HERE. THEY HAD ZOD STORED HERE.
WHAT OTHER ALIEN FORCES DO THEY HAVE HIDDEN--
AHHH!!
SMASSSHHHH!

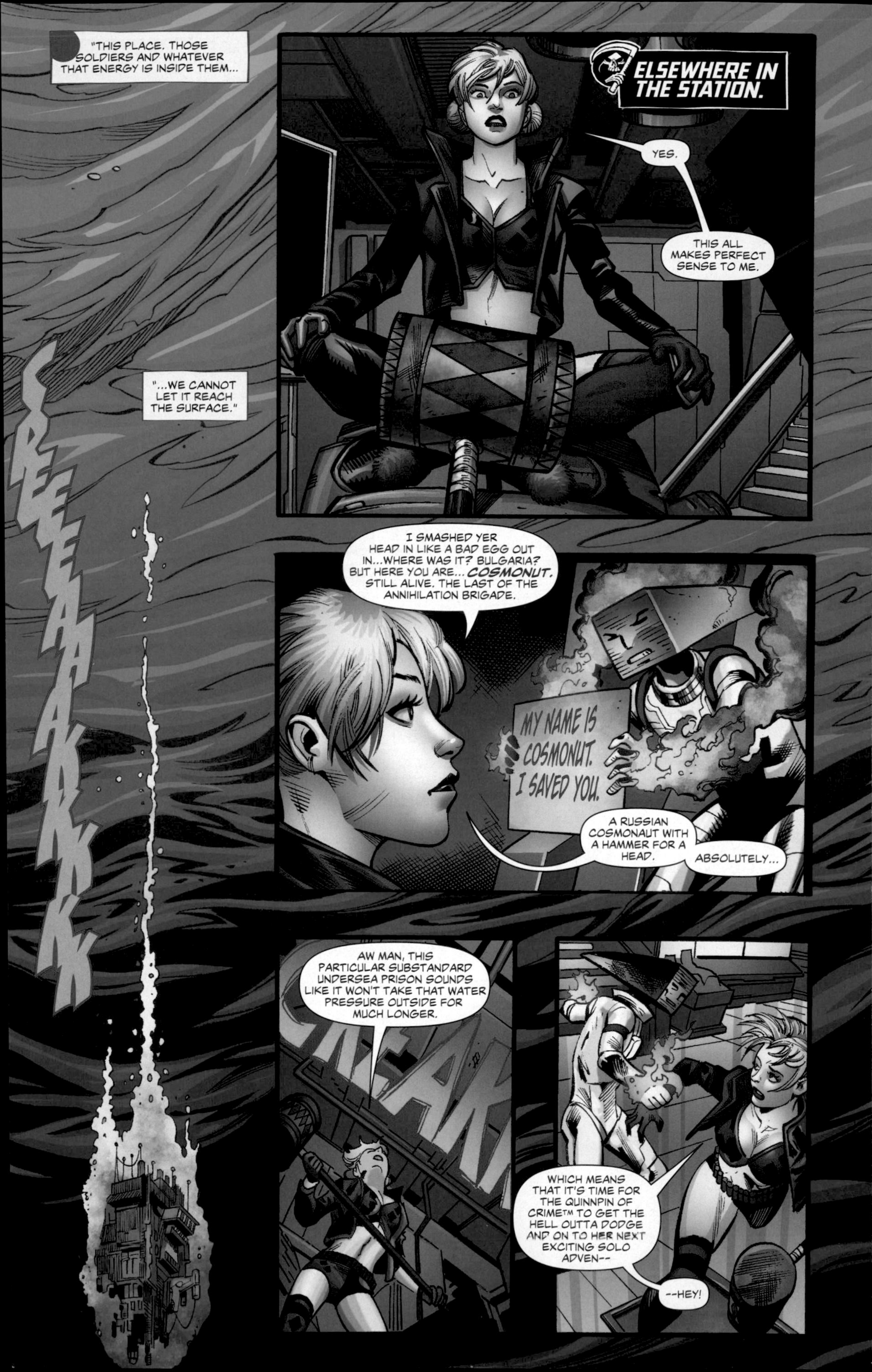
"THIS PLACE. THOSE SOLDIERS AND WHATEVER THAT ENERGY IS INSIDE THEM...
ELSEWHERE IN THE STATION.
YES.
THIS ALL MAKES PERFECT SENSE TO ME.
"...WE CANNOT LET IT REACH THE SURFACE."
I SMASHED YER HEAD IN LIKE A BAD EGG OUT IN...WHERE WAS IT? BULGARIA? BUT HERE YOU ARE... COSMONUT. STILL ALIVE. THE LAST OF THE ANNIHILATION BRIGADE.
MY NAME IS COSMONUT. I SAVED YOU.
A RUSSIAN COSMONAUT WITH A HAMMER FOR A HEAD.
ABSOLUTELY...
AW MAN, THIS PARTICULAR SUBSTANDARD UNDERSEA PRISON SOUNDS LIKE IT WON'T TAKE THAT WATER PRESSURE OUTSIDE FOR MUCH LONGER.
WHICH MEANS THAT IT'S TIME FOR THE QUINNPIN OF CRIME™ TO GET THE HELL OUTTA DODGE AND ON TO HER NEXT EXCITING SOLO ADVEN--
--HEY!

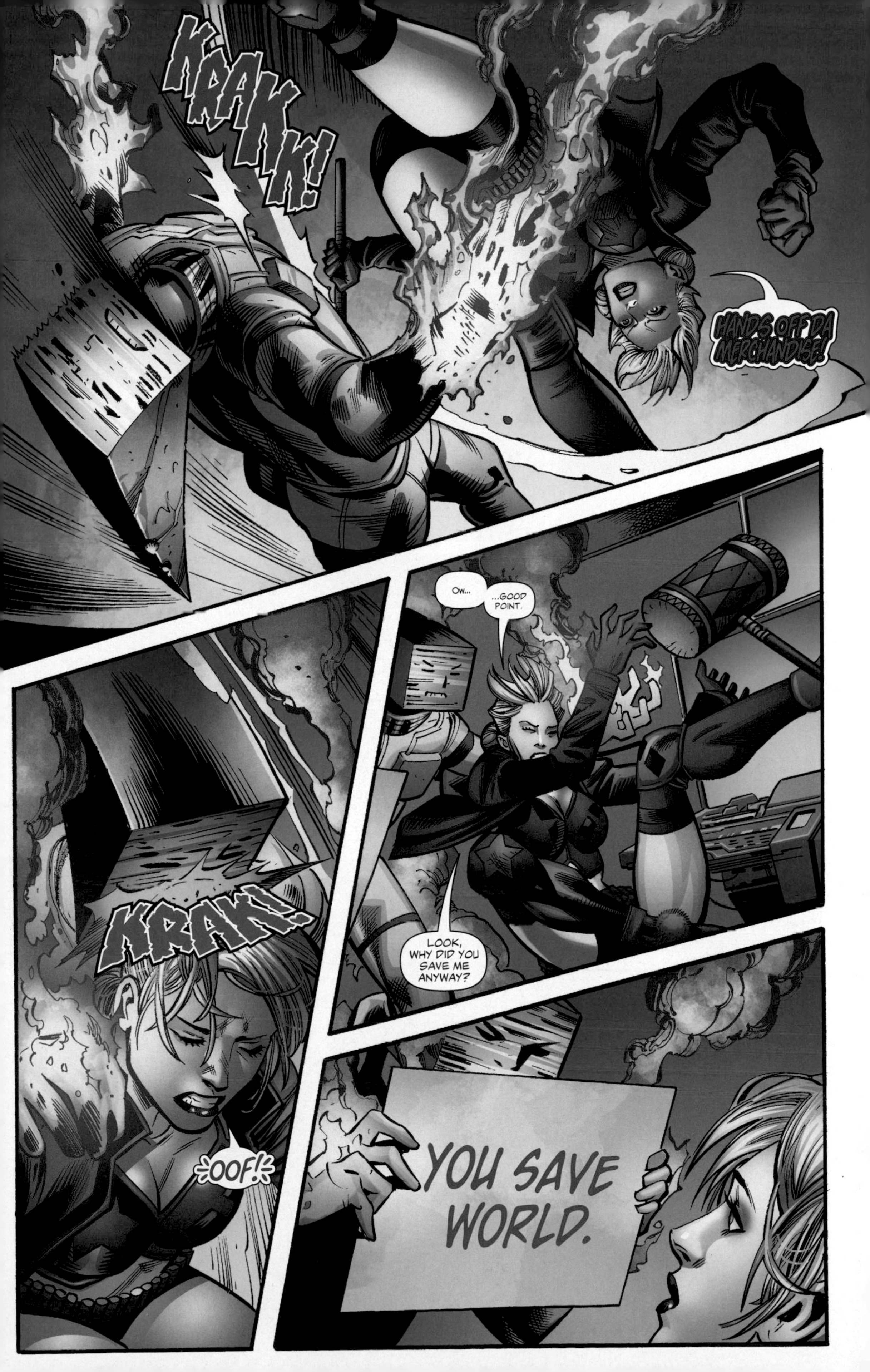
KRAKK!
HANDS OFF DA MERCHANDISE!
KRAK!
OOF!
OW...
...GOOD POINT.
LOOK, WHY DID YOU SAVE ME ANYWAY?
YOU SAVE WORLD.

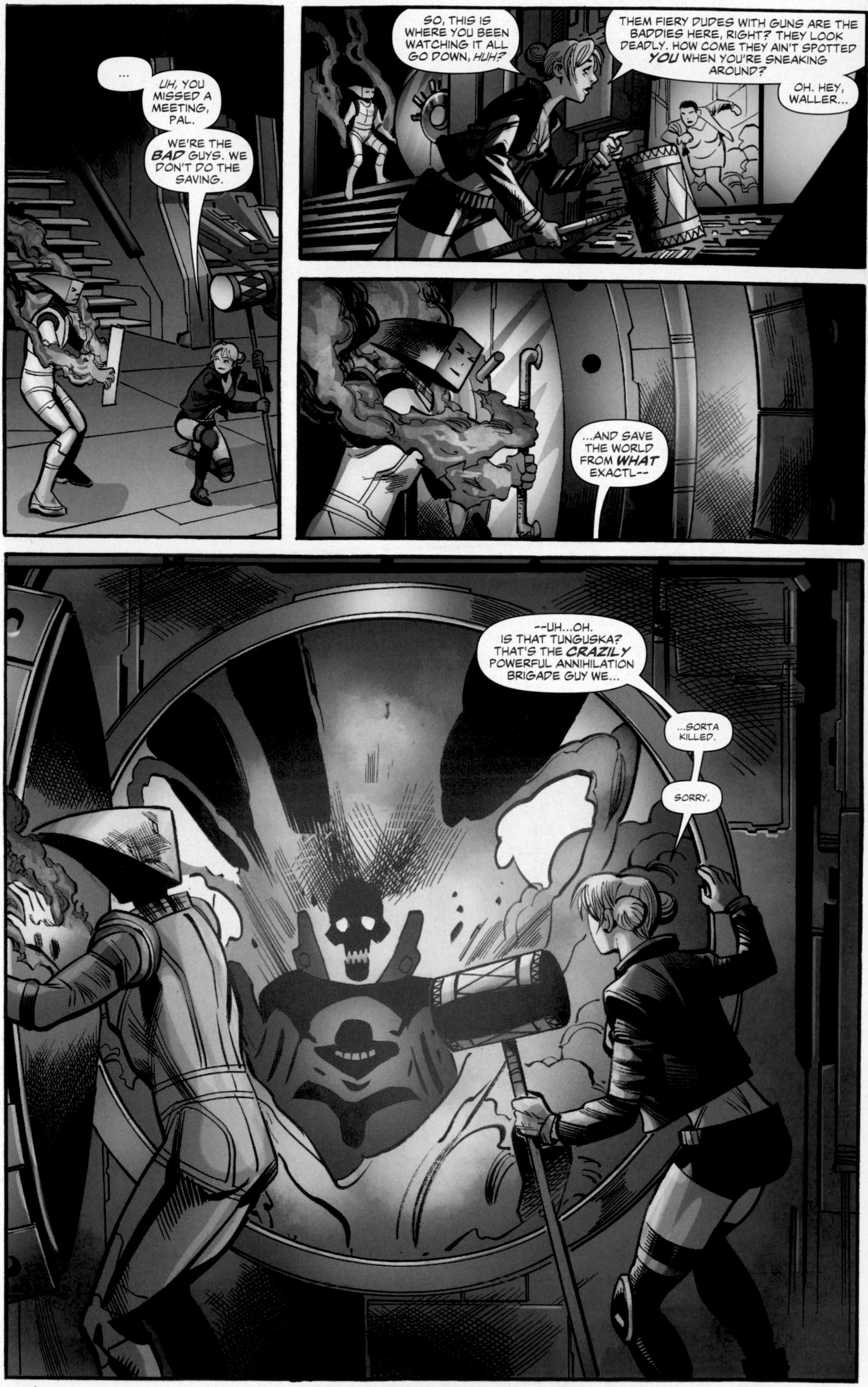
...
UH, YOU MISSED A MEETING, PAL.
WE'RE THE BAD GUYS. WE DON'T DO THE SAVING.
SO, THIS IS WHERE YOU BEEN WATCHING IT ALL GO DOWN, HUH?
THEM FIERY DUDES WITH GUNS ARE THE BADDIES HERE, RIGHT? THEY LOOK DEADLY. HOW COME THEY AIN'T SPOTTED YOU WHEN YOU'RE SNEAKING AROUND?
OH. HEY, WALLER...
...AND SAVE THE WORLD FROM WHAT EXACTL--
--UH...OH. IS THAT TUNGUSKA? THAT'S THE CRAZILY POWERFUL ANNIHILATION BRIGADE GUY WE...
...SORTA KILLED.
SORRY.

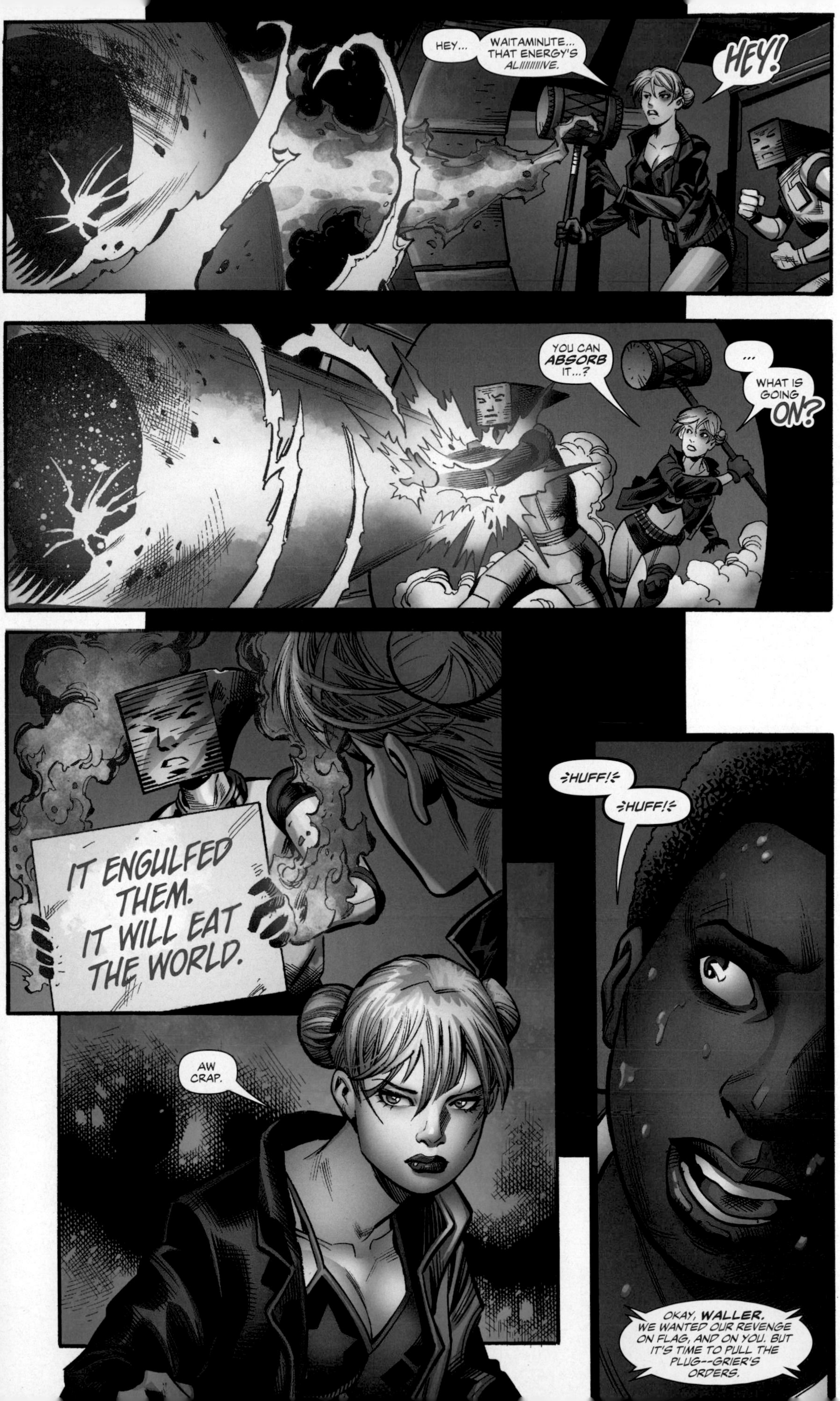
HEY...
WAITAMINUTE... THAT ENERGY'S ALIIIIIIIIVE.
HEY!
YOU CAN ABSORB IT...?
...
WHAT IS GOING ON?
IT ENGULFED THEM. IT WILL EAT THE WORLD.
AW CRAP.
HUFF!
HUFF!
OKAY, WALLER. WE WANTED OUR REVENGE ON FLAG, AND ON YOU. BUT IT'S TIME TO PULL THE PLUG--GRIER'S ORDERS.

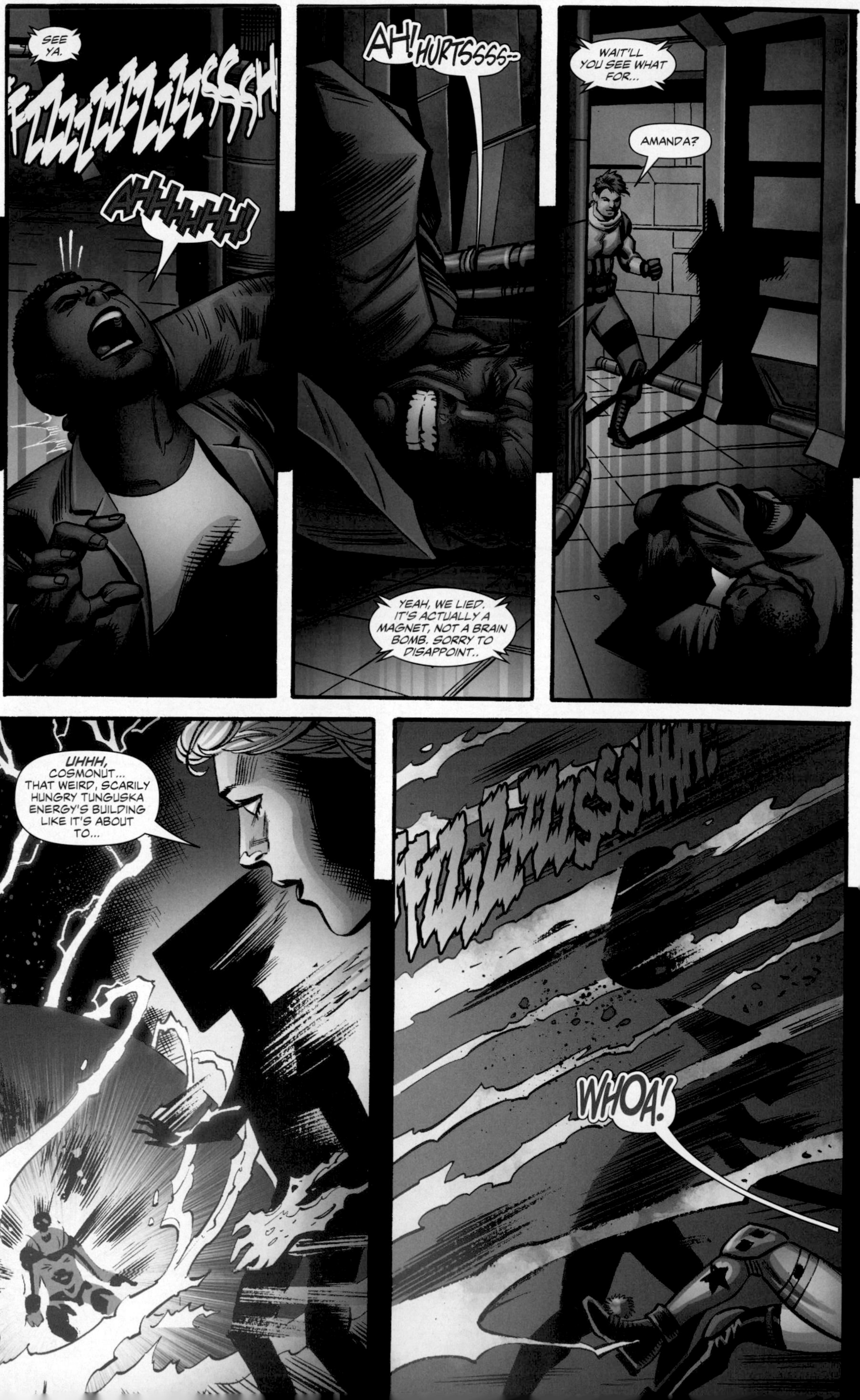
SEE YA.
FZZZZZZZZZZZZSSSH
AHHHHHH!
AH! HURTSSSS--
YEAH, WE LIED. IT'S ACTUALLY A MAGNET, NOT A BRAIN BOMB. SORRY TO DISAPPOINT..
WAIT'LL YOU SEE WHAT FOR...
AMANDA?
UHHH, COSMONUT... THAT WEIRD, SCARILY HUNGRY TUNGUSKA ENERGY'S BUILDING LIKE IT'S ABOUT TO...
WHOA!

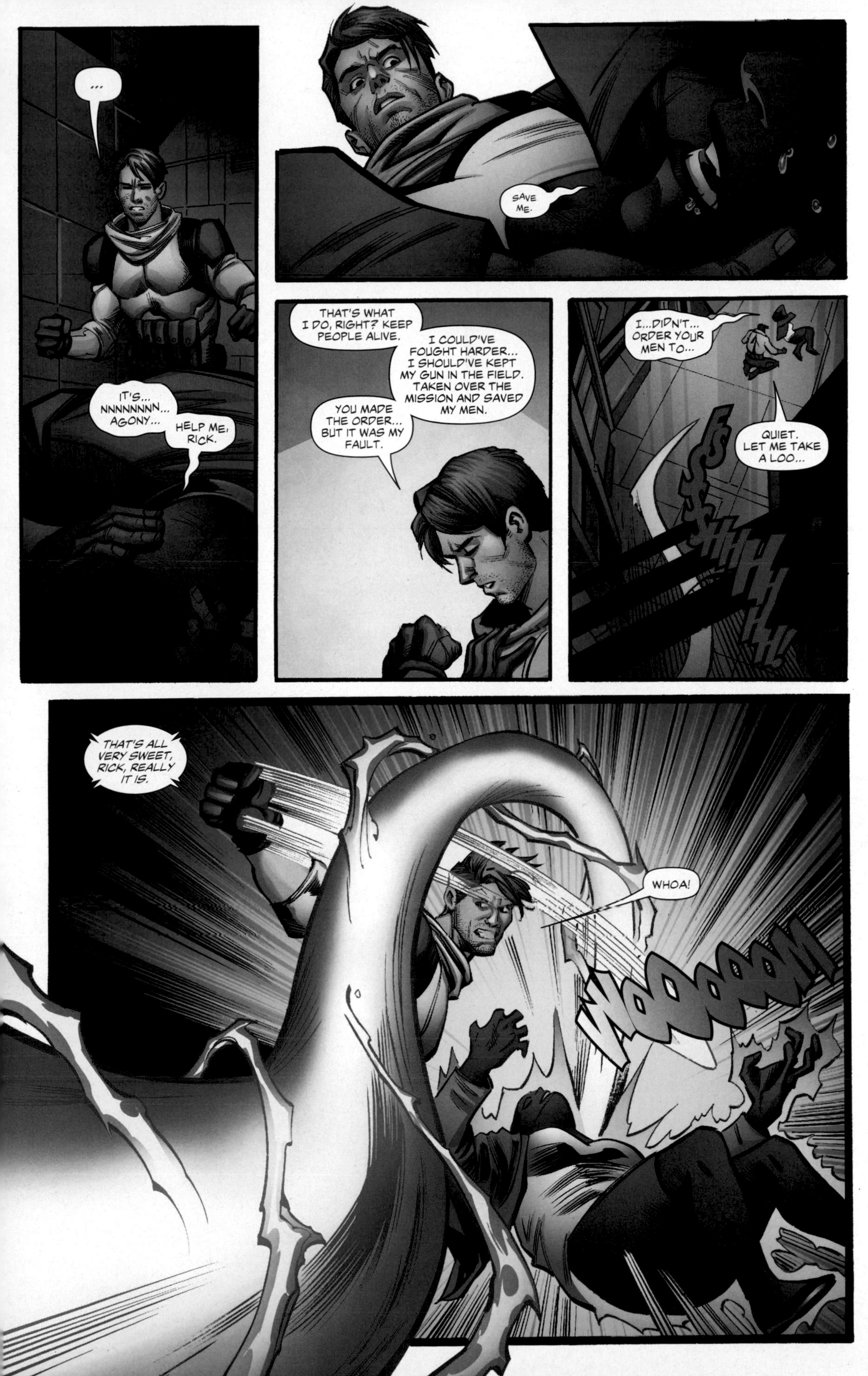
...
SAVE ME.
IT'S... NNNNNNNN... AGONY...
HELP ME, RICK.
THAT'S WHAT I DO, RIGHT? KEEP PEOPLE ALIVE.
I COULD'VE FOUGHT HARDER... I SHOULD'VE KEPT MY GUN IN THE FIELD. TAKEN OVER THE MISSION AND SAVED MY MEN.
YOU MADE THE ORDER... BUT IT WAS MY FAULT.
I...DIDN'T... ORDER YOUR MEN TO...
QUIET. LET ME TAKE A LOO...
SHHHHH!
THAT'S ALL VERY SWEET, RICK, REALLY IT IS.
WHOA!
WHOOOOOM!

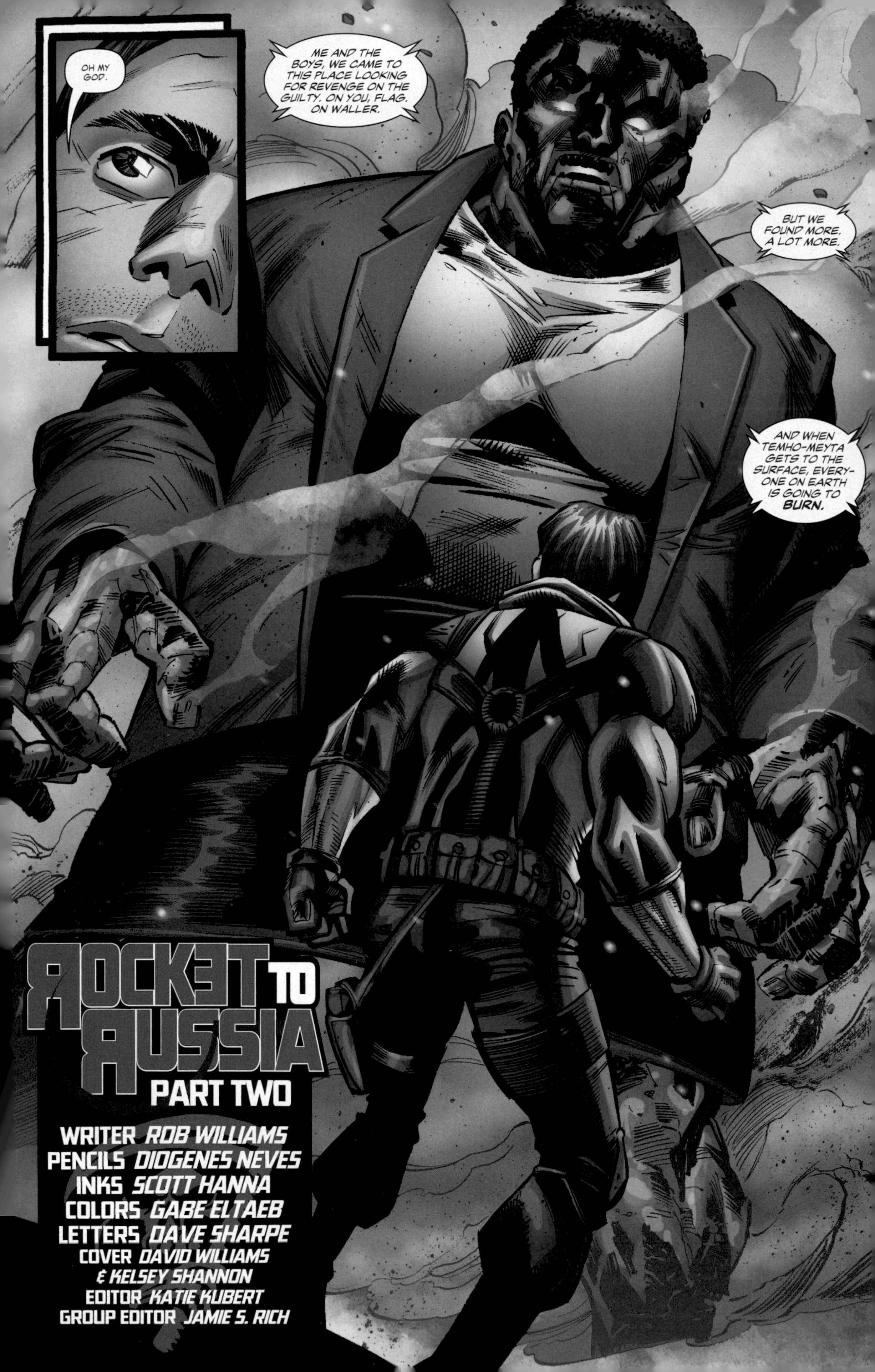
OH MY GOD.
ME AND THE BOYS, WE CAME TO THIS PLACE LOOKING FOR REVENGE ON THE GUILTY. ON YOU, FLAG. ON WALLER.
BUT WE FOUND MORE. A LOT MORE.
AND WHEN TEMHO-MEYTA GETS TO THE SURFACE, EVERY-ONE ON EARTH IS GOING TO BURN.
ROCKET TO RUSSIA
PART TWO
WRITER ROB WILLIAMS
PENCILS DIOGENES NEVES
INKS SCOTT HANNA
COLORS GABE ELTAEB
LETTERS DAVE SHARPE
COVER DAVID WILLIAMS & KELSEY SHANNON
EDITOR KATIE KUBERT
GROUP EDITOR JAMIE S. RICH

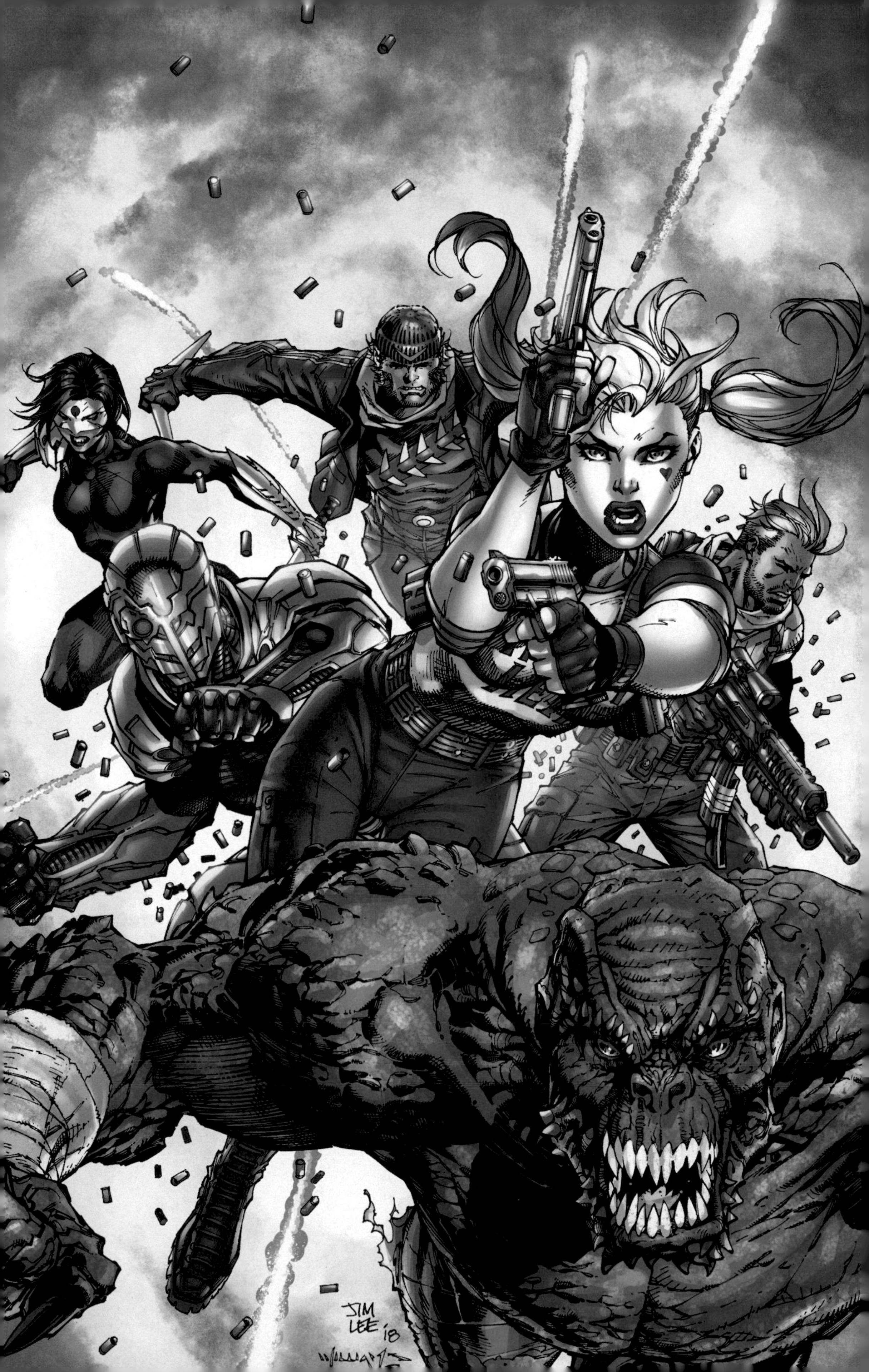
JIM
LEE '18

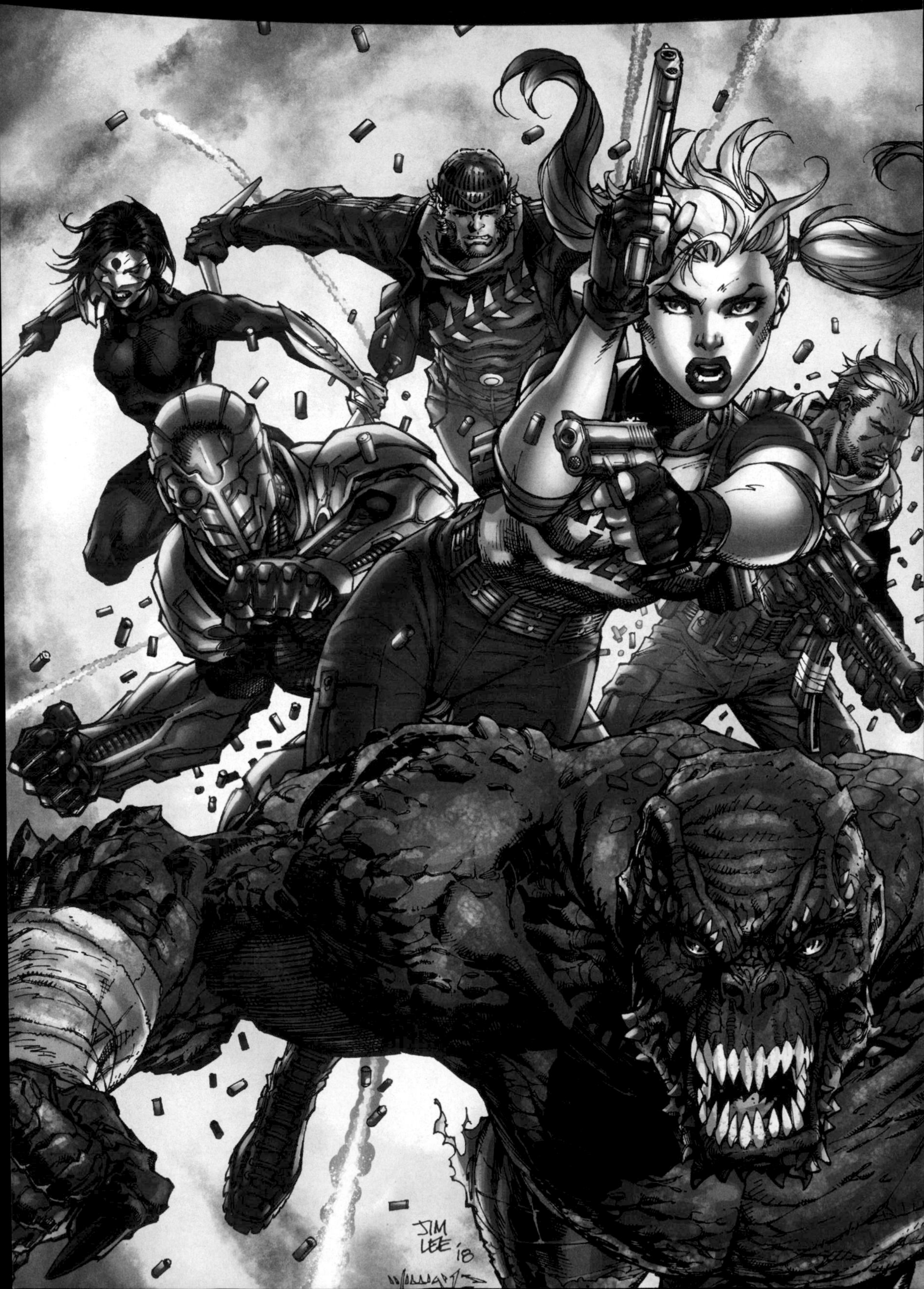
JIM LEE '18

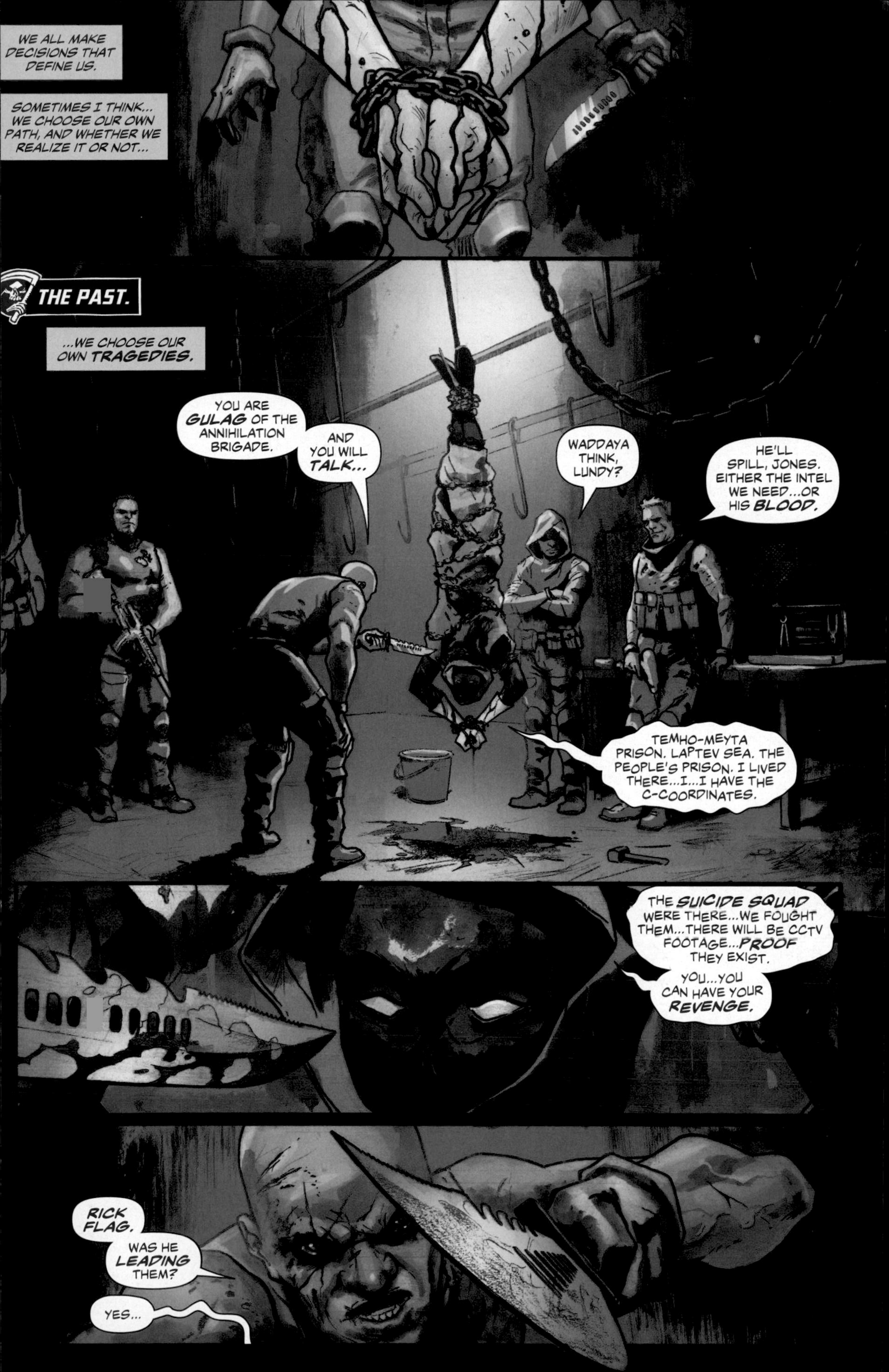
WE ALL MAKE DECISIONS THAT DEFINE US.
SOMETIMES I THINK... WE CHOOSE OUR OWN PATH, AND WHETHER WE REALIZE IT OR NOT...
THE PAST.
...WE CHOOSE OUR OWN TRAGEDIES.
YOU ARE GULAG OF THE ANNIHILATION BRIGADE.
AND YOU WILL TALK...
WADDAYA THINK, LUNDY?
HE'LL SPILL, JONES. EITHER THE INTEL WE NEED...OR HIS BLOOD.
TEMHO-MEYTA PRISON. LAPTEV SEA. THE PEOPLE'S PRISON. I LIVED THERE...I...I HAVE THE C-COORDINATES.
THE SUICIDE SQUAD WERE THERE...WE FOUGHT THEM...THERE WILL BE CCTV FOOTAGE...PROOF THEY EXIST.
YOU...YOU CAN HAVE YOUR REVENGE.
RICK FLAG.
WAS HE LEADING THEM?
YES...

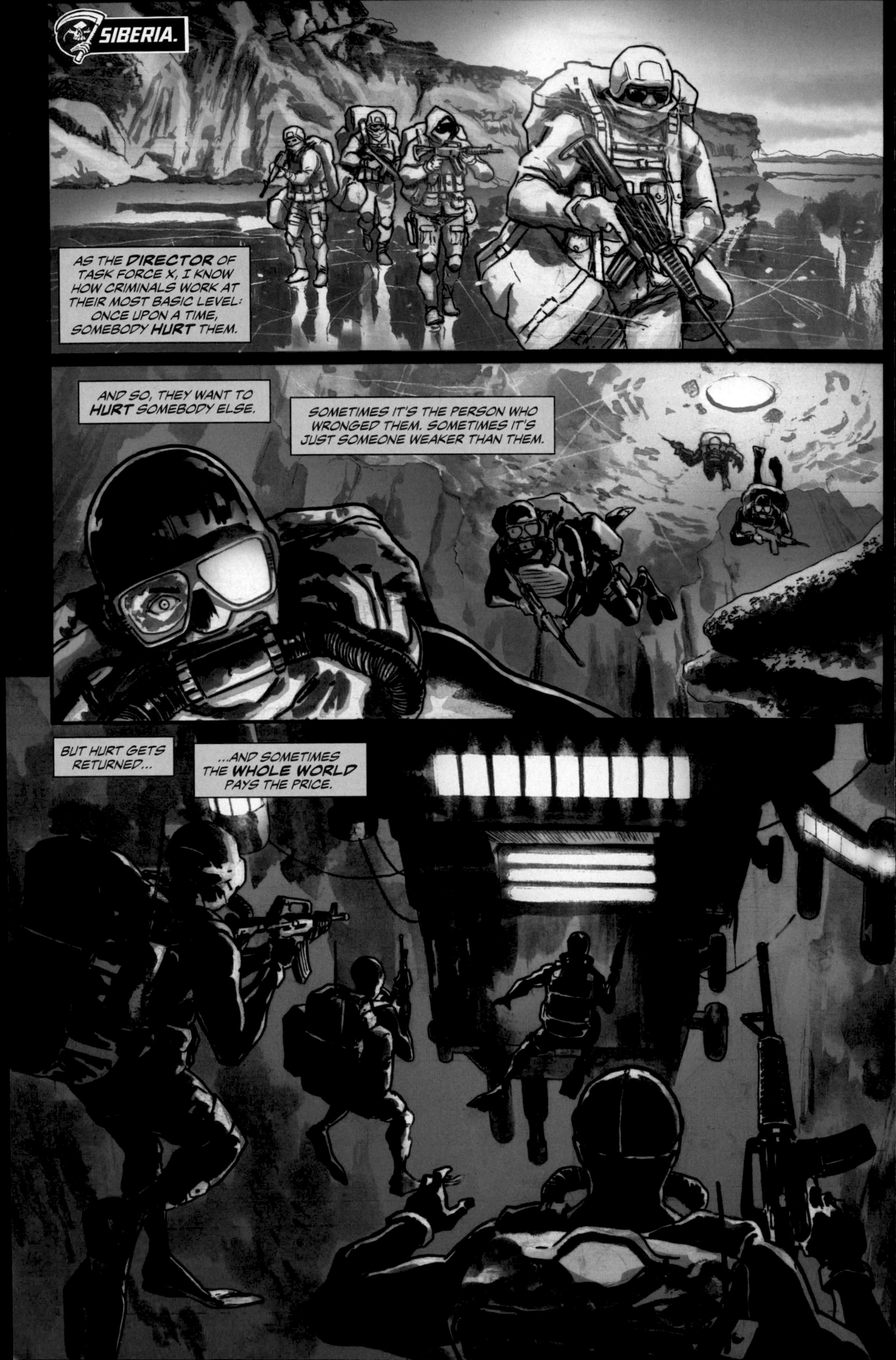

SIBERIA.
AS THE DIRECTOR OF TASK FORCE X, I KNOW HOW CRIMINALS WORK AT THEIR MOST BASIC LEVEL: ONCE UPON A TIME, SOMEBODY HURT THEM.
AND SO, THEY WANT TO HURT SOMEBODY ELSE.
SOMETIMES IT'S THE PERSON WHO WRONGED THEM. SOMETIMES IT'S JUST SOMEONE WEAKER THAN THEM.
BUT HURT GETS RETURNED...
...AND SOMETIMES THE WHOLE WORLD PAYS THE PRICE.

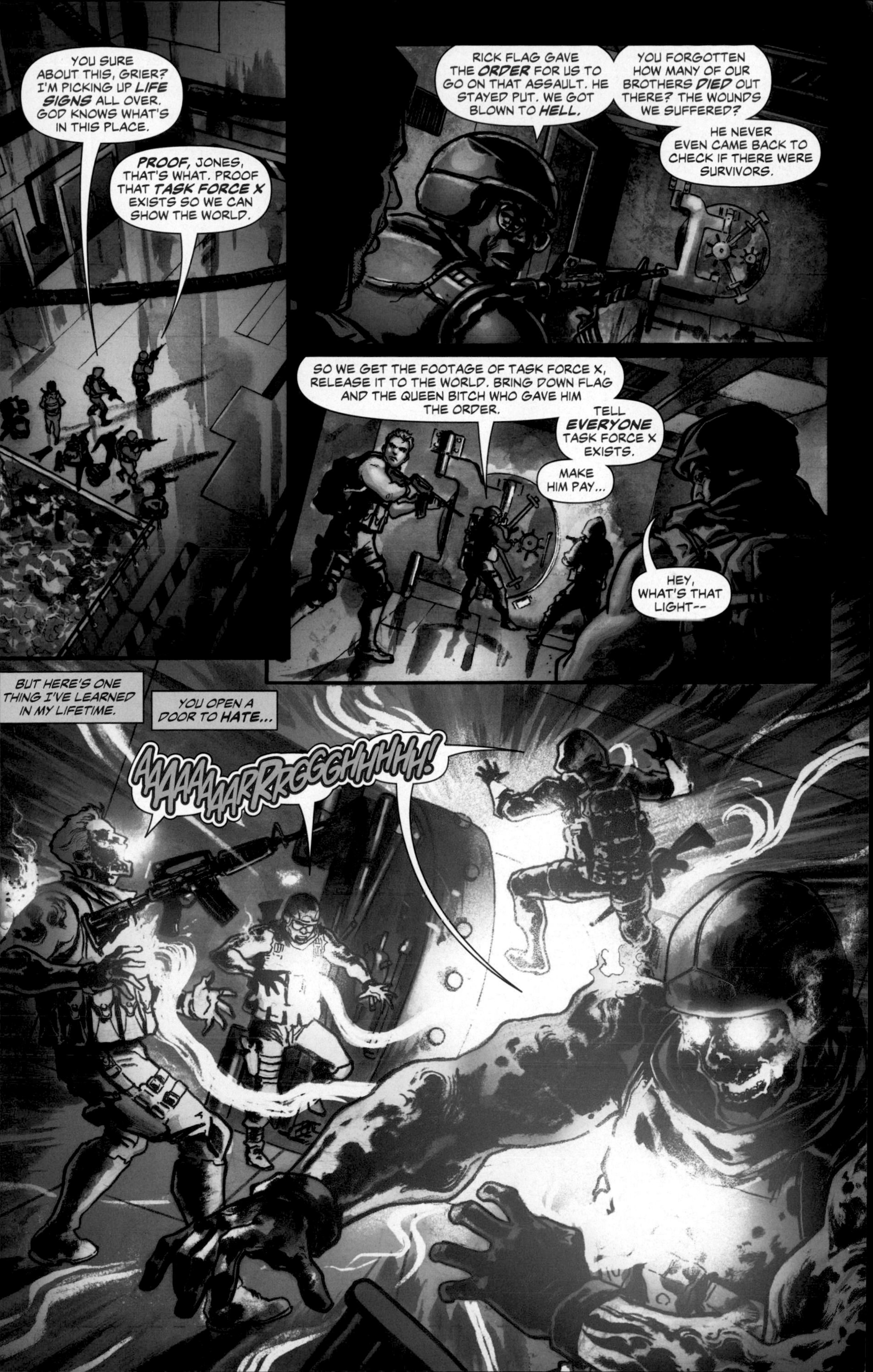

YOU SURE ABOUT THIS, GRIER? I'M PICKING UP LIFE SIGNS ALL OVER. GOD KNOWS WHAT'S IN THIS PLACE.
PROOF, JONES, THAT'S WHAT. PROOF THAT TASK FORCE X EXISTS SO WE CAN SHOW THE WORLD.
RICK FLAG GAVE THE ORDER FOR US TO GO ON THAT ASSAULT. HE STAYED PUT. WE GOT BLOWN TO HELL.
YOU FORGOTTEN HOW MANY OF OUR BROTHERS DIED OUT THERE? THE WOUNDS WE SUFFERED?
HE NEVER EVEN CAME BACK TO CHECK IF THERE WERE SURVIVORS.
SO WE GET THE FOOTAGE OF TASK FORCE X, RELEASE IT TO THE WORLD. BRING DOWN FLAG AND THE QUEEN BITCH WHO GAVE HIM THE ORDER.
TELL EVERYONE TASK FORCE X EXISTS.
MAKE HIM PAY...
HEY, WHAT'S THAT LIGHT--
BUT HERE'S ONE THING I'VE LEARNED IN MY LIFETIME.
YOU OPEN A DOOR TO HATE...
AAAAAAARRRRGGGHHHHH!

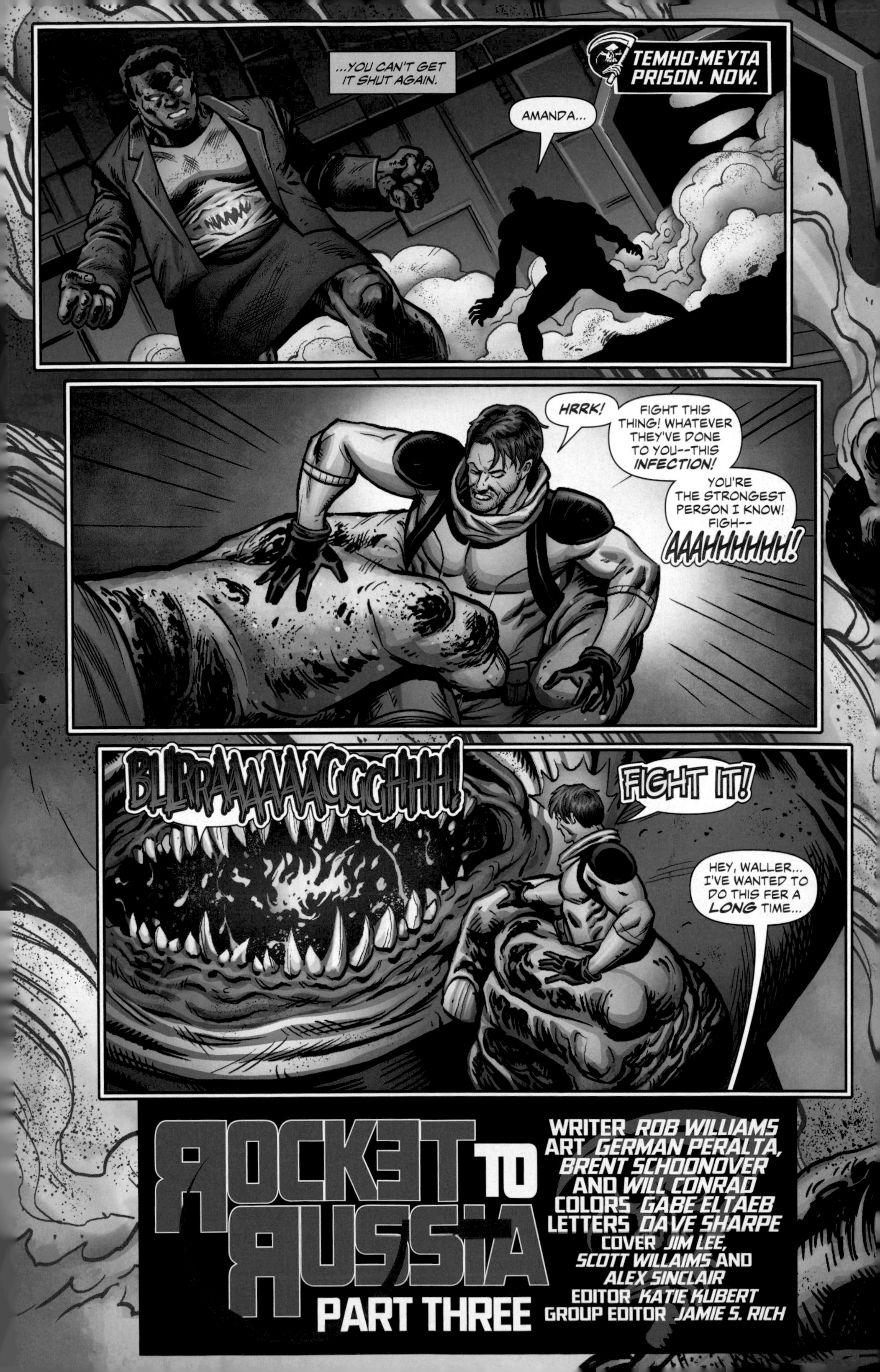
...YOU CAN'T GET IT SHUT AGAIN.
TEMHO-MEYTA PRISON. NOW.
AMANDA...
HRRK!
FIGHT THIS THING! WHATEVER THEY'VE DONE TO YOU--THIS INFECTION!
YOU'RE THE STRONGEST PERSON I KNOW! FIGH--
AAAHHHHHH!
BLLRRAAAAAAGGGHHH!
FIGHT IT!
HEY, WALLER... I'VE WANTED TO DO THIS FER A LONG TIME...
ROCKET TO RUSSIA
PART THREE
WRITER ROB WILLIAMS
ART GERMAN PERALTA, BRENT SCHOONOVER AND WILL CONRAD
COLORS GABE ELTAEB
LETTERS DAVE SHARPE
COVER JIM LEE, SCOTT WILLAIMS AND ALEX SINCLAIR
EDITOR KATIE KUBERT
GROUP EDITOR JAMIE S. RICH

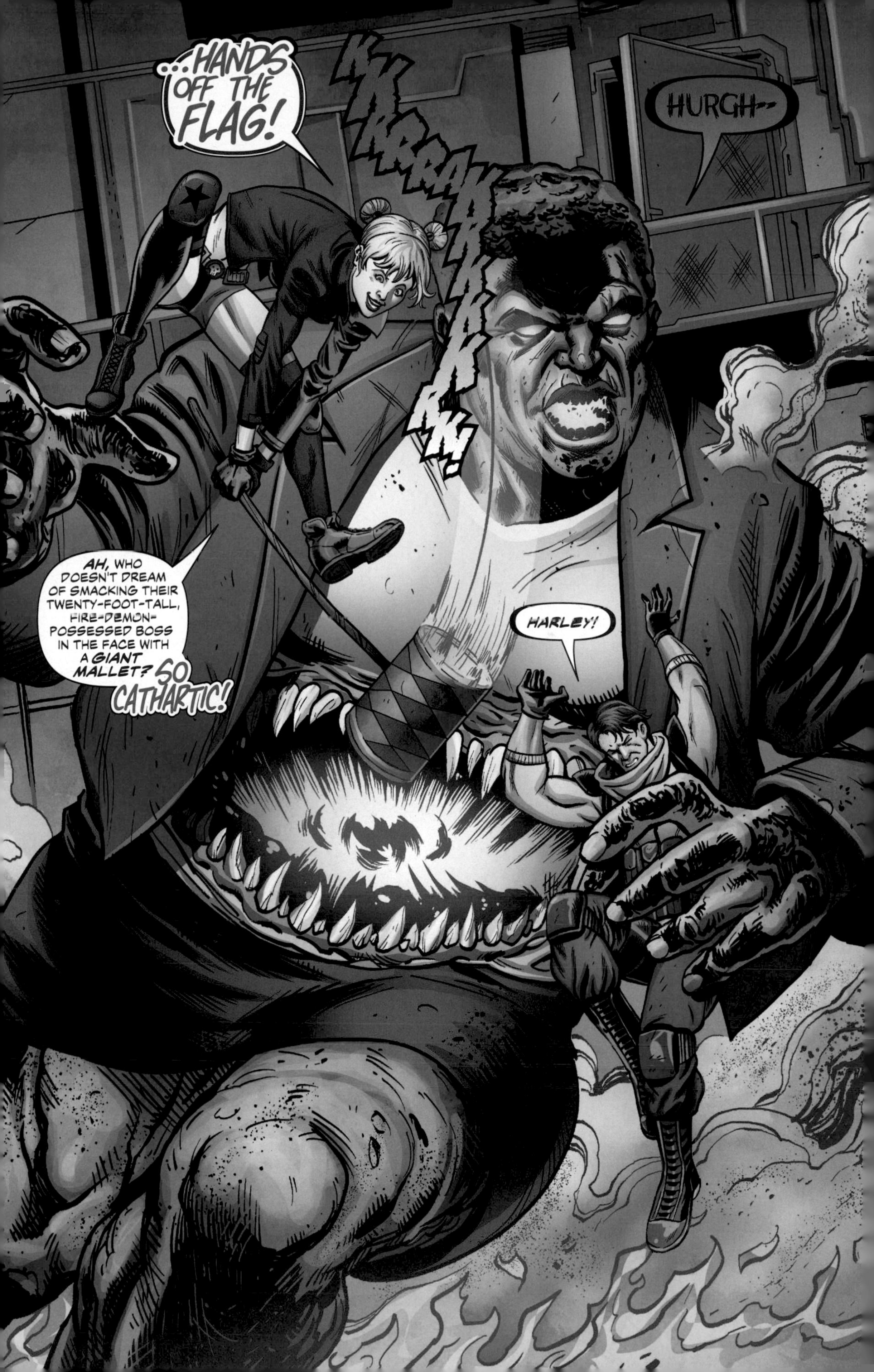
...HANDS OFF THE FLAG!
KKKRRAKKKKK!
HURGH--
AH, WHO DOESN'T DREAM OF SMACKING THEIR TWENTY-FOOT-TALL, FIRE-DEMON-POSSESSED BOSS IN THE FACE WITH A GIANT MALLET? SO CATHARTIC!
HARLEY!

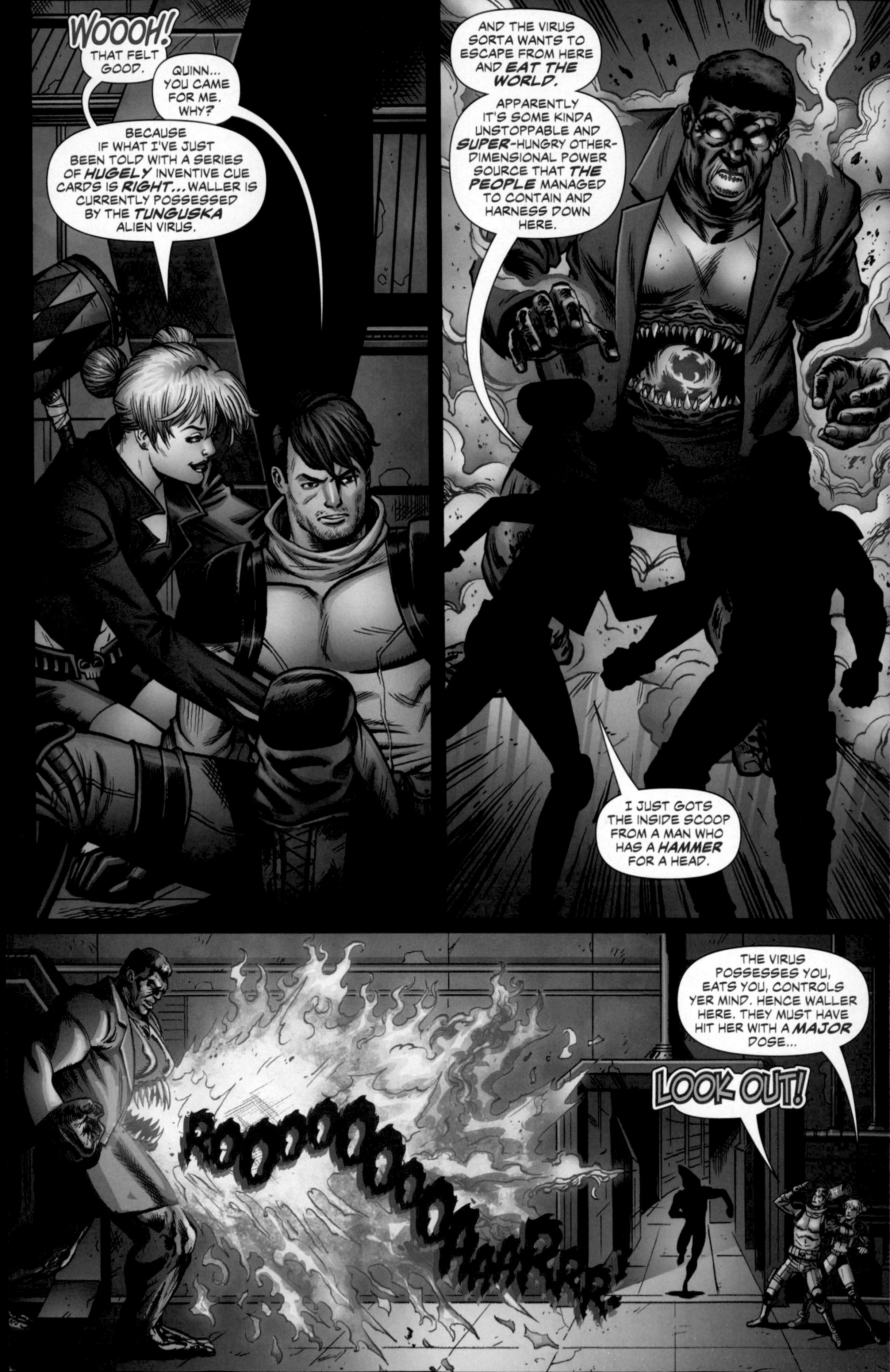
WOOOH! THAT FELT GOOD.
QUINN... YOU CAME FOR ME. WHY?
BECAUSE IF WHAT I'VE JUST BEEN TOLD WITH A SERIES OF HUGELY INVENTIVE CUE CARDS IS RIGHT... WALLER IS CURRENTLY POSSESSED BY THE TUNGUSKA ALIEN VIRUS.
AND THE VIRUS SORTA WANTS TO ESCAPE FROM HERE AND EAT THE WORLD.
APPARENTLY IT'S SOME KINDA UNSTOPPABLE AND SUPER-HUNGRY OTHER-DIMENSIONAL POWER SOURCE THAT THE PEOPLE MANAGED TO CONTAIN AND HARNESS DOWN HERE.
I JUST GOTS THE INSIDE SCOOP FROM A MAN WHO HAS A HAMMER FOR A HEAD.
THE VIRUS POSSESSES YOU, EATS YOU, CONTROLS YER MIND. HENCE WALLER HERE. THEY MUST HAVE HIT HER WITH A MAJOR DOSE...
LOOK OUT!
ROOOOOOOOOHARRR!

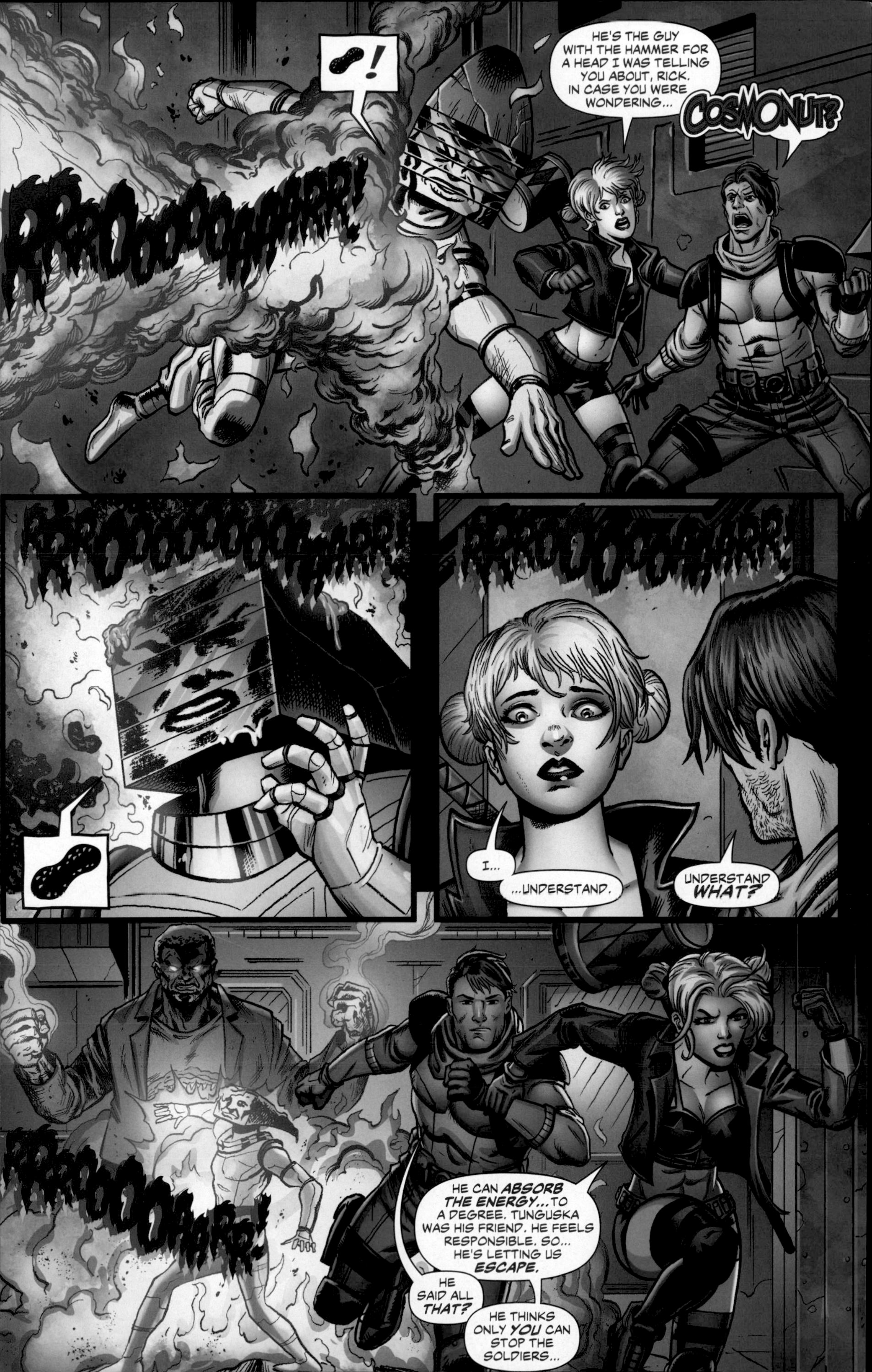

!
HE'S THE GUY WITH THE HAMMER FOR A HEAD I WAS TELLING YOU ABOUT, RICK. IN CASE YOU WERE WONDERING...
COSMONUT?
RRROOOOOHHRR!
RRROOOOOOOOHRR!
RRROOOOOOOHRR!
I...
...UNDERSTAND.
UNDERSTAND WHAT?
RRROOOOHRR!
HE CAN ABSORB THE ENERGY... TO A DEGREE. TUNGUSKA WAS HIS FRIEND. HE FEELS RESPONSIBLE. SO... HE'S LETTING US ESCAPE.
HE SAID ALL THAT?
HE THINKS ONLY YOU CAN STOP THE SOLDIERS...

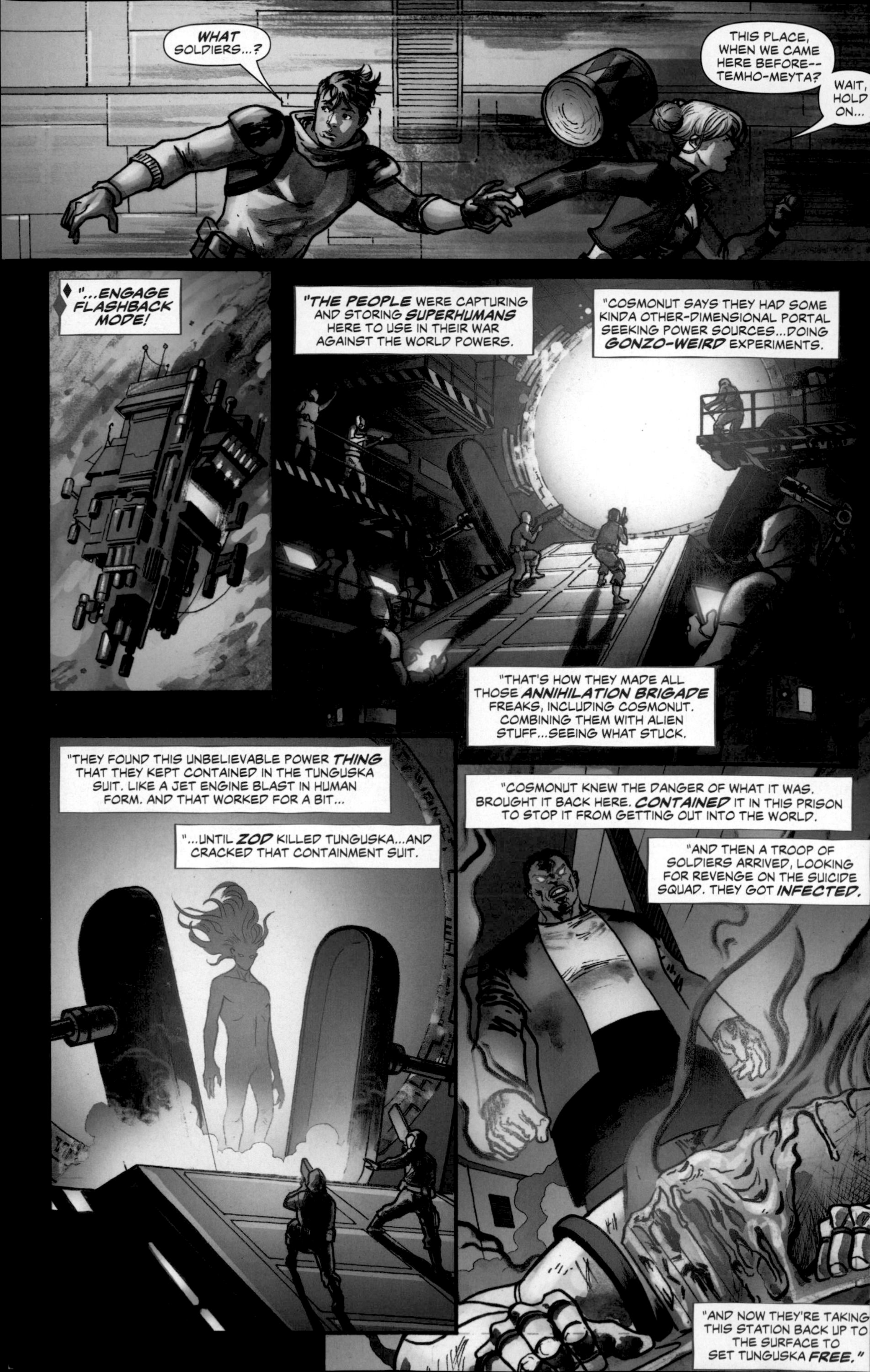
WHAT SOLDIERS...?
THIS PLACE, WHEN WE CAME HERE BEFORE-- TEMHO-MEYTA?
WAIT, HOLD ON...
"...ENGAGE FLASHBACK MODE!
"THE PEOPLE WERE CAPTURING AND STORING SUPERHUMANS HERE TO USE IN THEIR WAR AGAINST THE WORLD POWERS.
"COSMONUT SAYS THEY HAD SOME KINDA OTHER-DIMENSIONAL PORTAL SEEKING POWER SOURCES...DOING GONZO-WEIRD EXPERIMENTS.
"THAT'S HOW THEY MADE ALL THOSE ANNIHILATION BRIGADE FREAKS, INCLUDING COSMONUT. COMBINING THEM WITH ALIEN STUFF...SEEING WHAT STUCK.
"THEY FOUND THIS UNBELIEVABLE POWER THING THAT THEY KEPT CONTAINED IN THE TUNGUSKA SUIT. LIKE A JET ENGINE BLAST IN HUMAN FORM. AND THAT WORKED FOR A BIT...
"...UNTIL ZOD KILLED TUNGUSKA...AND CRACKED THAT CONTAINMENT SUIT.
"COSMONUT KNEW THE DANGER OF WHAT IT WAS. BROUGHT IT BACK HERE. CONTAINED IT IN THIS PRISON TO STOP IT FROM GETTING OUT INTO THE WORLD.
"AND THEN A TROOP OF SOLDIERS ARRIVED, LOOKING FOR REVENGE ON THE SUICIDE SQUAD. THEY GOT INFECTED.
"AND NOW THEY'RE TAKING THIS STATION BACK UP TO THE SURFACE TO SET TUNGUSKA FREE."

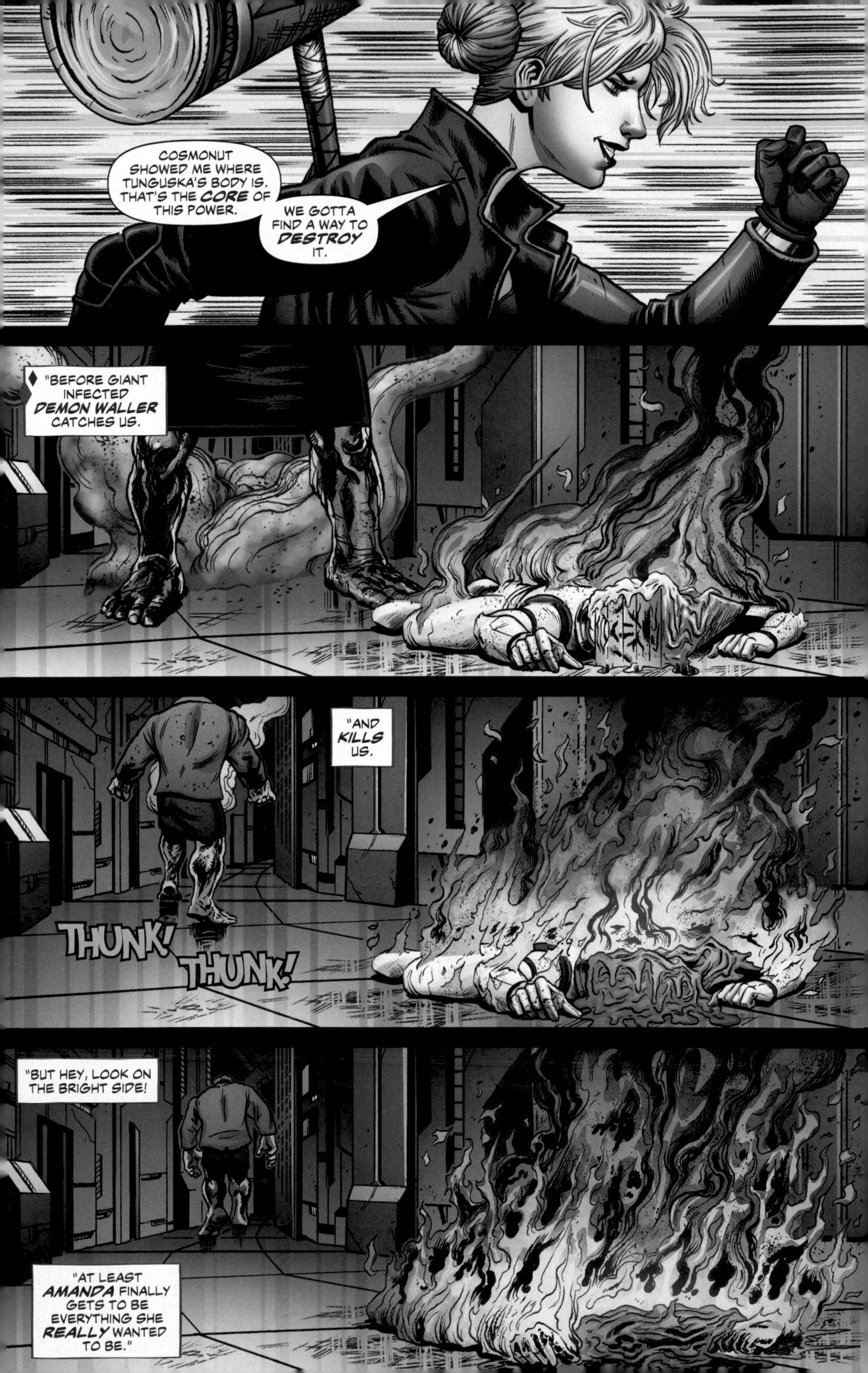
COSMONUT SHOWED ME WHERE TUNGUSKA'S BODY IS. THAT'S THE CORE OF THIS POWER.
WE GOTTA FIND A WAY TO DESTROY IT.
"BEFORE GIANT INFECTED DEMON WALLER CATCHES US.
"AND KILLS US.
THUNK! THUNK!
"BUT HEY, LOOK ON THE BRIGHT SIDE!
"AT LEAST AMANDA FINALLY GETS TO BE EVERYTHING SHE REALLY WANTED TO BE."

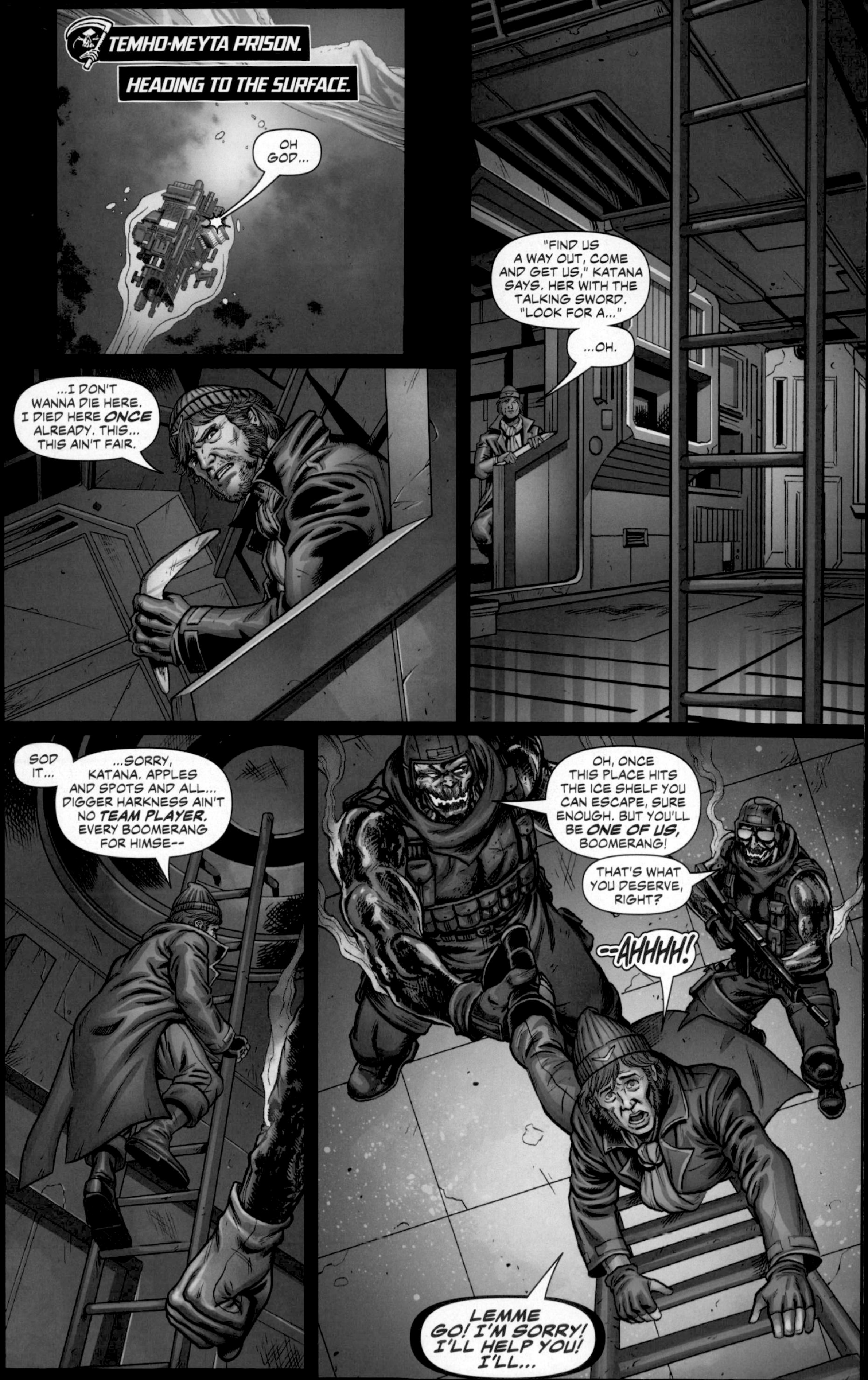
TEMHO-MEYTA PRISON.
HEADING TO THE SURFACE.
OH GOD...
"FIND US A WAY OUT, COME AND GET US," KATANA SAYS. HER WITH THE TALKING SWORD. "LOOK FOR A..."
...OH.
...I DON'T WANNA DIE HERE. I DIED HERE ONCE ALREADY. THIS... THIS AIN'T FAIR.
SOD IT...
...SORRY, KATANA. APPLES AND SPOTS AND ALL... DIGGER HARKNESS AIN'T NO TEAM PLAYER. EVERY BOOMERANG FOR HIMSE--
OH, ONCE THIS PLACE HITS THE ICE SHELF YOU CAN ESCAPE, SURE ENOUGH. BUT YOU'LL BE ONE OF US, BOOMERANG!
THAT'S WHAT YOU DESERVE, RIGHT?
--AHHHH!
LEMME GO! I'M SORRY! I'LL HELP YOU! I'LL...

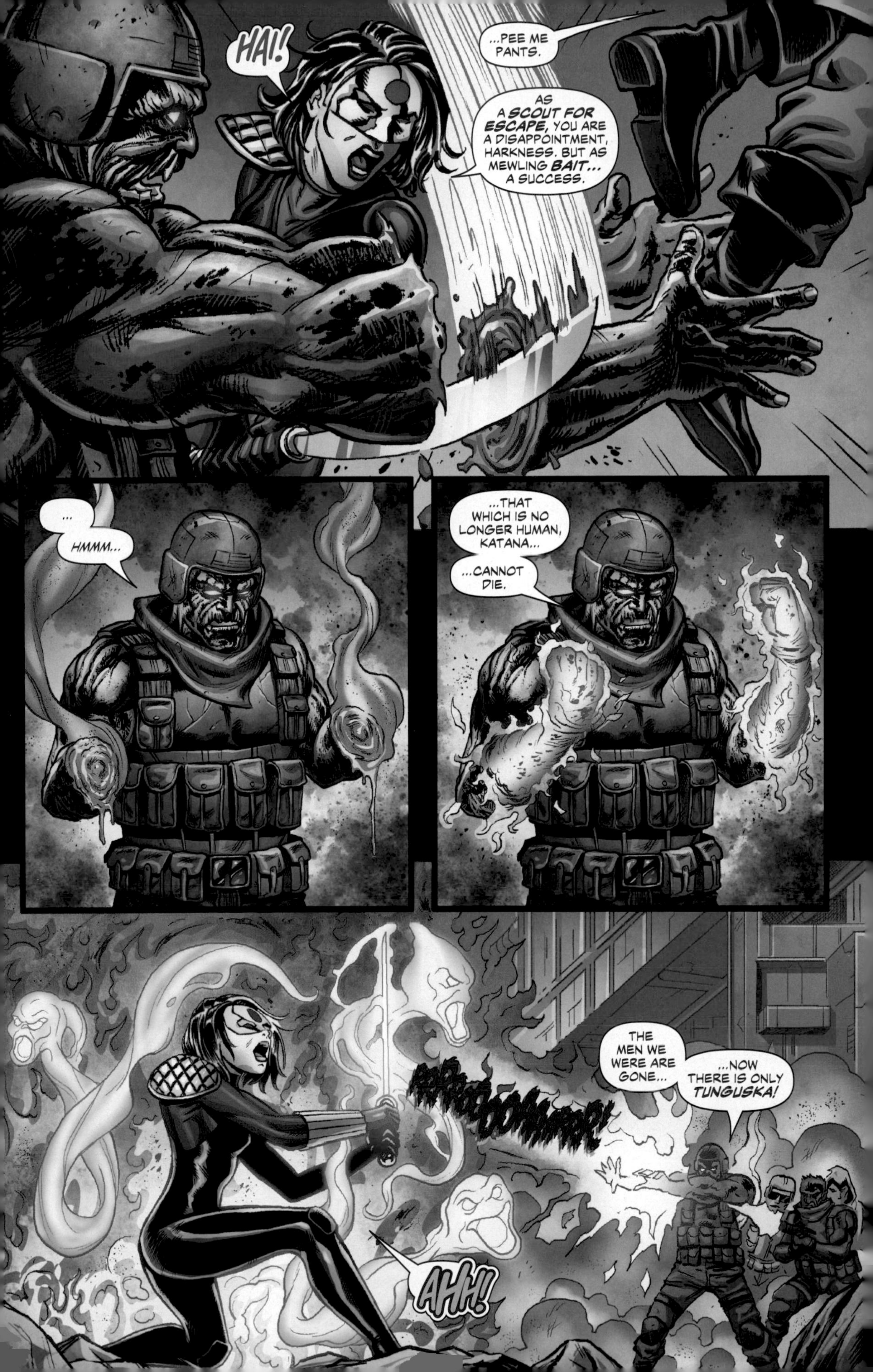
HAI!
...PEE ME PANTS.
AS A SCOUT FOR ESCAPE, YOU ARE A DISAPPOINTMENT, HARKNESS. BUT AS MEWLING BAIT... A SUCCESS.
... HMMM...
...THAT WHICH IS NO LONGER HUMAN, KATANA...
...CANNOT DIE.
THE MEN WE WERE ARE GONE...
...NOW THERE IS ONLY TUNGUSKA!
AHH!

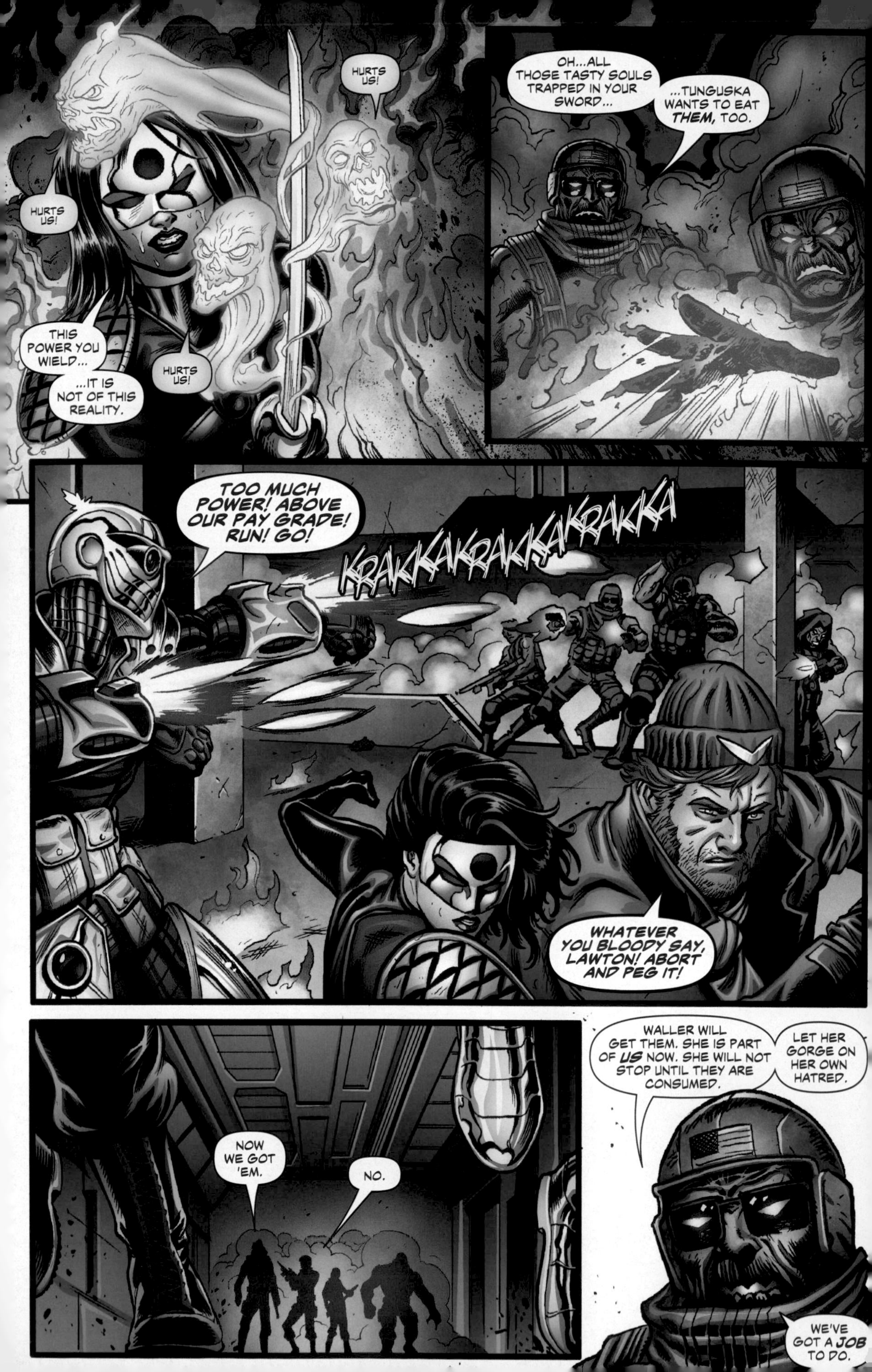
HURTS US!
HURTS US!
THIS POWER YOU WIELD...
...IT IS NOT OF THIS REALITY.
HURTS US!
OH...ALL THOSE TASTY SOULS TRAPPED IN YOUR SWORD...
...TUNGUSKA WANTS TO EAT THEM, TOO.
TOO MUCH POWER! ABOVE OUR PAY GRADE! RUN! GO!
KRAKKAKRAKKAKRAKKA
WHATEVER YOU BLOODY SAY, LAWTON! ABORT AND PEG IT!
NOW WE GOT 'EM.
NO.
WALLER WILL GET THEM. SHE IS PART OF US NOW. SHE WILL NOT STOP UNTIL THEY ARE CONSUMED.
LET HER GORGE ON HER OWN HATRED.
WE'VE GOT A JOB TO DO.

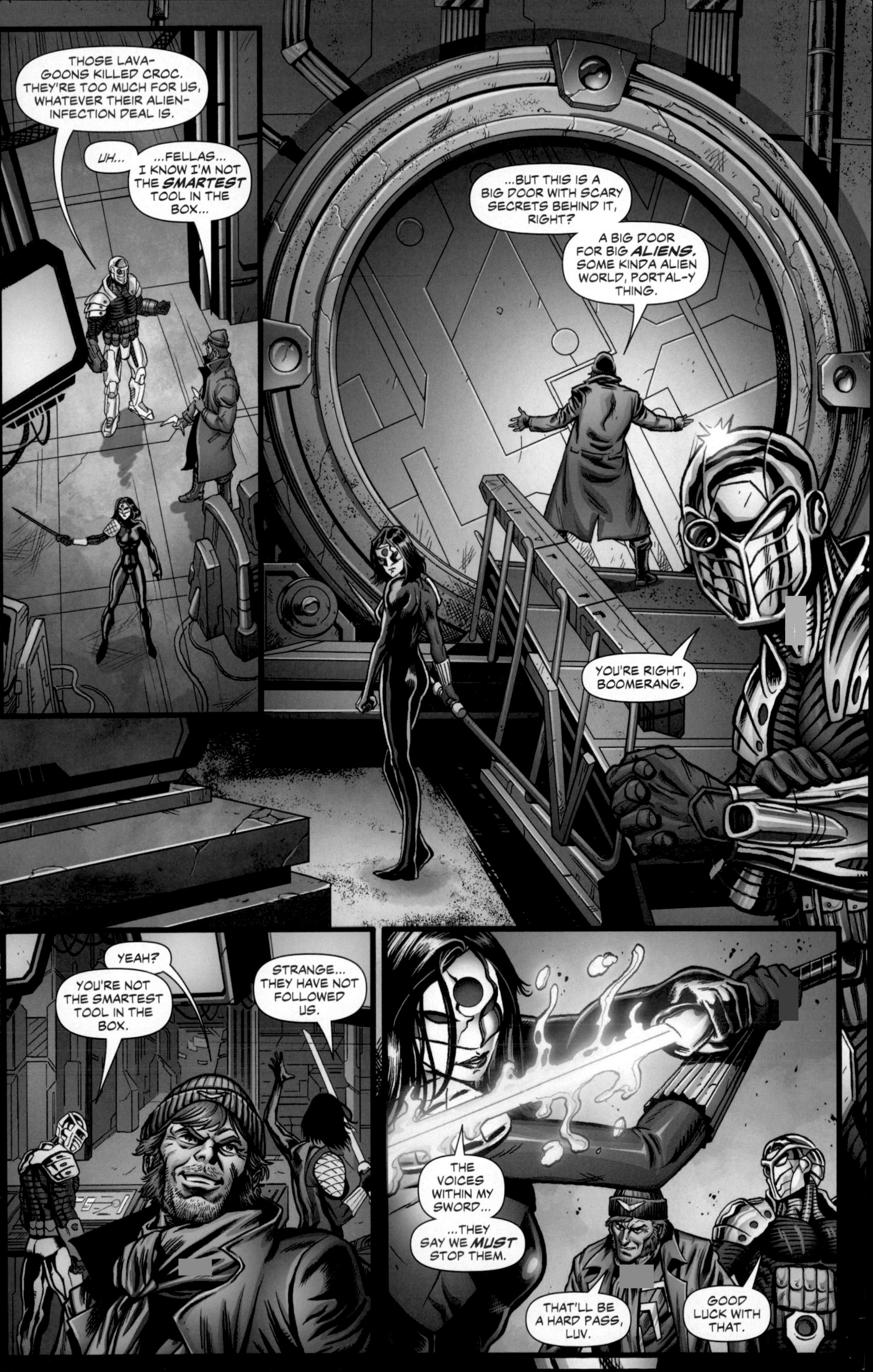
THOSE LAVA-GOONS KILLED CROC. THEY'RE TOO MUCH FOR US, WHATEVER THEIR ALIEN-INFECTION DEAL IS.
UH...
...FELLAS... I KNOW I'M NOT THE SMARTEST TOOL IN THE BOX...
...BUT THIS IS A BIG DOOR WITH SCARY SECRETS BEHIND IT, RIGHT?
A BIG DOOR FOR BIG ALIENS. SOME KINDA ALIEN WORLD, PORTAL-Y THING.
YOU'RE RIGHT, BOOMERANG.
YEAH?
YOU'RE NOT THE SMARTEST TOOL IN THE BOX.
STRANGE... THEY HAVE NOT FOLLOWED US.
THE VOICES WITHIN MY SWORD...
...THEY SAY WE MUST STOP THEM.
THAT'LL BE A HARD PASS, LUV.
GOOD LUCK WITH THAT.

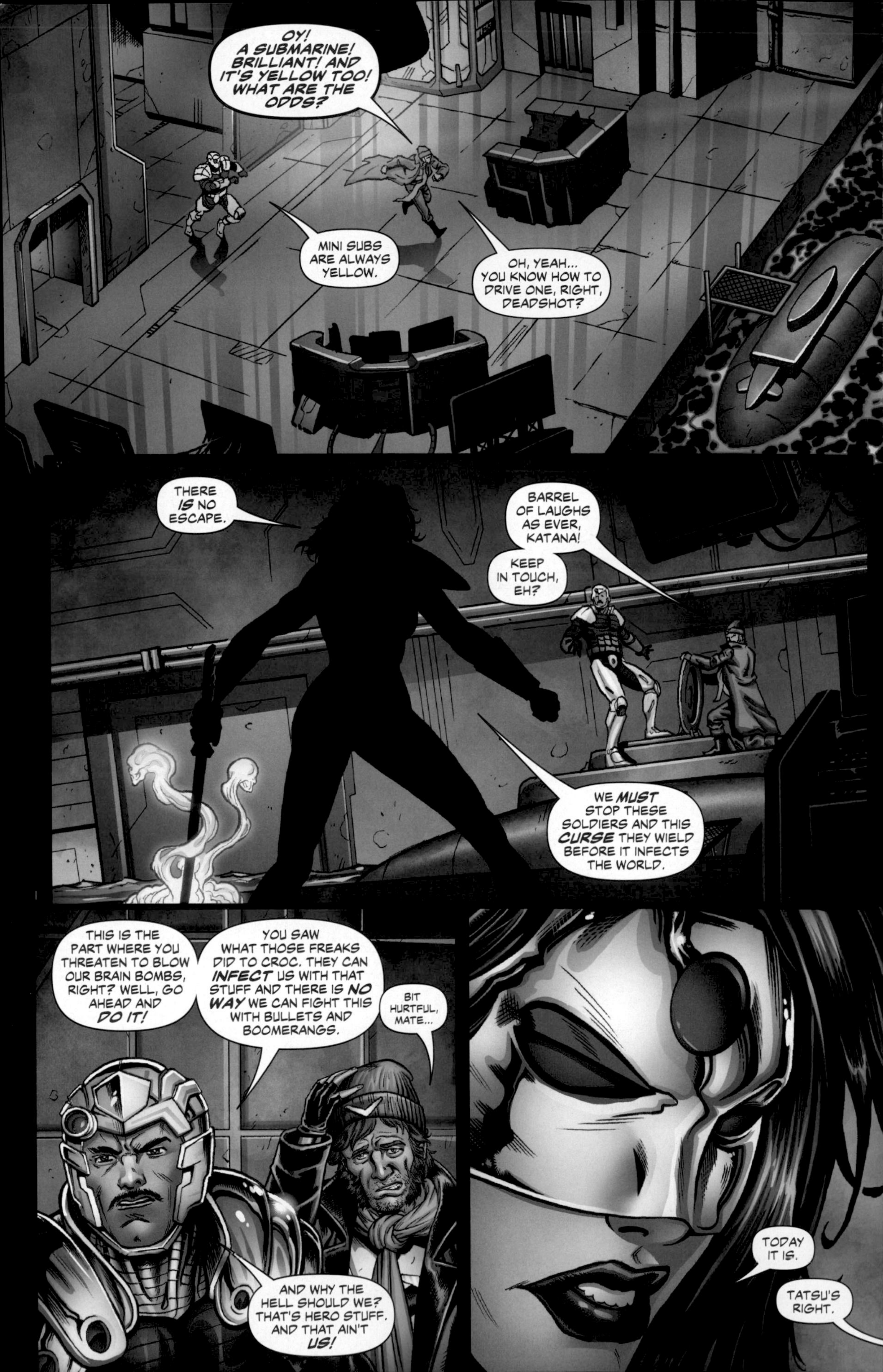
OY! A SUBMARINE! BRILLIANT! AND IT'S YELLOW TOO! WHAT ARE THE ODDS?
MINI SUBS ARE ALWAYS YELLOW.
OH, YEAH... YOU KNOW HOW TO DRIVE ONE, RIGHT, DEADSHOT?
THERE IS NO ESCAPE.
BARREL OF LAUGHS AS EVER, KATANA!
KEEP IN TOUCH, EH?
WE MUST STOP THESE SOLDIERS AND THIS CURSE THEY WIELD BEFORE IT INFECTS THE WORLD.
THIS IS THE PART WHERE YOU THREATEN TO BLOW OUR BRAIN BOMBS, RIGHT? WELL, GO AHEAD AND DO IT!
YOU SAW WHAT THOSE FREAKS DID TO CROC. THEY CAN INFECT US WITH THAT STUFF AND THERE IS NO WAY WE CAN FIGHT THIS WITH BULLETS AND BOOMERANGS.
BIT HURTFUL, MATE...
AND WHY THE HELL SHOULD WE? THAT'S HERO STUFF. AND THAT AIN'T US!
TODAY IT IS.
TATSU'S RIGHT.

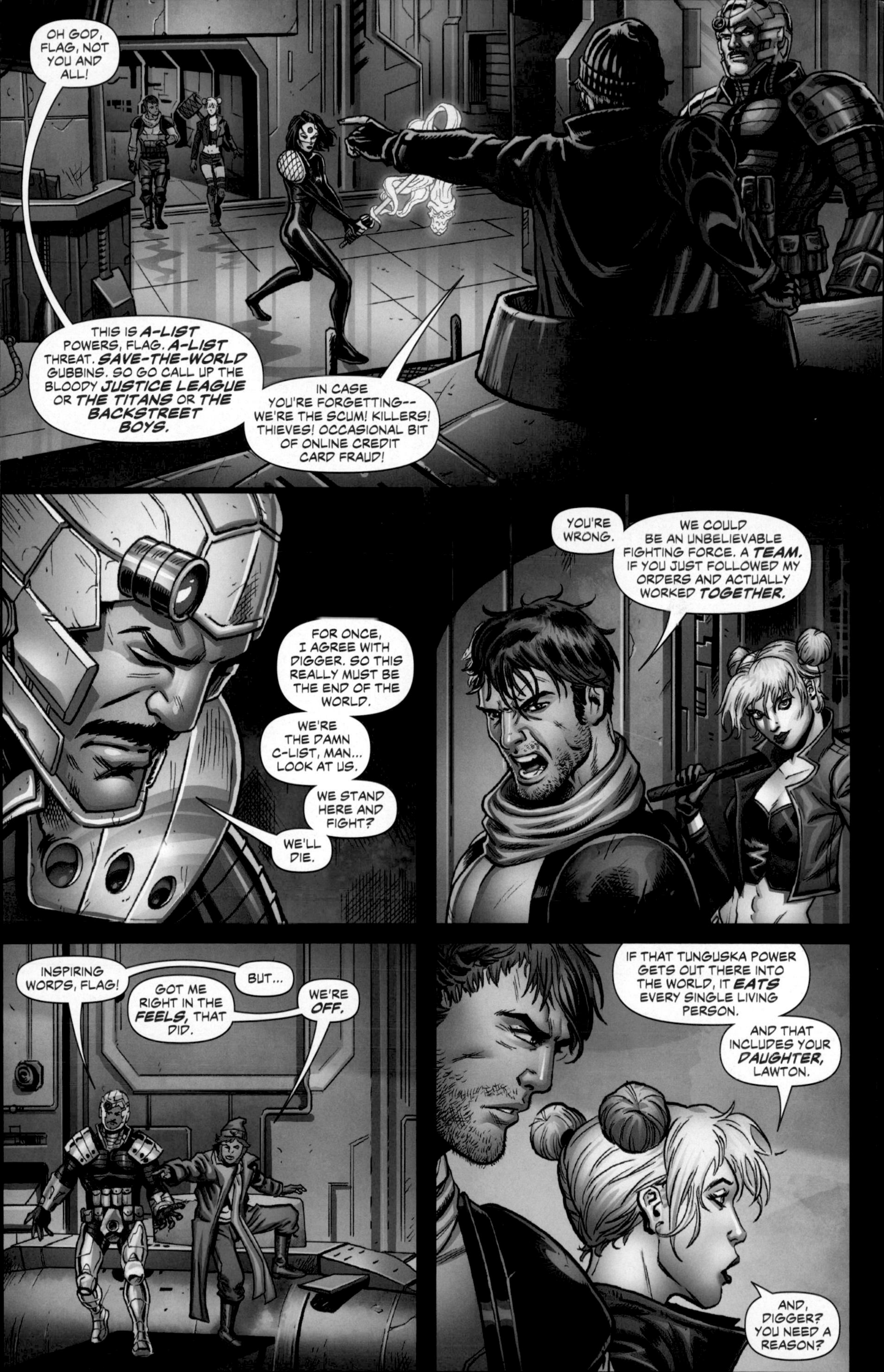
OH GOD, FLAG, NOT YOU AND ALL!
THIS IS A-LIST POWERS, FLAG. A-LIST THREAT. SAVE-THE-WORLD GUBBINS. SO GO CALL UP THE BLOODY JUSTICE LEAGUE OR THE TITANS OR THE BACKSTREET BOYS.
IN CASE YOU'RE FORGETTING-- WE'RE THE SCUM! KILLERS! THIEVES! OCCASIONAL BIT OF ONLINE CREDIT CARD FRAUD!
FOR ONCE, I AGREE WITH DIGGER. SO THIS REALLY MUST BE THE END OF THE WORLD.
WE'RE THE DAMN C-LIST, MAN... LOOK AT US.
WE STAND HERE AND FIGHT?
WE'LL DIE.
YOU'RE WRONG.
WE COULD BE AN UNBELIEVABLE FIGHTING FORCE. A TEAM. IF YOU JUST FOLLOWED MY ORDERS AND ACTUALLY WORKED TOGETHER.
INSPIRING WORDS, FLAG!
GOT ME RIGHT IN THE FEELS, THAT DID.
BUT...
WE'RE OFF.
IF THAT TUNGUSKA POWER GETS OUT THERE INTO THE WORLD, IT EATS EVERY SINGLE LIVING PERSON.
AND THAT INCLUDES YOUR DAUGHTER, LAWTON.
AND, DIGGER? YOU NEED A REASON?

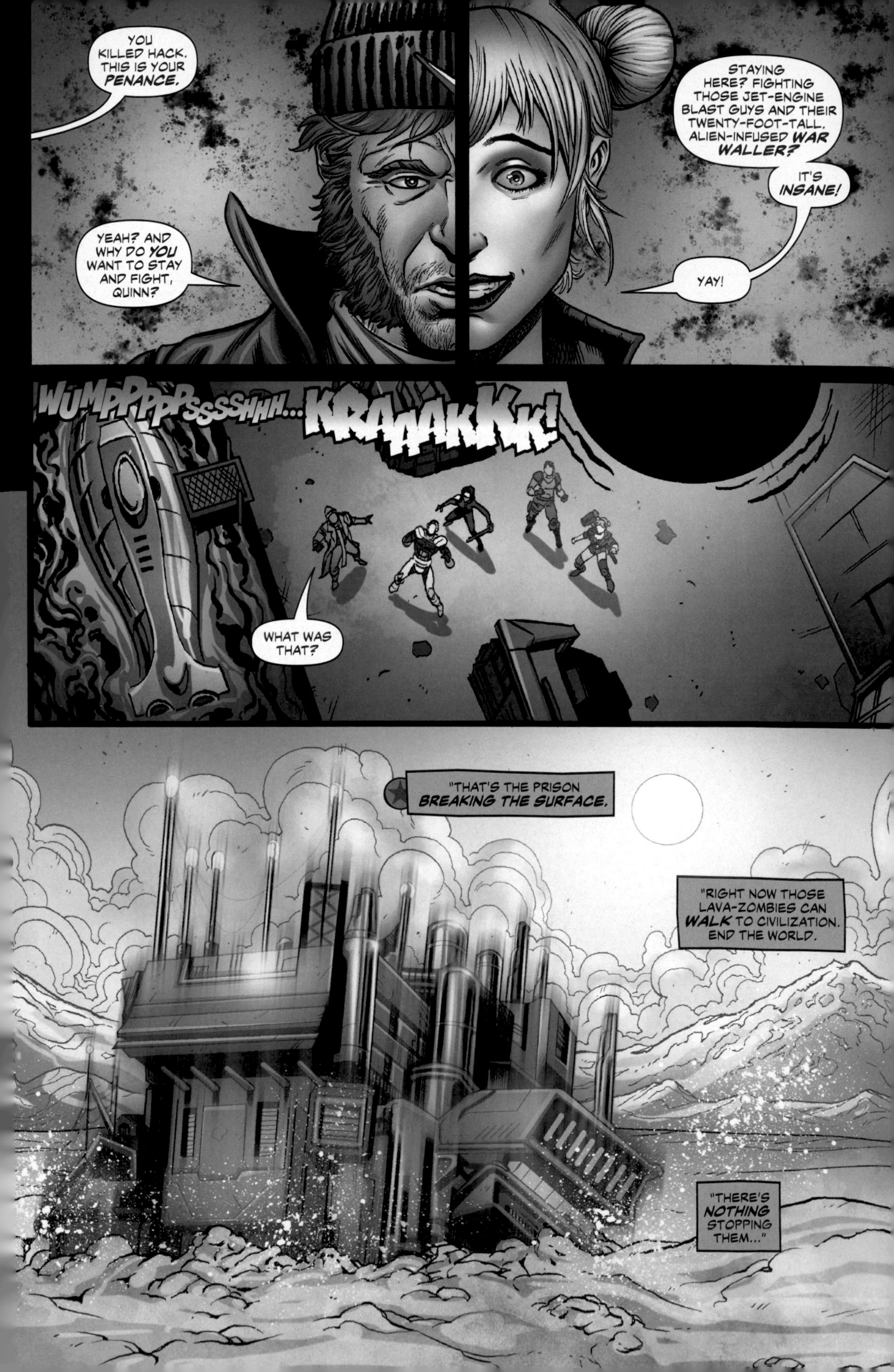

YOU KILLED HACK. THIS IS YOUR PENANCE.
STAYING HERE? FIGHTING THOSE JET-ENGINE BLAST GUYS AND THEIR TWENTY-FOOT-TALL, ALIEN-INFUSED WAR WALLER?
IT'S INSANE!
YEAH? AND WHY DO YOU WANT TO STAY AND FIGHT, QUINN?
YAY!
WUMPPPPPSSSSHHH...KRAAAKKKK!
WHAT WAS THAT?
"THAT'S THE PRISON BREAKING THE SURFACE.
"RIGHT NOW THOSE LAVA-ZOMBIES CAN WALK TO CIVILIZATION. END THE WORLD.
"THERE'S NOTHING STOPPING THEM..."

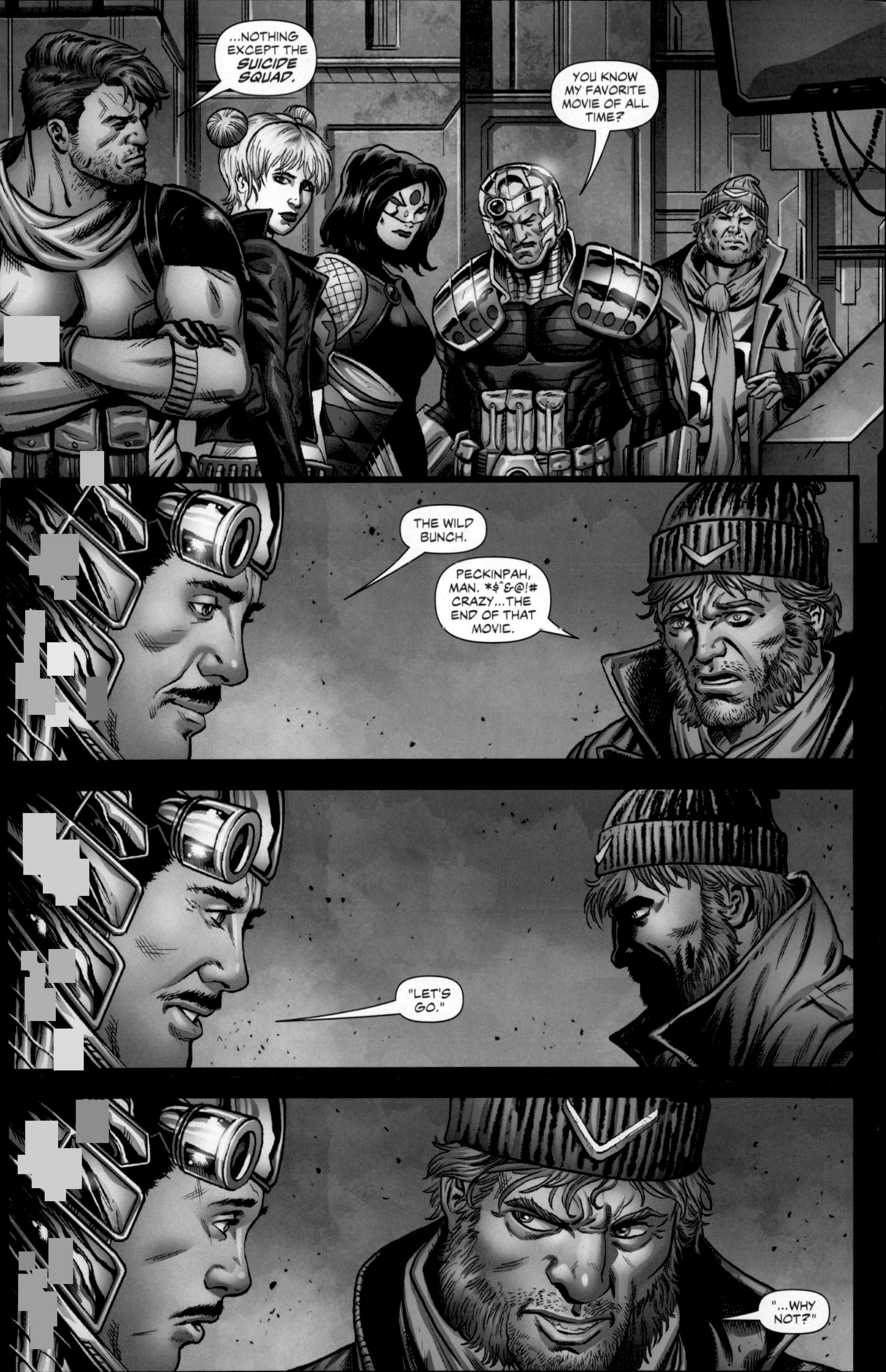
...NOTHING EXCEPT THE SUICIDE SQUAD.
YOU KNOW MY FAVORITE MOVIE OF ALL TIME?
THE WILD BUNCH.
PECKINPAH, MAN. *$^&@!# CRAZY...THE END OF THAT MOVIE.
"LET'S GO."
"...WHY NOT?"

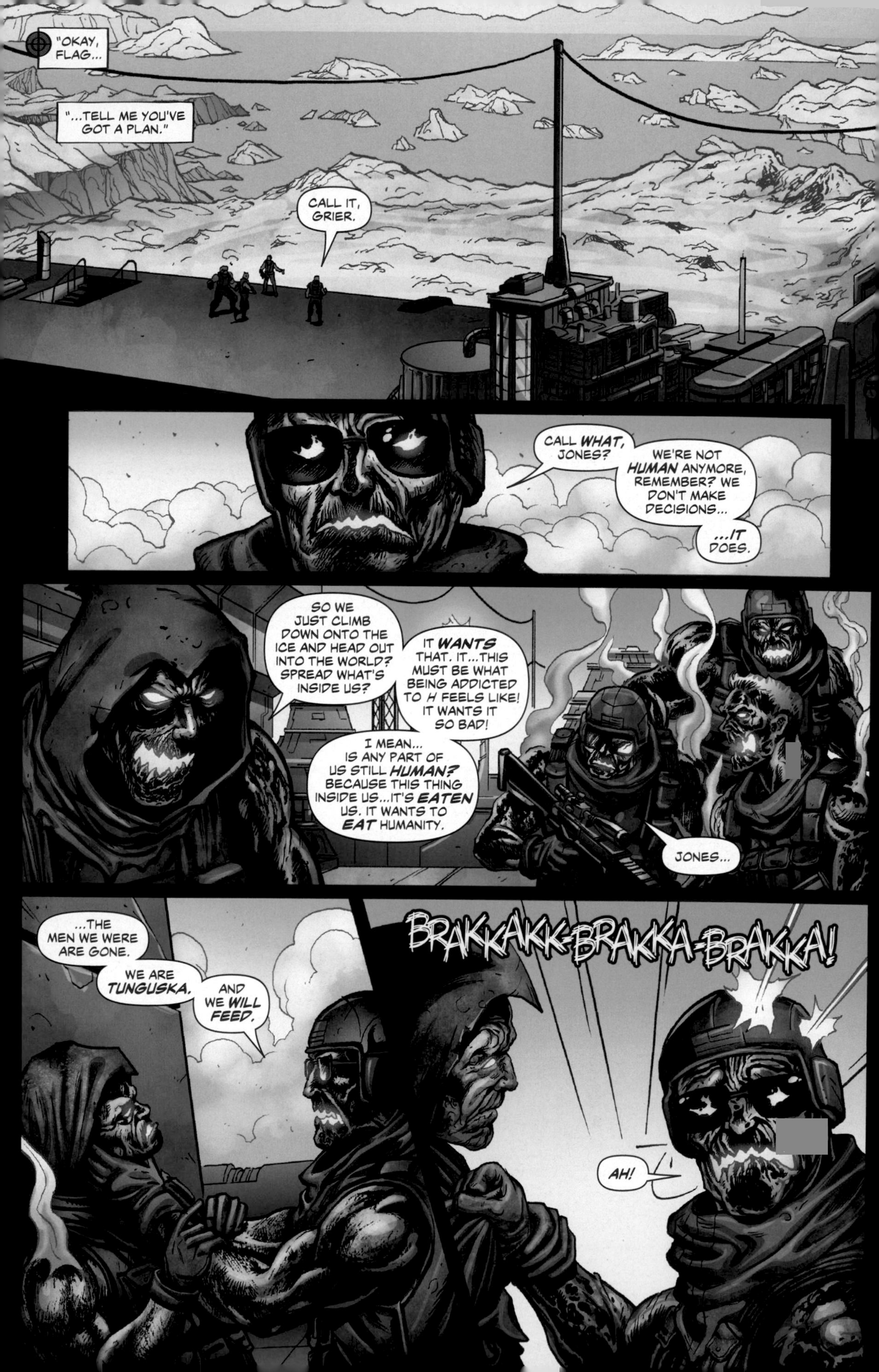
"OKAY, FLAG...
"...TELL ME YOU'VE GOT A PLAN."
CALL IT, GRIER.
CALL WHAT, JONES?
WE'RE NOT HUMAN ANYMORE, REMEMBER? WE DON'T MAKE DECISIONS...
...IT DOES.
SO WE JUST CLIMB DOWN ONTO THE ICE AND HEAD OUT INTO THE WORLD? SPREAD WHAT'S INSIDE US?
IT WANTS THAT. IT...THIS MUST BE WHAT BEING ADDICTED TO H FEELS LIKE! IT WANTS IT SO BAD!
I MEAN... IS ANY PART OF US STILL HUMAN? BECAUSE THIS THING INSIDE US...IT'S EATEN US. IT WANTS TO EAT HUMANITY.
JONES...
...THE MEN WE WERE ARE GONE.
WE ARE TUNGUSKA.
AND WE WILL FEED.
BRAKKAKK-BRAKKA-BRAKKA!
AH!

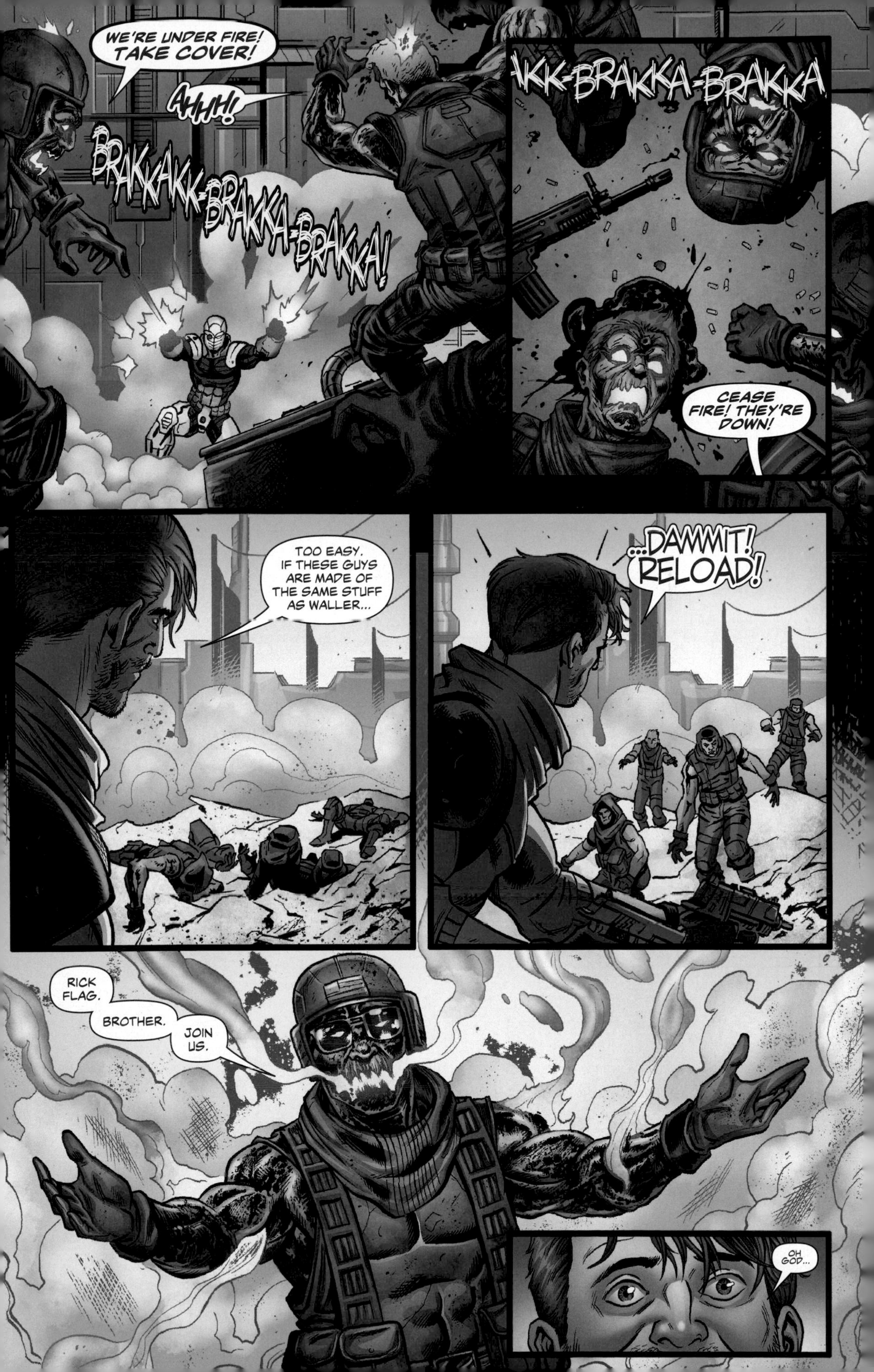
WE'RE UNDER FIRE! TAKE COVER!
AHHH!
BRAKKAKK-BRAKKA-BRAKKA!
AKK-BRAKKA-BRAKKA
CEASE FIRE! THEY'RE DOWN!
TOO EASY. IF THESE GUYS ARE MADE OF THE SAME STUFF AS WALLER...
...DAMMIT! RELOAD!
RICK FLAG.
BROTHER.
JOIN US.
OH GOD...

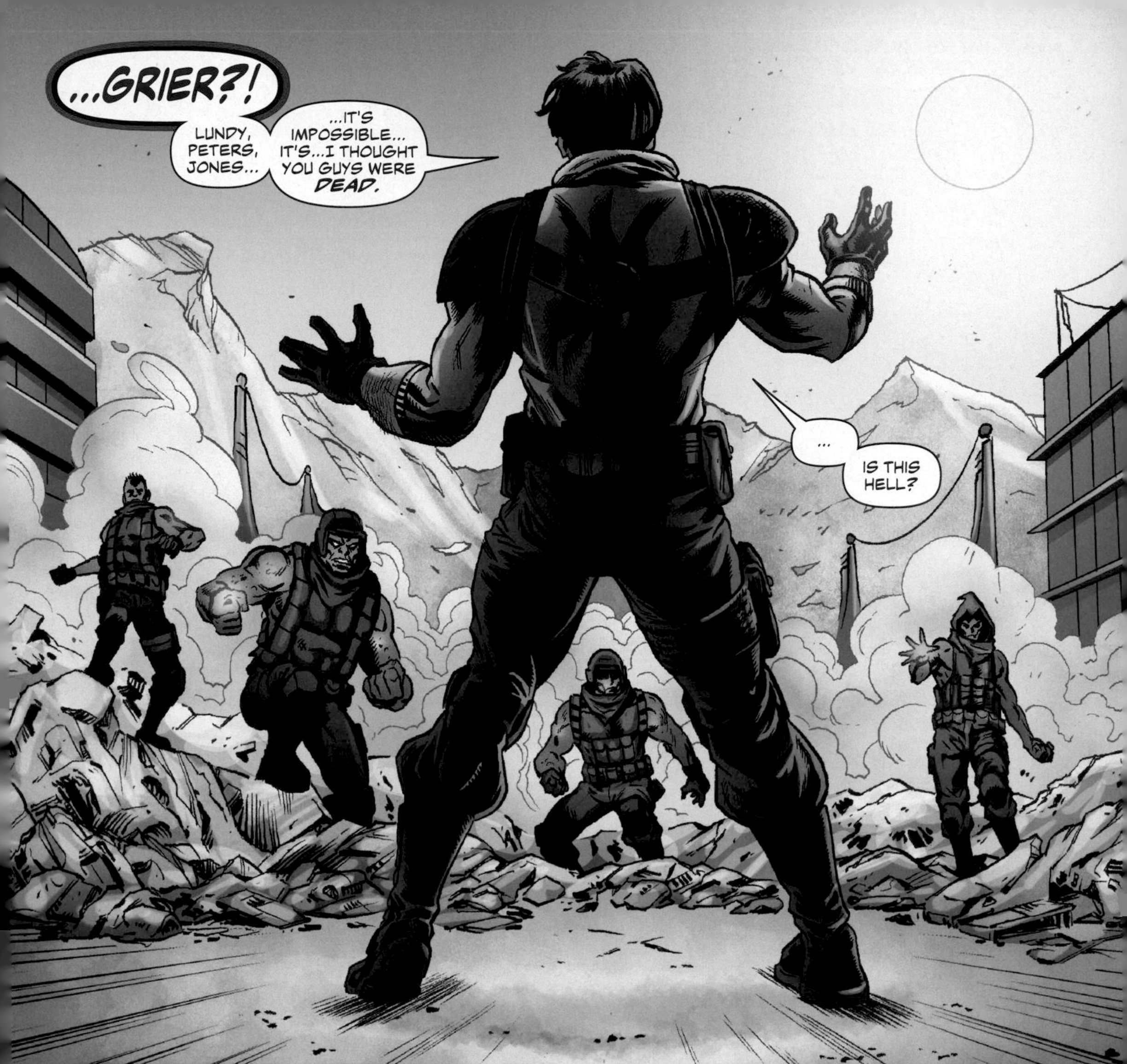
...GRIER?!
LUNDY, PETERS, JONES...
...IT'S IMPOSSIBLE... IT'S...I THOUGHT YOU GUYS WERE DEAD.
... IS THIS HELL?

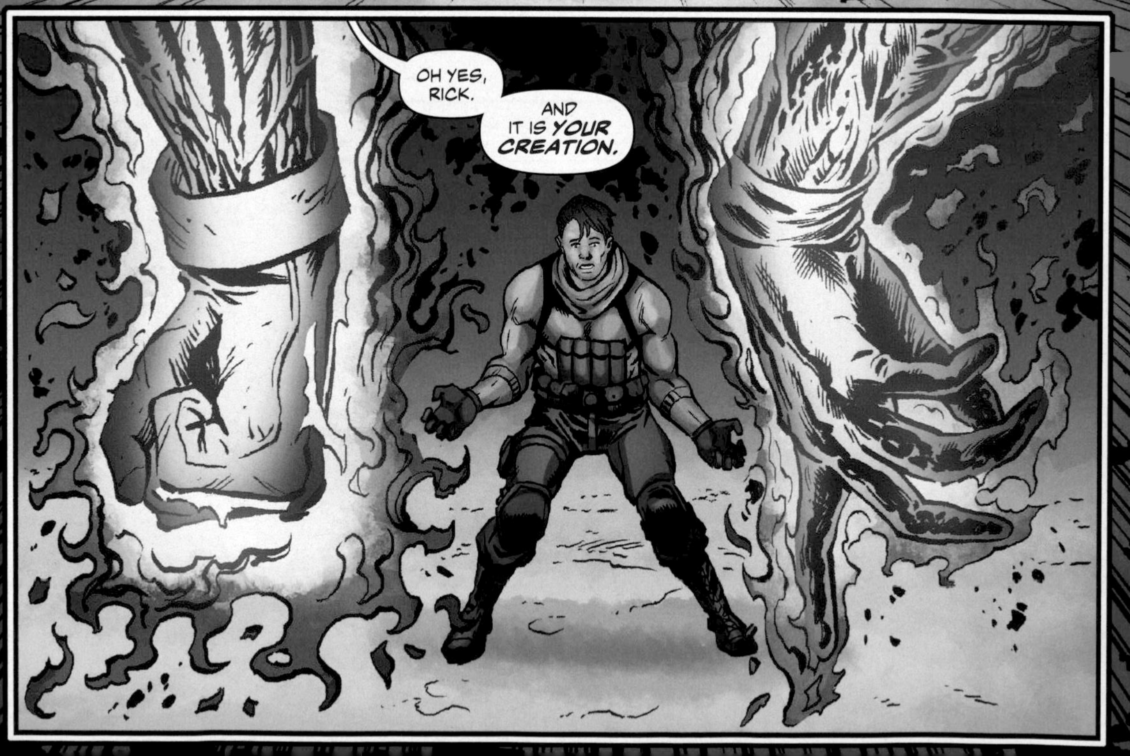
OH YES, RICK.
AND IT IS YOUR CREATION.

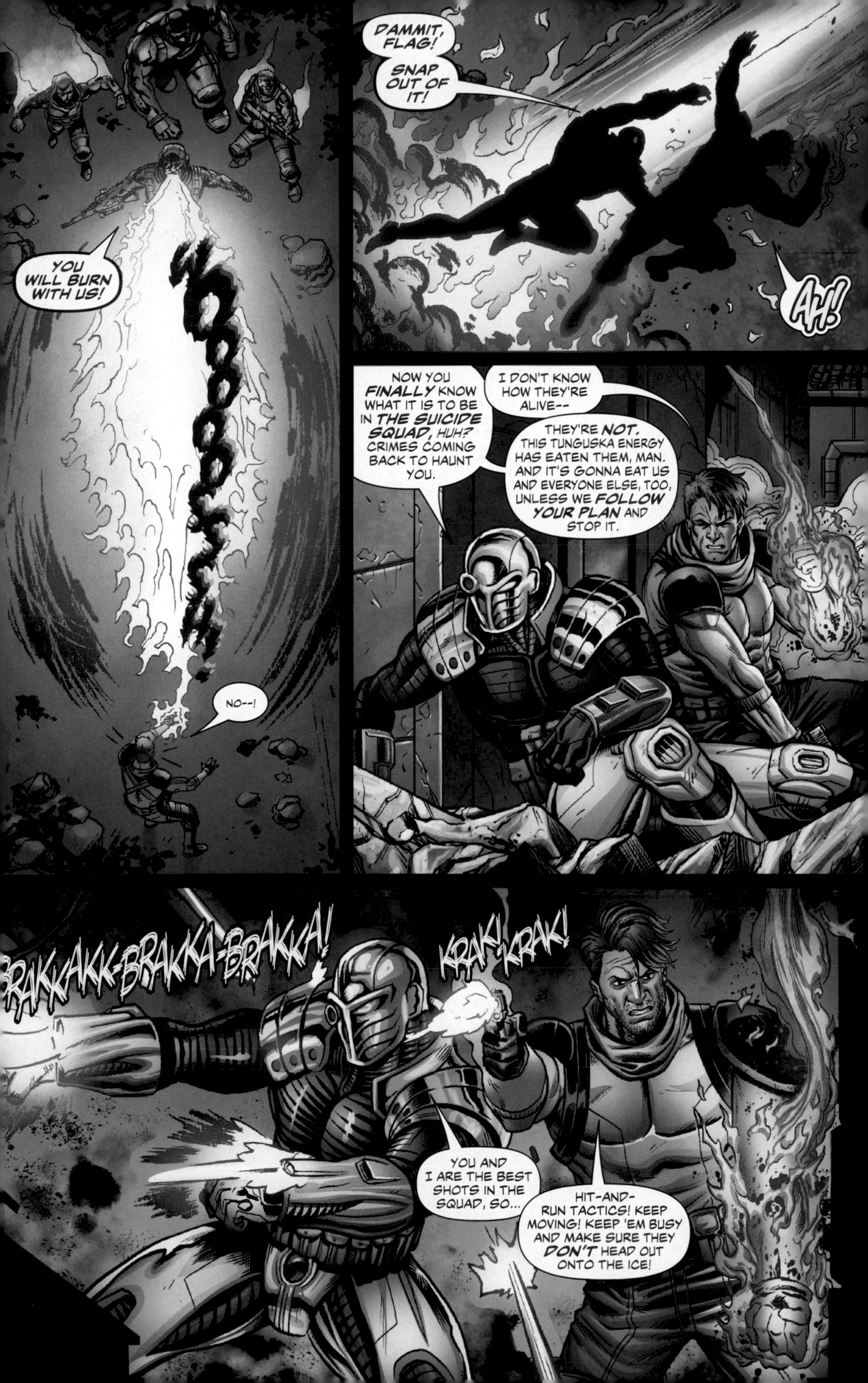
YOU WILL BURN WITH US!
NO--!
DAMMIT, FLAG!
SNAP OUT OF IT!
AH!
NOW YOU FINALLY KNOW WHAT IT IS TO BE IN THE SUICIDE SQUAD, HUH? CRIMES COMING BACK TO HAUNT YOU.
I DON'T KNOW HOW THEY'RE ALIVE--
THEY'RE NOT. THIS TUNGUSKA ENERGY HAS EATEN THEM, MAN. AND IT'S GONNA EAT US AND EVERYONE ELSE, TOO, UNLESS WE FOLLOW YOUR PLAN AND STOP IT.
BRAKKAKK-BRAKKA-BRAKKA-BRAKKA!
KRAK! KRAK!
YOU AND I ARE THE BEST SHOTS IN THE SQUAD, SO...
HIT-AND-RUN TACTICS! KEEP MOVING! KEEP 'EM BUSY AND MAKE SURE THEY DON'T HEAD OUT ONTO THE ICE!

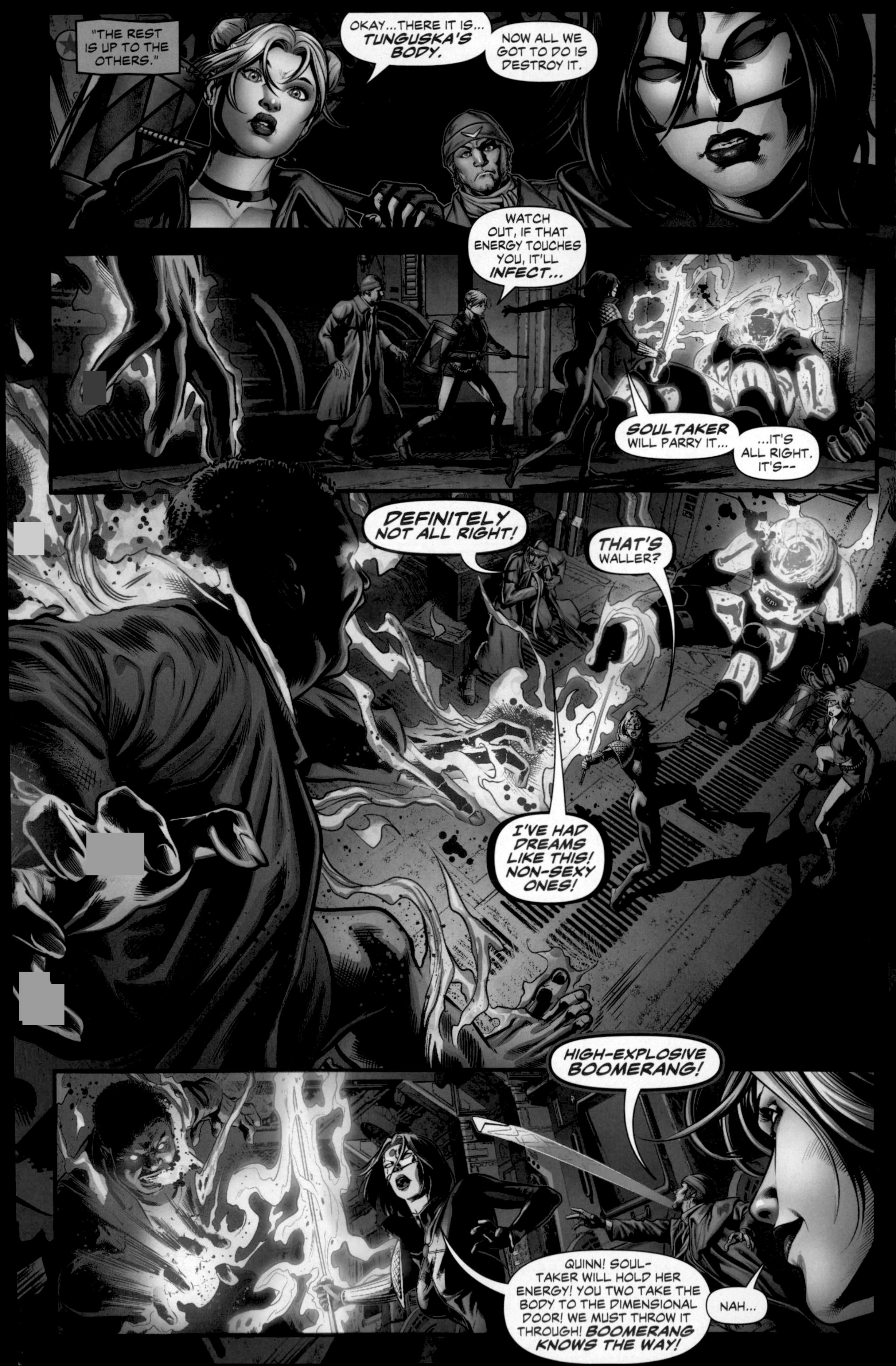
"THE REST IS UP TO THE OTHERS."
OKAY...THERE IT IS... TUNGUSKA'S BODY.
NOW ALL WE GOT TO DO IS DESTROY IT.
WATCH OUT, IF THAT ENERGY TOUCHES YOU, IT'LL INFECT...
SOULTAKER WILL PARRY IT...
...IT'S ALL RIGHT. IT'S--
DEFINITELY NOT ALL RIGHT!
THAT'S WALLER?
I'VE HAD DREAMS LIKE THIS! NON-SEXY ONES!
HIGH-EXPLOSIVE BOOMERANG!
QUINN! SOUL-TAKER WILL HOLD HER ENERGY! YOU TWO TAKE THE BODY TO THE DIMENSIONAL DOOR! WE MUST THROW IT THROUGH! BOOMERANG KNOWS THE WAY!
NAH...

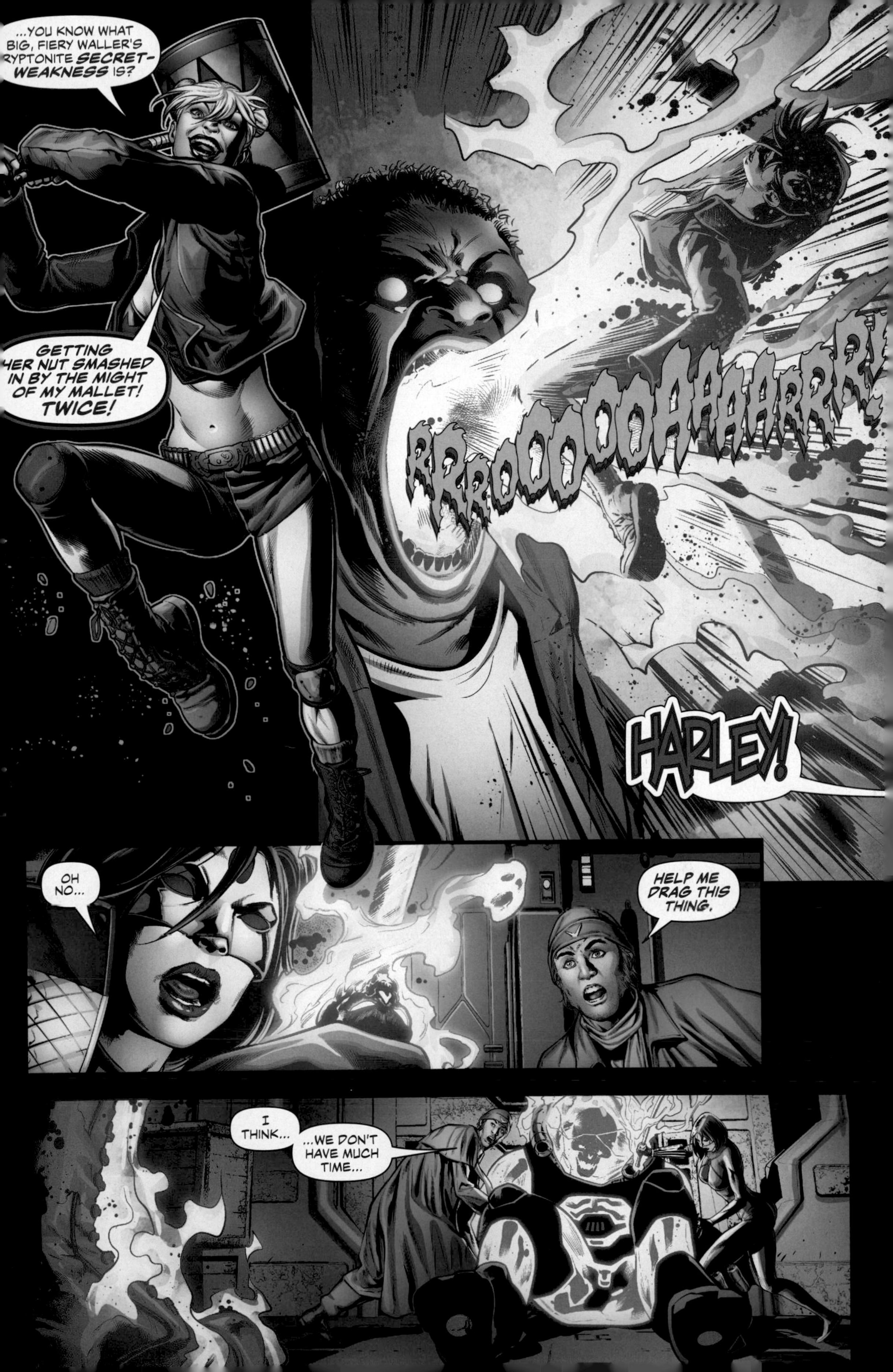
...YOU KNOW WHAT BIG, FIERY WALLER'S RYPTONITE SECRET-WEAKNESS IS?
GETTING HER NUT SMASHED IN BY THE MIGHT OF MY MALLET! TWICE!
RRROOOOOOAAAARRR
HARLEY!
OH NO...
HELP ME DRAG THIS THING.
I THINK...
...WE DON'T HAVE MUCH TIME...

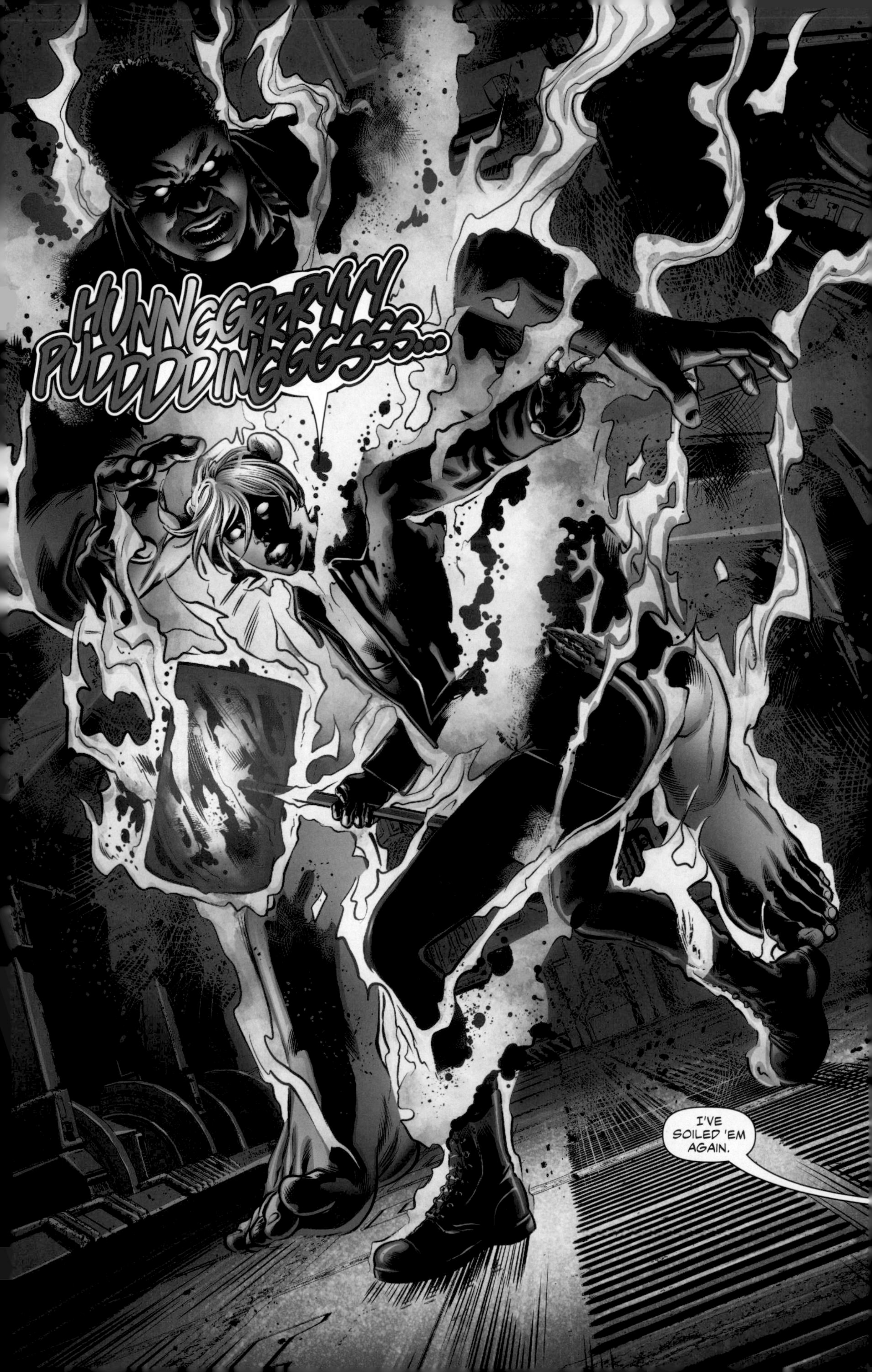
HUNNGRRRYYY PUDDDDINGGGSSS...
I'VE SOILED 'EM AGAIN.

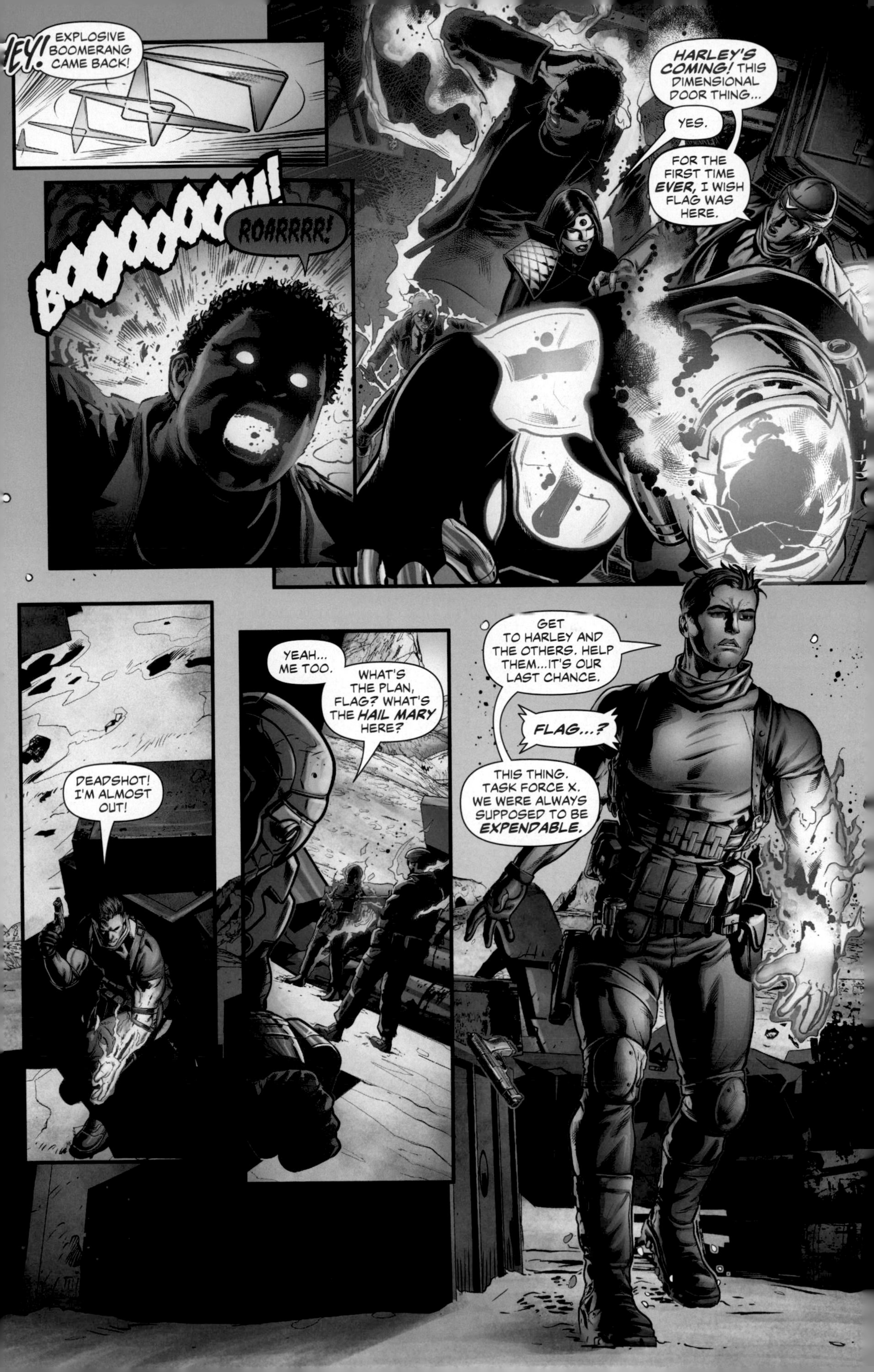

'EY! EXPLOSIVE BOOMERANG CAME BACK!
BOOOOOOOM!
ROARRRR!
HARLEY'S COMING! THIS DIMENSIONAL DOOR THING...
YES.
FOR THE FIRST TIME EVER, I WISH FLAG WAS HERE.
DEADSHOT! I'M ALMOST OUT!
YEAH... ME TOO.
WHAT'S THE PLAN, FLAG? WHAT'S THE HAIL MARY HERE?
GET TO HARLEY AND THE OTHERS. HELP THEM...IT'S OUR LAST CHANCE.
FLAG...?
THIS THING. TASK FORCE X. WE WERE ALWAYS SUPPOSED TO BE EXPENDABLE.

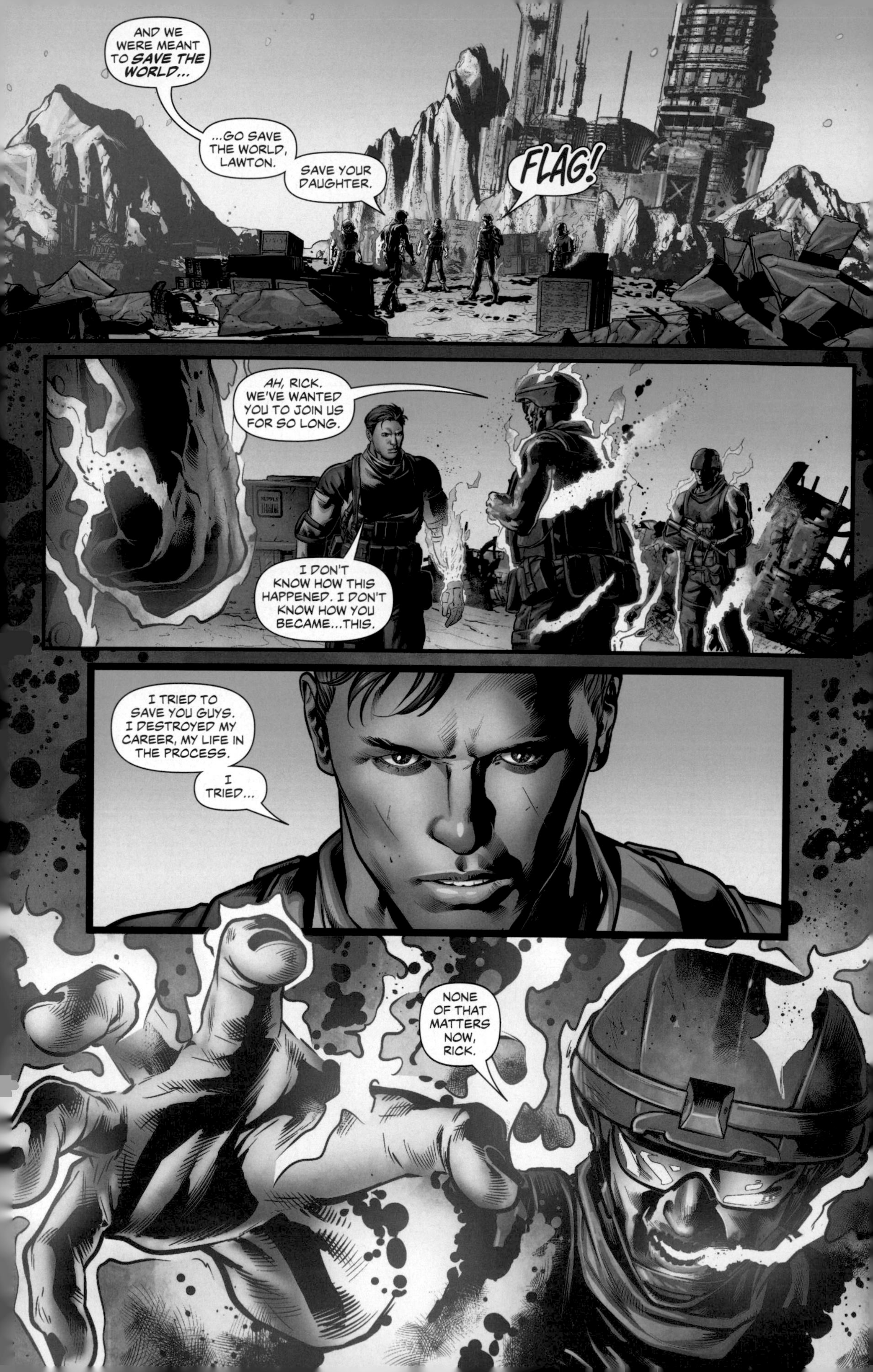
AND WE WERE MEANT TO SAVE THE WORLD...
...GO SAVE THE WORLD, LAWTON.
SAVE YOUR DAUGHTER.
FLAG!
AH, RICK. WE'VE WANTED YOU TO JOIN US FOR SO LONG.
I DON'T KNOW HOW THIS HAPPENED. I DON'T KNOW HOW YOU BECAME...THIS.
I TRIED TO SAVE YOU GUYS. I DESTROYED MY CAREER, MY LIFE IN THE PROCESS.
I TRIED...
NONE OF THAT MATTERS NOW, RICK.

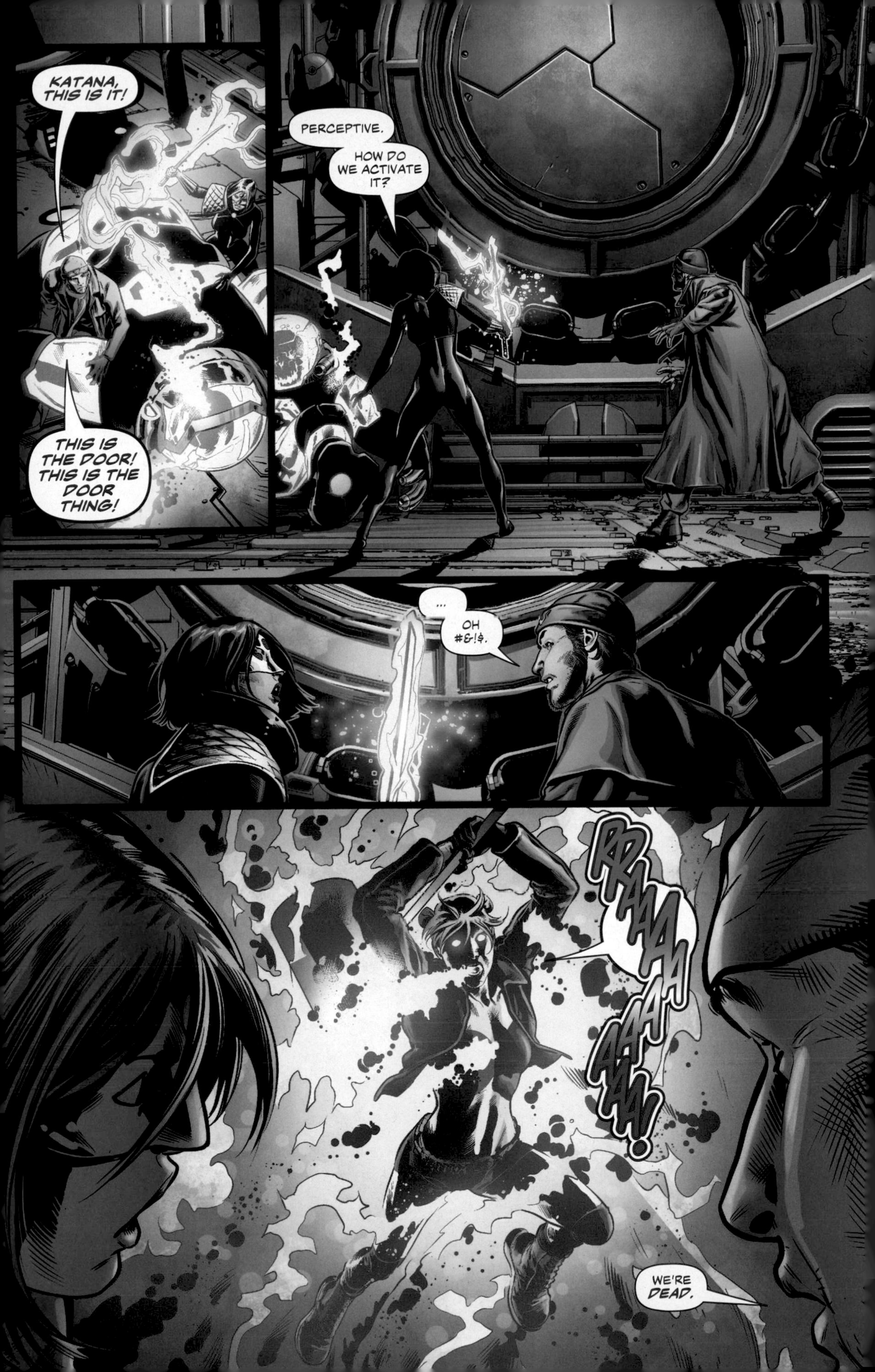
KATANA, THIS IS IT!
THIS IS THE DOOR! THIS IS THE DOOR THING!
PERCEPTIVE.
HOW DO WE ACTIVATE IT?
...
OH #&!$.
RRAAAAAAAAAAA!
WE'RE DEAD.

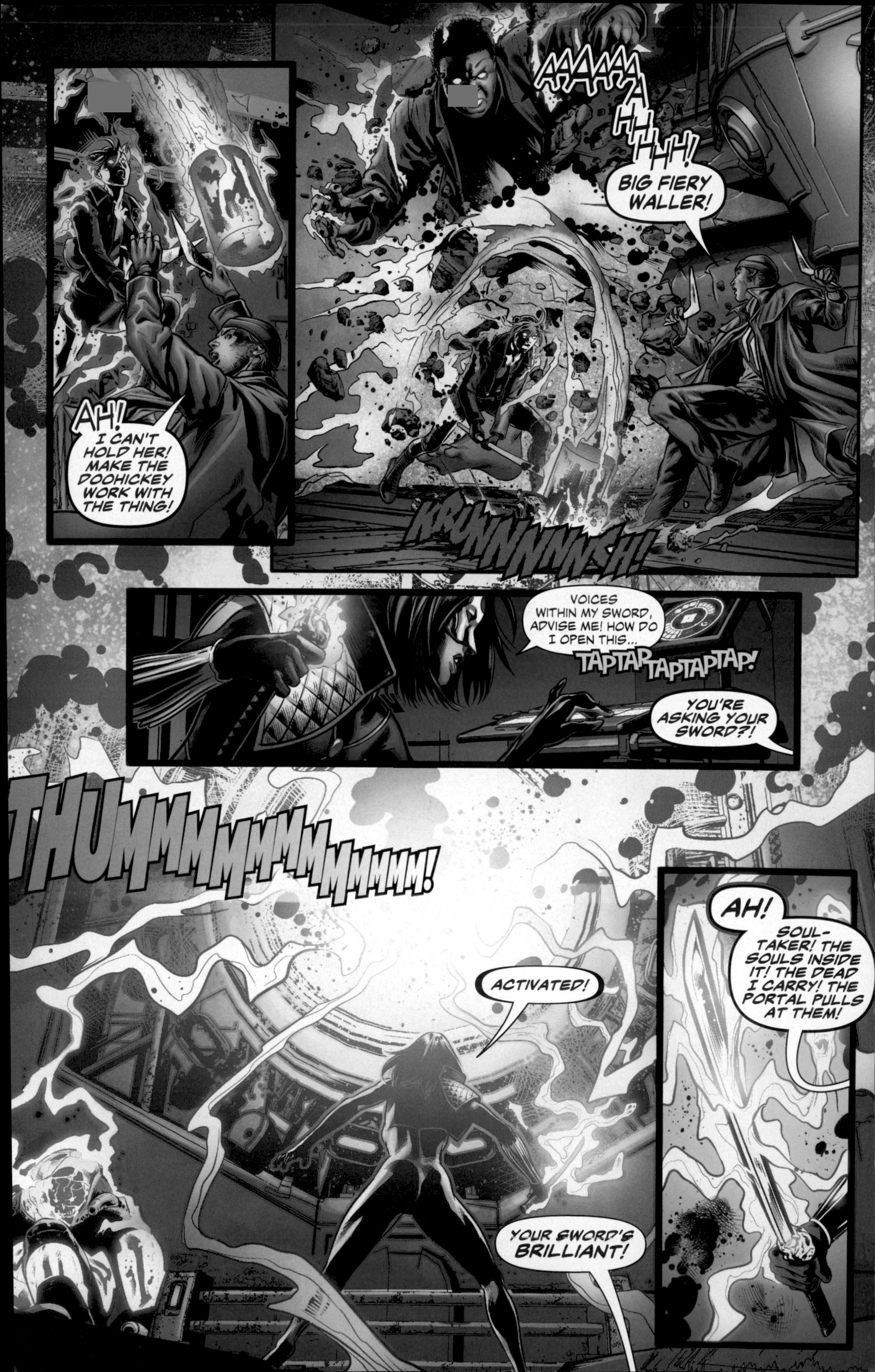
AAAAAAHHHHH!
BIG FIERY WALLER!
AH! I CAN'T HOLD HER! MAKE THE DOOHICKEY WORK WITH THE THING!
KRUNNNNNNSH!
VOICES WITHIN MY SWORD, ADVISE ME! HOW DO I OPEN THIS...
TAPTAPTAPTAPTAP!
YOU'RE ASKING YOUR SWORD?!
THUMMMMMMMMMMMMMMM!
ACTIVATED!
YOUR SWORD'S BRILLIANT!
AH!
SOUL-TAKER! THE SOULS INSIDE IT! THE DEAD I CARRY! THE PORTAL PULLS AT THEM!

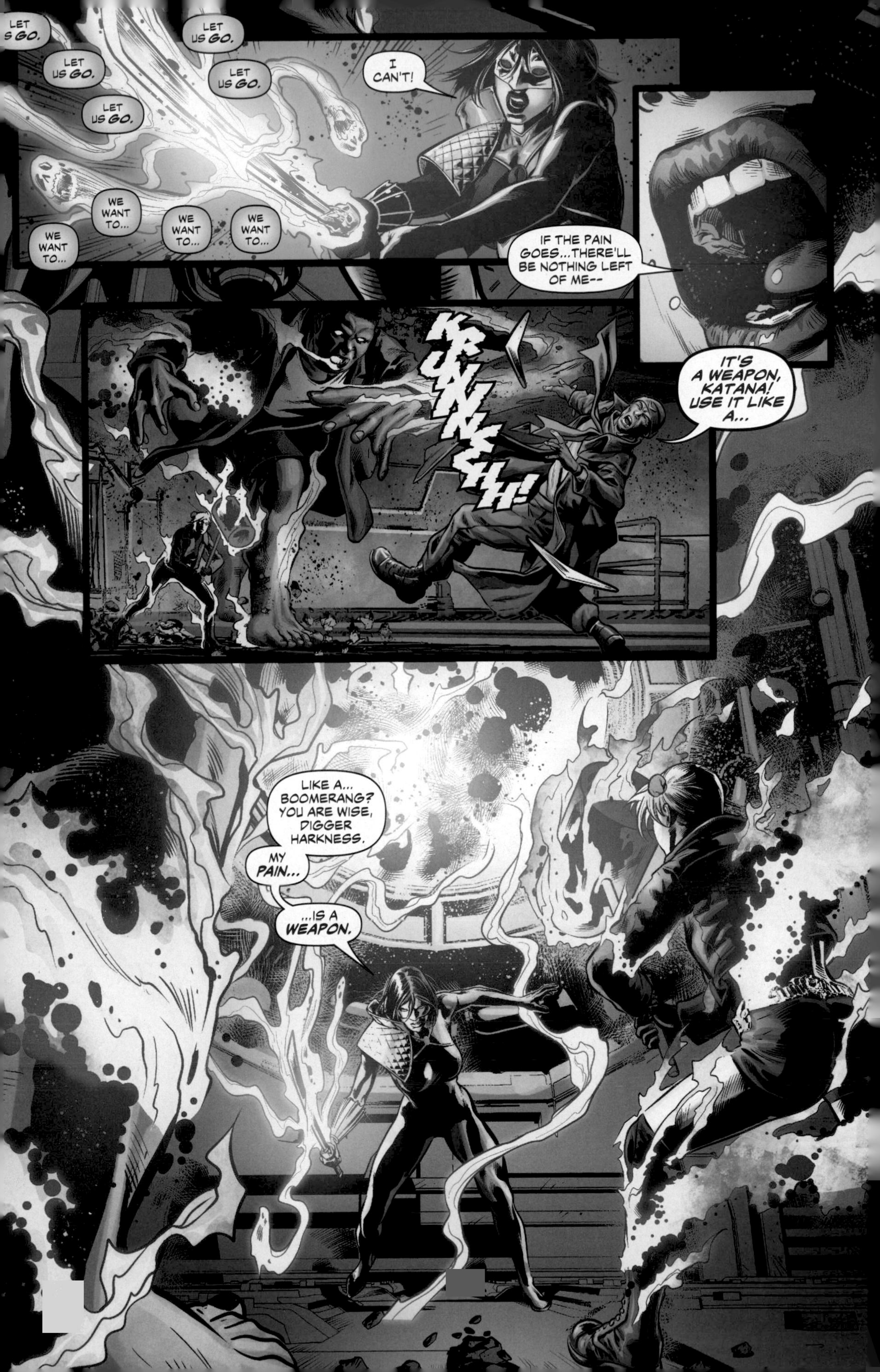
LET S GO.
LET US GO.
LET US GO.
LET US GO.
LET US GO.
I CAN'T!
WE WANT TO...
WE WANT TO...
WE WANT TO...
WE WANT TO...
IF THE PAIN GOES...THERE'LL BE NOTHING LEFT OF ME--
KRUNSHH!
IT'S A WEAPON, KATANA! USE IT LIKE A...
LIKE A... BOOMERANG? YOU ARE WISE, DIGGER HARKNESS.
MY PAIN...
...IS A WEAPON.

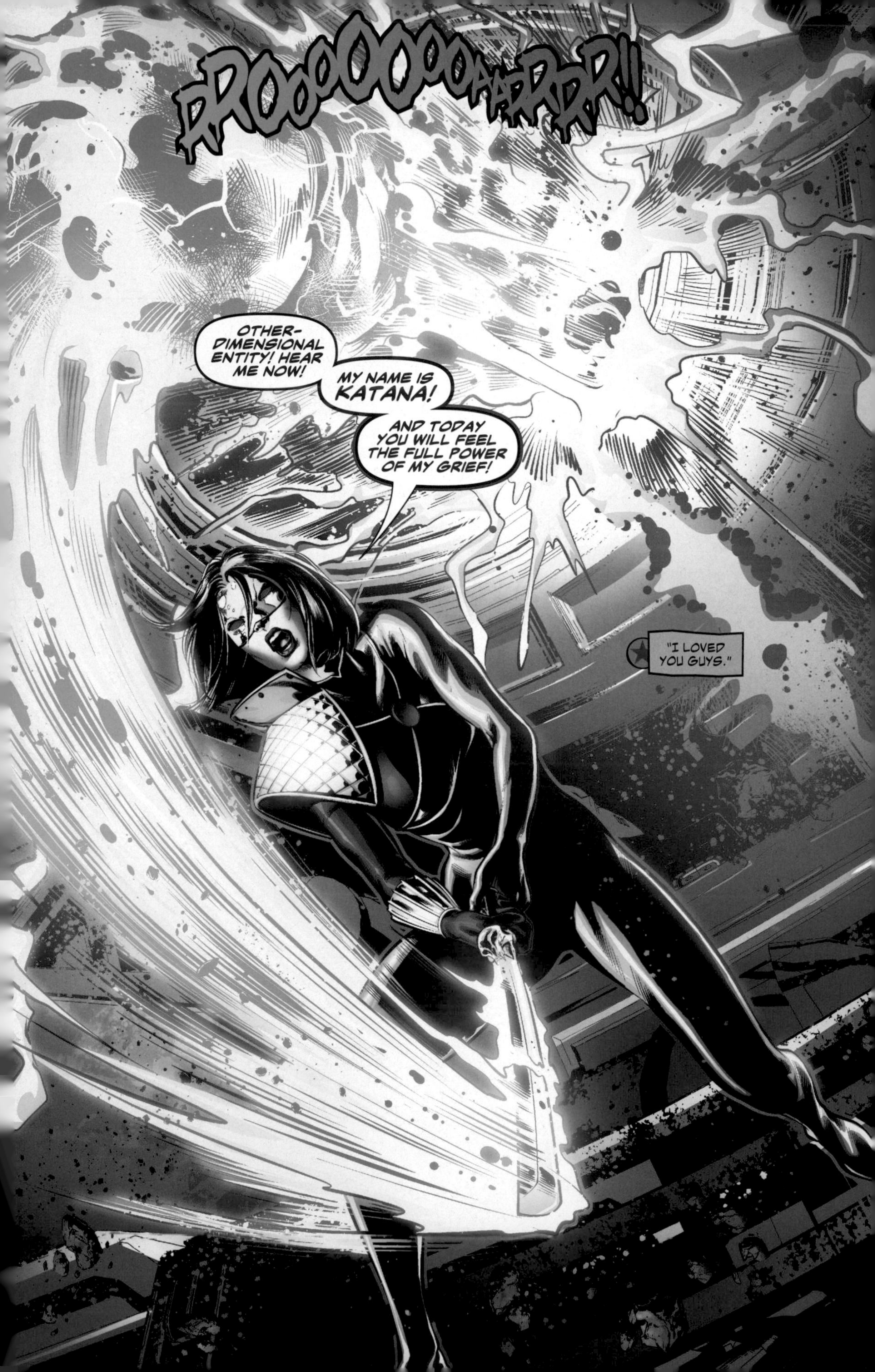
DROOOOOOOAARRDR!!
OTHER-DIMENSIONAL ENTITY! HEAR ME NOW!
MY NAME IS KATANA!
AND TODAY YOU WILL FEEL THE FULL POWER OF MY GRIEF!
"I LOVED YOU GUYS."

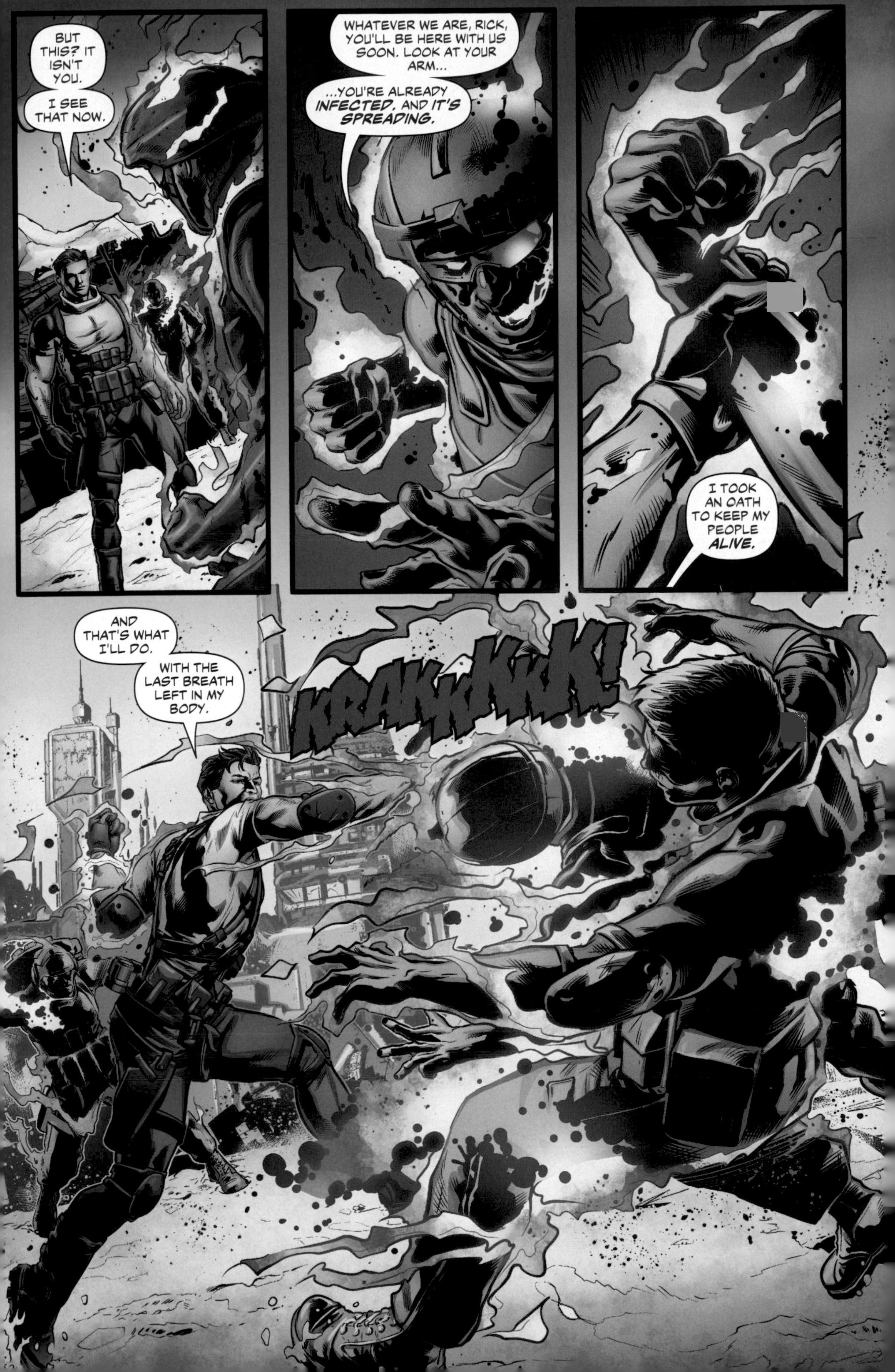
BUT THIS? IT ISN'T YOU.
I SEE THAT NOW.
WHATEVER WE ARE, RICK, YOU'LL BE HERE WITH US SOON. LOOK AT YOUR ARM...
...YOU'RE ALREADY *INFECTED.* AND *IT'S SPREADING.*
I TOOK AN OATH TO KEEP MY PEOPLE *ALIVE.*
AND THAT'S WHAT I'LL DO.
WITH THE LAST BREATH LEFT IN MY BODY.
KRAKKKKKK!

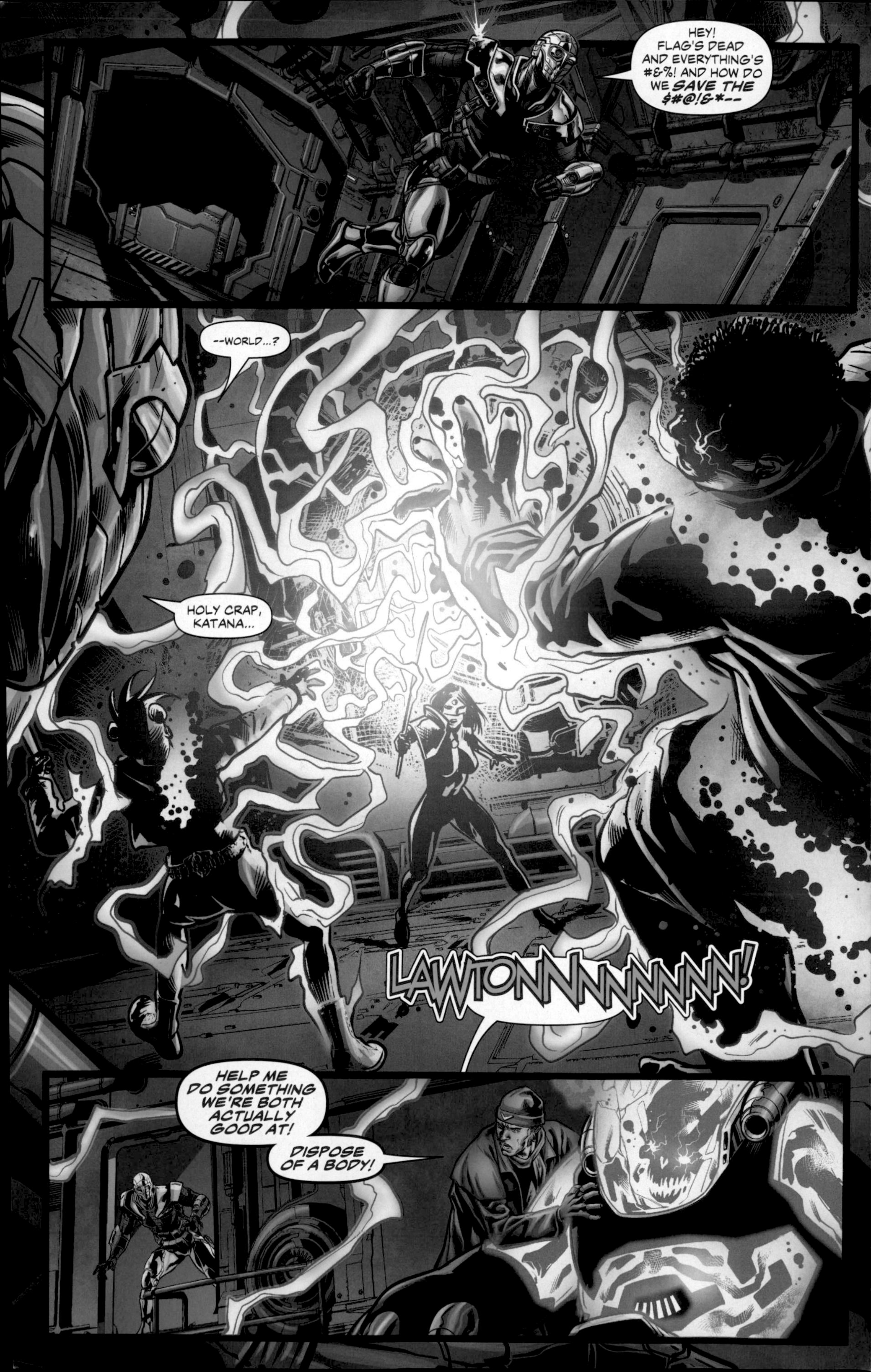
HEY! FLAG'S DEAD AND EVERYTHING'S #&%! AND HOW DO WE SAVE THE $#@!&*--
--WORLD...?
HOLY CRAP, KATANA...
LAWTONNNNNNNN!
HELP ME DO SOMETHING WE'RE BOTH ACTUALLY GOOD AT!
DISPOSE OF A BODY!

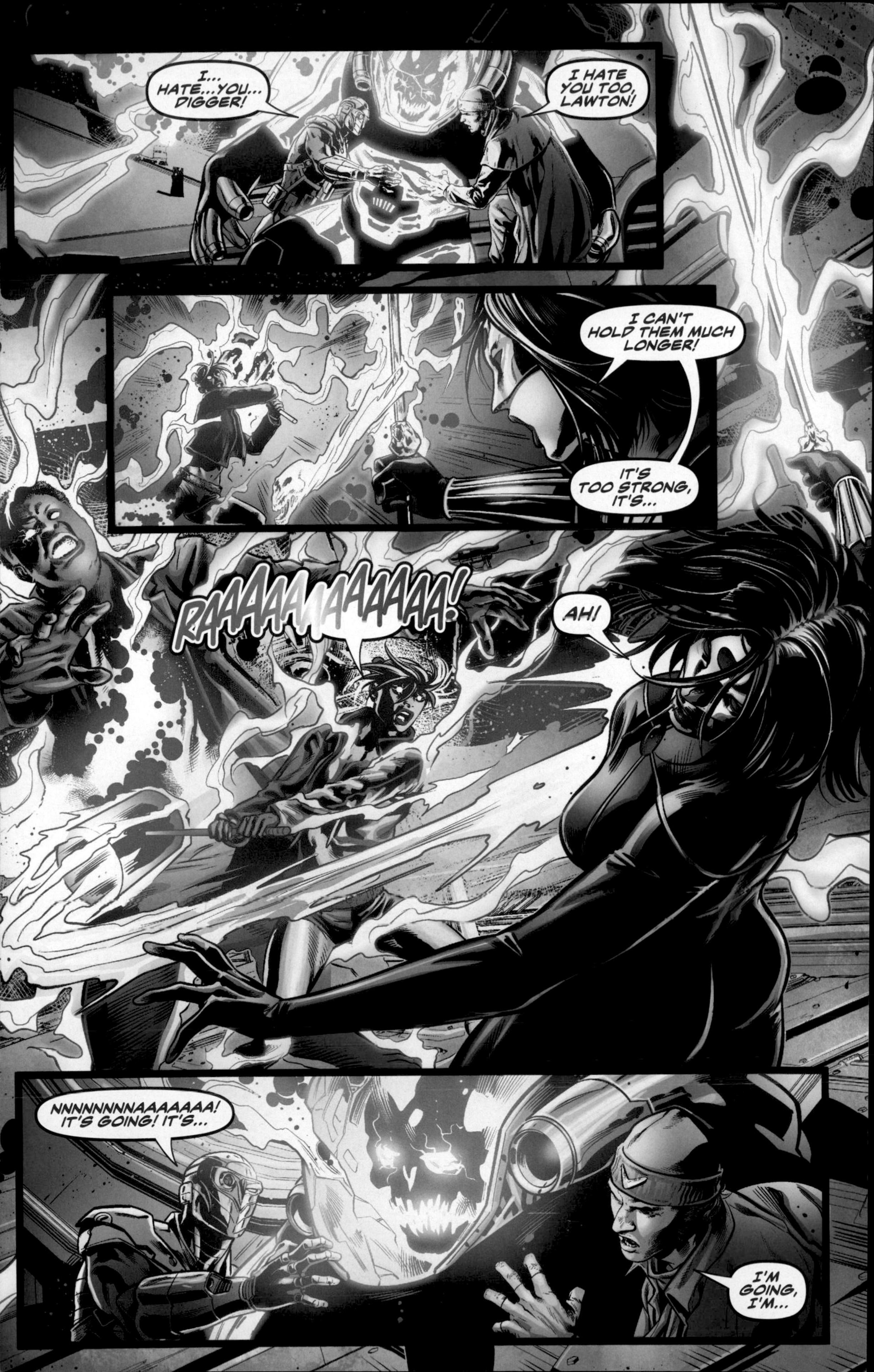
I... HATE...YOU... DIGGER!
I HATE YOU TOO, LAWTON!
I CAN'T HOLD THEM MUCH LONGER!
IT'S TOO STRONG, IT'S...
RAAAAAAAAAAAA!
AH!
NNNNNNNNAAAAAAA! IT'S GOING! IT'S...
I'M GOING, I'M...

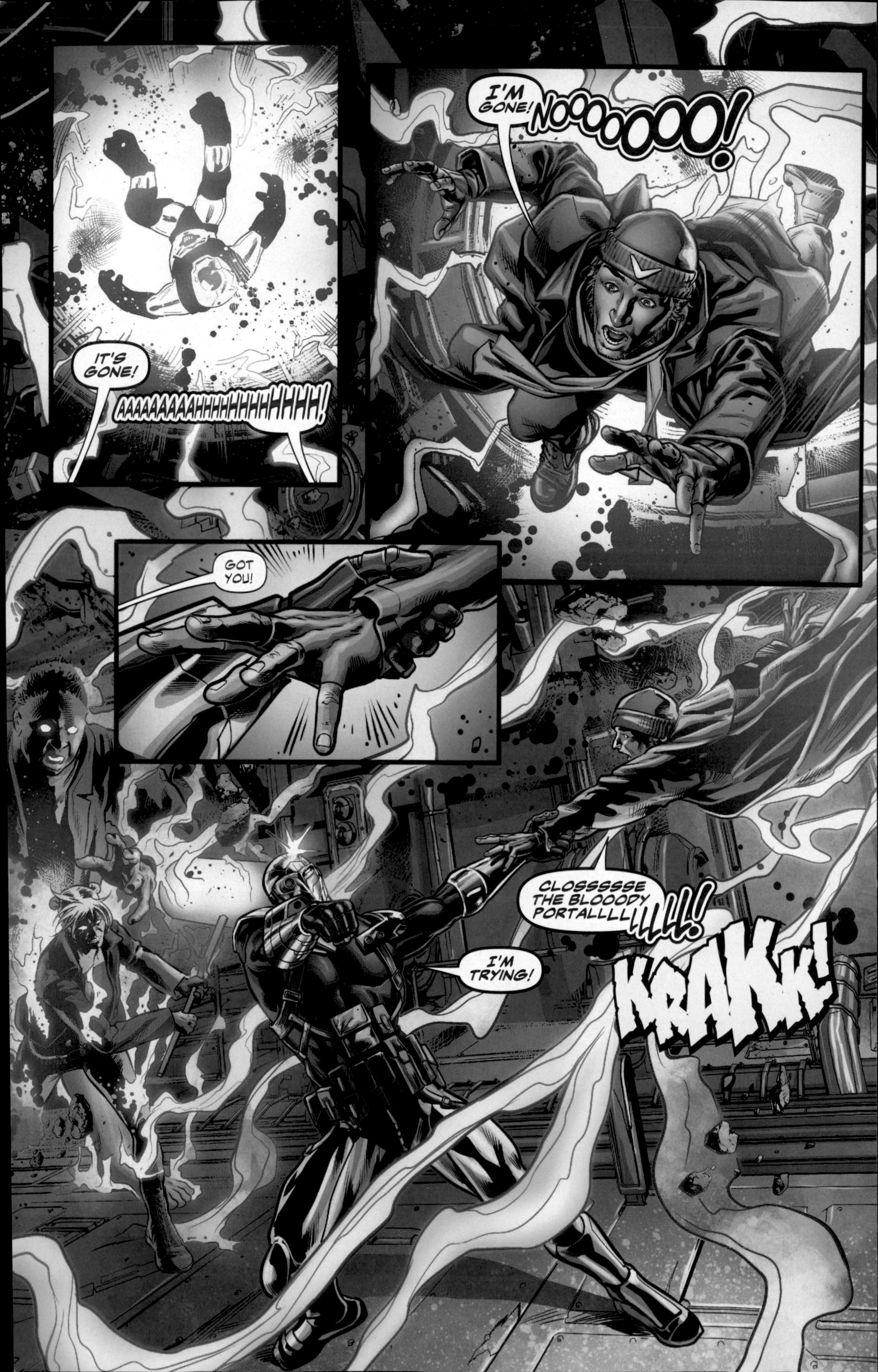
IT'S GONE!
AAAAAAAAAHHHHHHHHHHHH!
I'M GONE!
NOOOOOOOO!
GOT YOU!
CLOSSSSSE THE BLOOODY PORTALLLLLLLLL!
I'M TRYING!
KRAKK!

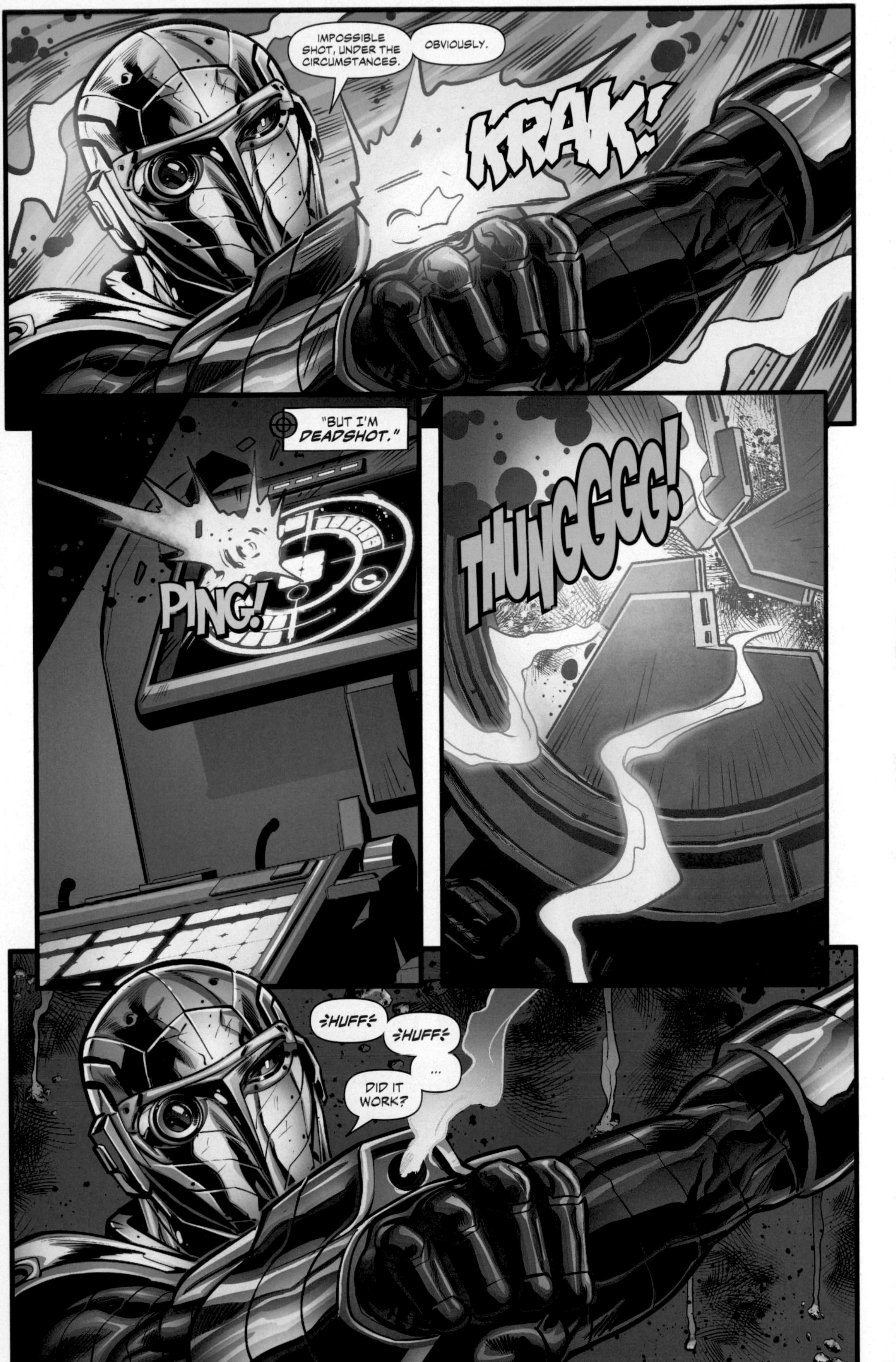
IMPOSSIBLE SHOT, UNDER THE CIRCUMSTANCES.
OBVIOUSLY.
KRAK!
"BUT I'M DEADSHOT."
PING!
THUNGGGG!
HUFF
HUFF
...
DID IT WORK?

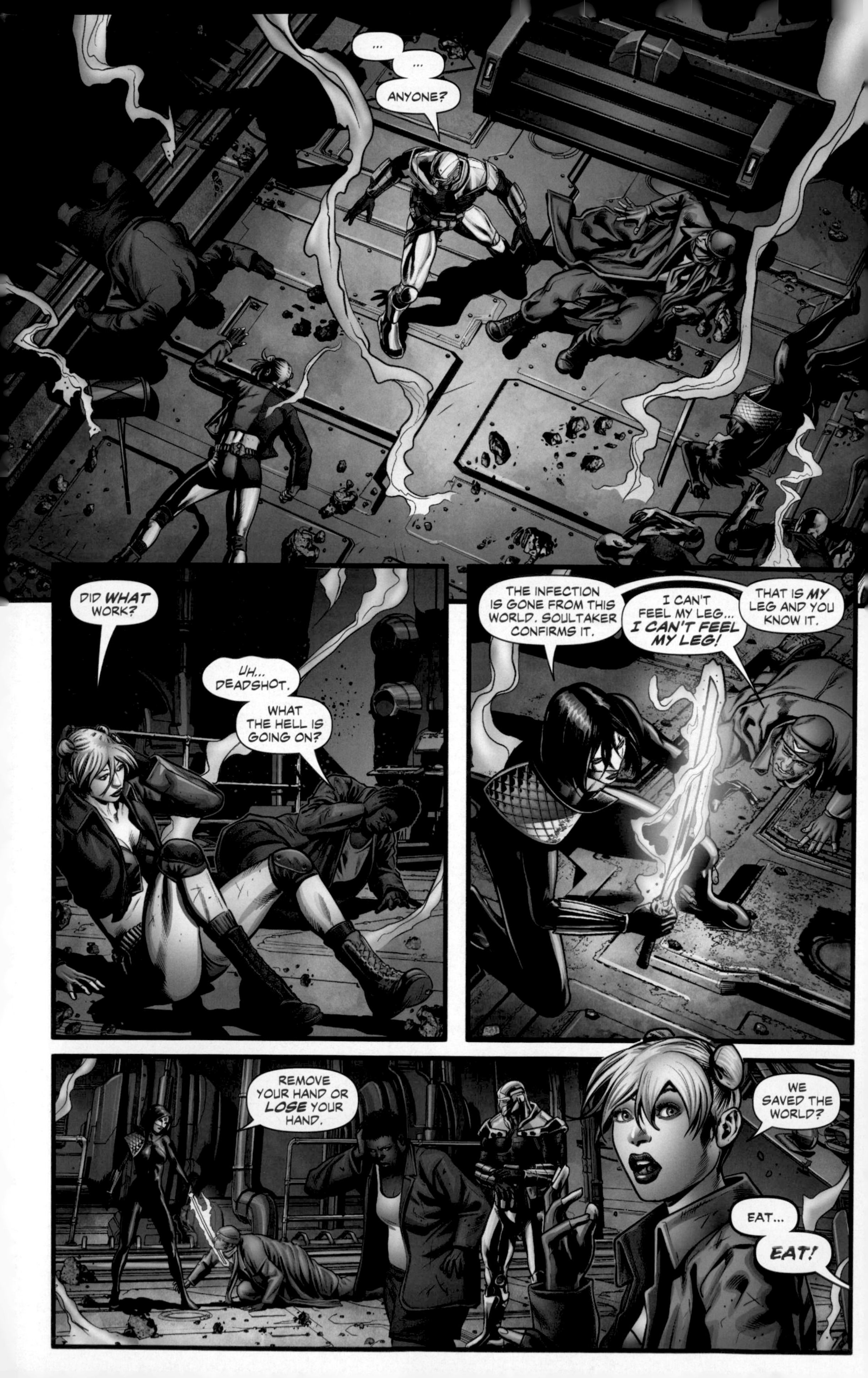
...
...
ANYONE?
DID *WHAT* WORK?
UH... DEADSHOT.
WHAT THE HELL IS GOING ON?
THE INFECTION IS GONE FROM THIS WORLD. SOULTAKER CONFIRMS IT.
I CAN'T FEEL MY LEG... *I CAN'T FEEL MY LEG!*
THAT IS *MY* LEG AND YOU KNOW IT.
REMOVE YOUR HAND OR *LOSE* YOUR HAND.
WE SAVED THE WORLD?
EAT...
EAT!

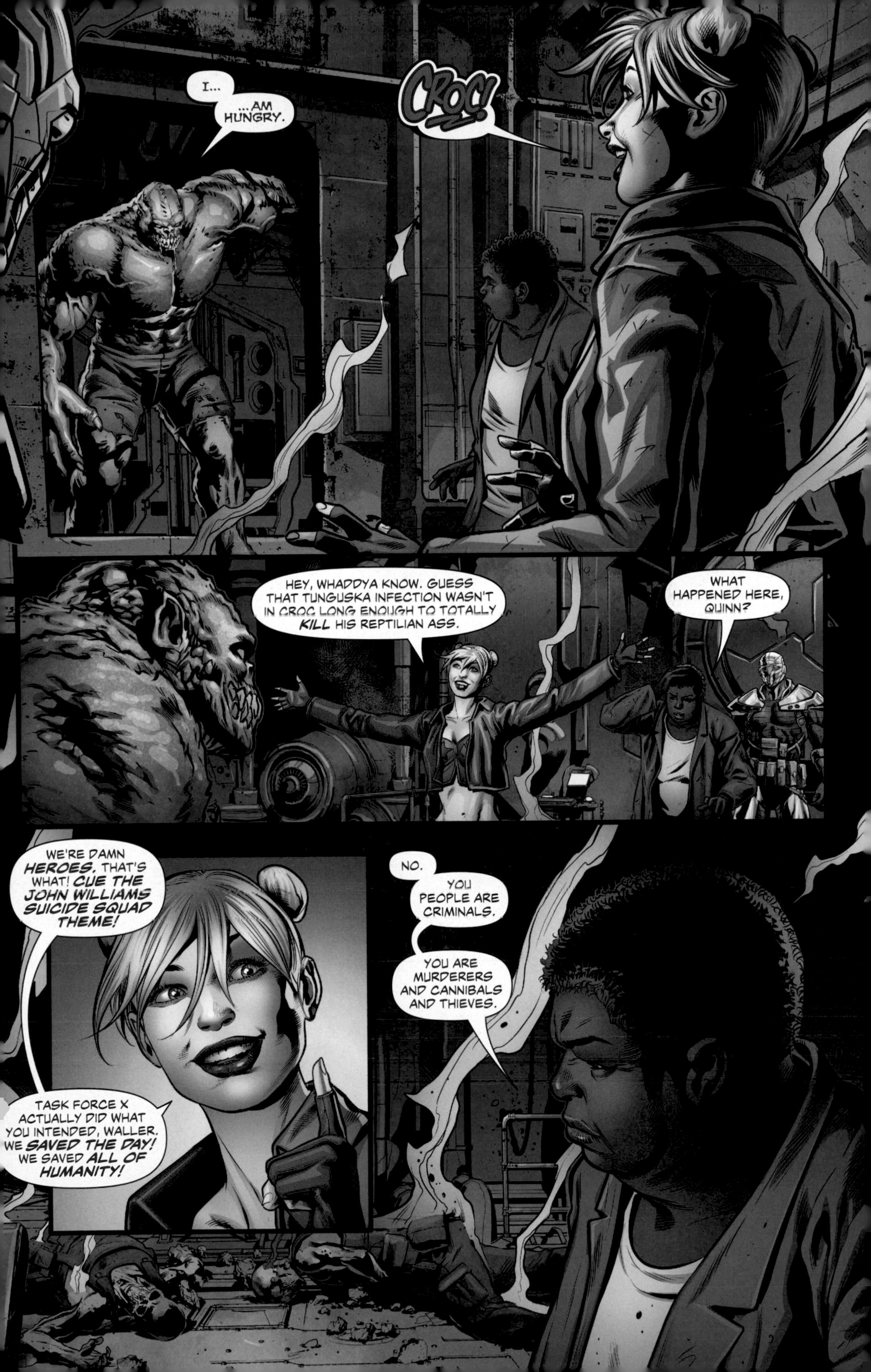
I...
...AM HUNGRY.
CROC!
HEY, WHADDYA KNOW. GUESS THAT TUNGUSKA INFECTION WASN'T IN CROC LONG ENOUGH TO TOTALLY KILL HIS REPTILIAN ASS.
WHAT HAPPENED HERE, QUINN?
WE'RE DAMN HEROES. THAT'S WHAT! CUE THE JOHN WILLIAMS SUICIDE SQUAD THEME!
TASK FORCE X ACTUALLY DID WHAT YOU INTENDED, WALLER. WE SAVED THE DAY! WE SAVED ALL OF HUMANITY!
NO.
YOU PEOPLE ARE CRIMINALS.
YOU ARE MURDERERS AND CANNIBALS AND THIEVES.

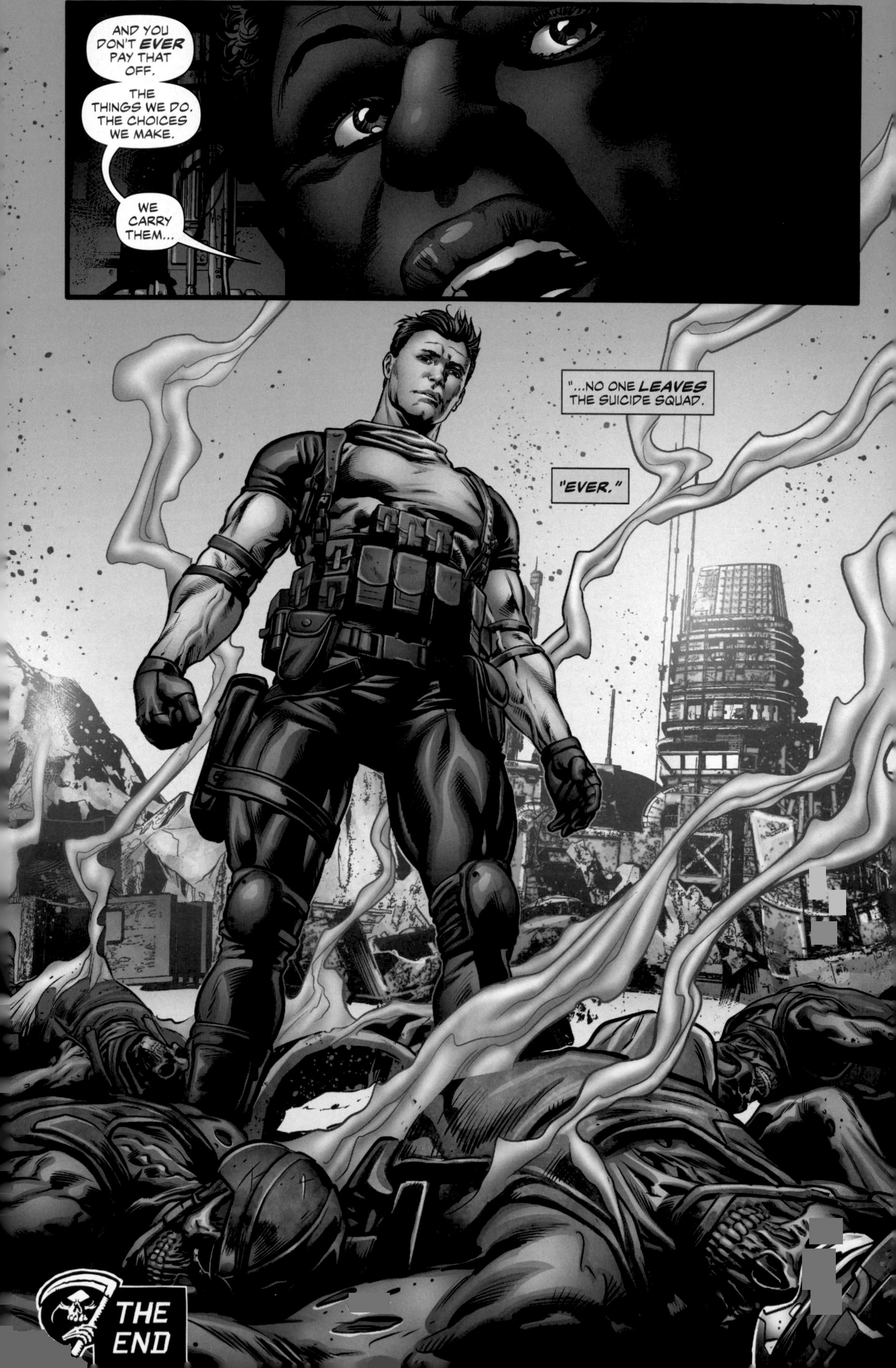
AND YOU DON'T **EVER** PAY THAT OFF.
THE THINGS WE DO. THE CHOICES WE MAKE.
WE CARRY THEM...
"...NO ONE **LEAVES** THE SUICIDE SQUAD.
"**EVER.**"
THE END

SUICIDE SQUAD #41 variant cover by FRANCESCO MATTINA

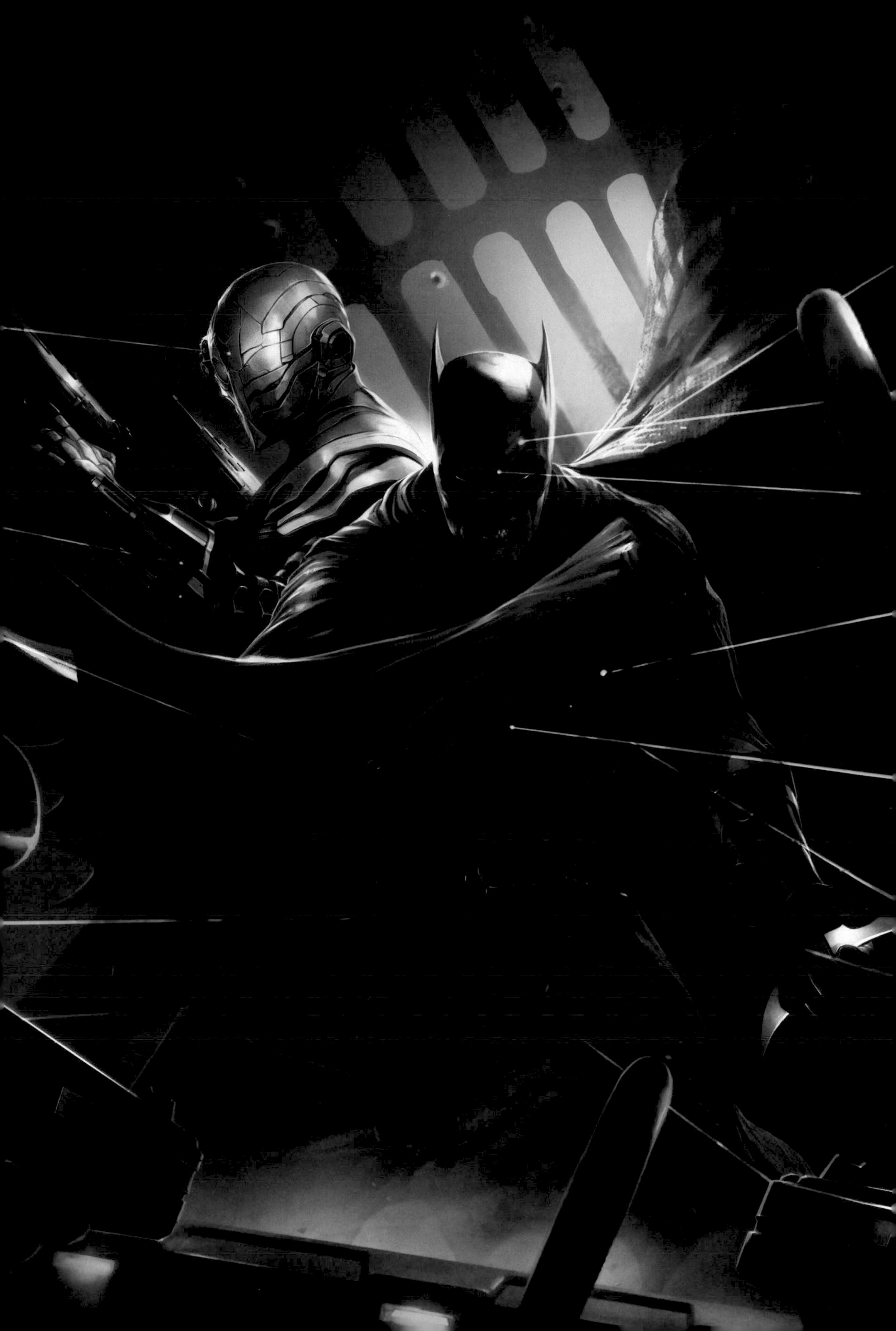

SUICIDE SQUAD #42 variant cover by FRANCESCO MATTINA

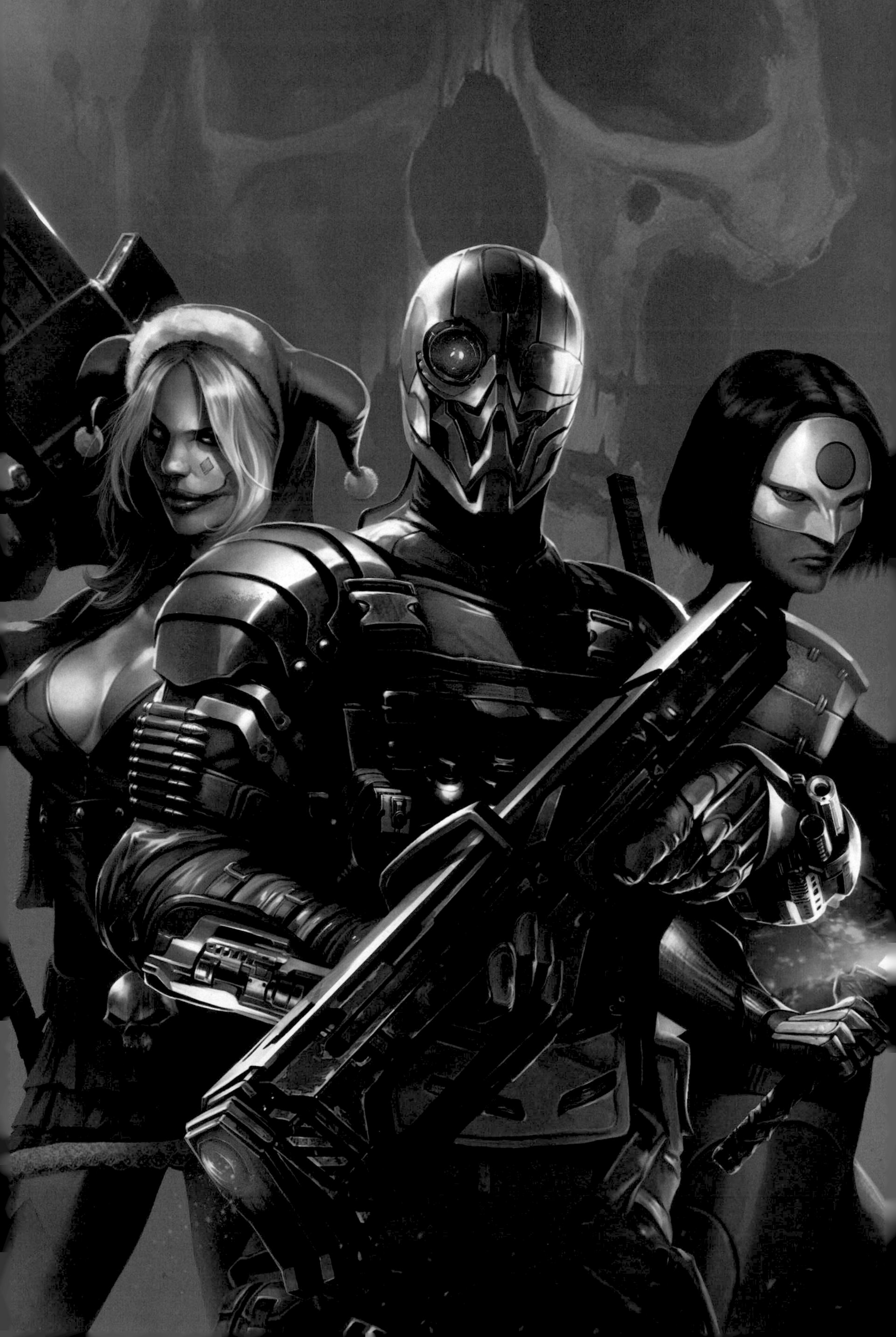

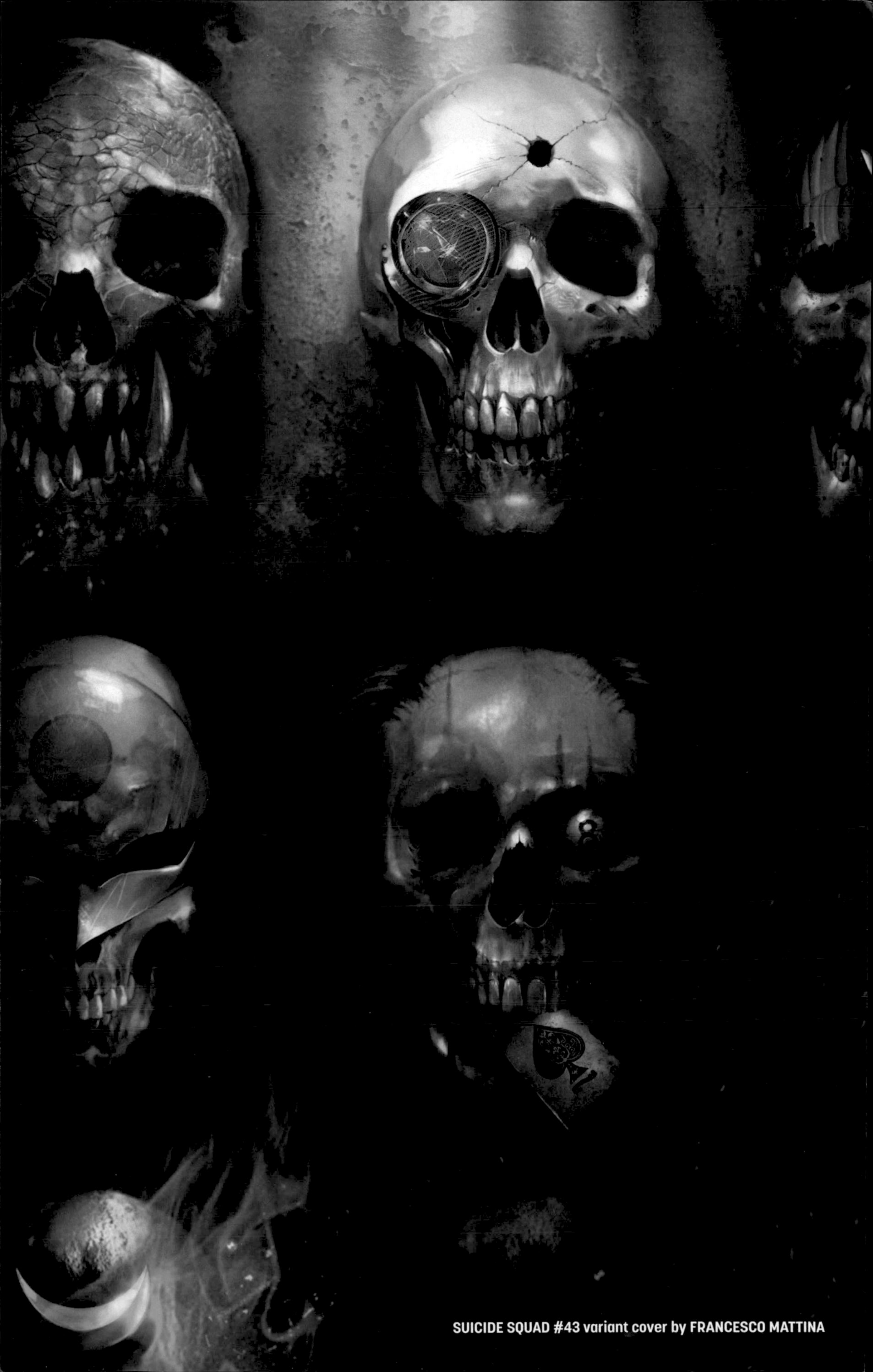

SUICIDE SQUAD #43 variant cover by FRANCESCO MATTINA

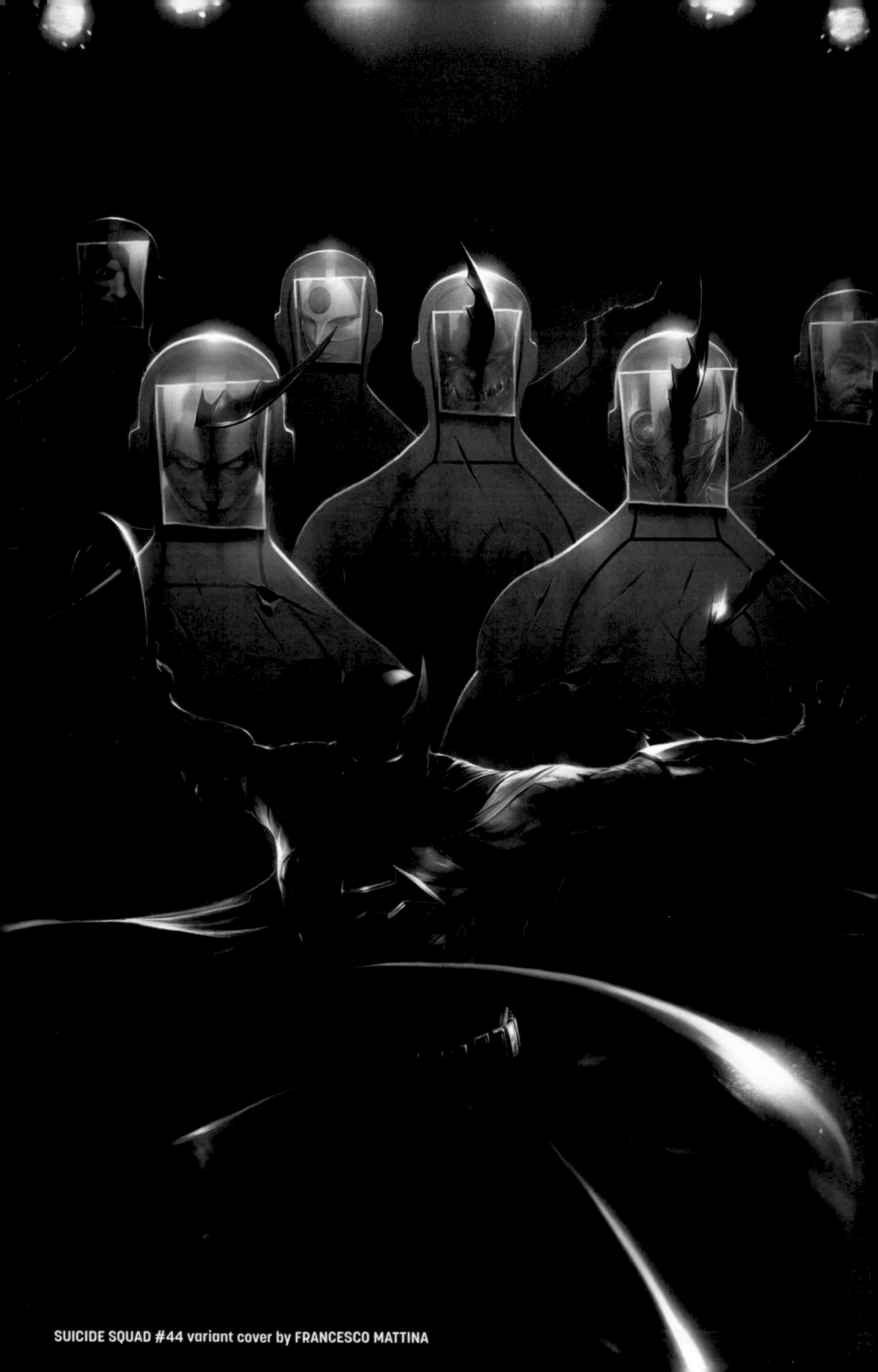

SUICIDE SQUAD #44 variant cover by FRANCESCO MATTINA

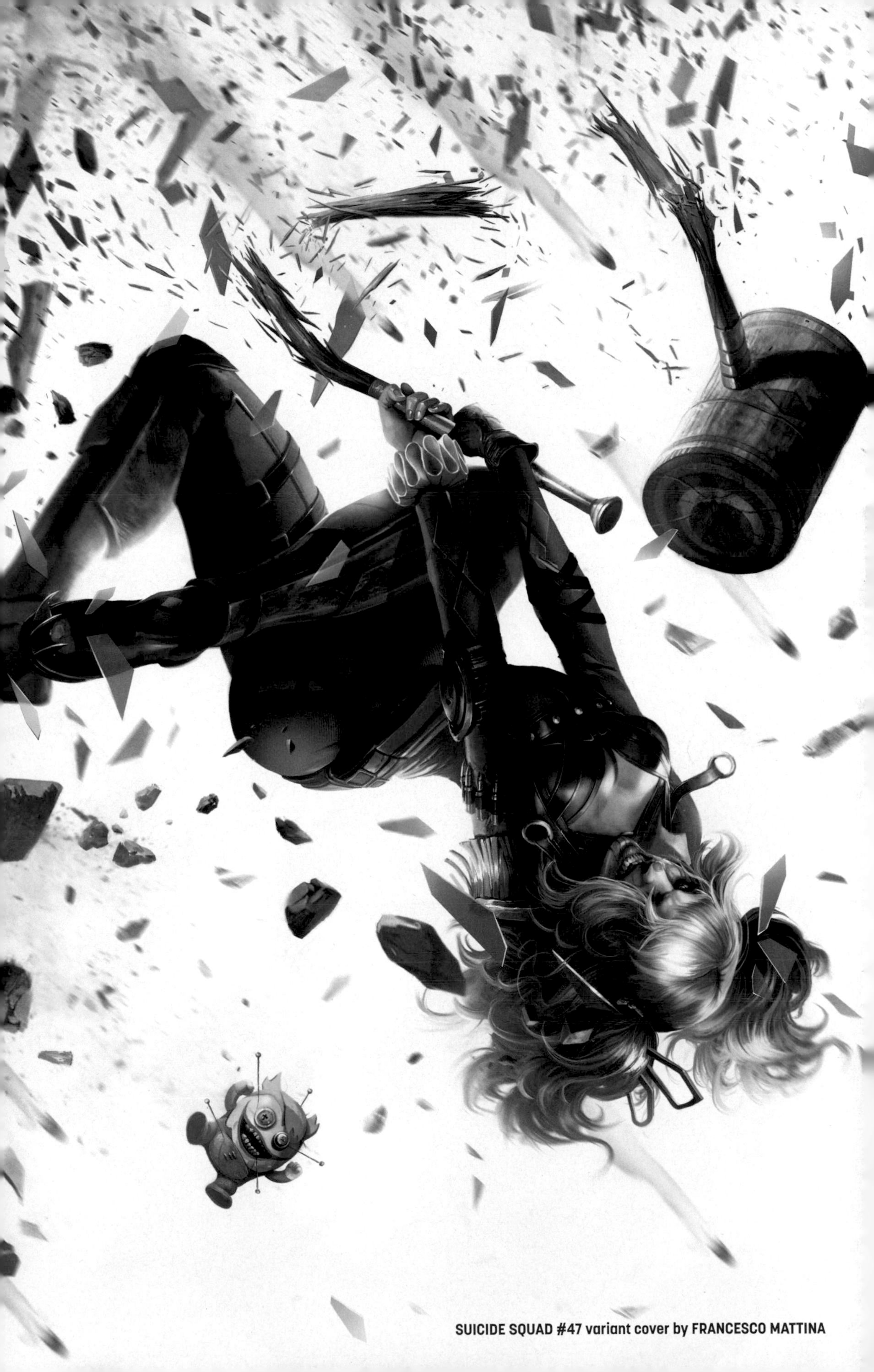

SUICIDE SQUAD #47 variant cover by FRANCESCO MATTINA

SUICIDE SQUAD #48
variant cover by FRANCESCO MATTINA

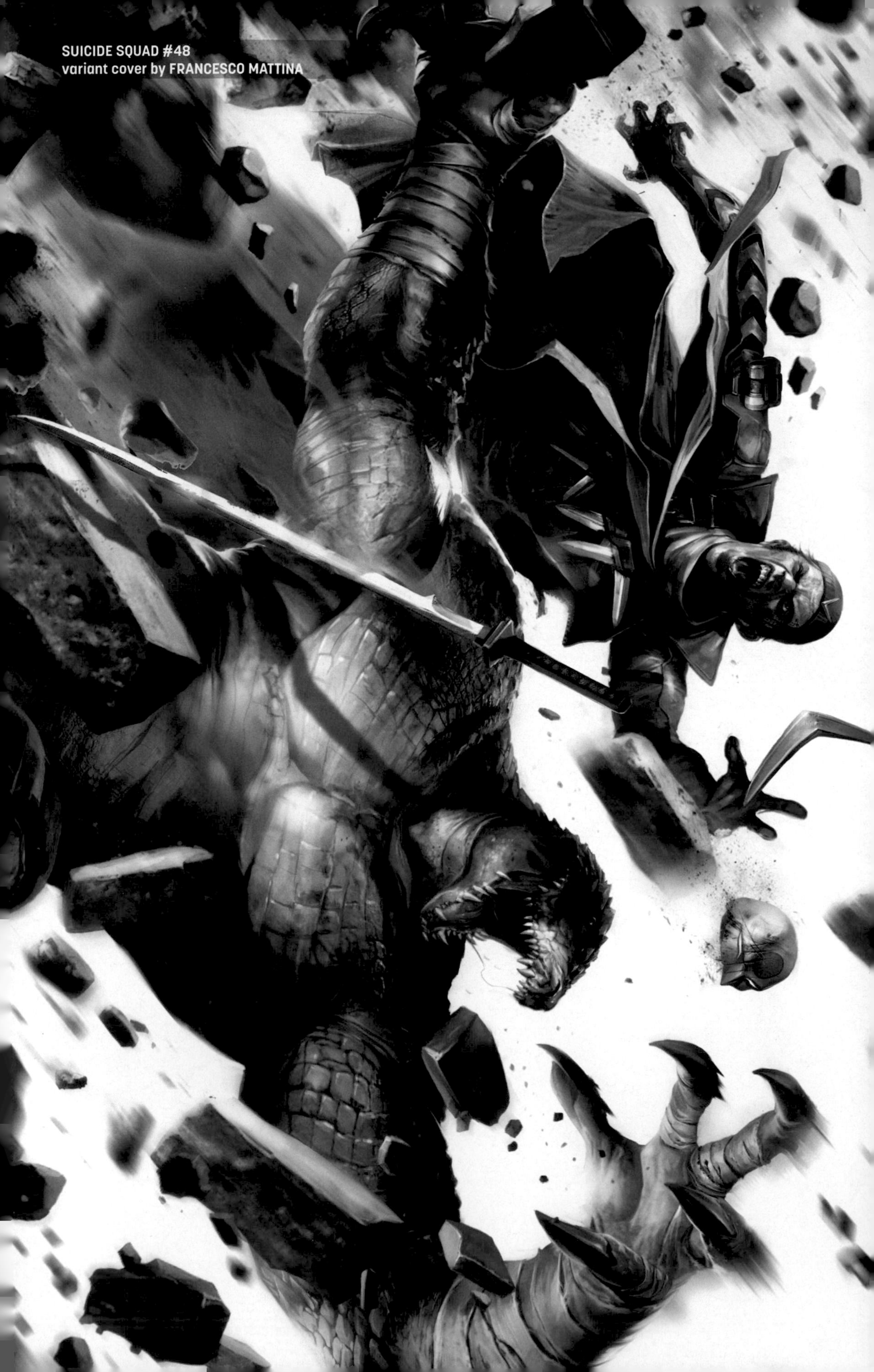

SUICIDE SQUAD #49 variant cover by FRANCESCO MATTINA

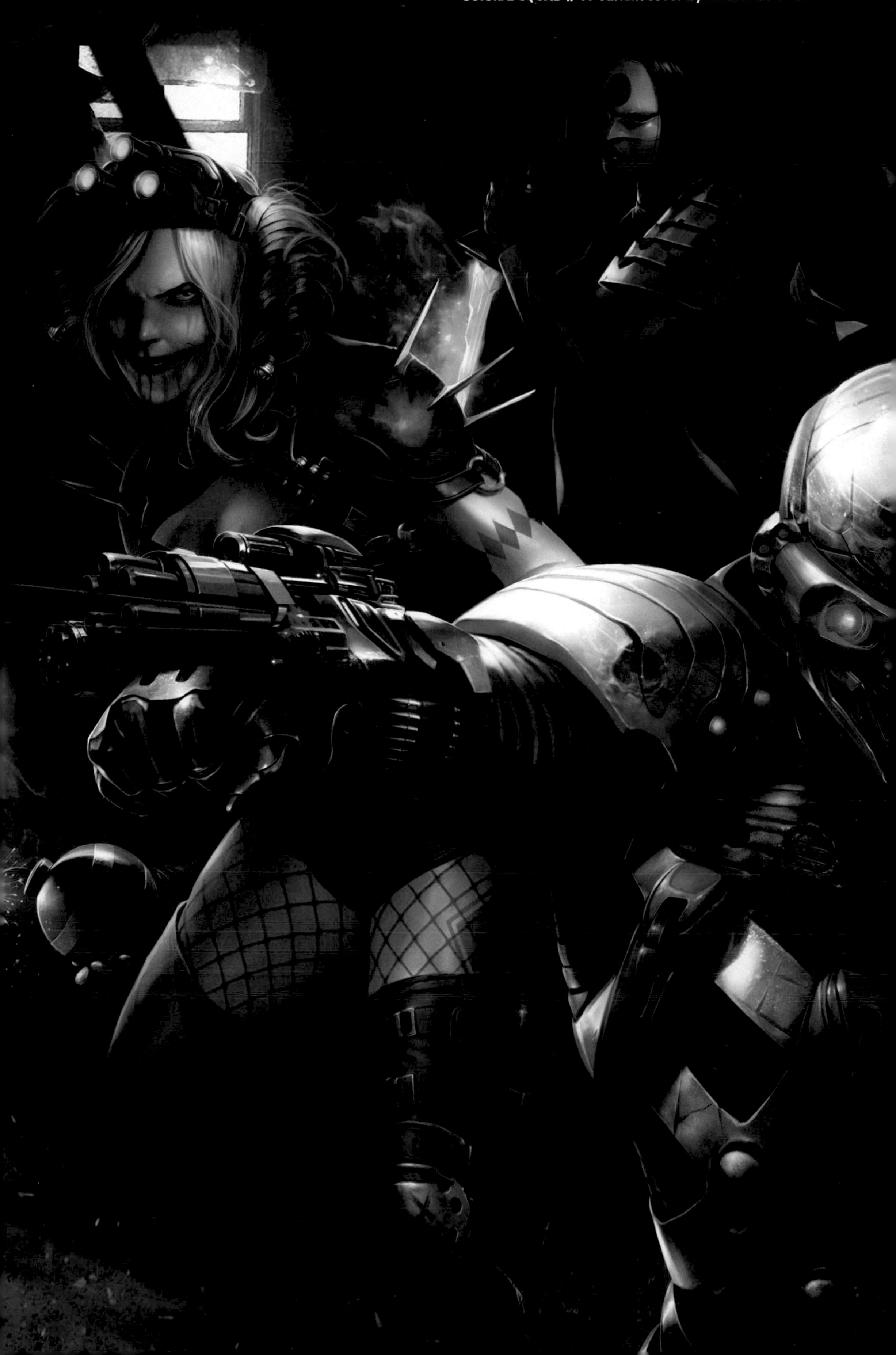

SUICIDE SQUAD #50 variant cover
by FRANCESCO MATTINA

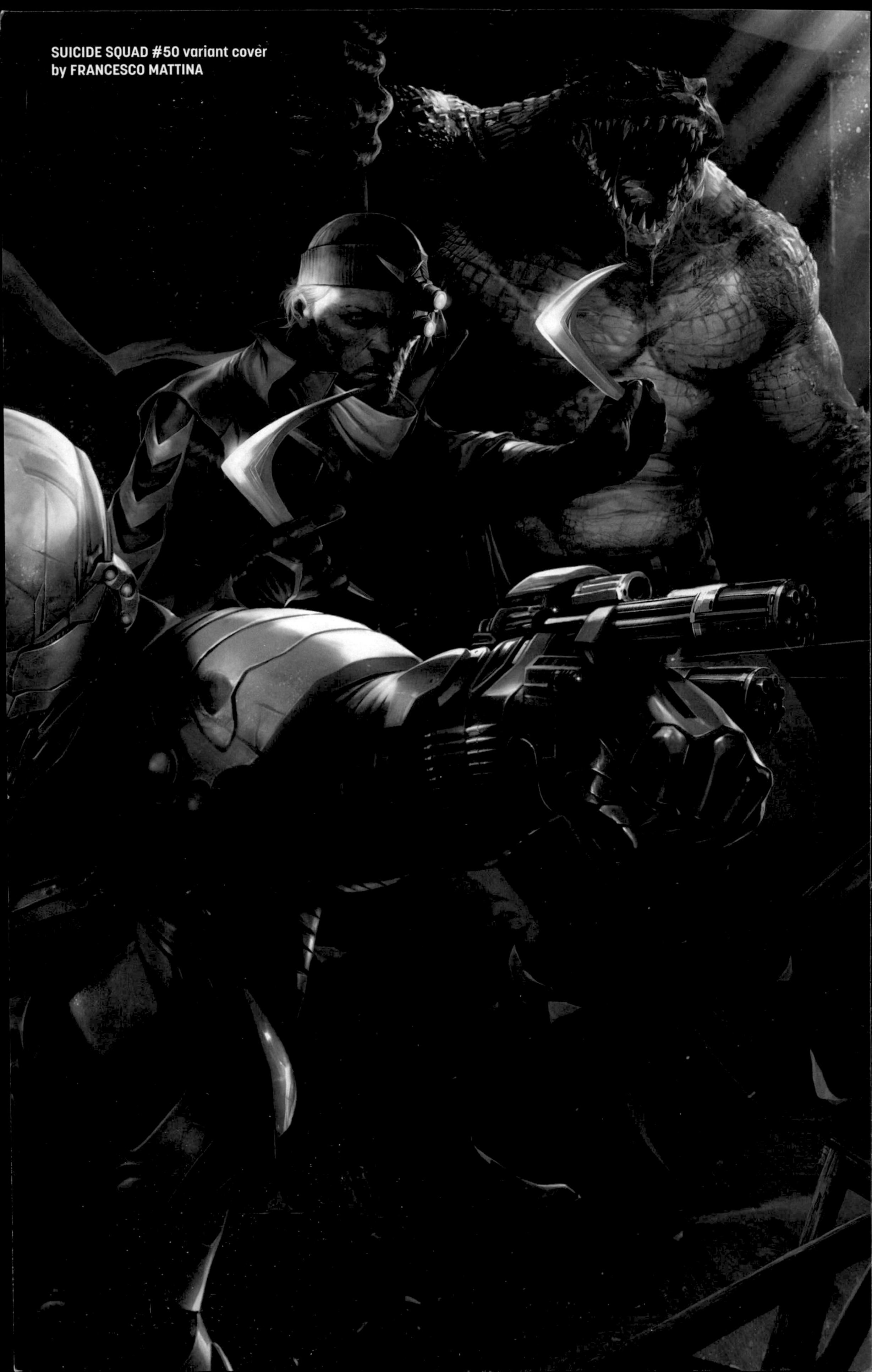